Applications of the Unified Protocol in Health Conditions

Applications of the Unified Protocol in Health Conditions

EDITED BY JORGE OSMA

AND

TODD J. FARCHIONE

OXFORD
UNIVERSITY PRESS

OXFORD
UNIVERSITY PRESS

Oxford University Press is a department of the University of Oxford. It furthers the University's objective of excellence in research, scholarship, and education by publishing worldwide. Oxford is a registered trade mark of Oxford University Press in the UK and certain other countries.

Published in the United States of America by Oxford University Press
198 Madison Avenue, New York, NY 10016, United States of America.

Library of Congress Cataloging-in-Publication Data
Names: Osma, Jorge, editor. | Farchione, Todd J., 1974– editor.
Title: Applications of the unified protocol in health conditions /
Jorge Osma and Todd J. Farchione.
Description: New York, NY : Oxford University Press, [2023] |
Includes bibliographical references and index.
Identifiers: LCCN 2023006162 (print) | LCCN 2023006163 (ebook) |
ISBN 9780197564295 (paperback) | ISBN 9780197564318 (epub) |
ISBN 9780197564325
Subjects: LCSH: Clinical health psychology. | Sick—Psychology.
Classification: LCC R726.7 .A662 2023 (print) | LCC R726.7 (ebook) |
DDC 610.1/9—dc23/eng/20230406
LC record available at https://lccn.loc.gov/2023006162
LC ebook record available at https://lccn.loc.gov/2023006163

DOI: 10.1093/oso/9780197564295.001.0001

Printed by Marquis Book Printing, Canada

CONTENTS

List of Figures vii
List of Tables ix
Foreword xi
About the Editors xv
Contributors xvii

1. Clinical Health Psychology: Foundations, History, and Future of a Promising Discipline and Profession 1
Rafael Ballester-Arnal, Maria Dolores Gil-Llario, and Cristina Giménez-García

2. The Unified Protocol for Transdiagnostic Treatment of Emotional Disorders and Physical Health Comorbidity: An Introduction 22
Todd J. Farchione, Daniella M. Spencer-Laitt, Shannon Sauer-Zavala, and David H. Barlow

3. Transdiagnostic Emotional Disorder Assessment and Case Formulation in Health Conditions 43
Anthony J. Rosellini, Jorge Osma, Carlos Suso, and Timothy A. Brown

4. The Unified Protocol for Transdiagnostic Treatment of Emotional Disorders in Type 2 Diabetes 69
Stephanie L. Leung, Todd J. Farchione, Elizabeth H. Eustis, Lindsey Pappalardo, and Jeffrey S. Gonzalez

5. Application of a Brief Unified Protocol Program in Group Format to People Living with HIV in a Public Health Unit 99
Alicia González-Baeza, Guadalupe Rua-Cebrian, Joanna Cano-Smith, Ignacio Pérez-Valero, and Jorge Osma

6. A Unified, Transdiagnostic Approach to Pain Management 131
Jenna Sandler Eilenberg and John D. Otis

7. Application of the Unified Protocol in Patients Who Have Undergone Bariatric Surgery 155
Vanesa Ferreres-Galán, Alba Quilez-Orden, Óscar Peris-Baquero, and Jorge Osma

8. Unified Protocol Application in Fertility Problems 177
Elena Crespo-Delgado, Verónica Martínez-Borba, Laura Andreu-Pejó, and Jorge Osma

9. Unified Protocol for Endometriosis 204
Laura A. Payne and Antje M. Barreveld

10. Cognitive–Behavioral Treatment for Anxiety and Depression in Parkinson's Disease: Efficacy and Clinical Application of the Unified Protocol 227
Gretchen O. Reynolds, Ryan Piers, and Alice Cronin-Golomb

11. Application of the Unified Protocol in Irritable Bowel Syndrome 257
Zahra Zanjani and Sanaz Joekar

12. Treating Depression and Anxiety Disorders Simultaneously in Patients with Cardiovascular Diseases Utilizing the Unified Protocol 285
Phillip J. Tully and Suzanne M. Cosh

13. The Unified Protocol for Smoking Cessation: Conceptual Basis and Integrated Treatment Approach 309
Amanda R. Mathew and Chelsea Cox

14. Unified Protocol Application in Patients with Long COVID-19 Condition 327
Verónica Martínez-Borba, Óscar Peris-Baquero, Laura Martínez-García, Jorge Osma, and Esther del Corral-Beamonte

Index 359

LIST OF FIGURES

3.1 Example MEDI profile. 50
4.1 Bidirectional relationship between diabetes symptomatology, affective components, and health behaviors. 77
4.2 Carmen conceptualization diagram. 80
8.1 Change in mood and anxiety during baseline (BL) and the UP-based prevention program. 195
8.2 Emotion dysregulation evolution during baseline (BL) and the UP-based preventive program. 195
9.1 Marla's OASIS scores over the course of 18 sessions. 221
10.1 Anxiety scores reported by Mr. X during baseline (2 weeks [B1–B2]) and post-treatment (immediate and 6-week follow-up [F1–F2]). BAI, Beck Anxiety Inventory; OASIS, Overall Anxiety Severity and Impairment Scale; STAI-S, State–Trait Anxiety Inventory–State; STAI-T, State–Trait Anxiety Inventory–Trait. 242
10.2 Scores reported by Mr X. during baseline, post-treatment, and 6-week follow-up assessments. 245
11.1 Changes in mood and anxiety during UP and 1-month follow-up. BL, baseline. 275
11.2 Changes in emotion regulation during UP and at 1-month follow-up. 276
13.1 Unified Protocol for smoking cessation: Conceptual model. 310
13.2 Case example data for (a) cigarettes per day and (b) smoking for affect regulation over the course of treatment. 321
14.1 MEDI scores at pretreatment assessment. AA, autonomic arousal; AVD, avoidance; DM, depressed mood; IC, intrusive cognitions; MEDI, Multidimensional Emotional Disorder Inventory; NT, neurotic temperament; PT, positive temperament; SOC, social anxiety; SOM, somatic anxiety; TRA, traumatic re-experiencing. 342
14.2 Change in depressive and anxiety symptoms at BL and during treatment. The dashed line indicates the clinical cut-off established for Spanish clinical populations (Osma et al., 2019). BL, baseline assessment; OASIS, Overall Anxiety Severity and Impairment Scale; ODSIS, Overall Depression Severity and Impairment Scale; T, weekly treatment assessment. 350

LIST OF TABLES

2.1 Modules Included in the Unified Protocol 28
3.1 Popular Transdiagnostic Emotional Disorder Questionnaires 48
3.2 Unified Protocol Case Formulation Form 52
3.3 A Case Formulation with the UP in Health Conditions: An Example with Chronic Pain 54
4.1 Baseline and Post-Treatment Descriptive Data 76
4.2 A Case Conceptualization with the UP in Type 2 Diabetes 88
4.3 Suggested Additional Considerations for UP Module Modifications for UP Treatment of T2D 92
5.1 A Case Formulation with the UP in a Woman Living with HIV 110
5.2 Normative Data and Direct Scores of Each Participant in Pretreatment, Post-Treatment, and 3-Month Follow-Up Assessments 119
5.3 Reliable Change Index of Each Participant Between Pretreatment and Post-Treatment and Between Pretreatment and 3-Month Follow-Up Assessments 121
6.1 A Case Conceptualization with the UP in Health Conditions 140
6.2 Outcome Measures 149
7.1 A Case Formulation Based on the UP 162
7.2 Assessment Protocol: Instruments and Constructs 167
7.3 Primary and Secondary Scores at Pretreatment and 6-Month Follow-Up for the Three Participants. 168
8.1 UP-PP Modules' Adaptations from the Original UP 182
8.2 Change in Psychological Factors from Pre-Assessment to 3-Month Follow Up 185
8.3 Case Conceptualization According to UP 189
8.4 Case Study Psychological Evolution from Pre-Assessment to 3-Month Follow-Up 194
9.1 A Case Conceptualization with the UP in Endometriosis 208
10.1 Case Formulation: UP for the Treatment of Depression in Parkinson's Disease 235
11.1 The Different Rome Criteria 258
11.2 UP-IBS Module Descriptions and Adaptations from the Original UP 265

11.3 A Case Conceptualization with the UP in Irritable Bowel Syndrome 267
12.1 Application of Transdiagnostic UP in CVD Populations Compared to Barlow's Original Model 289
12.2 A Case Conceptualization with the UP in Cardiovascular Disease 291
12.3 Self-Reported Psychological Rating Scale Outcomes for the Cardiovascular Case Study After Treatment with the UP 295
12.4 The Chest Pain Dilemma Matrix for the Case Example with CVD Treated with the UP 296
12.5 Change in Psychological Outcomes for Patients Randomized to Unified Protocol Versus Enhanced Usual Care in the CHAMPS Trial 298
13.1 Treatment Goals by Module 311
13.2 Session Content by Module 312
14.1 Description of the Psychological Measures Administered Throughout the Study 337
14.2 Evolution of Psycological Measures from Pre- to Post-Treatment Assessments 340
14.3 Case Conceptualization According to UP 343

FOREWORD

Psychological contributions to the severity and maintenance of physical disorders are vastly underestimated. For example, the leading causes of death in the United States by a very wide margin are heart disease and cancer, but some of the major contributing factors to these illnesses are psychological and behavioral. Thus, psychological factors account for substantially increased mortality from cardiovascular disease and cancer, and evidence-based psychological interventions increase survival rates in both conditions (Barlow et al., 2023; see Chapter 2, this volume). For the 38 million people suffering from AIDS around the world, behavioral and emotional factors, particularly the presence of emotional disorders, clearly contribute to HIV progression, at least partly through lowering compliance with medical regimens (see Chapter 5, this volume). It is also very clear that psychological and social factors have profound effects on brain structure and function. These factors seem to influence neurotransmitter activity, the secretion of neurohormones in the endocrine system, and even, at a more fundamental level, gene expression. In addition to cardiovascular disease and AIDS, psychological and social factors are important to a number of other disorders, including endocrinological disorders such as diabetes and a variety of disorders where immune system dysfunction is strongly implicated in addition to AIDS.

The tragedy of the ongoing COVIDovid-19 (SARS-CoV-2) pandemic that swept through the world in recent years continues to unfold. In 2020 the pandemic became the third leading cause of death in the United States, with a particularly devastating impact on people of color (Barlow et al., 2023), and similar increases in mortality were noted around the world. Anxious and depressive temperament predicted Covid related mental health burden even in those without a history of mental disorders at baseline (Moccia et al., 2020). Ironically, some public health behavioral practices necessarily put into place to reduce the spread of infection may have had untoward psychological consequences. For example, the prevalence of anxiety and depression nearly doubled during the pandemic. Based on evidence collected to date, social distancing that was necessarily imposed on the population by public health authorities to mitigate the spread of the virus was one of the major contributing factors to this increase in anxiety and depression (Ebrahimi et al., 2021; Spencer-Laitt et al., 2022). But more importantly, the damaging effects of social distancing were mediated by the temperament of neuroticism. Also, in those patients who developed anxiety and depression during Covid, the emotional distress persisted long after the remission of acute symptoms and may well be a major contributor to the ongoing problem of "long Covid" endured by 25% of the population initially infected with the virus, (Ebrahmi et al., 2021). Indeed, long Covid may be just one of a number of examples of chronic prolonged post-infection maladies, including most notably chronic fatigue syndrome. In these conditions, some evidence indicates that fundamental temperamental factors such as neuroticism contribute to the ongoing experience of many physical symptoms associated with the initial infection, as noted above. If future research confirms these hypotheses, the findings would have important treatment implications to relieve the considerable suffering associated with these post-infection syndromes.

We know now that neuroticism is highly prevalent not only in psychopathological conditions but in pathophysiological presentations comprising physical disorders. Indeed, several investigations have revealed that the economic burden of neuroticism when it accompanies both mental and physical disorders is staggeringly high, exceeding the costs of two-thirds of all physical disorders and exceeding the economic burden of major depressive disorder by a factor of 2.5 (Cuijpers et al., 2010; Lahey, 2009).

The goal of the Unified Protocol (UP) described in this book, and the principal mechanism of action of this intervention, is to reduce levels of neuroticism in the individual, thereby impacting clinical manifestations of more severe levels of this temperament. Of course, the UP was initially developed to target emotional disorders directly. The conceptual and theoretical development of this approach for anxiety, depressive, and related disorders, along with accumulated evidence for efficacy, is outlined briefly in cChapter 2 of this volume and presented in greater depth elsewhere (e.g., Sauer Zavala and& Barlow, 2021). Also published elsewhere is a more practical book on applications of the UP to various emotional disorders (Barlow & Farchione, 2018). This book, "Applications of the Unified Protocol in Health Conditions," is expertly edited by Drs. Jorge Osma and Todd Farchione, both of whom are international experts on the theory and application of the UP, serves a different and very welcome purpose. While clinicians whose business it is to treat disorders of emotion such as depression and the anxiety disorders are in fairly close communication with each other through the literature and attendance at meetings, the same cannot be said for clinicians treating the wide variety of physical disorders such as fertility problems, cancer, or pain management, who do not usually attend the same meetings or read the same literature. Thus, this book is focused on providing detailed practical advice on the applications of the evidence-based UP in a variety of cases spanning a large number of physical disorders, including those mentioned above. Also covered are principles of case formulation that would be particularly relevant to the contributing role of neuroticism in one disease process or another. A description of strategies for resolving typical roadblocks that a clinician might encounter during treatment and troubleshooting strategies is another important element of the text.

In view of the findings described above in the context of Covid, it would not be necessary for clinicians to diagnose the presence of a specific emotional disorder such as major depression or panic disorder to make this program useful. Rather, even those patients presenting with physical diseases or illnesses without diagnosable emotional disorders but whose conditions may be complicated by emotional overlay may benefit from applying the standardized modules in the UP. Another feature of this book that increases its value is a solid international lineup of authors from both Europe and the United States, along with close attention to integrating even broader multicultural factors in the formulation and treatment of these disorders. The systematic introduction of these interventions into hospitals and medical settings worldwide for specific disease processes, as outlined in the various chapters, should enhance the effectiveness of even the latest and most up-to-date medical inventions.

David H Barlow
Nantucket Island

REFERENCES

Barlow, D. H., Durand, V. M., & Hofmann, S. G. (2023). *Psychopathology: An integrative approach to mental disorders* (9th ed.). Cengage.

Barlow, D. H., & Farchione, T. J. (Eds.). (2018). *Applications of the unified protocol for transdiagnostic treatment of emotional disorders*. Oxford University Press.

Cuijpers, P., Smit, F., Penninx, B. W., de Graaf, R., ten Have, M., & Beekman, A. T. (2010). Economic costs of neuroticism: A population-based study. *Archives of General Psychiatry*, 67(10), 1086–1093. https://doi.org/10.1001/archgenpsychiatry.2010.130

Ebrahimi, O. V., Hoffart, A., & Johnson, S. U. (2021). Physical distancing and mental health during the COVID-19 pandemic: Factors associated with psychological symptoms and adherence to pandemic mitigation strategies. *Clinical Psychological Science*, 9(3), 489–506.

Lahey, B. B. (2009). Public health significance of neuroticism. *The American Psychologist*, 64(4), 241–256.

Moccia, L., Janiri, D., Pepe, M., Dattoli, L., Molinaro, M., De Martin, V., Chieffo, D., Janiri, L., Fiorillo, A., Sani, G., & Di Nicola, M. (2020). Affective temperament, attachment style, and the psychological impact of the COVID-19 outbreak: An early report on the Italian general population. *Brain, Behavior, and Immunity*, 87, 75–79.

Sauer-Zavala, S., & Barlow, D. H. (2021). *Neuroticism: A new framework for emotional disorders and their treatment*. New York: The Guilford Press.

Spencer-Laitt, D., Eustis, E. H., Barlow, D. H., & Farchione, T. J. (2022). The impact of COVID-19 related social distancing on mental health outcomes: A transdiagnostic account. *International Journal of Environmental Research and Public Health*, 19(11), 6596.

ABOUT THE EDITORS

Jorge Osma, PhD

Jorge Osma is Associate Professor in the Department of Psychology and Sociology at the University of Zaragoza. He received his clinical training at the Psychology Assistance Service at Jaume I University (Castellón, Spain) and was a member of the research group Labpsitec from 1999 to 2011 at the same university. During that time, he collaborated on several national and European funded research studies on the assessment and treatment of anxiety, mood, and related disorders, including some using information and communication technologies. He received his PhD from Jaume I University in 2009.

He has conducted research on the Unified Protocol (UP) since it was first published in 2011 and completed clinical training on the protocol at the Unified Protocol Institute (UPI) in 2015. He is committed to the dissemination of the UP in Spanish-speaking countries and recently developed a Spanish training program through the UPI and in collaboration with FIDAP (Research, Development and Application on Psychology of the Valencian Community Foundation, Spain).

He is currently the director of the research group IPES (Research on Personality, Emotion, and Health) at the Health Research Institute of Aragon. His research focuses on studying the efficacy of the UP for transdiagnostic treatment of emotional disorders and the development and refinement of more cost-effective delivery formats such as group, online, or blended, especially in public health settings. In recent years, he has been collaborating on different clinical studies applying the UP in health conditions such as HIV, obesity, infertility, or persistent COVID-19.

Todd J. Farchione, PhD

Todd J. Farchione is Research Associate Professor in the Department of Psychological and Brain Sciences at Boston University (BU). He received his doctorate from the University of California, Los Angeles (UCLA) and completed a clinical internship at the West Los Angeles VA Medical Center. Prior to joining the faculty at BU, he completed postdoctoral fellowships at the UCLA Neuropsychiatric Institute and Hospital and the Center for Anxiety and Related Disorders (CARD).

He currently directs a research group at CARD that focuses on understanding emotion and emotion regulation processes; identifying higher order, functional, psychopathological mechanisms; and dissemination of improved treatments for anxiety, mood, and commonly co-occurring disorders. He co-developed the UP for transdiagnostic treatment of emotional disorders and has made substantial contributions to the evaluation and refinement of the protocol since its inception. He has published extensively on the UP and on the nature and treatment of emotional disorders more broadly.

CONTRIBUTORS

Laura Andreu-Pejó
University Jaume I
Castellón, Spain
Health Research Institute of Aragon
Zaragoza, Spain

Rafael Ballester-Arnal
Full Professor of Clinical Health Psychology
Health Sciences Faculty
University Jaume I
Castellón, Spain

David H. Barlow
Department of Psychological and Brain Sciences
Center for Anxiety and Related Disorders
Boston University
Boston, MA, USA

Antje M. Barreveld
Department of Anesthesiology, Pain Management Services
Newton-Wellesley Hospital/Tufts University School of Medicine
Newton, MA, USA

Timothy A. Brown
Department of Psychological and Brain Sciences
Center for Anxiety and Related Disorders
Boston University
Boston, MA, USA

Joanna Cano-Smith
HIV Unit, Internal Medicine Service
Hospital Universitario La Paz
Madrid, Spain

Suzanne M. Cosh
School of Psychology
University of New England
Armidate, NSW, Australia

Chelsea Cox
Department of Psychology
University of Illinois at Chicago
Chicago, IL, USA

Elena Crespo-Delgado
University Jaume I
Castellón, Spain
Health Research Institute of Aragon
Zaragoza, Spain

Alice Cronin-Golomb
Department of Psychological and Brain Sciences
Boston University
Boston, MA, USA

Esther del Corral-Beamonte
Hospital Royo Villanova
Zaragoza, Spain

Jenna Sandler Eilenberg
Department of Psychological and Brain Sciences
Boston University
Boston, MA, USA

Elizabeth H. Eustis
Department of Psychological and Brain Sciences
Center for Anxiety and Related Disorders
Boston University
Boston, MA, USA

Todd J. Farchione
Department of Psychological and Brain Sciences
Boston University
Boston, MA, USA

Vanesa Ferreres-Galán
Mental Health Unit of the Hospital Comarcal de Vinaròs
Castellón, Spain
Health Research Institute of Aragón
Zaragoza, Spain

Maria Dolores Gil-Llario
Full Professor of Developmental and Educational Psychology
Faculty of Psychology
University of Valencia
Valencia, Spain

Cristina Giménez-García
Associate Professor of Clinical Health Psychology
Health Sciences Faculty
University Jaume I
Castellón, Spain

Jeffrey S. Gonzalez
Montefiore Medical Center/Albert Einstein College of Medicine
Bronx, NY, USA
Ferkauf Graduate School of Psychology
Bronx, NY, USA

Alicia González-Baeza
Biological and Health Psychology Department
Universidad Autónoma de Madrid
Madrid, Spain
HIV Unit, Internal Medicine Service
Hospital Universitario La Paz
Madrid, Spain

Sanaz Joekar
Assistant Professor
Department of Clinical Psychology
Medical Faculty
Kashan University of Medical Sciences
Kashan, Iran

Stephanie L. Leung
Montefiore Medical Center/Albert Einstein College of Medicine
Bronx, NY, USA

Verónica Martínez-Borba
University of Zaragoza
Teruel, Spain
Health Research Institute of Aragon
Zaragoza, Spain

Laura Martínez-García
University of Zaragoza Teruel, Spain
Health Research Institute of Aragón
Zaragoza, Spain

Amanda R. Mathew
Department of Preventive Medicine
Rush University Medical Center
Chicago, IL, USA

Jorge Osma
Department of Psychology and Sociology
University of Zaragoza
Teruel, Spain
Health Research Institute of Aragon
Zaragoza, Spain

John D. Otis
Research Associate Professor
Department of Psychological and Brain Sciences
Center for Anxiety and Related Disorders
Boston University
Boston, MA, USA

Lindsey Pappalardo
Ferkauf Graduate School of Psychology
Bronx, NY, USA

Laura A. Payne
Clinical and Translational Pain Research Laboratory
McLean Hospital/Harvard Medical School
Belmont, MA, USA

Ignacio Pérez-Valero
HIV Unit, Internal Medicine Service
Hospital Universitario La Paz
Madrid, Spain

Óscar Peris-Baquero
University of Zaragoza Teruel, Spain
Health Research Institute of Aragón
Zaragoza, Spain

Ryan Piers
Department of Psychological and Brain Sciences
Boston University
Boston, MA, USA

Alba Quilez-Orden
Mental Health Unit of Moncayo, Tarazona, Spain
Health Research Institute of Aragón
Zaragoza, Spain

Gretchen O. Reynolds
Department of Psychological and Brain Sciences
Boston University
Boston, MA, USA

Anthony J. Rosellini
Department of Psychological and Brain Sciences
Center for Anxiety and Related Disorders
Boston University
Boston, MA, USA

Guadalupe Rua-Cebrian
HIV Unit, Internal Medicine Service
Hospital Universitario La Paz
Madrid, Spain

Shannon Sauer-Zavala
Clinic for Emotional Health (CEH)
Department of Psychology
University of Kentucky
Kentucky, USA

Daniella M. Spencer-Laitt
Center for Anxiety and Related Disorders
Boston University
Boston, MA, USA

Carlos Suso
University Jaume I
Castellón, Spain

Phillip J. Tully
School of Medicine
The University of Adelaide, Australia
Adelaide, SA, Australia

Zahra Zanjani
Associate Professor
Department of Clinical Psychology
Medical Faculty
Kashan University of Medical Sciences
Kashan, Iran

1

Clinical Health Psychology

Foundations, History, and Future of a Promising Discipline and Profession

RAFAEL BALLESTER-ARNAL, MARIA DOLORES GIL-LLARIO, AND CRISTINA GIMÉNEZ-GARCÍA ■

INTRODUCTION

In 1978, the American Psychological Association (APA) founded a new division, Division 38 for Health Psychology, presided by Joseph Matarazzo, who defined this discipline as

> the aggregate of the specific educational, scientific, and professional contributions of the discipline of psychology to the promotion and maintenance of health, the prevention and treatment of illness, the identification of etiological and diagnostic correlates of health, illness, and related dysfunction, and to the analysis and improvement of the health care system and health policy formation. (Matarazzo, 1982, p. 4)

Since then, the growth of health psychology has been spectacularly fast, and currently it is a very consolidated subdiscipline, with future projected growth within psychology. Based on knowledge from different areas, such as basic psychology, clinical psychology, psychobiology, social psychology, and developmental psychology, health psychology uses the biopsychosocial model to understand the psychological factors that may influence health and disease.

The research on prevention and psychological intervention of "medical illnesses" has increased notably in the past three decades. Using the keyword "health psychology," a search of the PsychInfo database found that 274 papers

Rafael Ballester-Arnal, Maria Dolores Gil-Llario, and Cristina Giménez-García, *Clinical Health Psychology*
In: *Applications of the Unified Protocol in Health Conditions*. Edited by: Jorge Osma and Todd J. Farchione,
Oxford University Press. © Oxford University Press 2023. DOI: 10.1093/oso/9780197564295.003.0001

were published in 1985, just a few years after the discipline was founded. Five years later, in 1990, the number had increased to 531. In 2000, the number of papers published in just 1 year had almost tripled to 1,432. In 2011, 2,638 were published. Moreover, 5,039 articles were published in 2020. A total of 81,761 articles have been published in this field since it was founded. In addition, in relation to training, health psychology is now part of the psychology degree curriculum of most institutions in the Western world.

The current development of health psychology has been possible mostly due to three causes. From a historical viewpoint, health psychology is based on the biopsychosocial model developed after thousands of years during which other ways of understanding the relationship between mind and body prevailed—the supernatural, natural, moral, and biomedical models. Second, the current discipline owes much to contributions from other disciplines that made possible the crisis of confidence in the biomedical model and the formulation of the biopsychosocial model. In addition, in this area, it is necessary to highlight the significant contributions from authors such as T. Parsons from sociology or D. Mechanic from medical sociology. Third, none of this would have been possible if the social and sanitary conditions of our environment had not improved and we were not in a situation in which the most prevalent diseases are chronic conditions mostly associated with health habits that require a lifetime adaptation process. In this chapter, we review all factors that were essential for the birth of health psychology, as well as for the current conception of clinical health psychology as a subdiscipline and a health profession with an important present and a promising future.

MIND AND BODY: THE HISTORY OF A COMPLEX RELATIONSHIP

From the most ancient times, humans have tried to explain the causes of diseases and fight them with the resources based on their available knowledge and technology. Archeological remains show that 60,000 years ago, in the era in which Neanderthal man lived, there was already a special role for sick or injured people and a role for "healers" (Osmond & Siegler, 1979). In addition, in Greek mythology, there was a place for medicine. Asclepiades was the god of medicine. The myth holds that Asclepiades had two daughters: Panakeia (who cures everything) was the goddess in charge of curing diseases, and Hygieia (the goddess of health and hygiene) was responsible for public health and preventive medicine. The god expected his daughters to work harmoniously, but they competed more than they cooperated. When Hygieia was successful in preventing disease, what could Panacea do? When Panacea dominated popular and medical thought, what value was placed on Hygieia (Ballester, 1997)?

Nowadays, it seems logical for us to attribute a physical discomfort to an organic pathology, go to a health center, tell the doctor how we feel, undergo diagnostic tests based on the physical examination, take a box of antibiotics, go to the hospital, and undergo surgery. However, before reaching this point, the interpretation of the disease had to come a long way throughout human history.

The Supernatural Model: Spirits, Witchdoctors, and Shamans

In the beginning, humans attributed mysterious phenomena that occurred to them, including illness and death, to supernatural causes. The evidence suggests that in early societies, the mind, body, and even nature were considered an indivisible unit (Suls et al., 2010). In the supernatural model of health/disease, it was believed that a person became ill because demons or other spiritual forces had affected and controlled the person (Bishop, 1994). The individual could suffer the possession of an evil spirit or the flight of the soul, circumstances for which therapeutic measures such as exorcism, trepanation, and the restoration of the soul by certain rituals and dances were planned. This model prevailed for a very long time, from the first human beings until just a few thousand years ago, with testimonies from cultures such as ancient Mesopotamia; Assyrian culture, from which amulets such as the Imdugud amulet, that protected against evil spirits, are preserved; ancient Greece, from which there are remains such as the Asklepeion (sanatorium temple of the god Asklepios); and the ancient people of Israel, from whom humans incorporated the notion of illness as a consequence of sin, a possible challenge in which God tests the righteous person, etc.

However, we would be wrong to consider that during these millennia this type of belief overshadowed any other type of measure to prevent and cure diseases. These testimonies coincide in time with others, such as a Sumerian tablet considered the oldest medical document, dated to 3000 BC, in which medical recipes of the physicists of Nippur are described with cuneiform writing; remains showing soap making, sewerage systems, and the isolation of lepers in Mesopotamia; a drainage system in the Indus Valley; the well-known stela with the Code of Hammurabi that contains what could be the first regulation of medical practice in Babylon and possibly the world (dated 1740 BC); the famous Egyptian Papyrus of Ebers (1500 BC) containing a thousand recipes of remedies that were taken accompanied by psalms and rituals; the Smith Papyrus with Surgical Practices; another from Berlin with preventive measures; and many other testimonies.

The Natural Model: Philosophers–Healers

In line with the rational and philosophical thought in the 5th century BC in ancient Greece, an effort was made to find the natural causes of disease, which was a major change of course from the magical interpretation prior to scientific knowledge. Possibly the first proponent of this new model was Alcmaeon of Croton

(500 BC), from the Pythagorean school, who in his work *On Nature* described his dissections, the optic nerve, and the brain as the basis of intellectual activity. Alcmaeon expressed the idea that the balance of qualities preserved health, what he called "isonomia" versus the "monarchia" that represented disease. Nevertheless, this change in understanding disease was consolidated and had its greatest proponent in the "father of medicine," Hippocrates (460–377 BC), and his School of Cos, which produced the set of works called *Corpus Hippocraticum*. In his work, Hippocrates formulated a natural model of health/disease in which disease is caused by the imbalance (*dyscrasia*) of the elements in the body that, according to Empedocles, made up the cosmos, namely fire, land, water, and air. Each of these elements abounds in one of the body fluids. Accordingly, the fire is concentrated in the blood, the earth in the phlegm, the water in the yellow bile, and the air in the black bile. When these fluids are in imbalance, the organ where they are gets sick. If it is blood, it makes the heart sick; if it is phlegm, it makes the brain sick; if it is yellow bile, it makes the liver sick; and if it is black bile, it makes the spleen sick. This is the called theory of humors (Ballester, 1996). The therapy was aimed at restoring the health of the person by re-establishing the balance among the different humors, for which Hippocrates recommended following a proper diet and avoiding certain excesses. In addition to the humoral theory, Hippocrates is credited with diagnosis through observation and clinical experience, the beginning of the collection of medical records, and important aphorisms such as *primum non nocere* or the idea that the doctor only collaborates with nature in the recovery of the patient. Obviously, he is also credited with the famous Hippocratic Oath, which was probably written by one of his disciples.

The Greek philosophers, particularly Plato, were the first to propose that the mind and the body were two separate entities. The germ of this idea had already appeared in Hippocrates' work, and long before him, it seems that the separation between the world of matter and the spirit was developed by the Orphic religion and the cult of Dionysus, which in turned also influenced Pythagorean philosophy. However, it is also true that Greek culture and specifically the work of Plato and Aristotle assumed that mind and body influenced each other on a great variety of phenomena.

The Roman Empire took up the baton of the Greek view about health/disease and its position toward the mind/body dualism. Galen (2nd century AD), in addition to accepting the humoral theory of Hippocrates and the pneumatic theory of Diogenes of Apollonia, made important discoveries about the brain and the circulatory system, by means of the dissection of animals of many species. Galen consolidated the idea that diseases can be located in different pathologies that may occur in specific parts of the body (Sarafino & Smith, 2016), an idea that is directly related to the mechanism of the biomedical model. He defended that the perfect balance of humors did not exist and coined the concept of *diathesis* (a concept that is currently used with some nuance) when talking about the peculiar balance of humors that occurred in a person on which other factors acted.

The naturalistic conception of health and disease developed in Greece and Rome during this period had spread many years earlier and independently in Chinese culture. The key to understanding disease in this culture was the concept of equilibrium or balance among forces. Chinese culture considered a complete connection between mind and body, and a person's health was greatly influenced by their behavior and emotions. Currently, this emphasis on the mind–body interrelation is still present in Chinese medicine (Pachuta, 1989). The same is true of Egyptian medicine or Indian medicine with the concept of prana, equivalent to the chi (energy) of Chinese medicine.

The Moral Model: Clergy, Guilt, and Penances

After the fall of the Roman Empire and throughout the Middle Ages, the advancement and progress of medical knowledge slowed enormously, due in large part to the influence of the Church. The Church conceived the human being as a creature with a soul that separated the human from natural laws, subject only to the human's own designs and to the will of God. The body of the human was considered sacrosanct, and the dissection was dangerous for the one who performed it. The dissection of animals was also forbidden because they were also considered to have souls. Obstacles to observation blocked the development of anatomy and medicine for centuries (Sarafino & Smith, 2016). In this context, during the Middle Ages, the natural model of disease evolved into a moral model, according to which disease was often the punishment for morally reprehensible behavior. Once again, ideas about the demonic possessions of sick people's bodies gained relevance, thus returning medicine to the hands of priests, who sometimes had no other way to cure diseases other than corporal torture to cause the flight of the evil spirits, in addition to purges and bleeding. However, healing largely depended on the people's faith (Sanderson, 2018). Sick people were cared for in the first "hospitals," where they stayed with homeless and poor people.

Although the moral model seems very outdated, it is much more prevalent than is desirable. Recall that when the first cases of AIDS in people with homosexual practices emerged in the 1980s, many voices affirmed that humans were facing a new punishment from God (as in Sodom and Gomorrah) for those who carried out unnatural and perverse practices. This idea is also at the base of those who believe that alcoholic or drug-dependent patients should not benefit from receiving medical care because they are guilty of creating their condition (Ballester, 1996).

THE BIOMEDICAL MODEL

The current health system is framed within the biomedical model, which also assumes certain beliefs and values around health and disease.

The Origins of the Biomedical Model

Following the Middle Ages, during the Renaissance, the natural explanations about the disease returned. The humanism of Renaissance authors such as Leonardo da Vinci or Paracelsus returned the focus on man and his potential to explain the world around him, while doctors again assumed the responsibility of medicine. Later, in the 17th century, the philosopher René Descartes made a historical contribution to the problem of mind–body dualism—probably one of the most influential contributions on scientific thought. In his work, Descartes argued, as did the ancient Greeks, that the mind and the body are separate entities (Cartesian dualism); the mind belongs to the world of the *res cogitans* and the body to the *res extensa*. However, Descartes included three important innovations (Ballester, 1997). First, he conceived the body as a machine, composed of different parts, and described the mechanisms by which actions and sensations were produced. Disease, according to Descartes, occurred when some part of the machine broke or malfunctioned. The doctor's purpose was to diagnose where that failure had occurred and repair the machine. Second, Descartes proposed that the mind and body, although separate, could communicate by the pineal gland, located in the brain. Third, Descartes defended the idea that animals did not have a soul and that the soul of humans left the body when they died, and consequently, dissection could be an acceptable study method. Despite certain "romantic resistance," Cartesian thought prevailed in Western culture.

In the 18th and 19th centuries, medical knowledge advanced considerably due to important developments such as the invention of the microscope; the use of dissection in autopsies, with Morgagni's work; the development anatomoclinical neurology by Broca; advances in pathology, particularly due to the work of Virchow; and the studies of Pasteur and Koch in the field of bacteriology. In the mid-19th century, the field of surgery began to prosper, with the development of aseptic and anesthesia techniques. For the first time, rather than being major spreaders of infection, hospitals were places where the sick were cured. Moreover, the reputation of doctors, and people's confidence in their ability to heal, began to improve (Stone, 1979).

All these factors marked the beginning of a new way of understanding health and disease—the biomedical model—as well as the foundation of what could be called modern medicine (Bishop, 1994). Due to this new way of understanding and treating disease, death rates in Europe and the United States dropped considerably. In the 20th and 21st centuries, advances have continued and brought current medicine to a state that would have been unimaginable by our ancestors. The development of drugs or "miracle" medication such as penicillin and its derivatives, as well as vaccines for a wide variety of common diseases, together with the spectacular advances in surgical techniques and in medical technology have led to a revolution in health care. Currently, physicians are able to cure or significantly alleviate the suffering caused by diseases that once were fatal. Thus, what are the basic assumptions on which the biomedical model of the disease is based that have allowed this important advance in the healing of the sick?

The Basic Assumptions of the Biomedical Model

According to Engel (1977), one of the major critics of the biomedical model, the model is based on two assumptions: mind–body dualism and reductionism. The model assumes that the complex phenomenon of disease can be reduced to the language of chemistry and physics. The doctor concentrates on the physiological state of the person, considering the psychological and social ramifications of the disease as peripheral aspects (Engel, 1980).

In line with this model, therapeutic intervention must be guided by biological and mechanistic principles based on categorical or unicausal explanations. It is understood that a symptom is produced by a single type of cause, based on a biological disorder, and, consequently, the disease is eliminated by means of removing the underlying organic pathology (Ballester, 1997).

Undoubtedly, the biomedical model has assumed the status of cultural imperative because it has become so widespread both in the scientific field and among laypeople (Engel, 1977). Obviously, it must be recognized that in recent years, advances in the field of medical technology, following this model, have made it possible to diagnose organic pathologies with a level of certainty, haste, and precision that would have been unconceivable in the past. However, there are still challenges to be resolved—factors that are beyond X-rays, computerized axial tomography, or magnetic resonance—and aspects that need to be studied. The suffering of sick people and how they experience their illness should be considered within the field of medicine. This vision is what the biopsychosocial model aimed to provide (Ballester, 1997).

Criticism of the Biomedical Model

Many criticisms have been made of the biomedical model. Possibly one of the harshest was formulated by Engel in 1977, arguing that this model had become a dogma, something opposite to a reliable scientific model, due to its intransigence in considering, recognizing, and incorporating new ideas and concepts about the psychological, social, and cultural determinants of disease. Other authors, such as Fabrega (1973), Kleinman et al. (1978), Mechanic (1968/1978, 1980), Barondess (1979), Eisenberg (1980), and Cott (1986a, 1986b), also questioned the basis of the biomedical model. The following are some of the most common criticisms (Ballester, 1997):

1. The biomedical model does not pay attention to important determinants of health, such as public health measures, social conditions, and health behaviors.
2. Increasingly more studies show that the decision to seek medical help results more from discomfort or distress associated with everyday problems than from a specific organic pathology. Both the person's past experiences and their cultural background determine the process of seeking medical help, as was demonstrated by Zola (1973) and Mechanic (1968/1978).
3. Biomedicine does not pay enough attention to the patient's experience of sickness (illness), especially when there is no organic pathology and its treatment can sometimes worsen the discomfort, due to unnecessary medicalization (Cott, 1986a, 1986b). In fact, data indicate that more than 50% of visits made in primary care are for queries without an organic basis. McHugh and Vallis (1986) and Cott (1986a, 1986b) warned of the danger of "medicalizing" nonspecific demands from patients who do not have an organic referent, which leads to unnecessary diagnostic examinations and expensive and sometimes even harmful treatments. Cott formulated an interactive model in which the sickness or illness is the result of the reciprocal interaction between a disease and psychological and social variables. The assumption of this model requires forming multidisciplinary teams to deal with all aspects of the sickness, considering the patient as a whole.
4. The Western health system is much more based on hospitalization and acute treatment of diseases than on prevention and holistic treatment of the human being. In an era in which chronic diseases have displaced the prevalence of infectious diseases, and taking into account that most of these chronic diseases are the result of a certain lifestyle or harmful health habits, prevention at all levels (primary, secondary, and tertiary) takes on its full meaning. The importance of health behaviors has become so prominent in our time that Matarazzo (1984) coined the term "behavioral pathogens" to designate all behaviors—such as smoking, consuming alcohol, and overeating—that are responsible for some of the major public health problems.

THE BIOPSYCHOSOCIAL MODEL

Based on the criticisms about the biomedical model, the need for a more comprehensive model that considered the biological, psychological, and social factors involved in the disease, at the same level, seemed clear. The formulation of the biopsychosocial model in 1977 by Engel was the expression of a concern that had been present for many researchers.

The basic postulate of the biopsychosocial model, supported by the general systems theory (Bertalanffy, 1968), is that health and disease are the result of the interaction of biological, psychological, and social factors and, consequently, including these three factors when considering the determinants of a disease and its treatment is required. In this sense, the biopsychosocial model is opposed to mind–body dualism. Furthermore, this model maintains a position contrary to the reductionism with which the biomedical model solves the problem of mind–body dualism, maintaining that all factors are equally important in health and disease. Finally, it supports the idea that the relationship among these factors is not additive but, rather, interactive (Ballester, 1997).

According to the general systems theory, the human body is composed of interrelated systems, such as the cardiovascular system, the endocrine system, and the nervous system. In turn, each system is composed of various interrelated cells and tissues. In addition, the physical body is only one of the aspects of a person, and each person as a whole is a part of a larger system, which includes the family, the community, the society, and the biosphere. In the biopsychosocial model, studying the functioning of the person at the psychological and community level is as important as the analysis at the cellular level of the disease to avoid and combat the sickness.

The biopsychosocial model considers the patient as an active being in how the patient perceives and deals with their symptoms to achieve health. This conception of the patient as an active being is linked with the importance of individual responsibility in caring for one's own health and, therefore, the relevance of prevention and self-care in chronic diseases. Moreover, in this model, the conception of the human being as a global entity emphasizes that the health professional must consider the patient's emotions when explaining and treating disease, as well as in the doctor–patient relationship.

THE ORIGINS OF HEALTH PSYCHOLOGY

The formulation of the biopsychosocial model by Engel (1977), in which a series of concerns that had been present two or three decades earlier were specified, was a catalyst that accelerated research on the psychosocial factors associated with disease. In this sense, the biopsychosocial model contributed decisively to the constitution of the new discipline called *health psychology* (Ibáñez & Belloch, 1989). However, to understand how the role of psychology emerged in the field of health, it is necessary to discuss psychosomatic medicine, experimental psychophysiology, and behavioral medicine.

At the beginning of the 20th century, Sigmund Freud observed how some patients showed symptoms of physical illness in the absence of organic problems, and he considered that these symptoms were "converted" from unconscious emotional conflicts in what he called conversion hysteria. The symptoms included problems as varied as paralysis, deafness, blindness, or numbness in some part of the body. In the 1930s, the need to understand this type of problem motivated the study of the interaction between emotions and physiological processes, thus resulting in a new field of study called psychosomatic medicine, whose first publication, *Psychosomatic Medicine*, appeared in 1939. Its founders were researchers trained in medicine, including the psychoanalyst F. Alexander and the psychiatrist H. F. Dunbar. During the first 25 years, research focused on the psychoanalytic interpretation of a series of diseases considered "psychosomatic," such as ulcers, asthma, hypertension, migraines, and rheumatoid arthritis. In the 1960s, psychosomatic medicine generated a large number of investigations focused on the mind–body association, and high expectations were placed on this field of study. However, decades later, psychosomatic medicine was not as influential as predicted. Possible causes for this included that the research strategies mostly focused on case studies, with difficulties generalizing the results; the use of psychoanalytic concepts not validated empirically; and suspicion due to the lack of therapeutic specificity because the treatment of all psychosomatic conditions differed very little (Donker, 1991).

Another field of study that had an important impact on the subsequent development of health psychology was experimental psychophysiology, defined as the study of the physiological bases of psychological processes. This field of research had as its first antecedent the works of the physiologist Cannon (1935), who, interested in homeostasis, studied the physiological response of organisms to a threatening situation. However, Hans Selye was the one who developed the idea of the stress response. Based on research carried out with animal models, Selye demonstrated the physiological impact of certain behaviors and emotions, developing the formulation of the stress syndrome and general adaptation syndrome. The growing interest in psychophysiological reactions in humans made possible important technological advances in the measurement of different physiological parameters, such as muscle tension, skin temperature, and electrical activity of the skin and brain, which led to the development of biofeedback techniques.

The development of these techniques is considered crucial to the constitution of behavioral medicine in the early 1970s. In the beginning, it was considered as the field of study that brought together the information from the application of behavioral techniques, specifically biofeedback techniques in the field of medicine (Birk, 1973). However, because of the large diversity of disciplines that attempted to understand health and disease, such as anthropology, sociology, psychology, and biomedical sciences, a new discipline that integrated all the available knowledge was required (Schwartz & Weiss, 1978a). Following the Yale Conference in 1977, behavioral medicine was defined by Schwartz and Weiss (1978b) as

> the field concerned with the development of behavioral science knowledge and techniques relevant to the understanding of physical health and illness and the application of this knowledge and these techniques to prevention, diagnosis, treatment, and rehabilitation. Psychosis, neurosis, and substance abuse are included only insofar as they contribute to physical disorders as an end point. (p. 249)

THE CONSTITUTION OF HEALTH PSYCHOLOGY AS A SUBDISCIPLINE

As Rodin and Stone (1987) note, psychologists had been very active in the health system long before a field was labeled health psychology. However, except for some allusions to health by some "fathers of psychology," such as Wilhelm Wundt, William James (1922), or Stanley Hall (1904) (see Taylor, 1986/2017), the first semi-official action of organized psychology regarding the health system, specifically by the APA, was a roundtable at the annual meeting of the association in December 1911 to evaluate how psychology could contribute to education and medical practice. After that, the APA created a commission to study the situation and existing attitudes regarding the teaching of psychology in medical schools. Authors as relevant as Watson (1912) expressed the importance of psychological training for medical students to understand that their object of study was the whole person and not simply an organ or injury (Ballester, 2013).

However, the commission also verified that less than one-third of medical schools were providing this psychological training, and less than 10% had psychologists teaching medical students. The commission noted that there were major deficiencies in the understanding of the nature and psychology potential in the field of health, and it recommended that students receive both training in health psychology and traditional medical training (Rodin & Stone, 1987). In 1950, the University of Pittsburgh sponsored eight lectures on the relationship between psychology and medicine. The speakers described the end of a neglected period and an emerging collaboration between health professions and medical educators. Studies conducted after 1950 documented a sustained growth in the number of psychologists teaching in medical schools (Buck, 1961; Matarazzo, 1955; Mensch, 1953).

According to Rodin and Stone (1987), despite the fact that the incorporation of psychological competencies in medical practice through student instruction constituted the first focus of organized psychology, the entry of professional psychologists in the health care system has developed more quickly.

In relation to research, clinical psychology has long dealt with physical symptoms, although in a minor way. The first works focused on the application of therapy for issues that presented both physical and psychological symptoms (Olbrisch, 1977). In the 1930s, two articles were published about the "overusers" of health services. Throughout the 1940s and 1950s, strategies to improve some physical problems that may be influenced by vital stressors—the "psychosomatic illnesses"—were studied. The first studies on the psychological impact on patients undergoing surgery were published in the late 1950s. Olbrisch (1977) found that from the mid-1950s to 1970, only approximately three studies were published per year.

Rodin and Stone (1987) reviewed Psychological Abstracts published in the 1950s and 1960s. They found that in 1950, 136 articles were published covering topics related to health psychology. Most of them addressed pain, the effects of stress, and the psychological and behavioral determinants of sexual health. The total number of articles increased to 257 in 1960, with fewer articles on the subject of pain and more on health attitudes and behaviors, as well as a return to interest in the effects of psychological processes on physical health. All these studies were the starting point for the significant increase in the number of studies carried out in the 1970s and 1980s, when important institutional changes that determined the future of health psychology occurred (Ballester, 1997).

Specifically in June 1969, William Schofield published an article in *The American Psychologist* that triggered a period of rapid development in health psychology. He found that only 19% of the approximately 4,700 articles published between 1966 and 1967 dealt with topics that were not traditionally included in the mental health field. The most important consequence of Schofield's article was the appointment by the APA in 1973 of a working group led by Schofield on health research called the Task Force on Health Research. The task force carried out an exhaustive search among the Psychological Abstracts published from 1966 to 1973, focused on articles that did not fit within the mental health topics. The task force's conclusion was that psychologists had not perceived the potential of their work in producing improvements in health maintenance, the prevention of disease, and the provision of health care (APA, 1976). The task force developed a list of psychologists interested in health research, and they were invited to a conference at which Schofield's proposal of organizing as a section under the auspices of the Division of Psychologists in the Public Service, Division 18 of the APA, was discussed. The term Section on Health Research was chosen, and Schofield was its first elected president (Schofield, 1979). Soon thereafter, these psychologists thought that the development of the discipline would be greater if the status as an independent division within the APA was achieved. At the same time, another group of professionals created the Medical Psychologists Network, led by David Clayman, in order to bring together the increasing number of clinical psychologists working in medical institutions.

In the summer of 1978, members of the Health Research Section of the Medical Psychologists Network collected signatures to request that the APA classify it as a division. By the time the APA meeting was held in Toronto, they had collected more than 400 signatures, enough to approve the constitution of a new division, number 38, of the APA under the name Division of Health Psychology. At its first constitutional meeting, Joseph Matarazzo was elected president, and Clayman was elected secretary and treasurer (Taylor, 1986/2017). Matarazzo (1980) proposed the first definition of the new discipline—a definition that was widely agreed upon and according to which

> health psychology is the aggregate of the specific educational, scientific, and professional contributions of the discipline of psychology to the promotion and maintenance of health, the prevention and treatment of illness, the identification of etiologic and diagnostic correlates of health, illness, and related dysfunction. (p. 815)

To this definition, Matarazzo (1982) added soon after, about the functions of health psychology, "and to the analysis and improvement of the health care system and health policy formation" (p. 4).

One year after it was created, the division decided to publish a journal as a dissemination channel. In August 1980, Stone was appointed editor, and in January 1982, the first issue of *Health Psychology* was published. Finally, in May 1983, the Arden House Conference was held in order to analyze aspects related to the ideal training of health psychologists.

HEALTH PSYCHOLOGY, CLINICAL PSYCHOLOGY, AND CLINICAL HEALTH PSYCHOLOGY

Health psychology brings together the contributions of the different areas of psychology to the field of health: basic psychology, developmental and educational psychology, psychobiology, social psychology, clinical psychology, etc. All of them have made and continue to provide important contributions to the field of health (Morrison & Bennett, 2016). However, with regard to the establishment of the health psychology identity and its connections to other areas of psychology, a conflict with clinical psychology arose during its beginnings.

The first milestones that marked the beginnings of clinical psychology are not discussed in-depth here. Undoubtedly, the experimental studies performed in Germany by Wundt (1879) or in Russia by Bechterev (1886) (cited in Bernstein & Nietzel, 1980; Vander Weg & Suls, 2014) marked its beginnings as a scientific and experimental discipline. The first clinical psychologist is considered to be L. Witmer (1896) (cited in Bernstein & Nietzel, 1980), an American psychologist who focused on childhood disorders related to school performance. After that, the focus was on the evaluation of adults and the adoption of the psychodynamic approach (Brannon et al., 2018). The evolution and transformation of clinical psychology were driven especially by the social needs resulting from the two world wars, especially World War II (Lubek et al., 2018), which paved the way for the incorporation in university programs of the clinical psychology specialization (Friedman & Adler, 2014). Following the crisis of the psychodynamic model that dominated clinical psychology and criticisms in the 1950s and 1960s, new therapeutic approaches such as client-centered therapy (Rogers, 1951) and community psychology (Bennett et al., 1966) were developed. During this time of dissatisfaction, in which effective treatment techniques were demanded, behavior therapy emerged (Eysenck, 1964; Wolpe, 1958). By the 1970s, the fact that doctors and psychologists already had sufficient therapeutic resources to deal with most diseases (mental and physical) with some efficacy led to the development of behavioral medicine, under the assumption that clinical psychology could thus open up a new field of action, expanding it to the prevention and treatment of all disorders (Gentry, 1984).

At this point, what is the link between clinical psychology and clinical health psychology? Three decades ago, authors such as Sweet et al. (1991) preferred not to spend too much time making semantic distinctions between the different terms, simply referring to the activities of clinical psychologists in medical institutions. A similar dynamic is followed by some of the most prestigious manuals, including that by Hunter et al. (2014), whose title says nothing about health psychology: *Handbook of Clinical Psychology in Medical Settings*. In Spain, in the monograph edited by Pelechano (1996), some authors questioned the meaning of and need for a new discipline, health psychology, which would overlap in its content and interests with clinical psychology.

In their definition of health psychology, numerous authors (Brannon et al., 2018; Feuerstein et al., 2013; Friedman & Adler, 2014; Pickren & Degni, 2012; Taylor, 1986/2017; Vander Weg & Suls, 2014) include clinical psychology as one of the areas from which contributions are made to this discipline. According to Millon (1982), compared to the names medical psychology, behavioral medicine, and behavioral health, the name health psychology is the most appropriate because it gives a clear idea of the identity of the discipline and uses the term "health" rather than "illness" or "medicine." However, he considered that in health psychology, there is increased diversity in terms of professionals' training, orientations, and interests. Some, such as Stone, come from an orientation closer to social psychology and systems theory; others, such as Weiner, come from an orientation closer to psychophysiology; and others have an orientation closer to the psychology of learning, including Melamed and Siegel. Among the relationships between health psychology and other areas, Millon found the one with clinical psychology most interesting. According to Millon, it can be argued that these two significant areas of applied psychology are one and the same. Clinical psychology deviated in its evolution by following a dualistic mind–body model and limiting itself to people with "mental" problems. Health psychology emerged as an antidote to these deficiencies. According to Millon, clinical psychology differs from other applied areas by the fact that it is mainly oriented to help patients with problems. If the new content field of health psychology overlaps with the traditional interest of clinical psychology, a subspecialty of psychology will have been built that is applied (clinical) as well as conceptual (health). Millon (1982) calls this the "clinical health psychology" that would attend to both physical and mental problems, and he defines as

> the application of knowledge and methods from all substantive fields of psychology to the promotion and maintenance of mental and physical health of the individual and to the prevention, assessment, and treatment of all forms of mental and physical disorder in which psychological influences either contribute to or can be used to relieve an individual's distress or dysfunction. (p. 9)

In addition, authors such as Matarazzo and Carmody (1983) affirm that despite the fact that clinical psychology is a good platform to join the field of health, it is necessary to recognize that a large part of what health psychology is today derives from the contributions of experimental psychologists such as Miller and Skinner; psychophysiologists such as Lindsley and Lacey; social psychologists such as Schachter, Rodin, Singer, Leventhal, and Evans; and representatives from other areas of psychology.

In particular, for Belar and Deardorff (2009), the term clinical health psychology coined by Millon (1982) correctly includes the working area (health) and an emphasis on applied practice (clinical).

The perspective of Sherr (1996) is also interesting. In an editorial in the first issue of the journal *Psychology, Health & Medicine*, she clarifies the content of health psychology through a double-entry table: (a) problems that may be fundamentally psychological or medical and (b) the attention or care given to those problems that may be psychological or medical. Four areas emerge from this interaction: (a) the psychological treatment of psychological problems, traditionally occupied by clinical psychology; (b) the medical treatment of medical problems, which is the object of medicine; (c) the medical treatment of psychological problems, which psychiatry deals with; and (d) the psychological treatment of medical problems, which constitutes the field of health psychology.

We are in full agreement with the ideas of Rodin and Stone (1987), which include a very specific proposal complementing that of Millon (1982). Despite the fact that at a theoretical level, the idea of not distinguishing between mental and physical health is emphasized, psychologists and psychiatrists have restricted their practices, from their beginning until now, to psychopathological problems and serious behavioral disorders. At the same time, health psychology from the beginning focused mainly on health and physical illness, probably to take a stance and distance itself from the subdiscipline of clinical psychology. For Rodin and Stone (1987), from a theoretical standpoint, it is most logical to divide health psychology, as a branch of psychology related to or concerned with health, into clinical and nonclinical branches. Thus, there would be a clinical health psychology dealing with the applied aspect, both with the health promotion and the psychological treatment of any type of disorder, without distinctions that favor or maintain the mind–body dichotomy. In addition, a nonclinical health psychology would collect all the basic research on the psychological factors associated with health and disease from the different areas of psychology, such as psychobiology, basic psychology, developmental psychology, and educational psychology.

THE FUTURE OF HEALTH PSYCHOLOGY

Clinical health psychology and health psychology in general are very recent subdisciplines, so it is difficult to analyze their past with a perspective that only time provides. However, we can draw a few lines of what its future could be.

As Morrison and Bennett (2016) note, given the current importance of behavioral factors in health, ranging from primary to tertiary prevention and from health habits to adherence to treatments, it is necessary to reinforce the presence of the clinical health psychologist in the health system. Moreover, Burgess et al. (2020) call attention to schools, workplaces, and social services. Nevertheless, we must demonstrate to other health professionals and politicians the importance of our skills compared to other health professionals without the same skills. In addition, we must demonstrate that we are not optional professionals who will make the system more expensive but, rather, essential professionals who will ultimately reduce system costs and improve the quality of life of the population. For this purpose, it is essential that our interventions be supported by solid theories, based on evidence (Feuerstein et al., 2013), and that we train professionals with the appropriate skills to meet the needs of the health system.

Sarafino and Smith (2016) indicate that in addition to increasing efforts to prevent disease, future goals for health psychology should focus on continuing to improve techniques to help patients cope with disease and medical procedures, demonstrate their efficacy and efficiency (Wilson et al., 2019), demonstrate their profitability in the cost–benefit binomial (Shaffer et al., 2021), and increase the acceptance of psychologists in medical institutions. Gurung (2018), in particular, emphasizes the importance of paying more attention to the sociocultural aspects that influence people's health and illness behavior and, therefore, require adjustments to our interventions (Revenson & Gurung, 2018). The same is also the case for the developmental aspects, which would guide us to adjust our programs to the stages in the life span of recipients. Finally, Gurung insists that we utilize the opportunities that information and communication technologies offer us to provide health services that can reach the entire population, an aspect also mentioned by Hunter et al. (2014) and Wentink et al. (2018).

Other authors highlight the need for further analysis of the psychological influences on diseases in specific segments of the population based on age, gender (Arrospide et al., 2019; Homan, 2019), sexual orientation (Bostwick & Dotge, 2019; Norris et al., 2019), or sociocultural characteristics, because these may reveal specific aspects of interest (Reynaga-Abiko & Schiffner, 2014) or facilitate an unequal access to health. For this reason, clinical health psychologists must act from a perspective of social justice (Burnes & Christensen, 2020) and human rights (Patel, 2019).

For Brannon et al. (2018), just as Sarafino and Smith (2016) emphasized, the acceptance of psychologists in health centers by other health professionals constitutes the major challenge. They believe that the growth of opportunities for psychologists will depend on whether doctors, administrators, and other members of the hospital consider that psychologists are playing an important role in the care of patients. They also affirm that health psychology has other purposes, including increasing the period of healthier life by promoting the health in all segments of the population (Fleming & Baldwin, 2020), reducing inequalities in health, increasing access to preventive services, preparing interventions for a population in which the elderly will increasingly represent a greater percentage, and contributing to the control of health spending; Taylor (1986/2017) is in agreement.

In line with this last aspect and the need to reach a large percentage of the population, considering that many of emotional problems and coping strategies are common to numerous health conditions (e.g., in chronic diseases), the applications of the Unified Protocol for Transdiagnostic Treatment are very promising. This protocol also presents great versatility that allows for adjusting and personalizing the interventions depending on the medical situation of the patient.

CONCLUSION

It seems clear that the spirit that motivated and enveloped the origin and birth of health psychology has become widespread and naturalized. Whereas in the past it was necessary to demonstrate that a new subdiscipline within psychology was needed to deal with health promotion and to help people suffering from medical conditions, today the necessity of both the field of clinical health psychology and the professionals who work in it is rarely questioned. Whereas in the past it was necessary to demonstrate that mind and body were not two separate entities, there is currently an enormous amount of scientific evidence demonstrating their interaction. Whereas in the past it was necessary to convince the medical world and the general society that stress and many other psychological factors influence health, nowadays it is difficult to find someone who doubts this. Whereas in the past it was necessary to demonstrate that psychology had a whole arsenal of evidence-based interventions capable of improving the quality of life of the population, currently it is difficult to deny this reality, and trust in psychological treatments has increased. Increasingly more patients are demanding psychologists on the staff of health teams, and increasingly more doctors and nurses feel comfortable working with them and help vindicate the need for professionals who deal with the psychological aspects that accompany all diseases. Clinical health psychology has advanced in the only possible and dignified way, forgetting about sterile debates and concentrating on working and accumulating evidence of its strength, potential, and future. In just 40 years, health psychology has provided the field of psychology enormous social recognition, prestige, and a huge number of new fronts on which to act. Nevertheless, what we have achieved is nothing compared to the full potential that lies ahead for clinical health psychology.

REFERENCES

American Psychological Association Task Force on Health Research. (1976). Contributions of psychology to health research: Patterns, problems, and potentials. *The American Psychologist*, *31*, 263–274.

Arrospide, A., Machón, M., Ramos-Goñi, J. M., Ibarrondo, O., & Mar, J. (2019). Inequalities in health-related quality of life according to age, gender, educational level, social class, body mass index and chronic diseases using the Spanish value set for Euroquol 5D-5L questionnaire. *Health and Quality of Life Outcomes*, *17*(1), Article 69. https://doi.org/10.1186/s12955-019-1134-9

Ballester, R. (1996). Emociones y Psicología de la Salud. In F. Palmero & V. Codina (Eds.), *Trastornos Cardiovasculares: Influencia de los procesos emocionales* (pp. 27–63). Promolibro.

Ballester, R. (1997). *Introducción a la Psicología de la Salud: Aspectos conceptuales*. Promolibro.

Ballester, R. (2013). Psicología Clínica de la salud: Historia de la relación mente-cuerpo y nacimiento de una disciplina. In R. Ballester & M. D. Gil (Eds.), *Psicología Clínica de la Salud* (pp. 9–23). Pearson.

Barondess, J. (1979). Disease and illness: A crucial distinction. *American Journal of Medicine*, *66*, 375–376.

Belar, C. D., & Deardorff, W. W. (2009). *Clinical health psychology in medical settings*. American Psychological Association.

Bennett, C. C., Anderson, L. S., Hassol, L., Klein, D., & Rosenblum, G. (1966). Community psychology: A report of the Boston Conference on the Education of Psychologists for Community Mental Health. Boston University and South Shore Mental Health Center.

Bernstein, D. A., & Nietzel, M. T. (1980). *Introduction to clinical psychology*. McGraw Hill.

Bertalanffy, L. von. (1968). *General systems theory*. Braziller.

Birk, L. (1973). *Biofeedback: Behavioral medicine*. Grune & Stratton.

Bishop, G. D. (1994). *Health psychology: Integrating mind and body*. Allyn & Bacon.

Bostwick, W. B., & Dodge, B. (2019). Introduction to the special section on bisexual health: Can you see us now? *Archives of Sexual Behavior*, *48*(1), 79–87. https://doi.org/10.1007/s10508-018-1370-9

Brannon, L., Feist, J., & Updegraff, J. A. (2018). *Health psychology: An introduction to behavior and health*. Cengage.

Buck, R. L. (1961). Behavioral scientists in schools of medicine. *Journal of Health and Human Behavior*, *2*, 59–64.

Burgess, M. G., Brough, P., Biggs, A., & Hawkes, A. J. (2020). Why interventions fail: A systematic review of occupational health psychology interventions. *International Journal of Stress Management*, *27*(2), 195–207. https://doi.org/10.1037/str0000144

Burnes, T. R., & Christensen, N. P. (2020). Still wanting change, still working for justice: An introduction to the special issue on social justice training in health service psychology. *Training and Education in Professional Psychology*, *14*(2), 87–91. http://dx.doi.org/10.1037/tep0000323

Cannon, W. B. (1935). Stresses and strains of homeostasis. *American Journal of Medical Sciences*, *189*, 1–14.

Cott, A. (1986a). The disease–illness distinction: A model for effective and practical integration of behavioral and medical sciences. In S. McHugh & T. M Vallis (Eds.), *Illness behavior: A multidisciplinary model* (pp. 71–99). Plenum.

Cott, A. (1986b). Practical applications of the disease–illness distinction model: New concepts in health care delivery through the optimal integration of medical and behavioral sciences. *Canadian Journal of Public Health*, *77*, 51–58.

Donker, F. J. (1991). Medicina conductal y psicología de la salud. In G. Buela-Casal & V. E. Caballo (Eds.), *Manual de Psicología Clínica Aplicada* (pp. 3–13). Siglo XXI.

Eisenberg, L. (1980). What makes persons "patients" and patients "well"? *American Journal of Medicine*, *69*, 277–286.

Engel, G. L. (1977). The need for a new medical model: A challenge for biomedicine. *Science, 196*, 129–136.

Engel, G. L. (1980). The clinical application of the bio-psychosocial model. *American Journal of Psychiatry, 137*, 535–544.

Eysenck, H. J. (1964). *Experiments in behavior therapy*. Macmillan.

Fabrega, H. (1973). Toward a model of illness behavior. *Medical Care, 11*, 470–484.

Feuerstein, M., Labbe, E., & Kuczmierczyk, A. R. (2013). *Health psychology: A psychobiological perspective*. Plenum.

Fleming, M. L., & Baldwin, L. (2020). *Health promotion in the 21st century: New approaches to achieving health for all*. Routledge.

Friedman, H. S., & Adler, N. E. (2014). The intellectual roots of health psychology. In H. S. Friedman (Ed.), *The Oxford handbook of health psychology* (pp. 3–13). Oxford University Press.

Gentry, W. D. (1984). Behavioral medicine: A new research paradigm. In W. D. Gentry (Ed.), *Handbook of behavioral medicine* (pp. 1–12). Guilford.

Gurung, R. A. (2018). *Health psychology: Well-being in a diverse world*. SAGE.

Hall, C. S. (1904). *Health, growth and heredity*. Teachers' College Press.

Homan, P. (2019). Structural sexism and health in the United States: A new perspective on health inequality and the gender system. *American Sociological Review, 84*(3), 486–516. https://doi.org/10.1177/0003122419848723

Hunter, C. M., Hunter, C. L., & Kessler, R. K. (2014). *Handbook of clinical psychology in medical settings*. Springer.

Ibáñez, E., & Belloch, A. (1989). *Psicología y medicina*. Promolibro.

James, W. (1922). *On vital reserves: The energies of men; the gospel of relaxation*. Holt.

Kleinman, A., Eisenberg, L., & Good, B. (1978). Culture, illness and care: Lessons from anthropologic and cross-cultural research. *Annals of Medicine, 88*, 251–258.

Lubek, I., Ghabrial, M., Ennis, N., Crann, S., Jenkins, A., Green, M., Badali, J., Salmon, W., Moodley, J., Sulima, E., Yen, J., O'Doherty, K., & Barata, P. (2018). Notes on the development of health psychology and behavioral medicine in the United States. *Journal of Health Psychology, 23*(3), 492–505. https://doi.org/10.1177/1359105318755156

Matarazzo, J. D. (1955). The role of the psychologists in medical education and practice. *Human Organization, 14*, 9–14.

Matarazzo, J. D. (1980). Behavioral health and behavioral medicine: Frontiers for a new health psychology. *The American Psychologist, 35*, 807–817.

Matarazzo, J. D. (1982). Behavioral health's challenge to academic scientific and professional psychology. *The American Psychologist, 37*, 1–14.

Matarazzo, J. D. (1984). Behavior immunogens and pathogens in health and illness. In B. L. Hammonds & C. J. Scheirer (Eds.), *Psychology and health: The masters lecture series* (Vol. 3, pp. 9–43). American Psychological Association.

Matarazzo, J. D., & Carmody, T. P. (1983). Health psychology. In M. Hersen, A. E. Kazdin & A. S. Bellack (Eds.), *The clinical psychology handbook* (pp. 657–682). New York: Pergamon.

McHugh, S., & Vallis, T. M. (1986). Illness behaviour: Operationalization of the biopsychosocial model. In S. McHugh & T. M. Vallis (Eds.), *Illness behavior: A multidisciplinary model* (pp. 1–31). Plenum.

Mechanic, D. (1978). *Medical sociology*. Free Press. (Original work published 1968)
Mechanic, D. (1980). The experience and reporting of common physical complaints. *Journal of Health and Social Behavior, 21*, 146–155.
Mensch, I. N. (1953). Psychology in medical education. *The American Psychologist, 8*, 83–85.
Millon, T. (1982). On the nature of clinical health psychology. In T. Millon, C. Green, & R. Meagher (Eds.), *Handbook of clinical health psychology* (pp. 1–27) Plenum.
Morrison, V., & Bennett, P. (2016). Futures. In V. Morrison & P. Bennett (Eds.), *Introduction to health psychology* (pp. 520–642). Pearson.
Norris, A. L., Nelson, K. M., & Carey, M. P. (2019). HIV testing intentions and behaviors among 14–17-year-old sexual minority males. *AIDS Care, 31*(12), 1580–1584. https://doi.org/10.1080/09540121.2019.1612008
Olbrisch, M. E. (1977). Psychotherapeutic interventions in physical health: Effectiveness and economic efficiency. *The American Psychologist, 32*, 761–777.
Osmond, H., & Siegler, M. (1979). The sick role and aesculapian authority. *Alabama Journal of Medical Sciences, 17*(2), 197–201.
Pachuta, D. M. (1989). Chinese medicine: The law of five elements. In A. A. Sheikh & K. S. Sheikh (Eds.), *Eastern and Western approaches to healing: Ancient wisdom and modern knowledge* (pp. 64–90). Wiley.
Patel, N. (2019). Human rights-based approach to applied psychology. *European Psychologist, 24*(2), 113–124.
Pelechano, V. (1996). Psicología Clínica, Psicología de la Salud y la búsqueda del Santo Grial. In V. Pelechano (Ed.), *Psicología Clínica y/o Psicología de la Salud* (pp. 163–203). Promolibro.
Pickren, W. E., & Degni, S. (2012). A history of the development of health psychology. In H. S. Friedman (Ed.), *The Oxford handbook of health psychology* (pp. 15–40). Oxford University Press.
Revenson, T. A., & Gurung, R. A. (2018). *Health psychology*. Routledge.
Reynaga-Abiko, G., & Schiffner, T. (2014). Competency for diverse populations. In C. M. Hunter, C. L. Hunter, & R. Kessler (Eds.), *Handbook of clinical psychology in medical settings: Evidence-based assessment and intervention* (pp. 219–238). Springer.
Rodin, J., & Stone, G. C. (1987). Historical highlights in the emergence of the field. In G. C. Stone, S. M. Weiss, J. D. Matarazzo, N. E. Miller, J. Rodin, C. D. Belar, M. J. Follick, & J. E. Singer (Eds.), *Health psychology: A discipline and a profession* (pp. 15–26). University of Chicago Press.
Rogers, C. R. (1951). *Client-centered therapy*. Houghton Mifflin.
Sanderson, C. A. (2018). *Health psychology: Understanding the mind–body connection*. SAGE.
Sarafino, E. P., & Smith, T. W. (2016). *Health psychology: Bipsychosocial interactions*. Wiley.
Schofield, W. (1979). Clinical psychologists as health professionals. In G. C. Stone, N. E. Adlery, & F. Cohen (Eds.), *Health psychology: A handbook* (pp. 447–463). Jossey-Bass.
Schwartz, G. E., & Weiss, S. M. (1978a). Yale Conference on Behavioral Medicine: A proposed definition and statement of goals. *Journal of Behavioral Medicine, 1*, 3–12.
Schwartz, G. E., & Weiss, S. M. (1978b). Behavioral medicine revisited: An amended definition. *Journal of Behavioral Medicine*, 3, 249–251.

Shaffer, L. A., Robiner, W., Cash, L., Hong, B., Washburn, J. J., & Ward, W. (2021). Psychologists' leadership roles and leadership training needs in academic health centers. *Journal of Clinical Psychology in Medical Settings*, *28*, 252–261. https://doi.org/10.1007/s10880-020-09707-7

Sherr, L. (1996). Challenges for tomorrow. *Psychology, Health & Medicine*, *1*, 5–6.

Stone, G. C. (1979). Health and the health system: A historical overview and conceptual framework. In G. C. Stone, N. E. Adler, & F. Cohen (Eds.), *Health psychology: A handbook* (pp. 1–17. Jossey-Bass.

Suls, J. M., Davidson, K. W., & Kaplan, R. M. (2010). *Handbook of health psychology and behavioral medicine*. Guilford.

Sweet, J. J., Rozensky, R. H., & Tovian, S. M. (1991). Clinical psychology in medical settings: Past and present. In J. J. Sweet, R. H. Rozensky, & S. M. Tovian (Eds.), *Handbook of clinical psychology in medical settings* (pp. 3–9). Plenum.

Taylor, S. E. (2017). *Health psychology*. McGraw Hill. (Original work published 1986)

Vander Weg, M., & Suls, J. (2014). A history of clinical psychology in medical settings. In C. M. Hunter, C. L. Hunter, & R. Kessler (Eds.), *Handbook of clinical psychology in medical settings: Evidence-based assessment and intervention* (pp. 19–40). Springer.

Watson, J. B. (1912). Content of a course in psychology for medical students. *Journal of the American Medical Association*, *58*, 916–918.

Wentink, M. M., Prieto, E., de Kloet, A. J., Vliet Vlieland, T., & Meesters, J. (2018). The patient perspective on the use of information and communication technologies and e-health in rehabilitation. Disability and rehabilitation: *Assistive Technology*, *13*(7), 620–625. https://doi.org/10.1080/17483107.2017.1358302

Wilson, D. K., Christensen, A., Jacobsen, P. B., & Kaplan, R. M. (2019). Standards for economic analyses of interventions for the field of health psychology and behavioral medicine. *Health Psychology*, *38*(8), 669–671. https://doi.org/10.1037/hea0000770

Wolpe, J. (1958). *Psychotherapy by reciprocal inhibition*. Stanford University Press.

Zola, I. K. (1973). Pathways to the doctor: From person to patient. *Social Science and Medicine*, *7*, 677–689.

2

The Unified Protocol for Transdiagnostic Treatment of Emotional Disorders and Physical Health Comorbidity

An Introduction

TODD J. FARCHIONE, DANIELLA M. SPENCER-LAITT, SHANNON SAUER-ZAVALA, AND DAVID H. BARLOW ■

This chapter has three main purposes: (a) to introduce the functional model of emotional disorders, including the role of neuroticism; (b) to explain the relationship between this model of emotional disorders and physical health morbidities; and (c) to introduce the Unified Protocol for Transdiagnostic Treatment of Emotional Disorders (UP; Barlow et al., 2018) and set out the evidence for its use.

EMOTIONAL DISORDERS

For many years, commonalities between emotional disorders, including anxiety and depression, have been observed. Such commonalities are expressed in high rates of comorbidity and similar rates of treatment response, alongside shared neurobiological vulnerabilities. For example, a study of 1,127 patients found that 55% of patients with principal anxiety also met criteria for additional anxiety or depressive disorders at intake (Brown et al., 2001), a finding that was confirmed in a longitudinal study of 500 people over 15 years (Merikangas et al., 2003). Furthermore, treatment for one emotional disorder can, and often does,

Todd J. Farchione, Daniella M. Spencer-Laitt, Shannon Sauer-Zavala, and David H. Barlow, *The Unified Protocol for Transdiagnostic Treatment of Emotional Disorders and Physical Health Comorbidity* In: *Applications of the Unified Protocol in Health Conditions.* Edited by: Jorge Osma and Todd J. Farchione, Oxford University Press. © Oxford University Press 2023.
DOI: 10.1093/oso/9780197564295.003.0002

lead to symptoms improvement in other nontargeted conditions (e.g., Allen et al., 2010; Borkovec et al., 1995; Tsao et al., 2005), indicating that these treatments target common mechanisms. For example, one study found that overall comorbidity following treatment with cognitive–behavioral therapy for panic disorder reduced from 51% to 17% (Brown et al., 1995). Finally, neuroscientific research has revealed that emotional disorders are neurobiologically similar. For example, generalized anxiety disorder (GAD; Etkin et al., 2010; Paulesu et al., 2010), social anxiety disorder (Phan et al., 2006), specific phobias (Paquette et al., 2003; Straube et al., 2006), post-traumatic stress disorder (PTSD; Shin et al., 2005), and depression (Holmes et al., 2012) have all been associated with reduced higher cortical inhibition of amygdala overactivation.

These observed commonalities led to identification of key temperamental vulnerabilities underlying these conditions. Individuals with emotional disorders tend to have higher levels (Brown & Barlow, 2009) and frequency (Campbell-Sills et al., 2006) of negative affect. Indeed, neuroticism has been described as the tendency to experience intense and frequent negative emotions, along with the perception that the world is a threatening place that cannot be managed or controlled. This drives an aversion of and tendency to avoid stressful or challenging personally relevant events and outcomes, including the intense emotional experiences themselves. This aversion/avoidance can be considered an integral component of neuroticism (Barlow, 1988, 2002; Lilienfeld et al., 1993) and features prominently in a functional model of emotional disorders (Barlow et al., 2021).

Ultimately, the aversion/avoidance to emotions leads to more intense emotional experiences. For example, many individuals experience intrusive negative cognitions associated with negative emotions, but only some individuals find the thoughts intensely distressing and attempt to neutralize them through various strategies such as worrying and checking, consistent with obsessive–compulsive disorder (Rachman, 1978). Thus, Brown (2007) found that most of the temporal covariance among the features of anxiety and depression listed in the fifth edition of the *Diagnostic and Statistical Manual of Mental Disorders* (DSM-5; American Psychiatric Association [APA], 2013) could be explained by the dimensions of negative affect/neuroticism. That is, the expression of specific symptoms (i.e., somatic, cognitive, or interpersonal) in DSM-5-TR (APA, 2022) disorders is incidental and of secondary importance to the temperamental similarities between these conditions (Barlow et al., 2014). Although phenotypic expression of emotional disorders may be associated with specific learning experiences (Barlow, 2002), these disorders share a common psychopathological mechanism: neuroticism.

Neuroticism has been linked to a range of common mental health conditions (Clark et al., 1994; Khan et al., 2005; Krueger & Markon, 2011; Sher & Trull, 1994; Watson & Clark, 1994). In a meta-analysis using 33 population-based samples, Malouff and colleagues (2005) found large associations between neuroticism and mood disorders, anxiety disorders, somatoform disorders, schizophrenia, and eating disorders. Studies conducted after this meta-analysis also support this robust relationship between neuroticism and a range of common psychiatric diagnoses (e.g., Brown & Barlow, 2009; Chien et al., 2007; Khan et al., 2005; Merino et al., 2016; Weinstock & Whisman, 2006; Zinbarg et al., 2016). This trait has also been consistently linked to personality disorders (Clark et al., 1994; Clarkin et al., 1993; Costa & Widiger, 2002; Henry et al., 2001; Koenigsberg et al., 2001; Krueger & Markon, 2011; Larstone et al., 2002; Putnam & Silk, 2005; Samuel & Widiger, 2008; Saulsman & Page, 2004; Trull & Sher, 1994). For example, in a meta-analytic investigation, Saulsman and Page (2004) found moderate associations between this trait and borderline, avoidant, and dependent personality disorders. Neuroticism has also demonstrated relationships with drug and alcohol misuse (e.g., Kornør & Nordvik, 2007; Malouff et al., 2006, 2007; Rogers et al., 2019; Sher & Trull, 1994).

Neuroticism also significantly contributes to the co-occurrence of mental disorders. Indeed, the highest levels of this trait are observed in individuals with more than one form of psychopathology (Putnam & Silk, 2005). Specifically, in one study, neuroticism accounted for 20–45% of the comorbidity among emotional disorders (i.e., major depression, GAD, panic disorder, and phobias; Kessler et al., 2011), and others have demonstrated that a single higher order neuroticism factor accounts for the co-occurrence among these conditions (Brown, 2007; Griffith et al., 2010; Krueger, 1999). This has important public health implications because individuals with comorbid mental disorders are at an increased risk for experiencing more impairing symptoms and are more likely to seek costly mental health services (Kessler et al., 2005). Neuroticism, itself, is associated with greater use of both specific mental health services and primary care services for mental health problems, and this remains true even after controlling for the number of comorbid mental health disorders (Jylhä & Isometsä, 2006; ten Have et al., 2005). Higher levels of neuroticism predict a more chronic course of illness and a worse prognosis among those with emotional disorders (Clark et al., 1994; Kendler et al., 2006).

Finally, the economic burden associated with neuroticism is believed to outpace the combined cost attributed to common mental and physical disorders. Using data drawn from baseline (n = 7,076) and follow-up (n = 5,618) waves of the Netherlands Mental Health Survey and Incidence Study (Bijl et al., 1998), Cuijpers et al. (2010) determined that the economic burden of neuroticism itself is almost 2.5 times higher than for mood disorders (approximately $600 million per 1 million inhabitants) and surprisingly amounts to nearly two-thirds the expense of all somatic (physical) disorders. These results suggest that the effect of neuroticism on mental health care and population health far exceeds the cost of common mental disorders.

EMOTIONAL DISORDERS AND PHYSICAL HEALTH

There is notable comorbidity between physical illness and mental health concerns, with prevalence rates of mental disorders among individuals with chronic medical conditions reported at 36.6% (Daré et al., 2019). The specific prevalence of emotional disorders varies depending on medical diagnosis, but rates of emotional disorders are higher in individuals with physical health conditions compared to the general population. For example, in a study using data from more than 245,000 people from 60 countries, there was a 23% 1-year depression prevalence in individuals with one or two medical conditions compared to a 3.2% prevalence in the general population (Moussavi et al., 2017). Depression and anxiety disorders are associated with disrupted immune functioning (Maier & Watkins, 1998; Pace et al., 2006; Robles et al., 2005), abnormalities in cardiac functioning (Barger & Sydeman, 2005), and increased mortality among individuals with other risk factors for cardiac disease (Penninx et al., 2001; Robles et al., 2005). In addition, concurrent physical and mental disorders are associated with more physical symptoms, shorter lifetime, lower quality of life, and increased medical costs (Osma et al., 2021). Having both concerns is associated with lower psychological treatment adherence and treatment efficacy (Prince et al., 2007).

Therefore, mental disorders are strongly linked with both higher prevalence of medical conditions and high neuroticism (Currie & Wang, 2005; Robles et al., 2005; Sareen et al., 2005; Watkins et al., 2006). In addition, direct evidence relating neuroticism itself to physical health concerns is increasingly available. For example, researchers have demonstrated associations between neuroticism and a range of physical impairments, including cardiovascular disease (Suls & Bunde, 2005), atopic eczema (Buske-Kirschbaum et al., 2001), asthma (Huovinen et al., 2001), and irritable bowel syndrome (Spiller, 2007). Relationships between neuroticism and these conditions remain strong even when controlling for depression and other risk factors, such as social support (Bouhuys et al., 2004; Russo et al., 1997). The fact that neuroticism has been associated with both mental and physical disorders has been described as particularly important for public health (Lahey, 2009) because comorbidity among medical conditions and mental disorders has been linked to more complicated health problems, greater need for health services, and significantly poorer outcomes (Baune et al., 2007; McCaffery et al., 2006).

As with mental disorders, higher levels of neuroticism are associated with worse outcomes for medical conditions. For example, as levels of neuroticism increase, so does mortality from cardiovascular disease (Wilson et al., 2004, 2005); specifically, each increase of 1 *SD* in this trait was linked to a 10% greater risk of mortality, even when controlling for age, sex, socioeconomic status, smoking, alcohol consumption, physical activity, and initial health (Shipley et al., 2007). Similarly, among individuals with a cancer diagnosis, results from a 25-year longitudinal study revealed that patients with higher levels of neuroticism had a 130% greater death rate than those who were low in neuroticism (Nakaya et al., 2006). Neuroticism also predicts deterioration among patients with type 1 diabetes (Brickman et al., 1996). It is worth noting that individuals high in neuroticism are more likely to express unfounded medical complaints (Costa & McCrae, 1987), as well as to seek services following substantial worry (Goubert et al., 2004). Although these medical claims do not result in diagnoses, they still lead to patient suffering and costly health service use, highlighting the public health burden of this trait. Proposed mechanisms underscoring this risk include the trait's influence on health-related daily habits and medical practices, such as diet changes, exercise, and medication compliance (Suls & Bunde, 2005). Overall, neuroticism is linked to a greater risk of experiencing physical health problems, greater co-occurrence of physical and mental disorders, and a worse prognosis for those suffering.

THE EMOTIONAL DISORDERS FUNCTIONAL MODEL AND PHYSICAL ILLNESS

Although there is a large body of literature underscoring the relationship between neuroticism and the development of mental and physical health conditions (reviewed above), there is less elucidation on *how* this trait confers risk. The emotional disorders functional model was developed to articulate how neuroticism develops into anxiety, depressive, and related disorders (Barlow 1988, 1991, 2002). Specifically, individuals with a biological predisposition to experience negative emotions, as well as a psychological vulnerability emerging from developmentally early experiences expressed as a sense of unpredictability and uncontrollability over salient events (i.e., the neurotic temperament), come to view these affective experiences as aversive and engage in avoidant emotion regulation strategies (Barlow et al., 2014). Avoidant coping backfires, however, leading to more frequent and intense emotional experiences (Rassin, Muris, et al., 2000; Wegner et al., 1987) and symptoms (Abramowitz et al., 2001; Purdon, 1999). The specific provocation for negative emotions (e.g., uncertainty and a major decision) and coping strategy used (e.g., checking and reassurance seeking) may fall within the boundaries of discrete mental health conditions (e.g., GAD), yet aversive reactions to negative emotions are the transdiagnostic functional bridge that connects emotional experiences to disorder symptoms (i.e., avoidant coping).

The emotional disorders functional model also has implications for physical health conditions. Indeed, those higher in neuroticism are likely to be more distressed by an adverse health diagnosis (Kristoffersen et al., 2018; Menon et al., 2018); if that distress is met with an aversive reaction ("this is so uncomfortable," "I can't stand feeling this way"), individuals might be motivated to engage in coping that limits their contact with reminders of their illness (Livneh, 2009). Refusal to confront one's illness may affect the extent to which a patient engages in the health behaviors recommended by medical professionals to care for their condition. For example, patients with diabetes who report high levels of experiential avoidance are less likely to follow their doctor's recommendations (i.e., specialized diet plan, regular exercise, glucose monitoring, and daily medication) (Babler & Strickland, 2015; Hadlandsmyth et al., 2013). Similarly, individuals with chronic pain conditions who report high levels of neuroticism and aversive reactivity to emotions are more likely to describe their pain as severe (Kadimpati et al., 2015) and limit their mobility (Ramírez-Maestre et al., 2014), regardless of the objective severity of their injury. In addition, insofar as neuroticism itself is a risk factor for physical illnesses, targeting aversive reactions to a wide variety of negative emotions when they occur may reduce reliance on the avoidant emotion regulation strategies that, paradoxically, have been shown to lead to more frequent and intense emotional experiences (Rassin, Muris, et al., 2000; Wegner et al., 1987). When negative emotions become less frequent over time, and when these changes are sustained, this may constitute decreases in neuroticism (for a description of what constitutes trait change, see Magidson et al., 2014). Indeed, decreases in this trait may have far-reaching implications for both mental and physical illness.

TRANSDIAGNOSTIC TREATMENT

The term *emotional disorder*, therefore, is defined by commonalities in the mechanisms of emotion regulation and interpretation explained by the functional model described above. This functional model formed the rationale for the development of a unified, transdiagnostic approach to treatment named the Unified Protocol for Transdiagnostic Treatment of Emotional Disorders (UP; Barlow et al., 2016). Unlike most approaches that focus on symptoms of DSM-defined disorders, the UP addresses the temperamental constructs common to all emotional disorders, specifically emotion dysregulation associated with neuroticism and passive or ineffective coping styles such as emotion-motivated avoidant coping. By focusing on these common mechanisms, the UP is uniquely appropriate for treating comorbidity, reduces the training burden for mental health professionals, and is flexible and adaptable to different formats (e.g., group or online adaptations in addition to individual treatment) (Reinholt et al., 2017). As such, it is a scalable solution to a seemingly intractable problem of increasing access to empirically supported psychological treatments.

The UP aims to help patients understand and recognize their emotions and respond to them in more effective ways. It is typically conducted over the course of 12–16 sessions and comprises eight modules. It begins with two initial modules that target motivation, goal setting, and psychoeducation about the function of emotions; the latter serves to counter beliefs about the dangerousness of emotions. Then, the core five modules address mindful emotion awareness; cognitive flexibility to enhance abilities to generate alternatives to negative attributions about emotions expressed as aversive reactivity; modifying emotion-driven behaviors designed to avoid aversive emotional experiences; and exposure to intense emotional experiences, including through interoceptive exposure, which facilitates inhibitory learning and extinguishes distress associated with having intense emotions. The eighth and final module consists of relapse prevention. We briefly explain the content of each module below. The primary components of each module are summarized in Table 2.1.

Table 2.1 MODULES INCLUDED IN THE UNIFIED PROTOCOL

Module	Goals
1: Getting Started	Introduce the UP and its approach to managing emotions Establish goals for treatment Establish motivation to engage with treatment
2: Understanding Your Emotions	Understand the function of various emotions Understand the components of emotional experiences Learn to recognize and track emotional experiences
3: Mindful Emotion Awareness	Develop present-focused awareness of emotional experiences Learn to respond to emotions without judgment
4: Flexible Thinking	Understand the connections between thoughts and emotions Notice "automatic" thinking habits Develop more flexible ways of thinking
5: Emotional Behaviors	Identify and change unhelpful behaviors related to emotions Understand the role of avoidance in maintaining emotional behaviors
6: Facing Physical Sensations	Understand the role of physical sensations in emotional experiences Become more comfortable with the physical component of emotions Address negative thoughts associated with physical sensations Learn to face, rather than avoid, physical sensations associated with emotions
7: Emotion Exposures	Become more comfortable with emotions Practice flexible thinking Challenge automatic patterns of avoidance or other unhelpful behaviors
8: Relapse Prevention	Review skills learned throughout treatment Develop a plan for continued practice

Module 1: Goals and Motivation

The UP starts by drawing on motivational interviewing principles and techniques (Miller & Rollnick, 2013) to increase patients' motivation and readiness for change. Two exercises, a decisional balance exercise and a treatment goal-setting exercise, are used for this purpose. The decisional balance exercise requires patients to identify advantages and disadvantages of changing versus staying the same. In the goal-setting exercise, patients work with their therapist to identify areas they would most like to change and identify concrete goals for treatment. Potential obstacles to change are explored during these exercises. This module helps prepare patients for treatment but can be revisited at any time during treatment, as needed, to enhance treatment engagement.

Module 2: Understanding Emotions

Module 2 provides psychoeducation about the nature and function of emotions and was designed to help patients gain a greater awareness of their emotions and patterns of emotional responding. The therapist focuses on explaining the nature and adaptive function of emotions. As part of this discussion, the therapist introduces a three-component model that conceptualizes emotion as a dynamic interaction of cognitive, behavioral, and physiological aspects. Module 2 also introduces a framework for understanding emotional experiences, referred to by the acronym ARC. The ARC describes a sequence of events around emotions and includes the following components: *a*ntecedents, *r*esponse, and *c*onsequences. *Antecedents* are triggers (e.g., situations or events) of an emotional experience. These events trigger an emotional *response*, which corresponds to all cognitions, behaviors, and somatic sensations associated with the three-component model. Finally, the therapist works with their patient to understand the short- and long-term *consequences* of an emotional response. The therapist typically observes that the consequence of avoiding negative emotions serves to reduce negative emotions in the short term but ultimately perpetuates anxiety and distress because the patient does not learn that emotions can be tolerated.

Module 3: Mindful Emotion Awareness

The goal of Module 3 is for patients to develop a more present-focused, nonjudgmental view of their emotions. Patients often experience their emotions as confusing, overwhelming, and difficult to control. This module helps patients more clearly recognize the interaction that occurs between thoughts, feelings, and behaviors during an emotional experience. By utilizing mindfulness exercises, patients are taught to distinguish between their initial emotional reaction to a triggering event and subsequent reactions to their emotions, which tend to be negative and not present-focused. For instance, feeling deep sadness over a loss can lead to additional feelings of anxiety if a person experiences their sadness as intolerable (i.e., "I can't take it") or worry that their feelings will become more intense or never end. In this case, mindful emotion awareness would be used to help this individual connect with their feelings of sadness, as they occur, to gain a better understanding of the loss and how to best move forward.

Module 4: Cognitive Flexibility

Module 4 guides patients to think more flexibly. This module uses principles originated by Beck (1976) and modified in our setting throughout the decades (e.g., Craske & Barlow, 2022). Primarily, the therapist assists patients to recognize their (often anxious and negative) appraisals of certain situations and how these thoughts influence emotional experiences. This includes both automatic appraisals that happen quickly, while in the moment, and more generalizable (or core) cognitions that patients may have about themselves, such as "I am a failure" or "Bad things always happen to me," that can shape many emotional responses. The therapist identifies two thinking traps common to all emotional disorders: probability estimation (i.e., overestimating that a negative outcome is likely to occur) and catastrophizing (i.e., thinking that a potential outcome will be catastrophic). Patients are taught to identify these cognitive biases and encouraged to use standard cognitive reappraisal strategies to think more flexibly about external situations and internal events, including thoughts, memories, and emotions.

Module 5: Countering Emotional Behaviors

Module 5 targets emotion avoidance behaviors, or behaviors employed by patients in an attempt to avoid or suppress intense emotions. The therapist introduces three main types of emotion avoidance: behavioral avoidance, cognitive avoidance, and using safety signals. Behavioral avoidance includes directly avoiding certain places, people, or situations that produce strong emotions as well as behaviors that limit or reduce the intensity of emotion when a situation is unable to avoided. These more subtle avoidance behaviors might include behaviors such as not maintaining eye contact during a conversation to feel less awkward, texting or using email instead of meeting in person to avoid confrontation, or (in terms of positive emotion) not getting too excited about something to avoid being let down if things do not go as planned. A functional analysis can be used to help determine which behaviors serve to suppress or eliminate emotional experiences or are functionally related in some way. The second type of avoidance discussed in this module is cognitive avoidance, which includes mental activities such as distraction, mental rituals, pushing away distressing thoughts or memories, and reviewing or replaying prior events. We have also conceptualized repetitive negative thinking, including worry and rumination, as an example of emotion-motivated avoidant coping (Barlow et al., 2021; Sauer-Zavala & Barlow, 2021). For example, an anxious individual may worry excessively about future events (instead of focusing on the present) in a misguided effort to control something that is uncontrollable or predict an uncertain outcome. Finally, in this module, the therapist works with their patients to identify objects, and sometimes friends or other people, that make them feel more comfortable and secure or reduce arousal in potentially emotional situations. In the UP, these are referred to as safety signals and can take on many forms, including medication bottles; "lucky" charms; or even another person who can provide care, a sense of safety, or "moral support."

This module also focuses on identifying and altering *emotion-driven behaviors* (EDBs). EDBs is a term the UP coined to describe behavioral responses to emotions. In the emotion science literature, these responses were termed action tendencies (Barlow, 1988) and describe universal, evolutionary-favored behaviors motivated or driven by the emotion itself. EDBs can be adaptive and maladaptive. For instance, an adaptive EDB could be an individual standing up for themself in a situation in which they were being threatened, hurt, or directly wronged in some way. However, an EDB in this situation would be less adaptive if no clear physical or emotional harm had come to the person or they were grossly misreading the other person's intentions, but the emotion and behavior occurred anyway. In this module, patients learn to address emotional avoidance and EDBs by challenging patterns of avoidance and by developing and engaging in behaviors that are more appropriate than and different from maladaptive EDBs.

Module 6: Understanding and Confronting Physical Sensations

Module 6 aims to increase patients' tolerance of physical sensations that accompany emotional experiences and very frequently trigger these emotional experiences. The patient engages in interoceptive exposure exercises to elicit somatic sensations typically experienced during times of emotional distress; for example, hyperventilating, spinning, or running in place are used to provoke physical sensations in the respiratory, vestibular, and cardiovascular systems, respectively. The patient completes these exercises repeatedly, both in-session and for homework, with associated distress decreasing with repeated exposure and as the patient disconfirms the expectation that somatic sensations are dangerous or intolerable.

Module 7: Emotion Exposures

Emotion exposures, the final core module, draws on the concepts covered throughout the treatment. With the therapist, the patient develops in-session and out-of-session activities designed to expose them to emotion experiences uniquely based on the patient's presenting symptoms and patterns of avoidance. Often, these activities involve exposure to actual situations that the patient avoids, but they can also include internal somatic sensations, thoughts, and memories. Examples of emotion exposures include giving a public speech to elicit anxiety related to social evaluation concerns, riding an elevator to elicit fear/panic, imagining a past emotional event (often appropriate for PTSD or GAD), or watching a sad movie clip (for major depressive disorder). Through repeated exposures, the patient develops more adaptive appraisals and patterns of emotional responding. In this way, emotion exposures serve to regulate the emotional response provoked by intense emotional experiences.

Module 8: Relapse Prevention

In the final module, the focus is on reviewing the major treatment concepts and the patient's progress. Reasons for lack of improvement or difficulty in meeting treatment goals are discussed, as appropriate, including diagnostic error, lack of patient engagement, difficulty with knowledge acquisition, and unrealistic treatment goals. Strategies for preserving and extending treatment gains are also discussed.

EVIDENCE FOR THE UNIFIED PROTOCOL

A large randomized controlled trial revealed that the UP has equivalent efficacy compared to established gold standard single-disorder cognitive–behavioral therapy protocols in treating patients with principal anxiety disorders (Barlow et al., 2017); this equivalence was sustained at 12-month follow-up (Eustis et al., 2020). Recent meta-analyses (Carlucci et al., 2021; Sakiris & Berle, 2019) have confirmed that the UP significantly improves symptoms of internalizing disorders, with effect sizes comparable to those of single-disorder interventions. These meta-analyses also demonstrated that treatment with the UP leads to increases in adaptive emotion regulation strategies. Furthermore, a recent study showed that in a treatment-seeking sample with anxiety disorders and comorbid conditions, treatment with the UP was linked to significant reductions in the dimension of neuroticism itself (Sauer-Zavala et al., 2020).

As discussed in the following chapters, there is preliminary evidence that the UP is relatively efficacious in treating emotional sequelae such as anxiety and depression comorbid with medical conditions, specifically HIV (Allen et al., 2012), multiple sclerosis (Nazari et al., 2020), breast cancer (Mohammadizadeh et al., 2021), irritable bowel syndrome (IBS; Wurm et al., 2017), infertility (Mousavi et al., 2019), and Parkinson's disease (Reynolds et al., 2020), as well as chronic pain (Wurm et al., 2017). With respect to infertility, the UP may be as effective as mindfulness-based stress reduction (Mousavi et al., 2019).Gastrointestinal symptoms themselves may also be efficaciously treated by the UP (Mohsenabadi et al., 2018).

For example, in a randomized clinical trial of 64 patients with IBS, those treated with the UP had significant decreases in anxiety, depression, and gastrointestinal symptoms, as well as improvements in emotion regulation skills (Mohsenabadi et al., 2018). Notably, mediation analyses were conducted and reflected that improvements in emotion regulation mediated the effect of the intervention (UP) on changes in symptoms of emotional disorders as well as gastrointestinal distress (Mohsenabadi et al., 2018). This conclusion contributes to a body of evidence showing that patients with depression and anxiety, as well as patients with IBS, struggle with emotion dysregulation or use inefficient emotion regulation skills. In the case of IBS, this may lead to difficulties distinguishing emotions and physical symptoms. Overall, emotion dysregulation plays an important role in the maintenance of psychopathology, including that associated with physical conditions, and can be effectively treated with an emotion-focused intervention such as the UP.

CONCLUSION

Emotional disorders have considerable overlap, reflected in shared treatment response and common neurobiological underpinnings. This overlap has been explained by shared temperamental characteristics, particularly neuroticism. In a functional model, neuroticism is associated with aversive reactivity and emotion-motivated avoidant coping, serving to maintain negative emotional experience. Emotion dysregulation common to emotional disorders is also a component of some chronic physical health conditions, such as IBS. Indeed, there is a high comorbidity between chronic health conditions and emotional disorders, reflected in burdens on individuals and systems. Therefore, a transdiagnostic, emotion-focused approach such as the UP, which is scalable and easily adapted, is a suitable treatment for targeting the underlying mechanisms driving such co-occurring conditions.

The chapters that follow provide guidance to clinicians treating comorbid physical and emotional disorders using the UP. Chapter 3 is concerned with assessment and case formulation of comorbid physical and emotional disorders using transdiagnostic principles. Chapters 4 and 5 focus on the implementation of the UP in type 2 diabetes and for people living with HIV. Chapters 6–10 provide guidance on the use of the UP for chronic pain, fertility, patients who have undergone bariatric surgery, endometriosis, and Parkinson's disease. Chapters 11 and 12 examine the application of the UP to IBS and in the treatment of depression and anxiety disorders in patients undergoing treatment for cardiovascular diseases. Chapter 13 concerns the use of the UP to facilitate smoking cessation. Finally, Chapter 14 describes the application of the UP to treat anxiety and depressive symptoms or disorders in patients with long COVID-19 disease.

REFERENCES

Abramowitz, J. S., Tolin, D. F., & Street, G. P. (2001). Paradoxical effects of thought suppression: A meta-analysis of controlled studies. *Clinical Psychology Review*, *21*(5), 683–703. https://doi.org/10.1016/S0272-7358(00)00057-X

Allen, L. B., Tsao, J. C., Seidman, L. C., Ehrenreich-May, J., & Zeltzer, L. K. (2012). A unified, transdiagnostic treatment for adolescents with chronic pain and comorbid anxiety and depression. *Cognitive and Behavioral Practice*, *19*(1), 56–67. https://doi.org/10.1016/j.cbpra.2011.04.007

Allen, L. B., White, K. S., Barlow, D. H., Shear, M. K., Gorman, J. M., & Woods, S. W. (2010). Cognitive–behavior therapy (CBT) for panic disorder: Relationship of anxiety and depression comorbidity with treatment outcome. *Journal of Psychopathology and Behavioral Assessment*, *32*(2), 185–192. https://doi.org/10.1007/s10862-009-9151-3

American Psychiatric Association. (2013). *Diagnostic and statistical manual of mental disorders* (5th ed.). American Psychiatric Publishing.

American Psychiatric Association. (2022). *Diagnostic and statistical manual of mental disorders* (5th ed., text rev.). American Psychiatric Publishing.

Babler, E., & Strickland, C. J. (2015). Moving the journey towards independence: Adolescents transitioning to successful diabetes self-management. *Journal of Pediatric Nursing, 30*(5), 648–660. https://doi.org/10.1016/j.pedn.2015.06.005

Barger, S. D., & Sydeman, S. J. (2005). Does generalized anxiety disorder predict coronary heart disease risk factors independently of major depressive disorder? *Journal of Affective Disorders, 88*(1), 87–91. https://doi.org/10.1016/j.jad.2005.05.012

Barlow, D. H. (1988). *Anxiety and its disorders: The nature and treatment of anxiety and panic.* Guilford.

Barlow, D. H. (1991). Disorders of emotion. *Psychological Inquiry, 2*, 58–71.

Barlow, D. H. (2002). *Anxiety and its disorders: The nature and treatment of anxiety and panic* (2nd ed.). Guilford.

Barlow, D. H., Allen, L. B., & Choate, M. L. (2016). Toward a unified treatment for emotional disorders—Republished article. *Behavior Therapy, 47*(6), 838–853. https://doi.org/10.1016/j.beth.2016.11.005

Barlow, D. H., Curreri, A. J., & Woodard, L. S. (2021). Neuroticism and disorders of emotion: A new synthesis. *Current Directions in Psychological Science, 30*(5), 410–417. https://doi.org/10.1177/09637214211030253

Barlow, D. H., Farchione, T. J., Bullis, J. R., Gallagher, M. W., Murray-Latin, H., Sauer-Zavala, S., . . . Cassiello-Robbins, C. (2017). The Unified Protocol for transdiagnostic Treatment of Emotional Disorders compared with diagnosis-specific protocols for anxiety disorders: A randomized clinical trial. *JAMA Psychiatry*, 74, 875–884.

Barlow, D. H., Farchione, T. J., Sauer-Zavala, S., Murray-Latin, H., Ellard, K. K., Bullis, J. R., . . . Cassiello-Robbins, C. (2018). *The unified protocol for transdiagnostic treatment of emotional disorders: Therapist guide* (2nd ed.). Oxford University.

Barlow, D. H., Sauer-Zavala, S., Carl, J. R., Bullis, J. R., & Ellard, K. K. (2014). The nature, diagnosis, and treatment of neuroticism: Back to the future. *Clinical Psychological Science, 2*(3), 344–365. https://doi.org/10.1177/2167702613505532

Baune, B. T., Adrian, I., & Jacobi, F. (2007). Medical disorders affect health outcome and general functioning depending on comorbid major depression in the general population. *Journal of Psychosomatic Research, 62*(2), 109–118. https://doi.org/10.1016/j.jpsychores.2006.09.014

Beck, A. T. (1976). *Cognitive therapy and the emotional disorders.* International Universities Press.

Bijl, R. V., van Zessen, G., Ravelli, A., de Rijk, C., & Langendoen, Y. (1998). The Netherlands Mental Health Survey and Incidence Study (NEMESIS): Objectives and design. *Social Psychiatry and Psychiatric Epidemiology, 33*(12), 581–586. https://doi.org/10.1007/s001270050097

Borkovec, T. D., Abel, J. L., & Newman, H. (1995). Effects of psychotherapy on comorbid conditions in generalized anxiety disorder. *Journal of Consulting and Clinical Psychology, 63*(3), 479–483.

Bouhuys, A. L., Flentge, F., Oldehinkel, A. J., & van den Berg, M. D. (2004). Potential psychosocial mechanisms linking depression to immune function in elderly subjects. *Psychiatry Research, 127*(3), 237–245. https://doi.org/10.1016/j.psychres.2004.05.001

Brickman, A. L., Yount, S. E., Blaney, N. T., Rothberg, S. T., & De-Nour, A. K. (1996). Personality traits and long-term health status: The influence of neuroticism and conscientiousness on renal deterioration in type-1 diabetes. *Psychosomatics, 37*(5), 459–468. https://doi.org/10.1016/S0033-3182(96)71534-7

Brown, T. A. (2007). Temporal course and structural relationships among dimensions of temperament and DSM-IV anxiety and mood disorder constructs. *Journal of Abnormal Psychology, 116*(2), 313–328. https://doi.org/10.1037/0021-843X.116.2.313

Brown, T. A., Antony, M. M., & Barlow, D. H. (1995). Diagnostic comorbidity in panic disorder: Effect on treatment outcome and course of comorbid diagnoses following treatment. *Journal of Consulting and Clinical Psychology, 63*(3), 408–418. https://doi.org/10.1037/0022-006x.63.3.408

Brown, T. A., & Barlow, D. H. (2009). A proposal for a dimensional classification system based on the shared features of the DSM-IV anxiety and mood disorders: Implications for assessment and treatment. *Psychological Assessment, 21*(3), 256–271.

Brown, T. A., Campbell, L. A., Lehman, C. L., Grisham, J. R., & Mancill, R. B. (2001). Current and lifetime comorbidity of the DSM-IV anxiety and mood disorders in a large clinical sample. *Journal of Abnormal Psychology, 110*(4), 585–599. https://doi.org/10.1037/0021-843x.110.4.585

Buske-Kirschbaum, A., Geiben, A., & Hellhammer, D. (2001). Psychobiological aspects of atopic dermatitis: An overview. *Psychotherapy and Psychosomatics, 70*(1), 6–16. https://doi.org/10.1159/000056219

Campbell-Sills, L., Barlow, D. H., Brown, T. A., & Hofmann, S. G. (2006). Acceptability and suppression of negative emotion in anxiety and mood disorders. *Emotion, 6*(4), 587–595. https://doi.org/10.1037/1528-3542.6.4.587

Carlucci, L., Saggino, A., & Balsamo, M. (2021). On the efficacy of the Unified Protocol for Transdiagnostic Treatment of Emotional Disorders: A systematic review and meta-analysis. *Clinical Psychology Review, 87*, 101999. https://doi.org/10.1016/j.cpr.2021.101999

Chien, L.-L., Ko, H.-C., & Wu, J. Y.-W. (2007). The five-factor model of personality and depressive symptoms: One-year follow-up. *Personality and Individual Differences, 43*, 1013–1023. https://doi.org/10.1016/j.paid.2007.02.022

Clark, L. A., Watson, D., & Mineka, S. (1994). Temperament, personality, and the mood and anxiety disorders. *Journal of Abnormal Psychology, 103*(1), 103–116. https://doi.org/10.1037/0021-843x.103.1.103

Clarkin, J. F., Hull, J. W., Cantor, J., & Sanderson, C. (1993). Borderline personality disorder and personality traits: A comparison of SCID-II BPD and NEO-PI. *Psychological Assessment, 5*, 472–476. https://doi.org/10.1037/1040-3590.5.4.472

Costa, P. T., Jr., & McCrae, R. R. (1987). Neuroticism, somatic complaints, and disease: Is the bark worse than the bite? *Journal of Personality, 55*(2), 299–316. https://doi.org/10.1111/j.1467-6494.1987.tb00438.x

Costa, P. T., Jr., & Widiger, T. A. (2002). Introduction: Personality disorders and the five-factor model of personality. In P. T. Costa, Jr., & T. A. Widiger (Eds.), *Personality disorders and the five-factor model of personality* (2nd ed., pp. 3–14). American Psychological Association. https://doi.org/10.1037/10423-001

Craske, M. G., & Barlow, D. H. (2022). *Mastery of your anxiety and panic: Therapist guide* (5th ed.). Oxford University Press.

Cuijpers, P., Smit, F., Penninx, B. W. J. H., de Graaf, R., ten Have, M., & Beekman, A. T. F. (2010). Economic costs of neuroticism: A population-based study. *Archives of General Psychiatry, 67*(10), 1086–1093. https://doi.org/10.1001/archgenpsychiatry.2010.130

Currie, S. R., & Wang, J. (2005). More data on major depression as an antecedent risk factor for first onset of chronic back pain. *Psychological Medicine, 35*(9), 1275–1282. https://doi.org/10.1017/S0033291705004952

Daré, L. O., Bruand, P. E., Gérard, D., Marin, B., Lameyre, V., Boumédiène, F., & Preux, P. M. (2019). Co-morbidities of mental disorders and chronic physical diseases in developing and emerging countries: a meta-analysis. *BMC Public Health, 19*(1), 1–12. https://doi.org/10.1186/s12889-019-6623-6

Etkin, A., Prater, K. E., Hoeft, F., Menon, V., & Schatzberg, A. F. (2010). Failure of anterior cingulate activation and connectivity with the amygdala during implicit regulation of emotional processing in generalized anxiety disorder. *American Journal of Psychiatry, 167*(5), 545–554. https://doi.org/10.1176/appi.ajp.2009.09070931

Eustis, E. H., Gallagher, M. W., Tirpak, J. W., Nauphal, M., Farchione, T. J., & Barlow, D. H. (2020). The Unified Protocol compared with diagnosis-specific protocols for anxiety disorders: 12-month follow-up from a randomized clinical trial. *General Hospital Psychiatry*, 67, 58–61.

Goubert, L., Crombez, G., & Van Damme, S. (2004). The role of neuroticism, pain catastrophizing and pain-related fear in vigilance to pain: A structural equations approach. *Pain, 107*(3), 234–241. https://doi.org/10.1016/j.pain.2003.11.005

Griffith, J. W., Zinbarg, R. E., Craske, M. G., Mineka, S., Rose, R. D., Waters, A. M., & Sutton, J. M. (2010). Neuroticism as a common dimension in the internalizing disorders. *Psychological Medicine, 40*(7), 1125–1136. https://doi.org/10.1017/S0033291709991449

Hadlandsmyth, K., White, K. S., Nesin, A. E., & Greco, L. A. (2013). Proposing an acceptance and commitment therapy intervention to promote improved diabetes management in adolescents: A treatment conceptualization. *International Journal of Behavioral Consultation and Therapy, 7*(4), 12–16.

Henry, C., Mitropoulou, V., New, A. S., Koenigsberg, H. W., Silverman, J., & Siever, L. J. (2001). Affective instability and impulsivity in borderline personality and bipolar II disorders: Similarities and differences. *Journal of Psychiatric Research, 35*(6), 307–312.

Holmes, A. J., Lee, P. H., Hollinshead, M. O., Bakst, L., Roffman, J. L., Smoller, J. W., & Buckner, R. L. (2012). Individual differences in amygdala-medial prefrontal anatomy link negative affect, impaired social functioning, and polygenic depression risk. *Journal of Neuroscience, 32*(50), 18087–18100. https://doi.org/10.1523/jneurosci.2531-12.2012

Huovinen, E., Kaprio, J., & Koskenvuo, M. (2001). Asthma in relation to personality traits, life satisfaction, and stress: A prospective study among 11,000 adults. *Allergy, 56*(10), 971–977. https://doi.org/10.1034/j.1398-9995.2001.00112.x

Jylhä, P., & Isometsä, E. (2006). The relationship of neuroticism and extraversion to symptoms of anxiety and depression in the general population. *Depression and Anxiety, 23*, 281–289.

Kadimpati, S., Zale, E. L., Hooten, M. W., Ditre, J. W., & Warner, D. O. (2015). Associations between neuroticism and depression in relation to catastrophizing and pain-related anxiety in chronic pain patients. *PLoS One, 10*(4), e0126351. https://doi.org/10.1371/journal.pone.0126351

Kendler, K. S., Gatz, M., Gardner, C. O., & Pedersen, N. L. (2006). Personality and major depression: A Swedish longitudinal, population-based twin study. *Archives of General Psychiatry, 63*(10), 1113–1120. https://doi.org/10.1001/archpsyc.63.10.1113

Kessler, R. C., Chiu, W. T., Demler, O., & Walters, E. E. (2005). Prevalence, severity, and comorbidity of twelve-month DSM-IV disorders in the National Comorbidity Survey Replication (NCS-R). *Archives of General Psychiatry, 62*(6), 617–627. https://doi.org/10.1001/archpsyc.62.6.617

Kessler, R. C., Cox, B. J., Green, J. G., Ormel, J., McLaughlin, K. A., Merikangas, K. R., Petukhova, M., Pine, D. S., Russo, L. J., Swendsen, J., Wittchen, H.-U., & Zaslavsky, A. M. (2011). The effects of latent variables in the development of comorbidity among common mental disorders. *Depression and Anxiety, 28*(1), 29–39. https://doi.org/10.1002/da.20760

Khan, A. A., Jacobson, K. C., Gardner, C. O., Prescott, C. A., & Kendler, K. S. (2005). Personality and comorbidity of common psychiatric disorders. *British Journal of Psychiatry, 186*, 190–196. https://doi.org/10.1192/bjp.186.3.190

Koenigsberg, H. W., Harvey, P. D., Mitropoulou, V., New, A. S., Goodman, M., Silverman, J., Serby, M., Schopick, F., & Siever, L. J. (2001). Are the interpersonal and identity disturbances in the borderline personality disorder criteria linked to the traits of affective instability and impulsivity? *Journal of Personality Disorders, 15*(4), 358–370. https://doi.org/10.1521/pedi.15.4.358.19181

Kornør, H., & Nordvik, H. (2007). Five-factor model personality traits in opioid dependence. *BMC Psychiatry, 7*, Article 37. https://doi.org/10.1186/1471-244X-7-37

Kristoffersen, E. S., Aaseth, K., Grande, R. B., Lundqvist, C., & Russell, M. B. (2018). Psychological distress, neuroticism and disability associated with secondary chronic headache in the general population: The Akershus study of chronic headache. *Journal of Headache and Pain, 19*(1), Article 62. https://doi.org/10.1186/s10194-018-0894-7

Krueger, R. F. (1999). The structure of common mental disorders. *Archives of General Psychiatry, 56*(10), 921–926.

Krueger, R. F., & Markon, K. E. (2011). A dimensional-spectrum model of psychopathology: Progress and opportunities. *Archives of General Psychiatry, 68*(1), 10–11. https://doi.org/10.1001/archgenpsychiatry.2010.188

Lahey, B. B. (2009). Public health significance of neuroticism. *The American Psychologist, 64*(4), 241–256. https://doi.org/10.1037/a0015309

Larstone, R. M., Jang, K. L., Livesley, W. J., Vernon, P. A., & Wolf, H. (2002). The relationship between Eysenck's P-E-N model of personality, the five-factor model of personality, and traits delineating personality dysfunction. *Personality and Individual Differences, 33*, 25–37. https://doi.org/10.1016/S0191-8869(01)00132-5

Lilienfeld, S. O., Turner, S. M., & Jacob, R. G. (1993). Anxiety sensitivity: An examination of theoretical and methodological issues. *Advances in Behaviour Research and Therapy, 15*(2), 147–183.

Livneh, H. (2009). Denial of chronic illness and disability: Part I. Theoretical, functional, and dynamic perspectives. *Rehabilitation Counseling Bulletin, 52*(4), 225–236. https://doi.org/10.1177/0034355209333689

Magidson, J. F., Roberts, B., Collado-Rodriguez, A., & Lejuez, C. W. (2014). Theory-driven intervention for changing personality: Expectancy value theory, behavioral activation, and conscientiousness. *Developmental Psychology, 50*(5), 1442–1450. https://doi.org/10.1037/a0030583

Maier, S. F., & Watkins, L. R. (1998). Cytokines for psychologists: Implications of bi-directional immune-to-brain communication for understanding behavior, mood, and cognition. *Psychological Review, 105*(1), 83–107. https://doi.org/10.1037/0033-295X.105.1.83

Malouff, J. M., Thorsteinsson, E. B., Rooke, S. E., & Schutte, N. S. (2007). Alcohol involvement and the five-factor model of personality: A meta-analysis. *Journal of Drug Education, 37*(3), 277–294. https://doi.org/10.2190/DE.37.3.d

Malouff, J. M., Thorsteinsson, E. B., & Schutte, N. S. (2005). The relationship between the five-factor model of personality and symptoms of clinical disorders: A meta-analysis. *Journal of Psychopathology and Behavioral Assessment, 27*(2), 101–114. https://doi.org/10.1007/s10862-005-5384-y

Malouff, J. M., Thorsteinsson, E. B., & Schutte, N. S. (2006). The five-factor model of personality and smoking: A meta-analysis. *Journal of Drug Education, 36*(1), 47–58. https://doi.org/10.2190/9EP8-17P8-EKG7-66AD

McCaffery, J. M., Frasure-Smith, N., Dubé, M.-P., Théroux, P., Rouleau, G. A., Duan, Q., & Lespérance, F. (2006). Common genetic vulnerability to depressive symptoms and coronary artery disease: A review and development of candidate genes related to inflammation and serotonin. *Psychosomatic Medicine, 68*(2), 187–200. https://doi.org/10.1097/01.psy.0000208630.79271.a0

Menon, V., Shanmuganathan, B., Thamizh, J. S., Arun, A. B., Kuppili, P. P., & Sarkar, S. (2018). Personality traits such as neuroticism and disability predict psychological distress in medically unexplained symptoms: A three-year experience from a single centre. *Personality and Mental Health, 12*(2), 145–154. https://doi.org/10.1002/pmh.1405

Merikangas, K. R., Zhang, H., Avenevoli, S., Acharyya, S., Neuenschwander, M., & Angst, J. (2003). Longitudinal trajectories of depression and anxiety in a prospective community study: The Zurich Cohort Study. *Archives of General Psychiatry, 60*(10), 993–1000. https://doi.org/10.1001/archpsyc.60.9.993

Merino, H., Senra, C., & Ferreiro, F. (2016). Are worry and rumination specific pathways linking neuroticism and symptoms of anxiety and depression in patients with generalized anxiety disorder, major depressive disorder and mixed anxiety–depressive disorder? *PLoS One, 11*, e0156169. https://doi.org/10.1371/journal.pone.0156169

Miller, W. R., & Rollnick, S. (2013). *Motivational interviewing: Preparing people for change* (3rd ed.). Guilford.

Mohammadizadeh, H., Alimedi, M., Farnoodimehr, R., Ghaderi, S., & Sarallahi, M. (2021). The effectiveness of the Unified Protocol for emotional problems of women with breast cancer: A randomized clinical trial. *International Journal of Behavioral Sciences, 15*(3), 168–174.

Mohsenabadi, H., Zanjani, Z., Shabani, M. J., & Arj, A. (2018). A randomized clinical trial of the Unified Protocol for transdiagnostic treatment of emotional and gastro-intestinal symptoms in patients with irritable bowel syndrome: Evaluating efficacy and mechanism of change. *Journal of Psychosomatic Research, 113*, 8–15. https://doi.org/10.1016/j.jpsychores.2018.07.003

Mousavi, E., Hosseini, S., Bakhtiyari, M., Mohammadi, A., Isfeedvajani, M. S., Arani, A. M., & Sadaat, S. H. (2019). Comparing the effectiveness of the Unified Protocol transdiagnostic and mindfulness-based stress reduction program on anxiety and depression in infertile women receiving in vitro fertilisation. *Journal of Research in Medical and Dental Science, 7*(2), 44–51. https://doi.org/10.54905/disssi/v26i119/ms34e1964

Nakaya, N., Hansen, P. E., Schapiro, I. R., Eplov, L. F., Saito-Nakaya, K., Uchitomi, Y., & Johansen, C. (2006). Personality traits and cancer survival: A Danish cohort study. *British Journal of Cancer, 95*(2), 146–152. https://doi.org/10.1038/sj.bjc.6603244

Nazari, N., Sadeghi, M., Ghadampour, E., & Mirzaeefar, D. (2020). Transdiagnostic treatment of emotional disorders in people with multiple sclerosis: Randomized controlled trial. *BMC Psychology, 8*(1), 1–11. https://doi.org/10.1186/s40359-020-00480-8

Osma, J., Martínez-García, L., Quilez-Orden, A., & Peris-Baquero, Ó. (2021). Unified Protocol for the Transdiagnostic Treatment of Emotional Disorders in medical conditions: A systematic review. *International Journal of Environmental Research and Public Health, 18*(10), 5077. https://doi.org/10.3390/ijerph18105077

Pace, T. W. W., Mletzko, T. C., Alagbe, O., Musselman, D. L., Nemeroff, C. B., Miller, A. H., & Heim, C. M. (2006). Increased stress-induced inflammatory responses in male patients with major depression and increased early life stress. *American Journal of Psychiatry, 163*(9), 1630–1633. https://doi.org/10.1176/ajp.2006.163.9.1630

Paquette, V., Lévesque, J., Mensour, B., Leroux, J. M., Beaudoin, G., Bourgouin, P., & Beauregard, M. (2003). "Change the mind and you change the brain": Effects of cognitive–behavioral therapy on the neural correlates of spider phobia. *Neuroimage, 18*(2), 401–409. https://doi.org/10.1016/s1053-8119(02)00030-7

Paulesu, E., Sambugaro, E., Torti, T., Danelli, L., Ferri, F., Scialfa, G., Sberna, M., Ruggiero, G. M., Bottini, G., & Sassaroli, S. (2010). Neural correlates of worry in generalized anxiety disorder and in normal controls: A functional MRI study. *Psychological Medicine, 40*(1), 117–124. https://doi.org/10.1017/s0033291709005649

Penninx, B. W. J. H., Beekman, A. T. F., Honig, A., Deeg, D. J. H., Schoevers, R. A., van Eijk, J. T. M., & van Tilburg, W. (2001). Depression and cardiac mortality. *Archives of General Psychiatry, 58*(3), 221–227. https://doi.org/10.1001/archpsyc.58.3.221

Phan, K. L., Fitzgerald, D. A., Nathan, P. J., & Tancer, M. E. (2006). Association between amygdala hyperactivity to harsh faces and severity of social anxiety in generalized social phobia. *Biological Psychiatry, 59*(5), 424–429. https://doi.org/10.1016/j.biopsych.2005.08.012

Prince, M., Patel, V., Saxena, S., Maj, M., Maselko, J., Phillips, M. R., & Rahman, A. (2007). No health without mental health. *Lancet, 370*(9590), 859–877. https://doi.org/10.1016/s0140-6736(07)61238-0

Purdon, C. (1999). Thought suppression and psychopathology. *Behaviour Research and Therapy, 37*(11), 1029–1054. https://doi.org/10.1016/s0005-7967(98)00200-9

Putnam, K. M., & Silk, K. R. (2005). Emotion dysregulation and the development of borderline personality disorder. *Development and Psychopathology, 17*(4), 899–925. https://doi.org/10.1017/S0954579405050431

Rachman, S. (1978). *Fear and Courage*. Freemans.

Ramírez-Maestre, C., Esteve, R., & López-Martínez, A. (2014). Fear-avoidance, pain acceptance and adjustment to chronic pain: A cross-sectional study on a sample of 686 patients with chronic spinal pain. *Annals of Behavioral Medicine*, *48*(3), 402–410. https://doi.org/10.1007/s12160-014-9619-6

Rassin, E., Muris, P., Schmidt, H., & Merckelbach, H. (2000). Relationships between thought–action fusion, thought suppression and obsessive–compulsive symptoms: A structural equation modeling approach. *Behaviour Research and Therapy*, *38*(9), 889–897. https://doi.org/10.1016/S0005-7967(99)00104-7

Reinholt, N., Aharoni, R., Winding, C., Rosenberg, N., Rosenbaum, B., & Arnfred, S. (2017). Transdiagnostic group CBT for anxiety disorders: The Unified Protocol in mental health services. *Cognitive Behaviour Therapy*, *46*(1), 29–43. https://doi.org/10.1080/16506073.2016.1227360

Reynolds, G. O., Saint-Hilaire, M., Thomas, C. A., Barlow, D. H., & Cronin-Golomb, A. (2020). Cognitive-Behavioral Therapy for Anxiety in Parkinson's Disease. *Behavior Modification*, *44*(4), 552–579.

Robles, T. F., Glaser, R., & Kiecolt-Glaser, J. K. (2005). Out of balance. *Current Directions in Psychological Science*, *14*(2), 111–115. https://doi.org/10.1111/j.0963-7214.2005.00345.x

Rogers, A. H., Kauffman, B. Y., Bakhshaie, J., McHugh, R. K., Ditre, J. W., & Zvolensky, M. J. (2019). Anxiety sensitivity and opioid misuse among opioid-using adults with chronic pain. *American Journal of Drug & Alcohol Abuse*, *45*(5), 470–478. https://doi.org/10.1080/00952990.2019.1569670

Russo, J., Katon, W., Lin, E., Von Korff, M., Bush, T., Simon, G., & Walker, E. (1997). Neuroticism and extraversion as predictors of health outcomes in depressed primary care patients. *Psychosomatics*, *38*(4), 339–348. https://doi.org/10.1016/S0033-3182(97)71441-5

Sakiris, N., & Berle, D. (2019). A systematic review and meta-analysis of the Unified Protocol as a transdiagnostic emotion regulation based intervention. *Clinical Psychology Review*, *72*, 101751. https://doi.org/10.1016/j.cpr.2019.101751

Samuel, D., & Widiger, T. (2008). A meta-analytic review of the relationships between the five-factor model and DSM-IV-TR personality disorders: A facet level analysis. *Clinical Psychology Review*, *28*(8), 1326–1342. https://doi.org/10.1016/j.cpr.2008.07.002

Sareen, J., Cox, B. J., Clara, I., & Asmundson, G. J. (2005). The relationship between anxiety disorders and physical disorders in the U.S. National Comorbidity Survey. *Depression and Anxiety*, *21*(4), 193–202. https://doi.org/10.1002/da.20072

Sauer-Zavala, S., & Barlow, D. H. (2021). *Neuroticism: A new framework for emotional disorders and their treatment*. Guilford.

Sauer-Zavala, S., Fournier, J. C. Jarvi Steele, S., Woods, B. K., Wang, M., Farchione, T. J., & Barlow, D. H. (2020). Does the Unified Protocol really change neuroticism? Results from a randomized trial. *Psychological Medicine*, *51*(14), 2378–2387. https://doi.org/10.1017/s0033291720000975

Saulsman, L. M., & Page, A. C. (2004). The five-factor model and personality disorder empirical literature: A meta-analytic review. *Clinical Psychology Review*, *23*(8), 1055–1085. https://doi.org/10.1016/j.cpr.2002.09.001

Sher, K. J., & Trull, T. J. (1994). Personality and disinhibitory psychopathology: Alcoholism and antisocial personality disorder. *Journal of Abnormal Psychology, 103*(1), 92–102. https://doi.org/10.1037/0021-843X.103.1.92

Shin, L. M., Wright, C. I., Cannistraro, P. A., Wedig, M. M., McMullin, K., Martis, B., Macklin, M. L., Lasko, N. B., Cavanagh, S. R., Krangel, T. S., Orr, S. P., Pitman, R. K., Whalen, P. J., & Rauch, S. L. (2005). A functional magnetic resonance imaging study of amygdala and medial prefrontal cortex responses to overtly presented fearful faces in posttraumatic stress disorder. *Archives of General Psychiatry, 62*(3), 273–281. https://doi.org/10.1001/archpsyc.62.3.273

Shipley, B. A., Weiss, A., Der, G., Taylor, M. D., & Deary, I. J. (2007). Neuroticism, extraversion, and mortality in the UK Health and Lifestyle Survey: A 21-year prospective cohort study. *Psychosomatic Medicine, 69*(9), 923–931. https://doi.org/10.1097/PSY.0b013e31815abf83

Spiller, R. C. (2007). Role of infection in irritable bowel syndrome. *Journal of Gastroenterology, 42*(17), 41–47. https://doi.org/10.1007/s00535-006-1925-8

Straube, T., Glauer, M., Dilger, S., Mentzel, H. J., & Miltner, W. H. (2006). Effects of cognitive–behavioral therapy on brain activation in specific phobia. *Neuroimage, 29*(1), 125–135. https://doi.org/10.1016/j.neuroimage.2005.07.007

Suls, J., & Bunde, J. (2005). Anger, anxiety, and depression as risk factors for cardiovascular disease: The problems and implications of overlapping affective dispositions. *Psychological Bulletin, 131*(2), 260–300.

ten Have, M., Oldehinkel, A., Vollebergh, W., & Ormel, J. (2005). Does neuroticism explain variations in care service use for mental health problems in the general population? Results from the Netherlands Mental Health Survey and Incidence Study (NEMESIS). *Social Psychiatry and Psychiatric Epidemiology, 40*(6), 425–431. https://doi.org/10.1007/s00127-005-0916-z

Trull, T. J., & Sher, K. J. (1994). Relationship between the five-factor model of personality and Axis I disorders in a nonclinical sample. *Journal of Abnormal Psychology, 103*(2), 350–360.

Tsao, J. C., Mystkowski, J. L., Zucker, B. G., & Craske, M. G. (2005). Impact of cognitive–behavioral therapy for panic disorder on comorbidity: A controlled investigation. *Behaviour Research and Therapy, 43*(7), 959–970. https://doi.org/10.1016/j.brat.2004.11.013

Watkins, L. L., Blumenthal, J. A., Davidson, J. R. T., Babyak, M. A., McCants, C. B., & Sketch, M. H. (2006). Phobic anxiety, depression, and risk of ventricular arrhythmias in patients with coronary heart disease. *Psychosomatic Medicine, 68*(5), 651–656. https://doi.org/10.1097/01.psy.0000228342.53606.b3

Watson, D., & Clark, L. A. (1994). Introduction to the special issue on personality and psychopathology. *Journal of Abnormal Psychology, 103*, 3–5. https://doi.org/10.1037/h0092429

Wegner, D. M., Schneider, D. J., Carter, S. R., & White, T. L. (1987). Paradoxical effects of thought suppression. *Journal of Personality and Social Psychology, 53*(1), 5–13.

Weinstock, L. M., & Whisman, M. A. (2006). Neuroticism as a common feature of the depressive and anxiety disorders: A test of the revised integrative hierarchical model in a national sample. *Journal of Abnormal Psychology, 115*(1), 68–74. https://doi.org/10.1037/0021-843X.115.1.68

Wilson, R. S., Krueger, K. R., Gu, L., Bienias, J. L., Mendes de Leon, C. F., & Evans, D. A. (2005). Neuroticism, extraversion, and mortality in a defined population of older persons. *Psychosomatic Medicine*, *67*, 841–845. https://doi.org/10.1097/01.psy.0000190615.20656.83

Wilson, R. S., de Leon, C. F. M., Bennett, D. A., Bienias, J. L., & Evans, D. A. (2004). Depressive symptoms and cognitive decline in a community population of older persons. *Journal of Neurology, Neurosurgery & Psychiatry*, *75*(1), 126–129.

Wurm, M., Strandberg, E. K., Lorenz, C., Tillfors, M., Buhrman, M., Holländare, F., & Boersma, K. (2017). Internet delivered transdiagnostic treatment with telephone support for pain patients with emotional comorbidity: A replicated single case study. *Internet Interventions*, *10*, 54–64. https://doi.org/10.1016/j.invent.2017.10.004

Zinbarg, R. E., Mineka, S., Bobova, L., Craske, M. G., Vrshek-Schallhorn, S., Griffith, J. W., Wolitzky-Taylor, K., Waters, A. M., Sumner, J. A., & Anand, D. (2016). Testing a hierarchical model of neuroticism and its cognitive facets: Latent structure and prospective prediction of first onsets of anxiety and unipolar mood disorders during 3 years in late adolescence. *Clinical Psychological Science*, *4*(5), 805–824. https://doi.org/10.1177/2167702615618162

3

Transdiagnostic Emotional Disorder Assessment and Case Formulation in Health Conditions

ANTHONY J. ROSELLINI, JORGE OSMA,
CARLOS SUSO, AND TIMOTHY A. BROWN ■

Anxiety, mood, and other related emotional (or internalizing) disorders typically are assessed based on the presence or absence of criteria and symptoms defined in the *Diagnostic and Statistical Manual for Mental Disorders* (DSM; American Psychiatric Association, 2013). The DSM has served an important function by operationalizing emotional disorders in ways that have fostered diagnostic reliability and improved understanding of emotional disorder prevalence, risk, course, and treatment (Barlow, 2002). At the same time, the DSM is criticized for having poor construct validity by excessively discriminating symptoms and diagnostic categories that may reflect transdiagnostic mechanisms and dimensions (Brown & Barlow, 2009). Indeed, many DSM criteria and specifiers are shared across several emotional disorder categories (e.g., concentration problems due to depression, generalized anxiety, or post-traumatic stress; panic attacks caused by worry, reminders of past trauma, or occurring out-of-the-blue), and most individuals with emotional disorders have multiple diagnoses concurrently or over their lifetime (Brown et al., 2001). In addition, a large literature indicates that emotional disorder symptoms manifest along a continuum of severity rather than as diagnostic categories that are either present or absent (e.g., Haslam et al., 2020).

Emotional disorders also commonly co-occur with a range of physical health conditions, including diabetes and gastrointestinal and motor disorders, among others (see Sartorius et al., 2014). There are many challenges surrounding the assessment of emotional disorders among individuals with physical health conditions. Time constraints and lack of expertise may make it difficult for

Anthony J. Rosellini, Jorge Osma, Carlos Suso, and Timothy A. Brown, *Transdiagnostic Emotional Disorder Assessment and Case Formulation in Health Conditions* In: *Applications of the Unified Protocol in Health Conditions.* Edited by: Jorge Osma and Todd J. Farchione, Oxford University Press. © Oxford University Press 2023. DOI: 10.1093/oso/9780197564295.003.0003 physicians specializing in physical health issues to assess the heterogeneous spectrum of emotional disorder phenotypes (e.g., worry, panic, depression, and compulsive behaviors). In addition, many emotional disorders are defined in part by somatic and cognitive symptoms that can occur within the context of *either* physical or other mental disorders (e.g., fatigue, muscle tension, pain, sleep problems, and concentration difficulties). Difficulty distinguishing symptoms as due to a physical health condition, emotional disorder, or both reduces diagnostic reliability and complicates treatment planning.

In response to the aforementioned limitations of the DSM, alternate approaches to emotional disorder assessment and classification have been proposed with an emphasis on *transdiagnostic* dimensions that cut across traditional disorder categories. Given the high rates of comorbidity and symptom overlap between emotional and physical disorders, transdiagnostic approaches to emotional disorder assessment may be particularly useful among individuals with physical health conditions. Accordingly, the goals of this chapter are to (a) review leading transdiagnostic emotional disorder dimensions and assessment tools, (b) describe a transdiagnostic profile approach to emotional disorder classification, and (c) discuss specific recommendations and challenges surrounding the transdiagnostic assessment and case conceptualization of emotional disorders among individuals with health conditions.

TRANSDIAGNOSTIC EMOTIONAL DISORDER DIMENSIONS

Research has identified several dimensions of affect, cognition, and behavior (or some combination) that are associated with multiple emotional disorders as defined by the DSM (i.e., transdiagnostic dimensions). Consistent with leading alternative approaches to psychopathology assessment and classification, emotional disorder dimensions can be broadly categorized into higher and lower order constructs based on the nature and scope of transdiagnostic associations (Brown & Barlow, 2009; Kotov et al., 2017). Higher order dimensions include "trait"-like factors and mechanisms (e.g., temperament and emotion regulation) that influence the risk, expression (e.g., severity), and maintenance of a broad range of emotional disorder phenotypes. Lower order dimensions reflect narrower symptom expressions that can occur across multiple DSM emotional disorder categories and are more apt to fluctuate over time (cf. higher order dimensions).

Temperament and Personality

Heritable *neurotic/negative temperament* (NT) constructs such as neuroticism, negative affectivity, and behavioral inhibition are likely the most widely studied transdiagnostic emotional disorder dimensions (Barlow et al., 2014). These NT dimensions are defined broadly as one's general tendency to experience negative emotions (e.g., anxiety, depression, and anger) in response to perceived stress. High NT is associated with the presence and severity of all types of emotional disorder symptoms (Kotov et al., 2010), and prospectively predicts emotional disorder onset (Zinbarg et al., 2016) and course (Naragon-Gainey et al., 2013). NT also accounts for virtually all the shared variance across emotional disorders (Griffith et al., 2010) and thus is frequently identified as the core higher order emotional disorder dimension (cf. "internalizing spectra"; Kotov et al., 2017).

In addition to NT, a large literature exists on *positive temperament* (PT) constructs such as extraversion, positive affectivity, and behavioral activation. PT constructs are broadly defined as one's tendency to engage in social and goal-directed activities and experience positive emotions. Low PT is associated with the onset, severity, and chronicity of unipolar depression and social anxiety, whereas high PT is associated with mania (Johnson et al., 2012; Naragon-Gainey et al., 2013; Watson et al., 2019). High PT also appears to have benefits, including predicting long-term life satisfaction (Steel et al., 2008).

Both NT and PT prospectively predict a range of physical health behaviors and outcomes (Shipley et al., 2007). For instance, in a large community sample (N = 21,676), Charles and colleagues (2008) found that individuals with elevated neuroticism were more likely to have been diagnosed with musculoskeletal, neurological, gastrointestinal, and cardiovascular disorders over a 25-year follow-up. Accordingly, the assessment of NT and PT can inform the understanding of a patient's presenting emotional disorder symptoms (e.g., overall severity/comorbidity), likelihood of developing emotional disorder symptoms in the future (if currently asymptomatic), and overall prognosis of mental and physical health.

Higher Order Emotion Regulation Dimensions

Emotion regulation refers to the multifaceted process of monitoring, evaluating, and modifying emotions. A growing literature attests to the transdiagnostic relevance of cognitive and behavioral emotion regulation strategies used to prevent or reduce the intensity of negative emotions. Many "adaptive" and "maladaptive" emotion regulation strategies have been found to predict emotional disorder symptoms (Aldao, Nolen-Hoeksema, et al., 2010). For instance, experiential avoidance is a broad term defined as a general tendency to escape or avoid adverse internal experiences such as thoughts, memories, physiological sensations, and emotions (cf. avoidance/escape criteria for several DSM-defined emotional disorders). Research suggests that experiential avoidance is a temporally stable maladaptive emotional regulation strategy that prospectively predicts many different types of emotional disorder symptoms (Spinhoven et al., 2014).

Cognitive and behavioral suppression strategies also are associated with experiencing more severe emotional disorder symptoms (Aldao & Nolen-Hoeksema, 2010; Aldao, Nolen-Hoeksema, et al., 2010; Magee et al., 2012). Suppression can include attempts to inhibit (a) distressing thoughts or images (e.g., distraction or thought suppression) or (b) overt expressions of emotions or "acting on" emotions (i.e., expressive suppression). A related construct is mindfulness, which is broadly defined as one's awareness and acceptance of internal experiences and also is associated with a range of emotional disorder symptoms (Cash & Whittingham, 2010). In comparison, rumination and cognitive reappraisal are examples of more circumscribed cognitive emotion regulation dimensions associated with emotional disorders (Aldao, Nolen-Hoeksema, et al., 2010). Whereas *rumination* is defined as repetitive negative thoughts focused on past events, *reappraisal* refers to a one's ability to generate alternate thoughts or consider other possible outcomes (i.e., inversely associated with emotional disorder severity).

With respect to physical health outcomes, several studies have found experiential avoidance, suppression, rumination, and a lack of mindfulness and reappraisal to influence the experience of pain and associated clinical outcomes (Costa & Pinto-Gouveia, 2013; Feldner et al., 2006; Quartana & Burns, 2007; Renna et al., 2021). For instance, a growing literature suggests that rumination is associated with greater pain intensity, impairment (e.g., activity interference), and poorer perceived overall physical health (Sansone & Sansone, 2012). Assessing emotion regulation strategies may be particularly useful in treatment planning because some cognitive–behavioral interventions, including the Unified Protocol (Barlow et al., 2017), are organized into modules that target specific maladaptive strategies. For instance, emotion regulation could be assessed and modules prioritizing based on the most pronounced maladaptive strategies (e.g., targeting overt behavioral avoidance prior to rumination).

Mood and Anxiety Symptom Dimensions

Transdiagnostic lower order dimensions involve narrower symptom components that may occur in the context of several emotional disorders defined in the DSM and the *International Statistical Classification of Diseases and Related Health Problems* (World Health Organization, 2019; see Brown & Barlow, 2009; Kotov et al., 2017). Assessing narrower emotional disorder symptom dimensions is necessary for cognitive–behavioral treating planning (i.e., identifying key symptom targets/outcomes and risk management). Numerous transdiagnostic lower order dimensions have been identified in leading alternate models for emotional disorder assessment and classification, including situational fears, social interaction anxiety, intrusive thoughts, and traumatic re-experiencing (Brown & Barlow, 2009; Kotov et al., 2017). Some lower order emotional disorder dimensions may be particularly important to assess among individuals with physical health conditions because they (a) frequently co-occur with physical disorders and (b) may be due to, or exacerbated by, an organic cause. For example, depressed mood is common among individuals with physical health problems (e.g., cancer and pain; Bair et al., 2003; Pasquini & Biondi, 2007) but also can be caused or exacerbated by hypothyroidism (a medical condition). Depression also commonly co-occurs with other emotional disorders (Brown et al., 2001) and is important to assess for purposes of risk management (suicidality).

Several lower order anxiety dimensions may be relevant for individuals with physical disorders. Autonomic arousal, or the physiological symptoms of sympathetic nervous system activation (e.g., pounding heart and sweating), is most strongly related to panic disorder and post-traumatic stress disorder (Brown & McNiff, 2009), but it can occur within the context of any emotional disorder (see DSM-5 panic attack specifier) as well as a range of physical health conditions (e.g., hyperthyroidism and hyperhidrosis). Many DSM emotional disorders also are defined by other specific somatic symptoms that are common in a range of physical disorders (e.g., fatigue and appetite changes). In contrast to these somatic symptom dimensions, somatic anxiety is defined by worry and anxiety focused on health and physical symptoms (including autonomic arousal). Somatic anxiety is the core feature of somatic symptom and illness anxiety disorders but also is characteristic of panic disorder (Abramowitz et al., 2007) and obsessive–compulsive disorder (Hedman et al., 2017). Individuals with physical disorders, especially older adults, are more likely to worry about their health (El-Gabalawy et al., 2013).

Transdiagnostic Emotional Disorder Assessments

Many popular self-report questionnaires are designed to assess the aforementioned higher and lower order transdiagnostic emotional disorder dimensions (Table 3.1). Most self-report measures assess two or three emotional disorder dimensions. However, some can be used to assess a broad range of emotional disorder dimensions and thus can be efficient tools for determining clinical targets in need of functional analysis and treatment planning. For example, the 99-item Inventory of Depression and Anxiety Symptoms–II has 18 scales assessing lower order symptom dimensions such as depressed mood, mania, autonomic arousal, and social anxiety (Watson et al., 2012). Very few questionnaires are designed to assess both higher and lower order emotional disorder dimensions. As reviewed below, one exception is the Multidimensional Emotional Disorder Inventory (MEDI; Rosellini & Brown, 2019).

A DIMENSIONAL–CATEGORICAL PROFILE APPROACH TO EMOTIONAL DISORDER CLASSIFICATION

Many of the transdiagnostic dimensions reviewed above (or closely related constructs) are included in leading alternative approaches to psychopathology assessment and classification (e.g., Kotov et al., 2017). One such approach to emotional disorder classification, forwarded by Brown and Barlow (2009), proposes to assess a parsimonious set of transdiagnostic dimensions of temperament (e.g., NT and PT), mood (e.g., depression), anxiety foci (e.g., social, somatic, and

Table 3.1 POPULAR TRANSDIAGNOSTIC EMOTIONAL DISORDER QUESTIONNAIRES

Measure	Emotional Disorder Coverage/Subscales
Personality/Temperament	
NEO Personality Inventory Revised/ Five Factor Inventory (240/60 items; Costa & McCrae, 1992)	Neuroticism (NT); Extraversion (PT); Conscientiousness; Openness; Agreeableness; associated lower order facets (e.g., Anxiousness; Self-Consciousness; Excitement Seeking)
Behavioral Inhibition and Activation Scales (24 items; Carver & White, 1994)	Behavioral Inhibition (NT); Behavioral Activation (PT)
Positive and Negative Affect Schedule (20 items; Watson et al., 1988)	Negative Affectivity (NT); Positive Affectivity (PT)
Emotion Regulation	
Emotion Regulation Questionnaire (10 items; Gross & John, 2003)	Expressive Suppression; Cognitive Reappraisal
Ruminative Response Scale (22 items; Treynor et al., 2003)	Rumination; Depression; Brooding; Reflection
Multidimensional Experiential Avoidance Questionnaire (62 items; Gámez et al., 2011)	Behavioral Avoidance; Distress Aversion; Procrastination; Distraction/Suppression; Repression; Distress Endurance
Mood and Anxiety Symptom Dimensions	
Albany Panic and Phobia Questionnaire (27 items; Rapee et al., 1994)	Social Anxiety; Agoraphobia (situational fear); Interoceptive Fears (fear of internal sensations)
Depression Anxiety and Stress Scales (48/21 items; Lovibond & Lovibond, 1995)	Depression; Anxiety (autonomic arousal); Stress
Inventory of Depression and Anxiety Symptoms–II (99 items; Watson et al., 2012)	Dysphoria; Well-Being; Panic; Cleaning; Lassitude; Insomnia; Suicidality; Social Anxiety; Ill Temper; Mania; Euphoria; Claustrophobia; Ordering; Traumatic Avoidance; Traumatic Intrusions; Checking; Appetite Loss; Appetite Gain
Hybrid	
Multidimensional Emotional Disorder Inventory (49 items; Rosellini & Brown, 2019)	Neurotic Temperament; Positive Temperament; Depression; Autonomic Arousal; Somatic Anxiety; Social Anxiety, Intrusive Cognitions; Traumatic Re-experiencing; Avoidance
Minnesota Multiphasic Personality Inventory–3 (335 items; Ben-Porath & Tellegen, 2020)	Emotional Dysfunction (NT); Low Positive Emotions (PT); Demoralization; Somatic Complaints; Suicide Ideation; Helplessness; Stress; Worry; Compulsivity; Anxiety-Related Experiences; Anger Proneness; Behavior-Restricting Fears

NT, neurotic temperament construct; PT, positive temperament construct.

traumatic), and avoidance while maintaining broad coverage of anxiety, somatic symptom, obsessive–compulsive, trauma, mood, and related disorders defined in the DSM. The Brown and Barlow approach differs from others by also proposing to use the parsimonious set of transdiagnostic dimensions to operationalize data-driven emotional disorder profiles (i.e., categories). Indeed, although an array of dimensional scores is more useful for treatment planning, there are both clinical utility and practical need for categorical emotional disorder labels, including increased efficiency of communication between providers and confirming the "presence" of a disorder for insurance reimbursement. Specifically, Brown and Barlow argue for plotting dimensional scores into an emotional disorder "profile" and assigning a categorical label based on similarities with profiles identified in the population using empirical subtyping procedures.

Although some efforts have been made to identify data-driven emotional disorder profiles, studies have been limited by developing the profiles using a disparate array of self-report questionnaires (e.g., Rosellini & Brown, 2014). However, due to time restraints in certain clinical and research settings, it may not be possible to administer or score a broad suite of emotional disorder measures, particularly if the appointment is prioritizing the assessment/treatment of a physical health condition. We developed the MEDI to provide a brief but rich assessment of the transdiagnostic emotional disorder dimensions underscored in the Brown and Barlow (2009) approach and which can be plotted into a visual profile. The 49-item MEDI assesses nine emotional disorder dimensions: NT, PT, depressed mood, autonomic arousal, somatic anxiety, social anxiety, intrusive cognitions, traumatic re-experiencing, and avoidance. Importantly, MEDI items were generated using a transdiagnostic perspective. For example, items assessing intrusive cognitions are designed to broadly capture the experience of distressing, repetitive, and nonsensical thoughts/images (e.g., "I have thoughts or images that I find unacceptable") rather than specific thought content (e.g., contamination, violence, and loss of control) or associated behaviors (e.g., cleaning and checking). Initial psychometric findings for the MEDI are promising. The hypothesized nine-factor solution was supported in a large sample of emotional disorder outpatients (Rosellini & Brown, 2019). There also was strong evidence for the reliability and validity of the MEDI dimensions; all nine dimensions had acceptable scale reliability and concurrent validity with well-validated self-report measures and clinician-assigned diagnoses. Given its broad coverage of transdiagnostic emotional disorder dimensions, the MEDI may have general utility for clinicians and researchers interested in efficiently assessing a range of emotional disorder dimensions including in physical health care settings.

Example MEDI Profile

An example MEDI profile is presented in Figure 3.1. This type of "panic–somatic" profile (Rosellini & Brown, 2014) might characterize a patient with comorbid emotional disorders and physical health conditions. The highly elevated NT reflects a

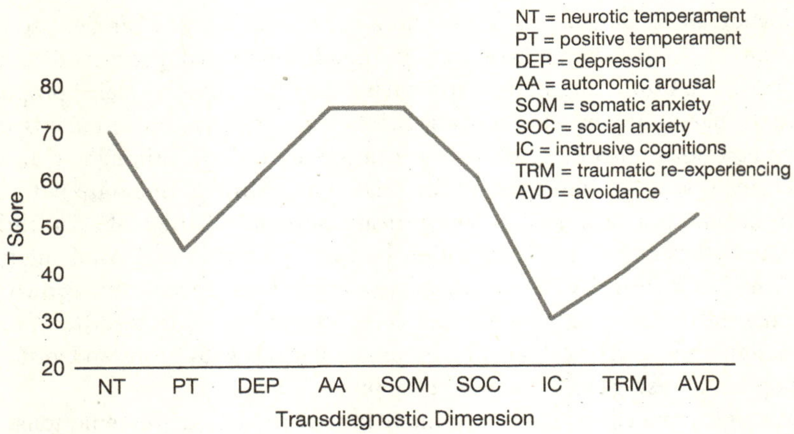

Figure 3.1 Example MEDI profile.

predisposition to negative affect and emotional disorder comorbidity, whereas the blunted PT captures a predispositional paucity of positive emotions and risk for depression and social anxiety. Accordingly, this profile is characterized by slight elevations on the depressed mood and social anxiety dimensions. However, the largest elevations are observed on the somatic anxiety and autonomic arousal dimension. These large elevations reflect severe health-related worry and associated physical symptoms (including possible panic attacks) and might be especially characteristic of individuals with co-occurring physical health conditions and emotional disorders such as panic disorder or somatic symptom disorder.

CASE FORMULATION IN HEALTH CONDITIONS

Case formulation is a fundamental tool for clinical and health psychologists. The goal is to organize information obtained during clinical assessment in a way that conceptualizes (hypothesizes) how different aspects of the patient's experience are related to and influence one another. Using a cognitive-behavioral perspective, case formulation involves attempting to explain a patient's psychopathology based on the posited mechanisms and interrelationships among their thoughts/beliefs, feelings, and behaviors, along with proximal and distal situational factors (i.e., current and past environment). This, in turn, can inform treatment planning by identifying specific intervention targets (e.g., deciding what symptoms, mechanisms, or skills should be prioritized).

The Unified Protocol for the Transdiagnostic Treatment of Emotional Disorders (UP) is a cognitive–behavioral intervention designed to address transdiagnostic mechanisms (e.g., neuroticism and emotion regulation) shared across the gamut of emotional disorders, including DSM-defined anxiety disorders (panic disorder, generalized anxiety disorder, social anxiety disorder, and agoraphobia), stress- and trauma-related disorders, obsessive–compulsive disorder and related disorders, and depressive disorders (major depressive disorder and dysthymia), among others (e.g., eating disorders; Bullis et al., 2019). Accordingly, case formulation using a UP (transdiagnostic) perspective requires the identification of commonalities in thoughts/beliefs, feelings, and behaviors across emotional disorders and associated symptoms (e.g., subclinical psychopathology).

Several examples of transdiagnostic processes are described in the UP treatment manual and can serve as a starting point for case conceptualization. First, many different emotional disorders are characterized by a range of different negative emotions that occur frequently and intensely, including anxiety, guilt, depression, and anger. Second, the experience of these negative emotions may either lead to or be exacerbated by a range of aversive cognitive reactions and processes, including (a) worry thoughts focused on the possibility of negative outcomes for oneself ("My heart is going to collapse," "I might not be able to breath") or others ("Something horrible is going to happen to my family"), (b) negative judgments about oneself ("I'm weak," "I won't be able to do it"), and (c) a reduced ability to remain present-focused. Third, virtually all emotional disorders also are characterized by attempts to downregulate frequent/intense emotional experiences and aversive cognitive reactions. Typically, attempts to downregulate involve "escape" behaviors (e.g., distraction or leaving a situation due to an intense emotional experience) or proactive avoidance (e.g., unwillingness to enter a situation or confront a stimuli because it will elicit an emotion; Barlow et al., 2017; Bullis et al., 2019).

The UP therapists guide/manual includes a helpful rubric for clinicians to use when conducting case formulation and treatment planning following a transdiagnostic perspective (Table 3.2). Specifically, this rubric guides clinicians to describe the patient's (a) presenting problems, (b) strong discomfort emotions, (c) aversive reactions to emotional experiences, and (d) avoidant coping (overt situational avoidance, subtle behavioral avoidance, cognitive avoidance, and safety signals). Consolidation of this information should, in turn, allow the clinician to adapt the UP modules/intervention to the specific personal and clinical characteristics of the patient (i.e., ideographic case conceptualization and treatment planning). These personalized adaptions of the UP and its modules can be outlined in the final section of the case formulation rubric named treatment plan. For additional recommendations surrounding UP case formulation, see Boettcher and Conklin (2018).

As discussed previously, emotional disorders and physical disorders are highly comorbid (Sartorius et al., 2014), higher order emotional disorder dimensions (temperament and emotion regulation) predict physical health outcomes (Charles et al., 2008; Shipley et al., 2007), and it is common for individuals to experience worry or depression in response to physical health problems (El-Gabalawy et al., 2013; Pasquini & Biondi, 2007). In addition, comorbidity of emotional disorders and physical health conditions may serve as a barrier to seek treatment (e.g., due to mobility issues) and negatively impact treatment efficacy (Prince et al., 2007), for example, by reducing medication adherence (e.g., diabetes patients; Das-Munshi et al., 2007). Accordingly, the case formulation of emotional disorders in

Table 3.2 Unified Protocol Case Formulation Form

<table>
<tr><td colspan="2">Presenting Problems</td></tr>
<tr><td>Strong Uncomfortable Emotions:</td><td>Aversive Reactions:</td></tr>
<tr><td colspan="2">Avoidant Coping

Situational Avoidance/Escape:

Subtle Behavioral Avoidance:

Cognitive Avoidance:

Safety Signals:</td></tr>
<tr><td colspan="2">Treatment Plan</td></tr>
</table>

people with medical conditions must include additional information above and beyond emotional disorder symptoms. In particular, we recommend expanded case formulation that includes both a description of the health condition and how the health condition (and its treatment) impacts the patient's life (in addition to formulating the interrelationships among emotions, reactions, and avoidance/escape behaviors). Specifically, the goals are to (a) assess how the health conditions and their treatments interfere in the patient's life across domains (e.g., physical functioning, work/studies, pleasurable activities, relationships, and spirituality); and (b) identify any associated uncomfortable emotions, aversive reactions, and related escape/avoidance behaviors.

After engaging in case formulation using this prescriptive, a treatment plan can be developed. It is particularly important to consider how to personalize and order the UP modules based on the case formulation. For instance, the psychoeducation module for an obese patient might include information about binge eating (e.g., leptin resistance), whereas psychoeducation for a patient living with HIV might include information about HIV/AIDS-related cognitive impairment. Alternatively, a patient who reports frequent avoidance/escape behaviors but minimal worry or distraction might benefit from engaging in emotional exposure prior to mindfulness or cognitive flexibility. If indicated, it also may be helpful to add modules from other treatment manuals (e.g., training in assertiveness or in problem-solving). In order to illustrate this approach to case formulation for comorbid EDs and health conditions, we describe a clinical case vignette with a chronic pain diagnosis and provide a detailed case formulation example and treatment plan (Table 3.3).

CASE EXAMPLE

M. is a 54-year-old man who works as an operator in a tile factory. M. started working in the tile sector as an operator at age 16 years. He has changed employers frequently because factories have been closing and merging due to the economic crisis. Unlike other colleagues, who have been losing their jobs as a result of this crisis, M. has kept his job. However, he fears that this will not last long as a result of his health problems. Specifically, M. began to experience pain in his lower back as a result of having to frequently lift heavy objects at work. Fifteen years ago, he was diagnosed with two herniated discs (L4–L5 and L5–S1). One of the hernias is displaced. As a result, in addition to his lower back pain, he feels a radiating pain down his left leg. He had surgery on his back 3 years ago in an effort to reduce his back pain. To his surprise, however, the pain returned strongly after a couple of weeks of some relief. Although he was on sick leave for a period due to his pain, his fear of retaliation from the company made him go back to work. Currently, he reports feeling a very strong anxiety due to the fear of being fired. The anxiety, however, is even stronger when he thinks of going to work every day with that pain. He sleeps very badly at night as he constantly ruminates about the bad luck he has had and how bad he is feeling at work due to the pain. He is waiting to be assessed for a permanent work disability, which he perceives would be the solution to all his problems. Although he continues to go to work, he has stopped interacting with his co-workers beyond working hours because he says that with his pain, he cannot socialize in typical ways (e.g., standing and talking at a bar). M. believes that, in general, people do not understand his situation. His wife is one exception. In fact, she is the one taking care of all the housework because he is unable to help due to the pain. He can no longer help around the house (e.g., setting the dinner table and washing dishes), which is bothersome to him because it means that his wife takes care of everything. In response, M. experiences thoughts of worthlessness and feelings of sadness, but anxiety and worry are what bothers him the most. He would like to stop thinking "about everything," but especially the pain and how it is impacting his life. He is currently taking medication for pain and sleep, which he thinks is helping. M. has restricted his activities to those either at home or at work—he barely leaves the house, with the exception of going to work. At home, he spends most of the time lying on the coach or in bed. He has

Table 3.3 A Case Formulation with the UP in Health Conditions: An Example with Chronic Pain

HEALTH CONDITION ANALYSIS						
Health condition description: Chronic low back pain with radiating pain into his left leg.						
How health condition (and its treatment) affects the patient's life?			**EMOTION ANALYSIS REGARDING HEALTH CONDITIONS AND ITS CONSEQUENCES**			
General life aspects		**Affectation/ interference** **0__________10** **Nothing Very Much**	**Strong uncomfortable emotions** Do patients feel strong emotions in any of these general life aspects?	**Intensity** **0__________10** **Nothing Extreme**	**Aversive reactions**	**Emotional behaviors** (Situational avoidance/ escape, subtle behavioral avoidance, cognitive avoidance, safety signals)
1. **Physical and basic necessities**	**Physical symptoms**: Dizziness and breathless when in high anxiety.	9	Anxiety	8	"I'm feeling worse and worse."	Rest in bed/coach
	Eat: Usually not hungry.	7	Depression and anger	7	"Why take care of me?"	Not preparing meals, ordering fast food
	Sex: Lost interest (painful, which causes him to ruminate and lose contact with the experience). Only under request by wife, which is becoming less frequent.	8	Depression and anger	6	"I'm not like I used to be"; "She is not enjoying sex with me as much as before."	Using pain to justify avoiding sex
	Sleep: Problems with falling sleep and maintaining sleep. He tends to watch TV until late on the coach.	9	Anxiety and anger	8	"I won't fall asleep."	Pills to sleep; avoids going to bed (TV until late); rumination about his situation

	Activity: Restricted to going to work. He no longer exercises.	9	Depression	7	"I cannot bear seeing my friends doing the same things I used to do."	Avoids physical activity; rest in bed/coach
	Energy: Very frequently fatigued, especially on working days.	8	Depression	7	"I'm not a useful person anymore"; "My wife is getting bored of me."	Rest in bed/coach
	Pain: Low back and left leg.	10	Anxiety and anger	9	"Feeling pain is intolerable for me."	Pain hypervigilance
	Medication side effects: Sedated.	7	Anger	7	"Why I have to suffer that much."	Poor medication adherence
	General: He can take care of himself (relatively autonomous in terms of self-hygiene and basic needs).	8				
2. **Work/studies**: He completed secondary education studies and then went to work. He has had similar positions as an operator since he was 16. He has never taken positions of high responsibility as he has always been reluctant to do so (he would feel anxiety if proposed).		8	Anxiety	8	"Nobody understand my situation"; "I feel the worst at work and it's not going to be better."	Request permanent work disability
3. **Daily life activities** (to buy, to cook, to clean, etc.): None. All performed by his wife.		10	Anxiety and depression	9	"I'm not a useful person anymore."	Ask wife for help or order delivery

(*continued*)

Table 3.3 CONTINUED

HEALTH CONDITION ANALYSIS					
Health condition description: Chronic low back pain with radiating pain into his left leg.					
How health condition (and its treatment) affects the patient's life?		**EMOTION ANALYSIS REGARDING HEALTH CONDITIONS AND ITS CONSEQUENCES**			
General life aspects	**Affectation/ interference** **0____10** **Nothing Very Much**	**Strong uncomfortable emotions** Do patients feel strong emotions in any of these general life aspects?	**Intensity** **0____10** **Nothing Extreme**	**Aversive reactions**	**Emotional behaviors** (Situational avoidance/ escape, subtle behavioral avoidance, cognitive avoidance, safety signals)
4. **Pleasant activities** (hobbies, sport, etc.): He watches TV and sometimes plays with puzzles.	8	Anxiety, anger, and depression	6	"Why me"; "I won't enjoy my hobbies anymore."	Does not exercise anymore (used to cycle and run); only joins some activities when not in pain or when pain medication is available
5. **Personal relationships** (couple, family, friends, etc.): His social interactions are very restricted. He tends to avoid people at work, as he perceives them as lacking empathy for his situation. He feels that he cannot keep up with the rhythm with his friends, so he blames his pain when they make plans to avoid joining them. He interacts with his wife, who is very understanding, and his two children (they do not live at home, so they interact less now). He used to visit his parents very often, but now that he is in pain he only goes to their place once every 2 weeks.	9	Anxiety, anger, and depression	9	"They are not empathic with my situation."	Defensive with others; avoids social interactions if possible; meets with other people who are sensitive to the problem or with whom he can cancel at last minute

6. **Spirituality**: Used to be religious. He claims to be catholic, but he does not pray or go to church anymore.	6	Depression	5	"Nothing can help me."	Minimizes the importance of faith; does not go to church; barely prays at home
7. **Life goals**: Not having pain ("If I didn't have pain, I could . . ."). When exploring what he would actually do if he managed to get rid of the pain, he responded that he would like to get a new job (as a concierge), exercise with friends, travel more with his wife, do more work at home, visit his children and do more activities with them, visit his parents more often, and start learning a new language (Portuguese).	9	Anxiety, anger, and depression	9	"I cannot do what I want because feeling this pain is horrible."	Restricts goals to non-painful ones; joins activities if escape or cancellation is easy
8. **Others**: None required.					
TREATMENT PLAN					
MODULE 1					
Setting the treatment goals and gaining motivation. Identify problem areas in the patient (work, social life, and household chorus). Set treatment goals. Treatment goals are not focused on reducing pain, but on learning emotion regulation strategies that will allow the patient to engage in behaviors that were previously avoided due to their emotional/physical implications. Motivation will focus on regaining valued activities. Explore costs and benefits of changing/staying the same (e.g., focusing on pain control only).					
MODULE 2					
Psychoeducation.Understanding emotions. Learning the function of emotions and how they develop. Emotions (anxiety and fear of pain) are barriers to patient engagement with valued activities. In this module, we will explain how emotions develop and what their function is (and what is not). Analysis of the emotional response (antecedent → emotional response → consequence). Identify emotional triggers (e.g., perceived misunderstanding of others, mistake made at work, or increase in pain).					

(continued)

Table 3.3 Continued

MODULE 3
Mindful emotional awareness. Pain and anxiety are usually avoided by the patient. Therefore, an effort will be made to encourage present-focused and nonjudgmental contact with both sensations (physical and emotional). Identify emotional/pain-related responses using mindfulness and awareness exercises to observe pain and its associated consequences (e.g., anxiety and anger) without running away from them.
MODULE 4
Cognitive flexibility. To analyze the relationship between automatic negative thoughts and his emotional/physical sensations and behaviors. The patient usually makes some rigid and automatic inferences/appraisals of events (e.g., "If I engage in this social activity, I will surely have pain and the others will not be empathetic about it. If this happens, it will be terrible and it will mean that other people are mean"). In this module, we will work on generating alternative thoughts (cognitive reappraisal) that make room for more diverse behavioral options ("If I engage in this social activity, I may or may not have pain and the others may or may not be more or less empathetic about it. I will probably have several ways of managing my pain if it does occur in the social situation").
MODULE 5
Identifying and countering emotional avoidance behaviors. We will identify emotional and pain behaviors (e.g., avoiding social interactions that could end in disappointment due to perceived lack of empathy) and learn their maladaptive role. Learn alternative actions incompatible with emotion/pain-avoidance-driven behaviors (e.g., actively report on his pain status and acknowledge the pain-related difficulties).
MODULE 6
Increasing awareness and confronting physical sensations. In this module, we will focus of the identification of physical sensations (e.g., pain, dizziness, and breathlessness) associated with intense emotions (e.g., sadness or anxiety). While some of these sensations are more chronic than others (i.e., pain), chronic pain is not a sign of damage/danger to the body. To confront physical sensations associated with difficult emotions, we will practice pain/dizziness-inducing exercises approved by his primary physician (e.g., climbing stairs, light weight lifting, and ball-passing).

MODULE 7
Emotional exposures. Understand the importance of emotional/painful exposure and setting a hierarchy to expose to previously avoided emotions, potentially painful activities, thoughts, memories, or places. We will conduct the exposures to tolerate the intense anxiety, sadness, or anger. For example, M. will need to confront different social situations, to talk about his pain, to increase health activities, etc.
MODULE 8
Relapse prevention. Recognizing accomplishments and looking to the future. Review the skills learned, review evolution, and promote generalization of skills to all contexts (home, family relations, hobbies, social life, and work). It will be necessary to establish a work plan in order to continue practicing the new emotion regulation strategies (e.g., mindfulness exercises regarding body symptoms) and to think in future risk situations to figure out how to deal with the intense emotions he will probably experience (e.g., some coworker says that he is faking his symptoms).
OTHER MODULES IF NECESSARY
M.may benefit from communication skills to facilitate the expression of his feelings and thoughts to other people (e.g., assertiveness).

no social activities, except for interactions with his wife, his two children (aged 25 and 23 years, both living outside the home), and his parents and parents-in-law. He avoids all other social activities.

EMOTIONAL DISORDER ASSESSMENT CHALLENGES AND TECHNOLOGY-BASED SOLUTIONS

To date, most research examining transdiagnostic emotional disorder constructs in the context of treatment has been limited by having few follow-up timepoints (e.g., pre-, mid-, and post-treatment) and assessing constructs retrospectively over relatively long episodes/periods. For instance, self-report questionnaires typically assess the frequency of using emotion regulation strategies "in general," whereas symptoms typically are assessed over a period of several weeks (Colombo, Fernández-Álvarez, Garcia-Palacios, et al., 2019). However, many emotional disorder dimensions may fluctuate and influence one another over much shorter time periods. Along these lines, research suggests that the impact of emotion regulation strategies on mood and anxiety is a dynamic process highly sensitive to contextual/situational factors (Aldao, 2013; Peeters et al., 2003). In addition, research has shown that retrospective assessment might be problematic because depressed individuals tend to overestimate negative affective states when evaluated retrospectively (e.g., mood-state distortion; Brown, 2007; Colombo, Suso-Ribera, et al., 2020). The assessment of behaviors, beliefs, and emotions more directly in the contexts in which they occur is likely to offer a more valid assessment of an individual's experiences (Rubenstein & Pugh, 2006).

Ecological Momentary Assessment

Ecological momentary assessment (EMA), also referred as experience sampling, is an alternative to retrospective assessment that aims to capture the dynamics of individuals in real-world settings. The word "ecological" denotes the focus of this methodology on assessing constructs directly in the real-life environments in which they occur (cf. in a lab or waiting room). The term "momentary" reflects the assessment of an individual's current (in vivo) thoughts, feelings, or behaviors, as opposed to past recalled experiences (Kirchner & Shiffman, 2013). Although EMA has existed for several decades, initial paper-and-pencil approaches (e.g., diaries) had significant compliance-related limitations, with many individuals completing EMA entries retrospectively rather than "in the moment" as directed (Stone et al., 2003).

With the increasing availability of smartphones and user-friendly dairy/assessment apps, the feasibility of EMA has dramatically improved during the past decade (Suso-Ribera et al., 2018). In addition, wearable devices and embedded biosensors have emerged as interesting alternatives to self-reports, for example, in the assessment of emotion regulation and downstream consequences in real-life settings (e.g., sleep patterns, physical activity, social interactions, electrical activity to derive heart rate variability, galvanic skin response, or temperature) (Colombo, Fernández-Álvarez, Patane, et al., 2020). Overall, EMA technologies, especially via smartphones, are appealing across health care settings due to their ubiquity, familiarity, and relative ease of use (Yang et al., 2019).

Smartphone-based EMA allows for the monitoring of events, thoughts, feelings, and behaviors in real-life settings using both prompted (e.g., receiving a notification or text message every hour requesting an EMA entry) and unprompted approaches (e.g., being directed to complete an EMA entry every time an event or emotional reaction occurs) (Kirchner & Shiffman, 2013). Accordingly, smartphone EMA can be used to overcome the aforementioned limitations associated with episodic, retrospective assessment conducted in non-ecological settings. For example, assessments can be designed to prevent retrospective assessment and backfilling by setting specific times when responses can be provided (Suso-Ribera et al., 2018). Importantly, a wide range of behaviors (e.g., medication compliance, self-injury, and avoidance), subjective experiences (e.g., mood, pain, and stress), and contextual data (e.g., environment, location, and social interactions) can be captured with EMA (Aan het Rot et al., 2012; Suso-Ribera et al., 2018), consistent with the aforementioned need to assess a broad range of transdiagnostic emotional disorder dimensions.

Clinical Applications

Ecological momentary assessment could have important clinical benefits in the case conceptualization and treatment planning of emotional disorders and co-occurring physical health problems. For example, EMA can be used for in vivo assessment of physical health symptoms, emotions, aversive reactions, and escape/avoidance behavior. EMA also can be used for the rapid detection of clinical deterioration (e.g., suicidality) or engaging in risky health behaviors (e.g., not taking medications) (Suso-Ribera et al., 2018), which can inform real-time interventions (i.e., ecological momentary intervention) (Myin-Germeys et al., 2016) or personalizing treatments (i.e., measurement-based care) (Gual-Montolio et al., 2020). Along these lines, EMA-based monitoring of emotional reactions and their antecedents and consequences (e.g., symptoms associated with current health condition) can be used to facilitate functional analysis and case conceptualization (cf. paper-and-pencil/retrospective self-monitoring), as well as in vivo exposure (e.g., tracking substance use disorders or heart rate during homework exposures) (McDevitt-Murphy et al., 2018). EMA-based assessment might be particularly useful in disentangling the temporal associations between physical health symptoms and emotional reactions, potentially informing points of intervention (e.g., when to implement a particular emotion regulation strategy) (Colombo, Fernández-Álvarez, et al., 2020). In addition, EMA may reduce the assessment burden on the clinician by making face-to-face interviewing more efficient (i.e., because ecologically relevant data are available a priori) (Santangelo et al., 2014).

Limitations of Ecological Momentary Assessment

Although a promising avenue for emotional disorder assessment, smartphone-based EMA has some noteworthy limitations. For example, similar to paper-and-pencil EMA, problems with compliance and data loss are common, especially in long-term assessments and very frequent daily sampling (Rodríguez-Blanco et al., 2018). In addition to sending reminders (e.g., text messages or push alerts) to the clients (Rofey et al., 2010), alarms can be sent to clinicians to notify them of missing data (Suso-Ribera et al., 2020). Nevertheless, the burden of EMA should be anticipated and minimized by thoughtfully selecting the optimal number of prompts/reminders to balance compliance with ecological validity. Economic incentives (Burke et al., 2017) or gamification (van Berkel et al., 2017) might be additional useful practices to increase completion rates. There also are issues surrounding data safety (e.g., how EMA data are stored to ensure that access by unwanted entities is controlled) and content validity (e.g., whether health care professionals participated in EMA content development) of EMA apps (Nicholas et al., 2015). In addition, there are very few clinical trials exploring the utility of EMA (Han & Lee, 2018). Thus, work is needed to (a) lay a foundation of acceptable data safety procedures for EMA technology (e.g., how the data are securely stored and how privacy is ensured), (b) involve mental health professionals in EMA content development, and (c) determine if EMA has value in routine clinical care (Suso-Ribera et al., 2020).

Technical problems also can occur when collecting EMA data (e.g., app updates and uncharged batteries), which must be monitored to minimize attrition and missing data (Colombo, Fernández-Álvarez, Patane, et al., 2019). Along these lines, the extent to which technology-supported EMA can be effectively implemented in routine care for emotional disorders or physical health conditions is still unclear. To date, the majority of studies implementing EMA in clinical samples have utilized an economic incentive to complete assessments and minimize dropouts (Gaudiano et al., 2015; Wen et al., 2017), which is not likely to be feasible and sustainable in routine care. More research using non-monetary forms of compliance motivation is needed to shed light on the feasibility of technology-based EMA for the assessment of emotional disorders in traditional (non-research) clinical settings.

CONCLUSION

Many individuals experience comorbid emotional disorders and physical health conditions. Fortunately, there are several tools available to aid clinicians in the assessment, case conceptualization, and treatment planning of these patients. Self-report questionnaires can be used to assess the higher order emotional disorder traits that prospectively predict physical health (e.g., neuroticism and emotion regulation), as well as the narrow emotional disorder symptom dimensions that often co-occur with physical disorders (e.g., depression and somatic anxiety). These data can then be combined with a clinician's functional analysis of a patient's emotions, thoughts, and behaviors using a systematic rubric of idiographic case conceptualization and treatment planning (see UP therapist guide and Table 3.3). At the same time, there are limitations associated with the retrospective assessment and case conceptualization of transdiagnostic emotional disorder dimensions (e.g., mood-state distortion). Although EMA is a promising approach to improving emotional disorder assessment and case formulation, significant efforts are needed to determine if, and how, EMA can be integrated into routine clinical care.

REFERENCES

Aan het Rot, M., Hogenelst, K., & Schoevers, R. A. (2012). Mood disorders in everyday life: A systematic review of experience sampling and ecological momentary assessment studies. *Clinical Psychology Review, 32*(6), 510–523.

Abramowitz, J. S., Olatunji, B. O., & Deacon, B. J. (2007). Health anxiety, hypochondriasis, and the anxiety disorders. *Behavior Therapy, 38*, 86–94.

Aldao, A. (2013). The future of emotion regulation research: Capturing context. *Perspectives on Psychological Science, 8*(2), 155–172.

Aldao, A., & Nolen-Hoeksema, S. (2010). Specificity of cognitive emotion regulation strategies: A transdiagnostic examination. *Behaviour Research and Therapy, 48*, 974–983.

Aldao, A., Nolen-Hoeksema, S., & Schweizer, S. (2010). Emotion-regulation strategies across psychopathology: A meta-analytic review. *Clinical Psychology Review, 30*, 217–237.

American Psychiatric Association. (2013). *Diagnostic and statistical manual of mental disorders* (5th ed.). American Psychiatric Publishing.

Bair, M. J., Robinson, R. L., Katon, W., & Kroenke, K. (2003). Depression and pain comorbidity: A literature review. *Archives of Internal Medicine, 163*, 2433–2445.

Barlow, D. H. (2002). *Anxiety and its disorders: The nature and treatment of anxiety and panic* (2nd ed.). Guilford.

Barlow, D. H., Farchione, T. J., Sauer-Zavala, S., Latin, H. M., Ellard, K. K., Bullis, J. R., Bentley, K. H., Boettcher, H. T., & Cassiello-Robbins, C. (2017). *Unified Protocol for transdiagnostic treatment of emotional disorders: Therapist guide*. Oxford University Press.

Barlow, D. H., Sauer-Zavala, S., Carl, J. R., Bullis, J. R., & Ellard, K. K. (2014). The nature, diagnosis, and treatment of neuroticism: Back to the future. *Clinical Psychological Science, 2*, 344–365.

Ben-Porath, Y. S., & Tellegen, A. (2020). *Minnesota Multiphasic Personality Inventory–3(MMPI-3)*. University of Minnesota Press.

Boettcher, H., & Conklin, L. R. (2018). Transdiagnostic assessment and case formulation: Rationale and application with the Unified Protocol. In D. H. Barlow & T. J. Farchione (Eds.), *Applications of the Unified Protocol for transdiagnostic treatment of emotional disorders* (pp. 17–37). Oxford University Press.

Brown, T. A. (2007). Temporal course and structural relationships among dimensions of temperament and DSM-IV anxiety and mood disorder constructs. *Journal of Abnormal Psychology, 116*(2), 313–328.

Brown, T. A., & Barlow, D. H. (2009). A proposal for a dimensional classification system based on the shared features of the DSM-IV anxiety and mood disorders: Implications for assessment and treatment. *Psychological Assessment, 21*, 256–271.

Brown, T. A., Campbell, L. A., Lehman, C. L., Grisham, J. R., & Mancill, R. B. (2001). Current and lifetime comorbidity of the DSM-IV anxiety and mood disorders in a large clinical sample. *Journal of Abnormal Psychology, 110*, 585–599.

Brown, T. A., & McNiff, J. (2009). Specificity of autonomic arousal to DSM-IV panic disorder and posttraumatic stress disorder. *Behaviour Research and Therapy, 47*(6), 487–493. https://doi.org/10.1016/j.brat.2009.02.016

Bullis, J. R., Boettcher, H., Sauer-Zavala, S., & Barlow, D. H. (2019). What is an emotional disorder? A transdiagnostic mechanistic definition with implications for assessment, treatment, and prevention. *Clinical Psychology Science and Practice, 26*(2), e12278.

Burke, L. E., Shiffman, S., Music, E., Styn, M. A., Kriska, A., Smailagic, A., Siewiorek, D., Ewing, L. J., Chasens, E., French, B., Mancino, J., Mendez, D., Strollo, P., & Rathbun, S. L. (2017). Ecological momentary assessment in behavioral research: Addressing technological and human participant challenges. *Journal of Medical Internet Research, 19*(3), e77.

Carver, C. S., & White, T. L. (1994). Behavioral inhibition, behavioral activation, and affective responses to impending reward and punishment: The BIS/BAS scales. *Journal of Personality and Social Psychology, 67*, 319–333.

Cash, M., & Whittingham, K. (2010). What facets of mindfulness contribute to psychological well-being and depressive, anxious, and stress-related symptomatology? *Mindfulness, 1*(3), 177–182. https://doi.org/10.1007/s12671-010-0023-4

Charles, S. T., Gatz, M., Kato, K., & Pedersen, N. L. (2008). Physical health 25 years later: The predictive ability of neuroticism. *Health Psychology, 27*(3), 369–378.

Colombo, D., Fernández-Álvarez, J., Garcia-Palacios, A., Cipresso, P., Botella, C., & Riva, G. (2019). New technologies for the understanding, assessment, and intervention of emotion regulation. *Frontiers in Psychology, 10*, 1261. doi:10.3389/fpsyg.2019.01261. eCollection 2019.

Colombo, D., Fernández-Álvarez, J., Patane, A., Semonella, M., Kwiatkowska, M., Garcia-Palacios, A., Cipresso, P., Riva, G., & Botella, C. (2019). Current state and future directions of technology-based ecological momentary assessment and intervention for major depressive disorder: A systematic review. *Journal of Clinical Medicine, 8*(4), 465. https://doi.org/10.3390/jcm8040465

Colombo, D., Fernández-Álvarez, J., Suso-Ribera, C., Cipresso, P., Valev, H., Leufkens, T., Sas, C., Garcia-Palacios, A., Riva, G., & Botella, C. (2020). The need for change: Understanding emotion regulation antecedents and consequences using ecological momentary assessment. *Emotion, 20*(1), 30–36. https://doi.org/10.1037/emo0000671

Colombo, D., Suso-Ribera, C., Fernández Álvarez, J., Cipresso, P., Garcia-Palacios, A., Riva, G., & Botella, C. (2020). Affect recall bias: Being resilient by distorting reality. *Cognitive Therapy and Research, 44*, 906–918.

Costa, P. T., & McCrae, R. R. (1992). *NEO PI-R professional manual*. Psychological Assessment Resources.

Costa, J., & Pinto-Gouveia, J. (2013). Experiential avoidance and self-compassion in chronic pain. *Journal of Applied Social Psychology, 43*, 1578–1591.

Das-Munshi, J., Stewart, R., Ismail, K., Bebbington, P. E., Jenkins, R., & Prince, M. J. (2007). Diabetes, common mental disorders, and disability: Findings from the UK National Psychiatric Morbidity Survey. *Psychosomatic Medicine, 69*(6), 543–550.

El-Gabalawy, R., Mackenzie, C. S., Thibodeau, M. A., Asmundson, G. J. G., & Sareen, J. (2013). Health anxiety disorders in older adults: Conceptualizing complex conditions in late life. *Clinical Psychology Review, 33*, 1096–1105.

Feldner, M. T., Hekmat, H., Zvolensky, M. J., Vowles, K. E., Secrist, Z., & Leen-Feldner, E. W. (2006). The role of experiential avoidance in acute pain tolerance: A laboratory test. *Journal of Behavior Therapy and Experimental Psychiatry, 37*, 146–158.

Gámez, W., Chmielewski, M., Kotov, R., Ruggero, C., & Watson, D. (2011). Development of a measure of experiential avoidance: The Multidimensional Experiential Avoidance Questionnaire. *Psychological Assessment, 23*, 692–713.

Gaudiano, B., Moitra, E., Ellenberg, S., & Armey, M. (2015). The promises and challenges of ecological momentary assessment in schizophrenia: Development of an initial experimental protocol. *Healthcare, 3*(3), 556–573.

Griffith, J. W., Zinbarg, R. E., Craske, M. G., Mineka, S., Rose, R. D., Waters, A. M., & Sutton, J. M. (2010). Neuroticism as a common dimension in the internalizing disorders. *Psychological Medicine, 40*, 1125–1136.

Gross, J. J., & John, O. P. (2003). Individual differences in two emotion regulation processes: Implications for affect, relationships, and well-being. *Journal of Personality and Social Psychology, 85*, 348–362.

Gual-Montolio, P., Martínez-Borba, V., Bretón-López, J. M., Osma, J., & Suso-Ribera, C. (2020). How are information and communication technologies supporting routine outcome monitoring and measurement-based care in psychotherapy? A systematic review. *International Journal of Environmental Research and Public Health, 17*(9), 3170.

Han, M., & Lee, E. (2018). Effectiveness of mobile health application use to improve health behavior changes: A systematic review of randomized controlled trials. *Healthcare Informatics Research, 24*(3), 207–226.

Haslam, N., McGrath, M. J., Viechtbauer, W., & Kuppens, P. (2020). Dimensions over categories: A meta-analysis of taxometric research. *Psychological Medicine, 50*(9), 1418–1432.

Hedman, E., Ljótsson, B., Axelsson, E., Andersson, G., Rück, C., & Andersson, E. (2017). Health anxiety in obsessive compulsive disorder and obsessive compulsive symptoms in severe health anxiety: An investigation of symptom profiles. *Journal of Anxiety Disorders, 45*, 80–86.

Johnson, S. L., Edge, M. D., Holmes, M. K., & Carver, C. S. (2012). The behavioral activation system and mania. *Annual Review of Clinical Psychology, 8*, 243–267.

Kirchner, T. R., & Shiffman, S. (2013). Ecological momentary assessment. In J. MacKillop & H. de Wit (Eds.), *The Wiley-Blackwell handbook of addiction psychopharmacology* (pp. 541–565). Wiley-Blackwell.

Kotov, R., Gámez, W., Schmidt, F., & Watson, D. (2010). Linking "big" personality traits to anxiety, depressive, and substance use disorders: A meta-analysis. *Psychological Bulletin, 136*, 768–821.

Kotov, R., Krueger, R. F., Watson, D., Achenbach, T. M., Althoff, R. R., Bagby, R. M., Brown, T. A., Carpenter, W. T., Caspi, A., Clark, L. A., Eaton, N. R., Forbes, M. K., Forbush, K. T., Goldberg, D., Hasin, D., Hyman, S. E., Ivanova, M. Y., Lynam,

D. R., Markon, K., . . . Zimmerman, M. (2017). The Hierarchical Taxonomy of Psychopathology (HiTOP): A dimensional alternative to traditional nosologies. *Journal of Abnormal Psychology, 126*, 454–477.

Lovibond, S. H., & Lovibond, P. F. (1995). *Manual for the Depression Anxiety Stress Scales* (2nd ed.). Psychology Foundation of Australia.

Magee, J. C., Harden, K. P., & Teachman, B. A. (2012). Psychopathology and thought suppression: A quantitative review. *Clinical Psychology Review, 32*, 189–201.

McDevitt-Murphy, M. E., Luciano, M. T., & Zakarian, R. J. (2018). Use of ecological momentary assessment and intervention in treatment with adults. *Focus, 16*(4), 370–375.

Myin-Germeys, I., Klippel, A., Steinhart, H., & Reininghaus, U. (2016). Ecological momentary interventions in psychiatry. *Current Opinion in Psychiatry, 29*(4), 258–263.

Naragon-Gainey, K., Gallagher, M. W., & Brown, T. A. (2013). Stable "trait" variance of temperament as a predictor of the temporal course of depression and social phobia. *Journal of Abnormal Psychology, 122*, 611–623.

Nicholas, J., Larsen, M. E., Proudfoot, J., & Christensen, H. (2015). Mobile apps for bipolar disorder: A systematic review of features and content quality. *Journal of Medical Internet Research, 17*(8), e198.

Pasquini, M., & Biondi, M. (2007). Depression in cancer patients: A critical review. *Clinical Practice and Epidemiology in Mental Health, 3*, 2.

Peeters, F., Nicolson, N. A., Berkhof, J., Delespaul, P., & DeVries, M. (2003). Effects of daily events on mood states in major depressive disorder. *Journal of Abnormal Psychology, 112*(2), 203–211.

Prince, M., Patel, V., Saxena, S., Maj, M., Maselko, J., Phillips, M. R., & Rahman, A. (2007). No health without mental health. *Lancet, 370*(9590), 859–877.

Quartana, P. J., & Burns, J. W. (2007). Painful consequences of anger suppression. *Emotion, 7*, 400–414.

Rapee, R. M., Craske, M. G., & Barlow, D. H. (1994). Assessment instrument for panic disorder that includes fear of sensation-producing activities: The Albany Panic and Phobia Questionnaire. *Anxiety, 1*, 114–122.

Renna, M. E., Shrout, M. R., Madison, A. A., Lustberg, M., Povoski, S. P., Agnese, D. M., Reinbolt, R. E., Wesolowski, R., Williams, N. O., Bhuvaneswari, R., Sardesai, S. D., Noonan, A. M., VanDeusen, J. B., Malarkey, W. B., & Kiecolt-Glaser, J. K. (2021). Worry and rumination in breast cancer patients: Perseveration worsens self-rated health. *Journal of Behavioral Medicine, 44*(2), 253–259.

Rodríguez-Blanco, L., Carballo, J. J., & Baca-García, E. (2018). Use of ecological momentary assessment (EMA) in non-suicidal self-injury (NSSI): A systematic review. *Psychiatry Research, 263*, 212–219.

Rofey, D. L., Hull, E. E., Phillips, J., Vogt, K., Silk, J. S., & Dahl, R. E. (2010). Utilizing ecological momentary assessment in pediatric obesity to quantify behavior, emotion, and sleep. *Obesity, 18*(6), 1270–1272.

Rosellini, A. J., & Brown, T. A. (2014). Initial interpretation and evaluation of a profile-based classification system for the anxiety and mood disorders: Incremental validity compared to DSM-IV categories. *Psychological Assessment, 26*, 1212–1224.

Rosellini, A. J., & Brown, T. A. (2019). The Multidimensional Emotional Disorder Inventory (MEDI): Assessing transdiagnostic dimensions to validate a profile approach to emotional disorder classification. *Psychological Assessment, 31*, 59–72.

Rubenstein, L. V., & Pugh, J. (2006). Strategies for promoting organizational and practice change by advancing implementation research. *Journal of General Internal Medicine, 21*(Suppl. 2), 58–64.

Sansone, R. A., & Sansone, L. A. (2012). Rumination: Relationships with physical health. *Innovations in Clinical Neuroscience, 9*, 29–34.

Santangelo, P., Bohus, M., & Ebner-Priemer, U. W. (2014). Ecological momentary assessment in borderline personality disorder: A review of recent findings and methodological challenges. *Journal of Personality Disorders, 28*(4), 555–576.

Sartorius, N., Holt, R. I., & Maj, M. (Eds.). (2014). *Comorbidity of mental and physical disorders*. Karger.

Shipley, B. A., Weiss, A., Der, G., Taylor, M. D., & Deary, I. J. (2007). Neuroticism, extraversion, and mortality in the UK Health and Lifestyle Survey: A 21-year prospective cohort study. *Psychosomatic Medicine, 69*, 923–931.

Spinhoven, P., Drost, J., de Rooij, M., van Hemert, A. M., & Penninx, B. W. (2014). A longitudinal study of experiential avoidance in emotional disorders. *Behavior Therapy, 45*, 840–850.

Steel, P., Schmidt, J., & Shultz, J. (2008). Refining the relationship between personality and subjective well-being. *Psychological Bulletin, 134*, 138–161.

Stone, A. A., Shiffman, S., Schwartz, J. E., Broderick, J. E., & Hufford, M. R. (2003). Patient compliance with paper and electronic diaries. *Controlled Clinical Trials, 24*(2), 182–199.

Suso-Ribera, C., Castilla, D., Zaragozá, I., Mesas, Á., Server, A., Medel, J., & García-Palacios, A. (2020). Telemonitoring in chronic pain management using smartphone apps: A randomized controlled trial comparing usual assessment against app-based monitoring with and without clinical alarms. *International Journal of Environmental Research and Public Health, 17*(18), 6568.

Suso-Ribera, C., Castilla, D., Zaragozá, I., Ribera-Canudas, M. V., Botella, C., & García-Palacios, A. (2018). Validity, reliability, feasibility, and usefulness of Pain Monitor: A multidimensional smartphone app for daily monitoring of adults with heterogeneous chronic pain. *Clinical Journal of Pain, 34*(10), 900–908.

Treynor, W., Gonzalez, R., & Nolen-Hoeksema, S. (2003). Rumination reconsidered: A psychometric analysis. *Cognitive Therapy and Research, 27*, 247–259.

van Berkel, N., Goncalves, J., Hosio, S., & Kostakos, V. (2017). Gamification of mobile experience sampling improves data quality and quantity. *Proceedings of the ACM on Interactive, Mobile, Wearable and Ubiquitous Technologies, 1*(3), 1–21.

Watson, D., Clark, L. A., & Tellegen, A. (1988). Development and validation of brief measures of positive and negative affect: The PANAS scales. *Journal of Personality and Social Psychology, 54*, 1063–1070.

Watson, D., O'Hara, M. W., Naragon-Gainey, K., Koffel, E., Chmielewski, M., Kotov, R., Stasik, S. M., & Ruggiero, C. J. (2012). Development and validation of new anxiety and bipolar symptom scales for an expanded version of the IDAS (the IDAS-II). *Assessment, 19*, 399–420.

Watson, D., Stanton, K., Khoo, S., Ellickson-Larew, S., & Stasik-O'Brien, S. M. (2019). Extraversion and psychopathology: A multilevel hierarchical review. *Journal of Research in Personality, 81*, 1–10.

Wen, C. K. F., Schneider, S., Stone, A. A., & Spruijt-Metz, D. (2017). Compliance with mobile ecological momentary assessment protocols in children and adolescents: A systematic review and meta-analysis. *Journal of Medical Internet Research, 19*(4), e132.

World Health Organization. (2019). *International statistical classification of diseases and related health problems* (11th ed.). https://icd.who.int

Yang, Y. S., Ryu, G. W., & Choi, M. (2019). Methodological strategies for ecological momentary assessment to evaluate mood and stress in adult patients using mobile phones: Systematic review. *Journal of Medical Internet Research, 21*(4), 1–11.

Zinbarg, R. E., Mineka, S., Bobova, L., Craske, M. G., Vrshek-Schallhorn, S., Griffith, J. W., Wolitzky-Taylor, K., Waters, A. M., Sumner, J. A., & Anand, D. (2016). Testing a hierarchical model of neuroticism and its cognitive facets: Latent structure and prospective prediction of first onsets of anxiety and unipolar mood disorders during 3 years in late adolescence. *Clinical Psychological Science, 4*, 805–824.

4

The Unified Protocol for Transdiagnostic Treatment of Emotional Disorders in Type 2 Diabetes

STEPHANIE L. LEUNG, TODD J. FARCHIONE, ELIZABETH H. EUSTIS, LINDSEY PAPPALARDO, AND JEFFREY S. GONZALEZ ■

PREVALENCE AND COST OF TYPE 2 DIABETES

Type 2 diabetes mellitus (T2D) affects approximately 30 million people in the United States and is the seventh leading cause of death (Centers for Disease Control and Prevention [CDC], 2020). Uncontrolled T2D is associated with a number of health risks, including increased risk of stroke, heart disease, kidney failure, and amputations (CDC, 2011, 2020). The United States spends approximately $245 billion per year on diabetes management (American Diabetes Association [ADA], 2018a,b). Lack of engagement with diabetes care regimens is prevalent (DiMatteo, 2004) and associated with poor health outcomes. In fact, diabetes self-management and medication adherence may be the central factors that explain discrepancies in the control of diabetes observed in clinical practice versus clinical treatment trials (Edelman & Polonsky, 2017).

Stephanie L. Leung, Todd J. Farchione, Elizabeth H. Eustis, Lindsey Pappalardo, and Jeffrey S. Gonzalez, *The Unified Protocol for Transdiagnostic Treatment of Emotional Disorders in Type 2 Diabetes* In: *Applications of the Unified Protocol in Health Conditions*. Edited by: Jorge Osma and Todd J. Farchione, Oxford University Press.
DOI: 10.1093/oso/9780197564295.003.0004

ANXIETY AND DEPRESSIVE SYMPTOMS AND DISORDERS ARE PREVALENT IN T2D

Individuals with diabetes are disproportionately likely to have mental health symptoms and disorders, the most common being anxiety and depression (Almawi et al., 2008; Chien & Lin, 2016; Mezuk et al., 2008; Peyrot & Rubin, 1997; Smith et al., 2018). A comprehensive review of psychiatric and psychosocial issues among individuals with diabetes highlighted depression and anxiety as important conditions consistently related to the prevalence of diabetes, its control and management, and treatment outcomes (Gonzalez et al., 2018). However, according to this review, far more research has focused on depression than anxiety, despite similar evidence of increased prevalence and association with poor health outcomes. Furthermore, no well-conducted treatment trials for anxiety in diabetes were identified. Having a T2D diagnosis may contribute to the development or worsening of anxiety disorders due to perceived burdens of disease management and the threat of complications (Bener et al., 2012; Maes et al., 1996; Peyrot & Rubin, 1997; Pouwer, 2009). Fear of hypoglycemia (glucose level <70 mg/dL; ADA, 2022) is an example of diabetes-specific emotional distress that can represent a clinically significant barrier to diabetes management, as an individual might purposefully eat excessively, or take less insulin than prescribed, to avoid possible aversive symptoms of hypoglycemia such as loss of consciousness (Wild et al., 2007). Anxiety and avoidance related to insulin use, often involving distress and apprehension about anticipated harms of insulin therapy, is a further example of a diabetes-specific affective construct that may interfere with appropriate intensification of therapy and adherence to insulin prescriptions in T2D (Polonsky, Fisher, Earles, et al., 2005). More broadly, diabetes-related distress (i.e., concern and fear about living with and managing diabetes) has been proposed as an important affective construct in diabetes care that is specific to living with the burdens of a chronic, life-threatening illness and demanding self-management regimen (Polonsky et al., 1995; Polonsky, Fisher, Earles, et al., 2005). Affective components of diabetes can range in severity (from situational distress to psychopathology) and may relate to diabetes-related stressors and the resources available to cope with them (Fisher et al., 2014; Gonzalez et al., 2011). Thus, there is a considerable evidence base establishing the importance of anxiety, depression, and diabetes-related distress in T2D. Although expert guidelines acknowledge the importance of addressing these issues in the management of T2D, evidence for a comprehensive treatment approach is currently lacking (Young-Hyman et al., 2016).

DIABETES SELF-MANAGEMENT IS A MAJOR EXPLANATORY PATHWAY FOR THE INFLUENCE OF AFFECTIVE COMPONENTS OF DIABETES ON DIABETES HEALTH OUTCOMES

Various plausible biobehavioral mechanisms have been proposed to account for relationships between affective components of diabetes and diabetes health outcomes (Gonzalez et al., 2018). These include shared metabolic pathways (e.g., persistent, high levels of autonomic arousal triggering excessive release of counterregulatory hormones, leading to insulin sensitivity and other issues), psychotropic medications that contribute to weight gain and subsequent glycemic dyscontrol (Baptista et al., 2002; Newcomer & Haupt, 2006), and unhealthy behaviors (e.g., cigarette smoking, overeating, and alcohol use; Chien & Lin, 2016). Given their close associations with affective components of diabetes and clear impact on treatment outcomes, health behaviors specific to self-management of diabetes may represent the most plausible of these potential pathways and are the most relevant to clinical practice (Young-Hyman et al., 2016). Daily management of diabetes may contribute to feelings of distress and anxiety (Maes et al., 2012) that, along with depression, are associated with poorer physical health and increased utilization of medical services, lower levels of adherence to diabetes self-management, higher incidence of uncontrolled diabetes, and increased rates of diabetes-related complications (Al-Hayek et al., 2012; Ciechanowski et al., 2000; de Groot et al., 2010; DiMatteo et al., 2000; Gonzalez et al., 2008; Lin et al., 2004; Lustman & Clouse, 2005; Surwit et al., 1992). The presence of symptoms related to anxiety and depression, such as problems with concentration and focus, preoccupation with negative thoughts about the self and one's future, and low energy and motivation, may directly impair one's ability to carry out complex tasks involved in diabetes management.

EXISTING DIABETES ADHERENCE AND SELF-MANAGEMENT PROGRAMS DO NOT ADDRESS THE AFFECTIVE COMPONENTS OF DIABETES IN A COMPREHENSIVE AND INTEGRATED MANNER

Self-management training and support programs exist for diabetes but have mostly focused on diabetes-specific outcomes. For example, a large systematic review of randomized controlled trials indicated that self-management programs demonstrate improvements in individuals' diabetes knowledge and glycemic control from pre–post intervention, with more mixed results for longer term follow-up (Norris et al., 2001). However, only one included study measured anxiety (Scott et al., 1984), highlighting the lack of research specific to anxiety. Although numerous treatment studies have evaluated psychological interventions for depression in the context of diabetes, with some evidence of benefits for glycemic control, these approaches have tended to focus only on depression and do not target the behavioral components of diabetes self-management (Baumeister et al., 2012; Markowitz et al., 2011). These approaches have largely failed to demonstrate any impact on measures of self-management or treatment adherence (Lin et al., 2006, 2012; Markowitz et al., 2011). In contrast, evidence suggests that integrative interventions that incorporate self-management training and support within the treatment of depression can positively impact self-management and glycemic control. One integrative intervention for T2D patients already taking antidepressant therapy found significant benefits for depression severity, adherence to antidepressant and anti-hyperglycemic medications, and glycemic control, compared to usual care (Bogner et al., 2012). Safren and colleagues (2010) developed another integrative treatment, Cognitive Behavioral Therapy for Adherence and Depression (CBT-AD), for depression and diabetes self-management. CBT-AD demonstrated significant beneficial impacts for clinician-rated depression severity and objectively measured glucose self-monitoring, medication adherence, and glycemic control in clinically depressed adults with T2D (Safren et al., 2014). Both integrative approaches involved ongoing monitoring and feedback of medication adherence based on electronic monitoring of medication bottle openings (Medication Event Monitoring System). Significant anxiety and diabetes distress were likely quite prevalent among participants in these trials but not reported. No interventions have been developed to comprehensively address the range of affective components typically seen in T2D, nor have they been designed to incorporate strategies to support successful diabetes self-management.

AN INTEGRATIVE APPROACH FOR ADDRESSING AFFECTIVE COMPONENTS AND BEHAVIORAL SELF-MANAGEMENT OF DIABETES IS NEEDED

Mental health issues are often overlooked or poorly addressed in settings in which diabetes care is provided. Patients with anxiety, depression, or other emotional disorders (i.e., disorders characterized by reactivity to emotions and avoidant coping; Bullis et al., 2019) are generally referred out to specialty mental health providers, who often lack the knowledge and experience necessary to provide high-quality care for people with diabetes (Bickett & Tapp, 2016; Young-Hyman et al., 2016). Despite collaborative efforts from the ADA and American Psychological Association to develop educational programs to help mental health providers better identify and treat diabetes-related issues (ADA, 2018b), the lack of comprehensive approaches that can address the broad spectrum of emotional disorders experienced by people with diabetes limits the potential impact of these initiatives. Although many evidence-based psychological treatments (EBPTs) for mental health disorders exist (Chambless & Ollendick, 2001; Layard & Clark, 2014), efforts to integrate them into clinical settings have been limited by the burden of training clinicians to competently administer multiple interventions for single disorders (Cook et al., 2009; Gray et al., 2013). As a result, clinicians often fail to use EBPTs to treat cases with more complex comorbidity in routine care, due to perceived lack of fit (Stirman et al., 2012), and instead rely on a more eclectic approach, limiting exposure to EBPTs (von Ranson et al., 2013). This problem extends to existing protocols for comorbid mental health problems and diabetes, which only target specific psychological disorders (e.g., depression; Safren et al., 2014). Transdiagnostic approaches offer one solution in that they can treat a wide range of presenting symptoms within one treatment protocol (Barlow et al., 2017), and they could be applied to treat diabetes self-management and a broad range of co-occurring mental health symptoms and disorders.

TRANSDIAGNOSTIC TREATMENT FOR COMORBID DIABETES AND DISTRESS

The Unified Protocol for Transdiagnostic Treatment of Emotional Disorders (UP) is an evidence-based cognitive–behavioral protocol for anxiety, depression, and related emotional disorders (Barlow et al., 2017, 2018; Casiello-Robbins et al., 2020; Eustis, Cardona, et al., 2020) that may fulfill this need in diabetes care. The UP consists of five core modules designed to target temperamental characteristics associated with neuroticism, particularly negative emotionality, and aversive reactions to emotional experiences when they occur (Boswell et al., 2013; Carl et al., 2014; Eustis, Gallagher, et al., 2020; Sauer-Zavala & Barlow, 2021; Sauer-Zavala et al., 2012, 2021). These shared underlying mechanisms are important to the development and maintenance of all anxiety, depressive, and related disorders (Barlow et al., 2014). To date, the potential generalizability of the UP as a practical solution to address common mental health issues in diabetes management has not yet been evaluated. This case study explores the potential application of the UP to directly address affective components of diabetes among adults with T2D, including emotional and behavioral challenges specific to diabetes—for example, fear of hypoglycemia, difficulty monitoring blood glucose levels, and disordered eating behavior. Diabetes-related distress, level of impaired functioning, depressive symptoms, and anxious symptoms were assessed pre- and post-intervention. A clinical psychologist in an integrated diabetes care clinic conducted the evaluation and administered the UP, with case consultation by one of the treatment developers.

CASE EXAMPLE

"Carmen" was a 56-year-old, partnered, Hispanic, heterosexual, cisgender woman who presented for an evaluation in an integrated diabetes care clinic with T2D and co-occurring anxiety and depressive symptoms. Carmen described a long-standing history of depression and anxiety during the 2 years prior to UP treatment. She related the onset of depression to a past back injury and ensuing chronic pain, which interfered with her ability to work. She noted feeling distressed about this change in her professional life and by her loss of independence—for example, reduced capability to cook due to low grip strength, limitations in mobility. Prior to starting the UP, Carmen tried to cope with bouts of depression by listening to music, dancing, crocheting, or engaging in household tasks.

At age 39 years, Carmen was diagnosed with T2D, later complicated by retinopathy (damage of the retina), which has been treated. She also had gastroesophageal reflux disease (GERD) and abdominal pain and bloating. She experienced symptoms that overlapped with a suboptimal eating pattern of inconsistent meals and frequent and excessive eating at night. At the time of assessment, she reported eating an excessive amount of food for 2 hours late at night, which appeared characteristic of binge eating disorder. Subsequently, she would stay awake until the food was digested and, after falling asleep, would gag or vomit, which was an effect of GERD and gastrointestinal symptoms. These episodes would occur approximately three times a week, accompanied by eating more rapidly than normal, eating when not hungry, and eating in response to experiencing negative emotions. Carmen described this pattern as ongoing for the 4 months prior to engaging in the UP. During UP treatment, she developed possible gastroparesis, a complication of T2D characterized by impaired stomach emptying. Carmen's gastrointestinal medical conditions created a complex picture of her binge eating pattern.

Carmen described previous engagement in optimal diabetes self-care when she was previously employed. At that time, she regularly consumed organic foods and vegetables, exercised, and practiced yoga. Stopping work, compounded by the COVID-19 pandemic (which began 10 months prior to initiation of UP treatment), impeded her ability to engage in these health behaviors because she was not leaving her home. She also reported forgetting to take diabetes medication, and at the beginning of UP treatment, she was starting to resolve this by tracking medication-taking with a calendar and the aid of her adult daughter.

In addition to being concerned about her physical health, Carmen also endorsed anxiety about her neighborhood environment (e.g., concern about safety due to witnessing multiple shootings over years' time) and social factors (e.g., low-income housing that constantly required maintenance). Carmen described since childhood being exposed to neighborhood violence and threats to her safety, which established a pattern of feeling she always had to be on the defensive. As an adult in her own home, she feared that a stranger would break in or that she would be endangered if she opened her apartment door to receive a package or take out the garbage; this led to reliance on her adult children's presence to ensure a feeling of safety. In addition, Carmen described that during childhood, she witnessed her mother using alcohol excessively, which often resulted in her mother's expressions of anger. Carmen noted these experiences as contributing to feelings of instability and difficulty coping with her own emotions, anger specifically.

Carmen reported a history of panic attacks that began years prior to starting UP treatment. She recalled her first panic attack occurring after a motor vehicle accident, which was followed by back spasm and feeling stuck and unable to walk, resulting in the reliance on a stranger and a friend to help her get home. Carmen stated that cardiac evaluation within a year prior to starting UP was negative for a medical explanation for her anxiety and panic. Her panic attacks were usually preceded by the feeling of her legs giving out and being unable to stand. Following the onset of panic attacks, Carmen was worried about having additional panic attacks and tended to avoid going out alone in fear that she would collapse without aid. During UP treatment, Carmen reported her most recent full-blown panic attack occurred a few months prior to the onset of UP treatment, in which she boarded a city bus with her daughter, then collapsed and was unable to get up. Carmen discussed a similar experience of her "legs giving out" at a store, although the panic symptoms presented later. She also described other panic-like episodes, although not full-blown panic attacks, when alone at night, to which she usually responded by going outside to get air and pacing, which she found helpful.

Carmen discussed the impact of anxiety on interpersonal relationships with her loved ones and with acquaintances alike. She would check on the whereabouts of her adult children excessively, as well as enter verbal conflicts with customer service representatives when faced with a barrier to a service or product she was trying to obtain. In addition, she recognized that her preoccupation with her loved ones' safety, feeling down about her reduced autonomy, and feeling sad about reminders that she was not working due to physical ailments impeded her ability to engage in personal goals such as re-entering the workforce. With concerns about possible falls and safety in the neighborhood, Carmen endorsed a fear of going out in public by herself, which was compounded by the stay-at-home order starting in March 2020 during the COVID-19 pandemic, 10 months prior to UP treatment onset. Therefore, Carmen became accustomed to a routine of diminished activity while alone in her home, which further fueled her negative thoughts and worry.

In addition to panic and agoraphobic avoidance, Carmen described low mood, primarily driven by unemployment and physical limitations, which engendered a sense of low autonomy. She also experienced reduced interest in hobbies such as crocheting, knitting, and socializing with friends and her adult children. Carmen was also plagued by sleep disturbance, namely difficulty with sleep onset and interference from racing thoughts. In addition, she endorsed low energy levels, problems with concentration, restlessness, and feelings of worthlessness and guilt. A year prior to starting UP treatment, Carmen experienced one incident of suicidal ideation and desire to die; she coped with this event by speaking with loved ones and developing a plan to present to the hospital if she felt in acute crisis. Over the course of UP treatment, Carmen maintained this safety plan when managing suicidal ideation, which occurred one time during treatment.

Carmen's primary medical history was significant for T2D (with retinopathy, treated with laser treatment and injections), hypertension, hypersensitivity lung disease, fibromyalgia, GERD, and gastroparesis. After psychological evaluation, Carmen met *Diagnostic and Statistical Manual of Mental Disorders*, fifth edition (DSM-5; American Psychiatric Association, 2013), criteria for panic disorder; other specified depressive disorder, depressive episode without sufficient symptoms; and binge eating disorder, mild. In addition, scores on self-report measures are displayed in Table 4.1. Carmen's baseline score on the Patient Health Questionnaire–9 (Kroenke et al., 2001), a widely used scale to assess depression, was 14, indicating moderate depressive symptoms. On the 7-item Generalized Anxiety Disorder Scale (Spitzer et al., 2006), which screens for generalized anxiety, Carmen's baseline score was 13, suggesting moderate symptoms of generalized anxiety. The Diabetes Distress Scale (DDS; Polonsky, Fisher, Earles, et al., 2005) assesses level of concern and fear related to having and managing diabetes. The cutoff for high diabetes distress is 3.0, and Carmen scored 5.71, which suggested high distress associated with diabetes (Fisher et al., 2012). The DDS also consists of four subscales (emotional burden, regimen distress, interpersonal

Table 4.1 Baseline and Post-Treatment Descriptive Data

	Baseline	End of Treatment
PHQ-9	14	4
GAD-7	13	4
DDS	5.71	2.18
WSAS	26	15

PHQ-9, Patient Health Questionnaire–9 (range, 0–27; clinical cutoff, ≥10); GAD-7, Generalized Anxiety Disorder 7-Item Scale (range, 0–21; clinical cutoff, ≥10); DDS, Diabetes Distress Scale (range, 1–6; clinical cutoff, >2.0); WSAS, Work and Social Adjustment Scale (range, 0–40).

distress, and physician distress; Polonsky, Fisher, Earles, et al., 2005). The Work and Social Adjustment Scale (WSAS; Mundt et al., 2002) is a measure of impairment in functioning. Carmen's score of 26 suggests moderately severe impairment.

TRANSDIAGNOSTIC CONCEPTUALIZATION

Consistent with guidelines provided in *Applications of the Unified Protocol for Transdiagnostic Treatment of Emotional Disorders* (Boettcher & Conklin, 2018), we conceptualized conditions as diagnosed above and patterns that maintained anxiety, anger, and lack of engagement in diabetes self-management from a transdiagnostic framework. The UP was developed to help individuals who frequently experience intense negative emotions, have aversive reactions to strong emotions, and often respond through patterns of avoidance. Processes of both diabetes distress and general emotional distress can affect individuals with T2D. People living with T2D may experience intense emotions such as anxiety and shame about blood glucose levels that are out of target range, which may lead to avoidance of blood glucose self-monitoring or health care visits. Fear of needles can inhibit finger sticks and insulin use. Emotional eating may result in high glycemic levels. Lack of engagement in health behaviors may contribute to poor diabetes outcomes. As individuals start to confront and increasingly be present with the negative emotions tied to having diabetes, they become more acclimated to tolerating the fluctuations in diabetes distress that can occur over time. They learn to cope with intense emotions and engage in diabetes self-care more optimally.

Carmen recognized ways in which anxiety negatively influenced her diabetes self-management. She described success with diabetes self-care as periods when she was regularly exercising, taking medications, and consuming a diet consisting of fresh produce. In contrast, she noted the interplay among anxiety, sad mood, physical symptoms, and abandonment of adaptive diabetes self-management

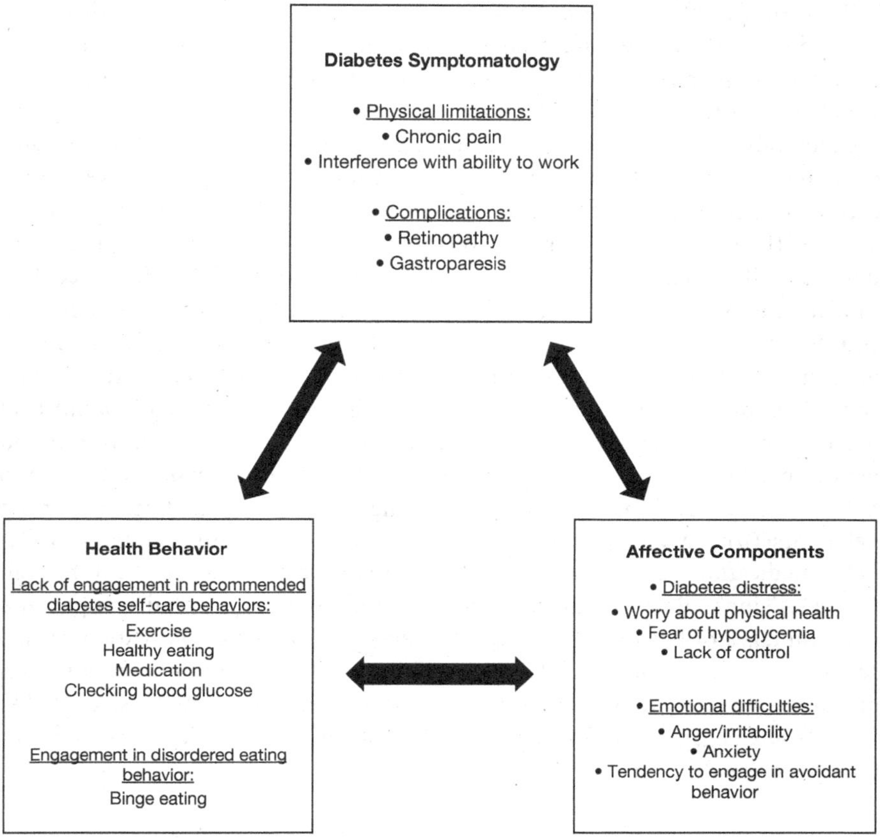

Figure 4.1 Bidirectional relationship between diabetes symptomatology, affective components, and health behaviors.

behaviors. Any reminder of her physical limitations would lead to avoidance of adaptive coping behaviors, in addition to self-isolation, irritability, and excessive worry, which posed as barriers to diabetes self-care behaviors including exercise and healthy eating (Figure 4.1).

TREATMENT

Module 1: Setting Goals and Maintaining Motivation

The first module of the UP sets the stage for treatment by employing motivational interviewing techniques to help patients establish goals and build motivation to engage in behavioral change (Miller & Rollnick, 2013). The components of this module are helpful for clarifying reasons to change and identifying obstacles and facilitators to goals among individuals with diabetes. People with

T2D often face physical limitations and decreased functioning from their premorbid state; as such, establishing goals that help them adapt to their new level of functioning can be helpful. This module was completed in one session, in which the therapist oriented Carmen to treatment, provided instructions for regular monitoring of anxiety and depression, and discussed the importance of homework. Motivational interviewing techniques were also employed to increase her readiness for change and promote self-efficacy to engage in behavior change. The therapist and Carmen collaboratively explored problems related to diabetes self-management and anxiety in the framework of the UP conceptual model. This exploration revealed unhelpful emotional response patterns that ran counter to how Carmen wanted to live her life. Namely, Carmen identified the problem of taking anger out on undeserving people, which reflected her frustration about her loss of independence. She also noted that anger would lead her to forget whether she took medications or insulin; in addition, frustration would result in low appetite and later binge eating. Carmen expressed a goal to better manage her diabetes by (a) maintaining a healthy diet and optimal eating behaviors; (b) engaging in yoga, meditation, and exercise; and (c) taking all diabetes medications as recommended. The therapist and Carmen worked through the "Decisional Balance" exercise in this module to explore advantages and disadvantages of her overarching goal to engage in diabetes self-care. Carmen identified several benefits of change, including that it will address chronic pain and allow her to regain her identity as an active person. She initially struggled to identify any negatives of working on her goals, then acknowledged that behavior change can be difficult.

Module 2: Understanding Emotions

Module 2, which focuses on the nature and function of emotions, was completed over the course of three sessions. Psychoeducation was provided on the three-component model of emotions in which cognitions, physical sensations, and behaviors factor into the experience of emotions. This model was applied to examples Carmen provided, particularly in relation to feelings of anger. Precipitating and maintaining factors of learned behaviors were also discussed. In Carmen's case, this included being conditioned to respond with defense and vigilance in the context of growing up in a rough neighborhood environment. Carmen also noted that her mother would model anger when she would drink alcohol excessively. Carmen recognized that with the view of anger as a negative and undesirable emotion, coupled with the fear of expressing her anger in the "wrong way," she developed a pattern of suppressing and internalizing anger, which was tied to sadness in the context of her loss of independence in recent years.

Antecedents, responses, and consequences of emotions (referred to as the "ARC" of emotion in the UP) were also explored. Carmen cited a specific example of frustration about her reduced independence due to her diabetes. In this example, she described a situation in which she was unable to open a jar of tomato sauce due to weakness and, as a result, had to ask one of her children for help. She noted feeling frustrated and remembered crying and being afraid when this happened. A sense of loss of control—for example, that one's diabetes is outside one's autonomy—is a common experience voiced by people with T2D. Likewise, those with diabetes often feel hopeless if they do not see a change in blood glucose control after performing recommended diabetes self-care behaviors, which can lead to avoidance of sustained engagement in these behaviors, thereby exacerbating blood glucose levels. Tracking reduced frequency of negative thoughts and lower levels of distress about functional changes that accompany diabetes might be useful to monitor over the course of UP treatment among those with T2D. In addition, tracking consistency and increased engagement in diabetes self-management behaviors (i.e., blood glucose self-monitoring, taking medications, maintaining healthy diet, and exercising) may also be useful. Through psychoeducation, these components of diabetes self-management were reviewed, and Carmen developed a reminder system to ensure that she adhered to her goal to take her medications as prescribed. In turn, progress on this goal also allowed her to regain a sense of control over her medical conditions.

Carmen also described examples of anxiety accompanied by catastrophic thoughts, short-term consequences of stomach pain, and long-term effects of anxiety lingering into the following day, which perpetuated the cycle of anxiety. For example, Carmen described one instance in which she experienced a panic attack while traveling in a cab, which caused her to feel anxious days later about an unrelated event—that is, when she did not receive an expected package in the mail. She identified common themes in both events: feeling "lost and no control" and thinking "I need to slow down and relax." Consistent with the framework of the UP, Carmen's perceived lack of control of her anxiety and her desire to control it were conceptualized as contributing to difficulties with her emotions (Figure 4.2). Over the course of this module and the subsequent one, Carmen practiced approaching her emotions in a more objective and nonjudgmental way. Carmen did well with this module and throughout UP treatment discussed times between sessions when she reflected on her emotions and how they impacted her behaviors.

Module 3: Mindful Emotion Awareness

Module 3 was completed in two sessions. In this module, the therapist provided education on using mindfulness to experience emotions in a present-focused, nonjudgmental manner. The goal of this module is to increase the patient's willingness to experience emotions without trying to avoid them by practicing present-focused awareness and nonjudgment of emotional experiences. These

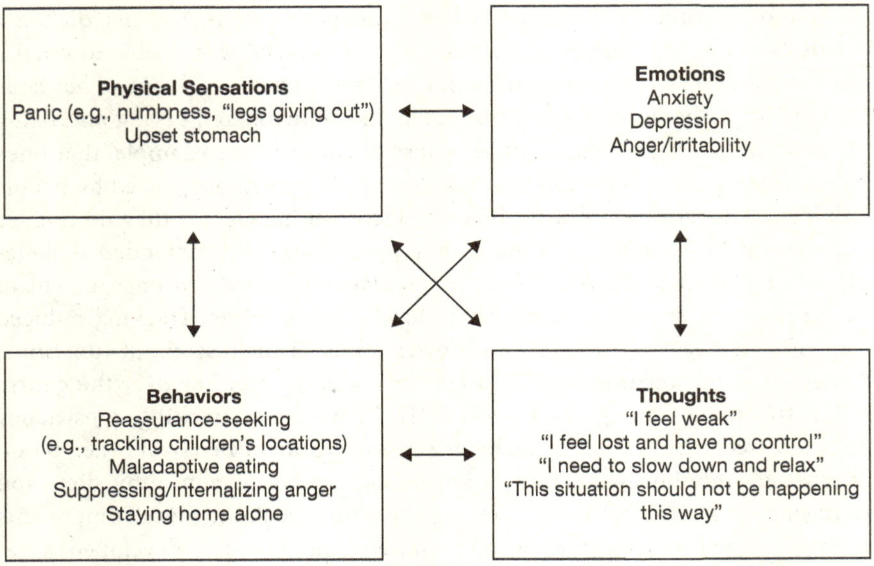

Figure 4.2 Carmen conceptualization diagram.

skills can also help facilitate the use of other CBT skills that are introduced later in the protocol.

Carmen found it beneficial to practice identifying and labeling emotions such as anger and sadness. She reflected on her past difficulty with opening the jar (described above) by recognizing she "felt weak, scared." She also expressed the thought, "Is it that serious?" which was discussed as a potential judgment about her emotional response to perceived failure. This cognition brought to light Carmen's tendency to frame situations in either a positive or a negative light, but always with the aim to strive for positivity. Upon reflection and review of Carmen's practice with mindful emotion awareness, she initially saw present-moment-focus as a way to avoid thinking about the past or future, which she was fearful might steer her toward negativity. The therapist and Carmen discussed the rationale for neutrality and lack of judgment when practicing mindful emotion awareness. For individuals with diabetes who are distressed by their reduced functioning, emphasis on the present moment can also help them notice when thoughts shift to the future or past and to gently bring their focus back to the present moment. Nonjudgment may also help with responding to challenges or setbacks in maintaining target blood glucose levels and diabetes self-care behaviors that may interrupt a critical and avoidant cycle and promote behavior change.

Carmen demonstrated the ability to actively apply mindfulness in her regular daily life outside of therapy. She practiced grounding when performing household chores. She also started routinely using meditation applications on her phone and practiced a meditation exercise twice per day.

Module 4: Cognitive Flexibility

Module 4 of the UP focuses on how thoughts influence emotions and vice versa. Patients are also taught to identify anxious and negative thinking patterns, learn ways to interrupt unhelpful thoughts, and generate other cognitions that allow for a more balanced and flexible thinking style. Over two sessions, the therapist and Carmen completed this module by using Socratic questioning, the downward arrow technique, and exploration of core beliefs to identify unhelpful thought patterns and examine their effect on Carmen's emotions and behaviors. This served as a springboard for finding more adaptive cognitions for Carmen to use in moments of intense emotion.

In this module, the therapist also taught Carmen about two types of cognitive distortions, or thinking traps: *jumping to conclusions*, or believing that a negative belief is true with little to no evidence, and *thinking the worst*, or automatically predicting the worst-case scenario will occur. The therapist and Carmen discovered that Carmen most often engaged in thinking the worst. For example, when a package she ordered did not arrive on schedule, she imagined that it was lost. She called the delivery company's customer service, and the customer service representative she spoke to could not provide specific details about the shipping status of Carmen's package. Carmen perceived the customer service representative as dismissive and disrespectful, which fueled catastrophic thoughts that her package would never arrive. Incredulous, she asked herself, "Am I really hearing this [from the customer service representative]?" as a heated reflexive reaction to the customer service representative's words, and then though to herself, "I'm not doing this." Carmen also identified the feeling of anger along with physical sensations of gastrointestinal distress—which, since childhood, often occurred in response to strong emotions in general—increased heart rate, and feeling hot. Carmen chose not to engage further with the customer service representative and abruptly ended the phone call without resolution. In this example, Carmen successfully recognized a negative emotion but then dismissed and left the upsetting interaction, which resulted in lack of resolution of the lost package. Increased practice with cognitive flexibility allowed Carmen to learn to respond to unhelpful thoughts in more productive ways. In later run-ins with strangers, Carmen exercised cognitive flexibility by recognizing that someone else's harsh tone might be more reflective of their own issues and not those of Carmen. This new way of thinking in turn allowed Carmen to move on from these interactions without stoking her own negative emotions.

In another example of practice with cognitive flexibility, Carmen was initially distressed following a gastroenterology visit during which gastroparesis was first diagnosed. As she considered the health encounter in hindsight, she felt she was not treated fairly in that her doctor did not recommend further medical testing, and instead, she had to initiate this question. After the visit, she wondered, "Why didn't [the doctor] recommend other tests? If I had good insurance, this wouldn't be happening." Carmen experienced this perceived slight as being related to her belief that she received poorer quality care from her current insurance plan. These thoughts caused considerable distress, which made it difficult for her to move forward with her care plan. After practicing cognitive flexibility, she became open to other ways of thinking about stressful situations and therefore was able to respond to distressing thoughts more calmly and achieved greater regulation of emotion. Carmen did better with this module as she continued to practice this skill in various situations.

Negative emotions such as shame among those with T2D is associated with lower attendance of medical appointments and reluctance to discuss self-care with a provider (Ritholz et al., 2014; Winkley et al., 2015). A common example of catastrophic thinking among those with T2D is fear of encountering shame and guilt when presenting to doctors' appointments if blood glucose levels are not within target range. These individuals may experience dread over attending the appointment and predict that they will receive negative news from their doctors, such as worsening of their medical condition. Thus, catastrophic thoughts about health care encounters might lead to avoidance of doctors' visits, which can lead to less medical care and, in turn, exacerbation of the physical condition. Learning and practicing cognitive flexibility would help these individuals adopt new thinking styles to better cope with challenging medical appointments and stay more engaged in health care, thus improving their management of T2D.

Many individuals with T2D also understandably have difficulty accepting their lower level of functioning compared to their premorbid state or struggle with receiving help from others. These thoughts can be tied to maladaptive thinking patterns about one's identity. Cognitive flexibility can provide more balanced views and perceptions about these individuals' disease, its impact on their identity and life, and personal ongoing strengths.

Module 5: Countering Emotional Behaviors

This module focuses on identifying patterns of maladaptive emotional responding, including avoidance of emotions (i.e., emotional behaviors). Unhelpful emotional response patterns include overt behavioral avoidance (e.g., avoiding public transportation due to fear of having a panic attack), subtle behavioral avoidance (e.g., using one's phone at a party to avoid small talk), cognitive avoidance (e.g., rumination), emotion-driven behaviors (e.g., lashing out at someone who triggered feelings of anger), and safety signals (e.g., bringing a loved one to an uncomfortable situation). Patients are taught how negative reinforcement perpetuates negative emotions. For example, Carmen reported emotional or binge eating, which is a common experience among those with T2D. The short-term reinforcement pattern of emotional eating might be that it alleviates distress or allows for short-term immediate coping with negative emotions, whereas long-term consequences include possible weight gain, frequent blood glucose readings above target range, and lack of resolution of distress. Learning the impact of binge eating patterns and emotions that underlie these behaviors allows for exploration of alternative actions for coping with negative emotions that lead to binge eating. The goal of this module is to guide patients in identifying alternative actions for responding to negative emotions and therefore institute a new way of responding to intense emotions.

This module was conducted over the course of three sessions. Carmen caught onto the concepts in this module well and self-initiated alternative actions with minimal instruction. She came to the realization that she was preoccupied with her adult children's whereabouts. Carmen recognized she was expending more energy worrying and trying to check that her children were safe, and it was taking effort and time away from her personal goals of pursuing hobbies and returning to work. Carmen uncovered a maladaptive pattern in which she would worry and ruminate about her children, then text them or track her daughter's location on a phone app to seek reassurance, which would temporarily assuage Carmen's concerns but annoy her children, leading to disagreement and conflict. In the long term, the rumination and reassurance-seeking also contributed to ongoing anxiety. Carmen planned alternative actions to seek employment and prioritize her health by engaging in exercise and meditation. Initially, Carmen was able to reduce her checking behavior by keeping the tracking app deleted, and instead she turned her attention to refining her resume and seeking job opportunities. She experienced less anxiety and also received positive feedback from her children. After some time, she fell back into the pattern of texting her daughter for updates, especially when her daughter would leave work at night. However, with continued practice focusing on her own goals and activities, Carmen did better with reducing reassurance-seeking.

Module 6: Understanding and Confronting Physical Sensations

The purpose of this module is to build awareness of physical sensations as one component of emotions and to increase tolerance of physical sensations via performance of interoceptive exposures. As people practice interoceptive exposures and change their interpretation of physical sensations, the distress around them tends to decrease. People with uncontrolled diabetes might experience frequent hyperglycemia, elevated blood glucose levels. Physical symptoms can include fatigue, headache, or shortness of breath. Generally, engagement in one's diabetes self-management regimen—regular exercise, consistent medication-taking, healthy diet, blood glucose monitoring, and adjusting insulin per a doctor's recommendation—will treat hyperglycemia. Establishing these behaviors takes time; therefore, it may take days or weeks to see fewer hyperglycemic events. During this time, interoceptive exposures, coupled with blood glucose checks to confirm if any physical symptoms might be related to hyperglycemia, might be helpful for those coping with symptoms of high blood glucose levels.

For people with T2D, it would be helpful to check blood glucose before practicing an interoceptive exposure to monitor possible real-time high or low blood glucose values. Hypoglycemia may be accompanied by shakiness, sweatiness, irritability, confusion, dizziness, and increased heart rate. In diabetes, it is paramount to treat hypoglycemia before all else. Furthermore, possible hypoglycemia unawareness (having low blood glucose without feeling symptoms) would be important for a patient to review with their medical provider before embarking on interoceptive exposure practice, as it increases the risk of severe hypoglycemic events and can be more difficult to treat earlier (Geddes et al., 2008; Henderson et al., 2003; Schopman et al., 2010).

Carmen did well with this module, which was conducted over the course of three sessions. She liked the idea of becoming more comfortable with physical sensations and was enthusiastic about the interoceptive exposures. In fact, she even might have been somewhat overzealous in one of her initial practices. She induced the sensation of numbness by holding books for 10 minutes, to the point her arms felt weak and gave out, dropping the books on her bed. The procedure of interoceptive exposure was re-reviewed, and Carmen was encouraged to start off with shorter durations of time engaging in the exposure—30 seconds or 1 or 2 minutes.

Module 7: Emotion Exposures

In this module, individuals are taught to confront emotionally provoking situations to increase comfort and tolerance with intense emotions and to practice using adaptive emotion-regulation skills. Full exposure to emotions thereby facilitates extinction of anxiety and distress associated with strong emotions. In Carmen's case, the "Emotion Exposures" module was taught before the module on physical sensations because at the time she was due to learn "Understanding and Confronting Physical Sensations," she was ill and experiencing multiple physical symptoms that would preclude purposeful induction of interoceptive exposures.

The therapist and Carmen completed the "Emotion Exposures" module over three sessions. The therapist guided Carmen in brainstorming emotion exposures that would provoke Carmen's anxiety yet would also be appropriate opportunities to practice new skills to cope with her emotions. For a couple years prior to starting UP treatment, Carmen was anxious about leaving her home by herself, as she was afraid that her legs would give out. Her anxiety was exacerbated by the onset of the COVID-19 pandemic within a year of starting the UP while she was compelled to stay at home, and she felt confined to the "four walls" of her apartment. Carmen identified exposure exercises in which she would have to leave the home. Carmen had even grown scared to open her apartment door to receive packages—she asked her neighbor to hold them for her—so she began with exposures in which she would not hastily leave her apartment for a task such as taking out garbage. With more exposure practice, she arrived at the point of receiving packages on behalf of her neighbor, exiting her apartment building, and traveling to other neighborhoods for meetings. During one of the exposures in which she ventured to a meeting, she felt anxious because strange men were greeting her, and she wondered if they were following her home. Carmen used mindful emotion awareness to recognize she was panicking and employed positive self-statements to explain to herself they might just be walking in the same direction. These proved helpful for calming her down and continuing home independently with less fear.

Fear, shame, and guilt are common negative emotions experienced by people with T2D during or in anticipation of health care encounters. Emotion exposure exercises might be developed to help people cope with these emotions. Shame and guilt might ensue when individuals try to stay engaged in their diabetes self-management plan but blood glucose values are still out of target range, and they fear they will disappoint their doctors. Sometimes individuals are fearful they are going to hear negative news during their doctors' visits, such as development of complications or recommendation to add a medication. Even worse, some individuals have experienced being directly shamed by their health care provider; this sometimes causes individuals to withdraw from medical services, which can jeopardize the long-term care and trajectory of their diabetes. Emotion exposures might include imagining or practicing conversations on these various topics with the therapist. In vivo exposures might include calling or sending a message to the doctor with a specific question about a topic an individual is dreading or raising a dreaded topic in a health care visit.

In addition to negative emotions related to health care encounters, anger is commonly experienced by individuals with T2D (Hatcher & Whittemore, 2006; Morris et al., 2005; Shiyanbola et al., 2018) and may be related to reduced functioning and independence, perceived unfairness of having diabetes, and exasperation with diabetes self-management. Emotion exposures around recognizing these realities of having diabetes may be helpful. In addition, fear, shame, and guilt may also accompany diabetes self-care behaviors such as medication-taking, blood glucose self-monitoring, dietary behavior, and exercise. Namely, people might feel ashamed and guilty for not engaging in such behaviors. This might lead to feelings of helplessness and desire to give up on T2D care, which can result in emotional eating or less engagement in diabetes self-care behaviors. Imaginal emotion exposures might involve setting aside time to deliberately allow oneself to experience negative emotions and thoughts (e.g., fears about future complications) rather than suppress them. An individual might practice situation-based exposures—for example, telling someone about missing medication doses to expose oneself to shame or guilt associated with deviating from the prescribed medication regimen. Behavioral experiments can also be incorporated into exposure practice. For someone who routinely avoids taking medication or checking their blood glucose levels, initial exposure exercises might include performing these behaviors once a week and then increasing frequency.

Module 8: Recognizing Accomplishments and Looking to the Future

The purpose of this module is to review progress over the course of UP treatment, plan for possible future difficulties, and discuss ways in which the patient can continue to use skills learned upon completion of treatment. In two sessions, the therapist and Carmen identified ways in which over time, Carmen engaged in more adaptive health behaviors, such as consistent medication-taking, exercise, and meditation. The therapist and Carmen also recognized Carmen's growth in how she perceived situations that previously made her anxious or agitated. In addition, Carmen noted improvement in her overall functioning and lower levels of anxiety and depressed mood. Carmen also overcame anxiety by ceasing checking behavior directed toward her children and by increasingly leaving her apartment for activities. Carmen identified future personal goals of completing a vocational rehabilitation program, seeking employment, and taking an international trip with her boyfriend in the following year.

CLINICAL OUTCOMES

Measures administered before and after treatment demonstrated reductions in scores across the board (Table 4.1). Post-treatment, symptoms of depression and anxiety were mild. Although DDS and WSAS indicated the presence of some emotional distress post-treatment, these scores still reflected a considerable reduction from baseline, which was consistent with Carmen's self-report during sessions and her progress on behavioral goals. These results, in conjunction with Carmen's reduced anxiety, might also reflect her increased comfort with her level of diabetes distress or impaired functioning.

Carmen also experienced improvements in diabetes outcomes. Before onset of UP treatment, Carmen's A1C was greater than 14.0%. Following treatment, her A1C was 11.7%. This reflects at least a 2.3% reduction in A1C over an 11-month period, which is a healthy pace for A1C to decline. An appropriate long-term goal might be an A1C below 7%, which is a generally recommended target with consideration of patient-specific factors to individually tailor A1C goal (ADA Professional Practice Committee, 2022). Likewise, blood glucose values she recorded in her logbook prior to starting the UP were in the range of 180 to the 300s. At the end of treatment, she reported her blood glucose levels were typically 138–284. Carmen's weight immediately prior to starting UP treatment is unknown. The most recent weight, measured at 3 months before onset of UP treatment, was 167 pounds. Her weight at 1 month following completion of the UP was 178 pounds. Weight fluctuations may be explained by several factors, including a body weight set point of approximately 178 pounds, evidenced by stable weight readings in the 170-pound range 10 years prior to UP treatment. Carmen's body might have returned to the set point of 178 pounds due to isolation and less physical activity during the COVID-19 pandemic, which started 10 months prior to initiation of UP treatment; in addition, her weight was 174 pounds at 2 months into the UP. Furthermore, a period of illness during the latter half of UP treatment also interrupted Carmen's exercise routine. Although Carmen did not experience overall weight loss following the UP, she expressed happiness and confidence around developing a regular exercise routine and reducing binge eating, which would be beneficial to long-term sustainability of behavior change.

Functionally, Carmen met several of her behavioral goals, including establishing consistency with her medication-taking plan, exercise, and healthy eating. Although her medication-taking plan started prior to beginning UP treatment, the UP might have helped her maintain this behavior and even enhance it over time, as she transitioned from writing down her medication-taking to entering the information in an app. Carmen also exhibited and reported improved coping with anger, depressed mood, and anxiety. By the end of UP treatment, she no longer met DSM-5 criteria for panic disorder, depressive disorder, or binge eating disorder.

CONCLUSION

This chapter presented a case study of the application of the UP for comorbid T2D and emotional disorders. The UP was well received as an integrated treatment approach to target aversive reactivity to strong negative emotions and associated avoidance (Table 4.2). This protocol may be easily trained and implemented in integrated diabetes centers, providing a possible one-stop shop for diabetes care rather than the siloed approach of receiving mental health treatment in a separate clinic. Training clinicians to deliver a single protocol that targets the features underlying the development and maintenance of comorbid emotional disorders and medical conditions may be more cost- and time-efficient. Considerations for the modification of the UP for T2D as described in this chapter might be helpful for mental health treatment providers who work with individuals with T2D (Table 4.3). Further integration of diabetes care and mental health care might come in the form of examining continuous glucose monitoring data to detect patterns between blood glucose readings and affect. This area warrants further investigation to understand feasibility and effectiveness in real-world settings.

Table 4.2 A Case Conceptualization with the UP in Type 2 Diabetes

HEALTH CONDITION ANALYSIS						
Health condition description: Female patient 56 years of age presenting with a history of type 2 diabetes complicated by retinopathy and gastroparesis. Prior to onset of UP treatment, the patient's hemoglobin A1c was >14.0% and blood glucose values were in the 180–300s range. The patient was referred by the treating endocrinology provider for anxiety and depressive symptoms and distress coping with chronic pain, inability to work, and loss of independence. The patient also presents with binge-eating episodes and an inconsistent meal pattern.						
How does the health condition (and its treatment) affect the patient's life?			**EMOTION ANALYSIS REGARDING HEALTH CONDITIONS AND ITS CONSEQUENCES**			
General life aspects		**Affectation/ interference** **0______10** **Nothing Very much**	**Strong uncomfortable emotions** Do patients feel strong emotions in any of these general life aspects?	**Intensity** **0______10** **Nothing Extreme**	**Aversive reactions**	**Emotional behaviors** (Situational avoidance/ escape, subtle behavioral avoidance, cognitive avoidance, safety signals)
Physical	**Eat:** Gastroesophageal reflux disease (GERD), abdominal pain, and bloating leading to inconsistent eating pattern; binge eating late at night, then waiting until food digested; then wake up gagging/vomiting Eating more rapidly than normal, eating when not hungry, and eating as a result of experiencing negative emotions	8 6	Worry Worry/guilt	10 6	Patient reported feeling distressed by her gastrointestinal symptoms, which led to irregular eating schedule and binge eating.	Binge eating late at night Using food to cope with intense emotions

Work	Unable to work	7	Guilt	8	Patient described feeling low self-esteem about leaving previous job due to physical limitations.	Distraction and thought suppression
Daily life activities	Not leaving apartment, not opening apartment door; not driving.	9	Anxiety, panic	10	Patient reported feeling afraid that something bad will happen to her if she opens apartment door, leaves apartment, drives.	Avoid going out alone
	Verbally aggressive toward customer service representatives	8	Anger, guilt	8	"This situation should not be happening this way."	Escape verbal arguments without resolution
	Cooking/eating	8	Shame, sadness	8	Patient reported a physical impact on preparing foods, which reminded her of physical shortcomings and lack of autonomy.	Relied less on fresh, whole foods; binge eating late at night
Personal relationships	Dependent on adult children	7	Shame/sadness	7	Patient described not having her own personal goals to focus on, which in turn led her to be excessively preoccupied with her adult children.	Self-critical when physical capacity fails her
	Preoccupied with knowing children's whereabouts	8	Anxiety	9		Frequently check daughter's location on tracking app
	Arguments with boyfriend	8	Anger/sadness	8		Escape verbal arguments without resolution

(continued)

Table 4.2 Continued

TREATMENT PLAN
MODULE 1
The first module of the UP sets the stage for treatment by employing motivational interviewing techniques to help patients establish goals and build motivation to engage in behavioral change. The components of this module help clarify values and identify obstacles and facilitators to goals among individuals with diabetes. People with T2D often face physical limitations and decreased functioning from their premorbid state; as such, establishing goals that help them adapt to their new level of functioning can be helpful. During this module, the therapist also orients the patient to treatment, provides instructions for regular monitoring of anxiety and depression, and discusses the importance of homework. Motivational interviewing techniques are employed to increase readiness for change and promote self-efficacy to engage in behavior change.
MODULE 2
The second module involves psychoeducation on the three-component model of emotions in which cognitions, physical sensations, and behaviors factor into the experience of emotions. An example of an experience commonly voiced by people with T2D is a sense of loss of control—for example, that one's blood glucose values are out of one's control—which can lead to feelings of sadness and anger. Likewise, those with diabetes often feel hopeless if they do not see a change in blood glucose control after performing recommended diabetes self-care behaviors, which can lead to avoidance of sustained engagement in these behaviors, thereby exacerbating blood glucose levels. Consideration is given to identify any other resultant emotion-driven behaviors that have adverse effects (e.g., binge eating). The case example reported negative thoughts related to feelings of sadness and disappointment about reduced physical and occupational functioning. Furthermore, physical symptoms associated with gastroparesis contributed to binge eating behavior.
MODULE 3
The third module focuses on mindfulness as a tool to experience emotion in a present-focused, nonjudgmental way. The purpose of this module was to (1) increase tolerance and acceptance of negative emotions, (2) decrease negative judgments about emotions, and (3) practice present-focused awareness to prepare the use of other skills that are taught later in therapy.
MODULE 4
The module on cognitive flexibility involves identification of anxious and negative thinking patterns, plus education on ways to interrupt unhelpful thoughts and generate other cognitions that allow for a more balanced thinking style. In turn, patients start to overcome their previous avoidant behaviors and to enhance acceptance of the physical impact of diabetes on their lives and functioning. The case example tended to *jump to conclusions*, which she managed to work through with skills learned in this module.

MODULE 5
The fifth module focuses on identifying patterns of maladaptive emotional responding, including avoidance of intense emotions. Patients are taught how negative reinforcement perpetuates negative emotions. Patients identify alternative actions for responding to negative emotions and therefore institute a new way of coping with intense emotions. This module offers an opportunity to explore the short-term reinforcement pattern of emotional eating (i.e., to alleviate distress or cope with negative emotions) and its long-term consequences (i.e., possible weight gain, frequent blood glucose readings above target range, lack of resolution of distress). Learning the impact of binge eating patterns and emotions that underlie these behaviors allows for exploration of alternative actions for coping with negative emotions that lead to binge eating. In the case example, the patient uncovered patterns associated with anxiety and reassurance-seeking (e.g., checking adult child's whereabouts on a location-tracking app), then identified alternative actions to cope (e.g., deleting app and instead focusing on patient's own personal goals).
MODULE 6
Module 6 involves psychoeducation on building awareness of how physical sensations occur with emotions and increasing tolerance of physical sensations via performance of interoceptive exposures. Some people with diabetes might experience frequent hyperglycemia (i.e., elevated blood glucose levels), which may be accompanied by physical symptoms of fatigue, headache, or shortness of breath. It may take weeks for an individual with T2D to establish optimal diabetes self-management behaviors (regular exercise, consistent medication-taking, healthy diet, blood glucose monitoring, and adjusting insulin per a doctor's recommendation), which will lead to less frequent hyperglycemia. During this time, interoceptive exposures, coupled with blood glucose checks to confirm if any physical symptoms might be related to hyperglycemia, might be helpful for those coping with symptoms of high blood glucose values. The case example used interoceptive exposures to learn to cope with panic symptoms of shakiness and sweatiness.
MODULE 7
Module 7 on emotion exposures focuses on teaching patients to confront anxiety-provoking situations to increase comfort and tolerance with intense emotions and to practice adaptive emotion-regulation skills. Fear, shame, and guilt are common negative emotions experienced by people with T2D during or in anticipation of health care encounters. Emotion exposure exercises might be developed to help people cope with these emotions. Emotion exposures might include imagining or practicing conversations on these various topics with the therapist. In vivo exposures might include calling or sending a message to the doctor with a specific question about a topic an individual is dreading or raising a dreaded topic in a health care visit. Emotion exposures for the case example focused on exercises in which she left the home to grow more comfortable with returning to routine activities.
MODULE 8
The purpose of the eighth module is to review progress over the course of UP treatment, plan for possible future difficulties, and discuss ways in which the patient can continue to use skills learned upon completion of treatment. The therapist and patient review gains from treatment and identify areas for continued and future practice of UP skills.

Table 4.3 Suggested Additional Considerations for UP Module Modifications for UP Treatment of T2D

UP Module	Description	Additional Considerations for T2D
Module 1: Setting goals and maintaining motivation	Use of motivational interviewing techniques to help patients establish goals and build motivation to engage in behavioral change	Address and normalize fluctuating motivation to engage in diabetes self-care over time
Module 2: Understanding emotions	Psychoeducation on the function and development of emotions, such as anxiety, sadness, anger, fear, and joy Identification of triggers, responses, and consequences of emotional responses Examination of short- and long-term consequences of emotional responses	Exploration of diabetes distress Using the three-component model and ARC, using examples specific to diabetes distress
Module 3: Mindful emotion awareness	Promote a neutral, present-focused, nonjudgmental perspective of emotions	Examine negative judgments about physical health and impact of T2D on daily functioning During meditation, if physical symptoms of hyperglycemia or hypoglycemia arise, encourage checking of blood glucose level to treat possible hypoglycemia if needed
Module 4: Cognitive flexibility	Identify negative thinking patterns and learn ways to interrupt unhelpful thoughts and generate other cognitions that allow for a more balanced, flexible thinking style	Address shame, guilt, or dread in anticipation of doctors' appointments Explore negative cognitions about oneself for having diabetes or difficulties related to the disease
Module 5: Countering emotional behaviors	Discover patterns of unhelpful emotional responding and develop more adaptive coping behaviors	Examine behaviors related to emotional eating, medication adherence issues, and scheduling and attending health care appointments
Module 6: Understanding and confronting physical sensations	Increase awareness and tolerance of physical sensations as integral to emotional experiences	Promote awareness of symptoms of hypo- and hyperglycemia and their relationship to emotions
Module 7: Emotion exposures	Confront emotional-provoking situations to increase comfort and tolerance with intense emotions and to practice adaptive emotion-regulation skills	Address emotions related to diabetes distress, potential physical limitations, and decreased functioning (e.g., developing tolerance to discomfort associated with new level of functioning)
Module 8: Recognizing accomplishments and looking to the future	Review progress over the course of treatment Plan for continued use of CBT skills in the future	De-emphasize A1c as sole marker of progress Encourage focus on emotional and behavioral functioning

REFERENCES

Al-Hayek, A. A., Robert, A. A., Alzaid, A. A., Nusair, H. M., Zbaidi, N. S., Al-Eithan, M. H., & Sam, A. E. (2012). Association between diabetes self-care, medication adherence, anxiety, depression, and glycemic control in type 2 diabetes. *Saudi Medical Journal, 33*(6), 681–683.

Almawi, W., Tamim, H., Al-Sayed, N., Arekat, M. R., Al-Khateeb, G. M., Baqer, A., Tutanji, H., & Kamel, C. (2008). Association of comorbid depression, anxiety, and stress disorders with type 2 diabetes in Bahrain, a country with a very high prevalence of type 2 diabetes. *Journal of Endocrinological Investigation, 31*(11), 1020–1024. https://doi.org/10.1007/BF03345642

American Diabetes Association. (2018a). Economic costs of diabetes in the U.S. in 2017. *Diabetes Care, 41*(5), 917–928. https://doi.org/10.2337/dci18-0007

American Diabetes Association. (2018b, September). *Mental health provider diabetes education program*. https://professional.diabetes.org/meeting/other/resources-mental-health-providers

American Diabetes Association. (2022). *Standards of Medical Care in Diabetes—2022* abridged for primary care providers. *Clinical Diabetes, 40*(1), 10–38. https://doi.org/10.2337/cd22-as01

American Diabetes Association Professional Practice Committee. (2022). 6. Glycemic targets: *Standards of Medical Care in Diabetes—2022. Diabetes Care, 45*(Suppl. 1), S83–S96. https://diabetesjournals.org/care/article/45/Supplement_1/S83/138927/6-Glycemic-Targets-Standards-of-Medical-Care-in

American Psychiatric Association. (2013). *Diagnostic and statistical manual of mental disorders* (5th ed.). American Psychiatric Publishing.

Baptista, T., Kin, N. M., Beaulieu, S., & de Baptista, E. A. (2002). Obesity and related metabolic abnormalities during antipsychotic drug administration: Mechanisms, management and research perspectives. *Pharmacopsychiatry, 35*(6), 205–219. https://doi.org/10.1055/s-2002-36391

Barlow, D. H., Cassiello-Robbins, C., Boettcher, H. T., Bentley, K. H., Bullis, J. R., Ellard, K. K., Murray Latin, H., Farchione, T. J., & Sauer-Zavala, S. (2018). *Unified Protocol for Transdiagnostic Treatment of Emotional Disorders: Workbook* (2nd ed.). Oxford University Press.

Barlow, D. H., Farchione, T. J., Bullis, J. R., Gallagher, M. W., Murray-Latin, H., Sauer-Zavala, S., Bentley, K. H., Thompson-Hollands, J., Conklin, L. R., Boswell, J. F., Ametaj, A., Carl, J. R., Boettcher, H. T., & Cassiello-Robbins, C. (2017). The Unified Protocol for Transdiagnostic Treatment of Emotional Disorders compared with diagnosis-specific protocols for anxiety disorders: A randomized clinical trial. *JAMA Psychiatry, 74*(9), 875–884. https://doi.org/10.1001/jamapsychiatry.2017.2164

Barlow, D. H., Sauer-Zavala, S., Carl, J. R., Bullis, J. R., & Ellard, K. K. (2014). The nature, diagnosis, and treatment of neuroticism: Back to the Future? *Clinical Psychological Science, 2*, 344–365.

Baumeister, H., Hutter, N., & Bengel, J. (2012). Psychological and pharmacological interventions for depression in patients with diabetes mellitus and depression. *Cochrane Database of Systematic Reviews*, 2012(12), CD008381. https://doi.org/10.1002/14651858.CD008381.pub2

Bener, A., Ghuloum, S., Al-Hamaq, A. O., & Dafeeah, E. E. (2012). Association between psychological distress and gastrointestinal symptoms in diabetes mellitus. *World Journal of Diabetes*, *3*(6), 123–129. https://doi.org/10.4239/wjd.v3.i6.123

Bickett, A., & Tapp, H. (2016). Anxiety and diabetes: Innovative approaches to management in primary care. *Experimental Biology and Medicine*, *241*(15), 1724–1731. https://doi.org/10.1177/1535370216657613

Boettcher, H., & Conklin, L. R. (2018). *Transdiagnostic assessment and case formulation: Rationale and application with the Unified Protocol.* In D. H. Barlow & T. J. Farchione (Eds.), *Applications of the Unified Protocol for Transdiagnostic Treatment of Emotional Disorders* (pp. 17–37). Oxford University Press.

Bogner, H. R., Morales, K. H., de Vries, H. F., & Cappola, A. R. (2012). Integrated management of type 2 diabetes mellitus and depression treatment to improve medication adherence: A randomized controlled trial. *Annals of Family Medicine*, *10*(1), 15–22. https://doi.org/10.1370/afm.1344

Boswell, J. F., Farchione, T. J., Sauer-Zavala, S., Murray, H. W., Fortune, M. R., & Barlow, D. H. (2013). Anxiety sensitivity and interoceptive exposure: A transdiagnostic construct and change strategy. *Behavior Therapy*, *44*(3), 417–431. https://doi.org/10.1016/j.beth.2013.03.006

Bullis, J. R., Boettcher, H., Sauer-Zavala, S., Farchione, T. J., & Barlow, D. H. (2019). What is an emotional disorder? A transdiagnostic mechanistic definition with implications for assessment, treatment, and prevention. *Clinical Psychology: Science and Practice*, 26(2), e12278. https://doi.org/10.1111/cpsp.12278

Carl, J. R., Gallagher, M. W., Sauer-Zavala, S. E., Bentley, K. H., & Barlow, D. H. (2014). A preliminary investigation of the effects of the Unified Protocol on temperament. *Comprehensive Psychiatry*, *55*(6), 1426–1434. https://doi.org/10.1016/j.comppsych.2014.04.015

Centers for Disease Control and Prevention. (2011). *National diabetes fact sheet, 2011.* https://stacks.cdc.gov/view/cdc/13329

Centers for Disease Control and Prevention. (2020). *National diabetes statistics report, 2020.* https://www.cdc.gov/diabetes/pdfs/data/statistics/national-diabetes-statistics-report.pdf

Chambless, D. L., & Ollendick, T. H. (2001). Empirically supported psychological interventions: Controversies and evidence. *Annual Review of Psychology*, *52*(1), 685–716. https://doi.org/10.1146/annurev.psych.52.1.685

Chien, I. C., & Lin, C. H. (2016). Increased risk of diabetes in patients with anxiety disorders: A population-based study. *Journal of Psychosomatic Research*, *86*, 47–52. https://doi.org/10.1016/j.jpsychores.2016.05.003

Ciechanowski, P. S., Katon, W. J., & Russo, J. E. (2000). Depression and diabetes: Impact of depressive symptoms on adherence, function, and costs. *Archives of Internal Medicine*, *160*(21), 3278–3285. https://doi.org/10.1001/archinte.160.21.3278

Cook, J. M., Biyanova, T., & Coyne, J. C. (2009). Barriers to adoption of new treatments: An internet study of practicing community psychotherapists. *Administration and Policy in Mental Health and Mental Health Services Research*, *36*(2), 83–90. https://doi.org/10.1007/s10488-008-0198-3

de Groot, M., Kushnick, M., Doyle, T., Merrill, J., McGlynn, M., Shubrook, J., & Schwartz, F. (2010). Depression among adults with diabetes: Prevalence, impact, and treatment options. *Diabetes Spectrum*, *23*(1), 15–18. https://doi.org/10.2337/diaspect.23.1.15

DiMatteo, M. R. (2004). Variations in patients' adherence to medical recommendations: A quantitative review of 50 years of research. *Medical Care, 42*(3), 200–209. https://doi.org/10.1097/01.mlr.0000114908.90348.f9

DiMatteo, M. R., Lepper, H. S., & Croghan, T. W. (2000). Depression is a risk factor for noncompliance with medical treatment: Meta-analysis of the effects of anxiety and depression on patient adherence. *Archives of Internal Medicine, 160*(14), 2101–2107. https://doi.org/10.1001/archinte.160.14.2101

Edelman, S. V., & Polonsky, W. H. (2017). Type 2 diabetes in the real world: The elusive nature of glycemic control. *Diabetes Care, 40*(11), 1425–1432. https://doi.org/10.2337/dc16-1974

Eustis, E. H., Cardona, N., Nauphal, M., Sauer-Zavala, S., Rosellini, A. J., Farchione, T. J., & Barlow, D. H. (2020). Experiential avoidance as a mechanism of change across cognitive–behavioral therapy in a sample of participants with heterogeneous anxiety disorders. *Cognitive Therapy and Research, 44*(2), 275–286. https://doi.org/10.1007/s10608-019-10063-6

Eustis, E. H., Gallagher, M. W., Tirpak, J. W., Nauphal, M., Farchione, T. J., & Barlow, D. H. (2020). The Unified Protocol compared with diagnosis-specific protocols for anxiety disorders: 12-month follow-up from a randomized clinical trial. *General Hospital Psychiatry, 67*, 58–61. https://doi.org/10.1016/j.genhosppsych.2020.08.012

Fisher, L., Gonzalez, J. S., & Polonsky, W. H. (2014). The confusing tale of depression and distress in patients with diabetes: A call for greater clarity and precision. Diabetic *Medicine, 31*(7), 764–772. https://doi.org/10.1111/dme.12428

Fisher, L., Hessler, D. M., Polonsky, W. H., & Mullan, J. (2012). When is diabetes distress clinically meaningful? Establishing cut points for the Diabetes Distress Scale. *Diabetes Care, 35*(2), 259–264. https://doi.org/10.2337/dc11-1572

Geddes, J., Schopman, J. E., Zammitt, N. N., & Frier, B. M. (2008). Prevalence of impaired awareness of hypoglycaemia in adults with type 1 diabetes. Diabetic *Medicine, 25*(4), 501–504. https://doi.org/10.1111/j.1464-5491.2008.02413.x

Gonzalez, J. S., Fisher, L., & Polonsky, W. H. (2011). Depression in diabetes: Have we been missing something important? *Diabetes Care, 34*(1), 236–239. https://doi.org/10.2337/dc10-1970

Gonzalez, J. S., Hood, K. K., Esbitt, S. A., Mukherji, S., Kane, N. S., & Jacobson, A. (2018). Psychiatric and psychosocial issues among individuals living with diabetes. In C. Cowie, S. Casagrande, A. Menke, M. Cissell, M. Eberhardt, J. Meigs, E. Gregg, W. Knowler, E. Barrett-Connor, D. Becker, F. Brancati, E. Boyko, W. Herman, B. Howard, K. Narayan, M. Rewers, & J. Fradkin (Eds.), Diabetes in America (3rd ed., Chapter 33, pp. 1-34). National Institute of Diabetes and Digestive and Kidney Diseases.

Gonzalez, J. S., McCarl, L. A., Wexler, D. J., Cagliero, E., Delahanty, L., Soper, T. D., Goldman, V., Knauz, R., & Safren, S. A. (2010). Cognitive Behavioral Therapy for Adherence and Depression (CBT-AD) in type 2 diabetes. *Journal of Cognitive Psychotherapy, 24*(4), 329–343. https://doi.org/10.1891/0889-8391.24.4.329

Gonzalez, J. S., Safren, S. A., Delahanty, L. M., Cagliero, E., Wexler, D. J., Meigs, J. B., & Grant, R. W. (2008). Symptoms of depression prospectively predict poorer self-care in patients with type 2 diabetes. Diabetic Medicine, *25*(9), 1102–1107. https://doi.org/10.1111/j.1464-5491.2008.02535.x

Gray, M., Joy, E., Plath, D., & Webb, S. A. (2013). Implementing evidence-based practice: A review of the empirical research literature. *Research on Social Work Practice, 23*(2), 157–166.

Hatcher, E., & Whittemore, R. (2006). Hispanic adults' beliefs about type 2 diabetes: Clinical implications. *Journal of the American Academy of Nurse Practitioners, 19*(10), 536–545.

Henderson, J. N., Allen, K. V., Deary, I. J., & Frier, B. M. (2003). Hypoglycaemia in insulin-treated type 2 diabetes: Frequency, symptoms and impaired awareness. Diabetic *Medicine, 20*(12), 1016–1021. https://doi.org/10.1046/j.1464-5491.2003.01072.x

Kroenke, K., Spitzer, R. L., & Williams, J. B. (2001). The PHQ-9: Validity of a brief depression severity measure. *Journal of General Internal Medicine, 16*(9), 606–613. https://doi.org/10.1046/j.1525-1497.2001.016009606.x

Layard, R., & Clark, D. M. (2014). *Thrive: The power of evidence-based psychological therapies*. Penguin.

Lin, E. H., Katon, W., Rutter, C., Simon, G. E., Ludman, E. J., Von Korff, M., Young, B., Oliver, M., Ciechanowski, P. C., Kinder, L., & Walker, E. (2006). Effects of enhanced depression treatment on diabetes self-care. *Annals of Family Medicine, 4*(1), 46–53. https://doi.org/10.1370/afm.423

Lin, E. H., Katon, W., Von Korff, M., Rutter, C., Simon, G. E., Oliver, M., Ciechanowski, P., Ludman, E. J., Bush, T., & Young, B. (2004). Relationship of depression and diabetes self-care, medication adherence, and preventive care. *Diabetes Care, 27*(9), 2154–2160. https://doi.org/10.2337/diacare.27.9.2154

Lin, E. H., Von Korff, M., Ciechanowski, P., Peterson, D., Ludman, E. J., Rutter, C. M., Oliver, M., Young, B. A., Gensichen, J., McGregor, M., McCulloch, D. K., Wagner, E. H., & Katon, W. J. (2012). Treatment adjustment and medication adherence for complex patients with diabetes, heart disease, and depression: A randomized controlled trial. *Annals of Family Medicine, 10*(1), 6–14. https://doi.org/10.1370/afm.1343

Lustman, P. J., & Clouse, R. E. (2005). Depression in diabetic patients: The relationship between mood and glycemic control. *Journal of Diabetes and Its Complications, 19*(2), 113–122. https://doi.org/10.1016/j.jdiacomp.2004.01.002

Maes, S., Leventhal, H., & de Ridder, D. T. D. (1996). Coping with chronic diseases. In M. Zeidner & N. S. Endler (Eds.), *Handbook of coping: Theory, research, applications* (pp. 221–251). Wiley.

Markowitz, S. M., Gonzalez, J. S., Wilkinson, J. L., & Safren, S. A. (2011). A review of treating depression in diabetes: Emerging findings. *Psychosomatics, 52*(1), 1–18. https://doi.org/10.1016/j.psym.2010.11.007

Mezuk, B., Eaton, W. W., Albrecht, S., & Golden, S. H. (2008). Depression and type 2 diabetes over the lifespan: A meta-analysis. *Diabetes Care, 31*(12), 2383–2390. https://doi.org/10.2337/dc08-0985

Miller, W. R., & Rollnick, S. (2013). *Motivational interviewing: Helping people change* (3rd ed.). Guilford.

Morris, J. E., Povey, R. C., & Street, C. G. (2005). Experiences of people with type 2 diabetes who have changed from oral medication to self-administered insulin injections: A qualitative study. *Practical Diabetes International, 22*(7), 239–243.

Mundt, J. C., Marks, I. M., Shear, M. K., & Greist, J. H. (2002). The Work and Social Adjustment Scale: A simple measure of impairment in functioning. *British Journal of Psychiatry, 180*, 461–464. https://doi.org/10.1192/bjp.180.5.461

Newcomer, J. W., & Haupt, D. W. (2006). The metabolic effects of antipsychotic medications. *Canadian Journal of Psychiatry, 51*(8), 480–491. https://doi.org/10.1177/070674370605100803

Norris, S. L., Engelgau, M. M., & Narayan, K. M. (2001). Effectiveness of self-management training in type 2 diabetes: A systematic review of randomized controlled trials. *Diabetes Care, 24*(3), 561–587. https://doi.org/10.2337/diacare.24.3.561

Peyrot, M., & Rubin, R. R. (1997). Levels and risks of depression and anxiety symptomatology among diabetic adults. *Diabetes Care, 20*(4), 585–590. https://doi.org/10.2337/diacare.20.4.585

Polonsky, W. H., Anderson, B. J., Lohrer, P. A., Welch, G., Jacobson, A. M., Aponte, J. E., & Schwartz, C. E. (1995). Assessment of diabetes-related distress. *Diabetes Care, 18*(6), 754–760. https://doi.org/10.2337/diacare.18.6.754

Polonsky, W. H., Fisher, L., Earles, J., Dudl, R. J., Lees, J., Mullan, J., & Jackson, R. A. (2005). Assessing psychosocial distress in diabetes: Development of the Diabetes Distress Scale. *Diabetes Care, 28*(3), 626–631. https://doi.org/10.2337/diacare.28.3.626

Pouwer, F. (2009). Should we screen for emotional distress in type 2 diabetes mellitus? Nature *Reviews Endocrinology, 5*(12), 665–671. https://doi.org/10.1038/nrendo.2009.214

Ritholz, M. D., Beverly, E. A., Brooks, K. M., Abrahamson, M. J., & Weinger, K. (2014). Barriers and facilitators to self-care communication during medical appointments in the United States for adults with type 2 diabetes. *Chronic Illness, 10*(4), 303–313. https://doi.org/10.1177/1742395314525647

Safren, S. A., Gonzalez, J. S., Wexler, D. J., Psaros, C., Delahanty, L. M., Blashill, A. J., Margolina, A. I., & Cagliero, E. (2014). A randomized controlled trial of cognitive behavioral therapy for adherence and depression (CBT-AD) in patients with uncontrolled type 2 diabetes. *Diabetes Care, 37*(3), 625–633.

Sauer-Zavala, S., & Barlow, D. H. (2021). *Neuroticism: A new framework for emotional disorders and their treatment*. Guilford.

Sauer-Zavala, S., Boswell, J. F., Gallagher, M. W., Bentley, K. H., Ametaj, A., & Barlow, D. H. (2012). The role of negative affectivity and negative reactivity to emotions in predicting outcomes in the Unified Protocol for the Transdiagnostic Treatment of Emotional Disorders. *Behaviour Research and Therapy, 50*(9), 551–557. https://doi.org/10.1016/j.brat.2012.05.005

Sauer-Zavala, S., Fournier, J. C., Jarvi Steele, S., Woods, B. K., Wang, M., Farchione, T. J., & Barlow, D. H. (2021). Does the Unified Protocol really change neuroticism? Results from a randomized trial. *Psychological Medicine, 51*(14), 2378–2387. https://doi.org/10.1017/S0033291720000975

Schopman, J. E., Geddes, J., & Frier, B. M. (2010). Prevalence of impaired awareness of hypoglycaemia and frequency of hypoglycaemia in insulin-treated type 2 diabetes. *Diabetes Research and Clinical Practice, 87*(1), 64–68. https://doi.org/10.1016/j.diabres.2009.10.013

Scott, R. S., Beaven, D. W., & Stafford, J. M. (1984). The effectiveness of diabetes education for non-insulin-dependent diabetic persons. *The Diabetes Educator, 10*(1), 36–39. https://doi.org/10.1177/014572178401000107

Shiyanbola, O. O., Ward, E. C., & Brown, C. M. (2018). Utilizing the common sense model to explore African Americans' perception of type 2 diabetes: A qualitative study. *PLoS One, 13*(11), e0207692.

Smith, K. J., Deschênes, S. S., & Schmitz, N. (2018). Investigating the longitudinal association between diabetes and anxiety: A systematic review and meta-analysis. *Diabetic Medicine*, *35*(6), 677–693. https://doi.org/10.1111/dme.13606

Spitzer, R. L., Kroenke, K., Williams, J. B., & Löwe, B. (2006). A brief measure for assessing generalized anxiety disorder: The GAD-7. *Archives of Internal Medicine*, *166*(10), 1092–1097. https://doi.org/10.1001/archinte.166.10.1092

Stirman, S. W., Kimberly, J., Cook, N., Calloway, A., Castro, F., & Charns, M. (2012). The sustainability of new programs and innovations: A review of the empirical literature and recommendations for future research. *Implementation Science*, *7*(1), 1–19. https://doi.org/10.1186/1748-5908-7-17

Surwit, R. S., Schneider, M. S., & Feinglos, M. N. (1992). Stress and diabetes mellitus. *Diabetes Care*, *15*(10), 1413–1422. https://doi.org/10.2337/diacare.15.10.1413

von Ranson, K. M., Wallace, L. M., & Stevenson, A. (2013). Psychotherapies provided for eating disorders by community clinicians: Infrequent use of evidence-based treatment. *Psychotherapy Research*, *23*(3), 333–343. https://doi.org/10.1080/10503307.2012.735377

Wild, D., von Maltzahn, R., Brohan, E., Christensen, T., Clauson, P., & Gonder-Frederick, L. (2007). A critical review of the literature on fear of hypoglycemia in diabetes: Implications for diabetes management and patient education. *Patient Education and Counseling*, *68*(1), 10–15. https://doi.org/10.1016/j.pec.2007.05.003

Winkley, K., Evwierhoma, C., Amiel, S. A., Lempp, H. K., Ismail, K., & Forbes, A. (2015). Patient explanations for non-attendance at structured diabetes education sessions for newly diagnosed type 2 diabetes: A qualitative study. *Diabetic Medicine*, *32*(1), 120–128. https://doi.org/10.1111/dme.12556

Young-Hyman, D., De Groot, M., Hill-Briggs, F., Gonzalez, J. S., Hood, K., & Peyrot, M. (2016). Psychosocial care for people with diabetes: A position statement of the American Diabetes Association. *Diabetes Care*, *39*(12), 2126–2140. https://doi.org/10.2337/dc16-2053

5

Application of a Brief Unified Protocol Program in Group Format to People Living with HIV in a Public Health Unit

ALICIA GONZÁLEZ-BAEZA, GUADALUPE RUA-CEBRIAN, JOANNA CANO-SMITH, IGNACIO PÉREZ-VALERO, AND JORGE OSMA

INTRODUCTION

The HIV Infection and Its Clinical Key Aspects

HIV is a retrovirus that can lead to progressive failure of the immune system. This retrovirus replicates as it enters vital cells, such as CD4+ T lymphocytes, and leads to their death, weakening the immune system (Moss & Bacchetti, 1989). Life-threatening conditions, such as serious opportunistic infections or severe immunodeficiency, could occur as a result of losing CD4+ T cells (Centers for Disease Control and Prevention [CDC], 2020).

People infected with HIV may experience different courses of progression. Soon after infection, people may experience the acute stage showing flu-like symptoms. Then, the infection often leads to a clinical latency or asymptomatic stage, in which people often show an absence of symptoms. If the infection is left untreated, over time, the immune system can be damaged significantly, leading to the most advanced stage—AIDS (Trilla et al., 1988). In fact, most untreated

Alicia González-Baeza, Guadalupe Rua-Cebrian, Joanna Cano-Smith, Ignacio Pérez-Valero, and Jorge Osma,
Application of a Brief Unified Protocol Program in Group Format to People Living with HIV in a Public Health Unit
In: *Applications of the Unified Protocol in Health Conditions.* Edited by: Jorge Osma and Todd J. Farchione,
Oxford University Press. © Oxford University Press 2023. DOI: 10.1093/oso/9780197564295.003.0005

people, approximately 80–90%, are diagnosed with AIDS within 7–12 years of infection (Zumla, 2010). However, a small proportion of people (5%) progress faster to AIDS, whereas others progress more slowly (4–7%) (Mellors et al., 1997; Poropatich & Sullivan, 2011).

Since 1996, antiretroviral therapy (ART) has been used to control viral replication and restore immune function to prevent HIV progression to AIDS and death; it also controls replication in peripheral fluids such as blood, vaginal fluid, or semen so that people on ART are unlikely to infect others. People who properly take ART usually remain aviremic or virologically suppressed and show undetectable HIV RNA copies in peripheral fluids, although no treatment eradicates the virus. Patients need to take ART daily to avoid viral replication and destruction of the immune system, which could begin again if the medication is stopped. Essentially, good adherence to ART is essential, and poor adherence leads to poor virological control.

Since the beginning of the epidemic, providing access to ART has been one of the greatest challenges for the World Health Organization. Unfortunately, ART is still not free in every country. Whereas 38 million people live with HIV worldwide, only approximately 26 million people (68%) had access to ART in 2020. Moreover, among people accessing treatment, approximately 88% were virological suppressed (United Nations Programme on HIV/AIDS, 2020). In the United States, for every 100 people living with HIV in 2018, 65% had access to ART, 50% were being monitored, and 56% achieved viral control (CDC, 2020b). In Spain, ART is free for everyone; most people living with HIV who follow medical monitoring receive ART (95%) and achieve viral control (90%) (Ministerio de Ciencia Innovación y Universidades, 2019).

The virus can be spread from one person to another through a variety of body fluids, such as blood, semen, vaginal fluid, or breast milk. Transmission occurs when fluids with HIV virus come into contact with membranes or damaged tissues of the non-HIV-positive person. The most common ways of HIV transmission are unprotected sex, shared needles, and mother-to-child transmission during pregnancy or birth. In the United States, new diagnoses are most often linked with sexual risk behaviors and intravenous drug use (CDC, 2020b). In Europe, the virus is spread most commonly through risky sexual behaviors, especially among men (European Centre for Disease Prevention and Control & World Health Organization, 2020). However, parenteral transmission is still prevalent in countries such as Spain (30–50%) due to the epidemic of parenteral drug use in the 1980s and 1990s (Díez et al., 2012), and studies show high frequencies of hepatitis C virus (HCV) in people living with HIV (González-García et al., 2005).

In summary, people living with HIV present multiple clinical situations and sociodemographic characteristics. Thus, clinical health psychologists must work with members of a heterogeneous HIV population who have acquired HIV in different ways and for whom access to treatment and the degree of adherence to ART vary. Thus, there are subgroups with specific needs, and their characteristics may vary widely between countries and particular settings.

Emotional Impact of HIV Infection

As described previously, people with access to treatment and good adherence have a good clinical prognosis, living with a good quality of life. However, several studies conducted in the United States and Europe indicate that emotional disorders (mood, anxiety, and related disorders) are more prevalent among people living with HIV compared to the general population (Bayón et al., 2012; Ciesla & Roberts, 2001). Depressive disorders occur in approximately one-third of this population. Furthermore, prevalences of 15.8% for generalized anxiety disorder, 10.5% for panic attack, and 14.8% for post-traumatic stress disorder have been reported (Bing et al., 2001; Olley et al., 2006).

Most people living with HIV must deal with multiple, potentially stressful, situations that can trigger negative emotions. Furthermore, significant emotional distress is often reported immediately before and after receiving an HIV diagnosis (Guzmán et al., 2012). Also, a wide range of triggers may occur throughout the disease process, such as those associated with antiretroviral treatment (starting daily dosage, effect sizes as body modifications or weight gain, change of antiretroviral regimens, etc.), hospitalizations, coping with social stigma, and disclosure stress or sexual difficulties (Martinez et al., 2012; Rendina et al., 2017).

As indicated previously, in the HIV population, several factors can be associated with emotional disorders. For instance, studies correlate having emotional disorders (e.g., depressive disorder) with more risky sexual behaviors (Carey et al., 2004); therefore, people with some emotional disorders are more vulnerable to HIV infection. Other studies have found HIV infection and some antiretroviral treatments may have neurotoxic effects that lead to disruption of the prefrontal cortex and paralimbic brain structures and may be associated with depressive symptoms (McIntosh et al., 2015; Mollan et al., 2014). Also, depression in people living with HIV may link with other factors, such as functional disability, comorbid conditions, female gender, drug abuse, exposure to violence, high neuroticism, low self-esteem, isolation, lack of support, and high HIV-related stigma (Nanni et al., 2015). Therefore, people with preexisting disorders appear to be at greater risk of being infected with HIV, and people with HIV appear to be at greater risk of presenting with emotional disorders.

Moreover, research studies associate the impact of emotional disorders with poor adherence to antiretroviral treatment and a worsening of immunological outcomes (Johnson et al., 2009; Nilsson Schönnesson et al., 2007). Other studies have found that chronic depression and stressful life events lead to a higher chance of HIV progression and death, despite antiretroviral adherence (Leserman, 2003). Thus, people living with HIV and emotional disorders or significant symptoms of depression or anxiety have a lower quality of life (Degroote et al., 2014).

PSYCHOLOGICAL TREATMENTS IN PEOPLE LIVING WITH HIV

Existing psychological interventions for people living with HIV are mainly based on cognitive–behavioral therapy (CBT) and deal with associated challenges and high levels of emotional disorders (Spies et al., 2013). Since the beginning of the epidemic, some interventions have focused on specific common symptoms or situations that cause stress, such as those developed to reduce the distress associated with recently diagnosed HIV (Yang et al., 2018) or HIV transmission risk behaviors (Kalichman et al., 2005), as well as to improve pain management (Moore et al., 2019), adherence to ART (Ballester, 2003; Joska et al., 2020), or body image and self-care (Blashill et al., 2017). Other treatments focus specifically on psychological disorders, including interventions for depressive disorders (Safren et al., 2016), substance use disorders (Moore et al., 2019), and post-traumatic stress disorders (Empson et al., 2017).

Although CBT interventions can be effective for specific disorders or situations that trigger stress, they may also present several issues for people living with HIV. The first important issue is the high level of comorbidity among different emotional disorders, which raises the question about which intervention is most appropriate to use first (Roca et al., 2009). Furthermore, therapies focused on dealing with particular stressors may have limited effects because people living with HIV are exposed to a wide range of situations that can trigger an intense emotional response (Martinez et al., 2012; Rendina et al., 2017). In addition, some people living with HIV have preexisted stigmas arising from drug use (Bayat et al., 2020) or sexual orientation (Chan & Mak, 2019; Rendina et al., 2017), which means that in addition to HIV-related stressor, they have to deal with other potentially stressful situations (Blashill et al., 2017).

Transdiagnostic interventions may help overcome these obstacles by focusing on sharing vulnerability factors and mechanisms contributing to the development and maintenance of a wide range of emotional disorders (Norton, 2012; Wilamowska et al., 2010). One example of a transdiagnostic intervention applied to people living with HIV is the HIV Anxiety Management/Reduction Treatment. This treatment is based on a transdiagnostic intervention for anxiety disorders developed by Norton (see Brandt et al., 2019) conducted in individual sessions. This intervention focuses on HIV-associated concerns, such as greater severity of HIV-related symptoms (e.g., muscle aches, nausea, and headaches), higher avoidant coping style, HIV medication nonadherence, and lower tolerance of distress (Brandt et al., 2015). In the study by Brandt et al. (2019), three participants living with HIV with a main diagnosis of anxiety disorder received the intervention over six individual sessions. The authors reported improved HIV medication adherence and quality of life in this small sample, as well as decreased anxiety, anxiety sensitivity, depression, and negative affect (Brandt et al., 2019).

A more recent transdiagnostic intervention is the Unified Protocol for Transdiagnostic Treatment of Emotional Disorders (UP), developed by Barlow and colleagues. The UP focuses on addressing difficulties in emotion regulation shared by a large range of emotional disorders (Barlow et al., 2017). The UP intervention aims to enhance tolerance of intense negative emotions (regardless of the trigger) and promote change in dysfunctional emotion regulation strategies (e.g., emotional behaviors) (Bullis et al., 2015). Furthermore, because of the UP's focus on addressing shared underlying mechanisms, as opposed to disorder-specific symptoms, it can be easily adapted according to the characteristics of the patients and population (Sauer-Zavala et al., 2020). The UP has already been adapted for a variety of applications, including emotional disorders comorbid to health conditions (e.g., cancer, Parkinson disease, and chronic pain), with encouraging preliminary results (Allen et al., 2012; Weihs et al., 2019).

We found only one study that adapted the UP to people living with HIV. This adaptation paired the UP with ESTEEM-SC (Effective Skills to Empower Effective Men–Sexual Compulsivity) over 10 individual sessions to 13 gay and bisexual men diagnosed with HIV with sexual compulsivity (Parsons et al., 2017). Positive results were reported. The protocol reduced emotion symptomatology, sexual risk behaviors, and sexual compulsivity.

Unfortunately, transdiagnostic interventions have scarcely been applied in people living with HIV and always in an individual format. Group UP intervention could be useful for addressing emotional disorders in this vulnerable population, particularly in community and public health settings in which resources are limited and the implementation of disorder-specific, individual interventions is challenging.

A BRIEF ADAPTATION OF THE UNIFIED PROTOCOL TO TREAT EMOTIONAL DISORDERS IN PEOPLE LIVING WITH HIV IN GROUP FORMAT

We developed an adaptation of the UP that included the core treatment modules of understanding emotions, increasing emotional awareness, improving cognitive flexibility, countering emotional behaviors, and practicing interoceptive and emotional exposures but was adjusted to be administered in a briefer five-session group format. In this adapted version, goal setting and motivation (Module 1 of the UP) were conducted for recruitment and participant inclusion, prior to starting the group. In all cases, patients were asked to read the complete protocol manual as homework during the treatment (Barlow et al., 2019). Group sessions lasted 120 minutes, and participants were assigned between-session "homework" tasks. Sessions 1–4 were conducted biweekly, and the fifth session was conducted after a month. The content of each session is detailed below.

Session 1: Understanding Your Emotions (Module 2 of the UP)

The primary objectives of this module were to learn the nature and function of emotions and their impact on daily life. This module also helped patients expand knowledge about their emotional response, including components, antecedents, and short- and long-term consequences of emotion-driven behaviors. The tasks during the session were focused on the psychoeducational dynamics to understand the adaptive nature of the emotions. Also, we explained the definition of emotional disorders and the ARC (antecedents, response, consequences) of their emotional experiences. In this session, people living with HIV usually described ARCs based on different emotions (i.e., anger, fear, shame, guilt, and anxiety) as they related to the impact of the HIV diagnosis, coping with the HIV status disclosure, or low self-perception due to belonging to minorities (HIV population; lesbian, gay, bisexual, or transgender population; or former intravenous drug users). Participants usually had similar shared background experiences and reflected on their thoughts, physical sensations, behaviors, and consequences. During this module, patients usually become more aware of their emotions and maladaptive emotion-driven behaviors (e.g., abandonment of rewarding activities, social avoidance, keeping secrets in significant social relationships, or rumination). As a homework assignment, patients were asked to track their emotions in highly emotional situations using the ARC for 2 weeks.

Session 2: Mindful Emotional Awareness (Module 3 of the UP)

The main objective of this module was to observe participants' daily emotional responses and reactions to emotions, with a mindful attitude of nonjudgment and present-focused awareness. The tasks during the session were focused on the psychoeducational dynamics to understand mindfulness from the review of the ARCs made at home, particularly focusing on the mind jumps to the past or future. We conducted the following exercises: "take a step back," a brief raising meditation, a brief mindful breathing meditation, and a brief music meditation. In this session, people living with HIV reflect on how they usually think about the future, which often generates anxiety—for example, thinking that others will reject them if they discover that they have been diagnosed with HIV or if they think they will develop serious side effects from the antiretroviral treatments. Some patients also become aware when their minds become too focused on the past. For example, a person who in the past felt rejected by his family or peers because of his sexual orientation may think "the same rejection will happen again" and mentally relive that situation in the presence of new antecedents. We observed a similar process in people with previous drug addiction history or belonging to other minorities.

For homework, each patient was asked to continue completing their ARC in new intense emotional situations. Furthermore, patients were asked to carry out informal meditation practices in daily activities (e.g., mindfulness during a shower or a meal) and complete the mindfulness practice form.

Session 3: Cognitive Flexibility (Module 4 of the UP)

The primary objectives of this module were to (a) understand how emotions and thoughts are associated with improving mental flexibility, (b) identify automatic thoughts, and (c) learn cognitive reappraisal. The tasks during the session were focused on psychoeducational dynamics to understand cognitive flexibility and the difference between "describing" and "interpreting" a situation. We conducted the "ambiguous image exercise" to introduce the importance of cognitions in emotional experiences and the concept of flexible thinking. We also helped patients identify common "thinking traps" and went through examples to help them practice flexible thinking. In this session, some participants become aware that their interpretations used to be that other people judge them or they tend to think that the worst is going to happen (e.g., rejection by HIV or other conditions, body image impact of treatments and other effect sizes, or they feel they will not be able to tolerate some future situation). Patients learn to generate alternative thoughts and more flexible interpretations. In our clinical experience, this appeared to be facilitated by the group format of treatment. For example, a patient believes with total certainty that his partner will reject him if he discloses his HIV status, and if this happens, he would not be able to handle his emotions. As the result of the group dynamic, other patients can share their feelings regarding this important aspect in relationships and/or can share their experiences in this regard and how they managed this situation. It is also possible that all the participants in the group think about possible alternative thoughts if they were in this exact situation. These group dynamics can help generate alternative thoughts and reduce the certainty of the negative automatic thoughts. Thereby, the patient would become aware of different outcomes and is able to think that "if the worst happened, I could handle it like some of my group partners did or I did in other situations" or "if he rejected me for this, he probably would not be a good partner in other areas." Psychologists should facilitate during the session that those participants who were previously exposed to typically feared situations related to disclosure of HIV or other stressors will share how they felt, what they thought, and how they handled the situation. In addition, it is interesting to highlight how they feel and think about it in the present. As a homework assignment, each participant continues completing their ARCs in new intense emotional situations and carries out informal meditation. They are asked to become aware of their "thinking traps" and to complete the correspondent practice form. We gave examples to provide guidance to do this homework based on related common concerns of people living with HIV and particularly thinking traps that were shared previously by the participants. Some frequent thinking traps were related to guilt about the HIV infection, including thoughts such as "I am permanently damaged [due to HIV or to Antiretroviral (ARV)]" or "I deserve to have HIV." These thoughts sometimes occur in gay people who recognize their internalized homophobia that is strengthened with an HIV diagnosis, and they also sometimes occur in people who have been diagnosed with HIV due to parenteral drug use. For example, a patient passively accepted all the decisions that his partner made without giving his point of view or opinion, thinking that he had no right to do so because his wife "had already done enough accepting his HIV condition." As a result, he felt inadequate all the time and "worthless." Through the questions in the practice form, we encouraged this person to challenge this thought at home, and we also asked the other patients if they had any suggestions for the person. Based on our experience, participants usually provide interesting questions, such as "If anyone in this group told you that he/she thinks is worthless, then what would you say to him/her?" "If you think that you are worthless and guiltier only because of HIV, then do you think everyone here is worthless and guilty too?" or "Can you tell us about other situations that show you are worthless?" Asking the group to propose topics that they think the other participants may explore at home is a powerful therapeutic tool that helps members of this population, who are not used to sharing their emotional states because of shame and guilt.

Session 4: Countering Emotional Behaviors, and Interoceptive and Emotion Exposures (Modules 5–7 of the UP)

The primary objectives of this module were to understand the relationship between a patient's emotional behaviors and their emotional difficulties and to understand emotional exposure as an adaptative mode of coping with emotional experiences. Tasks during the session were focused on psychoeducational dynamics to expand knowledge about avoidance of physical sensations, emotions, and situations and the short- and long-term consequences. We used "the white bear exercise." We used several examples from the *UP Workbook* to help patients identify their emotional behaviors and generate alternative (or opposite) behaviors to each one. The patients found it easier to track their own emotional behaviors and reflect on their consequences from the book examples. People living with HIV avoid intimacy and sexual intercourse, leading to a clear avoidance behavior. Sometimes, they feel an irrational fear and anxiety about infecting someone despite the almost nonexistent probability of doing so by patients well-treated with ARV. During the session, they come to understand the short-term relief of anxiety from avoiding intimacy and sexual intercourse and the long-term maladaptive emotional regulation strategy that reinforces the belief that isolation is the best strategy to be "safe" and "free of guilt." Other reasons for avoidance may be related to difficulties tolerating positive affect of feelings ("being loved or wanted despite HIV" or "not being able to be excited about anything") or low self-esteem, reinforced by the HIV diagnosis or related to previous internalized homophobia powered by the HIV diagnosis. They identify the short-term consequence they gain if they do not worry about their needs of joy, connection, or self-acceptance and also how they can experience negative long-term consequences by accepting their depression and their self-criticism. They also understand how cognitive rumination provides them short-term relief, believing that they are solving the problems but worsening their feelings in the long term.

In this session, following discussion of emotional behaviors, we focused on increasing patients' tolerance of intense emotions through exposure. As a first step, participants were asked to identify physical sensations associated with their intense emotions and then performed interoceptive exposure exercises (e.g., hyperventilation and running in the same place). Next, we helped participants complete a personal emotional exposure hierarchy that included situations, places, physical sensations, memories, thoughts, etc. that trigger an intense emotion, such as anxiety, shame, anger, or sadness. Examples include avoidance of anxiety about revealing serostatus or other aspects related to their history to someone significant, avoidance of anger with an inability to assert oneself, and avoidance of shame because of how they were infected or because how they are perceived by others when they reduce social contact. For example, some participants avoided the anxiety caused by thinking about social situations in which they should disclose their HIV status. Some of them mentioned the "fear to get too close to someone and then not being a good friend if do not tell that person that I have the HIV." To avoid deciding about their HIV status disclosure, they isolated themselves socially for years, progressively presenting more generalized anxiety in social situations. During session, they learned several resources: how avoidance led them to a higher long-term level of anxiety, how to tolerate the physical sensations associated with anxiety, and how to create a hierarchy of emotional exposure to different intense emotions that they had been avoiding. For homework, patients were encouraged to continue completing their ARC in new intense emotional situations, carry out informal meditation, and use cognitive flexibility. We also recommended continued practice of specific interoceptive exercises and asked patients to progress with completing exposures based on their personal hierarchy. We again asked the group to support others' hierarchy choices to take advantage of common emotional experiences between people living with HIV. A participant was encouraged by companions to change their behavior step by step, helped by the hierarchy: "Why don't you open yourself to go out with someone in the short term?" They suggested some steps such as going to a disco (something that the participant had not done for several years ago), talking to someone nice, or just joining a dating app.

Session 5: Recognize Achievements and Look to the Future (Module 8 of the UP)

The main objectives of this module were to review the treatment basis and skills learned in previous sessions, evaluate the progress since the beginning, identify skills for improvement and new goals, and develop a practice plan for the future for each participant. The tasks during the session were focused on psychoeducational dynamics to review modules and skills previously learned, group dynamics to complete the assessment and practice plan form, and anticipate difficulties and propose solutions among all participants. The module also included a farewell and closing time. As a homework assignment, each participant was encouraged to continue practicing all emotion regulation strategies they learned during the course of the program.

CASE EXAMPLE

S. is a 52-year-old Spanish heterosexual woman, a housewife, currently receiving government assistance for disability. She acquired HIV sexually, diagnosed 15 years ago, with controlled viremia for 12 years. S. lives with her 27-year-old daughter, who works as a veterinarian, and her 22-year-old son, who discontinued his academic studies and has been suffering from depression for 6 years. S. reports being infected with HIV by her ex-husband as he was her only sexual partner, and she reports being emotionally unstable since her diagnosis 15 years ago.

At initial intake, S. endorsed feelings of depression, which were exacerbated by a crisis in her almost 30-year marriage that led her to recently file for divorce. Her husband asked to end their marriage after revealing that he had been in a relationship with another woman for 5 years. She reported expressions such as "I always knew and put up with it," thinking she made many efforts to work on her marriage without success. She described feeling sad, empty, guilty, shameful, and worthless, adding to her high HIV-related stigma perception. She avoided telling anyone about the difficulties in her marriage.

The patient reported recurrent anxiety and worry about several areas of her life, including concerns about her relationship with her husband and feeling as though she needed to contact him every day even though he left the house, being ambivalent about her divorce, feeling overwhelmed by minor matters such as keeping up with housework, her still remaining visit to her lawyer to arrange papers for separation and divorce, and economic and tax issues.

She reported no social life apart from interaction with her ex-husband, her son and daughter, and some neighbors very occasionally. She occasionally visits her elderly mother, who has Alzheimer disease and lives in a nursing home. She reported that the past 7 years have been a challenge for her as her only brother died in 2012 after suffering from a long period of cancer. She also suffered two cerebral infarctions in 2015 and found out that she had human papillomavirus in 2016.

Her daughter and son do not know that their parents are living with HIV. S. reported that she would like to tell them but that her ex-husband is reluctant to do so. This issue is important to her because she fears that her children will disregard and be ashamed of her. She described feeling guilty for not telling them the truth but is struggling to tell them because she is feeling ashamed. Table 5.1 presents the complete case formulation of S.

Additional data regarding the S. case is provided in the following section. S. is Participant 3.

APPLICATION OF A BRIEF UNIFIED PROTOCOL PROGRAM IN PEOPLE LIVING WITH HIV: A CASE SERIES ANALYSIS

Participants

For the current analysis, we selected four participants who were included in our two first pilot groups. Note that one of the participants is S., described in the previous section. We selected these cases because they are representative of the heterogeneity of the people living with HIV in Spain. They differ with regard to the manner of transmission and time since HIV acquisition, comorbidities, treatment history, and sociodemographic characteristics. All of them completed all the treatment sessions and assessments, occurring at pretreatment, post-treatment, and 3 months after treatment was completed.

Clinical and sociodemographic characteristics of each participant at the pretreatment appointment are detailed below:

- Participant 1, a 23-year-old Spanish homosexual man, is a university degree student working on his final degree project who acquired HIV infection sexually only 2 months before beginning the group. He was receiving ART and showed a high level of adherence, good immunological status (CD4 = 648 cell/mm^3), and low viremia (382 copies/ml) with no history of AIDS or HCV diagnosis. He met criteria for a major depressive episode and social anxiety, with severe depressive (Beck Depression Inventory–II [BDI-II]) and anxiety (Beck Anxiety Inventory [BAI]) symptoms. He lived with his parents, whom he has not told that he has been diagnosed with HIV, and presented common fears in the first months of diagnosis, such as fear of HIV disclosure, fear of the efficacy and physical impact of antiretroviral treatment, and fear of not being able to travel to particular countries.
- Participant 2 is a 52-year-old Spanish heterosexual man who completed his studies until the age of 12 years. He was not actively working and was receiving a government assistance for disability. He acquired HIV from injection drug use. He was diagnosed 30 years ago with controlled HIV viremia for 6 years with a history of HCV diagnoses cured

Table 5.1 A Case Formulation with the UP in a Woman Living with HIV

HEALTH CONDITION ANALYSIS							
Health condition description: Woman living with HIV.							
How health condition (and its treatment) affect the patient's life?		**EMOTION ANALYSIS REGARDING HEALTH CONDITIONS AND ITS CONSEQUENCES**					
General life aspects		**Affectation/ Interference** **0________10** **Nothing Very much**	**Strong uncomfortable emotions** Do patients feel strong emotions in any of these general life aspects?	**Intensity** **0________10** **Nothing Extreme**	**Aversive reactions**	**Emotional behaviors** (Situational avoidance/ escape, subtle behavioral avoidance, cognitive avoidance, safety signals)
1. **Physical and basic necessities**	**Physical symptoms**: Feels clumsy, nervous, like crying, unable to calm herself.	8	Depression and anxiety	8	"I am worthless and I don't know what to do to feel better."	Stay at home Goes for a walk just with her dog
	Eat: Usually not hungry. Lost more than 2 kg in the last 3 months.	9	Depression and anxiety	9	"I don't feel I have to eat three times a day."	Avoids eating, not worried about diet
	Sex: Lost interest. She is in a divorce proceeding and is not in a relationship.	6	Shame	9	"I'm ugly and not interesting. I don't deserve to find someone."	Avoids meeting new people; uses the HIV diagnosis to justify not meeting new people
	Sleep: Rumination before falling asleep.	8	Anxiety	8	"If I don't sleep well, I'll lose my mind and get more nervous."	Catastrophic rumination about her insomnia and smartphone use until late at night

	Activity: Housekeeping and chores. Used to visit her mother once a week. Only talks to her son and daughter and occasionally to neighbors.	9	Depression and shame	8	"I am shameful, I will never have good things in my life again."	Avoidance of social activities Ruminates about HIV
	Energy: Usually fatigued.	8	Depression	9	"I am weak."	Watch TV and smartphone as a way to avoid physical activity
	Pain: In joints.	9	Depression and anger	9	"I cannot cope with this."	Ruminating about pain
	Medication side effects: Worry about cholesterol, osteoporosis, and insulin resistance.	7	Depression	7	"I am powerless and vulnerable."	Ruminating about being not healthy enough when she gets older; fear of being more prone to Alzheimer due to medication and antecedents
	General: She is an autonomous woman and can take care of herself, but with a deep sense of unhappiness, worthless and shame.	8				
2. **Work/studies**: Completed secondary education and always has worked as a housewife. Pensioner since HIV diagnosis.		9	Depression	9	"I am inadequate, not smart enough."	Rumination about being worthless; avoids advice about new activities such as learning English

(*continued*)

Table 5.1 Continued

HEALTH CONDITION ANALYSIS					
Health condition description: Woman living with HIV.					
How health condition (and its treatment) affect the patient's life?	**EMOTION ANALYSIS REGARDING HEALTH CONDITIONS AND ITS CONSEQUENCES**				
General life aspects	**Affectation/ Interference** **0______10** **Nothing Very much**	**Strong uncomfortable emotions** Do patients feel strong emotions in any of these general life aspects?	**Intensity** **0______10** **Nothing Extreme**	**Aversive reactions**	**Emotional behaviors** (Situational avoidance/ escape, subtle behavioral avoidance, cognitive avoidance, safety signals)
3. **Daily life activities** (to buy, to cook, to clean, etc.): She is in charge of all the housework.	9	Depression	9	"I can't choose what I want to do. Nobody cares about me."	Avoids asking for help; rumination about her workload
4. **Pleasant activities** (hobbies, sport, etc.): She watches TV, plays with her smartphone, and sometimes goes for a walk with her dog.	8	Depression	6	"I don't know what to do with my life."	Avoids going to dance, to walk with neighbors
5. **Personal relationships** (couple, family, friends, etc.): As she is in the divorce proceeding, she feels very alone. She has no social interactions beyond her children, her mother once a week, her ex-husband several times a week (a stressor for her), and some neighbors.	9	Guilt and shame	9	"I am afraid to be rejected by having HIV." "I am afraid of infecting someone."	Avoids telling their children that she lives with HIV Avoids social interactions if possible Procrastination of meetings with friends. Avoids visiting a lawyer to arrange her divorce

6. **Spirituality**: She is catholic, and she goes to church sometimes.	2	Shame and guilt	6	"Do not deserve spiritual care."	Does not go to church, or tries to go but gets away just before enter
7. **Life goals**: To feel independent from her ex-husband, to recover her joy, to be able to start a new romantic relationship, to go dancing with friends, to learn to swim, to learn English and to travel.	9	Depression, shame, and guilt	9	"I cannot do it alone. I don't get to succeed. I can't get what I want."	Joins activities if escape or cancellation is easy
8. **Others**: To tell her daughter and son that she lives with HIV.	10	Guilt and shame	10	"I am ashamed. I can't stand it. I should have done it before."	Avoids talk to their children naturally about HIV; rumination about what bad things may happen if she tells them the truth

	TREATMENT PLAN: FOCUS/APPLICATION OF CORE MODULES
SESSION	MODULE 1
1	Setting the treatment goals and gaining/maintaining motivation. The patient has moderate motivation for change. She wants to reduce her emotional distress but currently feels unable to make meaningful changes. She should raise awareness of the emotional impact in different areas: family issues (mainly disclosure her HIV condition), absence of social life, and absence of pleasant activities. We should establish with her the following treatment goals: decision-making about disclosure of her HIV condition to her children, increase social activity, learning regulation strategies to achieve these goals, and managing her physical and psychological symptoms. Motivation will address the exploration of costs and benefits of staying just as she is (e.g., focusing on guilt and shame to not trust her children).

(*continued*)

Table 5.1 Continued

	MODULE 2
1	Understanding your emotions. She will have to receive psychoeducation on adaptive nature of emotions. She must learn the functional nature of emotions, especially shame, guilt, sadness, and anxiety, which she considers negative and unwanted. She will learn how these emotions are an obstacle to living a positive life and achieving her goals—for example, how shame for living with HIV has reduced her social life and does not allow her to disclose her condition to significant others. She will discuss what is an emotional disorder to understand what are the maladaptive aspects of emotions. We will work on analyzing emotional responses (Antecedents, Responses, Consequences), especially with situations where she feels guilt and shame. She will learn to identify which are the antecedent of the emotional response, how she reacts, and which behaviors she performs. She also will learn to record the ARC of emotion, and break down each emotion into thoughts, sensations, and behaviors. She particularly should observe: thoughts associated with shame and guilt such as "my children will be angry with me, reject me and blame me for not avoiding it"; physical sensations experienced when feeling guilt or shame; behaviors such as hiding or not disclosing her serostatus, resulting in short-term relief but great long-term emotional distress (symptoms: anxiety, depression, loss of weight, sleep disorders, . . .). To generalize the knowledge that she will be acquiring in the session, she should complete ARCs of intense emotions as homework.
	MODULE 3
2	Mindful emotional awareness. She should develop mindful emotional awareness, through the observation of her daily emotional responses and her reactions to her own emotions. She will especially benefit from being nonjudgmental, due to her common engagement in rumination and cognitive responses to her shame and guilty emotional experiences ("I shouldn't feel like this," "this emotional experience is horrible," "I´m weak," . . .). She also will benefit from developing present-focused awareness because her thoughts are often focused on the past ("how could I not realize that he was cheating me," "I shouldn't have stayed with him,". . .) or future ("my children are going to reject me," "I can never be happy with the diagnosis," . . .). Reviewing her ARCs, she will be able to observe this type of cognitive response and thoughts related to self-judgment, judgment of emotion, and non-present-focused thoughts. In this module, we will also work to improve her ability to understand her emotional experiences in a more mindful way, using a brief raisin meditation and a brief music meditation to help her practice to "take a step back." To generalize the knowledge that she will acquire in the session, she should practice daily mindfulness practice and behavioral activation exercises based in listening to music.

	MODULE 4
3	Cognitive flexibility. Patient needs to gain a better understanding of the link between negative thoughts and emotions. She will particularly benefit from understanding how her emotional experiences are affected by the more common thinking traps: catastrophizing thoughts and jumping to conclusions (e.g., "If I tell my children that I am HIV positive, they will despise me for sure. And they will never talk to me again and I will be alone for my whole life. The whole family will know and I will be treated as a lousy person"). She will learn to generate alternative interpretations or appraisals (cognitive reappraisal) that allow greater cognitive flexibility (e.g., "If I tell my children that I am HIV-positive, they may react supporting me, they may first get mad for not telling them sooner, or they may completely reject me"; " If I tell them, I will have been loyal to my values and I will probably identify several reasons to explain why I was not strong enough to do it before or to manage their emotional response"; "I am not responsible for their reactions and feelings, but I can understand that they may need time to digest the information. I will have resources to regulate myself in the meantime"; "I will be able to tolerate my emotions regardless of how they respond").
	MODULE 5
4	Identifying and countering emotional avoidance behaviors. The patient has explicit behavioral avoidance in several areas that will be identified one by one: She stays at home most of the time and just goes out with her dog as a safety signal to relate to others or to simply get out beyond to do the weekly household shopping. She also avoids meeting new people, social interactions and pleasant activities, and she is spending a lot of time on her smartphone. Furthermore, she avoids visiting a lawyer to arrange her divorce. She also avoids eating regularly and struggles with maintaining a healthy diet. But, above all, her main avoidance is that she is keeping her HIV status a secret from her son and daughter. She also ruminates about that and other questions as a cognitive avoidance. It is important that she first identify and discuss her patterns of avoidance and become aware of the short- and long-term consequences of emotional behaviors (i.e., how they are tied to her emotions). She will then learn alternative behaviors (e.g., active self-care, activities she is prone to, like going to dance, going for a walk with neighbors, visiting a lawyer, telling the truth to her son and daughter).
	MODULE 6
4	Understanding and coping with physical sensations. She will identify how shame, guilt, and anxiety have associated physical sensations (e.g., feels clumsy, nervous, like crying, with stomachache or not hungry, fatigue, . . .). She has difficulties tolerating sensations of fatigue, stomach desire, and what she describes as "a desire to cry" because, when she feels them, she thinks she is weak and unable to handle her problems. She should learn to feel these sensations without interpreting or judging them. She will benefit from practicing interoceptive exercises that elicit these sensations (e.g., feeling heavy or tired wearing a heavy backpack for 5 minutes or feeling nauseous or full, drinking a lot of water, or wearing a tight belt).

(*continued*)

Table 5.1 CONTINUED

	MODULE 7
4	Understanding why emotional exposure is essential to cope with unpleasant emotional experiences. She will develop an emotion exposure hierarchy focused on increasing tolerance of emotions, including intense guilt and shame. Exposures will include spending time at a café near her house where some of her acquaintances may come by, walking by the park without her dog, going to church again, visiting a lawyer, and setting boundaries with her ex-husband. The highest step in the emotion exposure hierarchy will likely be "telling the truth about HIV to my son and daughter." Exposures will be conducted gradually during this module to help her change patterns of avoidance around intense emotions, including shame and guilt.
	MODULE 8
5	Relapse prevention. In the last session of treatment, we would like the patient to recognize achievements and look to the future. In this session, we will review treatment basis and skills. We will also evaluate the patient's progress since the beginning of the treatment, and identify areas for improvement. After reviewing the patient's progress in meeting her goals for treatment, she will develop a practice plan for continued practice of treatment skills across areas of her life (e.g., family, friends, activities, hobbies, etc.). The patient will likely continue to utilize ARCs to increase awareness of different antecedents, components of the emotional responses, and consequences in different situations. She may also continue to work on observation techniques, cognitive flexibility, and emotional exposure to generalize achievements. In this session, she should anticipate difficulties in the generalization and options to manage setbacks (e.g., although she will disclosure her serostatus to her children, she may wish to reveal it to another significant person in the future and she can anticipate how she will feel and her likely avoidance response. She can consider management alternatives). She should establish new goals based on previously achieved (e.g., she may continue to expose herself to social situations that make her feel embarrassed or she may be exposed to assertive communication with her ex-husband with better managing of unjustified guilt and fear).
	OTHER MODULES IF NECESSARY
	It may important in this case to discuss or develop: assertiveness skills and setting boundaries with others, and also to conduct some roleplaying exercises in session; psychoeducation on freedom to choose how to manage her privacy about HIV.

through antiviral treatments and no history of AIDS. He stopped using intravenous drugs such as heroin more than 20 years ago. He met criteria for a depressive major episode, with moderate depressive symptoms (BDI-II) and severe anxiety symptomatology (BAI). He lived with his wife in a cordial relationship, although it was one of his main concerns. He also reported a lack of impulse control associated with anger and avoidance to deal with situations causing anxiety.
- Participant 3 is case S. (see description in previous section).
- Participant 4 is a 59-year-old Peruvian homosexual man with primary studies, working for a rental apartment company. He acquired HIV sexually. He was diagnosed 16 years ago with controlled HIV viremia for 15 years and a history of AIDS but no history of HCV diagnosis. He met *Diagnostic and Statistical Manual of Mental Disorders*, fourth edition (DSM-IV; American Psychiatric Association, 1994), criteria for panic disorder and agoraphobia, and he had moderate depressive (BDI-II) and anxiety (BAI) symptoms. He reports intense anxiety symptoms due to situations related to leaving the house or taking a plane, describing high levels of avoidance.

Procedure

The study was carried out in an HIV clinic in Madrid, Spain, from June 2019 to April 2020. Patients who reported symptoms of anxiety and depression during their appointment with their HIV specialist doctor were offered to meet with a clinical and health psychologist for evaluation. The study included patients who were older than age 18 years with a history report of HIV, with a primary diagnosis of emotional disorder confirmed in the psychological screening evaluation. Patients were excluded if they reported severe mental health problems (psychotic disorders, maniac, hypomanic, etc.), suicidal risk, or recent drug abuse (the past 3 months considered); patients were also excluded if they received psychological therapy in the past year or initiated or changed psychopharmacological treatment during the past 3 months.

Two psychologists with 6 and 10 years of experience, respectively, received specialized training in the UP (20 hours) and were previously supervised by a certified specialist UP trainer.

All participants completed a screening visit and study assessments at pre- and post-treatment and 3-month follow-up. Assessment data were collected and managed using Research Electronic Data Capture (REDCap). The study was approved by the Research and Ethical Committee of the Hospital Universitario La Paz (Madrid), and all participants provided written informed consent.

Instruments

The Anxiety Disorders Interview Schedule for DSM-IV (ADIS-IV; Grisham et al., 2004; Spanish version by Botella & Ballester, 1997) was applied at the screening visit to determine the psychopathological diagnosis of the participants based on DSM-IV-TR criteria (American Psychiatric Association, 2000).

Once the inclusion criteria were met, all participants completed the pretreatment assessment. This evaluation was composed of self-administered questionnaires to assess anxiety and depressive symptoms (the Hospital Anxiety and Depression Scale; Zigmond & Snaith, 1983; Spanish version by Tejero et al., 1986), affectivity (the Positive and Negative Affect Schedule (Watson et al., 1988; Spanish adaptation by Sandín et al., 1999), quality of life (the Quality of Life Index–Spanish version; Mezzich et al., 2000), emotion regulation skills (the Difficulties in Emotion Regulation Scale; Gratz & Roemer, 2004; Spanish adaptation by Hervás & Jódar, 2008), daily interference (the Maladjustment Scale; Echeburúa et al., 2000), and traits of neuroticism and extroversion (the NEO-FFI Personality Inventory; Costa & McCrae, 1992, 1999).

Sociodemographic data such as gender, age, current work situation, and sexual orientation were obtained during the pretreatment interview. The HIV-related variables such as current viral load, CD4 cell count (cells/mm^3), time since HIV diagnosis, time since controlled HIV viremia (<50 copies/ml), AIDS diagnosis, infection by HCV, and mode of HIV transmission were recorded from the clinical records.

Results

The current analysis is a case study analysis of four participants. We aimed to describe the main sociodemographic and clinical characteristics of each participant and to evaluate the change obtained by each one at the end of the UP group treatment and at 3 months follow-up using the measures previously described.

Clinically significant change was calculated for each participant using the Reliable Change Index (RCI; Jacobson & Truax, 1991). The RCI provides a more objective measure of when participants return to normal functioning. Thus, means and standard deviations from the general Spanish population were used to calculate the RCI. We compared outcomes obtained at the pretreatment visit with those obtained at the post-treatment visit and 3-month follow-up for each participant.

Direct scores obtained on the individual tests across the different evaluation points are shown in Table 5.2, which also includes means and standard deviations from the general Spanish population by each measure. In this table, we observe change in scores from the pretreatment assessment to the 3-month follow-up.

Table 5.2 NORMATIVE DATA AND DIRECT SCORES OF EACH PARTICIPANT IN PRETREATMENT, POST-TREATMENT, AND 3-MONTH FOLLOW-UP ASSESSMENTS

Variable	Normative Data	P1			P2			P3			P4		
	M (*SD*)	Pre-T	Post-T	3MFU	Pre-T	Post-T	3MFU	Pre-T	Post-T	3MFU	Pre-T	Post-T	3MFU
HADS-A	8.08 (3.9)	16	8	12	11	8	5	15	4	4	11	7	4
HADS-D	4.46 (3.3)	11	4	6	11	6	2	12	6	2	7	4	1
QLI	6.98 (1.1)	5	7.1	5.5	4.6	6.5	7	5.5	8.3	10	6.5	8.6	9.5
MS	2.22 (1.66)	12	7	15	19	14	0	18	22	5	15	0	1
PANAS-PA	32.74 (8.31)	7	19	7	12	23	25	17	19	33	18	19	21
PANAS-NA	20.08 (7.63)	24	16	18	12	6	1	6	3	1	11	0	3
DERS total	58.4 (17.6)	92	73	80	67	68	47	78	54	39	58	52	46
DERS lack of emotional attention	9.60 (3.30)	6	4	8	8	8	10	7	13	8	12	14	14
DERS confusion	7.80 (3.10)	11	10	9	8	7	5	10	10	6	7	8	7
DERS rejection	14.70 (6.40)	26	20	26	16	18	9	32	10	10	16	10	9
DERS interference	10.10 (3.80)	19	17	16	16	16	13	17	11	6	7	6	6
DERS lack of control	16.20 (7.10)	30	22	21	19	19	10	12	10	9	16	14	10
NEO-FFI-N	20.53 (7.46)	35	41	37	33	31	24	33	26	9	27	16	18
NEO-FFI-E	31.72 (6.74)	29	27	25	21	25	26	24	27	37	16	29	29

DERS, Difficulties in Emotion Regulation Scale; HADS-A, Hospital Anxiety and Depression Scale (Anxiety subscale); HADS-D, Hospital Anxiety and Depression Scale (Depression subscale); MFU, 3-month follow-up; MS, Maladjustment Scale; NEO-FFI-E, NEO-FFI Personality Inventory (Extroversion subscale); NEO-FFI-E, NEO-FFI-N Personality Inventory (Neuroticism subscale); P, participant; PANAS-NA, Positive and Negative Affect Schedule (Negative Affect scale); PANAS-PA, Positive and Negative Affect Schedule (Positive Affect scale); Pre-T, pretreatment; Post-T, post-treatment; QLI, Quality of Life Index.

Table 5.3 shows comparisons between pretreatment, post-treatment, and 3-month follow-up measures. To determine if clinically significant changes occur across time, as a function of treatment, the RCI was calculated between pretreatment and post-treatment and between pretreatment and 3-month follow-up.

As can be observed in Tables 5.2 and 5.3, Participant 1 had significant improvement in measures of anxiety, depression, quality of life, maladjustment, emotional regulation, and neuroticism when comparing pretreatment and post-treatment scores. At 3-month follow-up, he maintained significant improvements in depression and lack of control in the emotion regulation subscale compared to pretreatment. Other measures showed a tendency to improve compared to pretreatment but were slightly worse than post-treatment (e.g., anxiety, negative affect, or the emotional regulation total score).

Compared to pretreatment, Participant 2 had significant improvement in measures of depression, quality of life, maladjustment, and positive affect at post-treatment. These improvements were maintained and extended to measures of anxiety, negative affect, emotional regulation, and neuroticism at 3-month follow-up.

Participant 3 had significant changes at post-treatment in measures of anxiety, depression, quality of life, and emotional regulation. Those improvements were maintained at the 3-month follow-up and extended to measures of daily interference, positive affect, neuroticism, and extraversion.

Participant 4 had significant improvement at post-treatment in measures of quality of life, daily interference, negative affect, emotional rejection, neuroticism, and extraversion. He maintained these improvements and significant change in measures of anxiety, depression, and lack of emotional control at 3-month follow-up.

CONCLUSION

To our knowledge, this is the first UP adaptation applied to people living with HIV in a brief group format in the Spanish Public Health System. Our results and our clinical experience lead us to believe that enhancing emotion regulation skills may be an effective means to improve emotional disorders. Although a larger clinical trial is needed to further assess the efficacy of the UP for this population, our initial results are quite promising. Adapting the UP for administration in a group format could help reduce stigma and isolation, both factors previously associated with emotional disorders in people living with HIV. The group setting could help normalize shared emotions triggered by thoughts or social situations related to HIV, sexual orientation, or drug use stigmas, as well as help participants share different ways of coping and be satisfied due to the social support perceived by their peers.

People living with HIV may have very different sociodemographic and biographic factors based on their mode of acquisition of HIV. However, we found

Table 5.3 Reliable Change Index of Each Participant Between Pretreatment and Post-Treatment and Between Pretreatment and 3-Month Follow-Up Assessments

Variable	Normative Data	P1		P2		P3		P4	
	M (*SD*)	Pre–Post	Pre–3 Month	Pre–Post	Pre–3 Month	Pre–Post	Pre–3 Month	Pre–Post	Pre–3 Month
HADS-A	8.08 (3.9)	−3.24[a]	−1.62	−1.22	−2.43[a]	−4.46[a]	−4.46[a]	−1.62	−2.84[a]
HADS-D	4.46 (3.3)	−3.06[a]	−2.18[a]	−2.19[a]	−3.94[a]	−2.62[a]	−4.37[a]	−1.31	−2.62[a]
QLI	6.98 (1.1)	3.61[a]	0.86	3.26[a]	4.12[a]	4.81[a]	7.73[a]	3.61[a]	5.15[a]
MS	2.22 (1.66)	−3.21[a]	1.93	−3.21[a]	−12.20[a]	2.57[a]	−8.35[a]	−9.63[a]	−8.99[a]
PANAS-PA	32.74 (8.31)	3.61[a]	0.00	3.31[a]	3.91[a]	0.60	4.81[a]	0.30	0.90
PANAS-NA	20.08 (7.63)	−2.14[a]	−1.61	−1.61	−2.94[a]	−0.80	−1.34	−2.94[a]	−2.14[a]
DERS total	58.4 (17.6)	−2.89[a]	−1.82	0.15	−3.04[a]	−3.64[a]	−5.92[a]	−0.91	−1.82
DERS lack of emotional attention	9.60 (3.30)	−0.82	0.82	0.00	0.82	2.47[a]	0.41	0.82	0.82
DERS confusion	7.80 (3.10)	−0.49	−0.97	−0.49	−1.46	0.00	−1.95	0.49	0.00
DERS rejection	14.70 (6.40)	−2.10[a]	0.00	0.70	−2.45[a]	−7.69[a]	−7.69[a]	−2.10[a]	−2.45[a]
DERS interference	10.10 (3.80)	−1.03	−1.55	0.00	−1.55	−3.10[a]	−5.68[a]	−0.52	−0.52
DERS lack of control	16.20 (7.10)	−2.66[a]	−2.99[a]	0.00	−2.99[a]	−0.66	−1.00	−0.66	−1.99[a]
NEOFFI-N	20.53 (7.46)	−0.67	0.45	−0.45	−2.01[a]	−1.56	−5.36[a]	−2.46[a]	−2.01[a]
NEOFFI-E	31.72 (6.74)	2.17[a]	−0.96	0.96	1.20	0.72	3.13[a]	3.13[a]	3.13[a]

[a]Less than ±1.96 (significant change in scores in the desired direction; i.e., improvement of scores until reaching a normalized score).

DERS, Difficulties in Emotion Regulation Scale; HADS-A, Hospital Anxiety and Depression Scale (Anxiety subscale); HADS-D, Hospital Anxiety and Depression Scale (Depression subscale); MS, Maladjustment Scale; NEO-FFI-E, NEO-FFI Personality Inventory (Extroversion subscale); NEO-FFI-E, NEO-FFI-N Personality Inventory (Neuroticism subscale); P, participant; PANAS-NA, Positive and Negative Affect Schedule (Negative Affect scale); PANAS-PA, Positive and Negative Affect Schedule (Positive Affect scale); Pre, pretreatment; Post, post-treatment; QLI, Quality of Life Index.

no significant barriers when applying the UP, despite the heterogeneous composition of the groups, consisting of people with different characteristics, such as gender, age, sexual orientation, history of intravenous drug use, and medical comorbidities. All participants reported high satisfaction levels regarding the group format. They highlighted the vicarious learning, meaning that they were able to learn from others about how to cope with their intense emotions despite the different triggers and backgrounds of the group members.

The UP focuses on addressing transdiagnostic mechanisms (e.g., lack of present focus, cognitive inflexibility, and avoidance) as opposed to specific symptoms (anxiety or depression), clinical presentations or diagnoses, or particularities of the population (e.g., gender, sexual orientation, and mode of transmission). Consequently, we found it unnecessary to include a substantial amount of new information or make special adaptations or add specific exercises to the UP in order to apply it successfully to people living with HIV. However, in this study, the therapists had expertise in the UP and considerable experience conducting psychological treatment with this population.

Our experience has also helped us to be aware of the benefit of extending a session to our program. We worked on the UP components of understanding emotional response, emotional awareness, cognitive flexibility, countering emotional behaviors, and interoceptive and emotional exposure and a review of contents previously learned in five sessions. However, we estimate that it would be beneficial to add one more session to ensure the correct practice of the emotional exposures (interoceptive, imagination, or in vivo), which will help guarantee all participants experience emotional tolerance to unwanted and strong emotions and will also allow all participants in larger groups to actively participate and share their experiences in each session.

Limitations and Barriers

Results of this study are limited due to the design of our pilot program and the methodological limitations of a case series more generally. Although our results are promising, we need to follow up our findings with a more rigorous clinical trial that includes a larger sample size and patients from other Spanish units and even worldwide.

Our experience in offering group treatment has been mainly positive, but some people living with HIV are not ready to start group therapy, for instance, due to great perceived stigma or social shame. We believe the efficacy of brief individual transdiagnostic treatments should be tested, which could help promote motivation and lower resistance to future participation in groups.

Furthermore, although we subjectively perceive a positive impact reducing stigma and isolation in our intervention groups, we did not evaluate these variables with standardized instruments. For this reason, we recommend including HIV-related stigma measures that allow evaluation of the impact of the intervention (self-stigma and perceived social stigma, loneliness, and isolation) to test the effect of future group interventions. Other measures of interest to include would be those associated with the mechanisms involved in the changes observed. Thus, we believe the effect of treatment on mindfulness, cognitive flexibility, and avoidance should be evaluated.

Future Directions

Due to the high rates of emotional disorders in people living with HIV and the existence of effective psychological treatments, we consider that it is essential to include clinical psychologists in HIV clinics as part of interdisciplinary teams, which would help in the identification, diagnosis, and treatment of emotional disorders. Furthermore, psychologists could train other health professionals to guarantee an appropriate intervention, in addition to empowering patients in their ability to detect and request help when they have emotional disorder symptoms.

One of the major challenges is increasing the capacity to detect emotional disorders and provide resources to apply cost-effective psychological treatments in the care of people living with HIV. This is consistent with the latest target of the World Health Organization that leads to improving their quality of life, which is added to other main targets such as increased access to antiretroviral treatment and higher levels of adherence to ART in many countries. We believe that the integration of clinical and health psychologists in HIV clinics and the development of transdiagnostic interventions can undoubtedly contribute to achieving this goal.

Moreover, our pilot groups were conducted face-to-face before the COVID-19 pandemic, although since then, we have had to switch to online groups. Although we do not present data in this work, our first experiences are mainly positive, but we have some considerations. Based on our experience, online treatments require more support materials, such as slides and platforms that allow, for example, responses to be written from the participants and that everyone can see; and the therapist should be more active in evoking common situations that can generate emotional regulation problems (mainly those associated to HIV stigma) and make a more explicit intervention to reduce the fear of non-confidentiality. Other limitations are related to the fact that some people do not have access to the internet, especially the elderly or those without economic resources, which is not unlikely in our population. In addition, some participants could not participate online due to scheduling issues. In this sense, our recent experiences have taught us that both online and face-to-face therapy may improve emotional disorders. Henceforth, we have the possibility to adapt our interventions based on the needs of people and external situations using face-to-face, online, or a mixed format.

Tips and Recommendations for Clinicians

The brief group format might be beneficial in a clinical setting with limited resources or for nongovernmental organizations specializing in the management of this population. However, we consider that more sessions and practice time for each emotional regulation skill could be more effective over time. Thus, we recommend extending the sessions as much as possible, even providing reinforcement in individual sessions in cases that require it (e.g., imaginary exposure for people with post-traumatic stress disorder).

We also recommend that clinical psychologists are trained and have experience in the intervention with people living with HIV, the application of the UP, and managing therapy groups. The experience working with people living with HIV implies working with a heterogeneous group of people—which thus implies having experience with specific population groups, such as lesbian, gay, bisexual, transgender, and queer (LGTBQ), ex-intravenous drug users, or immigrants—which can facilitate bias-free interventions and precise language use that can make participants feel confident and motivated during sessions.

Likewise, it would be useful for clinicians to acquire knowledge and expertise regarding the psychological implications of living with HIV and its emotional impacts, such as stigma, body image perception, sexual dysfunction, sleep disorders, and anxiety about infecting others. Moreover, clinicians must be knowledgeable about the pharmacological effects of antiretroviral drugs used to treat HIV infection; this is relevant due to the need of distinguishing between the drug effect and the etiological component of the emotional disorder. Therefore, UP interventions with this population need to integrate medical and psychological approaches.

We recommend that clinical psychologists be trained in the UP intervention to optimize the limited time in brief UP group interventions. For example, they should assess the most common triggers, emotional responses, and emotional behaviors of their patients (UP case formulation template) before starting. This knowledge will help clinicians redirect participants to the shared emotional regulation difficulties in every session (e.g., avoidance reactions) despite their differences. Through this therapeutic work, all participants will understand the necessity to learn a more adaptive set of emotional regulation skills to achieve their personal aims.

Finally, clinical psychologists must have group therapy training requiring a specific type of communication skills and techniques. Most important to working with people living with HIV is to create an accepting and nonjudgmental environment to start building a strong therapeutic alliance.

REFERENCES

Allen, L. B., Tsao, J. C. I., Seidman, L. C., Ehrenreich-May, J., & Zeltzer, L. K. (2012). A unified, transdiagnostic treatment for adolescents with chronic pain and comorbid anxiety and depression. *Cognitive and Behavioral Practice*, *19*(1), 56–67. https://doi.org/10.1016/j.cbpra.2011.04.007

American Psychiatric Association. (1994). *Diagnostic and statistical manual of mental disorders* (4th ed.).

American Psychiatric Association. (2000). *Diagnostic and statistical manual of mental disorders* (4th ed., text rev.).

Ballester, R. (2003). Eficacia terapéutica de un programa de intervención grupal cognitivo- compartamental para mejorar la adhesión al tratamiento y el estado emocional de pacientes con infección por VIH/SIDA. *Psicothema, 15*(4), 517–523.

Barlow, D. H., Farchione, T. J., Bullis, J. R., Gallagher, M. W., Murray-Latin, H., Sauer-Zavala, S., Bentley, K. H., Thompson-Hollands, J., Conklin, L. R., Boswell, J. F., Ametaj, A., Carl, J. R., Boettcher, H. T., & Cassiello-Robbins, C. (2017). The Unified Protocol for Transdiagnostic Treatment of Emotional Disorders compared with diagnosis-specific protocols for anxiety disorders: A randomized clinical trial. *JAMA Psychiatry, 74*(9), 875–884. https://doi.org/10.1001/jamapsychiatry.2017.2164

Barlow, D., Sauer-Zavala, S., Farchione, T., Murray, H., Ellard, K., Bullis, J., & Castellano-Robbins, C. (2019). *Unified Protocol for Transdiagnostic Treatment of Emotional Disorders (2nd ed.): Workbook* (J. Osma & E. Crespo, trans.). Alianza Editorial.

Bayat, A. H., Mohammadi, R., Moradi-Joo, M., Bayani, A., Ahounbar, E., Higgs, P., Hemmat, M., Haghgoo, A., & Armoon, B. (2020). HIV and drug related stigma and risk-taking behaviors among people who inject drugs: A systematic review and meta-analysis. *Journal of Addictive Diseases, 38*(1), 71–83. https://doi.org/10.1080/10550887.2020.1718264

Bayón, C., Ribera, E., Cabrero, E., Griffa, L., & Burgos, Á. (2012). Prevalence of depressive and other central nervous system symptoms in HIV-infected patients treated with HAART in Spain. *Journal of the International Association of Physicians in AIDS Care, 11*(5), 321–328. https://doi.org/10.1177/1545109712448217

Bing, E. G., Burnam, M. A., Longshore, D., Fleishman, J. A., Sherbourne, C. D., London, A. S., Turner, B. J., Eggan, F., Beckman, R., Vitiello, B., Morton, S. C., Orlando, M., Bozzette, S. A., Ortiz-Barron, L., & Shapiro, M. (2001). Psychiatric disorders and drug use among human immunodeficiency virus–infected adults in the United States. *Archives of General Psychiatry, 58*(8), 721–728. https://doi.org/10.1001/archpsyc.58.8.721

Blashill, A. J., Safren, S. A., Wilhelm, S., Jampel, J., Taylor, S. W., O'Cleirigh, C., & Mayer, K. H. (2017). Cognitive Behavioral Therapy for Body Image and Self-Care (CBT-BISC) in sexual minority men living with HIV: A randomized controlled trial. *Health Psychology, 36*(10), 937–946. https://doi.org/10.1037/hea0000505

Botella, C., & Ballester, R. (1997). *Trastorno de pánico: evaluación y tratamiento.* Martínez Roca.

Brandt, C. P., Bakhshaie, J., Zvolensky, M. J., Grover, K. W., & Gonzalez, A. (2015). The examination of emotion dysregulation as a moderator of depression and HIV-relevant outcome relations among an HIV+ sample. *Cognitive Behaviour Therapy, 44*(1), 9–20. https://doi.org/10.1080/16506073.2014.950323

Brandt, C. P., Paulus, D. J., Lopez-Gamundi, P., Green, C., Lemaire, C., & Zvolensky, M. J. (2019). HIV Anxiety Reduction/Management Program (HAMRT): Pilot randomized controlled trial. *AIDS Care, 31*(12), 1527–1532. https://doi.org/10.1080/09540121.2019.1597962

Bullis, J. R., Sauer-Zavala, S., Bentley, K. H., Thompson-Hollands, J., Carl, J. R., & Barlow, D. H. (2015). The Unified Protocol for Transdiagnostic Treatment of Emotional Disorders: Preliminary exploration of effectiveness for group delivery. *Behavior Modification, 39*(2), 295–321. https://doi.org/10.1177/0145445514553094

Carey, M. P., Carey, K. B., Maisto, S. A., Schroder, K. E. E., Vanable, P. A., & Gordon, C. M. (2004). HIV risk behavior among psychiatric outpatients: Association with psychiatric disorder, substance use disorder, and gender. *Journal of Nervous and Mental Disease, 192*(4), 289–296. https://doi.org/10.1097/01.nmd.0000120888.45094.38

Centers for Disease Control and Prevention. (2020, March 21). HIV in the United States and *dependent areas*. https://www.cdc.gov/hiv

Chan, R. C. H., & Mak, W. W. S. (2019). Cognitive, regulatory, and interpersonal mechanisms of HIV stigma on the mental and social health of men who have sex with men living with HIV. *American Journal of Men's Health, 13*(5). https://doi.org/10.1177/1557988319873778

Ciesla, J. A., & Roberts, J. E. (2001). Meta-analysis of the relationship between HIV infection and risk for depressive disorders. *American Journal of Psychiatry, 158*(5), 725–730. https://doi.org/10.1176/appi.ajp.158.5.725

Costa, P. T., & McCrae, R. R. (1992). *Revised NEO Personality Inventory (NEO-PI-R) and NEO Five-Factor Inventory (NEO-FFI): Professional manual.* Psychological Assessment Resources.

Costa, P. T., & McCrae, R. R. (1999). *Inventario de Personalidad NEO Revisado (NEO PI-R).* Inventario NEO reducido de Cinco Factores (NEO-FFI): *Manual profesional.* TEA.

Degroote, S., Vogelaers, D., & Vandijck, D. M. (2014). What determines health-related quality of life among people living with HIV: An updated review of the literature. *Archives of Public Health, 72*(1), Article 40. https://doi.org/10.1186/2049-3258-72-40

Díez, M., Oliva, J., Sánchez, F., Vives, N., Cevallos, C., Izquierdo, A.; groupo SINIVIH. (2012). Incidence of new HIV diagnoses in Spain, 2004–2009. *Gaceta Sanitaria, 26*(2), 107–115. https://doi.org/10.1016/j.gaceta.2011.07.023

Echeburúa, E., Gargallo, P., & Fernández-Montalvo, J. (2000). Escala de inadaptación (EI): Propiedades psicométricas en contextos clínicos. *Análisis y Modificación de Conducta, 26*(107), 325–340.

Empson, S., Cuca, Y. P., Cocohoba, J., Dawson-Rose, C., Davis, K., & Machtinger, E. L. (2017). Seeking Safety group therapy for co-occurring substance use disorder and PTSD among transgender women living with HIV: A pilot study. *Journal of Psychoactive Drugs, 49*(4), 344–351. https://doi.org/10.1080/02791072.2017.1320733

European Centre for Disease Prevention and Control & World Health Organization. (2020, January). HIV/AIDS surveillance in Europe *2019: 2018 data*. https://doi.org/10.2900/611648

González-García, J. J., Mahillo, B., Hernández, S., Pacheco, R., Diz, S., García, P., Esteban, H., Arribas, J. R., Quereda, C., Rubio, R., Díez, J., Moreno, S., & Vázquez-Rodríguez, J. J. (2005). Prevalences of hepatitis virus coinfection and indications for chronic hepatitis C virus treatment and liver transplantation in Spanish HIV-infected patients: The GESIDA 29/02 and FIPSE 12185/01 multicenter study. Enfermedades infecciosas y microbiologia *clinica, 23*(6), 340–348. https://doi.org/10.1157/13076173

Gratz, K. L., & Roemer, L. (2004). Multidimensional assessment of emotion regulation and dysregulation: Development, factor structure, and initial validation of the

Difficulties in Emotion Regulation Scale. *Journal Psychopathology and Behavioral Assessment*, *26*, 41–54. https://doi.org/10.1023/B:JOBA.0000007455.08539.94

Grisham, J. R., Brown, T. A., & Campbell, L. A. (2004). The Anxiety Disorders Interview Schedule for DSM-IV (ADIS-IV). In M. J. Hilsenroth, D. L. Segal, & M. Hersen (Eds.), *Comprehensive handbook of psychological assessment, Vol. 2: Personality assessment* (pp. 163–177). Wiley.

Guzmán, R., Bermúdez, J., López, E. T., & Sulvarán, O. M. (2012). Impacto psicosocial asociado al diagnóstico de infección por vih/SIDA. *Psicología y Salud*, *22*(2), 163–172.

Hervás, G., & Jódar, R. (2008). Adaptación al castellano de la Escala de Dificultades en la Regulación Emocional. *Clínica y Salud*, *19*(2), 139–156.

Jacobson, N. S., & Truax, P. (1991). Clinical significance: A statistical approach to defining meaningful change in psychotherapy research. *Journal of Consulting and Clinical Psychology*, *59*(1), 12–19. https://doi.org/10.1037/0022-006X.59.1.12

Johnson, C. J., Heckman, T. G., Hansen, N. B., Kochman, A., & Sikkema, K. J. (2009). Adherence to antiretroviral medication in older adults living with HIV/AIDS: A comparison of alternative models. *AIDS Care*, *21*(5), 541–551. https://doi.org/10.1080/09540120802385611

Joska, J. A., Andersen, L., Rabie, S., Marais, A., Ndwandwa, E.-S., Wilson, P., King, A., & Sikkema, K. J. (2020). COVID-19: Increased risk to the mental health and safety of women living with HIV in South Africa. *AIDS and Behavior*, *24*(10), 2751–2753. https://doi.org/10.1007/s10461-020-02897-z

Kalichman, S. C., Rompa, D., & Cage, M. (2005). Group intervention to reduce HIV transmission risk behavior among persons living with HIV/AIDS. *Behavior Modification*, *29*(2), 256–285. https://doi.org/10.1177/0145445504272603

Leserman, J. (2003). HIV disease progression: Depression, stress, and possible mechanisms. *Biological Psychiatry*, *54*(3), 295–306. https://doi.org/10.1016/S0006-3223(03)00323-8

Martinez, J., Lemos, D., Hosek, S., & the Adolescent Medicine Trials Network. (2012). Stressors and sources of support: The perceptions and experiences of newly diagnosed Latino youth living with HIV. *AIDS Patient Care and STDs*, *26*(5), 281–290. https://doi.org/10.1089/apc.2011.0317

McIntosh, R. C., Rosselli, M., Uddin, L. Q., & Antoni, M. (2015). Neuropathological sequelae of human immunodeficiency virus and apathy: A review of neuropsychological and neuroimaging studies. Neuroscience & *Biobehavioral Reviews*, *55*, 147–164. https://doi.org/10.1016/j.neubiorev.2015.04.008

Mellors, J. W., Muñoz, A., Giorgi, J. V., Margolick, J. B., Tassoni, C. J., Gupta, P., Kingsley, L. A., Todd, J. A., Saah, A. J., Detels, R., Phair, J. P., & Rinaldo, C. R. J. (1997). Plasma viral load and CD4+ lymphocytes as prognostic markers of HIV-1 infection. *Annals of Internal Medicine*, *126*(12), 946–954. https://doi.org/10.7326/0003-4819-126-12-199706150-00003

Mezzich, J. E., Ruipérez, M. A., Pérez, C., Yoon, G., Liu, J., & Mahmud, S. (2000). The Spanish version of the Quality of Life Index: Presentation and validation. *Journal of Nervous and Mental Disease*, *188*(5), 301–305. https://doi.org/10.1097/00005053-200005000-00008

Ministerio de Ciencia Innovación y Universidades. (2019). Encuesta Hospitalaria de pacientes con infección por el VIH. Resultados 2018. Análisis de la evolución 2003–2018. https://www.mscbs.gob.es/ciudadanos/enfLesiones/enfTransmisibles/sida/vigilancia/Encuesta_hospitalaria2019.pdf

Mollan, K. R., Smurzynski, M., Eron, J. J., Daar, E. S., Campbell, T. B., Sax, P. E., Gulick, R. M., Na, L., O'Keefe, L., Robertson, K. R., & Tierney, C. (2014). Association between efavirenz as initial therapy for HIV-1 infection and increased risk for suicidal ideation or attempted or completed suicide. *Annals of Internal Medicine, 161*(1), 1. https://doi.org/10.7326/M14-0293

Moore, A. A., Lake, J. E., Glasner, S., Karlamangla, A., Kuerbis, A., Preciado, D., Jenkins, J., Dominguez, B. X., Candelario, J., Liao, D. H., Tang, L., & Reid, M. C. (2019). Establishing the feasibility, acceptability and preliminary efficacy of a multi-component behavioral intervention to reduce pain and substance use and improve physical performance in older persons living with HIV. *Journal of Substance Abuse Treatment, 100*, 29–38. https://doi.org/10.1016/j.jsat.2019.02.003

Moss, A. R., & Bacchetti, P. (1989). Natural history of HIV infection. *AIDS, 3*(2), 55–61. https://doi.org/10.1097/00002030-198902000-00001

Nanni, M. G., Caruso, R., Mitchell, A. J., Meggiolaro, E., & Grassi, L. (2015). Depression in HIV infected patients: A review. *Current Psychiatry Reports, 17*(1), 530. https://doi.org/10.1007/s11920-014-0530-4

Nilsson Schönnesson, L., Williams, M. L., Ross, M. W., Bratt, G., & Keel, B. (2007). Factors associated with suboptimal antiretroviral therapy adherence to dose, schedule, and dietary instructions. *AIDS and Behavior, 11*(2), 175–183. https://doi.org/10.1007/s10461-006-9160-0

Norton, P. J. (2012). *Group cognitive–behavioral therapy of anxiety: A transdiagnostic treatment manual.* Guilford.

Olley, B. O., Seedat, S., & Stein, D. J. (2006). Persistence of psychiatric disorders in a cohort of HIV/AIDS patients in South Africa: A 6-month follow-up study. *Journal of Psychosomatic Research, 61*(4), 479–484. https://doi.org/https://doi.org/10.1016/j.jpsychores.2006.03.010

Parsons, J. T., Rendina, H. J., Moody, R. L., Gurung, S., Starks, T. J., & Pachankis, J. E. (2017). Feasibility of an emotion regulation intervention to improve mental health and reduce HIV transmission risk behaviors for HIV-positive gay and bisexual men with sexual compulsivity. *AIDS and Behavior, 21*(6), 1540–1549. https://doi.org/10.1007/s10461-016-1533-4

Poropatich, K., & Sullivan, D. J. J. (2011). Human immunodeficiency virus type 1 long-term non-progressors: The viral, genetic and immunological basis for disease non-progression. *Journal of General Virology, 92*(Pt. 2), 247–268. https://doi.org/10.1099/vir.0.027102-0

Rendina, H. J., Gamarel, K. E., Pachankis, J. E., Ventuneac, A., Grov, C., & Parsons, J. T. (2017). Extending the Minority Stress Model to incorporate HIV-positive gay and bisexual men's experiences: A longitudinal examination of mental health and sexual risk behavior. *Annals of Behavioral Medicine, 51*(2), 147–158. https://doi.org/10.1007/s12160-016-9822-8

Roca, M., Gili, M., Garcia-Garcia, M., Salva, J., Vives, M., Garcia Campayo, J., & Comas, A. (2009). Prevalence and comorbidity of common mental disorders in primary care. *Journal of Affective Disorders, 119*(1–3), 52–58. https://doi.org/10.1016/j.jad.2009.03.014

Safren, S. A., Bedoya, C. A., O'Cleirigh, C., Biello, K. B., Pinkston, M. M., Stein, M. D., Traeger, L., Kojic, E., Robbins, G. K., Lerner, J. A., Herman, D. S., Mimiaga, M. J., & Mayer, K. H. (2016). Cognitive behavioural therapy for adherence and depression in patients with HIV: A three-arm randomised controlled trial. *Lancet HIV, 3*(11), 529–538. https://doi.org/10.1016/S2352-3018(16)30053-4

Sandín, B., Chorot, P., Lostao, L., Joiner, T. E., Santed, M. A., & Valiente, R. M. (1999). Escalas PANAS de afecto positivo y negativo: Validación factorial y convergencia transcultural. *Psicothema, 11*(1), 37–51.

Sauer-Zavala, S., Bentley, K. H., Steele, S. J., Tirpak, J. W., Ametaj, A. A., Nauphal, M., Cardona, N., Wang, M., Farchione, T. J., & Barlow, D. H. (2020). Treating depressive disorders with the Unified Protocol: A preliminary randomized evaluation. *Journal of Affective Disorders, 264*, 438–445. https://doi.org/10.1016/j.jad.2019.11.072

Spies, G., Asmal, L., & Seedat, S. (2013). Cognitive–behavioural interventions for mood and anxiety disorders in HIV: A systematic review. *Journal of Affective Disorders, 150*(2), 171–180. https://doi.org/10.1016/j.jad.2013.04.018

Tejero, A., Guimerá, E. M., Farré, J., & Peri, J. M. (1986). Uso Clínico Del HAD (Hospital Anxiety and Depression Scale) en Población Psiquiátrica: Un Estudio de Su Sensibilidad, Fiabilidad Y Validez. *Revista del Departamento Psiquiatría, 12*, 233–238.

Trilla, A., Mensa, J., & Gatell, J. M. (1988). Infeccion por el Virus de la Inmunodeficiencia Humana y SIDA. In C. Rozman (Ed.), *Medicina interna* (pp. 2341–2352). Doyma.

United Nations Programme on HIV/AIDS. (2020). Fact *sheet*—World AIDS *Day* 2020. https://www.unaids.org/sites/default/files/media_asset/UNAIDS_FactSheet_en.pdf

Watson, D., Clark, L. A., & Tellegen, A. (1988). Development and validation of brief measures of positive and negative affect: The PANAS scales. *Journal of Personality and Social Psychology, 54*(6), 1063–1070. https://doi.org/10.1037/0022-3514.54.6.1063

Weihs, K. L., McConnell, M. H., Wiley, J. F., Crespi, C. M., Sauer-Zavala, S., & Stanton, A. L. (2019). A preventive intervention to modify depression risk targets after breast cancer diagnosis: Design and single-arm pilot study. *Psycho-Oncology, 28*(4), 880–887. https://doi.org/10.1002/pon.5037

Wilamowska, Z. A., Thompson-Hollands, J., Fairholme, C. P., Ellard, K. K., Farchione, T. J., & Barlow, D. H. (2010). Conceptual background, development, and preliminary data from the Unified Protocol for Transdiagnostic Treatment of Emotional Disorders. *Depression and Anxiety, 27*(10), 882–890. https://doi.org/10.1002/da.20735

Yang, J. P., Simoni, J. M., Dorsey, S., Lin, Z., Sun, M., Bao, M., & Lu, H. (2018). Reducing distress and promoting resilience: A preliminary trial of a CBT skills intervention among recently HIV-diagnosed MSM in China. *AIDS Care, 30*(5), 39–48. https://doi.org/10.1080/09540121.2018.1497768

Zigmond, A. S., & Snaith, R. P. (1983). The Hospital Anxiety and Depression Scale. *Acta Psychiatrica Scandinavica, 67*(6), 361–370. https://doi.org/10.1111/j.1600-0447.1983.tb09716.x

Zumla, A. (2010). Mandell, Douglas, and Bennett's principles and practice of infectious diseases. *Lancet: Infectious Diseases, 10*(5), 303–304. https://doi.org/10.1016/S1473-3099(10)70089-X

6

A Unified, Transdiagnostic Approach to Pain Management

JENNA SANDLER EILENBERG AND JOHN D. OTIS ■

INTRODUCTION

Pain is defined as an unpleasant sensory and emotional experience associated with actual or potential tissue damage, or described in terms of such damage. When pain persists for longer than 3 months, it is considered chronic pain (International Association for the Study of Pain, 2017). Chronic pain can be caused by a number of events in a person's life, including normal degenerative changes that occur as a person ages, injury caused by accidents or illness, or traumas experienced as a result of domestic violence or military combat. Chronic pain conditions affect at least 116 million adults in the United States at a cost of $560–$635 billion annually in direct medical treatment costs and lost productivity due to pain (Gaskin & Richards, 2012; Institute of Medicine, 2011). A survey conducted by the U.S. Centers for Disease Control and Prevention indicated that 19.6% of adults endorsed having "pain most days or every day" for the past 6 months (QuickStats, 2017). Pain is one of the most frequent reasons that people seek medical care, with common types of chronic pain conditions including low back pain, knee pain, headache, arthritis, multiple sclerosis, fibromyalgia, and shingles.

The experience of chronic pain can have a significant impact on many domains of a person's life, including their ability to maintain employment, engage in hobbies, exercise, and establish or maintain relationships. Chronic pain can be a stressful experience that can increase a patient's vulnerability to experience other psychological disorders, such as depression and anxiety (Woo, 2010). Pain can also contribute to maladaptive health behaviors such as alcohol or drug use, poor

Jenna Sandler Eilenberg and John D. Otis, *A Unified, Transdiagnostic Approach to Pain Management* In: *Applications of the Unified Protocol in Health Conditions*. Edited by: Jorge Osma and Todd J. Farchione, Oxford University Press. © Oxford University Press 2023. DOI: 10.1093/oso/9780197564295.003.0006 diet, or inadequate sleep, all of which can intensify the experience of pain and contribute to the expression of other psychological vulnerabilities. Conversely, the presence of co-occurring psychological conditions (e.g., anxiety, depression, or post-traumatic stress disorder [PTSD]) can contribute to poorer pain treatment outcomes, including functional limitations, impaired social functioning, higher unemployment, and reduced treatment satisfaction (Bair et al., 2003, 2008). Thus, understanding factors that maintain or contribute to the experience of pain is a critical topic of research.

Emotional disorders are highly prevalent in patients with chronic pain, and they can impact an individual's experience of pain. For example, depression prevalence rates range from 30% to 54% in chronic pain samples (Banks & Kerns, 1996; Elliott et al., 2003), and depression is associated with more frequent pain complaints and impairment (Bair et al., 2003). Rates of anxiety are as high as 45% in pain populations (Kroenke et al., 2013; Staerkle et al., 2004). Anxiety and fear play an important role in the experience of pain, with one study finding that for patients with low back pain, anxiety accounted for 32% of the disability and 14% of the severity of the pain (Staerkle et al., 2004). Pain and emotional disorders share common neurobiological circuits. For example, correlations exist between brain responses involved during pain catastrophizing (i.e., the tendency to respond to pain stimuli with exaggerated negative interpretations and expected outcomes) and brain responses involved in the modulation of pain, including the dorsolateral prefrontal, insula, and anterior cingulate cortices (Seminowicz & Davis, 2006). In addition, studies have found that inducing a depressed mood state and negative pain-specific cognitions is associated with increased pain unpleasantness and increased activity in the prefrontal cortex, subgenual anterior cingulate cortex, and hippocampus (Berna et al., 2010). Evidence of overlapping structures involved in pain and negative cognitions may explain how the presence of an emotional disorder may impact processing of painful stimuli.

Based on a biopsychosocial model of chronic pain, a number of cognitive–behavioral approaches to the treatment of chronic pain have been developed (Otis, 2007a, 2007b; Thorn, 2017; Turk & Fritz, 2005). Cognitive–behavioral approaches to pain management focus on teaching the patient strategies for modifying negative thoughts; tools for changing maladaptive behaviors that often contribute to, exacerbate, and maintain the experience of pain; and methods for reintegrating previously avoided activities back into their everyday routines. Although cognitive–behavioral therapy (CBT) is now considered to be the "gold standard" psychological treatment approach for chronic pain, symptoms related to other co-occurring emotional disorders can significantly complicate and interfere with many aspects of treatment, including setting goals, becoming motivated to participate in treatment, and making plans to begin exercise (Kerns & Haythornthwaite, 1988). For example, it is not uncommon for patients with pain and anxiety to catastrophize and worry about the meaning of pain, to avoid activities for fear of pain during physical movement, or to socially isolate themselves from friends and family. Similarly, patients with pain and co-occurring depression may report that they understand the benefits of setting therapy goals but also report that they lack the motivation to take the first step toward achieving them. Given the high comorbidity rates of chronic pain and emotional disorders, and the negative impact of emotional disorders on the experience of pain and its treatment, it is clear that patients who suffer from pain and co-occurring emotional disorders such as depression or anxiety would benefit greatly from learning more adaptive emotion regulation strategies for managing negative emotions that could be used across a variety of situations and contexts, including pain-specific situations (e.g., difficulty exercising due to pain) and other everyday situations (e.g., difficulty managing the negative moods that can affect relationships and also can exacerbate pain).

A UNIFIED, TRANSDIAGNOSTIC APPROACH TO PAIN MANAGEMENT

One treatment approach that may have the potential to address shared mechanisms across chronic pain and comorbid emotional disorders is the Unified Protocol for the Transdiagnostic Treatment of Emotional Disorders (UP; Barlow et al., 2018a, 2018b). The UP was developed based on research suggesting that there is a considerable overlap in symptoms across emotional disorders. The UP targets common vulnerabilities across disorders, including high levels of negative affect and reliance on maladaptive emotion regulation strategies. Recent studies suggest that these common vulnerabilities play an influential role in the development and maintenance of chronic pain.

According to the biopsychosocial model of pain, the experience of chronic pain is multifaceted, representing interactions among biological, psychological, and social dimensions (Gatchel et al., 2007). Increased recognition of the multidimensional nature of pain has led to a proliferation of research to further understand the mechanisms by which psychological factors influence the pain experience. According to Melzack and Wall's (1965) gate control theory of pain, the dorsal horn of the spinal cord acts as a gate that regulates processing of pain-related information by the central nervous system. Affective and cognitive factors, such as negative mood states or pain catastrophizing, are posited to influence the opening and closing of this gate, consequently modulating the relationship between tissue damage and pain perception. Such factors intensify the perception of pain by opening the gate and allowing more pain signals to the brain (Melzack & Wall, 1965). For example, anticipatory anxiety before an experimental pain task (e.g., cold pressor task) predicts higher self-reported pain intensity during the task (Tsao et al., 2004). Chronic pain patients with a high level of negative affect tend to engage in pain catastrophizing (Quartana et al., 2009). High levels of negative affect are also associated with a bias toward recalling negative past events and pain-related past events (Gamsa, 1994; Liu et al., 2013). One of the psychological factors that contributes to the transition from acute to chronic pain is the ensuing cycle in which intensified perception of pain leads to more negative thoughts about pain, which in turn leads to heightened sensitivity to future pain experiences (Nicholas et al., 2011).

Catastrophic thinking about pain also increases the tendency to engage in escape behavior at low thresholds of painful stimuli (Eccleston & Crombez, 1999). Patients with chronic pain engage in ongoing escape behavior, which leads to widespread avoidance of and disengagement from activities. Escape and avoidance behavior function as a way to control or suppress uncomfortable strong emotions or sensory experiences. Whereas some avoidance of situations that trigger pain may be adaptive, widespread avoidance often backfires and leads to heightened pain sensitivity and pain catastrophizing (Asmundson et al., 2012). For example, a study found that individuals who were asked to suppress thoughts about pain prior to a laboratory-based pain task reported higher pain intensity and more intrusive thoughts about pain than individuals who were asked to actively monitor their thoughts about pain (Cioffi & Holloway, 1993; Sullivan et al., 1997). This aligns well with the UP's focus on targeting avoidant reactions that provide relief in the short term but ultimately serve to maintain disorder symptoms. For instance, in panic disorder, avoidance of situations that trigger fear of a panic attack relieves anxiety in the short term but exacerbates anxiety about having a future panic attack. Avoidance of feared situations prevents opportunities to disconfirm beliefs about the danger associated with the potential threat and about one's inability to cope with the accompanying anxiety. Instead, avoidance results in increased fear that begins to generalize to a growing number of situations. For someone with panic disorder, this might lead to an inability to tolerate enclosed spaces, such as public transportation or elevators, and consequently an inability to function in everyday life situations, such as commuting to work. Patients with chronic pain often engage in a similar cycle of avoidance. For example, someone with back pain may avoid situations that they expect will trigger pain, such as exercise. In the short term, this avoidance leads to relief because they did not have to face the situation they feared would trigger pain. However, in the long term, this fear may generalize to any form of physical activity, which could lead to heightened pain sensitivity, social isolation, physical deconditioning, and interference with tasks of daily living. Therefore, helping patients re-engage in activities that are important to them is often a key treatment target in CBT for chronic pain (Eccleston & Crombez, 1999).

The UP was also developed to address the high comorbidity rates across disorders. In a nationally representative sample, prevalence of a comorbid mood disorder with chronic pain was 21.7% and prevalence of a comorbid anxiety disorder was 35.1%; both are significantly higher than rates in the general population (McWilliams et al., 2003). Comorbid psychiatric conditions are associated with greater pain intensity and a more refractory illness course (e.g., Burns et al., 1998; Holzberg et al., 1996). Research has found that anxiety disorders are more likely to precede onset of the chronic pain condition, whereas depressive disorders are more likely to follow onset of chronic pain. Researchers have postulated that the co-occurrence of anxiety disorders and chronic pain can be explained by shared vulnerabilities such as high anxiety sensitivity, selective attention to threatening stimuli, and reduced threshold for alarm (Asmundson & Katz, 2009). In addition, a study of the neural correlates of pain found that in patients with major depressive disorder (MDD), anticipatory anxiety prior to a pain task led to increased activation in areas of the brain associated with emotional reactivity. This same pattern was not found in individuals without MDD, suggesting that activation of these areas of the brain may interfere with the ability to cope with pain (Strigo et al., 2008). These data suggest that treating chronic pain without addressing symptoms of underlying anxiety and mood disorders may limit the long-term effectiveness of treatment. The UP provides a framework for addressing the common symptoms that maintain anxiety and mood disorders and chronic pain, such as fear, avoidance, arousal, and negative affect. Given the strong links between chronic pain and comorbid psychiatric conditions, the potential for broad treatment response across disorders is especially important in this population.

THE UNIFIED PROTOCOL FOR TRANSDIAGNOSTIC TREATMENT OF EMOTIONAL DISORDERS

The UP consists of five core modules that target characteristics underlying all anxiety, depressive, and related disorders: (a) mindful emotion awareness, (b) cognitive flexibility, (c) identifying and preventing patterns of emotion avoidance, (d) increasing awareness and tolerance of emotion-related physical sensations, and (e) interoceptive and situational emotion-focused exposures.

The UP's mindful emotion awareness module introduces the concept of nonjudgmental, present-focused awareness with the goal of observing emotions mindfully as they arise instead of trying to control or suppress them. Mindfulness-based interventions in chronic pain patients have been shown to increase pain acceptance and tolerance and decrease stress even without modifying the pain itself (Chiesa & Serretti, 2011). One possible mechanism by which mindfulness-based interventions may mitigate the impact of pain on quality of life is by inhibiting the interruptive nature of pain. Because of its importance for survival, pain serves as the body's warning signal, interrupts ongoing processes, and demands immediate attention. Individuals with chronic pain demonstrate an attentional bias toward pain-related cues, which is associated with indices of poorer quality of life. In a randomized clinical trial of a mindfulness-based intervention compared to an active control condition, chronic pain patients who were randomized to the mindfulness-based intervention exhibited significant reductions in pain-related attentional biases, demonstrating the potential utility of mindfulness in the treatment of chronic pain (Garland & Howard, 2013).

The UP's cognitive flexibility module teaches cognitive reappraisal skills, emphasizing two common cognitive distortions: catastrophizing and jumping to conclusions. An abundance of research has demonstrated the influence of pain-related cognitions on the perceived intensity of pain, disability, and mood among chronic pain patients. Modifying maladaptive appraisals and beliefs about pain stimuli has been shown to reduce perceived severity of pain and improve functioning (Burns et al., 2012). Reductions in catastrophic thinking about pain have been found to predict improvement in pain-related outcomes across various treatment modalities (e.g., pain education program, CBT, and physical training program). In CBT specifically, reductions in catastrophic thinking about pain have also been found to predict improvements in depressive symptoms (Burns et al., 2012), demonstrating the potential for the UP to provide benefit to patients in pain-related symptoms as well as mood and emotional functioning.

In the third core module of the UP, patients are taught to identify emotion-driven behaviors that prevent them from fully experiencing and processing strong emotions and to respond more adaptively in the future. Emotion-driven behaviors include subtle behavioral avoidance (e.g., procrastination), cognitive avoidance (e.g., daydreaming), or safety signals (e.g., an object or person that someone may keep with them during situations that evoke strong emotions). In chronic pain, as postulated by the fear-avoidance model, catastrophic interpretations of pain signals can prompt pain-related fear, which then leads to emotion-driven behaviors meant to avoid perceived danger. In the case of chronic pain, pain is typically no longer a sign of actual danger, and thus emotion-driven behaviors have lost their adaptive value (Volders et al., 2015). Instead, emotion-driven behaviors perpetuate cycles of pain and disability. Examples of emotion-driven behaviors in chronic pain include doing certain activities less frequently or in a different way, such as carrying fewer groceries at a time or holding a grab bar in the shower (subtle behavioral avoidance); spending significant effort trying not to pay attention to the pain (cognitive avoidance); or reliance on people or objects during situations expected to cause pain, such as constantly carrying pain medications (safety signal). As is the case with emotional disorders, engaging in emotion-driven behaviors interferes with extinction of pain-related fear. For example, a chronic pain patient who always carries pain medication may learn that engaging in physical activity does not cause the expected pain outcome, but this new learning may be contingent on the presence of the pain medication. In the absence of pain medication being immediately available, the expectancy that physical activity can cause pain may be reactivated (den Hollander et al., 2010).

The fourth core module of the UP targets the physical sensations associated with strong emotions (e.g., breathlessness in the face of strong anxiety). The module offers psychoeducation about the influence of the patient's subjective interpretations of bodily cues on mood, thoughts, and behaviors, and it provides the opportunity to repeatedly induce certain physical sensations to increase the patient's tolerance of them. Pain is often preceded by other physiological sensations, such as muscle twitches, gastrointestinal sensations, mild pain, or general discomfort or fatigue, that can become conditioned stimuli eliciting escape or avoidance behavior. These physical sensations become particularly salient when there are no clear environmental triggers or predictors of pain. In chronic pain patients, such interoceptive conditioning can result in widespread avoidance of physiological arousal. Unfortunately, the resulting physical deconditioning may lead to increased physiological arousal (e.g., heavy breathing and heart racing) at lower levels of physical activity, leading to a negative spiral of avoidant behavior (De Peuter et al., 2011). Accumulating evidence has demonstrated the efficacy of interoceptive exposures in treatment for chronic pain. In one study, a 4-week interoceptive exposure treatment plus daily practice reduced pain severity in a group of patients with co-occurring chronic pain and PTSD (Wald et al., 2010). In another study, patients were instructed to focus on pain sensations for at least 15 minutes and were asked to practice this attentional focus daily for 3 weeks. Results demonstrated increased pain acceptance and decreased pain-related distress (Flink et al., 2009). Of note, a significant number of studies also demonstrate the beneficial effects of distraction on pain severity and pain-related distress, which is conceptually the opposite of exposure. Although research has found evidence for the efficacy of both interoceptive exposure and distraction, it is unclear whether one method is superior to the other in reducing pain-related distress and disability (Flink et al., 2009).

In the final core module of the UP, patients engage in exposure exercises designed to increase their tolerance of uncomfortable emotional and sensory experiences. In vivo exposures have the potential to reduce the threat value of pain by providing opportunities to disconfirm beliefs that drive pain-related fear. For example, re-engaging in physical activity provides an opportunity for a chronic pain patient to identify feared consequences (e.g., injury) and test whether the feared consequences occur during the exposure. Exposures also provide opportunities for patients to learn about their ability to cope with uncomfortable emotional or sensory experiences. A randomized clinical trial examined the efficacy of a transdiagnostic emotion-focused exposure treatment for chronic pain and comorbid anxiety and depression. The exposure treatment was compared to an internet-based CBT pain management program. The results indicated that patients in the exposure treatment group had significantly better long-term outcomes in pain interference and depressive symptoms relative to the internet-based CBT group (Boersma et al., 2019). These data suggest that in vivo exposures for chronic pain may be an essential ingredient for long-term treatment success.

Taken together, evidence suggests several advantages of a unified approach targeting the underlying, shared mechanisms that are central to the development of both chronic pain and emotional disorders. First, using a unified, transdiagnostic treatment approach for patients with chronic pain may produce more comprehensive and longer lasting symptom improvements across a range of emotional disorders as well as pain-related symptoms. Preliminary support for the use of a unified approach to treating pain and emotional disorders was demonstrated by Allen et al. (2012), who described the application of a modified version of the UP for two adolescents with pain and emotional disorders. The results indicated that both participants demonstrated improvements at post-treatment, some of which were more evident at the 3-month follow-up (Allen et al., 2012). Second, using a transdiagnostic treatment approach that focuses on a single set of core therapeutic principles rather than several diverse protocols would simplify the training of therapists treating patients with chronic pain. A global needs assessment in pain psychology revealed a shortage of mental health providers who feel comfortable treating chronic pain despite high levels of interest and need (Darnall et al., 2016). A transdiagnostic treatment approach has the potential to address these workforce gaps. In addition, this approach to the treatment of pain and emotional disorders would potentially be much more cost-effective, would simplify the dissemination of evidence-based treatments, and would broaden the reach of treatment to those who need it most.

CASE EXAMPLE

Background and Presenting Problem

Carolina is a 30-year-old Caucasian/Latinx female who works in retail and is also a part-time graduate student in business. She identifies as bisexual; she does not currently have a romantic partner but is actively dating. She describes her family relationships as somewhat strained due to her parents' marital discord, their reliance on Carolina for financial and emotional support, and their disapproval of her sexual identity. Carolina slipped on ice 2 years ago, at which time she broke her right ankle and sprained her knee. After the injury, she wore a cast on her ankle for 8 weeks and then participated in physical therapy for 8 additional weeks. After the completion of physical therapy, she began re-engaging in her usual daily activities. However, approximately 3 months ago, Carolina began re-experiencing pain in her knee and ankle. At this time, she was under significant stress due to her mother being hospitalized with COVID-19 (her mother has since recovered). Carolina was examined by her primary care physician and orthopedic physician, and X-rays were obtained, all of which revealed that her injuries appeared fully healed. Her primary care physician recommended psychological treatment for her symptoms. Carolina presented to our center, reporting that she is looking for help with managing her pain. She reports experiencing pain daily and notes that her pain increases over the course of the day, ranging from 1 to 8 on a scale of 10, with an average rating of 4. Carolina has noticed that her pain is exacerbated by stress and believes that her pain reflects the intersection of a physical and emotional problem. Specifically, she reports increased pain during her exam periods at school, during the holidays when she is required to work extra hours at her job, and when she is experiencing interpersonal difficulties. Strategies that temporarily alleviate her pain include taking a hot bath, using a compression bandage on her ankle, and elevating her foot. Carolina endorsed moderate worry about how serious the physical problem may be, specifically worrying that the pain will not go away and she will be unable to function well. These symptoms interfere because she has been reducing her shifts at work and suffering financially as a result. She also has been avoiding physical activity and having more difficulty falling asleep at night. Carolina has noticed that she has been experiencing low mood in the last few weeks, which has also led to a decrease in her motivation to engage in social activities. Carolina is bothered by these symptoms because she feels increasingly isolated and is concerned about her job security if she continues to miss work.

In addition to pain-related fear, Carolina endorsed excessive and difficult-to-control worry about her school/career (e.g., completing school tasks well, moving up in her career, making connections with other professionals, and obtaining positive recommendations from her supervisors and professors). She also worries excessively about finding a long-term romantic partner and about family relationships. Carolina described physical symptoms associated with this worry, including difficulty concentrating, muscle tension, fatigue, and sleep difficulties. Based on the initial assessment at our center using the Anxiety Disorders Interview Schedule for DSM-5 (ADIS-5-L), Carolina was assigned a principal diagnosis of somatic symptom disorder, with predominant pain, moderate. A secondary diagnosis of generalized anxiety disorder was assigned to capture her excessive, difficult-to-control worry and associated physical symptoms, which predated her pain. Symptoms of major depressive disorder were also present at a subclinical level, with onset soon after her pain recurrence.

Transdiagnostic Case Conceptualization

As evidenced by her long-standing excessive and difficult-to-control worry across a variety of domains, Carolina exhibited a predisposition to high levels of neuroticism. Although her ankle and knee injury had healed, Carolina's predisposition to high negative affect increased her risk for chronic pain following an injury. When her mother became seriously ill, Carolina's high stress levels combined with these vulnerabilities triggered a resurgence of her pain. Of note, Carolina also described her tendency to express anxiety and stress symptoms somatically because it feels more acceptable to express physical distress than emotional distress in her culture. Her worries that her pain was a sign of a more serious physical problem and that her pain will never go away led her to begin avoiding long shifts at work, physical activity, and social activities that she feared might exacerbate her pain. Pain-related worries contributed to difficulties concentrating on her schoolwork, increased irritability, and trouble falling asleep at night. This pain-related fear also contributed to feelings of hopelessness and low mood. Her avoidance of physical activity likely led to physical deconditioning, which made it more likely for her to experience injury and pain at lower levels of activity. The aim of the UP was to target the underlying fear and avoidance that led Carolina to become isolated and inactive, with the goal of preventing further disability. Table 6.1 presents a detailed summary of the case conceptualization.

Table 6.1 A Case Conceptualization with the UP in Health Conditions

HEALTH CONDITION ANALYSIS							
Health condition description: Chronic knee and ankle pain in right leg post-recovery from an injury in which she broke her ankle and sprained her knee after slipping on ice. Injury occurred 2 years ago; treatment involved cast and physical therapy. Resurgence of pain 3 months ago with no clear medical cause.							
How does the health condition (and its treatment) affect the patient's life?				**EMOTION ANALYSIS REGARDING HEALTH CONDITIONS AND ITS CONSEQUENCES**			
General life aspects		**Affectation/ interference** **0________10** **Nothing Very much**	**Strong uncomfortable emotions** Do patients feel strong emotions in any of these general life aspects?	**Intensity** **0________10** **Nothing Extreme**	**Aversive reactions**	**Emotional behaviors** (Situational avoidance/escape, subtle behavioral avoidance, cognitive avoidance, safety signals)	
1. Physical and basic necessities	**Physical symptoms**: Increased pain when stressed or anxious.	7	Anxiety, depression, anger	6	"I can't handle anything anymore."	Takes ibuprofen on stressful days in anticipation of pain	
	Eat: Poor eating habits. Tends to have a decreased appetite when experiencing pain flare-up, sometimes increased appetite when stress and anxiety is high.	4	Depression and anger	4	"What's the point in eating well if I'm going to be in pain anyway?"	Only cooks simple meals that take little time to prepare	
	Sex: Avoids due to pain-related fear.	4	Anxiety	4	"Sex is going to hurt, I won't enjoy it."	Cuts off relationships before there is an expectation of sex	

	Sleep: Difficulty falling asleep at night. Worries a lot when lying bed.	8	Anxiety	9	"I will feel angry and frustrated tossing and turning trying to fall asleep."	Does not get in bed until she is completely exhausted
	Activity: Avoids physical activity due to pain-related fear. Decreasing shifts at work and limiting social activities that involve walking or standing.	10	Anxiety, depression, anger	10	"My co-workers and friends think I'm lazy and weak."	Distances herself from co-workers and friends by declining invitations and restricting communication
	Energy: Experiencing fatigue, especially during periods of stress.	6	Depression	5	"I'm not able to be productive anymore."	Ruminates about how the fatigue affects her performance
	Pain: Right knee and ankle pain that increases over the course of the day, ranging from 1 to 8 on a scale of 10, with an average rating of 4.	9	Anxiety, anger	10	"Pain will never go away."	Wears compression bandage and carries ibuprofen; pain hypervigilance
	Medication side effects: None.	0	None	0		
	General: Currently functioning moderately well, but concerned about increasing limitations.	4				

(*continued*)

Table 6.1 Continued

HEALTH CONDITION ANALYSIS					
Health condition description: Chronic knee and ankle pain in right leg post-recovery from an injury in which she broke her ankle and sprained her knee after slipping on ice. Injury occurred 2 years ago; treatment involved cast and physical therapy. Resurgence of pain 3 months ago with no clear medical cause.					
How does the health condition (and its treatment) affect the patient's life?			**EMOTION ANALYSIS REGARDING HEALTH CONDITIONS AND ITS CONSEQUENCES**		
General life aspects	**Affectation/ interference** **0____10** **Nothing Very much**	**Strong uncomfortable emotions** Do patients feel strong emotions in any of these general life aspects?	**Intensity** **0____10** **Nothing Extreme**	**Aversive reactions**	**Emotional behaviors** (Situational avoidance/escape, subtle behavioral avoidance, cognitive avoidance, safety signals)
2. Work/studies: Completed bachelor's degree and currently a part-time graduate student in business. First in her family to go to college and feels a lot of pressure to succeed. Works full-time in a retail job to help pay for tuition and living expenses. She has been calling out sick a lot recently due to pain-related anxiety.	8	Anxiety	8	"I'm a failure." "I'm going to let my family down."	Perfectionism with work and school
3. Daily life activities (to buy, to cook, to clean, etc.): Lives with two roommates in a rented apartment. Takes care of her own cooking, splits cleaning responsibilities with roommates.	5	Depression	4	"I can't keep up with life responsibilities."	Avoids household chores when feeling overwhelmed; defensive with roommates when they bring it to her attention
4. Pleasant activities (hobbies, sport, etc.): Watching Netflix, photography, walking outside	8	Depression	8	"I don't deserve time to do my hobbies."	Does not walk outside often; uses Netflix as a distraction

5. Personal relationships (couple, family, friends, etc.): Social interactions are increasingly restricted. Declines social events if she expects it will involve much standing or walking. Low mood has also led to reduced motivation to engage in social activities. Parents live in another state, but rely on her for financial and logistical support (they speak limited English).	8	Anxiety, depression	8	"They won't understand what I'm going through."	Anger outbursts, especially at her mother; uses work/school obligations as an excuse to cancel plans with friends
6. Spirituality: Practices Buddhist meditation regularly, but otherwise does not endorse religious or spiritual practices.	2	None	1		
7. Life goals: To live a pain-free life. Also would like to find a partner to share her life with. Feels external pressure from her family to succeed academically but also has her own desire to start a nonprofit that provides financial and job counseling to recent immigrants.	8	Anxiety, depression, anger	8	"My pain makes me feel hopeless about the future." "Why is this happening to me?"	Restricts goals to those that do not cause pain
8. Others					

TREATMENT PLAN
MODULE 1
Setting treatment goals and assessing motivation for change. Therapist will work with patient to identify problem areas and set treatment goals. Treatment goals will not explicitly focus on reducing pain, but on learning emotion regulation and coping strategies that will allow patient to re-engage in behaviors that were previously avoided due to pain-related fears. Therapist will work collaboratively with patient to complete decisional balance exercise to explore costs and benefits of changing/staying the same.

(*continued*)

Table 6.1 CONTINUED

MODULE 2
Psychoeducation.In addition to discussing the functional nature of emotions and introducing the three-component model, the therapist will introduce education about chronic pain. This includes discussion about the function of pain; the cycle of pain, distress, and disability; and the gate control theory of pain. The therapist will explain that acute pain is key to survival, as it alerts us to the presence of tissue damage. However, when pain persists over time, it leads to negative beliefs about pain, which leads to avoidance of activities that trigger pain-related fear, which in turn leads to physical deconditioning that can lower the threshold at which pain is perceived. Discussion of the gate theory of pain will demonstrate the mechanisms by which thoughts, behaviors, and mood can influence perceptions of pain.
MODULE 3
Mindful emotion awareness. During the mindfulness module, Carolina will be instructed to focus on noticing her emotions about pain without judging them. It will be important to work with her to address her judgment and frustration about her pain (e.g., feeling like she should be able to push through the pain). Mindful emotion awareness sessions will focus on helping Carolina recognize that she can't predict the future and that future-focused thoughts happen at the expense of what's happening right now. She will practice anchoring in the present when she notices her future-oriented pain thoughts coming up and will learn to re-focus her attention on the fact that her pain is bearable in the present moment.
MODULE 4
Cognitive flexibility. Carolina will identify frequent thinking traps both related and unrelated to her pain. Pain-related cognitions include "My pain makes me weak" and "My ankle will never feel better." She will work on identifying periods of time when her ankle pain has subsided, which will help her challenge the belief that her pain is constant and unending. Carolina will be asked to consider other people in her life who experience chronic pain, in an effort to challenge some of the beliefs she has about her own pain experience. Carolina and the therapist will also discuss whether she would be able to cope with the pain if it doesn't go away. Carolina will also work on identifying and challenging negative automatic thoughts related to work and school performance. She will be encouraged to identify links between these negative automatic thoughts and her pain (e.g., she puts a lot of pressure on herself in every domain of her life, which heightens her stress and is ultimately not helpful).
MODULE 5
Identifying and countering emotional avoidance behaviors. Carolina will learn to identify the emotion-driven behaviors that provide relief in the short term but contribute to her symptoms in the long term. For example, she endorses snapping at family members (especially her mother) because of frustration with her pain. While expressing anger provides an outlet for releasing this frustration, it exacerbates her pain in two ways: by increasing muscle tension that physically worsens her pain and by opening the pain gate and allowing more pain signals to the brain. She will also identify the links between perfectionism with schoolwork and pain-related consequences. One of Carolina's primary goals of therapy is to re-engage in physical activity (specifically walking) because she feels her lack of exercise is making her pain worse and also contributing to social isolation. She avoids any social situations in which she is expected she may have to walk or stand for long periods of time. In addition to this overt avoidance, she always wears a compression bandage on her ankle when she leaves the house and carries ibuprofen in her bag in case she notices any small hint of pain while she is out.

MODULE 6
Increasing awareness and confronting physical sensations. In addition to the interoceptive exercises offered in the UP, the therapist will guide Carolina through interoceptive exposures focused on pain sensations. As outlined previously in Flink et al. (2009), Carolina will be asked to focus her attention on her pain sensations while engaging in graded exercises (sitting, standing, walking, and jumping) for approximately 15 minutes. She will be instructed to focus on the sensations without trying to change them or distract herself from them. For homework, she will practice focusing on her pain sensations during her daily activities and to track her pain intensity and distress level during each practice. These exercises will also help her notice how often she uses distraction as a coping strategy when she notices any physical cues of pain. This will provide an opportunity for the therapist to discuss with Carolina the pros and cons of distraction for pain (i.e., for acute pain, distraction can often be a helpful coping strategy, but for chronic pain, constant distraction can backfire and reinforce pain-related fear).
MODULE 7
Emotion exposures. Carolina's exposure hierarchy will focus on her ultimate goal of re-engaging in physical activity. Prior to beginning situational exposures, the therapist will consult with Carolina's primary care physician to gauge whether graded physical activity exposures are safe and whether there are any exposures they should specifically avoid. In the beginning, Carolina may experience increased pain as she begins spending more time on her feet. The therapist will inform her this may happen, and they will discuss the idea of "good pain" (e.g., muscle soreness after a workout indicating that the exercise was working as intended). It will also give Carolina an opportunity to examine beliefs about her ability to cope with pain.
MODULE 8
Relapse prevention. Session will focus on highlighting progress and accomplishments, reviewing the skills learned, and discussing ways to promote generalization of skills. Therapist and patient will collaboratively establish a plan for continuing to practice skills introduced in treatment and identify strategies for future situations that may require Carolina to approach rather than avoid intense emotions.
OTHER MODULES IF NECESSARY
Two additional sessions will be added to the UP core modules: one session focused on relaxation and the other focused on sleep behaviors. The therapist will provide in-depth relaxation training. Because the stress response can trigger pain, the therapist will discuss the physical symptoms associated with the sympathetic nervous system and describe how activation of the parasympathetic nervous system using relaxation techniques can counteract the stress response. Carolina will practice diaphragmatic breathing in-session and outside of session to reduce muscle tension and physiological arousal. As Carolina, like many chronic pain patients, is struggling with sleep, the therapist will spend one session introducing basic sleep hygiene techniques.

Treatment Overview

Psychoeducation and Treatment Rationale

In addition to discussing the functional nature of emotions and introducing the three-component model, the therapist introduced education about chronic pain. This included discussion about the function of pain; the cycle of pain, distress, and disability; and the gate control theory of pain. The therapist explained that acute pain is key to survival because it alerts people to the presence of tissue damage. However, when pain persists over time, it leads to negative beliefs about pain, which leads to avoidance of activities that trigger pain-related fear, which in turn leads to physical deconditioning that can lower the threshold at which pain is perceived. Discussion of the gate theory of pain demonstrated the mechanisms by which thoughts, behaviors, and mood can influence perceptions of pain. Carolina acknowledged the influence of stress, negative cognitions, and mood on her pain symptoms. She reported that her highest levels of pain occur when she gets in bed each night, a time when she also notices her worries frequently spiraling out of control. The therapist explained to Carolina that this treatment is not explicitly focused on reducing her pain but, rather, improving her ability to cope with and accept her pain. The hope is that as she learns to better cope with her pain, she will also notice improvements in the pain itself.

Mindful Emotion Awareness

During the mindful emotion awareness module, Carolina uncovered the fact that she frequently judges herself for feeling frustrated about her pain. She felt that her mother was recovering from COVID-19 and others in the world were experiencing significantly worse physical problems, and she should have a higher pain tolerance. She also described feeling at times like the "pain is in her head" due to the fact that her physicians did not find any physical cause for the symptoms. She consequently felt like her pain symptoms were not legitimate and judged herself for not being able to push through the pain. During the mindfulness exercises, she focused on noticing her emotions about pain without judging them. She continued to challenge these judgments in the cognitive flexibility module.

Carolina noticed that she spends a lot of time thinking about how her pain is going to feel later in the day. While she is at work, she is often focused on how spending so much time on her feet is going to make her feel miserable when she gets home. Mindful emotion awareness sessions focused on helping Carolina recognize that she cannot predict the future and that these future-focused thoughts happen at the expense of what is happening right now. She practiced anchoring in the present when she noticed her future-oriented pain thoughts coming up and was able to refocus her attention on the fact that her pain was bearable in the present moment. Carolina reported that increasing her present-focused awareness helped her change her attitude toward work and gradually reduce her missed workdays.

Cognitive Flexibility

In the cognitive flexibility module, Carolina identified frequent thinking traps both related and unrelated to her pain. Pain-related cognitions included "My pain makes me weak" and "My ankle will never feel better." During the session, she was able to identify brief periods of time when her ankle pain subsided, such as when she spent the weekend with someone she recently started dating. This helped challenge her belief that her pain is constant and unending. Carolina talked about her mother who has fibromyalgia and a good friend who has Lyme disease, both of whom experience chronic pain. She recognized that she does not believe either of them to be weak because of their pain; in fact, she sees them as strong women who have fulfilling lives despite their pain. Although she felt her pain was different because it was idiopathic pain, she acknowledged that she was holding a different standard for herself than for others. She also recounted the conversations with her physicians and remembered that they had told her that chronic pain following an ankle injury is very common. Emphasizing this part of these conversations normalized the pain and helped her feel that her complaints were more legitimate. Carolina and the therapist also discussed whether she would be able to cope with the pain if it does not go away. She noted all the things she has accomplished while experiencing pain and acknowledged that "although it would be super frustrating, I will survive." Carolina also brought up negative automatic thoughts related to work and school performance. Examples included "I'm 30 years old. I should have figured out my career by now" and "My boss doesn't think I'm competent." She linked these thoughts to her pain by recognizing that she puts a lot of pressure on herself in every domain of her life, which heightens her stress and is ultimately not helpful.

Identifying and Preventing Patterns of Emotional Avoidance

Carolina identified the emotion-driven behaviors that have provided relief in the short term but contributed to her symptoms in the long term. For example, she endorsed "snapping" at family members (especially her mother) because of frustration with her pain. Although expressing anger provided an outlet for releasing this frustration, it exacerbated her pain in two ways: by increasing muscle tension that physically worsened her pain and by opening the pain gate and allowing more pain signals to the brain. In addition to pain-related consequences, Carolina's anger outbursts led to strained relationships with her parents and subsequent feelings of guilt for lashing out. She also identified perfectionism with her schoolwork as an emotion-driven behavior with significant impacts on her pain. Carolina often pushed herself to do schoolwork until the point of complete exhaustion. As a result, she used the weekends to recover and often needed to miss work on weekend days. The therapist helped Carolina conceptualize her perfectionism as avoidance of failure or making mistakes. One of Carolina's primary goals of therapy was to re-engage in physical activity (specifically walking) because she felt her lack of exercise was making her pain worse and also contributing to social isolation. She reported that she avoided any social situations in which she expected she may have to walk or stand for long periods of time. In addition to this overt avoidance, she always wore a compression bandage on her ankle when she left the house and carried ibuprofen in her bag in case she noticed any small hint of pain while she was out.

Increasing Awareness and Tolerance of Emotion-Related Physical Sensations

During the interoceptive exposure exercises offered in the UP, Carolina appeared to fully engage in them; however, they generally did not cause distress. She reported that she felt safe in the therapy space and felt in control despite the discomfort elicited by the exercises. In addition to these exercises, the therapist guided Carolina through interoceptive exposures focused on pain sensations. As outlined in Flink et al. (2009), Carolina was asked to focus her attention on her pain sensations while engaging in graded exercises (sitting, standing, walking, and jumping) for approximately 15 minutes. She was instructed to focus on the sensations without trying to change them or distract herself from them. For homework, she was asked to practice focusing on her pain sensations during her daily activities and to track her pain intensity and distress level during each practice. Although her pain intensity did not change across the exposure practices, her level of distress reduced over time. These exercises also helped her notice how often she uses distraction as a coping strategy when she notices any physical cues of pain. This provided an opportunity for the therapist to discuss with Carolina the pros and cons of distraction for pain (i.e., for acute pain, distraction can often be a helpful coping strategy, but for chronic pain, constant distraction can backfire and reinforce pain-related fear).

Interoceptive and Situational Emotion-Focused Exposures

Carolina's exposure hierarchy was focused on her ultimate goal of re-engaging in physical activity. Prior to beginning situational exposures, the therapist consulted with Carolina's primary care physician to gauge whether graded physical activity exposures were safe and whether there were any exposures they should specifically avoid. The primary care physician had no concerns and gave permission to move forward. Carolina worked toward walking for increasingly longer stretches, and she also worked toward peeling back her safety behaviors (removing her compression bandage and leaving her ibuprofen at home). Once she felt relatively comfortable walking alone, she planned social exposures in which she met friends for an activity involving walking or standing (e.g., walk in the park). After a few exposures, Carolina brought up the fact that she uses specialty orthotics in her shoes and wanted to wear a different pair of shoes on a date but feared this would make her pain unbearable. She used a session to practice walking exposures wearing this desired pair of shoes and to evaluate the accuracy of her fear. Once she had successfully completed numerous exposures, she also began taking short showers instead of baths at home. In the beginning, Carolina experienced increased pain as she began spending more time on her feet. The therapist had informed her this would likely happen, and they discussed the idea of "good pain" (e.g., muscle soreness after a workout indicating that the exercise was working as intended). It also gave Carolina an opportunity to examine beliefs about her ability to cope with pain.

Additional Modifications to the UP

Two additional sessions were added to the UP core modules: one session focused on relaxation and the other focused on sleep behaviors. The therapist provided in-depth relaxation training. Because the stress response can trigger pain, the therapist discussed the physical symptoms associated with the sympathetic nervous system and described how activation of the parasympathetic nervous system using relaxation techniques can counteract the stress response. Carolina practiced diaphragmatic breathing in-session and outside of session to reduce muscle tension and physiological arousal. She found these breathing exercises particularly helpful in preparing her body for sleep at night. Because Carolina, like many chronic pain patients, was struggling with sleep, the therapist also spent one session introducing basic sleep hygiene techniques.

Routine Outcome Monitoring

Prior to beginning treatment, Carolina completed the Pain Anxiety Symptom Scale, Pain Catastrophizing Scale, and Brief Pain Inventory (see Table 6.2 for pre- and post-treatment scores). The Pain Anxiety Symptom Scale is a 20-item questionnaire that measures pain-specific anxiety and has four subscales. Each item is rated on a scale from 0 (never) to 5 (always). Carolina's pretreatment scores indicated elevated levels of cognitive anxiety and fearful thinking responses consistent

Table 6.2 Outcome Measures

	Pretreatment Scores	**Post-Treatment Scores**
Pain Anxiety Symptom Scale		
Total	24	20
Cognitive	12	9
Escape/avoidance	3	4
Fear	9	6
Physiological anxiety	0	1
Pain Catastrophizing Scale	29	7.5
Brief Pain Inventory–Short Form[a]		
Worst pain in past week	5	5
Average pain in past week	6	3
Pain interference	5	2

[a]Scale is 0–10, where higher scores indicate worse symptoms.

with chronic pain patients in the measure's validation sample (McCracken & Dhingra, 2002). At post-treatment, both of these subscale scores had decreased to below the mean score in the measure's validation sample. The Pain Catastrophizing Scale is a 13-item questionnaire that measures automatic negative appraisals associated with pain. Each item is rated on a scale from 0 (not at all) to 4 (all the time) (Sullivan et al., 1995). Carolina's scores decreased substantially from pre- to post-treatment, indicating an improvement in her ability to engage in more balanced thinking patterns related to her pain. Last, Carolina completed the Brief Pain Inventory–Short Form (Cleeland & Ryan, 1994). Changes from pre- to post-treatment demonstrated that despite continued pain flare-ups, Carolina's reported interference with general activities such as mood, work, relationships, and sleep improved by the end of the treatment. Finally, she reported satisfaction with treatment, stating that she felt more confident in her ability to manage her pain. She noted that she had re-engaged in many social activities and felt more connected to her friends. Carolina requested a referral to a supportive therapist to continue longer term therapy related to her family of origin and relationship with her parents.

CONCLUSION

Given the high prevalence of chronic pain, and given that comorbidity tends to be the "norm" rather than the "exception" in patients with pain, novel treatments such as the UP have the potential to offer a more comprehensive approach to treatment, producing more long-lasting change. Although limited research has examined the use of the UP with chronic pain patients, accumulating evidence demonstrates the efficacy of individual components of the UP protocol in treatment of chronic pain. Despite clinical practice guidelines, psychological treatment is often a last resort for individuals suffering from chronic pain. Many have already sought treatment from a myriad of providers (physicians, physical therapists, massage therapists, chiropractors, etc.) and tried various medical treatments (surgery, medications, etc.) before they access psychological services. Therefore, it is important for the therapist to (a) validate their previous treatment experiences, (b) provide a strong rationale for the use of a transdiagnostic evidence-based psychological treatment, (c) explore the patient's expectancies for treatment, and (d) instill hope about treatment outcomes. As illustrated in the case of Carolina, it is critical that therapists tailor their treatment using the UP to the particular patients' needs; thus, this treatment should be implemented flexibly. Modifications to the UP such as the addition of relaxation techniques and sleep hygiene may be particularly important for adapting the UP for chronic pain. In addition, it may be important to work in collaboration with the patient's medical team (physician, physical therapist, etc.) to ensure that exposures and other treatment activities are safe for the patient.

Further research building upon the promising preliminary study by Allen et al. (2012) is needed to determine the efficacy of the UP treatment for patients with chronic pain and co-occurring conditions. Furthermore, it is critical to determine the longevity of changes experienced by patients with pain who receive the UP; thus, long-term follow-up assessments should be incorporated in future research. It is clear that the transdiagnostic treatment approach offered by the UP has many advantages, from simplifying the training of therapists treating patients with pain to improved clinical outcomes for patients.

REFERENCES

Allen, L. B., Tsao, J. C., Seidman, L. C., Ehrenreich-May, J., & Zeltzer, L. K. (2012). A unified, transdiagnostic treatment for adolescents with chronic pain and comorbid anxiety and depression. *Cognitive and Behavioral Practice, 19*(1), 56–67.

Asmundson, G. J., & Katz, J. (2009). Understanding the co-occurrence of anxiety disorders and chronic pain: State-of-the-art. *Depression and Anxiety, 26*(10), 888–901.

Asmundson, G. J., Parkerson, H. A., Petter, M., & Noel, M. (2012). What is the role of fear and escape/avoidance in chronic pain? Models, structural analysis and future directions. *Pain Management, 2*(3), 295–303.

Bair, M. J., Robinson, R. L., Katon, W., & Kroenke, K. (2003). Depression and pain co-morbidity: A literature review. *Archives of Internal Medicine, 163*, 2433–2445.

Bair, M. J., Wu, J., Damush, T. M., Sutherland, J. M., & Kroenke, K. (2008). Association of depression and anxiety alone and in combination with chronic musculoskeletal pain in primary care patients. *Psychosomatic Medicine, 70*, 890–897.

Banks, S. M., & Kerns, R. D. (1996). Explaining high rates of depression in chronic pain: A diathesis-stress framework. *Psychological Bulletin, 119*, 95–110.

Barlow, D. H., Farchione, T. J., Sauer-Zavala, S., Murray Latin, H., Ellard, K., Bullis, J., Bentley, K., Boettcher, H., & Cassiello-Robbins, C. (2018a). *Unified Protocol for Transdiagnostic Treatment of Emotional Disorders: Therapist Guide* (2nd ed.). Oxford University Press.

Barlow, D. H., Sauer-Zavala, S., Farchione, T. J., Murray Latin, H., Ellard, K., Bullis, J., Bentley, K., Boettcher, H., & assiello-Robbins, C. (2018b). *Unified Protocol for Transdiagnostic Treatment of Emotional Disorders: Workbook* (2nd ed.). Oxford University Press.

Berna, C., Leknes, S., Holmes, E. A., Edwards, R. R., Goodwin, G. M., & Tracy, I. (2010). Induction of depressed mood disrupts emotion regulation neurocircuitry and enhances pain unpleasantness. *Biological Psychiatry, 67*, 1083–1090.

Boersma, K., Södermark, M., Hesser, H., Flink, I. K., Gerdle, B., & Linton, S. J. (2019). Efficacy of a transdiagnostic emotion-focused exposure treatment for chronic pain patients with comorbid anxiety and depression: A randomized controlled trial. *Pain, 160*(8), 1708–1718.

Burns, J. W., Day, M. A., & Thorn, B. E. (2012). Is reduction in pain catastrophizing a therapeutic mechanism specific to cognitive–behavioral therapy for chronic pain? *Translational Behavioral Medicine, 2*(1), 22–29.

Burns, J. W., Johnson, B. J., Mahoney, N., Devine, J., & Pawl, R. (1998). Cognitive and physical capacity process variables predict long-term outcome after treatment of chronic pain. *Journal of Consulting and Clinical Psychology*, *66*(2), 434–439.

Chiesa, A., & Serretti, A. (2011). Mindfulness based cognitive therapy for psychiatric disorders: A systematic review and meta-analysis. *Psychiatry Research*, *187*(3), 441–453.

Cioffi, D., & Holloway, J. (1993). Delayed costs of suppressed pain. *Journal of Personality and Social Psychology*, *64*(2), 274–282.

Cleeland, C. S., & Ryan, K. M. (1994). Pain assessment: Global use of the Brief Pain Inventory. *Annals of the Academy of Medicine, Singapore, 23*(2), 129–138.

Darnall, B. D., Scheman, J., Davin, S., Burns, J. W., Murphy, J. L., Wilson, A. C., Kerns, R. D., & Mackey, S. C. (2016). Pain psychology: A global needs assessment and national call to action. *Pain Medicine*, *17*(2), 250–263.

De Peuter, S., Van Diest, I., Vansteenwegen, D., Van den Bergh, O., & Vlaeyen, J. W. (2011). Understanding fear of pain in chronic pain: Interoceptive fear conditioning as a novel approach. *European Journal of Pain*, *15*(9), 889–894.

Eccleston, C., & Crombez, G. (1999). Pain demands attention: A cognitive–affective model of the interruptive function of pain. *Psychological Bulletin*, *125*(3), 356–366.

Elliott, T. E., Renier, C. M., & Palcher, J. A. (2003). Chronic pain, depression, and quality of life: Correlations and predictive value of the SF-36. *Pain Medicine*, *4*(4), 331–339.

Flink, I. K., Nicholas, M. K., Boersma, K., & Linton, S. J. (2009). Reducing the threat value of chronic pain: A preliminary replicated single-case study of interoceptive exposure versus distraction in six individuals with chronic back pain. *Behaviour Research and Therapy*, *47*(8), 721–728.

Gamsa, A. (1994). The role of psychological factors in chronic pain: I. A half century of study. *Pain*, *57*(1), 5–15.

Garland, E. L., & Howard, M. O. (2013). Mindfulness-oriented recovery enhancement reduces pain attentional bias in chronic pain patients. *Psychotherapy and Psychosomatics*, *82*(5), 311–318.

Gaskin, D. J., & Richard, P. (2012). The economic costs of pain in the United States. *Journal of Pain*, *13*(8), 715–724.

Gatchel, R. J., Peng, Y. B., Peters, M. L., Fuchs, P. N., & Turk, D. C. (2007). The biopsychosocial approach to chronic pain: Scientific advances and future directions. *Psychological Bulletin*, *133*(4), 581–624.

Hollander, M. D., De Jong, J. R., Volders, S., Goossens, M. E., Smeets, R. J., & Vlaeyen, J. W. (2010). Fear reduction in patients with chronic pain: A learning theory perspective. *Expert Review of Neurotherapeutics*, *10*(11), 1733–1745.

Holzberg, A. D., Robinson, M. E., Geisser, M. E., & Gremillion, H. A. (1996). The effects of depression and chronic pain on psychosocial and physical functioning. *Clinical Journal of Pain*, *12*(2), 118–125.

Institute of Medicine Committee on Advancing Pain Research, Care, and Education. (2011). *Relieving pain in America: A blueprint for transforming prevention, care, education, and research.* National Academies Press.

International Association for the Study of Pain. (2017). *Classification of Chronic Pain: Descriptions of Chronic Pain Syndromes and Definitions of Pain Terms* (2nd ed.). IASP Press.

Kerns, R. D., & Haythornthwaite, J. A. (1988). Depression among chronic pain patients: Cognitive-behavioral analysis and effect on rehabilitation outcome. *Journal of Consulting and Clinical Psychology, 56*(6), 870–876.

Kroenke, K., Outcalt, S., Krebs, E., Bair, M. J., Wu, J., Chumbler, N., & Yu, Z. (2013). Association between anxiety, health-related quality of life and functional impairment in primary care patients with chronic pain. *General Hospital Psychiatry, 35*(4), 359–365.

Liu, X., Li, L., Xiao, J., Yang, J., & Jiang, X. (2013). Abnormalities of autobiographical memory of patients with depressive disorders: A meta-analysis. *Psychology and Psychotherapy, 86*(4), 353–373.

McCracken, L. M., & Dhingra, L. (2002). A short version of the Pain Anxiety Symptoms Scale (PASS-20): preliminary development and validity. *Pain Research & Management, 7*(1), 45–50.

McWilliams, L. A., Cox, B. J., & Enns, M. W. (2003). Mood and anxiety disorders associated with chronic pain: An examination in a nationally representative sample. *Pain, 106*(1–2), 127–133.

Melzack, R., & Wall, P. D. (1965). Pain mechanisms: A new theory. *Science, 150*(3699), 971–979.

Nicholas, M. K., Linton, S. J., Watson, P. J., Main, C. J., & "Decade of the Flags" Working Group. (2011). Early identification and management of psychological risk factors ("yellow flags") in patients with low back pain: A reappraisal. *Physical Therapy, 91*(5), 737–753.

Otis, J. D. (2007a). *Managing chronic pain: A cognitive-behavioral therapy approach, therapist guide*. Oxford University Press.

Otis, J. D. (2007b). *Managing chronic pain: A cognitive-behavioral therapy approach, patient workbook*. Oxford University Press.

Quartana, P. J., Campbell, C. M., & Edwards, R. R. (2009). Pain catastrophizing: A critical review. *Expert Review of Neurotherapeutics, 9*(5), 745–758.

QuickStats: Age-adjusted percentage of adults aged ≥18 years who were never in pain, in pain some days, or in pain most days or every day in the past 6 months, by employment status—National Health Interview Survey, United States, 2016. (2017). *MMWR Morbidity and Mortality Weekly Report, 66*(29), 796.

Seminowicz, D. A., & Davis, K. D. (2006). Cortical responses to pain in healthy individuals depends on pain catastrophizing. *Pain, 120*, 297–306.

Staerkle, R., Mannion, A. F., Elfering, A., Junge, A., Semmer, N. K., Jacobshagen, N., Grob, D., Dvorak, J., & Boos, N. (2004). Longitudinal validation of the Fear-Avoidance Beliefs Questionnaire (FABQ) in a Swiss–German sample of low back pain patients. *European Spine Journal, 13*(4), 332–340.

Strigo, I. A., Simmons, A. N., Matthews, S. C., Arthur, D., & Paulus, M. P. (2008). Association of major depressive disorder with altered functional brain response during anticipation and processing of heat pain. *Archives of General Psychiatry, 65*(11), 1275–1284.

Sullivan, M. J. L., Bishop, S. R., & Pivik, J. (1995). The Pain Catastrophizing Scale: Development and validation. *Psychological Assessment, 7*(4), 524–532.

Sullivan, M. J., Rouse, D., Bishop, S., & Johnston, S. (1997). Thought suppression, catastrophizing, and pain. *Cognitive Therapy and Research, 21*(5), 555–568.

Thorn, B. (2017). *Cognitive therapy for chronic pain: A step-by-step guide* (2nd ed.). Guilford.

Tsao, J. C., Myers, C. D., Craske, M. G., Bursch, B., Kim, S. C., & Zeltzer, L. K. (2004). Role of anticipatory anxiety and anxiety sensitivity in children's and adolescents' laboratory pain responses. *Journal of Pediatric Psychology*, *29*(5), 379–388.

Turk, D. C., & Fritz, W. (2005). *The pain survival guide: How to reclaim your life*. American Psychological Association.

Volders, S., Boddez, Y., De Peuter, S., Meulders, A., & Vlaeyen, J. W. (2015). Avoidance behavior in chronic pain research: A cold case revisited. *Behaviour Research and Therapy*, *64*, 31–37.

Wald, J., Taylor, S., Chiri, L. R., & Sica, C. (2010). Posttraumatic stress disorder and chronic pain arising from motor vehicle accidents: Efficacy of interoceptive exposure plus trauma-related exposure therapy. *Cognitive Behaviour Therapy*, *39*(2), 104–113.

Woo, A. K. (2010). Depression and anxiety in pain. *Reviews in Pain*, *4*(1), 8–12.

Application of the Unified Protocol in Patients Who Have Undergone Bariatric Surgery

VANESA FERRERES-GALÁN, ALBA QUILEZ-ORDEN,
ÓSCAR PERIS-BAQUERO, AND JORGE OSMA ■

INTRODUCTION

Obesity is a chronic disease characterized by an increase in body fat reserves, which is generally estimated by the body mass index (BMI). BMI is calculated as body weight (in kilograms) divided by height measured squared (in meters squared). In adults (ages 18 years or older), overweight is defined by a BMI greater than 25, and obesity is defined by a BMI greater than 30 (Yumuk et al., 2015). Obesity has become a serious public health problem globally due to its high prevalence. In fact, more than 1.9 billion adults are overweight, and of these, more than 650 million people are obese, representing 13% of the world's adult population (World Health Organization [WHO], 2020).

The causes of obesity are complex and multifactorial, involving interactions between biological, behavioral, social, and environmental factors (Yumuk et al., 2015). It presents high rates of comorbidity with different physical (myocardial infarction, arterial hypertension, stroke, etc.) and mental health alterations, increasing the probability of developing anxiety or mood disorders by 25% (Castaneda et al., 2019) and thus affecting different areas of functioning of people who suffer from it and reducing their quality of life (Spirou et al., 2020).

Vanesa Ferreres-Galán, Alba Quilez-Orden, Óscar Peris-Baquero, and Jorge Osma, *Application of the Unified Protocol in Patients Who Have Undergone Bariatric Surgery* In: *Applications of the Unified Protocol in Health Conditions*. Edited by: Jorge Osma and Todd J. Farchione, Oxford University Press. © Oxford University Press 2023.
DOI: 10.1093/oso/9780197564295.003.0007

Obesity carries very high costs for health systems, accounting for approximately 8.4% of the total cost of medical care (Organisation for Economic Co-operation and Development, 2019). As such, significant effort has been made to develop treatments for weight loss in patients with obesity, including interventions such as lifestyle modifications (caloric restriction, increased physical activity, and behavior modification), pharmacotherapy, or surgical interventions (Sarwer & Heinberg, 2020). Currently, bariatric surgery (BS) is the most widely used procedure worldwide and has been shown to be effective in reducing weight in severely obese patients (Spirou et al., 2020). BS is associated with a wide range of patient health benefits, including significant weight loss, improvement in many comorbid health conditions, and increased quality of life (Lauren et al., 2020). However, in the long term, 20–50% of operated patients regain weight (Cassin et al., 2016), and it is estimated that patients recover approximately 10% of their weight during the first 10 years following the intervention. In addition, other negative consequences associated with BS are related to dermal sequels that remain after the intervention, which cause a reduction in quality of life, especially in social activities and self-image (Sarwer & Heinberg, 2020).

PSYCHOLOGICAL TREATMENTS FOR PEOPLE WITH OBESITY OR WHO HAVE UNDERGONE BARIATRIC SURGERY

Anxiety, mood, and eating disorders are the most prevalent mental health conditions in BS candidates, and they are highly associated with early weight regain after BS (Hjelmesæth et al., 2019; Sarwer & Heinberg, 2020). The presence of these psychological conditions suggests the need for psychological assessment and intervention as a fundamental part of multidisciplinary work that should be done with these patients (Sarwer & Heinberg, 2020).

Psychological interventions, especially those that use techniques such as psychoeducation, goal setting, self-monitoring, normalization of eating patterns, stimulus control, cognitive restructuring, and relapse prevention, have resulted in improvements in the psychopathology of eating disorders (binge eating, emotional eating, dissatisfaction with body image, etc.). Cognitive–behavioral therapy (CBT) has demonstrated the most improvement in the psychopathology of eating behavior and general psychological functioning (Lauren et al., 2020).

Treatment adherence is another factor to be considered. The rate of dropout and non-attendance at post-BS follow-up appointments is approximately 72% (Toussi et al., 2009). Among the various factors proposed to explain this situation are weight loss at the beginning of treatment, lower BMI, and better mood (e.g., Burgess et al., 2017). In terms of psychological aspects, lower levels of depression, stress, anxiety, and negative affect are the best predictors of adherence to treatment (Chang et al., 2009). Therefore, psychological interventions should also focus on addressing these factors to ensure successful adherence.

Interventions based on CBT have been developed to treat specific diagnoses, which results in some limitations, often derived from the high comorbidity between psychological disorders or the condition of subclinical symptoms or unspecified disorders (Brown et al., 2001). As such, specific psychological treatments may not be the most cost-effective because they are unable to attend to the different forms of psychopathology (McManus et al., 2010).

Finally, there are other limitations, especially in public health systems, in applying specific intervention protocols because health professionals must specialize in each of the interventions, which means an increased cost for training professionals and a greater expense for the health care system. All these limitations make it difficult to disseminate and implement evidence-based psychological interventions in health settings (Barlow et al., 2018).

To address the previously mentioned limitations, different transdiagnostic interventions have been developed with the fundamental objective of identifying the etiological and maintenance mechanisms shared by different types of psychological disorders (Sauer-Zavala et al., 2017). Fairburn et al. (2003) developed a transdiagnostic model that identified four central dimensions shared by the different eating disorders: clinical perfectionism, low self-esteem, emotional intolerance, and interpersonal difficulties. Based on this conception, they develop improved CBT for eating disorders (Fairburn, 2008).

Considering that eating disorders, along with depression and anxiety, are the most prevalent disorders in BS candidates (Sarwer & Heinberg, 2020), and these factors are most associated with early weight regain after BS (Hjelmesæth et al., 2019), it would be interesting to determine what these health conditions have in common in order to address them together from a transdiagnostic perspective. In this sense, neuroticism was proposed by Brown and Barlow (2009) as the core dimension shared by emotional disorders (which include anxiety, mood, and related disorders) that contributes to their etiology, course, and maintenance. Neuroticism is also associated with a greater presence of health problems and thus with a greater frequency of use of medical services (Lahey, 2009). In addition, neuroticism is associated with worse outcomes after BS (Oltmanns et al., 2020). Therefore, finding an intervention focused on the treatment of this specific personality dimension could have advantages for post-BS patients.

The Unified Protocol for the Transdiagnostic Treatment of Emotional Disorders (UP) is a CBT-based intervention that explicitly addresses neuroticism through adaptive emotional regulation strategy training (Osma et al., 2021; Sauer-Zavala et al., 2021). Because it is a transdiagnostic treatment, it addresses comorbid disorders, subclinical symptomatology, and unspecified disorders (Barlow et al., 2018).

One of strengths of the UP is its flexibility and versatility, which allows it to be adapted to different disorders, patients, contexts, and formats. For example, clinicians can increase the duration of any of the modules or change their order (Sauer-Zavala et al., 2019). These characteristics are especially relevant for the application of the UP in public health systems, in addition to being able to be applied in a group format. Using the UP, several patients can be attended to at the same time, reducing the waiting list for therapy. Moreover, this format helps develop social support networks among the participants, who exchange experiences, thus increasing the social support perceived by them (Yalom & Leszcz, 2005).

The UP has considerable empirical support, significantly improving symptoms after the intervention with effect sizes that are at least comparable to those obtained by specific interventions for each emotional disorder (Sakiris & Berle, 2019) and even obtaining greater efficacy for the treatment of neuroticism (Sauer-Zavala et al., 2021), which is particularly prevalent in this health condition. These data have been obtained by applying the UP in different formats (individual, group, face-to-face, and online), and there is also encouraging preliminary data regarding its application in different health conditions (e.g., cancer and HIV) (Cassiello-Robbins et al., 2020; Osma, Martínez-García, et al., 2021). In relation to eating disorders, a pilot study applied the UP to treat emotional disorders in residential eating disorder programs, showing a reduction in anxiety and depression symptoms (Thompson-Brenner et al., 2019).

Despite its positive results, the UP has not yet been applied to emotional symptoms or emotional disorders in post-BS patients. Therefore, in this chapter, we present an adaptation of the UP applied in group format in post-BS patients. We also provide preliminary data of a pilot study conducted in a public mental health unit in Spain together with a clinical case formulation.

UNIFIED PROTOCOL ADAPTATION FOR PATIENTS AFTER BARIATRIC SURGERY

Taking into account the versatility offered by the UP to modify the number and order of both modules and sessions, here we present a proposed adaptation of the UP for patients after BS in public health settings.

Module 1: Setting Goals and Maintaining Motivation

People who have undergone BS usually have the general goal of maintaining post-BS weight loss and have a high motivation for change. This is especially true for patients who have struggled with losing weight and have been "stuck" at a particular weight despite ongoing efforts. For this reason, it can help to clarify the role of psychological factors in the development and maintenance of overeating. In this module, we introduce the concept of emotional eating and how emotions and emotion regulation can negatively affect weight. Accordingly, information regarding emotional eating and its conceptualization as an emotion-driven behavior (EDB) can be discussed. We recommend personalizing goals for each patient considering individual characteristics and clinical presentation. When discussing motivation to change, and identifying specific steps for each treatment goal, we mention that some changes can be achieved in a short period of time (e.g., doing physical exercise), whereas others may require longer periods of time (e.g., to lose weight). Clinicians should also try to identify intense emotions that are triggered by other experiences not directly associated with eating patterns, weight loss, or body image (e.g., interpersonal difficulties, social interaction, and work issues). The decisional balance exercise in this module is conducted as in the original manual (Barlow et al., 2018).

Module 2: Understanding Your Emotions

In the original UP, patients learn about the function of both negative (e.g., anxiety, sadness, and guilt) and positive emotions (e.g., happiness and hope). We also discuss several other emotions that are not contained in the original UP such as boredom (a state of mind that can provoke intense emotions). In addition, we have found it helpful to discuss the function of what we describe as "justified guilt/shame" versus "non-justified guilt/shame" that some individuals can feel because of social and media pressure about body image, body shape, and weight (that is not always related to health). In this module, we also stress how binge eating and continued snacking are EDBs and consider short- and long-term consequences of these behaviors (i.e., reducing emotional distress short term and increasing feelings of guilt and increasing weight long term). We ask participants to specifically observe their emotional eating patterns to help them identify the association between binge eating or snacking and emotions such as stress, anxiety, and guilt, or states such as boredom. In these patients, sometimes positive emotions can also trigger nonadaptive EDBs such as drinking too much alcohol or binge eating (e.g., "My boss told me that I am doing a great job and I felt really happy and I could not stop thinking about eating something delicious to celebrate it").

Module 3: Mindful Emotion Awareness

In this module, we generally follow the procedures of the original UP manual. However, we emphasize the importance of intense emotion and associated physical sensations that may be directly linked to a sense of hunger. This observation can help patients differentiate "real hunger" (i.e., hunger based on a physical need) from an "emotional sense of hunger." Finally, in this module, mindful emotion awareness is often used to increase awareness of eating and to help patients better observe the sensory qualities (i.e., smell, touch, and taste) of different foods. These exercises can be helpful because practicing conscious eating facilitates focusing on all factors related to eating behavior from a nonjudgmental attitude ("I am eating too much" or "I should eat more than that"). In addition, this practice facilitates a slower intake, which is healthier and can also help people observe their sense of satiety to stop eating.

Module 4: Cognitive Flexibility

This module focuses on the anxious and negative thoughts related to strong emotions, including those associated with eating behaviors, self-image, and weight. Examples include "If I eat, the discomfort is more manageable," "Being fat is not a matter of weight, I always feel that way," "People think that I'm fat," and "Everything will be fine once I lose all the weight I need to." Patients learn cognitive flexibility, which involves using different questions to help patients evaluate situations in a more objective and adaptive manner. This includes helping patients accept current aspects of their physical appearance (weight and self-image) and develop new, more balanced ways of thinking about themselves and weight loss. For example, a patient in our clinic developed the following thought: "My skin is soft and lacks firmness, but this is normal after all the weight I have lost and I can work to improve it with exercise. Despite this, it will last some time. I should focus on the things I can do and my abilities. I am more valuable than a body."

Module 5: Countering Emotional Behaviors

This module is applied in the same way as in the original UP; however, we emphasize emotional behaviors (including EDBs) that are closely related to eating patterns and self-image. This might include wearing loose and dark clothes; avoiding showing their bodies; not eating in public; avoiding seeing their reflection in mirrors; and binge eating, isolation, or distraction.

Module 6: Understanding and Confronting Physical Sensations

The aim of this module is to help patients tolerate the physical sensations they have associated with intense and unpleasant emotions. Patients with higher scores on anxiety sensitivity will benefit the most from this module. A very relevant physical sensation to work on with these patients is hunger. It would be interesting to develop exercises to expose this sensation in order to learn to identify and tolerate it. In order to design the interoceptive exposures, clinicians should consider the current physical state of the patients to guarantee their safety during the exercises. Following BS, some patients can have difficulty with certain body movements or mobility restrictions for a while.

Module 7: Putting It into Practice—Emotion Exposures

In this module, patients put into practice all emotion regulation strategies they have learned to help them tolerate the intense and unpleasant emotions while keeping their personal goals in mind. In general, for these patients, intense emotions (anxiety, depression, guilt, shame, or happiness) are mostly associated with eating and image issues. However, patients also focus on other other vital areas of their lives, including work, family, or romantic relationships. Emotion exposures include all stimuli that can trigger intense emotions.

Module 8: Moving UP from Here: Recognizing Accomplishments and Looking to Your Future

This module can be applied following the guidelines established in the original UP. However, we also recommend a longer follow-up period for these patients, at least until 36 months after treatment, consistent with the existing literature (Spirou et al., 2020).

CASE EXAMPLE

An example case formulation following a transdiagnostic perspective, consistent with the UP, is shown in Table 7.1. This patient, Patricia (pseudonym), is a 51-year-old woman who lives with her partner and has three sons (aged 30, 28, and 23 years). Her education level consists of vocational training. She underwent BS 6 months before starting the intervention (April 2018); BS was successful (weight reduction goals have been achieved, improving her health condition). However, at the time of UP treatment, the participant met criteria for a diagnosis of adjustment disorder (F43.23; fifth edition of the *Diagnostic and Statistical Manual of Mental Disorders* [American Psychiatric Association, 2013]) reactive to BS changes.

She did not present with a previous psychological history nor had she received prior psychological treatment. The patient was referred by her endocrinologist for mood-related symptoms. During the initial evaluation, the patient described a "constant anxiety but not related to any specific problem." The patient reported satisfaction and general stability in family, social, personal, and work areas. She recognized that her anxiety could be related to physical changes she experienced following BS.

APPLICATION OF THE UP IN POST-BARIATRIC SURGERY PATIENTS: A CASE SERIES ANALYSIS

Objective

The aim of the present study is to preliminarily evaluate the acceptance, satisfaction, adherence, and clinical utility of the UP applied in a group format to three post-BS patients with an emotional disorder or subclinical emotional symptoms receiving treatment in a public mental health unit.

Table 7.1 A Case Formulation Based on the UP

HEALTH CONDITION ANALYSIS						
Health condition description: Patricia has a medical diagnosis of morbidly obese and for this reason received bariatric surgery (BS). Psychological treatment began 6 months after BS, and at that time the patient met criteria for a diagnosis of adaptive disorder reactive to BS changes.						
How health condition (and its treatment) affects the patient's life?			**EMOTION ANALYSIS REGARDING HEALTH CONDITIONS AND ITS CONSEQUENCES**			
General life aspects		**Affectation/ interference** **0______10** **Nothing Very much**	**Strong uncomfortable emotions** Do patients feel strong emotions in any of these general life aspects?	**Intensity** **0______10** **Nothing Extreme**	**Aversive reactions**	**Emotional behaviors** (Situational avoidance/ escape, subtle behavioral avoidance, cognitive avoidance, safety signals)
1. Physical and basic necessities	**Eat**: She eats out of hours, especially sweets and after lunch and dinner. Also when she feels more anxious.	7 8	Anxiety Sadness	8 8	"I am desperate for food." "I'm going to get fat again."	**Emotion-driven behavior**: She uses food to regulate herself when she is emotionally upset.
	Pain: None.					
	Medication side effects: None.					
	General: She feels constant anxiety but not related to any specific problem.	8	Anxiety	8	"I don't know what's wrong with me." "I may never be the same again."	**Emotion-driven behavior**: She eats when she feels intense emotions.
2. Work/studies	The symptomatology affects her work to the extent that she is unable to enjoy it due to the high anxiety that she experiences.	8 7 6	Anxiety Sadness Blame	8 7 8	"I have always enjoyed my job and now I can't." "I will not be able to perform adequately at work."	**Emotion-driven behavior:** She always brings food to work to eat if she is feeling emotionally active.

3. Daily life activities (to buy, to cook, to clean, etc.)	She maintains all her activities but with difficulty because of anhedonia and anxiety. She sleeps less because she has high anxiety while sleeping.	8 9	Sadness Anxiety	8 8	"What's wrong with me?" "It's all too hard for me."	**Situational avoidance:** She makes excuses to stay at home. She goes to sleep later.
4. Pleasant activities	She has reduced her activities, and the ones she does, she does not enjoy them as before.	7	Sadness	6	"It no longer makes sense to do what I was doing."	**Situational avoidance:** She has reduced her activity (e.g., she goes out less with her friends).
5. Personal relationships	She continues to maintain her contacts and social activities, although less frequently due to lack of interest and high levels of anxiety.	6 7	Sadness Anxiety	6 6	"If they see me so anxious, they'll worry about me." "I'm better at home. I'm more relaxed."	**Situational avoidance:** She often makes excuses to avoid meeting. She looks for places where she feels safer.
6. Life goals	She wants to regain the emotional balance she had previously.	8	Concern	8	"I may never go back to the way I was." "Now that I'm losing weight, I'm worse than ever."	**Situational and behavioral avoidance:** Avoidance of social and pleasurable activities she used to do.
TREATMENT PLAN						
MODULE 1						
Based on Patricia's clinical assessment, she might aim to enjoy working again, to go out with her friends as she used to do, to sleep better, and to avoid binge eating in order to maintain her weight after the BS. She has a high motivation for treatment, so it will be necessary to explain in depth the barriers to change and the benefits to maintain their actual functioning to help her to be aware of these aspects prior to starting treatment.						

(*continued*)

Table 7.1 Continued

MODULE 2
In this module, Patricia will learn the functionality of all emotions and we will discuss antecedents and consequences of their emotional experiences (anxiety and sadness). We will focus specially on her binge eating behavior pattern to identify the main antecedents, thoughts, physical sensations, and emotion-driven behaviors, and we will also discuss the short- and long-term consequences.
MODULE 3
In this module, Patricia will be trained to become aware of her emotional experiences (anxiety, sadness, and blame). Patricia said that when she feels anxiety, she tends to get trapped and blocked by it, and the only way to start feeling better is eating or being alone. She will practice to remain in the present moment without judging and to observe the intense emotions without reacting. She will also learn to be anchored and to maintain the aims in her mind despite the intense emotions she is feeling. We can also practice meditation exercises through mindful eating and food exercises.
MODULE 4
Patricia will have to identify her thinking traps especially focused on catastrophizing and advance the future negatively. Some thoughts she will identify will be: “I may never go back to the way I was,” “It’s all too hard for me,” or “It’s not worth the effort. ” She will learn the link between her thoughts and the other parts of the emotional experience, including the emotion-driven behavior of binge eating. She will benefit from training in generating alternative thoughts that could be more adaptive to her.
MODULE 5
Throughout this module, Patricia will identify her emotional behaviors and the negative consequences they have produced in her life. She will think in alternative or opposite behaviors to each one. In Patricia’s case, some alternative behaviors will probably be to go out with friends, to not stop working, or to avoid eating when not necessary.
MODULE 6
Patricia experiences high levels of anxiety, so in this session she will be encouraged to practice interoceptive exposures in order to learn to tolerate the physical sensations associated with anxiety, such as tachycardia, hyperventilation, and others.
MODULE 7
During this module, we will work especially on exposure to intense anxiety and sadness. Some of the examples that can be worked on with Patricia will be performing pleasant activities that she sometimes avoided and managing situations in which she felt anxious and sad, without having to use food to regulate herself.
OTHER MODULES IF NECESSARY
According to the characteristics of the patient’s problem, it will be necessary to work on emotional eating and self-image (self-esteem) transversally throughout all the intervention modules.

Participants

The inclusion criteria were (a) age older than 18 years; (b) being a candidate for BS or post-BS patient; (c) presenting with symptoms of anxiety and/or depression or meeting criteria for at least one emotional disorder, as assessed by the MINI International Neuropsychiatric Interview (Sheehan et al., 1998); (d) speak Spanish or Catalan fluently; and (e) be willing to commit to attending sessions for the duration of treatment. The exclusion criterion was having a serious condition (e.g., severe mental disorder or risk of suicide or substance use) that requires prioritization for treatment so that an interaction between the two interventions cannot be ruled out.

The total sample of the study comprised three participants, whose clinical and sociodemographic characteristics are provided next.

Participant 1

Participant 1 is a 56-year-old woman, married and with one son (aged 22 years). She has an educational level of vocational training and is currently unemployed. She underwent BS 6 months before starting UP treatment (April 2019) and achieved successful results (weight reduction goals have been achieved, improving her health condition). She presented with a diagnosis of adjustment disorder not directly related to the BS process but, rather, because of problems in her family relationships. She did not report a previous psychological history, and she was referred to the group by her family doctor in October 2019. The participant also presented with hyperphagia, an excessive increase in the sensation of appetite and uncontrolled food intake. She was constantly anxious, had conciliation and maintenance insomnia, and also had irritable mood. The patient was seeking treatment so she could better manage these symptoms. She noticed that her eating patterns were dysregulated, and she was concerned about gaining weight again and thus losing the results she had achieved through BS.

Participant 2

Participant 2 is a 55-year-old woman, married and with three children. She has a basic education level, and she works in the domestic field. She received BS 15 months before starting UP treatment (July 2018); she obtained satisfactory results from the surgery. The participant presented with a principal diagnosis of dysthymia and a secondary diagnosis of unspecified eating disorder.

She had been treated at the Mental Health Unit (MHU) for many years (since June 2014) prior to beginning the study. At first, she met criteria for a diagnosis of dysthymia, and she received psychopharmacological treatment with follow-up by the psychiatrist. Progressively, the participant's mood improved, as did the symptoms of the unspecified eating disorder (specifically, binge-eating was reduced). However, despite the fact that binge eating decreased in frequency, it never fully resolved. In January 2016, she was proposed as a BS candidate but did not pass the psychiatric evaluation due to the persistence of binges, so she was referred to the psychologist to work on the pattern of food intake and be reevaluated in the future. Throughout 2017, she worked with the psychologist on different techniques, such as food registrations and awareness. Gradually, the binges decreased, and she also experienced weight loss, which were necessary requirements for BS. She underwent BS in April 2018. Although the results of BS were mainly positive, the emotional symptoms associated with the diagnosis of dysthymia remained, as did some maladaptive eating patterns. For all these reasons, she was referred to the group intervention.

Participant 3

Participant 3 is Patricia, whose case was described previously.

Procedure

The current intervention was carried out in the Spanish National Health System, specifically in the MHU of the Hospital Comarcal de Vinaròs (Castellón). The participants were recruited from the sample of a larger study; for more information, see Ferreres et al. (2022) . We used a convenience sampling method for this pilot study. Participation was voluntary and without financial reward. The clinician informed participants about the study, verified that they met the inclusion criteria, and administered the evaluation battery in pencil-and-paper format. After the evaluation, the psychologist and co-therapist (both trained to apply the UP in a group format) started the intervention. The intervention consisted of nine 2-hour weekly sessions in group format (one session for Modules 1–6 and 8 and two sessions for Module 7).

The assessment was conducted at pretreatment, post-treatment, and 6-months follow-up.

Measures

The assessment measures used in the study are shown in Table 7.2.

Results

Feasibility and Satisfaction with the Intervention Received

Participants 1 and 2 attended all intervention sessions, and participant 3 missed two. Therefore, the average of participants' attendance was eight sessions (*SD* = 1.15; range: 7–9), leading to a 92.59% attendance rate. No participant dropped out during treatment or follow-up. Results of the Satisfaction with Treatment Questionnaire (STQ) show high levels of satisfaction with the UP. Two participants rated the quality of the program received as "good," and the other one rated it as "excellent." All participants affirmed that UP was the type of intervention they expected "in general" (two participants) or "totally" (one participant). All of them said that they would recommend the UP program to people who

Table 7.2 Assessment Protocol: Instruments and Constructs

Instrument	Construct Evaluated
Mini-International Neuropsychiatric Interview (MINI; Sheehan et al., 1998)	Major psychiatric disorders based on the DSM-IV criteria
Primary outcomes	
Overall Anxiety Severity and Impairment Scale (OASIS; Norman et al., 2006; Spanish validation by Osma et al., 2019)	Severity and impairment associated with anxiety symptoms
Overall Depression Severity and Impairment Scale (ODSIS; Bentley et al., 2014; Spanish validation by Osma et al., 2019)	Severity and impairment associated with depressive symptoms
Body mass index (BMI)	Body mass divided by the square of the body height
Secondary outcomes	
NEO-FFI Personality Inventory (NEO-FFI; Costa & McCrae, 199; Manga et al., 2004)	Neuroticism and extraversion
Difficulties in Emotion Regulation Scale (DERS; Gratz & Roemer, 2004; Spanish validation by Hervás & Jódar, 2008)	Different factors of emotional dysregulation
Quality of Life Index (QLI; Lorente et al., 2002; Mezzich et al., 2000)	Quality of life
Maladjustment Inventory (MI; Echeburúa et al., 2000)	Extent to which the person's current problems are affecting the different areas of their life
Satisfaction with Treatment Questionnaire (STQ; ad hoc)	Satisfaction with the treatment received

needed similar help. One participant answered that the UP had helped her "quite" and two participants answered "a lot" to face their problems more effectively. Finally, two participants affirmed that they would "probably" choose the UP if they needed help again, whereas the other one chose the alternative "totally."

In general, qualitative assessment showed that participants viewed the group format as being a very positive aspect (Participant 1: "A very welcoming atmosphere has developed and we have been able to show all our emotions"; Participant 2: "The best has been the interest of the companions"; and Participant 3: "It has helped me to know that there are more people who have the same problem as me"). Furthermore, participants did not identify significant barriers to applying the UP in a public health system, but they proposed increasing the number of sessions and including topics related to nutrition and physical activity to further improve the intervention.

Clinical Changes in Each Participant

Table 7.3 shows the pretreatment and 6-month follow-up results for each of the participants. In addition, for measures in which the normative mean was taken as

Table 7.3 PRIMARY AND SECONDARY SCORES AT PRETREATMENT AND 6-MONTH FOLLOW-UP FOR THE THREE PARTICIPANTS.[a]

		P1			P2			P3		
	M (*SD*)	Pre	6-M FU	RCI	Pre	6-m FU	RCI	Pre	6-m FU	RCI
Primary outcomes										
OASIS	—	9	2	—	7	5	—	3	1	—
ODSIS	—	3	0	—	5	0	—	8	0	—
BMI	—	27.5	26.2	—	29.5	28.1	—	27.3	23	—
Secondary outcomes										
Neuroticism	21.58 (7.48)	30	12	−4.01[b]	40	36	−3.79[b]	28	15	−2.90[b]
Extraversion	32.05 (6.64)	34	37	0.73	17	16	3.66[b]	20	20	0,00
QLI	6.98 (1.10)	6.40	9.00	4.47[b]	3.90	5.10	4.98[b]	6.90	7.90	1.72
MI	2.22 (1.66)	19	0	−12.20[b]	22	9	−11.56[b]	5	0	−3.21[b]
DERS	59.10 (17.50)	117	44	−11.09[b]	107	74	−5.31[b]	54	44	−1.52

[a]Mean and standard deviation of the normative sample and RCI.

[b]Less than ±1.96 (significant change in scores in the desired direction; i.e., improvement of scores until reaching a normalized score).

BMI, body mass index; DERS, Difficulties in Emotion Regulation Scale; MI, Maladjustment Inventory; OASIS, Overall Anxiety Severity and Impairment Scale; ODSIS, Overall Depression Severity and Impairment Scale; P, participant; Pre, pretreatment; QLI: Quality of Life Index; RCI, Reliable Change Index; 6-M FU, 6-month follow-up.

a reference for clinical improvement, a Reliable Change Index (RCI) is included. The RCI evaluates the clinically significant change obtained to identify which variables for which the participants have approximated the scores of a normative sample. A clinically significant change was considered to have occurred when the participants once again obtain scores that reflect normal functioning, and this is manifested by absolute values of the RCI equal to or greater than 1.96 (Jacobson & Truax, 1991).

At the 6-month follow-up, a generalized decrease or a positive tendency in the expected direction is observed across all study outcomes. Regarding the primary outcomes (emotional symptomatology and weight), all participants evidenced a decrease in anxiety and depressive symptoms from pretest to 6-month follow-up, all participants normalized their scores for depression symptoms, and Participants 1 and 2 also normalized their scores for anxiety symptoms. Also, participants did not gain weight, showing a BMI that was maintained at 6-month follow-up.

Regarding secondary outcomes, Participant 1 evidenced reliable change on measures of neuroticism, quality of life, interference, and emotional dysregulation, with scores in the normal range at post-treatment. Participant 2 also showed improvement across all variables assessed. Finally, Participant 3 evidenced normalized scores on neuroticism and interference.

Summary of Preliminary Results

Emotional symptoms frequently occur following BS. In addition, many people who have undergone BS suffer changes at a physical and functional level, such as drastic weight loss, problems with body image satisfaction, and mood changes or stress (Jumbe et al., 2017). Cognitive–behavioral interventions such as the UP are needed to address the psychological well-being of post-BS patients (Spirou et al., 2020).

Of all the results obtained in this study, the high attendance rate stands out in comparison with those of other studies that also have applied CBT-based interventions (e.g., Cassin et al., 2016). The STQ results show high satisfaction with the treatment received, which generally coincides with that obtained in other psychosocial interventions. The feedback from participants was very positive, based on the qualitative data we collected. None of the participants identified obstacles to implementing this intervention in a public health context. The participants provided suggestions that could help improve future interventions, such as presenting more information on topics directly related to BS (nutritional information, physical activity, self-image, etc.) and increasing the number of sessions (from 9 to 12). In addition, general clinical improvement was observed, with all participants reporting a decrease in scores of anxiety and depression, neuroticism, emotional dysregulation and interference, and an increase in quality of life.

CONCLUSION

Obesity is one of the most prevalent public health problems throughout the world (National Health and Medical Research Council, 2013). Throughout this chapter, we noted the importance of considering psychological interventions for people with a history of obesity and who have undergone BS. The role of clinical health psychologists is essential to improving both physical and psychological outcomes in these patients. Considering the clinical comorbidity that typically occurs in post-BS patients (anxiety, depression, eating disorders, etc.; Sarwer & Heinberg, 2020), we believe that the UP can be a useful intervention. The results described in this chapter are encouraging and provide preliminary support for the clinical utility of the UP to treat emotional disorders and/or subclinical symptoms in post-BS patients.

In addition to the direct benefits derived for post-BS patients, the transdiagnostic framework of the UP allows it to be applied to a range of comorbid emotional symptoms/disorders and is well suited for group application. This may make the UP a more cost-effective option for health systems that provide services for obesity and patients seeking treatment post-BS. However, the greatest advantage of the UP is that it aids in the maintenance of improvements that have already been obtained through BS (Sarwer & Heinberg, 2020), directly addressing patients' psychological needs by improving their functioning and quality of life through specialized care.

Limitations/Barriers Observed

The results of this preliminary evaluation are promising, and the UP appeared to perform extremely well. However, there are some limitations. The first limitation relates to the group format. For our purposes, the reduced number of sessions did not allow us to carefully attend to some important concepts, such as those related to physical activity or self-esteem. Next, in this pilot study, we believe it would have been helpful for patients to have a more specific UP workbook that includes content which specifically addresses difficulties experienced by these patients, including physical activity, binge eating, and body image, and different forms for personalizing aspects of the treatment in this regard (e.g., recording weekly weight and physical activity, and recording thoughts related to their body, shape, and self-esteem).

We also noted limitations inherent to treating post-BS patients. Working on emotions with these patients can be difficult because they sometimes have unrealistic expectations regarding the intervention and may assume that BS by itself is the solution to their obesity problem and ignore that having regulated habits is essential to maintain the success of the intervention. Because the physiological changes induced by the operation are significant, patients can experience less motivation for change after BS (although motivation increases when weight loss stagnates and psychological problems usually reappear), so it is necessary to work on motivation and adjustment of expectations (Lauren et al., 2020). Many patients' low awareness about the relationship between food and emotional regulation can also make it difficult to work on psychological aspects.

Another problem is that due to obesity, these patients have may have difficulty attending sessions in hospitals or MHUs. It is often difficult for these patients to use transportation, and in general their mobility is limited. In these cases, it would be helpful to offer treatment in an alternative format, such as telehealth or an online treatment.

Future Directions

There are different lines of work to provide higher quality health care to post-BS patients through the application of the UP. First, there is a need to develop studies with more rigorous research designs, such as randomized controlled clinical trials with larger sample sizes and longer term follow-up. Second, more information is needed regarding the appropriate length of the intervention in order to achieve the expected goals and also regarding whether using both individual and group sessions could be beneficial.

Third, although the weight loss achieved due to BS tends to improve the physical appearance of patients, many of them report continued body dissatisfaction after BS associated with sagging skin throughout the body and dermatological problems. Many patients undergo plastic surgery to solve these problems, but scars may appear later, which can negatively affect body satisfaction and self-esteem (Sarwer & Heinberg, 2020). For this reason, it would be very interesting for future adaptations of the UP to add content about self-esteem, especially related to body image.

Fourth, despite the fact that this chapter is focused on the application of the UP in post-BS patients, it would be very interesting to develop a line of research in which this intervention is applied in patients who are candidates for BS; in fact, there is already a protocol that raises this possibility (Quilez-Orden et al., 2020). This is essential because there are different studies that explain how the presence of a psychopathological history prior to BS predicts worse outcomes post-BS (Oltmanns et al., 2020). It would be especially interesting to apply the UP before BS because the most prevalent disorders among patients undergoing BS are anxiety disorders (24%), mood disorders (31.5%), and eating disorders (50%) (Sarwer & Heinberg, 2020). The presence of these disorders in BS candidates is associated with poor weight loss or early recovery after BS (Hjelmesæth et al., 2018). Applying an intervention specifically designed to improve emotion regulation strategies in people with obesity waiting for BS can have important advantages. It could improve their prognosis post-BS and perhaps, if they achieve greater regulation of their eating behaviors, prevent the need to undergo the operation. In addition, for those undergoing BS, other aspects could also be addressed, such as adjustment of expectations and providing patients help to follow the dietary guidelines for the operation.

Fifth, another very interesting line of research would be to apply the UP completely online or even in a self-applied format so that it is more accessible and can reach patients who, due to their obesity, have mobility problems or patients who, due to the location of their home or the means of transportation, have difficulty getting to an MHU. In addition, technological tools could be integrated to aid in the acquisition of healthy habits because they would facilitate the recording of physical activity performed, hours of sleep, food intake, or weight change in a more ecological and comfortable manner.

What seems clear is that increased training in adaptive emotional regulation skills, at the level of both prevention and intervention, could prevent obesity conditions in people so that they would not require surgical intervention.

Tips/Advice to Clinicians

Clinicians must focus on the relationship between food and emotions in these types of patients. Analyzing this relationship is essential to understanding how poor weight loss or recovery is related to emotional dysregulation problems. Thus, it will be much easier to carry out the case formulation taking into account the specific aspects of the emotional response that should be worked on and to make it easier for the patient to become aware of them. Note that it is necessary to use a multidisciplinary approach in treating these patients. This includes training them in specific aspects related to diet and physical activity, and it often involves consulting other health professionals. It is also necessary to work on adjusting expectations, especially with regard to body image and self-esteem, and to include them in the different UP exercises so that patients become aware of and accept the changes that have been occurring in their bodies. Patients must be reminded that BS is the first step in their change process and that they will have to work hard to maintain their initial success.

REFERENCES

American Psychiatric Association. (2013). *Diagnostic and statistical manual of mental disorders* (5th ed.). American Psychiatric Publishing.

Barlow, D. H., Farchione, T. J., Sauer-Zavala, S., Latin, H. M., Ellard, K. K., Bullis, J. R., Bentley, K. H., Boettcher, H. T., & Cassiello-Robbins, C. (2018). *Unified Protocol for Transdiagnostic Treatment of Emotional Disorders: Therapist guide* (2nd ed.). Oxford University Press.

Bentley, K. H., Gallagher, M. W., Carl, J. R., & Barlow, D. H. (2014). Development and validation of the Overall Depression Severity and Impairment Scale. *Psychological Assessment, 26*(3), 815–830.

Brown, T. A., & Barlow, D. H. (2009). A proposal for a dimensional classification system based on the shared features of the DSM-IV anxiety and mood disorders: Implications for assessment and treatment. *Psychological Assessment, 21*(3), 256–271.

Brown, T. A., Campbell, L. A., Lehman, C. L., Grisham, J. R., & Mancill, R. B. (2001). Current and lifetime comorbidity of the DSM-IV anxiety and mood disorders in a large clinical sample. *Journal of Abnormal Psychology, 110*(4), 585–599.

Burgess, E., Hassmén, P., & Pumpa, K. L. (2017). Determinants of adherence to lifestyle intervention in adults with obesity: A systematic review. *Clinical Obesity, 7*(3), 123–135.

Cassiello-Robbins, C., Southward, M. W., Tirpak, J. W., & Sauer-Zavala, S. (2020). A systematic review of Unified Protocol applications with adult populations: Facilitating widespread dissemination via adaptability. *Clinical Psychology Review, 78*, 101852.

Cassin, S. E., Sockalingam, S., Du, C., Wnuk, S., Hawa, R., & Parikh, S. V. (2016). A pilot randomized controlled trial of telephone-based cognitive behavioural therapy for preoperative bariatric surgery patients. *Behaviour Research and Therapy, 80*, 17–22.

Castaneda, D., Popov, V. B., Wander, P., & Thompson, C. C. (2019). Risk of suicide and self-harm is increased after bariatric surgery—A systematic review and meta-analysis. *Obesity Surgery, 29*(1), 322–333.

Chang, M. W., Brown, R., & Nitzke, S. (2009). Participant recruitment and retention in a pilot program to prevent weight gain in low-income overweight and obese mothers. *BMC Public Health, 9*(1), 1–11.

Costa, P. T., & McCrae, R. R. (1999). *Revised NEO Personality Inventory (NEO-PI-R) and NEO Five-Factor Inventory (NEO-FFI)*. TEA Ediciones.

Echeburúa, E., De Corral, P., & Fernández-Montalvo, J. (2000). Escala de inadaptación (EI): Propiedades psicométricas en contextos clínicos. *Análisis y Modificación de Conducta, 26*(107), 325–340.

Fairburn, C. G. (2008). *Cognitive behavior therapy and eating disorders*. Guilford.

Fairburn, C. G., Cooper, Z., & Shafran, R. (2003). Cognitive behaviour therapy for eating disorders: A "transdiagnostic" theory and treatment. *Behaviour Research and Therapy, 41*(5), 509–528.

Ferreres-Galán, V., Quilez-Orden, A., & Osma, J. (2022). Application of the unified protocol for transdiagnostic treatment of emotional disorders in post-bariatric surgery patients: An effectiveness and feasibility study in group format. *Annals of Psychology, 38*, 219–231.

Gratz, K. L., & Roemer, L. (2004). Multidimensional assessment of emotion regulation and dysregulation: Development, factor structure, and initial validation of the Difficulties in Emotion Regulation Scale. *Journal of Psychopathology and Behavioral Assessment, 26*(1), 41–54.

Hervás, G., & Jódar, R. (2008). The Spanish version of the Difficulties in Emotion Regulation Scale. *Clinica y Salud, 19*(2), 139–156.

Hjelmesæth, J., Asberg, A., Andersson, S., Sandbu, R., Robertsen, I., Johnson, L. K., Angeles, P. C., Hertel, J. K., Skovlund, E., Heijer, M., Ek, A.-L., Krogstad, V., Karlsen, T.-I., Christensen, H., Andersson, T. B., & Karlsson, C. (2018). Impact of body weight, low energy diet and gastric bypass on drug bioavailability, cardiovascular risk factors and metabolic biomarkers: Protocol for an open, non-randomised, three-Armed single centre study (COCKTAIL). *BMJ Open, 8*(5), e021878.

Hjelmesæth, J., Rosenvinge, J. H., Gade, H., & Friborg, O. (2019). Effects of cognitive behavioral therapy on eating behaviors, affective symptoms, and weight loss after bariatric surgery: A randomized clinical trial. *Obesity Surgery, 29*(1), 61–69.

Jacobson, N. S., & Truax, P. (1991). Clinical significance: A statistical approach to defining meaningful change in psychotherapy research. *Journal of Consulting and Clinical Psychology, 59*, 12–19.

Jumbe, S., Hamlet, C., & Meyrick, J. (2017). Psychological aspects of bariatric surgery as a treatment for obesity. *Current Obesity Reports, 6*(1), 71–78.

Lahey, B. B. (2009). Public health significance of neuroticism. *The American Psychologist, 64*(4), 241–256.

Lauren, A. D., Sijercic, I., & Cassin, S. E. (2020). Preoperative and post-operative psychosocial interventions for bariatric surgery patients: A systematic review. *Obesity Reviews, 21*(4), e12926.

Lorente, E., Ibáñez, M. I., Moro, M., & Ruipérez, M. A. (2002). Índice de Calidad de Vida: estandarización y características psicométricas en una muestra española. *Psiquiatría y Salud Integral, 2*(2), 45–50.

Manga, D., Ramos, F., & Morán, C. (2004). The Spanish norms of the NEO Five-Factor Inventory: New data and analyses for its improvement. *International Journal of Psychology and Psychological Therapy, 4*(3), 639–648.

McManus, F., Shafran, R., & Cooper, Z. (2010). What does a transdiagnostic approach have to offer the treatment of anxiety disorders? *British Journal of Clinical Psychology, 49*(4), 491–505.

Mezzich, J. E., Ruipérez, M. A., Pérez, C., Yoon, G., Liu, J., & Mahmud, S. (2000). The Spanish version of the Quality of Life Index. *Journal of Nervous and Mental Disease, 188*(5), 301–305.

National Health and Medical Research Council. (2013). *Clinical practice guidelines for the management of overweight and obesity in children and adolescents.*

Norman, S. B., Cissel, S. H., Means-Christensen, A. J., & Stein, M. B. (2006). Development and validation of an Overall Anxiety Severity and Impairment Scale. *Depression and Anxiety, 23*(4), 245–249.

Oltmanns, J. R., Rivera, J., Cole, J., Merchant, A., & Steiner, J. P. (2020). Personality psychopathology: Longitudinal prediction of change in body mass index and weight post-bariatric surgery. *Health Psychology, 39*(3), 245–254.

Organisation for Economic Co-operation and Development. (2019). *The heavy burden of obesity: The economics of prevention.*

Osma, J., Martínez-García, L., Quilez-Orden, A., & Peris-Baquero, O. (2021). Unified Protocol for the Transdiagnostic Treatment of Emotional Disorders in medical conditions: A systematic review. *International Journal of Environmental Research and Public Health, 18*, 5077.

Osma, J., Peris-Baquero, O., Suso-Ribera, C., Sauer-Zavala, S., & Barlow, D. H. (2021). Predicting and moderating the response to the Unified Protocol: Do baseline personality and affective profiles matter? *Cognitive Therapy and Research, 45*, 817–830. https://doi.org/10.1007/s10608-021-10208-6

Osma, J., Quilez-Orden, A., Suso-Ribera, C., Peris-Baquero, O., Norman, S. B., Bentley, K. H., & Sauer-Zavala, S. (2019). Psychometric properties and validation of the Spanish versions of the overall anxiety and depression severity and impairment scales. *Journal of Affective Disorders, 252*, 9–18.

Quilez-Orden, A., Ferreres-Galán, V., & Osma, J. (2020). Feasibility and clinical usefulness of the Unified Protocol in online group format for bariatric surgery candidates: Study protocol for a multiple baseline experimental design. *International Journal of Environmental Research and Public Health, 17*(17), 1–18.

Sakiris, N., & Berle, D. (2019). A systematic review and meta-analysis of the Unified Protocol as a transdiagnostic emotion regulation based intervention. *Clinical Psychology Review, 72*, 1017–1051.

Sarwer, D. B., & Heinberg, L. J. (2020). A review of the psychosocial aspects of clinically severe obesity and bariatric surgery. *The American Psychologist, 75*(2), 252–264.

Sauer-Zavala, S., Cassiello-Robbins, C., Ametaj, A. A., Wilner, J. G., & Pagan, D. (2019). Transdiagnostic treatment personalization: The feasibility of ordering Unified Protocol modules according to patient strengths and weaknesses. *Behavior Modification, 43*(4), 518–543.

Sauer-Zavala, S., Fournier, J. C., Steele, S. J., Woods, B. K., Wang, M., Farchione, T. J., & Barlow, D. H. (2021). Does the Unified Protocol really change neuroticism? Results from a randomized trial. *Psychological Medicine, 51*(14), 2378–2387.

Sauer-Zavala, S., Gutner, C. A., Farchione, T. J., Boettcher, H. T., Bullis, J. R., & Barlow, D. H. (2017). Current definitions of "transdiagnostic" in treatment development: A search for consensus. *Behavior Therapy, 48*(1), 128–138.

Sheehan, D. V., Lecrubier, Y., Sheehan, K. H., Amorim, P., Janavs, J., Weiller, E., Hergueta, T., Baker, R., & Dunbar, G. C. (1998). The Mini-International Neuropsychiatric Interview (M.I.N.I.): The development and validation of a structured diagnostic psychiatric interview for DSM-IV and ICD-10. *Journal of Clinical Psychiatry, 59*, 34–57.

Spirou, D., Raman, J., & Smith, E. (2020). Psychological outcomes following surgical and endoscopic bariatric procedures: A systematic review. *Obesity Reviews, 21*(6), e12998.

Thompson-Brenner, H., Boswell, J. F., Espel-Huynh, H., Brooks, G., & Lowe, M. R. (2019). Implementation of transdiagnostic treatment for emotional disorders in residential eating disorder programs: A preliminary pre–post evaluation. *Psychotherapy Research, 29*(8), 1045–1061.

Toussi, R., Fujioka, K., & Coleman, K. J. (2009). Pre- and postsurgery behavioral compliance, patient health, and postbariatric surgical weight loss. *Obesity, 17*(5), 996–1002.

World Health Organization. (2020). Obesity and overweight. https://www.who.int/news-room/fact-sheets/detail/obesity-and-overweight#:~:text=%2Fm2).-,Adults,than%20or%20equal%20to%2030

Yalom, I. D., & Leszcz, M. (2005). *The theory and practice of group psychotherapy*. Basic Books.

Yumuk, V., Tsigos, C., Fried, M., Schindler, K., Busetto, L., Micic, D., & Toplak, H. (2015). European guidelines for obesity management in adults. *Obesity Facts*, *8*(6), 402–424.

8

Unified Protocol Application in Fertility Problems

ELENA CRESPO-DELGADO, VERÓNICA MARTÍNEZ-BORBA, LAURA ANDREU-PEJÓ, AND JORGE OSMA ■

INTRODUCTION

Fertility Problems: Definition and Prevalence Rates

Conceiving a child can be one of the most important events in many people's lives, but sometimes this can be challenging because of recurrent fertility-related problems. Infertility is a chronic reproductive system illness, defined by the inability to achieve a pregnancy after at least 12 months of regular unprotected sexual intercourse (Zegers-Hochschild et al., 2010). Studies estimate that infertility affects 186 million people worldwide, although it is difficult to determine exact global rates because of significant variability between epidemiological studies carried out in different countries throughout the world (Inhorn & Patrizio, 2014). Nevertheless, there is clearly a need for assisted reproduction treatments (ART) worldwide (Adamson et al., 2018). In previous decades, problems related to fertility were believed to be inherent to women. Today, evidence shows that this is not the case and that both men and women can contribute to infertility. In fact, 20–35% of all cases of infertility are due to a combination of male and female factors (Agarwal et al., 2015; Centers for Disease Control and Prevention [CDC], 2019a), and in 15–30% of patients, infertility remains unexplained (Gelbaya et al., 2014). Indeed, infertility is a complex phenomenon that affects both men and women. Furthermore, it affects not only heterosexual couples but also single individuals, same-sex couples, and lesbian, gay, bisexual, transgender, queer, and

Elena Crespo-Delgado, Verónica Martínez-Borba, Laura Andreu-Pejó, and Jorge Osma, *Unified Protocol Application in Fertility Problems* In: *Applications of the Unified Protocol in Health Conditions.* Edited by: Jorge Osma and Todd J. Farchione, Oxford University Press. © Oxford University Press 2023. DOI: 10.1093/oso/9780197564295.003.0008 other persons (LGBTQ+) who may wish to have children. In 2018, 39.6% of all U.S. births were to unmarried women (CDC, 2019b). In recent years, there has also been an increase in LGBTQ+ people seeking fertility treatments (e.g., Wingo et al., 2018).

The etiology of infertility is multifactorial and includes biological, environmental, lifestyle, and reproductive disease factors as well as age (La Marca & Mastellari, 2020; Tarín et al., 2015; Vander Borght & Wyns, 2018). For this reason, the consensus recommendation is that the tests for the diagnosis of infertility should start immediately when the person who is trying to conceive has a history of medical, sexual, or reproductive problems, advanced age, or physical findings that suggest the possibility of impaired reproduction (Fernando Zegers-Hochschild et al., 2017).

Assisted Reproduction Treatments (Intrauterine Insemination and In Vitro Fertilization)

Assisted reproductive treatments involve a progression in implementation that can range from scheduled sexual intercourse to complex treatments such as intrauterine insemination (IUI) with or without medication for ovarian hyperstimulation and in vitro fertilization (IVF; Smith et al., 2011). IUI is one of the techniques widely used in the United States and Europe (Boulet et al., 2019; Calhaz-Jorge et al., 2020), especially in couples with unexplained infertility, because it is lower cost and less invasive than IVF (Farquhar & Marjoribanks, 2018). IUI is a relatively simple procedure in which semen (couple or donor) is processed in the laboratory and then inserted into the uterine cavity using a small catheter at the time of ovulation. Unfortunately, pregnancy after IUI is not always guaranteed, with the probability to achieve a pregnancy of approximately 17% in a stimulated cycle (Ayeleke et al., 2020).

Scientific Evidence of Fertility Problems and the Emotional Impact of ART

The existing literature indicates that women with an infertility diagnosis may be at greater risk of developing other associated health problems, namely psychological disorders (Hanson et al., 2017). In fact, women report higher rates of depression and anxiety after ART compared to levels prior to treatment (Lakatos et al., 2017). Specifically, up to 65% of women under ART present anxiety or depression symptoms and a range of emotional disorders (Cox et al., 2006), compromising the cost-effectiveness and continuity of ART (Kiesswetter et al., 2020).

Due to the aforementioned high prevalence and impact of emotional disorders during ART, there is a need to implement prevention programs to address anxiety and depression and limit the development of emotional disorders in women undergoing these treatments.

PSYCHOLOGICAL ASPECTS IN WOMEN UNDERGOING ART

Psychological Interventions

Several systematic reviews have shown that psychosocial interventions, mainly those based on psychosocial, cognitive–behavioral therapy (CBT), or mind–body interventions (mindfulness-based programs), are effective in improving psychological stress, anxiety, and depression symptoms and marital functioning in infertile couples (Abdolahi et al., 2019; Frederiksen et al., 2015; Gaitzsch et al., 2020). Given the effectiveness of these programs, in the past decade there has been increased development and implementation of psychological interventions for people with fertility problems, using a variety of approaches and treatment formats. For example, interventions in group format such as the Mindfulness-Based Program for Infertility, CBT, or counseling have been shown to be effective for anxious and/or depressive symptomatology (Frederiksen et al., 2015). Another example is the use of information and communication technologies. A number of studies have demonstrated that an online education/support (i.e., a brief online education program about infertility distress) and CBT program with strategies specifically for infertility-related problems (stress, ruminations, sadness, grief, and relationship problems) could improve anxiety and depression symptoms, infertility distress, sexual concerns, distress related to living without children, and clarity in decision-making in infertile women (Cousineau et al., 2008; Sexton et al., 2010; van Dongen et al., 2016). These programs also have good patient acceptability, which has led to their inclusion in existing clinical guidelines (van Dongen et al., 2016).

Implementation Barriers and Limitations of Psychological Interventions During ART

Despite the preponderance of evidence supporting the effectiveness of ART, existing reviews and meta-analytic studies have some limitations, including methodological discrepancies, variability in quality of study design, and the fact that there are few longitudinal studies (Abdolahi et al., 2019; Frederiksen et al., 2015; Gaitzsch et al., 2020). For example, there are discrepancies in study design (e.g., randomized control studies vs. uncontrolled studies) that may affect the quality of study results. In addition, some studies utilized small samples and failed to report the type of ART delivered (i.e., IUI or IVF) or when it occurred (i.e., first IUI cycle or first IFV cycle). There are also important limitations related to psychological interventions more broadly. Most are symptom-focused interventions, mainly related to stress, depression, and/or anxiety. Despite some studies including other measures of improvement (i.e., marital function or quality of life; Gaitzsch et al., 2020), this is typically not the primary focus of these interventions.

Furthermore, there are differences in the timing of the interventions (before vs. during cycles), the number of sessions (i.e., 5 CBT sessions vs. 15 CBT sessions), the duration of the intervention (i.e., a 4-week body mass index program vs. a 16-week CBT intervention), the format (mostly individual or group and very few online interventions), and the assessment instruments used (specific vs. general). Finally, preventive interventions are rare.

Unified Protocol as a "Preventive Intervention as Usual" Alternative

Existing interventions for emotional disorders (e.g., CBT) have ample evidence for addressing specific diagnoses (e.g., major depressive disorder). However, high comorbidity between emotional disorders often complicates treatment decisions and leads clinicians to apply two treatments simultaneously (McManus et al., 2010); treat the main presenting difficulty and expect improvement in secondary conditions; or apply a separate treatment afterwards (i.e., sequentially), which is inefficient and requires significant clinical resources (Barlow et al., 2004).

An alternative to these treatment approaches is the Unified Protocol for Transdiagnostic Treatment of Emotional Disorders (UP; Barlow et al., 2004), which focuses on addressing shared etiological and maintenance mechanisms among the different emotional disorders, such as high neuroticism and low extraversion, anxiety sensitivity, or intolerance of uncertainty (Rosellini & Brown, 2019). In addition, in terms of implementation and dissemination of evidence-based psychological treatments, this approach is likely more cost-effective and scalable than traditional CBT approaches because mental health practitioners only have to learn one treatment for all emotional disorders (Barlow et al., 2004) as opposed to a variety of different disorder-specific protocols. The main objective of the UP is to train patients in new adaptive emotion regulation skills to better tolerate and respond to intense emotions and improve their quality of life (Barlow et al., 2018).

The UP has already been applied in the treatment of different emotional disorders with positive results (Barlow et al., 2017), and it has been shown to be effective for addressing comorbidity (e.g., Steele et al., 2018). There is also some initial support for using the UP as a prevention program (Sauer-Zavala et al., 2021). Furthermore, previous studies have adapted the UP to address psychological disturbances that affect women with perinatal depression (Crespo-Delgado et al., 2020) or other health conditions more prevalent in women (Osma et al., 2021). However, literature about the efficacy of the UP in the prevention of emotional disorders during fertility treatments is scarce. In fact, it seems that health systems tend to underestimate the importance of addressing psychological well-being during that process; therefore, there is a lack of mental health professionals in fertility units accompanying women throughout this (usually) long and often emotionally difficult treatment.

Unified Protocol Application in Fertility Problems

Applying the UP to women undergoing IUI requires some modifications to the protocol. Table 8.1 details the UP–Prevention Program (UP-PP) adaptations that our team developed.

UP CLINICAL UTILITY AND VIABILITY FOR EMOTIONAL DISORDERS PREVENTION IN WOMEN UNDERGOING ART IN A REPRODUCTIVE HUMAN UNIT

Study Description

A pilot study was conducted between September 2019 and November 2020 to explore an adapted version of the UP (UP-PP) to prevent the onset of emotional disturbances in women undergoing IUI in a human reproductive unit (HRU) in a Spanish public hospital. A detailed description of the study procedures and results can be consulted in Martínez-Borba et al. (2022).

Procedure

The Ethics Committee of the Hospital Universitario General de Castellón approved this study and all procedures. Hospital staff of the HRU in this hospital gave general information about the UP-PP to the women attending the unit and invited these women to participate in the study in order to learn skills to regulate their emotions during the IUI process and reduce the risk of them developing an emotional disorder. Women who agreed to participate were contacted by a psychologist for an interview in order to provide additional information about the UP-PP and to determine whether the women met inclusion criteria for the study. The inclusion criteria consisted of the following: (a) not meeting criteria for an emotional disorder at the time of study enrollment (because it was a prevention program), as assessed with the Mini-International Neuropsychiatric Interview (MINI) interview (Sheehan et al., 1998; see description below); (b) being able to attend to all program sessions; and (c) having received at least one IUI. Women were excluded if they presented a mental health disorder or risk of suicide. After this initial interview, women who met inclusion criteria and wanted to participate in the study were sent an email to respond to pre-assessment (see Assessment Instruments) through the Qualtrics online platform. The same questionnaires administered at pre-assessment were also sent at post-assessment and two follow-up assessments, at 1 and 3 months following the end of treatment.

Table 8.1 UP-PP Modules' Adaptations from the Original UP

Module 1: Setting goals and maintaining motivation	**Adjusting expectations: Emotional changes and emotion regulation during ART**. In this module, before setting goals and explaining how to maintain motivation, it is important to examine the emotional changes that usually occur during fertility treatments, as well as the ways in which emotion, and difficulties in emotion regulation, can occur before, during, and after pregnancy. It is also important to analyze women's expectations about IUI because there is a lack of information about the emotional changes that often occur during this procedure. In addition, it is important to examine and clarify expectations regarding the UP-PP. Finally, myths about pregnancy, labor, postpartum, and motherhood are also discussed in this first module because women undergoing IUI treatment often idealize and have misconceptions regarding those states.
Module 2: Understanding emotions	**What do our emotions tell us? Analysis of emotional experiences**. In this module, psychoeducation about emotions and their functions is explored just like in the original UP manual but with specific examples of emotion-provoking situations that are more relevant to women going through fertility treatment (i.e., antecedent: meeting pregnant women in the supermarket; physical response: palpitations and shortness of breath; cognitive response: "I will never get pregnant"; behavioral response: avoiding the supermarket).
Module 3: Mindful emotion awareness	**Living in the present to facilitate change.** In this module, mindful emotion awareness is applied in accordance with content from the original UP.
Module 4: Cognitive flexibility	**My mind doesn't help me: Worries, doubts, and fears.** This module focuses on thoughts. The main objective is to help women identify maladaptive thinking patterns and learn how to think more flexibly. There is not a specific modification of the UP manual in this regard, but we use specific fertility examples (i.e., "My life has no meaning if I am not a mother").
Module 5: Countering emotional behaviors	**My Ladder of opportunity: Behavior guided by my goals and values**. The aim of this module is to explain emotional behaviors and their consequences and also start thinking about how to change them. The first adaptation suggested is to give the Rokeach Values Survey (Rokeach, 1973) to women in order to think about their own goals and values in the different relevant areas of their life besides motherhood (i.e., work, social, couple, family, and personal areas), identify emotional behaviors and change them for other behaviors guided by their personal goals and values, and use these behaviors when they experience intense emotions. The second adaptation was adding Problem-Solving Solution to help women determine whether emotions are justified (problem-solving application: evaluate their options and choose the more appropriate in that moment) or not (cognitive flexibility).
Module 6: Recognizing accomplishments and looking to the future	**Emotional release valves: Meaningful activities and assertive communication**. This module can also be adapted to improve well-being by adding future "pleasant activities" according to women's personal goals and values. In this module, women can also learn how to anticipate difficult situations and assertive communication techniques to be used with familiars, partners, friends, and co-workers because difficult conversations could emerge during the following months and the subsequent ART.

Participants

The study sample was composed of five Spanish women (mean age = 33.80 years; *SD* = 4.09; range: 28–39). Almost all participants had a stable relationship (*n* = 4), all of them were currently employed, and all had at least a high education level (university studies). The number of artificial inseminations ranged between 1 and 3 (*M* = 2, *SD* = 1.00). Two women had no masculine partner, so time trying to get pregnant ranged between 6 and 12 months (*M* = 9, *SD* = 4.24). The remaining participants (*n* = 3) had masculine partners, and the origin of fertility problems was unknown (*n* = 2) or female (*n* = 1). In these cases, time trying to get pregnant ranged between 20 and 36 months (*M* = 26.67, *SD* = 8.33). No participant had previous children.

UP-PP Online Adaptation

The UP-PP consists of one individual session and five 2-hour group sessions. Treatment was conducted weekly and occurred over 6 weeks. UP-PP was originally developed as a face-to-face treatment. However, due to the COVID-19 pandemic, after the second session, the program administration was changed to be provided completely online through Zoom video calls.

The modules described previously were explained during group online sessions. After each session, women received an email with a homework reminder and the manual with the module content.

Assessment Instruments

- MINI (Ferrando et al., 1998; Sheehan et al., 1998): This semistructured clinical interview explores psychiatric disorders according to criteria from the fourth edition of the *Diagnostic and Statistical Manual of Mental Disorders* (American Psychiatric Association [APA], 1994).
- Overall Anxiety/Depression Severity and Impairment Scales (OASIS/ODSIS; Bentley et al., 2014; Norman et al., 2006; Osma, Quilez-Orden, et al., 2019): These scales were designed to evaluate the frequency, intensity, and interference of anxiety and depressive symptoms during the last week. Total scores range between 0 and 20; higher scores represent higher anxiety/depressive symptoms. The cutoff point for clinical samples in Spain is 10 (Osma, Quilez-Orden, et al., 2019).
- Positive and Negative Affect Schedule (PANAS; Sandín et al., 1999; Watson et al., 1988): The PANAS consists of 20 adjectives that evaluate positive (10 items) and negative (10 items) emotional experiences. Total scores range from 10 to 50, with higher scores representing higher positive and negative emotional experiences.

- Fertility Quality of Life Tool (FertiQol; Boivin et al., 2011): The FertiQol consists of 34 items that evaluate quality of life related to fertility treatments. Total scores range between 0 and 136 points, with higher scores representing better quality of life.
- Difficulties in Emotion Regulation Scale (DERS; Gratz & Roemer, 2004; Hervás & Jódar, 2008): DERS is composed of 28 items assessing emotional regulation deficits. It can be divided into five subscales: (a) inattention (i.e., "I am attentive to my feelings"), (b) confusion (i.e., "I have no idea how I am feeling"), (c) rejection (i.e., "When I'm upset, I become angry with myself for feeling that way"), (d) interference (i.e., "When I'm upset, I have difficulty focusing on other things"), and (e) lack of control (i.e., "I experience my emotions as overwhelming and out of control"). It is also possible to obtain a global dysregulation score. Total scores range between 28 and 140, with higher scores indicating greater difficulties in emotion regulation.
- Program satisfaction: This measure was designed by our research team and includes ad hoc questions. In this chapter, satisfaction with the intervention format and contents is reported. Items were rated from 0 to 10, with higher scores indicating higher satisfaction. Program satisfaction was only assessed at post-assessment.

Results

Change in Mood: Anxiety and Depressive Symptoms

As shown in Table 8.2, both anxiety and depressive symptoms decreased from pre- to post-assessment and slightly increased at two follow-up assessments. However, these differences were nonsignificant (all $p > .050$), which means that anxiety and depressive symptoms remained at nonclinical levels. The maximum score reported by our sample was 4.4 in anxiety symptoms at 1-month follow-up and 2.8 in depressive symptoms at 3-month follow-up, which are far below the clinical cutoff point for OASIS and ODSIS established in Spanish populations (<10 points; Osma, Quilez-Orden, et al., 2019).

Change in Affect: Positive and Negative Scales

High positive affect scores were found across all assessments. As shown in Table 8.2, despite a small decrease at follow-up compared to pre-assessment, these differences were nonsignificant both at 1-month follow up ($z = -0.37, p = .715$) and at 3-month follow-up ($z = -0.67, p = .500$).

Negative affect decreased from pre- to post-assessment, then increased at 1-month follow-up, and again decreased in the last assessment. The lowest mean score was obtained at 3-month follow-up. Reductions in negative affect from pre-assessment to 3-month follow-up were significant ($z = -2.03, p = .042$).

Table 8.2 CHANGE IN PSYCHOLOGICAL FACTORS FROM PRE-ASSESSMENT TO 3-MONTH FOLLOW UP

Measure	CCO/ND [*M* (*SD*)]	Descriptive Data				Comparisons					
		Pre M (*SD*)	Post M (*SD*)	1-M FU M (*SD*)	3-M FU M (*SD*)	Pre–Post		Pre–1-M FU		Pre–3-M FU	
						Z	*p*	*Z*	*p*	*Z*	*p*
Anxiety symptoms	CCO = 10	2.60 (2.88)	2.20 (1.48)	4.40 (3.05)	4.00 (3.08)	−0.56	.577	−0.95	.343	−0.81	.416
Depressive symptoms	CCO = 10	1.80 (2.49)	0.80 (1.78)	1.80 (4.02)	2.80 (4.76)	−1.34	.180	0.00	.999	−0.45	.655
Positive affect	ND [32.52 (8.46)]	38.40 (10.19)	38.40 (12.54)	36.60 (7.30)	36.40 (9.29)	0.01	.999	−0.37	.715	−0.67	.500
Negative affect	ND [20.61 (7.73)]	21.00 (8.86)	18.00 (8.97)	22.40 (8.20)	15.80 (4.09)	−1.84	.066	−0.41	.686	**−2.03**	.042
Quality of life	ND [68 (range: 46–87)]	91.25 (26.17)	95.00 (11.40)	100.25 (13.10)	85.75 (17.44)	−0.73	.465	−0.37	.715	−0.37	.715
Global dysregulation	ND [59.1 (17.50)]	52.80 (20.92)	44.00 (7.11)	44.60 (11.44)	45.00 (8.80)	−0.67	.500	−0.94	.345	−0.95	.343
Inattention	—	9.80 (1.79)	9.20 (3.11)	10.0 (3.74)	9.60 (3.65)	−0.71	.480	−0.27	.785	−0.38	.705
Confusion	—	6.00 (1.23)	5.80 (1.30)	5.60 (1.95)	6.00 (1.73)	−0.37	.713	−0.37	.715	−0.37	.713
Rejection	—	15.00 (11.00)	11.00 (3.81)	10.40 (4.22)	11.00 (4.30)	−0.55	.581	−0.921	.357	−0.41	.686
Interference	—	8.60 (4.08)	6.60 (0.55)	7.40 (2.41)	6.80 (1.92)	−0.68	.498	−0.55	.581	−0.81	.416
Lack of control	—	13.40 (5.68)	11.40 (2.41)	11.20 (2.17)	11.60 (2.07)	−1.13	.257	−1.13	.257	−0.41	.680

CCO, clinical cutoff; ND, normative data; Post, post-assessment; Pre, pre-assessment; 1-M-Follow-Up, 1-month follow-up assessment; 3-M follow-up, 3-month follow-up assessment.

SOURCE: Martínez-Borba et al. (2022).

Change in Quality of Life Related to Fertility Problems

Quality of life gradually increased from pre-assessment to 1-month follow-up (see Table 8.2). In the last assessment, when most participants ($n = 4$) finished the IUI without a positive result, scores of quality of life decreased; however, scores on this measure were still within the normative range (46–87).

Change in Emotion Dysregulation

As shown in Table 8.2, the rejection and lack of control subscales had higher scores at pre-assessment. A tendency to improve was observed not only in these two subscales but also in emotion interference. Regarding inattention and confusion, both subscales remained relatively stable across all assessments. On the other hand, global emotion dysregulation has its highest score at pre-assessment compared to post-assessment and the two follow-ups. Although there appear to be clear improvements in emotion dysregulation, these observed differences were not significant (all $p > .050$).

Program Satisfaction

At post-assessment, women were asked to rate the delivery format and the UP-PP contents. First, format satisfaction was measured. In general, women indicated high satisfaction with online and face-to-face formats ($n = 4$), whereas only one participant favored the face-to-face format compared with the online format. Most participants ($n = 3$) would prefer group and face-to-face format in a future emotion regulation program.

Second, women were also asked to rate their level of satisfaction with each of the skills learned during the UP-PP. The highest scores were reported for the thoughts identification ($M = 9.4$; $SD = 0.55$; range: 9–10); learning about emotion components: thoughts, physical sensations, and behaviors ($M = 9.4$; $SD = 0.89$; range: 8–10); and assertive communication skills ($M = 9.4$; $SD = 1.34$; range: 7–10) modules. Lower scores were reported for a module focusing on adopting alternative behaviors, although mean level satisfaction was still generally high ($M = 8.8$; $SD = 1.30$; range: 7–10).

Preliminary Conclusion at the Group Level

In light of our results, it seems that the UP-PP could serve as a preventive program for women undergoing IUI. Specifically, our results showed that women included in this study (a) did not develop any emotional disorders despite undergoing IUI during treatment or the 3-month follow-up period, (b) maintained baseline positive affect and quality of life scores during IUI, (c) maintained nonclinical levels of negative affect and continued to demonstrate good emotion regulation, and (d) were satisfied with the UP-PP.

First, the fact that women did not develop clinical anxiety and depressive symptoms is especially relevant because, as previously noted, women often report higher rates of depression and anxiety after ART compared to levels prior to treatment (Lakatos et al., 2017). These women did not report an increase in anxiety and depressive symptoms despite facing stressful situations associated with fertility treatments, namely not getting pregnant after all possible IUI treatments or suffering abortions (one participant), in addition to difficulties related to the COVID-19 pandemic (i.e., involuntary discontinuation of fertility treatments, job loss, economic difficulties, familiar and social distancing, etc.), which may have worsened their overall level of stress (Vaughan et al., 2020).

Second, the UP-PP included some modules focused on enhancing life satisfaction, namely motivation enhancement and emotional awareness (Gallagher et al., 2013), that could help promote positive affect and improve quality of life. In this sense, women who get unfavorable results after undergoing all possible IUI treatments face additional stressors (e.g., deciding to continue with other private and costly treatment options or agreeing not to become parents) that can damage positive affect and quality of life. For this reason, and based on our preliminary results, the reinforcement of these modules could be particularly relevant in these cases. Our results are consistent with other findings that support the development of coping skills to improve positive and decrease negative affect as a means of building resilience for future stressors (Kraaij et al., 2009). We suggest that throughout our adapted UP-PP, women can learn adaptive emotion regulation strategies to better manage stressful situations and the intense emotions they experience during fertility treatments.

Finally, the participants reported high satisfaction and acceptability not only with the UP-PP but also with the online format delivery. Our preliminary results suggest that delivering the UP-PP in a group format via the internet may be feasible in public health settings.

CASE EXAMPLE

The case study we discuss here was one of the participants of the pilot study described above. "M." is a 35-year-old Spanish woman in a stable relationship for 6 years, living together with her husband for the past 5 years. Neither M. nor her husband had previous children. M. did not provide previous medical or mental health history.

Fertility Problems Development

M. was first diagnosed with hypothyroidism in 2009 and polycystic ovaries in 2011. In 2018, she and her husband planned their pregnancy, and after 14 months of regular sexual intercourse without achieving a pregnancy, they decided to consult with a specialist in the HRU in a Spanish public hospital. Both were examined, and M. was diagnosed with endometriosis, a condition that reduces the probability of achieving a pregnancy (Parasar et al., 2017). The ART established by the doctor in charge of the HRU was three cycles of ovarian hyperstimulation plus IUI with her partner's sperm. At the first contact with psychologists responsible for the UP-PP, she had already undergone one cycle of IUI. During the UP-PP, she underwent one additional IUI in her HRU. Finally, between 1-month and 3-month follow-up assessments, she received the last IUI possible in her case. In total, she received three IUI from pre-assessment to 3-month follow-up. At the end of the study, she had to decide whether to continue with IVF or discontinue fertility treatments.

Case Formulation with the UP

M.'s presenting complaints are described in Table 8.3. Her fertility problems were interfering with several areas of her life, including physical and basic necessities (i.e., balanced diet, pain control, medication side effects, etc.), work, daily life activities, pleasant activities, personal relationships, and life goals. Although she sometimes reported strong emotion intensity and moderate to extreme interference, as can be expected in a preventive program, her general functioning was adequate, and no disturbances were detected.

Psychological Assessments Conducted Before, During, and After UP-PP Application

This individual case included 17 assessment points. First, one assessment was conducted before the UP-PP started (pre-assessment). At pre-assessment, M. was administered the measures described previously (OASIS, ODSIS, PANAS, FertiQol, and DERS). Next, M.'s progress in mood and emotion dysregulation was assessed daily before the UP-PP started (baseline period [BL]) and weekly thereafter, during acute intervention. BL consisted of 7 consecutive assessments conducted during 7 days prior to initiating UP-PP. Because repeated measures were used, instead of administering complete questionnaires, during baseline and weekly UP-PP assessments, three questions for mood (happiness, sadness, and anxiety) and two questions for emotion dysregulation (attention and confusion) were administered.

Finally, the same measures administered at pre-assessment (OASIS, ODSIS, PANAS, FertiQoL, and DERS) were also administered immediately after the UP-PP (post-assessment) and at two follow-up points (1- and 3-month follow-ups).

Table 8.3 Case Conceptualization According to UP

HEALTH CONDITION ANALYSIS						
Health condition description: The patient presents fertility problems, described as the impossibility of achieving pregnancy after 12 months of regular sexual relations without using any contraceptive method. In her case, fertility problems are caused by female problems. Specifically, she presented polycystic ovaries (she presented ovarian cysts and menstrual irregularities) and endometriosis (characterized in her case by difficulties in getting pregnant and menstrual pain).						
How health condition (and its treatment) affects the patient's life?			**EMOTION ANALYSIS REGARDING HEALTH CONDITIONS AND ITS CONSEQUENCES**			
General life aspects		**Affectation/ interference** **0____10** **Nothing Very much**	**Strong uncomfortable emotions** Do patients feel strong emotions in any of these general life aspects?	**Intensity** **0____10** **Nothing Extreme**	**Aversive reactions**	**Emotional behaviors** (Situational avoidance/ escape, subtle behavioral avoidance, cognitive avoidance, safety signals)
1. **Physical and basic necessities**	**Eat**: No time for lunch due to laboral schedules.	4	Frustration	5	"If I do not get pregnant it is my fault because I do not eat enough."	**Subtle avoidance behaviors**: Not talking to her boss to ask for permission to have time for dinner.
	Obsessive thoughts about the necessity to control food to increase the probability to get pregnant.	5	Anxiety	6	"I should control everything I eat."	Checking if every aliment is recommended when trying to get pregnant.
	Pain: Painful medical procedures (i.e., blood extraction, regular self-inject) both previous and during artificial insemination.	6	Anxiety	7	Tachycardia and suffocation	**Avoidance/ escape**: "If it continues this way I will stop the artificial inseminations."
	Intense pain during menstrual cycle (due to endometriosis).	6	Frustration	4	"If I had known all these medical procedures I would have never started them."	

(*continued*)

Table 8.3 Continued

HEALTH CONDITION ANALYSIS						
Health condition description: The patient presents fertility problems, described as the impossibility of achieving pregnancy after 12 months of regular sexual relations without using any contraceptive method. In her case, fertility problems are caused by female problems. Specifically, she presented polycystic ovaries (she presented ovarian cysts and menstrual irregularities) and endometriosis (characterized in her case by difficulties in getting pregnant and menstrual pain).						
How health condition (and its treatment) affects the patient's life?			**EMOTION ANALYSIS REGARDING HEALTH CONDITIONS AND ITS CONSEQUENCES**			
General life aspects		**Affectation/ interference** 0____10 Nothing Very much	**Strong uncomfortable emotions** Do patients feel strong emotions in any of these general life aspects?	**Intensity** 0____10 Nothing Extreme	**Aversive reactions**	**Emotional behaviors** (Situational avoidance/ escape, subtle behavioral avoidance, cognitive avoidance, safety signals)
	Medication side effects: mood fluctuations associated with hormonal drugs. During some IUI, she faced the impossibility to finally conduct the IUI due to hyperstimulation.	5 4	Anger, sadness Sadness, helplessness	5 5	"Maybe I am not prepared to be mum." All these efforts are useless."	**Cognitive avoidance**: Rumination about stopping medication and fertility treatments.
	General: High general dissatisfaction associated with medical procedures (i.e., blood extractions, self-injection of hormonal treatment, or information provided by sanitarians).	6	Regret, annoyance	6	"The clinical staff do not worry about us."	**Impulsiveness**: Hostile behaviors with clinical staff. **Subtle avoidance behaviors**: Not asking doubts during medical appointments.
2. **Work**	She had to ask for permission for assistance with ART medical procedures. She thought she could not request more time to eat or to rest when she was in pain due to menstrual cycles and procedures.	3	Frustration, guilt	4	"They will judge me as a I am a women and I want to get pregnant." "Maybe I lose my job."	She used to eat unhealthy meals when she got home in the afternoon. **Avoidance/escape**: Not talking with her co-workers about fertility problems

3. **Daily life activities** (to buy, to cook, to clean, etc.)	Intrusive thoughts when shopping at supermarket.	4	Sadness, apathy	4	Desire to cry; stomach discomfort	**Subtle avoidance behaviors**: Not going through the baby section of the supermarket. **Safety signal**: Chatting with the mobile when she is near the baby section.
4. **Pleasant activities** (hobbies, sport, etc.)	She loved animals and her desire was to have a dog training school and a riding school. However, because of fertility treatments, she was so tired and discouraged to do activities related with animals.	3	Disappointment, worthlessness	4	"I will never get my desire to have my own riding school." "I am unable to do all my obligations."	**Subtle avoidance behaviors**: Procrastinating meeting a friend who has a riding school and avoiding activities with her dogs. **Cognitive avoidance:** Using TV as a distractor to keep from thinking.
5. **Personal relationships** (couple, family, friends, etc.)	Fluctuations in mood related to the hormonal treatment have caused troubles in communication with her husband.	4	Sadness	5	"I do not understand my emotions." "They should know how I feel."	**Subtle avoidance behaviors**: Not talking with her husband, family, and friends about her feelings.
	Not knowing how to respond when family and friends talk about children.	5	Shame, guilt	6	"I should feel happier about my friend's pregnancy."	**Avoidance/escape**: Did not meet friends and familiars who had children or may ask about pregnancies and motherhood.

(*continued*)

Table 8.3 Continued

<table>
<tr><td colspan="7">HEALTH CONDITION ANALYSIS</td></tr>
<tr><td colspan="7">Health condition description: The patient presents fertility problems, described as the impossibility of achieving pregnancy after 12 months of regular sexual relations without using any contraceptive method. In her case, fertility problems are caused by female problems. Specifically, she presented polycystic ovaries (she presented ovarian cysts and menstrual irregularities) and endometriosis (characterized in her case by difficulties in getting pregnant and menstrual pain).</td></tr>
<tr><td colspan="3">How health condition (and its treatment) affects the patient's life?</td><td colspan="4">EMOTION ANALYSIS REGARDING HEALTH CONDITIONS AND ITS CONSEQUENCES</td></tr>
<tr><td colspan="2">General life aspects</td><td>Affectation/ interference
0______10
Nothing Very much</td><td>Strong uncomfortable emotions
Do patients feel strong emotions in any of these general life aspects?</td><td>Intensity
0______10
Nothing Extreme</td><td>Aversive reactions</td><td>Emotional behaviors
(Situational avoidance/ escape, subtle behavioral avoidance, cognitive avoidance, safety signals)</td></tr>
<tr><td>6. Life goals</td><td>Despite the fact that she was engaged in all medical procedures and treatments prescribed by clinical staff to get pregnant, she did not obtain a positive outcome.</td><td>5</td><td>Frustration, sadness</td><td>6, 4</td><td>"I will never get pregnant."

"If I do not get pregnant I will be useless."</td><td>The frustration of not achieving her life goals resulted in the desire to stop fertility treatment.</td></tr>
<tr><td colspan="7">TREATMENT PLAN</td></tr>
<tr><td colspan="7">MODULE 1: Setting goals and maintaining motivation: Adjusting expectations—Emotional changes and emotional regulation during ART</td></tr>
<tr><td colspan="7">During the first session, expectations about fertility treatments and also about maternity will be discussed. First, given that M. presented negative expectations about fertility treatments (i.e., "All these efforts are useless") during the session, the proportion of women who achieve a pregnancy during IUI will be discussed as well as other options to become a mother (i.e., in vitro fertilization or adoption) in order to promote more positive but realistic expectations that favor engagement with fertility treatment. Second, to facilitate the correct adjustment to negative results during IUI and due to the maladaptive thought about maternity she presented (i.e., "If I do not get pregnant I will be useless"), her role as a woman in other vital areas will be reinforced to create a life with meaning regardless of maternity.</td></tr>
</table>

MODULE 2: Understanding emotions: What do our emotions tell us? Analysis of emotional experiences
Psychoeducation about emotions will be explained to provide M. more knowledge about them and consequently improve her control of her emotional response facing stressors. She reported, "I do not understand my emotions." For instance, she explained that she did not know why she argued with her husband when she was sad. After the three components of emotional response are explained (i.e., cognitive, physical, and behavioral components), she may learn that some antecedents (i.e., hormonal drug effects) produce emotional responses (i.e., sadness and frustration) and the behavior associated (i.e., argue with her husband) could have short- and long-term consequences (i.e., difficulties in communication with her partner).
MODULE 3: Mindful emotion awareness: Living in the present to facilitate change
During the mindful exercises, she will learn how to observe and describe her emotional response with a nonjudgmental approach. She will specifically practice in order to not judge herself ("I am unable to do all my obligations"), others ("Clinical staff do not worry about us"), and her own emotions ("I should feel happier about my friends' pregnancy").
MODULE 4: Cognitive flexibility: My mind doesn't help me—Worries, doubts, and fears
In this session, she will learn about her own maladaptive thoughts (i.e., probability overestimations and catastrophizing; "I will never get pregnant"), and she will practice to be more flexible (e.g., "I am not sure whether I will get pregnant, but it is a good opportunity to try it" or "If I will never get pregnant, I would have other maternity options").
MODULE 5: Countering emotional behavior: My ladder of opportunity—Behavior guided by my goals and values
Before the UP program, M. conducted several emotional behaviors. During this module, she will list all these behaviors (i.e., not asking doubts to clinical staff or not meeting with friends/familiars), and she will program alternative action. For example, she will be recommended to write a list of doubts to ask at the next medical visit, and she may phone her sister.
MODULE 6: Recognizing accomplishments and looking to the future: Emotional release valves—Meaningful activities and assertive communication
During this module, M. will be encouraged to reinforce the activities she was doing at the present time (i.e., "spending time with her dogs"), and then she will include an activity that she was recently procrastinating, namely going to riding school. After this, she will introduce a past activity (i.e., reading books), and she will propose a future activity to be included in next months (i.e., go skating with her husband). In addition, she will learn and practice assertive communication skills to ask for permission from her boss to have time for dinner.
OTHER MODULES IF NECESSARY
In Module 5, problem-solving skills will be added to the UP contents to be applied when the emotions of M. are justified. Not having time for lunch is a real problem that needed to be addressed. She will evaluates her options (changing her job, staying in her job but talking first to her boss, staying in her job and continuing with no time for lunch, asking for a reduction in working hours, etc.), and then she will decide the best option considering short- and long-term consequences.

Psychological Status of the Patient Prior to the UP-PP Application

At pre-assessment, M. did not meet criteria for a mental disorder diagnosis (based on the MINI diagnostic interview). As shown in Table 8.4, scores demonstrated no mood disturbances at pre-assessment. All scores remained under the clinical cutoff of 10 points in OASIS and ODSIS scales (Osma, Quilez-Orden, et al., 2019). M. reported high positive affect and low negative affect on the PANAS. In addition, quality of life was high at pre-assessment, as measured by the FertiQol questionnaire. Finally, she reported minimal difficulties in emotion regulation, with the highest scores on the attention, interference, and lack of control subscales.

Changes in Mood and Emotion Dysregulation During UP-PP

Figure 8.1 shows mood during baseline and over the course of UP-PP, with the horizontal line indicating UP-PP initiation. As observed, mood improved from BL to UP-PP session 6. Specifically, happiness during BL assessment oscillated from 1 to 7 points (M = 5.00), whereas during treatment scores ranged between 6 and 9 points (M = 8.3). The contrary tendency was observed for sadness and anxiety. Sadness symptomatology ranged between 0 and 9 points during BL (M = 2.28). During treatment, however, sadness scores decreased, ranging between 0 and 3 points (M = 0.5). Anxiety scores ranged between 0 and 6 both at BL and during treatment. However, mean scores decreased from BL (M = 1.85) to UP-PP session

Table 8.4 Case Study Psychological Evolution from Pre-Assessment to 3-Month Follow-Up

Measure	CCO/ND [*M* (*SD*)]	Pre	Post	1-M FU	3-M FU
Anxiety symptoms	CCO = 10	0	0	6	2
Depressive symptoms	CCO = 10	0	0	0	0
Positive affect	ND [32.52 (8.46)]	49	40	30	38
Negative affect	ND [20.61 (7.73)]	15	14	24	13
Quality of life	ND [68 (range: 46–87)]	86	89	81	80
Global dysregulation	ND [59.1 (17.50)]	51	42	47	46
Inattention	—	11	9	13	13
Confusion	—	5	5	5	5
Rejection	—	7	7	7	9
Interference	—	14	7	8	6
Lack of control	—	14	14	14	13

CCO, clinical cutoff; ND, normative data; Post, post-assessment; Pre, pre-assessment; 1-M FU, 1-month follow-up assessment; 3-M FU, 3-month follow-up assessment.

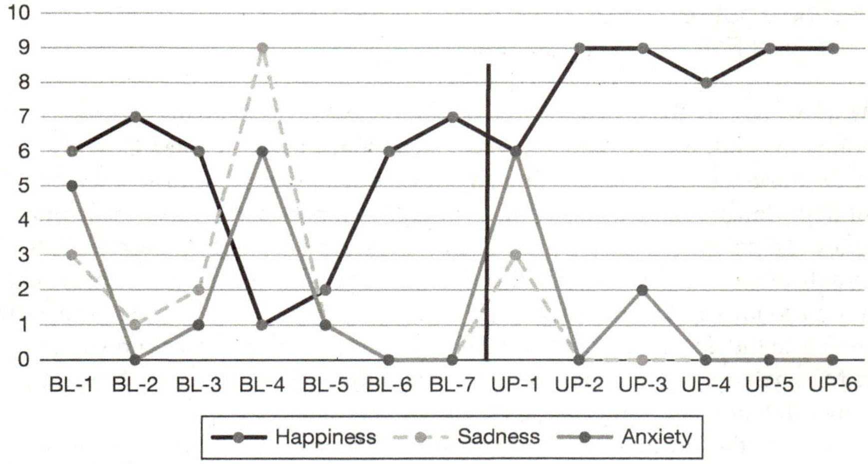

Figure 8.1 Change in mood and anxiety during baseline (BL) and the UP-based prevention program.

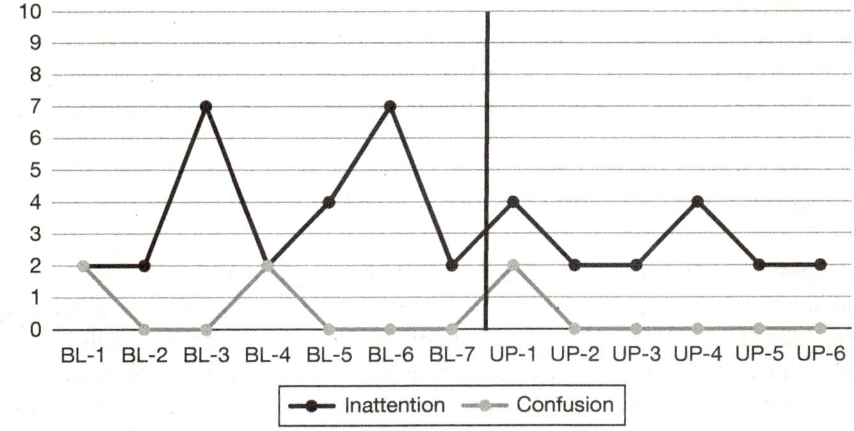

Figure 8.2 Emotion dysregulation evolution during baseline (BL) and the UP-based preventive program.

6 ($M = 1.33$). The observed tendency was that mood remained more stable during UP-PP than during BL.

As observed in Figure 8.2, scores on a measure of emotion dysregulation also generally improved during treatment, compared to the BL assessment period. Emotion inattention ranged between 2 and 7 ($M = 3.71$) at BL, whereas during the UP-PP scores ranged between 2 and 4 points ($M = 2.67$). With regard to emotion confusion, the mean scores decreased from BL ($M = 0.57$; range: 0–2) to UP-PP ($M = 0.33$; range: 0–2).

Psychological Evolution After Finishing the UP-PP: Post- and Follow-Up Assessments

As observed in Table 8.4, mood scores remained at subclinical levels (<10 points for both anxiety and depressive symptoms; Osma, Quilez-Orden, et al., 2019) during all assessments. First, depressive symptoms remained stable across all four longitudinal assessments. Anxiety symptoms increased at 1-month follow-up coinciding with issues in her work, and they again decreased at 3-month follow-up. Second, positive affect decreased from pre-assessment to 1-month follow-up but then increased at 3-month follow-up to levels that were similar to those at the end of treatment. Negative affect followed a similar pattern as M.'s anxiety symptoms, increasing at 1-month follow-up but then decreasing at 3-month follow-up, compared to pre-assessment scores.

On the other hand, during pre-, post-, and follow-up assessments, quality of life oscillated between 80 and 89 points (of a total of 136). Scores on this measure increased from pre- to post-assessment and then slightly decreased at 1- and 3-month follow-up when M. had unsuccessfully completed all possible IUI. At that time, she used the problem-solving technique from the UP-PP to decide whether to continue with IVF or stop trying to get pregnant. She and her partner decided to undergo IVF despite the associated high economic cost. With respect to emotion dysregulation, scores were maintained across most subscales, namely inattention, confusion, rejection, and lack of control, whereas interference and global dysregulation scores improved from pre-assessment to 3-month follow-up.

Program Satisfaction and Case Study Conclusions

M. reported high satisfaction with all UP-PP contents. In addition, she reported that she liked session structure: sharing their feelings and experiences, learning new skills to face their daily difficult situations, and practicing these skills in their real context. She also reported gratefulness for receiving psychological assistance during IUI because she believed that clinical staff in the HRU did not adequately attend to her worries and fears related to the fertility process. In addition, she noted that it was important for her to receive this assistance during fertility treatment.

She concluded that "this program helped me to manage my emotions during fertility processes, but also to generalize this knowledge to other contexts such as my job and family." In this sense, at the end of the program and at follow-up assessments, positive results were found not only in quantitative measures (i.e., her scores on administered questionnaires) but also for behaviors and attitudes manifested by M. For example, after the 1-month follow-up, she asked for permission to have time for lunch at work. She also talked about her and her husband's infertility problems with a co-worker, which she was unable to share with others previously because of the strong emotion it would cause, and reported she felt supported and understood as a result. Regarding familiar relationships, she explained that she engaged in less avoidance, met her family more frequently, and stopped avoiding conversations about motherhood and children.

CONCLUSION

Overall, it appears that a brief UP-PP delivered through video calls and in a group format could be a feasible and useful prevention measure during IUI to reduce the emergence of emotional disorders/anxiety and depressive symptoms. The positive results obtained regarding affect and quality of life in our pilot study are likely associated with the incorporation of new treatment content such as pleasant activities, assertive skills, and problem-solving. Promising results have been found when a preventive UP group program was delivered in other public health services in Spain (Osma, Suso-Ribera, et al., 2019). Therefore, we believe that the UP-PP presented in this chapter could also be feasible and useful in other HRUs (i.e., private centers).

Limitations/Barriers Observed

Emotion regulation skills during assisted reproduction treatments are fundamental for managing stress associated with fertility treatments (Galhardo et al., 2013). However, in Spain, there is an important gap in standardized protocols for emotional disorder prevention during these treatments, and psychologists are not included in HRUs. As a result, women undergoing ART are rarely offered a multidisciplinary service that includes psychological interventions.

Another important barrier observed during UP-PP implementation was the format of delivery. Group sessions potentially allow more women to benefit from psychological services because more women are able to be reached at every point. However, the group format made scheduling difficult at times because of participants' work schedules and other responsibilities. In addition, as described previously, group sessions were conducted through online video calls in order to overcome restrictions on face-to-face contact due to the COVID-19 pandemic. The inclusion of this technology allowed us to reduce obstacles related to geographical displacement to the hospital; however, video calls still require all group members to be present at a specific time, which may be difficult under some conditions.

It is important to note that when women were specifically asked about their preference for in-person versus internet-based treatment, three of them reported they would choose the in-person face-to-face format. In our immediate context, which is the public health system in Spain, online psychological interventions are rarely offered, and services still rely on face-to-face programs.

Future Directions

After carrying out this study, the first aspect we believe that needs to be considered for the future is that it is necessary to provide multidisciplinary services to women undergoing IUI because ART are focused solely on the physical procedure, as opposed to associated emotional components. In this sense, it is highly convenient to increase the visibility and importance of psychological processes during ART in HRUs. Therefore, it will be necessary to offer preventive emotion regulation-based programs such as the UP-PP to all women receiving ART. In order to do so, policy changes must occur, such as incorporating clinical and health psychologists in HRUs.

To overcome barriers in access to mental health care and improve emotional disorder prevention programs, it is necessary to consider cultural differences (i.e., translation of materials into other languages and availability of internet access). Another way to overcome these barriers in access to treatment is to promote information and communication technologies. One simple solution would be to deliver online group sessions and extend the use of technologies (i.e., mobile applications) to develop completely self-administered programs that could be accessed anytime and anywhere depending on women's availability in order to reach women who, due to work schedules, cannot commit to online group sessions. For example, integrating online devices (i.e., video calls, web pages, and mobile applications) in the real context in which women receive ART would facilitate access to treatment. In this regard, it would be necessary to promote the use of these technologies by health care professionals treating these women to motivate them and improve adherence to these devices, especially when they are self-administered.

Finally, it is necessary to accumulate more scientific evidence in the field of preventive psychological interventions during ART using more robust empirical designs (e.g., randomized controlled trials and long follow-ups) because evidence is still scarce. It is also advisable to study the efficacy, acceptance, and feasibility of incorporating a partner in psychological prevention interventions. This could increase adherence to treatment and facilitate partner/social support and communication during assisted reproduction treatments.

Tips/Advice to Clinicians

Some of the barriers we identified in the development of this study allowed us to make some changes and improvements to the program and also to propose future lines of research. The first modification in our UP-PP was to include an additional session. The length of the program was modified in accordance with women's opinions and in agreement with psychologist experience. Future groups will include seven, as opposed to six, UP-PP group sessions. During the sixth session, women will propose pleasant activities to be included in their daily routines and also learn a problem-solving technique. It is important to include this skill in order to evaluate alternative solutions and select the most appropriate one when the woman is faced with a real problem and, consequently, unpleasant emotion is probably justified. Session 7 will focus on communication skills and assertiveness before moving on to more standard content from Module 8 of the UP, which reinforces achievements and helps participants plan future steps. In our experience, the inclusion of a problem-solving technique and assertiveness skills helps women improve their ability to correctly manage difficult situations and improve their interpersonal relationships in their most proximal context, namely their partner, family, or friends. For this reason, we encourage clinicians to include this content in their intervention programs.

In addition, we think it is also important to include the partner, or the most proximal family member, in psychological programs for women undergoing ART. This could help expand the support women receive during these treatments, increase detection of emotional symptoms/emotional disorders in the partner or family context, and also help improve interpersonal relationships. Finally, given that fertility problems affect not only heterosexual couples but also single and LGBTQ+ individuals, clinicians who provide psychological interventions should attend to these differences when programs are developed and implemented. In this way, examples of situations (e.g., M. argues with her husband) exposed during group sessions and in manuals should provide diverse examples (e.g., M. argues with her wife partner, family, or friend) that enable all participants in the group to feel represented.

REFERENCES

Abdolahi, H., Ghojazadeh, M., Abdi, S., Farhangi, M., Nikniaz, Z., & Nikniaz, L. (2019). Effect of cognitive behavioral therapy on anxiety and depression of infertile women: A meta-analysis. *Asian Pacific Journal of Reproduction*, *8*(6), 251–259. https://doi.org/10.4103/2305-0500.270102

Adamson, G. D., de Mouzon, J., Chambers, G. M., Zegers-Hochschild, F., Mansour, R., Ishihara, O., Banker, M., & Dyer, S. (2018). International Committee for Monitoring Assisted Reproductive Technology: World report on assisted reproductive technology, 2011. *Fertility and Sterility*, *110*(6), 1067–1080. https://doi.org/10.1016/j.fertnstert.2018.06.039

Agarwal, A., Mulgund, A., Hamada, A., & Chyatte, M. R. (2015). A unique view on male infertility around the globe. *Reproductive Biology and Endocrinology*, *13*(1), Article 37. https://doi.org/10.1186/s12958-015-0032-1

American Psychiatric Association. (1994). Diagnostic and statistical manual of mental disorders (4th ed.).

Ayeleke, R. O., Asseler, J. D., Cohlen, B. J., & Veltman-Verhulst, S. M. (2020). Intrauterine insemination for unexplained subfertility. *Cochrane Database of Systematic Reviews*, 2020(3), CD001838. https://doi.org/10.1002/14651858.CD001838.pub6

Barlow, D. H., Allen, L., & Choate, M. (2004). Toward a unified treatment for emotional disorders. *Behavior Therapy*, *35*, 205–230.

Barlow, D. H., Farchione, T. J., Bullis, J. R., Gallagher, M. W., Murray-Latin, H., Sauer-Zavala, S., Bentley, K. H., Thompson-Hollands, J., Conklin, L. R., Boswell, J. F., Ametaj, A., Carl, J. R., Boettcher, H. T., & Cassiello-Robbins, C. (2017). The Unified Protocol for Transdiagnostic Treatment of Emotional Disorders compared with diagnosis-specific protocols for anxiety disorders: A randomized clinical trial. *JAMA Psychiatry*, *74*(9), 875–884. https://doi.org/10.1001/jamapsychiatry.2017.2164

Barlow, D. H., Sauer-Zavala, S., Farchione, T., Murray, H., Ellard, K., Bullis, J., & Castellano-Robbins, C. (2018). *Protocolo Unificado para el Tratamiento Transdiagnóstico de los Trastornos Emocionales (2 ed.): Manual del terapeuta (Jorge Osma y Elena Crespo, trad, 2019).* Alianza Editorial.

Bentley, K., Gallagher, M., & Barlow, D. (2014). Development and validation of the Overall Depression Severity and Impairment Scale. *Psychological Assessment*, *26*(3), 815–830. https://doi.org/10.1037/a0036216

Boivin, J., Takefman, J., & Braverman, A. (2011). The Fertility Quality of Life (FertiQoL) tool: Development and general psychometric properties. *Fertility and Sterility*, *96*(2), 409–415.e3. https://doi.org/10.1016/j.fertnstert.2011.02.046

Boulet, S. L., Kawwass, J., Session, D., Jamieson, D. J., Kissin, D. M., & Grosse, S. D. (2019). US state-level infertility insurance mandates and health plan expenditures on infertility treatments. *Maternal and Child Health Journal*, *23*(5), 623–632. https://doi.org/10.1007/s10995-018-2675-y

Calhaz-Jorge, C., De Geyter, C. H., Kupka, M. S., Wyns, C., Mocanu, E., Motrenko, T., Scaravelli, G., Smeenk, J., Vidakovic, S., & Goossens, V. (2020). Survey on ART and IUI: Legislation, regulation, funding and registries in European countries. *Human Reproduction Open*, *2020*(1). https://doi.org/10.1093/hropen/hoz044

Centers for Disease Control and Prevention. (2019a). Reproductive *health*: Infertility *FAQs*. https://www.cdc.gov/reproductivehealth/infertility

Centers for Disease Control and Prevention. (2019b). *Unmarried childbearing*. https://www.cdc.gov/nchs/fastats/unmarried-childbearing.htm

Cousineau, T. M., Green, T. C., Corsini, E., Seibring, A., Showstack, M. T., Applegarth, L., Davidson, M., & Perloe, M. (2008). Online psychoeducational support for infertile women: A randomized controlled trial. *Human Reproduction*, *23*(3), 554–566. https://doi.org/10.1093/humrep/dem306

Cox, S. J., Glazebrook, C., Sheard, C., Ndukwe, G., & Oates, M. (2006). Maternal self-esteem after successful treatment for infertility. *Fertility and Sterility*, *85*(1), 84–89. https://doi.org/10.1016/j.fertnstert.2005.07.1287

Crespo-Delgado, E., Martínez-Borba, V., & Osma, J. (2020). The Unified Protocol for Transdiagnostic Treatment of Perinatal Depression: A case study. *Clinical Case Studies*, 19(6), 491–508. https://doi.org/10.1177/1534650120951266

Farquhar, C., & Marjoribanks, J. (2018). Assisted reproductive technology: An overview of Cochrane Reviews. Cochrane Database of Systematic Reviews, 2018(8), CD010537. https://doi.org/10.1002/14651858.CD010537.pub5

Ferrando, L., Bober, J., Gibert, M., Soto, M., & Soto, O. (1998). M.I.N.I Mini International Neuropsychiatric Interview: Versión en español 5.0.0.DSM-IV. Insituto IAP.

Frederiksen, Y., Farver-Vestergaard, I., Skovgård, N. G., Ingerslev, H. J., & Zachariae, R. (2015). Efficacy of psychosocial interventions for psychological and pregnancy outcomes in infertile women and men: A systematic review and meta-analysis. *BMJ Open*, *5*(1), e006592. https://doi.org/10.1136/bmjopen-2014-006592

Gaitzsch, H., Benard, J., Hugon-Rodin, J., Benzakour, L., & Streuli, I. (2020). The effect of mind–body interventions on psychological and pregnancy outcomes in infertile women: A systematic review. *Archives of Women's Mental Health*, *23*(4), 479–491. https://doi.org/10.1007/s00737-019-01009-8

Galhardo, A., Cunha, M., Pinto-Gouveia, J., & Matos, M. (2013). The mediator role of emotion regulation processes on infertility-related stress. *Journal of Clinical Psychology in Medical Settings*, *20*(4), 497–507. https://doi.org/10.1007/s10880-013-9370-3

Gallagher, M., Sauer-Zavala, S., Boswell, J., Carls, J., Bullis, J., Farchione, T., & Barlow, D. (2013). The impact of the Unified Protocol for emotional disorders on quality of life. *International Journal of Cognitive Therapy*, *6*(1), 57–72. https://doi.org/10.1521/ijct.2013.6.1.57

Gelbaya, T. A., Potdar, N., Jeve, Y. B., & Nardo, L. G. (2014). Definition and epidemiology of unexplained infertility. *Obstetrical and Gynecological Survey*, *69*(2), 109–115. https://doi.org/10.1097/OGX.0000000000000043

Gratz, K. L., & Roemer, L. (2004). Multidimensional assessment of emotion regulation and dysregulation: Development, factor structure, and initial validation of the Difficulties in Emotion Regulation Scale. *Journal of Psychopathology and Behavioral Assessment*, *26*(1), 41–54. https://doi.org/10.1023/B:JOBA.0000007455.08539.94

Hanson, B., Johnstone, E., Dorais, J., Silver, B., Peterson, C., & Hotaling, J. (2017). Infertilidad femenina, diagnósticos asociados a la infertilidad y comorbilidades: Una revisión. *Revista de Reproducción Asistida y Genética*, *34*(2), 167–177.

Hervás, G., & Jódar, R. (2008). The Spanish version of the Difficulties in Emotion Regulation Scale. *Clinica y Salud*, *19*(2), 139–156.

Inhorn, M. C., & Patrizio, P. (2014). Infertility around the globe: New thinking on gender, reproductive technologies and global movements in the 21st century. *Human Reproduction Update*, *21*(4), 411–426. https://doi.org/10.1093/humupd/dmv016

Kiesswetter, M., Marsoner, H., Luehwink, A., Fistarol, M., Mahlknecht, A., & Duschek, S. (2020). Impairments in life satisfaction in infertility: Associations with perceived stress, affectivity, partnership quality, social support and the desire to have a child. *Behavioral Medicine*, *46*(2), 130–141. https://doi.org/10.1080/08964289.2018.1564897

Kraaij, V., Garnefski, N., & Schroevers, M. J. (2009). Coping, goal adjustment, and positive and negative affect in definitive infertility. *Journal of Health Psychology*, *14*(1), 18–26. https://doi.org/10.1177/1359105308097939

Lakatos, E., Szigeti, J., Ujma, P., Sexty, R., & Balog, P. (2017). Anxiety and depression among infertile women: A cross-sectional survey from Hungary. *BMC Women's Health*, *17*(1), Article 48. https://doi.org/10.1186/s12905-017-0410-2

La Marca, A., & Mastellari, E. (2020). Infertility. In F. Petraglia & B. Fauser (Eds.), *Female reproductive dysfunction: Endocrinology* (pp. 211–233). Springer. https://doi.org/10.1007/978-3-030-14782-2_11

Martínez-Borba, V., Osma, J., Crespo-Delgado, E., Andreu-Pejó, L., & Monferrer-Serrano, A. (2022). Prevention of emotional disorders and symptoms under health conditions : A pilot study using the Unified Protocol in a fertility unit. *Anales de Psicologia*, *38*(1), 25–35.

McManus, F., Shafran, R., & Cooper, Z. (2010). What does a transdiagnostic approach have to offer the treatment of anxiety disorders? *British Journal of Clinical Psychology*, *49*, 491–505.

Norman, S. B., Hami Cissell, S., Means-Christensen, A. J., & Stein, M. B. (2006). Development and validation of an Overall Anxiety Severity and Impairment Scale (OASIS). *Depression and Anxiety*, *23*(4), 245–249. https://doi.org/10.1002/da.20182

Osma, J., Martínez-García, L., Quilez-Orden, A., & Peris-Baquero, Ó. (2021). Unified Protocol for the Transdiagnostic Treatment of Emotional Disorders in medical conditions: A systematic review. *International Journal of Environmental Research and Public Health*, *18*(10), Article 5077. https://doi.org/10.3390/ijerph18105077

Osma, J., Quilez-Orden, A., Suso-Ribera, C., Peris-Baquero, O., Norman, S., Bentley, K., & Sauer-Zavala, S. (2019). Psychometric properties and validation of the Spanish versions of the Overall Anxiety and Depression Severity and Impairment Scales. *Journal of Affective Disorders*, *252*, 9–18. https://doi.org/10.1016/j.jad.2019.03.063

Osma, J., Suso-Ribera, C., & Peris-Baquero, O. (2019). Eficacia del Protocolo Unificado en formato grupal para el tratamiento transdiagnóstico de los trastornos emocionales en unidades de salud mental pública españolas. In Aplicaciones del Protocolo Unificado para el tratamiento transdiagnóstico de la disregulación emocional (pp. 203–220). Alianza Editorial.

Parasar, P., Ozcan, P., & Terry, K. L. (2017). Endometriosis: Epidemiology, diagnosis and clinical management. *Current Obstetrics and Gynecology Reports*, *6*(1), 34–41. https://doi.org/10.1007/s13669-017-0187-1

Rosellini, A. J., & Brown, T. A. (2019). The Multidimensional Emotional Disorder Inventory (MEDI): Assessing transdiagnostic dimensions to validate a profile approach to emotional disorder classification. *Psychological Assessment*, *31*(1), 59–72. https://doi.org/10.1037/pas0000649

Sandín, B., Chorot, P., Lostao, L., Joiner, T. E., Santed, M. A., & Valiente, R. M. (1999). Escalas PANAS de afecto positivo y negativo: Validacion factorial y convergencia transcultural. *Psicothema*, *11*(1), 37–51.

Sauer-Zavala, S., Tirpak, J. W., Eustis, E. H., Woods, B. K., & Russell, K. (2021). Unified Protocol for the Transdiagnostic Prevention of Emotional Disorders: Evaluation of a brief, online course for college freshmen. *Behavior Therapy*, *52*(1), 64–76. https://doi.org/10.1016/j.beth.2020.01.010

Sexton, M. B., Byrd, M. R., O'Donohue, W. T., & Jacobs, N. N. (2010). Web-based treatment for infertility-related psychological distress. *Archives of Women's Mental Health*, *13*(4), 347–358. https://doi.org/10.1007/s00737-009-0142-x

Sheehan, D., Lecrubier, Y., Sheehan, K., Amorim, P., Janavs, J., Weiller, E., Hergueta, T., Baker, R., & Dunbar, G. (1998). The Mini-International Neuropsychiatric Interview (M.I.N.I.): The development and validation of a structured diagnostic psychiatric interview for DSM-IV and ICD-10. *Journal of Clinical Psychiatry*, *59*(20), 22–33.

Smith, J. F., Eisenberg, M. L., Millstein, S. G., Nachtigall, R. D., Sadetsky, N., Cedars, M. I., & Katz, P. P. (2011). Fertility treatments and outcomes among couples seeking fertility care: Data from a prospective fertility cohort in the United States. *Fertility and Sterility*, *95*(1), 79–84. https://doi.org/10.1016/j.fertnstert.2010.06.043

Steele, S. J., Farchione, T. J., Cassiello-Robbins, C., Ametaj, A., Sbi, S., Sauer-Zavala, S., & Barlow, D. H. (2018). Efficacy of the Unified Protocol for transdiagnostic treatment of comorbid psychopathology accompanying emotional disorders compared to treatments targeting single disorders. *Journal of Psychiatric Research, 104*, 211–216. https://doi.org/10.1016/j.jpsychires.2018.08.005

Tarín, J. J., García-Pérez, M. A., Hamatani, T., & Cano, A. (2015). Infertility etiologies are genetically and clinically linked with other diseases in single meta-diseases. Reproductive Biology and Endocrinology, *13*(1), Article 31. https://doi.org/10.1186/s12958-015-0029-9

Vander Borght, M., & Wyns, C. (2018). Fertility and infertility: Definition and epidemiology. *Clinical Biochemistry, 62*, 2–10. https://doi.org/10.1016/j.clinbiochem.2018.03.012

van Dongen, A., Nelen, W., IntHout, J., Kremer, J., & Verhaak, C. (2016). e-Therapy to reduce emotional distress in women undergoing assisted reproductive technology (ART): A feasibility randomized controlled trial. *Human Reproduction, 31*(5), 1046–1057. https://doi.org/10.1093/humrep/dew040

Vaughan, D. A., Shah, J. S., Penzias, A. S., Domar, A. D., & Toth, T. L. (2020). Infertility remains a top stressor despite the COVID-19 pandemic. *Reproductive Biomedicine Online, 41*(3), 425–427. https://doi.org/10.1016/j.rbmo.2020.05.015

Watson, D., Clark, L. A., & Tellegen, A. (1988). Development and validation of brief measures of positive and negative affect: The PANAS scales. *Journal of Personality and Social Psychology, 54*(6), 1063. https://doi.org/10.1037/0022-3514.54.6.1063

Wingo, E., Ingraham, N., & Roberts, S. C. M. (2018). Reproductive health care priorities and barriers to effective care for LGBTQ people assigned female at birth: A qualitative study. *Women's Health Issues, 28*(4), 350–357. https://doi.org/10.1016/j.whi.2018.03.002

Zegers-Hochschild, F., Adamson, G., de Mouzon, J., Ishihara, O., Mansour, R., Nygren, K., Sullivan, E., Van der Poel, S., & the World Health Organization. (2010). Glosario de terminología en Técnicas de Reproducción Asistida (TRA). In *Red Latioamericana de Reproducción Asistida.* World Health Organization.

Zegers-Hochschild, F., Adamson, G. D., Dyer, S., Racowsky, C., de Mouzon, J., Sokol, R., Rienzi, L., Sunde, A., Schmidt, L., Cooke, I. D., Simpson, J. L., & van der Poel, S. (2017). The International Glossary on Infertility and Fertility Care, 2017. *Fertility and Sterility, 108*(3), 393–406. https://doi.org/10.1016/j.fertnstert.2017.06.005

9

Unified Protocol for Endometriosis

LAURA A. PAYNE AND ANTJE M. BARREVELD

WHAT IS ENDOMETRIOSIS?

Endometriosis, defined by the presence of ectopic endometrial tissue implanted outside of the uterus, affects approximately 10% of reproductive-age women. A disease largely characterized by pain, pain from endometriosis can be attributed to nerve infiltration, neuronal innervation of lesions, proinflammatory cytokines, prostaglandins, chemokines, and other substances (Berkley et al., 2005; Godin et al., 2021; Stratton & Berkley, 2011). The prevalence of chronic pelvic pain secondary to endometriosis is estimated to be approximately 25–30% (Guo & Wang, 2006; Mowers et al., 2016). Approximately 15,000 annual emergency department visits in the United States are attributed to endometriosis (Agarwal et al., 2020), leading to significant economic impacts on the individual, society, and the health care system.

Endometriosis is diagnosed by symptoms and can be confirmed surgically by laparoscopic-assisted visualization and biopsy (Ballard et al., 2010). The pain experience is unique to every woman, regardless of the extent of ectopic tissue implants (Gruppo Italiano per lo Studio dell'Endometriosi, 2001). Symptoms of endometriosis are most commonly painful menses (dysmenorrhea) and excessive menstrual bleeding (menorrhagia). Other symptoms may include pain during intercourse (dyspareunia); painful bowel movements or urination; infertility; and generalized pelvic/abdominal, back, and muscle (myofascial) pain. Treatment of endometriosis is multimodal and individualized and may include oral analgesics or topical agents, hormone therapy, surgical or interventional management, physical therapy, cognitive–behavioral therapy (CBT), nutritional approaches, and other alternative therapies.

Laura A. Payne and Antje M. Barreveld, *Unified Protocol for Endometriosis* In: *Applications of the Unified Protocol in Health Conditions*. Edited by: Jorge Osma and Todd J. Farchione, Oxford University Press. © Oxford University Press 2023.
DOI: 10.1093/oso/9780197564295.003.0009

EMOTIONAL SYMPTOMS

Pain from endometriosis can negatively impact every aspect of a woman's life, with physical, sexual, fertility, social, financial, and psychological consequences. Women with this disease often present with higher levels of daily stress, somatic symptoms, fatigue, depression, and anxiety compared to those without endometriosis (Chen et al., 2016; Laganà et al., 2015). Although women are twice as likely as men to experience depression (at rates of approximately 10% in women versus 5% in men) (Brody et al., 2018), approximately 15% of women with endometriosis, or greater than 30% of women versus the general female population, suffer from depression (Chen et al., 2016; Warzecha et al., 2020). Addressing all aspects of a woman's pain experience, including her mental health, is critical to improving her daily quality of life and function.

RELEVANCE OF THE UNIFIED PROTOCOL FOR ENDOMETRIOSIS

Despite its well-established efficacy for chronic pain conditions (e.g., Ehde et al., 2014; Williams et al., 2020), CBT approaches have not commonly been evaluated for women with endometriosis specifically (Evans et al., 2019; Mikocka-Walus et al., 2021). Women are most likely to seek treatment for endometriosis due to symptoms of pain and infertility (As-Sanie et al., 2019), and CBT approaches to pain management can be very useful for many women with these symptoms. In a study that included five focus groups of 17 women who had undergone surgery for endometriosis, 100% of participants indicated that CBT should be included as part of the standard of care for women following laparoscopic surgery (Boersen et al., 2021). In addition, there is a growing consensus that CBT for chronic pelvic pain, of which endometriosis is often a cause for women, is a critical tool that should be offered to patients in addition to standard medical approaches (Katz et al., 2021; Urits et al., 2020).

Although women with endometriosis often present with comorbid depression and anxiety, CBT for chronic pain focuses primarily on pain management strategies. Failure to recognize and address the emotional sequelae of this chronic pain condition is a limitation of some psychological treatment approaches. Like other pain conditions, endometriosis must be conceptualized within the biospsychosocial framework (Dunselman et al., 2014; Van Niekerk et al., 2019), and the studies that have address endometriosis-related symptoms beyond pain have demonstrated improvements in emotional symptoms, well-being, and daily functioning (Hansen et al., 2017; Kold et al., 2012). However, the emotional symptoms that often accompany dysmenorrhea, dyspareunia, and infertility associated with endometriosis additionally require sufficient attention during the treatment process. For these reasons, the Unified Protocol for Transdiagnostic Treatment of Emotional Disorders (UP; Barlow et al., 2017a, 2017b) is ideally suited to address the emotional needs of women with endometriosis, as its focus is on the importance of emotion recognition and adaptive responding.

The UP has been adapted for chronic pain and extensively described elsewhere (e.g., Payne, 2017). The emotion regulation strategies utilized for chronic pain diagnoses may be similarly applied in the case of endometriosis. However, due to the common experience of shame, guilt, and fear around sexual functioning and infertility in endometriosis (Fritzer et al., 2013, 2016; Kennedy, 1991), as well as the lack of public and professional recognition of this debilitating condition (As-Sanie et al., 2019), providers utilizing the UP have the opportunity to use it for additional contexts and situations to guide emotion exposures. As described in the case below, only a portion of the intervention was targeting pain management, and the rest instead focused on the emotions that "Marla" struggled with as a result of the biological and psychosocial concomitants of endometriosis.

CASE EXAMPLE

Marla was a 32-year-old, married, White woman who presented to her gynecologist with a long history of menstrual pain and difficulty getting pregnant. She reported that she started menarche at age 14 years and always had painful periods (referred to as dysmenorrhea) that she had mostly managed with over-the-counter medications such as ibuprofen and naproxen. Starting in her 20s, Marla also noted that she occasionally experienced abdominal pain independently from menstruation, but she did not view it as a chronic problem. In the past few years, however, Marla had more pelvic pain and stated that she began to experience symptoms of urinary frequency and urgency, which were also most bothersome when she was menstruating.

Marla's primary concern was that she and her husband had been trying to conceive a child over the past year, and she had not been able to get pregnant. She reported that she felt anxious about her fertility, as her family was quite large (she had four brothers), and there was an expectation that she would also have many children. Marla said that she and her husband had been timing intercourse to when she believed she was ovulating, but this had been somewhat difficult because her menstrual cycles were irregular. She also mentioned that she had always experienced pain during sexual intercourse (known as dyspareunia), so there were often cycles where she avoided sex completely because it was too painful. This resulted in a number of arguments between Marla and her husband, as he did not understand why sometimes she felt a lot of pain during intercourse and other times did not. Marla reported that she felt guilt and anxiety about her pain and difficulty having penetrative intercourse with her husband. In addition, she experienced guilt and shame about not fulfilling her family's expectations about having a family.

Marla was diagnosed with endometriosis following a laparoscopic procedure conducted by her gynecologist. Her physician was not able to remove all endometrial tissue, and Marla experienced ongoing pelvic pain, dysmenorrhea, and dyspareunia following the procedure. Her gynecologist suggested that Marla would benefit from a cognitive–behavioral approach to help her manage feelings of anxiety, guilt, and shame, as well as help her better manage pain.

Application of the UP

Marla and her therapist met for an initial session for an introduction to the treatment and to conduct a functional assessment of Marla's symptoms (the complete conceptualization of the case is shown in Table 9.1). Given her physical symptoms of chronic pelvic pain, along with emotional symptoms of anxiety, guilt, and shame, Marla was an ideal candidate for the UP's transdiagnostic approach to address both pain-related and emotional dysfunction. Initially, Marla was unsure how a psychological intervention would help her pain and functioning, so this initial session focused on reflecting the ways that anxiety and related emotions were limiting her life and interfering in her relationships. Although the full functional assessment was not yet communicated with her in this first session, Marla's therapist was taking note of how these emotions were leading to attempts to avoid, suppress, and escape from how she was feeling, which were further contributing to suffering and pain.

Module 1: Setting Goals and Maintaining Motivation (One Session)

In the next session, Marla and her therapist focused on exploring motivation for treatment. The therapist utilized the skills of "rolling with resistance" by not challenging Marla's reluctance about therapy. Instead, the therapist encouraged her to think of their work together as one additional tool that may help Marla on her journey to decrease pain and improve her functioning. Marla's concerns about therapy were acknowledged as valid, and the therapist also spent time exploring some of her fears that she would not improve. This helped strengthen the relationship between Marla and the therapist by allowing Marla to discuss her concerns openly and without judgment.

The Treatment Goals Form is typically assigned for a first homework assignment, although Marla's therapist thought she could use some help getting started on the form in session. Furthermore, beginning to identify treatment goals together can help facilitate the development of the therapeutic relationship, and it guided Marla to consider what would be observable, measurable, and reasonable expectations for her treatment. As is not uncommon, Marla first identified the goals of (a) eliminating pain and (b) getting pregnant. The therapist explained that although the goals are understandable and measurable to some extent, they may be outside the scope of what can be achieved in treatment. Instead, Marla and her therapist spent time exploring why these goals were important and how

Table 9.1 A Case Conceptualization with the UP in Endometriosis

HEALTH CONDITION ANALYSIS						
Health condition description: Endometriosis with chronic dysmenorrhea (menstrual pain) and dyspareunia (pain during sex). Some additional symptoms of bladder sensitivity (urgency and frequency).						
How health condition (and its treatment) affects the patient's life?			**EMOTION ANALYSIS REGARDING HEALTH CONDITIONS AND ITS CONSEQUENCES**			
General life aspects		**Affectation/ interference** **0____10** **Nothing Very much**	**Strong uncomfortable emotions** Do patients feel strong emotions in any of these general life aspects?	**Intensity** **0____10** **Nothing Extreme**	**Aversive reactions**	**Emotional behaviors** (Situational avoidance/escape, subtle behavioral avoidance, cognitive avoidance, safety signals)
1. **Physical and basic necessities**	**Physical symptoms**: Increased pain when experiencing panic; chronic stress contributes to overall pelvic pain and dyspareunia.	6	Panic, anxiety	8	"If I'm in pain, I have to get help immediately."	Goes to the ER; takes NSAIDs when feeling any symptoms
	Eat: Generally healthy eating habits.	2	None	0	—	—
	Sex: Infrequent penetrative intercourse with partner due to significant pain during penetration; limited engagement in nonpenetrative sexual activities; anxiety about communicating about sex.	9	Anxiety, guilt, anger, sadness	10	"I've done something wrong because I can't even have sex with my husband."	Avoids talking to husband about painful intercourse; avoids other forms of sexual intimacy
	Sleep: Occasionally disrupted sleep with some insomnia (approximately 2X/month).	1	None	0	—	—
	Activity: Previously very active; recently has limited running and other physical activity due to pain.	5	Guilt	4	"Something is wrong with me because I can't even move my body."	Avoids exercise and some physical activity
	Energy: Periodically fatigued due to pelvic pain.	3	Guilt	3	"My body doesn't work well."	Avoids activities that feel strenuous

	Pain: Chronic pelvic pain (1–2X/week) and more frequent during menstruation. Pain is often experienced at a 3 or 4, but can be as high as a 9 or 10. Pain during intercourse is rated at a 7. Bladder sensitivity is rated at a 3.	6	Panic, guilt, anxiety, shame	8	"Being in pain means I've done something wrong."	Shuts down in conversations or disengages; excessive rest; will go to the ER for severe pain episodes
	Medication side effects: None.	0	None	0	—	—
	General: Overall high functioning, but experiencing significant impairments in interpersonal relationships, including with husband and family members.	6	Anxiety, guilt, shame	6	"I just feel bad."	Disengages from activities, people, and emotions when feeling overwhelmed
2. **Work/studies**: Completed some college coursework and worked in sales for a department store prior to meeting her husband. Since being married, she has not worked and focused on starting a family and taking care of her own elderly family members.		2	Anxiety	2	—	—
3. **Daily life activities** (to buy, to cook, to clean, etc.): Lives with her husband. She takes responsibility for most household activities, including grocery shopping, cooking for both of them, cleaning the house, and paying bills.		3	Anxiety, guilt	4	"I am a failure as a wife when I can't even take care of our home."	Avoids or procrastinates on some household activities; will order take-out instead of cooking; lets items "pile up" around the house
4. **Pleasant activities** (hobbies, sport, etc.): Used to enjoy running. Now focuses on some decorating projects and watching movies with her husband.		5	Anxiety	4	"If I exercise and I feel pain, I could be ruining my chances of having children."	Uses distraction (phone); avoids most physical exercise; very cautious body movements; often puts hand on stomach area

(*continued*)

Table 9.1 CONTINUED

HEALTH CONDITION ANALYSIS					
Health condition description: Endometriosis with chronic dysmenorrhea (menstrual pain) and dyspareunia (pain during sex). Some additional symptoms of bladder sensitivity (urgency and frequency).					
How health condition (and its treatment) affects the patient's life?		**EMOTION ANALYSIS REGARDING HEALTH CONDITIONS AND ITS CONSEQUENCES**			
General life aspects	**Affectation/ interference** **0______10** Nothing Very much	**Strong uncomfortable emotions** Do patients feel strong emotions in any of these general life aspects?	**Intensity** **0______10** Nothing Extreme	**Aversive reactions**	**Emotional behaviors** (Situational avoidance/escape, subtle behavioral avoidance, cognitive avoidance, safety signals)
5. **Personal relationships** (couple, family, friends, etc.): Husband, large extended family, core group of friends. Has significant difficulty communicating emotions and discussing pain and infertility in these relationships.	10	Guilt, anxiety, anger	10	"My family will be really upset with me if I can't have children."	Avoids eye contact; avoids discussing pregnancy, fertility, and pain with friends and family; will avoid seeing friends
6. **Spirituality**: Raised Catholic but is no longer practicing.	0	None	0	—	—
7. **Life goals**: Have a family with children of her own. She feels substantial pressure from her family to have many children, and this has superseded any other goals she may have for herself.	9	Anxiety, guilt, frustration	10	"I'll never have a baby."	Focuses exclusively on goals related to pregnancy; avoids pregnancy-related topics in conversations; will search the internet for infertility information; obsessively using ovulation predictor test kits
8. **Others**: N/A					

TREATMENT PLAN
MODULE 1
The therapist and Marla will need to reconsider her initial goals, which are specific but not necessarily achievable through the UP. Marla will identify treatment goals that are manageable and achievable, focusing on increasing activity and improving communication and relationships with her husband, family, and friends. Motivation strategies will focus on "rolling with resistance," as Marla is somewhat skeptical of how therapy will be able to help her with her initial goals of therapy.
MODULE 2
The therapist will begin this module with an introduction to the nature and function of emotions, as well as a description of the biopsychosocial model of pain, including how stress and emotions impact physical experiences. The therapist will explain how current conceptualizations of pain no longer attribute pain to either a medical or psychological cause. Rather, the experience of pain is determined by many different factors. The therapist will then introduce the ARC of Emotions and discuss how behaviors in response to emotions (and pain) can have an impact on those very emotions and sensations in the short and long term. Marla's therapist will encourage her to see the connection between her tendency to avoid things that caused physical or emotional distress and how that makes her feel overall in her life.
MODULE 3
The therapist should be careful to de-emphasize the goal of relaxation in this module, although Marla may find many of the exercises very relaxing. These practices may help improve sleep and overall functioning, which can lead to additional behavioral changes and higher levels of energy. The therapist will also want to highlight the skills of anchoring in the present to help Marla realize her tendency to emotionally withdraw from friends and family when she feels uncomfortable (anxious or guilty). This skill will help her stay focused on the present moment.
MODULE 4
The therapist will first introduce the concept of interpretations, which will help Marla understand the meaning of her feelings of anxiety and guilt related to her pain. Marla and her therapist will focus on her interpretations that she had done something "bad" or "wrong," or that she was bad and how chronic feelings of guilt and anxiety also lead to interpreting situations in a way that is consistent with those emotions. This will be particularly relevant in Marla's interactions with her husband around sexual intercourse. When Marla experiences pain during intercourse, she feels guilty and makes the interpretation that her husband is angry with her or disappointed with her. She then avoids future sexual interactions and also avoids talking to her husband about it. Identification of thinking traps will help Marla examine the evidence that her husband is angry or disappointed with her. The therapist can help Marla identify several alternative interpretations, including that her husband is confused about her behavior. This practice will help Marla recognize the impact of her interpretations and allow her to engage with more balanced thoughts. The therapist will also help Marla identify core beliefs ("I'm unlovable") that will further highlight how Marla's interpretations affect how she feels.

(*continued*)

Table 9.1 Continued

MODULE 5
The therapist will plan to focus on Marla's extensive array of emotion-driven behaviors (EDBs), particularly involving overt avoidance and subtle emotional avoidance. Marla understandably experiences anxiety and fear related to her interpretations that others will reject her or be disappointed by her; however, her reactions to the anxiety and fear in the short term (reduction of anxiety/fear) actually reinforced the interpretations and negative emotions in the long term. The therapist will identify how responding to feelings of guilt by either "shutting down" or apologizing excessively actually makes her feel somewhat more in control in the short term but will give her brain the implicit feedback that she has done something wrong in the long term. The therapist will also discuss how her EDB of going to the emergency room when in pain led to increased stress, anxiety, and pain.
MODULE 6
Exposure to physical sensations will be a challenging but very helpful module. Marla will likely be very anxious about the practice of eliciting physical sensations because of her fear that it will trigger pain. However, the therapist will help Marla recall the value of previous exposures. The therapist will explain that it is essential that they activate some of the sensations that Marla is fearful of so that they can practice changing her responses and reversing the cycle of anxiety. The therapist will not try to help her stay calm during these exercises, and should verbally and nonverbally communicate that the panic attack is not dangerous or an emergency.
MODULE 7
Marla and the therapist will have a variety of situations and contexts to choose from when designing the emotion exposure hierarchy. From physical activities to social activities to interpersonal interactions, the situations that can serve as exposures may range from producing mild to severe anxiety. The therapist may choose to begin with a universally challenging assertiveness practice, such as asking to use the restroom in a coffee shop without making a purchase. Subsequent exposures can involve *not* going to the ER immediately when experiencing intense pain, engaging in regular exercise, and spending more time with friends. Variations of these exposures can also make them more or less challenging, as needed (e.g., spending an hour with a friend versus spending a whole day with a group of friends).
MODULE 8
The therapist will review Marla's accomplishments and the most important skills she learned in treatment. They will discuss the importance of continued practice, and the value of trying to fully address all of the situations on her hierarchy. The therapist will remind Marla that pain symptoms may fluctuate over time and to continue to focus on the behavioral changes that Marla has control over.
OTHER MODULES IF NECESSARY
The therapist may offer Marla an additional joint session with Marla's husband to discuss her progress and to ideally focus on communicating more effectively, particularly regarding sexual intimacy.

her life would look differently if these goals were achieved. Marla said that if she felt less guilt and shame, she would be more open with her family, especially her oldest brother, about what she was going through with endometriosis and fertility difficulties. She would also be more active in her life and consider exercising more and taking dance classes. She also wanted to spend more time with her friends, even though many were pregnant or already had children, which is why Marla had been avoiding them. Marla also noted that she wanted her relationship with her husband to improve, but she was not sure how to work on this. She and the therapist identified what seemed like two top problems—pain that limits her activities and guilt/shame that interferes in her relationships. For each of these top problems, two goals were specified. For the top problem of pain, Marla identified the goals of taking a dance class and running a 5K race. For the top problem of guilt/shame, Marla and her therapist agreed that one goal would be to engage in at least one social activity with a friend per week and to have a conversation with her husband about her endometriosis and pain during sexual intercourse. For homework, Marla was asked to complete the Decisional Balance Worksheet to help identify the motivating reasons for change, as well as some of the obstacles she may face in the process.

It is important to note that the goals identified on Marla's Treatment Goals Form do not comprehensively address the top problems she identified (e.g., there was no goal about communicating with her family members). This is to be expected, as attempting to identify goals that tackle all aspects of the top problems would be overwhelming and likely unachievable in the acute phase of treatment. However, working toward the identified goals may produce change in other areas related to the top problem. At the conclusion of treatment, Marla and her therapist will review her functioning in these areas and determine new goals for Marla to work on by herself in the long term.

Module 2: Understanding Emotions (Two Sessions)

Learning about the functional and adaptive nature of emotions was critical for Marla, as is the case for many individuals who experience chronic and significant medical conditions. Often, we attempt to identify a difference between conditions with a "medical" cause (which then requires a medical intervention) and conditions with a "psychological" cause that require a psychological intervention. This distinction is both outdated and inaccurate; we now know that any chronic condition involves biological, psychological, and social components, and each of these must be sufficiently addressed to facilitate healing and recovery. For Marla, chronic feelings of frustration, guilt, and anxiety contributed to chronic stress, which further exacerbated her pain and symptoms. The focus of this module was to help Marla understand that the emotions she experienced were completely understandable, given the context in which they occurred and her response to them.

Marla's therapist presented the idea that emotions are adaptive and help motivate us to take the necessary action to protect ourselves or meet our needs. This concept proved difficult for Marla to accept because she had always viewed the guilt and anxiety she felt as entirely problematic. When the three-component model of emotions was introduced, she struggled to identify her thoughts (e.g., she stated "I just feel bad"), physical sensations, or behaviors. To work around this challenge, Marla's therapist used some examples that were not specifically relevant to Marla, such as experiencing anxiety when speaking in front of a group of people. This technique helped Marla to see that components of an emotional experience (i.e., thoughts, physical sensations, and behaviors) were interacting in a way that caused her to feel worse in certain situations. For homework, she provided an example of this model from when she avoided seeing her friends due to feeling sad that she has not been able to get pregnant. Marla was able to acknowledge that the situation triggered thoughts such as "I'll never have a baby," physical sensations of dread and fatigue, and then attempts to avoid her friends or at least talking about having a family. The ARC of Emotions and the short-term (feeling relief due to avoiding the discomfort of being confronted with her friends' children) and long-term (feeling more anxious and sad about her own difficulties as well as increasingly disconnected and unsupported by her friends) consequences of this behavior were discussed to help Marla understand why her attempts to avoid situations and conversations to feel better had left her actually feeling much worse.

Module 3: Mindful Emotion Awareness (Two Sessions)

The concept of mindful, nonjudgmental emotion awareness was presented in Module 3. Marla's completion of the ARC of Emotions in the previous sessions had proved to be helpful in increasing her awareness of her reactions, particularly her behavioral responses to emotions. The information in this module built upon those developing skills by introducing the idea of purposely noticing emotions in the present moment. The first exercise to practice this skill focused on the therapist reading a guided meditation from the UP workbook, which Marla made an audio recording of so she could listen on her own. Marla reported that the exercise was very relaxing and enjoyable, although her therapist was careful to explain that paying attention to uncomfortable emotions will not necessarily be relaxing. Instead of relaxation as a goal, her therapist encouraged Marla to focus on the daily practice as a goal, regardless of how she felt. Due to the extent of the material in this module, Marla's therapist focused only on the guided meditation for this first session of Module 3.

When she returned the following week, Marla reported that she had practiced the guided meditation daily. This commitment to practice is especially important, and she and the therapist discussed how Marla had been able to make the time to follow through with the plan. Marla reported that she started waking up approximately 15–20 minutes earlier than usual, and she felt better in the morning, despite anticipating the contrary. This experience in and of itself was used to illustrate the skill of emotion awareness and staying in the present moment. By noticing how Marla felt in the present moment in the morning (instead of what she believed she would feel), she was able to look at her experience to give her this important information (i.e., she felt a bit more engaged and energetic by waking up slightly earlier in the morning). Marla's therapist then continued the in-session practice on mindful emotion awareness by purposely eliciting emotions in response to both sad and happy music. The sad music that Marla's therapist chose was an instrumental song; the happy music was a well-known pop song. Importantly, Marla was not informed about the specific songs beforehand, as it is often the case that music can elicit many different emotions, even those contrary to what would be expected. After the mindful mood induction practice, the skills for practicing anchoring in the present were introduced. Marla found this skill particularly useful, as she noticed that her mind would start racing as soon as she felt her pain increasing. The process of anchoring in the present helped Marla "check in" with her body, as well as her thoughts and behaviors, and realign her behaviors to what was actually happening in the present moment. This skill could be particularly useful when Marla was interacting with her family. Often, she was afraid that her family members would ask her about starting a family or say something about her getting pregnant and would preemptively "shut down" by either disengaging from the conversation or leaving the room. Marla and her therapist discussed how anchoring in the present could allow her to both recognize her fear and anxiety in that moment and also choose her behavior based on what was happening in the moment (i.e., if the group was not asking about her plans to have a baby, then Marla could remain engaged in the conversation). Marla planned to practice anchoring in the present, as well as the mindful mood induction, for homework.

Module 4: Cognitive Flexibility (Two Sessions)

Module 4 began with a review of the nature and function of thoughts, and psychoeducation around the idea that thoughts are our brains' interpretations of situations based on what we know about the world through our past experiences, our neurobiological makeup, and information we have learned. Marla's therapist explained how Marla's interpretation of situations often led to her feeling guilt or anxiety, as she was often interpreting that she had done something wrong or that something "bad" was going to happen. Marla also brought up that she often anticipated experiencing pain from certain activities (e.g., sexual intercourse and strenuous exercise), which would also trigger anxiety about those activities. Importantly, Marla's therapist also introduced her to the other aspect of cognitions, which is that how she *feels emotionally* will influence her *interpretations of a situation.* In this sense, Marla's chronic feelings of guilt, shame, and anxiety were also leading her to interpret situations as examples of her having done something wrong or something bad that was going to happen. For instance, Marla would often withdraw from her family or get angry and frustrated when she perceived that someone had made a critical remark about her. Marla was able to acknowledge that she may be more likely to interpret their comments as critical or negative *because* she was already feeling guilty and ashamed. This realization that her emotions had an impact on her thoughts proved to be an important turning point for Marla, as she was able to come to terms with the possibility that her interpretations did not necessarily match what her family was communicating. The nature of interpretations was then further described in terms of thinking traps. Marla recognized that she often engaged in "jumping to conclusions," such that she was already reacting to a situation she thought was going to happen in her mind, but before anything had actually happened. Marla and her therapist practiced coming up with alternative interpretations of situations using questions to help promote cognitive flexibility. For example, when Marla recognized the automatic interpretation, "My father is disappointed with me when he asked why I was so quiet," she was able to examine the evidence for and against that interpretation and reflect on her past experience to consider if that was the case. Then, she came up with the alternative interpretation of "My father has always expressed how proud he is of me, and it seems unlikely that he's disappointed by me because of this one interaction we had."

At the following session, Marla's therapist reviewed Marla's practice of cognitive flexibility and helped her generate additional appraisals for each of the situations she listed. They then spent the remainder of the session using the Downward Arrow form to help identify and explore some of Marla's core beliefs. Using examples from the homework form, Marla and her therapist first identified a thought of "My family will be really upset with me if I can't have children," which then meant that "My family will distance themselves from me, or maybe even shut me out." This thought meant that Marla would not have any support from her family and that she would be alone. Marla identified that this interpretation meant "I caused this, and I must be unlovable." Then Marla and her therapist explored the nature of this core belief (i.e., "I am unlovable") in terms of its history and in what situations it is triggered. For homework, Marla began tracking the situations in which she felt anxious, guilty, or shameful and reflected on whether the core belief of "I'm unlovable" was contributing to her reactions.

Module 5: Countering Emotional Behaviors (One Session)

The importance of Module 5 in introducing clients to emotional behaviors cannot be understated, and for Marla, it was critical that she become more aware of the behaviors she was engaging in that were contributing to the cycle of guilt, shame, anxiety, and pain. This was particularly relevant because Marla had recently experienced an intense episode of pelvic pain, which led her to go to the emergency department. She was treated with nonsteroidal anti-inflammatory drugs, which Marla later realized she probably could have taken herself at home. Instead, her panic and anxiety about worsening pain resulted in spending many hours at the hospital, leaving both her and her husband exhausted, which triggered feelings of intense shame and guilt.

Marla's therapist reviewed all the different types of emotional behaviors and some examples of each, and Marla was easily able to identify patterns of overt avoidance (e.g., avoiding sexual intercourse and avoiding conversations with her family), subtle behavioral avoidance (e.g., "shutting down" when feeling guilty and engaging in excessive planning/information seeking when she was feeling anxious), and cognitive avoidance (e.g., distracting herself with activities or playing on her phone). As is often the case, Marla did not seem to use any safety signals, and she had trouble identifying any emotion-driven behaviors (EDBs). Marla's therapist pointed out that her behavior of immediately going to the hospital when she experienced pain recently may have been an example of an EDB. Marla was panicking due to the unusually high levels of pain and sought out emergency care as a result. However, Marla had trouble recognizing her behavior as an EDB; she continued to focus on the idea that high levels of pain indicated an emergency. As with many individuals who experience chronic pain, the emotional aspect of pain (often fear) results in the EDB of urgently seeking help. Marla's therapist validated how Marla was feeling and then carefully encouraged her to consider that despite being in tremendous pain, her life was not in danger in any way. In fact, Marla had experienced this level of pain at other times in her life. During this discussion, the therapist observed that Marla began to disconnect and "shut down," such that she was responding in single-word answers to questions and avoiding eye contact. This provided a valuable opportunity for Marla's therapist to point out that she was engaging in EDBs in session and encouraged Marla to instead express what she was feeling. Marla hesitated, but after repeated encouragement and probing, she voiced that she felt angry at the therapist for what she perceived as the therapist criticizing her response to her pain. Marla's therapist remained quiet, which gave Marla the opportunity to fully explore these emotions without interruption. Marla then was able to make the connection that she also experienced anger with her family members when she felt they were critical or pressured her, and she recognized that this feeling had been present long before the issue of her being able to have children. Marla also recognized that she felt angry with her husband when she perceived pressure from him to have sexual intercourse, which led to her emotionally disconnecting from him instead of expressing her feelings. They discussed Marla's subtle emotional avoidance of "shutting down" in response to anger as a strategy she had learned earlier in her life when she did not have the capacity to express her emotions to her adult family members. However, this emotional behavior was no longer helpful for her in that situation, so Marla's therapist encouraged her to continue to explore her tendency to disconnect and consider how she was feeling at the time. She agreed to practice this and to record what an alternative response to a similar situation would be for homework.

Module 6: Understanding and Confronting Physical Sensations (One Session)

Although Marla had been practicing various forms of emotion exposure throughout her treatment thus far, Module 6 involved deliberately provoking uncomfortable physical sensations. When Marla's therapist introduced the rationale for exposure to physical sensations and the associated emotions, Marla expressed that she was very anxious about these procedures. Given her experience of chronic pain due to endometriosis, she was highly sensitized to physical changes in her body, and any sensation she believed would lead to pain and discomfort was avoided. The therapist reminded Marla of how valuable her exposures to emotion in past sessions had been, even though they were uncomfortable. Marla hesitantly agreed to proceed with the symptom induction test in session.

The first exercise involved hyperventilation, and Marla was able to complete the full 60 seconds and reported only moderate distress. Similarly, she completed the spinning and breathing through a thin straw exercises with mild to moderate distress. Marla's therapist suggested they try a slightly more challenging exercise that would elicit sensations similar to pelvic pain. Marla reported that she often felt pressure on her abdominal area that was a dull, aching pain. So, she and the therapist designed an exercise in which Marla placed several heavy books on her abdomen. She was able to tolerate it for 15 seconds and then requested the books be removed. Marla reported that her distress about the symptoms was an "8" out of 10, and she was very fearful of the pain she felt. As she was discussing it, Marla became even more anxious and began to experience a panic attack. The therapist encouraged Marla to use the skills she had been learning—to engage in anchoring in the present and to counter any emotional behaviors she may want to engage in. After several minutes, the panic symptoms subsided, and Marla was able to process this experience with the therapist. She acknowledged that during the panic attack, she recognized that her interpretations shifted such that she began to think she was having a medical emergency. However, Marla recalled when she had previously gone to the emergency department during a particularly significant pain episode and was able to remember that she was not in any danger in this present moment. As a result, Marla found this experience in session to be helpful in creating a greater feeling of control of her behaviors in response to her symptoms. Marla was asked to practice this exercise for homework.

Interestingly, Marla avoided doing any of the exercises at home over the following week. She reported that even though the experience was helpful in session, she was nervous about doing the exercise around her husband or her family because she thought she might feel "out of control." Marla and her therapist both agreed that this was an example of overt avoidance, but Marla was still unwilling to practice the exercise at home. In the spirit of "rolling with resistance," her therapist agreed to move forward in the treatment protocol rather than getting stuck on ensuring that she complete this one exercise.

Module 7: Emotion Exposures (Eight Sessions)

At the beginning of Module 7, Marla and her therapist worked on developing her Emotion Exposure Hierarchy while they reviewed the skills she had learned thus far, as well as repeatedly coming back to the idea that exposure to the emotion and the modification of her behavioral response was the only way to help Marla balance her emotions and help them function more adaptively. Marla was able to generate a variety of situations for the hierarchy. These included exercise (specifically running for 5 minutes, running for 1 mile, and then running for 3 miles), social activities (e.g., going out with one close friend, going out with a group of friends, and going out with a group of friends who had children where that was likely to be the primary topic of conversation), and communication (e.g., talking with a friend about her infertility, attending an endometriosis support group, and talking with her cousin about her pain). Very challenging situations included talking with her husband about the pain she experiences during intercourse and talking with her mother and father about infertility. Marla's therapist also encouraged Marla to include conducting the physical sensation exercise (placing heavy books on her abdomen) at home, as well as an imaginal exposure of writing a narrative about never being able to have children. Marla made it clear she did not want to engage in these exposures, and her therapist agreed that she did not have to, but it would still be helpful to have them on the list. This strategy can be a helpful tool for individuals who are very reluctant to engage in certain exposures at first but may reconsider once they have gained some momentum with less challenging exposures.

The first in-session exposure focused on assertiveness practice. This was helpful for several reasons. First, many of Marla's situations on her hierarchy were not conducive to practicing in session. Second, assertiveness practice is challenging for most individuals, so it is a useful practice to utilize with many clients, including those without specific concerns about social interactions. For Marla, practicing asserting herself also triggered feelings of guilt, so this was relevant to her specific emotions. At the session, Marla and her therapist worked through the first half of the Record of Emotion Exposure Practice before the exposure. Then, they went outside to conduct an exposure of asking to use the restroom at a local coffee shop without purchasing anything. As they entered the coffee shop, the therapist stayed in the background so that it appeared Marla was by herself. Marla was able to ask to use the restroom; however, the staff said she could not use the restroom without making a purchase. Marla thanked them and left the shop. Back in the office, they processed what happened during the exposure and completed the remainder of the Record of Emotion Exposure Practice. Her therapist congratulated Marla on asking the staff to use the restroom, and they discussed that in the future, Marla could practice further asserting herself with the staff. For homework, they agreed that she would first focus on the exercise situations in her hierarchy and try running for 5 minutes.

The next several sessions continued in a similar fashion. Marla completed in-session exposures either directly related to her presenting concerns or instead provoked emotions that she generally found uncomfortable. For out-of-session practice, Marla completed most of the exercise situations on her hierarchy relatively quickly. She was feeling better physically as a result and signed up for a dance class, which helped her achieve two of her identified treatment goals. She had several unexpected pain episodes and was able to use the anchoring in the present skills to keep herself grounded in the present moment instead of going to the hospital. However, she continued to struggle with communication around her pain and infertility. Marla was still avoiding talking with her husband about her pain, and she continued to disengage emotionally from her family. During one session, Marla's therapist suggested she write a letter to her husband describing her pain and the pressure she felt around sexual intercourse. Marla completed the letter for homework and read it aloud at the next session as her in-session exposure. Marla was tearful and expressed anger and sadness during her reading of the letter. Although she was not able to express these feelings to her husband directly, she did find it helpful to identify and describe the emotions.

Module 8: Recognizing Accomplishments and Looking to the Future (One Session)

At the final session, Marla and her therapist reviewed the skills she learned and her progress over the course of treatment. Interestingly, Marla reported that the experience of having a panic attack in session following the symptom induction test of placing heavy books on her abdomen was the most significant experience in therapy. Although it was prior to the repeated emotion exposures in Module 7, she found that making the connection between her fear and anxiety and her pain was the moment she kept remembering when reflecting on her work. After describing this, Marla's therapist asked her if she wanted to try the exposure again. Marla agreed, and she lay down and placed the heavy books on her abdomen herself. She reported high levels of anxiety ("7" out of 10), and she engaged in the exercise for 45 seconds this time and reported that she experienced pain, but it was more manageable when she did not feel as fearful.

Marla and her therapist additionally identified some long-term goals for her to work on. She was planning a weekend vacation with her sister-in-law, and Marla's goal was to share more about her infertility and frustration during that trip. This low-pressure activity with a family member seemed like a good next step, although Marla identified the long-term goal of communicating her infertility and diagnosis of endometriosis to each of her immediate family members. Although she had not identified a goal of increasing intimacy with her husband at the beginning of treatment, Marla reported that she wanted to explore ways of being intimate with her husband in addition to sexual intercourse.

Marla's therapist reminded her that, like emotions, pain varies with many different aspects of living, including stress and biological factors. They discussed how Marla could approach future pain flare-ups and what steps she could take to implement the skills she found most helpful. When Marla left the session, she acknowledged she had a lot to continue to work on, but she believed she developed a foundation of gaining greater balance in her life and the tools she needed to more effectively manage her pain and emotions.

TREATMENT OUTCOME

Prior to the first session of treatment, Marla completed self-report questionnaires designed to measure symptoms relevant to her presentation. She completed the

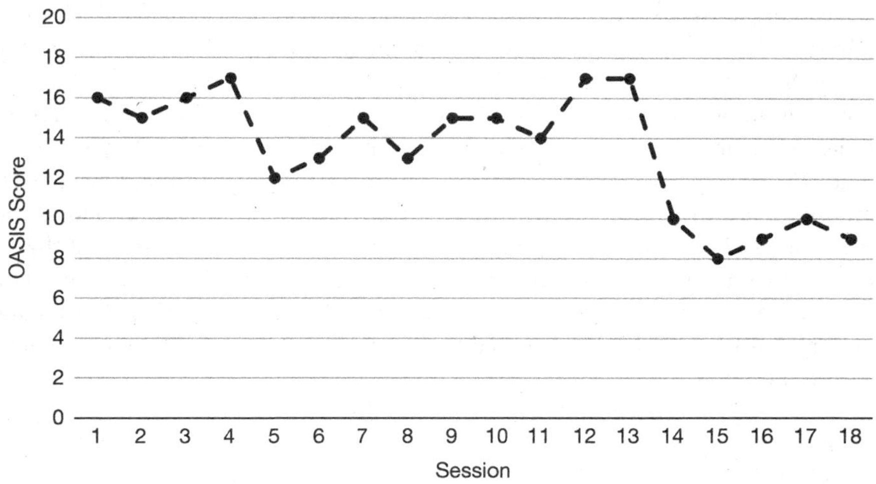

Figure 9.1 Marla's OASIS scores over the course of 18 sessions.

30-item Endometriosis Health Profile (EHP-30; Jones et al., 2001, 2004, 2006), which includes five core subscales (pain, control and powerlessness, emotions, social support, and self-image), as well as optional additional subscales that Marla completed (sexual intercourse and infertility), with subscale scores each ranging from 0 (excellent health) to 100 (worst possible health). In addition, Marla completed a measure from the UP workbook—the Overall Anxiety Severity and Impairment Scale (OASIS; Campbell-Sills et al., 2009; Norman et al., 2006)—prior to each session (Figure 9.1).

At baseline, Marla's scores on the EHP-30 core subscales ranged from 50 (pain subscale) to 65 (self-image). Not surprisingly, her scores on the sexual intercourse and infertility subscales were 73 and 80, respectively. Her OASIS score at baseline was 16 (out of 20), reflecting severe anxiety. At the final treatment session, Marla's EHP-30 scores suggested improvement in several domains. The pain subscale was lower (35), as was the self-image subscale (40). The sexual intercourse and infertility subscales also showed some improvement (60 and 64, respectively), but these areas were still very significant for Marla and would require continued practice and emotion exposures. Her OASIS score decreased to 9, suggesting she had made considerable improvements in her anxiety symptoms and related impairment.

EFFICACY/CLINICAL UTILITY

Although the UP has not been formally tested in individuals with endometriosis, evidence from published papers suggests that the UP does successfully target the affective components of endometriosis. In a group format, participants with infertility demonstrated improvement in anxiety and depressive symptoms compared to a waiting list condition (Mousavi et al., 2019). In addition, adults with chronic pain also demonstrated improvement in anxious and depressive symptoms following 10 sessions of internet-based delivery of the UP (Wurm et al., 2017). Common underlying factors that play a role in endometriosis, such as experiential avoidance, are also addressed through the strategies in the UP (Khakpoor et al., 2019). In particular, dysregulated (unexpressed) anger in individuals with endometriosis may be an important target of treatment. A study employing a multiple-baseline across-subjects single-case experimental design showed that a specific treatment skill taught in the UP—mindful emotion awareness—resulted in reductions of dysregulated anger (Cassiello-Robbins et al., 2020). These data suggest that the UP has the potential to directly target the affective components of endometriosis.

DISCUSSION

Endometriosis is a chronic and complex health condition that is associated with high rates of anxiety and depression (As-Sanie et al., 2019). The case described in this chapter—Marla—demonstrates how facilitating adaptive emotion regulation through emotional awareness, cognitive reappraisal, and exposure to emotions can have substantial positive effects on psychosocial and emotional functioning. Marla applied these skills in relation to her actual experience of pain (the symptom induction test); however, the use of skills was often applied to her emotions of guilt and shame. This is not to say that her pain was "caused" by guilt and shame. Rather, the goal of psychological interventions must be to address the entire biopsychosocial experience of an individual with endometriosis (Till et al., 2019).

Directions for Future Research

Future research should focus on the direct evaluation of the UP for chronic health conditions specific to women, such as endometriosis. Greater awareness and innovation are needed to address the emotional and psychosocial needs of this chronic and disabling condition. In addition, future work exploring the utility of the UP for addressing guilt and shame would also provide a valuable contribution to the applicability of the UP across a range of different emotional and physical symptoms.

Limitations

The UP of course does have limitations in its breadth of application to chronic health conditions, such as endometriosis. Because endometriosis is an underrecognized and underresearched health condition, individuals with this condition will benefit from a provider that has an appreciation for the emotional implications of potential infertility, surgical recovery, and lack of recognition from health care providers or family members. It would be impossible to describe all the important factors specific to endometriosis in the UP manual; in this case, it would be helpful for providers to ensure they are familiar with the symptoms associated with endometriosis, as well as the treatment approaches. For example, although not a part of the case described in this chapter, many women face difficult decisions with regard to surgical removal of the uterus to alleviate pain. This decision and the implications of the decision will result in often complex feelings of sadness, frustration, and loss. Having a clear understanding of these and other emotions for those with endometriosis will greatly facilitate application of the UP.

Advice for Clinicians

Working with individuals who have chronic pain can be challenging because many are often deeply entrenched in the cycle of pain and emotions. Most important, providers must communicate an attitude of empathic support and belief in the client's experience as valid and understandable. This will facilitate all interventions and skills administered in the UP. Clinicians opting to utilize the UP for chronic pain conditions, such as endometriosis, would benefit from focusing on addressing emotions such as anger, guilt, and shame, which are all common to the experience of chronic pain.

REFERENCES

Agarwal, S. K., Soliman, A. M., Bond, J. C., & Epstein, A. J. (2020). National patterns of emergency department use for women with endometriosis, 2006–2015. *Journal of Women's Health*, *29*(3), 420–426. doi:10.1089/jwh.2019.7879

As-Sanie, S., Black, R., Giudice, L. C., Gray Valbrun, T., Gupta, J., Jones, B., Laufer, M., Milspaw, A., Missmer, S., Norman, A., Taylor, R., Wallace, K., Williams, Z., Yong, P., & Nebel, R. A. (2019). Assessing research gaps and unmet needs in endometriosis. *American Journal of Obstetrics and Gynecology*, *221*(2), 86–94. doi:10.1016/j.ajog.2019.02.033

Ballard, K., Lane, H., Hudelist, G., Banerjee, S., & Wright, J. (2010). Can specific pain symptoms help in the diagnosis of endometriosis? A cohort study of women with chronic pelvic pain. *Fertility and Sterility*, *94*(1), 20–27. doi:10.1016/j.fertnstert.2009.01.164

Barlow, D. H., Farchione, T. J., Sauer-Zavala, S., Murray Latin, H., Ellard, K. K., Bullis, J. R., Bentley, K. H., Boettcher, H. T., & Cassiello-Robbins, C. (2017a). *Unified Protocol for Transdiagnostic Treatment of Emotional Disorders: Therapist guide* (2nd ed.). Oxford University Press.

Barlow, D. H., Farchione, T. J., Sauer-Zavala, S., Murray Latin, H., Ellard, K. K., Bullis, J. R., Bentley, K. H., Boettcher, H. T., & Cassiello-Robbins, C. (2017b). *Unified Protocol for Transdiagnostic Treatment of Emotional Disorders: Workbook* (2nd ed.). Oxford University Press.

Berkley, K. J., Rapkin, A. J., & Papka, R. E. (2005). The pains of endometriosis. *Science, 308*(5728), 1587–1589. doi:10.1126/science.1111445

Boersen, Z., de Kok, L., van der Zanden, M., Braat, D., Oosterman, J., & Nap, A. (2021). Patients' perspective on cognitive behavioural therapy after surgical treatment of endometriosis: A qualitative study. *Reproductive Biomedicine Online, 42*(4), 819–825. doi:10.1016/j.rbmo.2021.01.010

Brody, D. J., Pratt, L. A., & Hughes, J. P. (2018, February). Prevalence of depression among adults aged 20 and over: United States, 2013–2016. *NCHS Data Brief* (303), 1–8.

Campbell-Sills, L., Norman, S. B., Craske, M. G., Sullivan, G., Lang, A. J., Chavira, D. A., Bystritsky, A., Sherbourne, C., Byrne, P., & Stein, M. B. (2009). Validation of a brief measure of anxiety-related severity and impairment: the Overall Anxiety Severity and Impairment Scale (OASIS). *Journal of Affective Disorders, 112*(1–3), 92–101. doi:10.1016/j.jad.2008.03.014

Cassiello-Robbins, C., Sauer-Zavala, S., Brody, L. R., & Barlow, D. H. (2020). Exploring the effects of the mindfulness and countering emotional behaviors modules from the Unified Protocol on dysregulated anger in the context of emotional disorders. *Behavior Therapy, 51*(6), 933–945. doi:10.1016/j.beth.2019.12.007

Chen, L. C., Hsu, J. W., Huang, K. L., Bai, Y. M., Su, T. P., Li, C. T., Yang, A. C., Chang, W.-H., Chen, T. J., Tsai, S.-J., & Chen, M. H. (2016). Risk of developing major depression and anxiety disorders among women with endometriosis: A longitudinal follow-up study. *Journal of Affective Disorders, 190*, 282–285. doi:10.1016/j.jad.2015.10.030

Dunselman, G. A., Vermeulen, N., Becker, C., Calhaz-Jorge, C., D'Hooghe, T., De Bie, B., Heikinheimo, O., Horne, A., Kiesel, L., Nap, A., Prentice, A., Saridogan, E., & Nelen, W.; European Society of Human Reproduction and Embryology. (2014). ESHRE guideline: Management of women with endometriosis. *Human Reproduction, 29*(3), 400–412. doi:10.1093/humrep/det457

Ehde, D. M., Dillworth, T. M., & Turner, J. A. (2014). Cognitive–behavioral therapy for individuals with chronic pain: Efficacy, innovations, and directions for research. *The American Psychologist, 69*(2), 153–166. doi:10.1037/a0035747

Evans, S., Fernandez, S., Olive, L., Payne, L. A., & Mikocka-Walus, A. (2019). Psychological and mind–body interventions for endometriosis: A systematic review. *Journal of Psychosomatic Research, 124*, 109756. doi:10.1016/j.jpsychores.2019.109756

Fritzer, N., Haas, D., Oppelt, P., Renner, S., Hornung, D., Wölfler, M., Ulrich, U., Fischerlehner, G., Sillem, M., & Hudelist, G. (2013). More than just bad sex: Sexual dysfunction and distress in patients with endometriosis. *European Journal of Obstetrics, Gynecology, and Reproductive Biology, 169*(2), 392–396. doi:10.1016/j.ejogrb.2013.04.001

Fritzer, N., Tammaa, A., Haas, D., Oppelt, P., Renner, S., Hornung, D., Wolfler, M., Ulrich, U., & Hudelist, G. (2016). When sex is not on fire: A prospective multicentre study evaluating the short-term effects of radical resection of endometriosis on quality of sex life and dyspareunia. *European Journal of Obstetrics, Gynecology, and Reproductive Biology, 197*, 36–40. doi:10.1016/j.ejogrb.2015.11.007

Godin, S. K., Wagner, J., Huang, P., & Bree, D. (2021). The role of peripheral nerve signaling in endometriosis. *FASEB bioAdvances, 3*(10), 802–813. doi:10.1096/fba.2021-00063

Gruppo Italiano per lo Studio dell'Endometriosi. (2001). Relationship between stage, site and morphological characteristics of pelvic endometriosis and pain. *Human Reproduction, 16*(12), 2668–2671. doi:10.1093/humrep/16.12.2668

Guo, S. W., & Wang, Y. (2006). The prevalence of endometriosis in women with chronic pelvic pain. *Gynecologic and Obstetric Investigation, 62*(3), 121–130. doi:10.1159/000093019

Hansen, K. E., Kesmodel, U. S., Kold, M., & Forman, A. (2017). Long-term effects of mindfulness-based psychological intervention for coping with pain in endometriosis: A six-year follow-up on a pilot study. *Nordic Psychology, 69*(2), 100–109. doi:10.1080/19012276.2016.1181562

Jones, G., Jenkinson, C., & Kennedy, S. (2004). Evaluating the responsiveness of the Endometriosis Health Profile Questionnaire: The EHP-30. *Quality of Life Research, 13*(3), 705–713. doi:10.1023/B:QURE.0000021316.79349.af

Jones, G., Jenkinson, C., Taylor, N., Mills, A., & Kennedy, S. (2006). Measuring quality of life in women with endometriosis: Tests of data quality, score reliability, response rate and scaling assumptions of the Endometriosis Health Profile Questionnaire. *Human Reproduction, 21*(10), 2686–2693. doi:10.1093/humrep/del231

Jones, G., Kennedy, S., Barnard, A., Wong, J., & Jenkinson, C. (2001). Development of an endometriosis quality-of-life instrument: The Endometriosis Health Profile-30. *Obstetrics and Gynecology, 98*(2), 258–264. doi:10.1016/s0029-7844(01)01433-8

Katz, L., Fransson, A., & Patterson, L. (2021). The development and efficacy of an interdisciplinary chronic pelvic pain program. *Canadian Urological Association Journal, 15*(6), e323–e328. doi:10.5489/cuaj.6842

Kennedy, S. (1991). What is important to the patient with endometriosis? *British Journal of Clinical Practice Supplement, 72*, 8–10; discussion 11–13.

Khakpoor, S., Mohammadi Bytamar, J., & Saed, O. (2019). Reductions in transdiagnostic factors as the potential mechanisms of change in treatment outcomes in the Unified Protocol: A randomized clinical trial. *Research in Psychotherapy, 22*(3), 379. doi:10.4081/ripppo.2019.379

Kold, M., Hansen, T., Vedsted-Hansen, H., & Forman, A. (2012). Mindfulness-based psychological intervention for coping with pain in endometriosis. *Nordic Psychology, 64*, 2–16. doi:10.1080/19012276.2012.693727

Laganà, A. S., Condemi, I., Retto, G., Muscatello, M. R., Bruno, A., Zoccali, R. A., Triolo, O., & Cedro, C. (2015). Analysis of psychopathological comorbidity behind the common symptoms and signs of endometriosis. *European Journal of Obstetrics, Gynecology, and Reproductive Biology, 194*, 30–33. doi:10.1016/j.ejogrb.2015.08.015

Mikocka-Walus, A., Druitt, M., O'Shea, M., Skvarc, D., Watts, J. J., Esterman, A., Tsaltas, J., Knowles, S., Harris, J., Dowding, C., Parigi, E., & Evans, S. (2021). Yoga, cognitive–behavioural therapy versus education to improve quality of life and reduce healthcare costs in people with endometriosis: A randomised controlled trial. *BMJ Open, 11*(8), e046603. doi:10.1136/bmjopen-2020-046603

Mousavi, E., Hosseini, S., Bakhtiyari, M., Mohammadi, A., Isfeedvajani, M. S., Arani, A. M., & Sadaat, S. H. (2019). Comparing the effectiveness of the Unified Protocol transdiagnostic and mindfulness-based stress reduction program on anxiety and depression in infertile women receiving in vitro fertilisation. *Journal of Research in Medical and Dental Science, 7*(2), 44–51.

Mowers, E. L., Lim, C. S., Skinner, B., Mahnert, N., Kamdar, N., Morgan, D. M., & As-Sanie, S. (2016). Prevalence of endometriosis during abdominal or laparoscopic hysterectomy for chronic pelvic pain. *Obstetrics and Gynecology, 127*(6), 1045–1053. doi:10.1097/aog.0000000000001422

Norman, S. B., Cissell, S. H., Means-Christensen, A. J., & Stein, M. B. (2006). Development and validation of an Overall Anxiety Severity and Impairment Scale (OASIS). *Depression and Anxiety, 23*(4), 245–249. doi:10.1002/da.20182

Payne, L. A. (2017). The Unified Protocol for chronic pain. In D. H. Barlow & T. J. Farchione (Eds.), *Applications of the Unified Protocol for Transdiagnostic Treatment of Emotional Disorders* (pp. 215–230). Oxford University Press.

Stratton, P., & Berkley, K. J. (2011). Chronic pelvic pain and endometriosis: Translational evidence of the relationship and implications. *Human Reproduction Update, 17*(3), 327–346. doi:10.1093/humupd/dmq050

Till, S. R., As-Sanie, S., & Schrepf, A. (2019). Psychology of chronic pelvic pain: Prevalence, neurobiological vulnerabilities, and treatment. *Clinical Obstetrics and Gynecology, 62*(1), 22–36. doi:10.1097/grf.0000000000000412

Urits, I., Callan, J., Moore, W. C., Fuller, M. C., Renschler, J. S., Fisher, P., . . . Viswanath, O. (2020). Cognitive behavioral therapy for the treatment of chronic pelvic pain. *Best Practice & Research: Clinical Anaesthesiology, 34*(3), 409–426. doi:10.1016/j.bpa.2020.08.001

Van Niekerk, L., Weaver-Pirie, B., & Matthewson, M. (2019). Psychological interventions for endometriosis-related symptoms: A systematic review with narrative data synthesis. *Archives of Women's Mental Health, 22*(6), 723–735. doi:10.1007/s00737-019-00972-6

Warzecha, D., Szymusik, I., Wielgos, M., & Pietrzak, B. (2020). The impact of endometriosis on the quality of life and the incidence of depression: A cohort study. *International Journal of Environmental Research and Public Health, 17*(10), 3641. doi:10.3390/ijerph17103641

Williams, A. C. C., Fisher, E., Hearn, L., & Eccleston, C. (2020). Psychological therapies for the management of chronic pain (excluding headache) in adults. *Cochrane Database of Systematic Reviews, 8*(8), CD007407. doi:10.1002/14651858.CD007407.pub4

Wurm, M., Klein Strandberg, E., Lorenz, C., Tillfors, M., Buhrman, M., Holländare, F., & Boersma, K. (2017). Internet delivered transdiagnostic treatment with telephone support for pain patients with emotional comorbidity: A replicated single case study. *Internet Interventions, 10*, 54–64. doi:10.1016/j.invent.2017.10.004

10

Cognitive–Behavioral Treatment for Anxiety and Depression in Parkinson's Disease

Efficacy and Clinical Application of the Unified Protocol

GRETCHEN O. REYNOLDS,
RYAN PIERS, AND ALICE CRONIN-GOLOMB ■

PARKINSON'S DISEASE: CLINICAL CHARACTERISTICS

Parkinson's disease (PD) is second only to Alzheimer's disease as the most common of the neurodegenerative disorders, affecting 10 million people worldwide (Saeed et al., 2017), with typical onset between ages 65 and 70 (Tysnes & Storstein, 2017). PD prevalence increases with age, afflicting 1% of the population older than age 60 (Tysnes & Storstein, 2017). In 2010, 680,000 adults were estimated to have PD in the United States, with that number expected to rise to 1,238,000 by 2030 (Marras et al., 2018). PD is associated with significant disability as well as economic and social burden, and it is one of the fastest growing neurologic disorders, with the global number of individuals with PD doubling between 1990 and 2016 (Dorsey et al., 2018; Kowal et al., 2013).

PD has traditionally been considered a classic movement disorder, first described as the "shaking palsy" by James Parkinson in 1817 (Donaldson, 2015). Clinically, PD is diagnosed based on the presence of four cardinal motor signs—resting tremor, bradykinesia, rigidity, and postural instability/gait dysfunction—and it is associated with dopaminergic loss in the substantia nigra (Jankovic, 2008) and the presence of α-synuclein-containing Lewy neurites and/or Lewy bodies (Braak et al., 2004). PD is now believed to develop in six neuropathological

Gretchen O. Reynolds, Ryan Piers, and Alice Cronin-Golomb, *Cognitive–Behavioral Treatment for Anxiety and Depression in Parkinson's Disease* In: *Applications of the Unified Protocol in Health Conditions.* Edited by: Jorge Osma and Todd J. Farchione, Oxford University Press. © Oxford University Press 2023. DOI: 10.1093/oso/9780197564295.003.0010 stages, starting in the brainstem and olfactory bulb, before progressing through the midbrain and eventually compromising the cortex (Braak et al., 2002, 2004). In addition to the classic motor symptoms, a constellation of non-motor symptoms also emerge over the course of the disease with significant impact on quality of life and daily functioning (Cronin-Golomb, 2013). The range of non-motor symptoms in PD includes depression, anxiety, apathy, hallucinations, cognitive impairment, sleep disruption, and dysautonomia, many of which may be associated with compromise of non-dopaminergic systems in the early stages of the disease (Chaudhuri et al., 2006; Poewe, 2008). PD affects more men than women (Miller & Cronin-Golomb, 2010), and the disease typically progresses over the course of 7–14 years, with older age and dementia diagnosis associated with increased mortality (Macleod et al., 2014).

ANXIETY IN PARKINSON'S DISEASE

Anxiety affects up to 30–40% of individuals with PD, and it may manifest as generalized anxiety, social anxiety, phobias, panic disorder, and/or episodic anxiety in the context of PD motor fluctuations (Broen et al., 2016; Lutz et al., 2016; Pontone et al., 2009). Anxiety may occur years before the onset of motor symptoms and may be related to underlying dopaminergic, noradrenergic, and serotoninergic dysfunction (Prediger et al., 2012).

DEPRESSION IN PARKINSON'S DISEASE

Depression affects 40–50% of persons with PD (PwPD; Bonnet et al., 2012; Marsh, 2013; Reijnders et al., 2008) and is considered a core neuropsychiatric symptom. PD depression is associated with fatigue, sleep disturbance, physical and cognitive decline, falls, and maladjustment to disease progression, and it is a strong predictor of poor quality of life (Bryant et al., 2012; Fan et al., 2016; Schrag, 2006; Starkstein et al., 1992; Voss & Richard, 2011; Yamanishi et al., 2013). Depression often co-occurs with mild cognitive impairment (MCI) and dementia in PD, and depression is the most common neuropsychiatric symptom in PD with MCI (Monastero et al., 2013). Those with PD depression exhibit cognitive deficits in executive functioning and working memory, verbal fluency, abstract reasoning, and episodic and semantic memory (Costa et al., 2006; Fernandez et al., 2009; Klepac et al., 2010; Santangelo et al., 2009; Stefanova et al., 2006).

Depression, anxiety, and other non-motor symptoms associated with brainstem processes often precede the development of motor symptoms in PD, sometimes by up to 20 years (Jacob et al., 2010; Shiba et al., 2000), and constitute the PD prodrome (Mahlknecht et al., 2015). Apathy in PD, presumably arising from mesolimbic dopaminergic denervation (Pagonabarraga et al., 2015; Tremblay et al., 2015), may also be associated with higher depression scores, impaired cognition, more severe motor symptoms, greater disability, and reduced quality of life

(Barone et al., 2009; den Brok et al., 2015; Pedersen et al., 2009; Starkstein et al., 2009). Taken together, there is consensus that depression in PD is a downstream effect of PD neuropathology.

Acknowledging the pathological contributions to PD neuropsychiatric symptoms does not discount the psychosocial reactions and stress associated with the disease, such as social anxiety, sadness, or withdrawal in response to motor symptoms, which are potential targets for interventions.

PSYCHOSOCIAL FACTORS

Diagnosis of Parkinson's Disease

Receiving a diagnosis of PD is a life-changing event. Because PD is progressive and neurodegenerative, living with the condition is burdensome and demanding, both for PwPD and their care partners (Phillips, 2006). Physical and cognitive disability, and perception of disease progression, may limit PwPD's pursuit of long-term goals, a core component of identity formation and maintenance (Carver & Scheier, 2001). PD may create a large discrepancy between one's perceived "actual self" (one's current self-concept) and "ideal self" (one's aspirations), leading to a "despised self" (self-hatred) and the development of psychopathology such as depression (Horner & Paris, 1999). Furthermore, in response to stressful life events related to PD, individuals may ruminate on what they cannot control (e.g., the progression of the disease and the deterioration of their mobility, independence, and cognition). Indeed, chronic or uncontrollable stressors are particularly likely to lead to rumination (Watkins, 2008), and having a ruminative response style is linked to subsequent increases in depressive symptoms (Nolen-Hoeksema & Davis, 1999), increased risk for the development of depression (Abela & Hankin, 2011), and longer duration of depressive episodes (Robinson & Alloy, 2003). One longitudinal study found that rumination mediated the association between stressful life events and symptoms of depression (Michl et al., 2013), highlighting the importance of psychological interventions that target rumination for PwPD.

Disease-Specific Stigma

Individuals with PD commonly experience disease-specific stigma (Hermanns, 2013), which in turn adversely impacts quality of life and activities of daily living (Ma et al., 2016; Salazar et al., 2019). Facial masking, for example, is a motor consequence of PD that is associated with negative social perceptions by others (Tickle-Degnen et al., 2011). There appears to be a strong relation between self-perceived stigma and depression in PD. One study found that higher levels of depression predicted self-perceived stigma for both men and women with PD, and that depression mediated the relation between stigma perception and activities of daily living (Salazar et al., 2019). Individuals with stigma-related stressors experience more rumination (Hatzenbuehler et al., 2009), which, as noted above, increases risk for the development of depression (Abela & Hankin, 2011) and longer duration of depressive episodes (Robinson & Alloy, 2003).

EMOTIONAL AND COGNITIVE FACTORS

Emotion Representation Deficits

Emotion representation deficits are characteristic of PD (Enrici et al., 2015). One of the structures affected in PD is the prefrontal cortex (PFC), a region responsible for complex decision-making, planning, and inhibitory control (Kolb et al., 2012; Siddiqui et al., 2008). The medial orbitofrontal cortex, a subdivision of the PFC, is associated with theory of mind (ToM) or the capacity of an individual to understand that another's behavior is motivated by their own independent thoughts, feelings, emotions, desires, intentions, and beliefs (Spreng et al., 2008). Studies have found that PwPD exhibit deficits on ToM tasks, including ones in which participants are asked to identify false beliefs (Mengelberg & Siegert, 2003) and infer mental states from observed facial expressions (Suzuki et al., 2006; Yoshimura et al., 2005). ToM impairment increases risk of depression, decreases quality of life, and contributes to psychosocial impairment beyond that attributed to depression (Bodden et al., 2010; Bora et al., 2006; Fett et al., 2011; Irani et al., 2012).

Emotion Regulation Deficits

Individuals with PD also may experience emotion regulation difficulties (Enrici et al., 2015). Some PwPD exhibit increased difficulty controlling anger and feelings of disgust compared to healthy adults, and these deficits are associated with compromised daily life and social functioning (Ille et al., 2016). In non-PD studies, compared to persons without depression, those with depression more often exhibited maladaptive emotion regulation strategies, such as avoidance, rumination, and suppression, and less often exhibited adaptive emotion strategies, such as acceptance, problem-solving, and reappraisal (Visted et al., 2018). In PD and other populations, the association between depression and maladaptive emotion regulation is likely bidirectional. That is, depression could lead to poor emotion regulation, and poor emotion regulation could lead to depression, and it is likely that the two processes occur simultaneously.

Autobiographical Memory Deficits

Autobiographical memory deficits are observed in PD (Smith et al., 2010; Smith & Souchay, 2013) due, in part, to reductions in activity in frontostriatal neural circuitry (Lewis et al., 2003). Autobiographical memory comprises personally experienced past events and serves many important functions, including mood regulation, foresight, and the formation of individual identity (Cohen, 1996; van den Hoven & Eggen, 2008). Autobiographical memory deficits may lead to processing biases (e.g., overgeneralization and reduced salience of positive information) that contribute to the development and maintenance of depressive symptoms (Sumner et al., 2010). In turn, depressive disorders are associated with less specific and more overgeneralized autobiographical memories (Liu et al., 2013). Three mechanisms through which depressive disorders may impact autobiographical memory have been proposed: capture and rumination (intense and prolonged negative self-focus and sensitivity to negative emotion), functional avoidance (conceptualization of negative experiences as general events to avoid associated emotion), and impaired executive control (impaired recollection of events and inability to form appropriate hypotheses based on evidence) (Williams et al., 2007). Deficits in autobiographical memory occur in PD as a downstream effect of PD neuropathology and may contribute to depressive symptoms. Having comorbid depression may also exacerbate autobiographical memory deficits, leading to a harmful cycle.

CURRENT TREATMENT OF ANXIETY AND DEPRESSION IN PARKINSON'S DISEASE

Non-motor symptoms in PD, and anxiety and depression in particular, often have a greater impact on quality of life than the motor symptoms (Hanna & Cronin-Golomb, 2011; Quelhas & Costa, 2009; Schrag, 2006), yet they remain inadequately diagnosed and treated (Pontone et al., 2013; Prediger et al., 2012). Indeed, despite the high prevalence and negative impact of anxiety on quality of life in PD, there remains little evidence base to guide treatment (Djamshidian & Friedman, 2014). Polypharmacy is common to treat the multiple motor and non-motor symptoms of the PD (e.g., sleep disruption and autonomic dysfunction), often with side effects, and many PwPD prefer not to add antidepressants to other disease-specific medications (Mintzer & Burns, 2000; Qato et al., 2008). Furthermore, clinical trials of antidepressant medications reveal only marginal to modest clinical significance for the treatment of depression in the general population (Pigott et al., 2010) and in PD (Troeung et al., 2013), and to date, there have been no randomized controlled trials for the treatment of anxiety in PD (Seppi et al., 2019). Dopaminergic therapy, commonly used for the treatment of motor symptoms in PD, may alleviate anxiety in some PwPD, whereas others may respond to selective serotonin reuptake inhibitors (SSRIs), tricyclic antidepressants, monoamine oxidase inhibitors (MAOIs), or benzodiazepines. However, MAOIs and benzodiazepines, in particular, can be associated with serious side effects, including hypertensive crisis and psychomotor and cognitive symptoms (Khatri et al., 2020). In a meta-analysis of placebo-controlled trials for depression and/or anxiety in PD, antidepressants yielded a large, but nonsignificant, secondary effect on anxiety in PD (Troeung et al., 2013). It is also important to note that these pharmacologic treatments were not specifically designed for use in PD (Connolly & Fox, 2014), and many older adults may wish to avoid adding another medication to their regimen (Novaes et al., 2017).

Given the high prevalence and negative impact of depression and anxiety in PD, the mixed efficacy of antidepressants for these symptoms, and hesitancy of PwPD to take antidepressants, evidence-based psychological treatments may become the first-line treatment for depression and anxiety in PD. It is well established that cognitive–behavioral therapy (CBT) is an effective treatment for depression in older adults (Chand, 2013; Serfaty et al., 2009), with evidence of above-average effect sizes (Pinquart et al., 2007; Pinquart & Sorensen, 2001) and maintenance of treatment gains at follow-up (Jayasekara et al., 2015; Serfaty et al., 2009). This potential efficacy and lack of adverse side effects has led to studies examining the potential of nonpharmacologic interventions, including CBT and mindfulness-based therapies, for the treatment of anxiety and depression in PD (Dissanayaka et al., 2016; Yang et al., 2012). CBT has been shown to be an effective treatment for depression in PD, with positive effects maintained at follow-up (Dobkin et al., 2019; Dobkin, Menza, Allen, Gara, et al., 2011; Dobkin, Menza, Allen, Tiu, et al., 2011; Troeung et al., 2014). CBT has also been found to reduce anxiety in PD, across a variety of settings and treatment modalities (e.g., individual, group, in-person, phone/internet-delivered), although additional research trials are needed with adequate control groups and larger sample sizes (Kraepelien et al., 2015; Troeung et al., 2014; Veazey et al., 2009; Zhang et al., 2020).

THE UNIFIED PROTOCOL AS A TREATMENT FOR DEPRESSION AND ANXIETY IN PARKINSON'S DISEASE

Considering the heterogeneity of emotional symptoms in PD, high prevalence, and the frequent comorbidity among anxiety and depression (Goldman & Postuma, 2014; Schrag & Taddei, 2017), the transdiagnostic Unified Protocol (UP) is well-suited to simultaneously target a range of affective symptoms (Barlow et al., 2014) and perhaps also positively impact other non-motor symptoms, such as sleep and cognition, in PD. The UP consists of eight treatment modules: five core modules to target emotional processing (present-focused awareness, cognitive flexibility, emotional avoidance and emotion-driven behaviors, awareness and tolerance of physical sensations, and interoceptive and situational emotion exposures), along with modules on motivation, psychoeducation, and relapse prevention. There are many reasons why PwPD might find the UP particularly helpful for addressing emotional symptoms. The psychoeducation component provides individuals with information related to the etiology and maintenance of depressive and anxiety disorders, specifically the contribution of thoughts, physical sensations, and behaviors to emotional experience. To tailor this component for use in PD, clinicians may discuss the experience of sadness PwPD feel when confronted with physical limitations related to PD. PwPD may also find psychoeducation on the non-motor symptoms in PD validating and helpful for better understanding their emotions and patterns of emotional responding. By cultivating nonjudgmental, present-focused awareness, individuals may enhance emotion regulation and reduce frequency and intensity of rumination. Responding to executive deficits in flexibility and working memory often seen in PD (Kehagia et al., 2010), cognitive restructuring may increase flexibility in thinking about one's experience and target processing biases (e.g., overestimation of likelihood of negative outcomes and events, catastrophizing, and reduced salience of positive information) commonly experienced by PwPD and depression. Finally, through exposure therapy, the UP encourages individuals to "lean in" and "sit with" their unpleasant emotional experience to facilitate new learning. The process of expectancy violation teaches them that their most feared outcomes do not occur, subsequently decreasing experiential avoidance. Exposure therapy may also help PwPD cope with the feelings of uncertainty that pervade the experience of living with the disease (Bogosian et al., 2017) and increase discomfort tolerance, which is negatively related to depression (Harrington, 2006). The UP also offers the flexibility to tailor treatment to a range of presentations of anxiety in PD—such as excessive social anxiety related to motor symptoms, generalized worry about PD, health, or other topics, and/or physiological symptoms of anxiety—via nonjudgmental, present-focused awareness, cognitive restructuring, and interoceptive and emotion-based exposures. In summary, the components of the UP may help PwPD to manage mood and anxiety symptoms while also preparing them to navigate difficult challenges they may face in the future.

CASE EXAMPLE: UP FOR THE TREATMENT OF DEPRESSION IN PARKINSON'S DISEASE

B. is a 56-year-old non-Hispanic White cisgender woman who was diagnosed with PD approximately 7 years ago (at age 49). B. holds an associate's degree and for most of her life worked as a corporate event manager until she decided to retire prematurely due to her diagnosis of PD. Since her retirement, B. has worked as a homemaker, but she frequently misses her job as a corporate events manager and feels that she has trouble finding "purpose" at times, which negatively affects her mood. B. is happily married to her husband and has close loving relationships with her three adult children. She describes her husband and children as all very supportive of her and her journey with PD. B. also has several good friends and enjoys golfing with them and her husband during the summer. B. was recently diagnosed with major depressive disorder, moderate severity, based on criteria in the fifth edition of the *Diagnostic and Statistical Manual of Mental Disorders* (DSM-5; American Psychiatric Association, 2013). Specifically, B. endorsed five clinically significant symptoms of depression over the prior 2-week period: depressed mood, significant weight gain, increased need for sleep, fatigue/loss of energy, and difficulty making decisions/impaired concentration.

B. did not meet criteria for any additional diagnoses. Since her diagnosis of PD, B. has struggled with "separating myself from PD" (i.e., she has difficulty thinking of herself as "just B.," as opposed to "B. with PD"). The motor symptoms of PD, particularly tremor, serve as "constant reminders" of her diagnosis, and B. finds these symptoms severely distressing. B. takes PD medication daily to manage the motor symptoms; however, significant tremor (particularly in her right arm) is apparent when medication effects wear off. B. often feels "self-conscious and ashamed" when she displays motor symptoms in public, particularly during social interactions and around others she does not know well, and chooses to hide her symptoms as best she can in these circumstances or leaves or avoids the situation entirely. B. believes that she must hide her motor symptoms from others because she does not want to be "perceived as weak" or "make people uncomfortable or sad for me." A recent example of this is her decision to not attend a hike with her husband and their friends due to fear that she would experience motor dysfunction. Since her diagnosis, whenever B. experiences a positive event in her life, it is frequently met by the thought "but I have PD," which significantly interferes with her ability to remain in the present moment and experience the full extent of positive emotions. Furthermore, when confronted with difficult emotions (e.g., sadness, anger, and fear), B. frequently engages in avoidance coping and distraction (e.g., by watching TV). B. also struggles with "overwhelming fatigue," a symptom that she and her neurologist believe is due to PD, which "feels different than other types of fatigue" and "like I'm 500 pounds." This fatigue, which she experiences approximately one or two times per week, causes B. significant impairment and distress, as she spends most of her day in bed and very few items on her daily "to-do list" get accomplished. When experiencing "overwhelming fatigue," B. often becomes self-critical (e.g., she repeatedly says to herself "I'm useless"). B. also frequently experiences difficulty falling asleep due to worry about her future with PD (e.g., "My family is going to have to take care of me and I'm going to be an overwhelming burden to them"). Moreover, B. experiences poor sleep quality, a common symptom of PD, which causes her to feel exhausted in the morning and very fatigued throughout the day regardless of how many hours she slept the night before (see the complete case formulation in Table 10.1).

CASE EXAMPLE: UP FOR THE TREATMENT OF ANXIETY IN PARKINSON'S DISEASE

Mr. X is a 79-year-old, Caucasian man with 18 years of education and an 8-year history of PD. During the intake, he reported symptoms of social anxiety and limited-symptom panic attacks, and he expressed interest in improving his "resistance to anxiety." He first experienced rapid breathing attacks approximately 6 or 7 years prior, initially triggered by an increase in his dose of parkinsonian medication (carbidopa/levodopa). The dosage was then reduced, but rapid breathing attacks persisted, albeit at a slightly lower severity. Within the past year, he had started to identify these attacks as manifestations of anxiety, characterized by a

Table 10.1 Case Formulation: UP for the Treatment of Depression in Parkinson's Disease

HEALTH CONDITION ANALYSIS					
Health condition description: Parkinson's disease					
How does a health condition (and its treatment) affect the patient's life?			**EMOTION ANALYSIS REGARDING HEALTH CONDITIONS AND ITS CONSEQUENCES**		
General life aspects	**Affectation/ interference** **0______10** **Nothing Very much**	**Strong uncomfortable emotions.** Do patients feel strong emotions in any of these general life aspects?	**Intensity** **0______10** **Nothing Extreme**	**Aversive reactions**	**Emotional behaviors** (Situational avoidance/escape, subtle behavioral avoidance, cognitive avoidance, safety signals)
Physical and basic necessities **Physical symptoms**: Motor symptoms (e.g., tremor). Finds these symptoms severely distressing and often feels "self-conscious and ashamed" when she displays motor symptoms in public, particularly during social interactions and in the company of others she does not know well.	9	Anxiety, depression, fear, shame	9	Thinks that others will perceive her as weak or be uncomfortable or sad for her	Hides symptoms, avoids or leaves social interactions
Sleep: Problems with falling sleep due to worry about future with PD. *Note*: Also experiences poor sleep quality, a common symptom of PD, which causes her to feel exhausted in the morning and very fatigued throughout the day regardless of how many hours she slept the night before.	8	Anxiety, depression	5	Unhelpful worry, rumination	Cognitive avoidance and distraction (e.g., watching TV)
Energy: Very frequently fatigued, which limits activity level. Experiences "overwhelming fatigue" 1–2 times per week, which is incapacitating.	9	Depression, anxiety, anger	8	Becomes self-critical because of inability to be productive	Stays in bed for most of the day

(*continued*)

Table 10.1 Continued

HEALTH CONDITION ANALYSIS					
Health condition description: Parkinson's disease					
How does a health condition (and its treatment) affect the patient's life?			**EMOTION ANALYSIS REGARDING HEALTH CONDITIONS AND ITS CONSEQUENCES**		
General life aspects	**Affectation/ interference** **0______10** **Nothing Very much**	**Strong uncomfortable emotions.** Do patients feel strong emotions in any of these general life aspects?	**Intensity** **0______10** **Nothing Extreme**	**Aversive reactions**	**Emotional behaviors** (Situational avoidance/escape, subtle behavioral avoidance, cognitive avoidance, safety signals)
Work/studies: Retired early because of diagnosis of PD.	5	Depression, sadness	8	Misses working and often feels sadness because she is not working	Cognitive avoidance and distraction (e.g., watching TV)
Daily life activities (to buy, to cook, to clean, etc.): Unable to find motivation to do daily life activities and items on her "to-do list" at times, and feels completely unable to perform these activities when experiencing "overwhelming fatigue."	9	Depression, anxiety, anger	8	Becomes self-critical because of inability to be productive	Stays in bed for most of the day
Pleasant activities (hobbies, sport, etc.): Sometimes avoids pleasant activities (e.g., hike with her husband and their friends) due to fear of experiencing motor dysfunction.	5	Anxiety, depression	4	Decides pleasant activity not worth risk	Does not attend pleasant activity she enjoys

Personal relationships (couple, family, friends, etc.): Chooses not to attend social interactions at times when PD medications are wearing off. Often feels "self-conscious and ashamed" when she displays motor symptoms in public, particularly in the company of others she does not know well, and chooses to hide her symptoms as best she can in these circumstances or leaves or avoids the setting entirely.	9	Anxiety, depression, fear, shame	9	Thinks that others will perceive her as weak or be uncomfortable or sad for her	Hides symptoms, avoids or leaves social interactions
Spirituality: No impact. Catholic, but does not practice.	N/A	N/A	N/A	N/A	N/A
Life goals: Career goals and trajectory halted because of early retirement. Frequently misses working and feels that she has trouble finding "purpose" at times, which negatively affects her mood.	6	Depression, sadness	5	Unhelpful rumination affects mood and limits daily function	Cognitive avoidance and distraction (e.g., watching TV)
TREATMENT PLAN					
MODULE 1					
Goal-Setting and Motivation Therapist will work with patient to identify problem areas and treatment goals. They will discuss how diagnosis of PD and associated challenges (e.g., difficulty falling asleep at night due to worry about future with PD) have interfered with patient's life and caused distress. Treatment goals will focus on learning strategies to manage worry, helping facilitate acceptance of "this disease they didn't ask for," and helping the patient reengage in behaviors that patient has avoided due to fear of experiencing motor symptoms of PD (e.g., during social interactions, during pleasant activities). Therapist and patient will collaboratively complete decisional balance exercise exploring the costs and benefits of changing/staying the same.					

(continued)

Table 10.1 CONTINUED

MODULE 2		
Emotion Psychoeducation Therapist will provide psychoeducation regarding the functional nature of emotions and introduce the three-component model. Throughout the session, therapist will look for opportunities to validate and normalize the difficult emotional experience related to having PD (e.g., sadness, anger, anxiety, fear). Therapist will ask patient to give examples of how strong uncomfortable emotions are interfering with her life. Using the ARC model, therapist will emphasize the importance of evaluating the short- and long-term consequences of current thoughts/physical sensations/behavioral responses as a way to promote future adaptive responses and a functional coexistence with PD.		
MODULE 3		
Mindful Emotion Awareness Patient will learn the importance of taking a nonjudgmental, present-focused approach to thoughts, feelings, and behavioral urges during difficult emotional experiences (e.g., when experiencing motor symptoms of PD). Patient will be instructed to approach and acknowledge motor symptoms of PD without judging them in order to develop her emotion regulation ability and acceptance. Patient will also practice recognizing when she is experiencing unhelpful worry about her future with PD. Patient will use the mindful emotion awareness meditation as a proactive and reactive coping strategy (e.g., every night before bed, in response to worry about future with PD) and the anchoring in the present skill to redirect her attention to the present moment.		
MODULE 4		
Cognitive Flexibility Patient will learn to identify negative unhelpful thoughts related to PD. Patient will practice using cognitive flexibility to challenge negative unhelpful thoughts by thinking of other interpretations.		
Situation/Trigger	**Automatic Thought(s)**	**Other Interpretations(s)**
Experience motor symptoms (e.g., tremor in right arm)	"If others see my motor symptoms I'll be perceived as weak."	"Most of the time I feel people treat me the same when they see my motor symptoms. It is unlikely that others perceive me as weak. It is more likely that they perceive me as strong for living for PD."
Experience motor symptoms (e.g., tremor in right arm)	"If others see my motor symptoms, they'll be uncomfortable or sad for me."	"Most of the time people seem comfortable when they see my motor symptoms. I have no evidence that people are sad for me. When people ask about my motor symptoms, it is usually coming from a place of curiosity and not judgment."

"Overwhelming fatigue"	"I'm useless."	"I have accomplished much in my life. The fatigue is related to having PD and means nothing about me as a person. I have goals for the future. I am a good mother, friend, and partner to my husband."
In bed at night before falling asleep	"My family is going to have to take care of me and I'm going to be an overwhelming burden to them."	"My family may need to take care of me. It may be difficult for them, but I know they will always love me and be willing to do whatever they can."
Patient and therapist will discuss how patient will cope if the worst-possible scenarios do come true.		
MODULE 5		
Countering Emotional Behaviors Patient will learn to identify emotional behaviors that provide relief in the short term but are unhelpful in the long term. Patient will practice countering emotional behaviors with helpful alternative action and evaluate the short- and long-term consequences of engaging in this alternative action.		

Emotional Behavior	Alternative Action
Avoidance of pleasant activities due to fear of motor dysfunction	Attend pleasant activities despite fear of motor dysfunction
Watching TV to distract from negative emotions	Approach, rather than avoid, negative emotion
Staying in bed for most of the day	Get out of bed and make best effort at being productive

MODULE 6
Understanding and Confronting Physical Sensations Therapist will help patient identify physical sensations associated with strong uncomfortable emotions (e.g., heaviness, racing heart, chest pressure, pit in stomach, muscle tension). Therapist will describe and demonstrate interoceptive exposures and have patient practice inducing physical sensations. Therapist will only have patient practice interoceptive exposures that are appropriate and safe given extent of patient's motor disability due to PD. Therapist will utilize alternative interoceptive exposure exercises if deemed appropriate and safe (e.g., spinning in chair instead of spinning in circles). Patient will practice interoceptive exposure exercises between sessions.

(*continued*)

Table 10.1 CONTINUED

MODULE 7
Emotion Exposures Emotion exposures will focus on approaching situations that patient believes will bring on strong uncomfortable emotions due to having PD (e.g., not leaving or avoiding social interactions if exhibiting motor symptoms; not trying to hide motor symptoms during social interactions; not avoiding pleasant activities, e.g., hike with her husband and their friends, due to fear of experiencing motor dysfunction). Patient will conduct emotion exposures within sessions and between sessions and discuss substance use disorders, expectancy violations, and what she learned from the exposures with therapist.
MODULE 8
Relapse Prevention Therapist will summarize UP modules/skills and patient progress made through treatment. Patient and therapist will collaboratively create practice plan to continue skill work in future. Patient and therapist will discuss anticipated challenges of patient continuing skill work and problem-solve if possible.
OTHER MODULES IF NECESSARY

sudden rush of panic with shortness of breath or "rapid breathing," trembling or shaking, and fear of losing control. These attacks initially occurred out of the blue but now also occurred after sitting for a long time and in situations that required focus, such as being alone and having to complete an effortful task (e.g., dressing and walking). He reported having up to 30 of these limited-symptom attacks within the past month, unrelated to PD medication use. As a result, he was frequently avoiding social/public situations (e.g., community chorus and restaurants) and endorsed high distress about these symptoms.

Regarding social anxiety, he endorsed fear and avoidance of social situations within the past 2 years, correlating with progression of PD symptoms. He expressed the most fear and avoidance of eating in public, initiating/maintaining a conversation, and attending parties, and he believed he had become more of a "hermit." He worried that he would not be able to respond or perform quickly enough, in part due to PD symptoms, and that he will appear "different from everyone else," which may trigger feelings of panic/anxiety. He also reported concern that social interactions could be "very unsatisfying for both people" if he is unable to respond adequately. He had previously seen a psychiatrist and neurologist, and he had tried several different medications for anxiety symptoms without benefit, including imipramine (for several months), Ativan, as well as citalopram, which he discontinued after 18 days due to significant side effects. He was not currently taking any psychotropic medications, and he had been on his current medication regimen for PD and other medical conditions for the past 2 years. He did not report any recent experience with CBT, defined as eight sessions within the past 5 years.

He completed 12 weeks of treatment (~50- to 60-minute sessions) and received all eight of the UP modules. Few modifications were made to the treatment, although psychoeducation about anxiety within the context of PD was incorporated as needed. Regarding specific strategies, he reported that the anchoring in the present technique helped to alleviate feelings of panic. Cognitively, he endorsed concern about being "less fun and less self-sufficient" in social situations and worry that he will not be able to respond quickly enough or handle questions in the context of PD symptoms (e.g., hyperactive salivary gland) and anxiety; we challenged these thoughts by de-catastrophizing (e.g., "Even if I have to slow down and clear my throat, I will be able to engage in conversation or return to it later") and generating more flexible, realistic appraisals (e.g., "I don't know how others are experiencing the social interaction, and they may be understanding and supportive of my taking the time to engage in meaningful conversation"), in order to interrupt panic or anxiety symptoms. For interoceptive- and emotion-based exposures, we first practiced rapid, deep breathing and straw breathing; he then chose a complex topic to present in session, while the therapist presented opposing arguments and required him to persuade her otherwise as part of Module 7 (exposures). We also completed an in-session conversation exposure, in which he spoke with a person he had never met (one of the therapist's colleagues).

Treatment was completed as part of a research study (Reynolds et al., 2020), which included weekly tracking of anxiety and depressive symptoms during

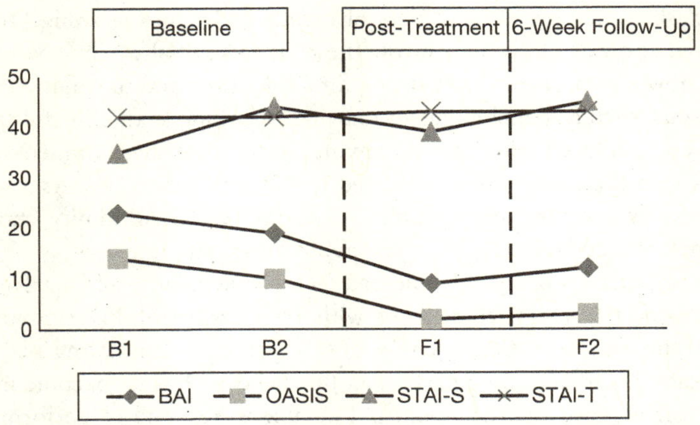

Figure 10.1 Anxiety scores reported by Mr. X during baseline (2 weeks [B1–B2]) and post-treatment (immediate and 6-week follow-up [F1–F2]). BAI, Beck Anxiety Inventory; OASIS, Overall Anxiety Severity and Impairment Scale; STAI-S, State–Trait Anxiety Inventory–State; STAI-T, State–Trait Anxiety Inventory–Trait. Adapted from Reynolds et al. (2020).

baseline and treatment phases, using the Beck Anxiety Inventory (BAI; Beck & Steer, 1993), the Overall Anxiety Severity and Impairment Scale (OASIS; Norman et al., 2006), and the State–Trait Anxiety Inventory (STAI; Spielberger et al., 1983) for tracking of anxiety symptoms (Figure 10.1), as well as the Geriatric Depression Scale (GDS; Yesavage et al., 1982), the Overall Depression Severity and Impairment Scale (ODSIS; Bentley et al., 2014), and the Beck Depression Inventory–II (BDI-II; Beck et al., 1996) for tracking of depressive symptoms (described in text below). Mr. X reported stable anxiety symptoms during the baseline phase across all measures. Upon introduction of the intervention, his BAI and OASIS scores trended downward until a spike in symptoms during the middle of treatment, which coincided with several missed sessions due to winter weather and a slight adjustment in his parkinsonian medications (increased dose of carbidopa/levodopa) to address motor symptoms. Upon resuming regular weekly sessions (weeks 7–11), his anxiety symptoms decreased, until a slight increase on the BAI during the end of treatment, which coincided with the most difficult exposures, as well as a bout of bronchitis in the 2 weeks preceding session 12. In comparison to the baseline phase, changes in the level of both the BAI and OASIS during the treatment phase indicated a positive effect of the intervention, which was significant at post-treatment, with the low OASIS score also maintained at 6-week follow-up. No significant changes were observed at post-treatment or follow-up on the STAI, perhaps due to floor effects, because most of his scores fell below the suggested cut score for older adults of 54 or 55 (Kvaal et al., 2005); the trait scale of the STAI is also less responsive to change than the state scale (Julian, 2011).

At post-treatment, Mr. X reported improved symptoms of other specified anxiety disorder (limited-symptom panic attacks) and social anxiety disorder on the diagnostic interview, and he no longer met criteria for either diagnosis at post-treatment or follow-up. He reported having experienced 10 limited-symptom panic attacks in the last month (vs. 30 at intake) and believed that he was better able to tolerate symptoms when they occurred with significantly reduced interference and distress. He also reported that the rapid breathing episodes were less intense with a slower pace to his breathing. Regarding social anxiety, he reported only mild anxiety related to certain social settings (e.g., slight concern of maintaining conversation, asking others to change behavior, and being slow in public restrooms) with minimal avoidance/interference and distress. The interview results were consistent with his self-report on measures of panic disorder and social anxiety, with significant post-treatment decreases on the Panic Disorder Severity Scale (Shear et al., 2001) and Anxiety Sensitivity Index (Reiss et al., 1986), which persisted at follow-up. He reported nonsignificant improvements at post-treatment on the Social Interaction Anxiety Scale (Mattick & Clarke, 1998) and Social Phobia Inventory (Connor et al., 2000), perhaps due to floor effects.

Mr. X did not meet criteria for a depressive disorder at the intake, and his depression scores on two self-report measures (BDI-II and ODSIS) dropped during the baseline phase, thereby limiting interpretation of these measures at post-treatment and follow-up. However, on the remaining measure of depression, which is designed for use in older adults (GDS), he showed no significant changes during baseline but improvements at post-treatment and follow-up, suggesting some positive effect of the intervention on mild, subclinical symptoms of depression. At post-treatment and follow-up, he also demonstrated significant improvements on secondary outcomes of apathy, quality of life, fear of falling, and sleep. There were no significant treatment effects on motor symptoms or cognition in preliminary analyses. He reported extreme acceptability and satisfaction with the intervention, reporting maximum satisfaction on the Client Satisfaction Questionnaire (Larsen et al., 1979), and believed that the intervention helped him "recalibrate" his emotions and reduce the intensity of anxiety/panic breathing episodes, initially triggered by PD medication adjustments. He reported using cognitive strategies to "adjust my emotional response to more sensibly respond to what is happening in the moment and not . . . be a victim of runaway emotions that are logically inappropriate for what is taking place." He found the interoceptive and emotional exposures most helpful, and he made one suggestion that participants be provided with a hard copy of the workbook or organized binder of handout materials in the future (rather than printed copies of handouts each week).

FEASIBILITY AND CLINICAL UTILITY OF THE UP FOR TREATMENT OF ANXIETY AND DEPRESSION IN PARKINSON'S DISEASE

We evaluated the feasibility and clinical utility of the UP for the treatment of anxiety in PD using a single-case, multiple-baseline experimental design (Reynolds et al., 2020). Participants were nine individuals with mild to moderate idiopathic PD who met diagnostic criteria for an anxiety disorder as defined in the DSM-5 (American Psychiatric Association, 2013): mean age = 61 years (range: 33–79);

mean education = 17 years (range: 14–20); five women, four men; all Caucasian, non-Hispanic; and mean PD duration = 6.6 years (range: 1.6–15.4). Participants presented with a range of anxiety diagnoses at baseline, including generalized anxiety disorder, panic disorder, social anxiety, and agoraphobia; two also met criteria for comorbid dysthymia or major depressive disorder. Participants were required to be stable on psychotropic medications for at least 6 weeks prior to the intake and throughout the study. Relevant exclusion criteria included the presence of another chronic medical, psychiatric, or neurologic illness; current substance use; dementia; average "off" time >50% of the day (periods when PD medication wears off, resulting in worsening symptoms); recent CBT experience; or concurrent psychosocial treatment. After completion of the baseline phase (2, 4, or 6 weeks), treatment consisted of 12 weekly sessions (~50–60 minutes each) of CBT, following the standard UP protocol, followed by a post-treatment assessment and 6-week follow-up. There was also the option for a 20- to 30-minute meeting with a study partner at the halfway point of treatment to review relevant concepts and facilitate homework practice (completed by seven of nine participants). Of note, the protocol was amended halfway through the study to allow for telehealth therapy sessions to reduce participant burden and boost recruitment. Of the nine participants, five completed therapy sessions in person and four completed them remotely via secure videoconferencing.

Primary outcome measures included weekly self-report ratings of anxiety and depression during the baseline and intervention phases (BAI, BDI-II, OASIS, ODSIS, STAI, and GDS). Based on visual inspection and reliable change indices, seven of the nine participants reported significantly reduced anxiety and/or depression at post-treatment, with most reductions maintained at 6-week follow-up. Occasional spikes in anxiety scores were related to specific treatment components (e.g., implementation of exposures) or external factors, such as psychosocial stressors, illness, or missed treatment sessions. Treatment effects on secondary outcome measures (e.g., apathy, quality of life, motor symptoms, sleep, and cognition) were highly variable across participants. There was preliminary evidence of reduced fear of falling, but minimal and/or inconsistent effects on quality of life, motor symptoms, freezing of gait, apathy, sleep, pain, and cognition. The treatment was feasible with high adherence and retention, and participants reported high levels of treatment satisfaction and acceptability. In addition, the four telehealth participants generally reported that the treatment seemed natural and allowed them to be absorbed in sessions as they occurred.

In summary, this exploratory study was the first to evaluate the utility and feasibility of the UP for the treatment of anxiety in PD. Results indicated that the UP, delivered in 12 individual sessions (either in person or via secure videoconferencing), significantly reduced anxiety and/or comorbid depressive symptoms among adults with mild to moderate PD at post-treatment and/or 6-week follow-up, regardless of treatment modality.

A clinical trial is currently being conducted by our group evaluating the feasibility, acceptability, and preliminary efficacy of the UP delivered via telehealth for treatment of depression in PD (Piers et al., 2022). The case formulation in this chapter describes the 12-week treatment with one study participant, B., with PD and major depressive disorder. Following treatment with the UP, B. completed a post-treatment assessment 1 week after finishing treatment and a follow-up assessment 6 weeks after the post-treatment assessment (Figure 10.2). At post-treatment and 6-week follow-up, B. no longer met criteria for major depressive disorder by DSM-5 criteria and reported significantly fewer symptoms of depression (as measured by the BDI-II; Beck et al., 1996). B.'s scores at post-treatment and 6-week follow-up also indicated (a) a reduction in beliefs about the unacceptability of experiencing or expressing negative emotions (as measured by the Beliefs About Emotions Scale; Rimes & Chalder, 2010), (b) an increase in use of cognitive reappraisal and reduction in use of expressive suppression to regulate emotions (as measured by the Emotion Regulation Questionnaire; Gross & John, 2003), and (c) a reduction in experiential avoidance (as measured by the Brief Experiential Avoidance Questionnaire; Gámez et al., 2014). B's scores on these three measures may explain, at least in part, her improvement after treatment with the UP.

Of note, baseline, post-treatment, and 6-week follow-up data were collected during the COVID-19 pandemic, which negatively impacted sleep and associated motor and non-motor symptoms, as well as quality of life, among many PwPD (Kumar et al., 2020). When asked about the degree to which she had been affected by COVID-19, B. reported "moderate impact" (at baseline), "moderate-to-severe

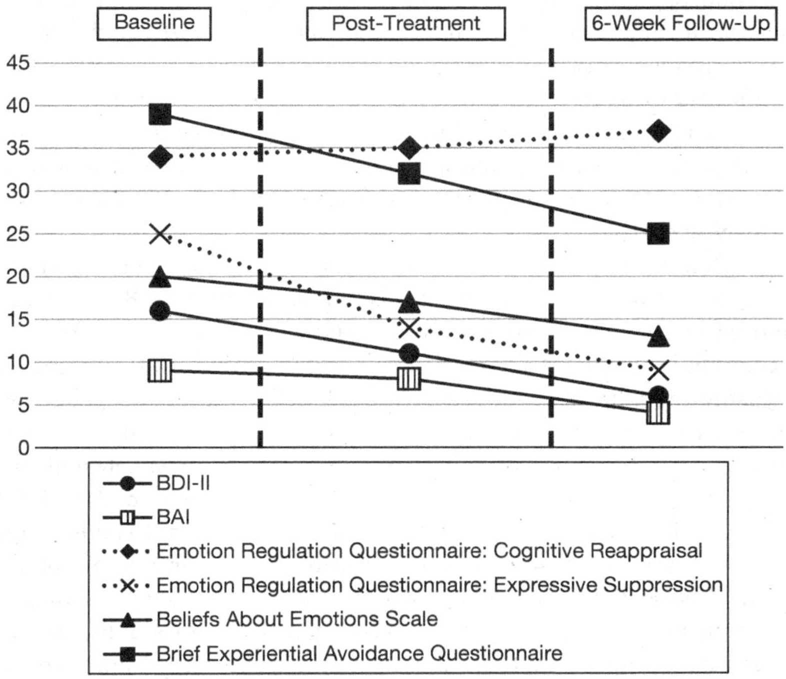

Figure 10.2 Scores reported by Mr. X. during baseline, post-treatment, and 6-week follow-up assessments.

impact" (at post-treatment), and "mild impact" (at 6-week follow-up) on a single-item questionnaire created to assess the personal impact of COVID-19. Despite the degree to which COVID-19 was impacting B.'s life at post-treatment and 6-week follow-up, depression treatment was successful and gains were maintained at 6-week follow-up, providing further evidence of the UP's efficacy for treatment of depression in PD. For more information about this clinical trial, see our published case study (Piers et al., 2022).

CONCLUSION

The previously discussed findings provide promising preliminary evidence of the feasibility and clinical utility of the UP for treatment of anxiety and depression in PD and also highlight the potential of telehealth in this population. Limitations include reduced generalizability because the nine-person sample consisted of highly educated, Caucasian individuals in the mild to moderate stages of PD (Reynolds et al., 2020). Future research should aim to replicate these findings in larger, randomized trials and also enroll a more diverse sample with regard to race, ethnicity, education level, and socioeconomic status. Systematic examination of the potential effects of the UP on secondary outcomes in PD, including cognition, sleep, fear of falling, and motor function, as they relate to emotional symptoms, would also be valuable. Continued development of telehealth delivery of CBT is also warranted, given promising preliminary findings in PD (Dobkin et al., 2011; Piers et al., 2022; Reynolds et al., 2020) and high interest in telehealth approaches to mental health treatment among PwPD (Dobkin et al., 2013). Telehealth may expand access to psychological treatment among PwPD, particularly for those who may experience motor disability, reliance on others for transportation, lack of local resources, care partner burden, and/or perceived stigma, all of which may act as barriers to attending in-person sessions (Dobkin et al., 2013; Koychev et al., 2017; Maffoni et al., 2017; Salazar et al., 2019).

Future clinical treatment and research should also consider the potential impact of apathy on treatment outcomes. Apathy is common in PD (den Brok et al., 2015), and indeed, one of the nonresponders in our study (Reynolds et al., 2020) presented with comorbid generalized anxiety disorder and dysthymia and endorsed significant apathy and difficulty with motivation at baseline. At follow-up, he reported that he was trying to keep up with CBT strategies and acknowledged the need to practice the strategies more often, but he continued to procrastinate and struggle with apathy and amotivation. In this context, future adaptations of the UP for tailored use in PD may include (a) optional modules or content to address apathy; (b) increased care partner involvement if available, particularly for out-of-session practice; (c) presentation of treatment handouts in a more organized, streamlined format, perhaps including weekly bullet points of major themes/skills, particularly for those with cognitive symptoms; and (d) systematic tracking of homework completion, perhaps in collaboration with the PwPD and care partner.

Regarding other PD-specific adaptations when using the UP, clinicians must determine the extent of the person's motor dysfunction prior to beginning interoceptive exposure and not ask them to engage in exercises that may put their safety at risk. For example, "spinning in circles" may be inappropriate because PwPD are prone to falls (Allen et al., 2013). Clinicians may elect to use alternative interoceptive exposure exercises if they are deemed appropriate and safe (e.g., spin in a chair that swivels to induce the same physiological effect), but they should always exercise extreme caution when planning interoceptive exposure exercises. Some PwPD may be unable to write neatly or efficiently because of their motor disability. If this is the case, clinicians should offer to document their responses on worksheets during session and, with their consent, ask a spouse, care partner, or family member if they would be willing to assist the PwPD with documentation between sessions. If the PwPD lives alone or an assistant is unavailable, documentation via audio or video recorder may be an alternative solution.

Taken together, the UP is feasible for use in PD, with promising evidence of clinical efficacy for the treatment of anxiety and depression. It has the potential for both in-person and telehealth delivery, providing PwPD with foundational coping skills to best manage emotional and behavioral challenges throughout the disease course and optimize quality of life.

REFERENCES

Abela, J., & Hankin, B. (2011). Rumination as a vulnerability factor to depression during the transition from early to middle adolescence: A multiwave longitudinal study. *Journal of Abnormal Psychology, 120*, 259–271.

Allen, N. E., Schwarzel, A. K., & Canning, C. G. (2013). Recurrent falls in Parkinson's disease: A systematic review. *Parkinson's Disease, 2013*, 906274. doi:10.1155/2013/906274

American Psychiatric Association. (2013). *Diagnostic and statistical manual of mental disorders* (5th ed.). American Psychiatric Publishing. https://doi.org/10.1176/appi.books.9780890425596

Barlow, D., Sauer-Zavala, S., Carl, J., Bullis, J., & Ellard, K. (2014). The nature, diagnosis, and treatment of neuroticism: Back to the future. *Clinical Psychological Science, 2*, 344–365.

Barone, P., Antonini, A., Colosimo, C., Marconi, R., Morgante, L., Avarello, T. P., Bottacchi, E., Cannas, A., Ceravolo, G., Ceravolo, R., Cicarelli, G., Gaglio, R. M., Giglia, R. M., Iemolo, F., Manfredi, M., Meco, G., Nicoletti, A., Pederzoli, M., Petrone, A., . . . Dotto, P. D. (2009). The PRIAMO study: A multicenter assessment of nonmotor symptoms and their impact on quality of life in Parkinson's disease. *Movement Disorders, 24*(11), 1641–1649. https://doi.org/10.1002/mds.22643

Beck, A., & Steer, R. (1993). *Beck Anxiety Inventory manual*. Psychological Corporation.

Beck, A., Steer, R., & Brown, G. (1996). *Manual for the Beck Depression Inventory–II*. Psychological Corporation.

Bentley, K. H., Gallagher, M. W., Carl, J. R., & Barlow, D. H. (2014). Development and validation of the Overall Depression Severity and Impairment Scale. *Psychological Assessment, 26*(3), 815–830. https://doi.org/10.1037/a0036216

Bodden, M. E., Mollenhauer, B., Trenkwalder, C., Cabanel, N., Eggert, K. M., Unger, M. M., Oertel, W. H., Kessler, J., Dodel, R., & Kalbe, E. (2010). Affective and cognitive theory of mind in patients with Parkinson's disease. *Parkinsonism & Related Disorders, 16*(7), 466–470. https://doi.org/10.1016/j.parkreldis.2010.04.014

Bogosian, A., Hurt, C., Vasconcelos, E. S. D., Hindle, J., McCracken, L., & Cubi-Molla, P. (2017). Distant delivery of a mindfulness-based intervention for people with Parkinson's disease: The study protocol of a randomised pilot trial. *Pilot and Feasibility Studies, 3*(4). https://pilotfeasibilitystudies.biomedcentral.com/articles/10.1186/s40814-016-0117-4

Bonnet, A. M., Jutras, M. F., Czernecki, V., Corvol, J. C., & Vidailhet, M. (2012). Nonmotor symptoms in Parkinson's disease in 2012: Relevant clinical aspects. *Parkinson's Disease, 2012*, 198316. https://doi.org/10.1155/2012/198316

Bora, E., Eryavuz, A., Kayahan, B., Sungu, G., & Veznedaroglu, B. (2006). Social functioning, theory of mind and neurocognition in outpatients with schizophrenia; Mental state decoding may be a better predictor of social functioning than mental state reasoning. *Psychiatry Research, 145*(2), 95–103. https://doi.org/10.1016/j.psychres.2005.11.003

Braak, H., Del Tredici, K., Bratzke, H., Hamm-Clement, J., Sandmann-Keil, D., & Rüb, U. (2002). Staging of the intracerebral inclusion body pathology associated with idiopathic Parkinson's disease (preclinical and clinical stages). *Journal of Neurology, 249*(3), iii1–iii5. https://doi.org/10.1007/s00415-002-1301-4

Braak, H., Ghebremedhin, E., Rüb, U., Bratzke, H., & Del Tredici, K. (2004). Stages in the development of Parkinson's disease-related pathology. *Cell and Tissue Research, 318*(1), 121–134. https://doi.org/10.1007/s00441-004-0956-9

Broen, M. P. G., Narayen, N. E., Kuijf, M. L., Dissanayaka, N. N. W., & Leentjens, A. F. G. (2016). Prevalence of anxiety in Parkinson's disease: A systematic review and meta-analysis. *Movement Disorders, 31*(8), 1125–1133. https://doi.org/10.1002/mds.26643

Bryant, M. S., Rintala, D. H., Hou, J. G., Rivas, S. P., Fernandez, A. L., Lai, E. C., & Protas, E. J. (2012). The relation of falls to fatigue, depression and daytime sleepiness in Parkinson's disease. *European Neurology, 67*(6), 326–330. https://doi.org/10.1159/000335877

Carver, C. S., & Scheier, M. F. (2001). *On the self-regulation of behavior*. Cambridge University Press.

Chand, S. (2013). How to adapt CBT for older adults. *Current Psychiatry, 12*, 10–15.

Chaudhuri, K. R., Healy, D. G., & Schapira, A. H. V. (2006). Non-motor symptoms of Parkinson's disease: Diagnosis and management. *Lancet Neurology, 5*, 235–245.

Cohen, G. (1996). *Memory in the real world*. Psychology Press.

Connolly, B., & Fox, S. H. (2014). Treatment of cognitive, psychiatric, and affective disorders associated with Parkinson's disease. *Neurotherapeutics, 11*(1), 78–91. https://doi.org/10.1007/s13311-013-0238-x

Connor, K., Davidson, J., Churchill, L., Sherwood, A., Foa, E., & Weisler, R. (2000). Psychometric properties of the Social Phobia Inventory (SPIN). *British Journal of Psychiatry, 176*, 379–386.

Costa, A., Peppe, A., Carlesimo, G. A., Pasqualetti, P., & Caltagirone, C. (2006). Major and minor depression in Parkinson's disease: A neuropsychological investigation. *European Journal of Neurology, 13*(9), 972–980. https://doi.org/10.1111/j.1468-1331.2006.01406.x

Cronin-Golomb, A. (2013). Emergence of nonmotor symptoms as the focus of research and treatment of Parkinson's disease: Introduction to the special section on nonmotor dysfunctions in Parkinson's disease. *Behavioral Neuroscience, 127*(2), 135–138. https://doi.org/10.1037/a0032142

den Brok, M., van Dalen, J., van Gool, W., Moll van Charante, E., de Bie, R., & Richard, E. (2015). Apathy in Parkinson's disease: A systematic review and meta-analysis. *Movement Disorders, 30*(6), 759–769.

Dissanayaka, N. N. W., Idu Jion, F., Pachana, N. A., O'Sullivan, J. D., Marsh, R., Byrne, G. J., & Harnett, P. (2016). Mindfulness for motor and nonmotor dysfunctions in Parkinson's disease. *Parkinson's Disease, 2016*, 7109052. https://doi.org/10.1155/2016/7109052

Djamshidian, A., & Friedman, J. H. (2014). Anxiety and depression in Parkinson's disease. *Current Treatment Options in Neurology, 16*(4), Article 285. https://doi.org/10.1007/s11940-014-0285-6

Dobkin, R. D., Mann, S., Interian, A., Gara, M., & Menza, M. (2019). Cognitive behavioral therapy improves diverse profiles of depressive symptoms in Parkinson's disease. *International Journal of Geriatric Psychiatry, 34*, 722–729.

Dobkin, R. D., Menza, M., Allen, L. A., Gara, M. A., Mark, M. H., Tiu, J., Bienfait, K. L., & Friedman, J. (2011). Cognitive–behavioral therapy for depression in Parkinson's disease: A randomized, controlled trial. *American Journal of Psychiatry, 168*(10), 1066–1074. https://doi.org/10.1176/appi.ajp.2011.10111669

Dobkin, R. D., Menza, M., Allen, L. A., Tiu, J., Friedman, J., Bienfait, K. L., Gara, M. A., & Mark, M. H. (2011). Telephone-based cognitive–behavioral therapy for depression in Parkinson disease. *Journal of Geriatric Psychiatry and Neurology, 24*(4), 206–214. https://doi.org/10.1177/0891988711422529

Dobkin, R. D., Rubino, J. T., Friedman, J., Allen, L. A., Gara, M. A., & Menza, M. (2013). Barriers to mental health care utilization in Parkinson's disease. *Journal of Geriatric Psychiatry and Neurology, 26*(2), 105–116.

Donaldson, I. (2015). James Parkinson's *Essay on the Shaking Palsy*. *Journal of the Royal College of Physicians of Edinburgh, 45*(1), 84–86. https://doi.org/10.4997/JRCPE.2015.118

Dorsey, E. R., Elbaz, A., Nichols, E., Abd-Allah, F., Abdelalim, A., Adsuar, J. C., Ansha, M. G., Brayne, C., Choi, J.-Y. J., Collado-Mateo, D., Dahodwala, N., Do, H. P., Edessa, D., Endres, M., Fereshtehnejad, S.-M., Foreman, K. J., Gankpe, F. G., Gupta, R., Hankey, G. J., . . . Murray, C. J. L. (2018). Global, regional, and national burden of Parkinson's disease, 1990–2016: A systematic analysis for the Global Burden of Disease Study 2016. *Lancet Neurology, 17*(11), 939–953. https://doi.org/10.1016/S1474-4422(18)30295-3

Enrici, I., Adenzato, M., Ardito, R. B., Mitkova, A., Cavallo, M., Zibetti, M., Lopiano, L., & Castelli, L. (2015). Emotion processing in Parkinson's disease: A three-level study on recognition, representation, and regulation. *PLoS One, 10*(6), e0131470. https://doi.org/10.1371/journal.pone.0131470

Fan, J.-Y., Chang, B.-L., & Wu, Y.-R. (2016). Relationships among depression, anxiety, sleep, and quality of life in patients with Parkinson's disease in Taiwan. *Parkinson's Disease, 2016*, 4040185. https://doi.org/10.1155/2016/4040185

Fernandez, H., See, R., Gary, M., Bowers, D., Rodriguez, R., Jacobson, C., & Okun, M. (2009). Depressive symptoms in Parkinson disease correlate with impaired global and specific cognitive performance. *Journal of Geriatric Psychiatry and Neurology, 22*, 223–227.

Fett, A.-K. J., Viechtbauer, W., Dominguez, M.-G., Penn, D. L., van Os, J., & Krabbendam, L. (2011). The relationship between neurocognition and social cognition with functional outcomes in schizophrenia: A meta-analysis. *Neuroscience & Biobehavioral Reviews, 35*(3), 573–588. https://doi.org/10.1016/j.neubiorev.2010.07.001

Gámez, W., Chmielewski, M., Kotov, R., Ruggero, C., Suzuki, N., & Watson, D. (2014). The Brief Experiential Avoidance Questionnaire: Development and initial validation. *Psychological Assessment, 26*(1), 35–45. https://doi.org/10.1037/a0034473

Goldman, J. G., & Postuma, R. (2014). Premotor and nonmotor features of Parkinson's disease. *Current Opinion in Neurology, 27*(4), 434–441. https://doi.org/10.1097/WCO.0000000000000112

Gross, J. J., & John, O. P. (2003). Individual differences in two emotion regulation processes: Implications for affect, relationships, and well-being. *Journal of Personality and Social Psychology, 85*(2), 348–362. https://doi.org/10.1037/0022-3514.85.2.348

Hanna, K. K., & Cronin-Golomb, A. (2011). Impact of anxiety on quality of life in Parkinson's disease. *Parkinson's Disease, 2012*, 640707. https://doi.org/10.1155/2012/640707

Harrington, N. (2006). Frustration intolerance beliefs: Their relationship with depression, anxiety, and anger, in a clinical population. *Cognitive Therapy and Research, 30*(6), 699–709. https://doi.org/10.1007/s10608-006-9061-6

Hatzenbuehler, M. L., Nolen-Hoeksema, S., & Dovidio, J. (2009). How does stigma "get under the skin"? The mediating role of emotion regulation. *Psychological Science, 20*(10), 1282–1289. https://doi.org/10.1111/j.1467-9280.2009.02441.x

Hermanns, M. (2013). The invisible and visible stigmatization of Parkinson's disease. *Journal of the American Association of Nurse Practitioners, 25*, 563–566.

Horner, A. J., & Paris, B. (1999). Visions of the self: Karen Horney's *Vision of the Self*. *American Journal of Psychoanalysis, 59*, 157–166.

Ille, R., Wabnegger, A., Schwingenschuh, P., Katschnig-Winter, P., Kögl-Wallner, M., Wenzel, K., & Schienle, A. (2016). Intact emotion recognition and experience but dysfunctional emotion regulation in idiopathic Parkinson's disease. *Journal of the Neurological Sciences, 361*, 72–78. https://doi.org/10.1016/j.jns.2015.12.007

Irani, F., Seligman, S., Kamath, V., Kohler, C., & Gur, R. C. (2012). A meta-analysis of emotion perception and functional outcomes in schizophrenia. *Schizophrenia Research, 137*(1), 203–211. https://doi.org/10.1016/j.schres.2012.01.023

Jacob, E. L., Gatto, N. M., Thompson, A., Bordelon, Y., & Ritz, B. (2010). Occurrence of depression and anxiety prior to Parkinson's disease. *Parkinsonism & Related Disorders, 16*(9), 576–581. https://doi.org/10.1016/j.parkreldis.2010.06.014

Jankovic, J. (2008). Parkinson's disease: Clinical features and diagnosis. *Journal of Neurology, Neurosurgery & Psychiatry, 79*(4), 368–376. https://doi.org/10.1136/jnnp.2007.131045

Jayasekara, R., Procter, N., Harrison, J., Skelton, K., Hampel, S., Draper, R., & Deuter, K. (2015). Cognitive behavioural therapy for older adults with depression: A review. *Journal of Mental Health, 24*(3), 168–171. https://doi.org/10.3109/09638237.2014.971143

Julian, L. J. (2011). Measures of anxiety. *Arthritis Care & Research, 63*(S11), S467–S472. https://doi.org/10.1002/acr.20561

Kehagia, A. A., Barker, R. A., & Robbins, T. W. (2010). Neuropsychological and clinical heterogeneity of cognitive impairment and dementia in patients with Parkinson's disease. *Lancet Neurology*, *9*(12), 1200–1213. https://doi.org/10.1016/S1474-4422(10)70212-X

Khatri, D. K., Choudhary, M., Sood, A., & Singh, S. B. (2020). Anxiety: An ignored aspect of Parkinson's disease lacking attention. *Biomedicine & Pharmacotherapy*, *131*, 110776. https://doi.org/10.1016/j.biopha.2020.110776

Klepac, N., Hajnšek, S., & Trkulja, V. (2010). Cognitive performance in nondemented nonpsychotic Parkinson disease patients with or without a history of depression prior to the onset of motor symptoms. *Journal of Geriatric Psychiatry and Neurology*, *23*(1), 15–26. https://doi.org/10.1177/0891988709351831

Kolb, B., Mychasiuk, R., Muhammad, A., Li, Y., Frost, D. O., & Gibb, R. (2012). Experience and the developing prefrontal cortex. *Proceedings of the National Academy of Sciences of the USA*, *109*(Suppl. 2), 17186–17193. https://doi.org/10.1073/pnas.1121251109

Kowal, S. L., Dall, T. M., Chakrabarti, R., Storm, M. V., & Jain, A. (2013). The current and projected economic burden of Parkinson's disease in the United States. *Movement Disorders*, *28*(3), 311–318. https://doi.org/10.1002/mds.25292

Koychev, I., & Okai, D. (2017). Cognitive–behavioural therapy for non-motor symptoms of Parkinson's disease: A clinical review. *Evidence-Based Mental Health*, *20*(1), 15–20.

Kraepelien, M., Svenningsson, P., Lindefors, N., & Kaldo, V. (2015). Internet-based cognitive behavioral therapy for depression and anxiety in Parkinson's disease—A pilot study. *Internet Interventions*, *2*(1), 1–6. https://doi.org/10.1016/j.invent.2014.11.006

Kumar, N., Gupta, R., Kumar, H., Mehta, S., Rajan, R., Kumar, D., Kandadai, R. M., Desai, S., Wadia, P., Basu, P., Mondal, B., Juneja, S., Rawat, A., Meka, S. S., Mishal, B., Prashanth, L. K., Srivastava, A. K., & Goyal, V. (2020). Impact of home confinement during COVID-19 pandemic on sleep parameters in Parkinson's disease. *Sleep Medicine*, *77*, 15–22. https://doi.org/10.1016/j.sleep.2020.11.021

Kvaal, K., Ulstein, I., Nordhus, I. H., & Engedal, K. (2005). The Spielberger State–Trait Anxiety Inventory (STAI): The state scale in detecting mental disorders in geriatric patients. *International Journal of Geriatric Psychiatry*, *20*(7), 629–634.

Larsen, D. L., Attkisson, C. C., Hargreaves, W. A., & Nguyen, T. D. (1979). Assessment of client/patient satisfaction: Development of a general scale. *Evaluation and Program Planning*, *2*(3), 197–207. https://doi.org/10.1016/0149-7189(79)90094-6

Lewis, S. J. G., Dove, A., Robbins, T. W., Barker, R. A., & Owen, A. M. (2003). Cognitive impairments in early Parkinson's disease are accompanied by reductions in activity in frontostriatal neural circuitry. *Journal of Neuroscience*, *23*(15), 6351–6356. https://doi.org/10.1523/JNEUROSCI.23-15-06351.2003

Liu, X., Li, L., Xiao, J., Yang, J., & Jiang, X. (2013). Abnormalities of autobiographical memory of patients with depressive disorders: A meta-analysis. *Psychology and Psychotherapy*, *86*(4), 353–373. doi:10.1111/j.2044-8341.2012.02077.x

Lutz, S. G., Holmes, J. D., Ready, E. A., Jenkins, M. E., & Johnson, A. M. (2016). Clinical presentation of anxiety in Parkinson's disease: A scoping review. *OTJR: Occupational Therapy Journal of Research*, *36*(3), 134–147. https://doi.org/10.1177/1539449216661714

Ma, H.-I., Saint-Hilaire, M., Thomas, C. A., & Tickle-Degnen, L. (2016). Stigma as a key determinant of health-related quality of life in Parkinson's disease. *Quality of Life Research*, *25*(12), 3037–3045. https://doi.org/10.1007/s11136-016-1329-z

Macleod, A. D., Taylor, K. S. M., & Counsell, C. E. (2014). Mortality in Parkinson's disease: A systematic review and meta-analysis. *Movement Disorders, 29*(13), 1615–1622. https://doi.org/10.1002/mds.25898

Maffoni, M., Giardini, A., Pierobon, A., Ferrazzoli, D., & Frazzitta, G. (2017). Stigma experienced by Parkinson's disease patients: A descriptive review of qualitative studies. *Parkinson's Disease, 2017*, 7203259. https://doi.org/10.1155/2017/7203259

Mahlknecht, P., Seppi, K., & Poewe, W. (2015). The concept of prodromal Parkinson's disease. *Journal of Parkinson's Disease, 5*(4), 681–697. https://doi.org/10.3233/JPD-150685

Marras, C., Beck, J. C., Bower, J. H., Roberts, E., Ritz, B., Ross, G. W., Abbott, R. D., Savica, R., Van Den Eeden, S. K., Willis, A. W., & Tanner, C. (2018). Prevalence of Parkinson's disease across North America. *NPJ Parkinson's Disease, 4*(1), Article 21. https://doi.org/10.1038/s41531-018-0058-0

Marsh, L. (2013). Depression and Parkinson's disease: Current knowledge. *Current Neurology and Neuroscience Reports, 13*(12), Article 409. https://doi.org/10.1007/s11910-013-0409-5

Mattick, R. P., & Clarke, J. C. (1998). Development and validation of measures of social phobia scrutiny fear and social interaction anxiety. *Behaviour Research and Therapy, 36*(4), 455–470. https://doi.org/10.1016/S0005-7967(97)10031-6

Mengelberg, A., & Siegert, R. (2003). Is theory-of-mind impaired in Parkinson's disease? *Cognitive Neuropsychiatry, 8*(3), 191–209. https://doi.org/10.1080/13546800244000292

Michl, L. C., McLaughlin, K. A., Shepherd, K., & Nolen-Hoeksema, S. (2013). Rumination as a mechanism linking stressful life events to symptoms of depression and anxiety: Longitudinal evidence in early adolescents and adults. *Journal of Abnormal Psychology, 122*(2), 339–352. https://doi.org/10.1037/a0031994

Miller, I. N., & Cronin-Golomb, A. (2010). Gender differences in Parkinson's disease: Clinical characteristics and cognition. *Movement Disorders, 25*(16), 2695–2703. https://doi.org/10.1002/mds.23388

Mintzer, J., & Burns, A. (2000). Anticholinergic side-effects of drugs in elderly people. *Journal of the Royal Society of Medicine, 93*, 457–462.

Monastero, R., Di Fiore, P., Ventimiglia, G. D., Camarda, R., & Camarda, C. (2013). The neuropsychiatric profile of Parkinson's disease subjects with and without mild cognitive impairment. *Journal of Neural Transmission, 120*(4), 607–611. https://doi.org/10.1007/s00702-013-0988-y

Nolen-Hoeksema, S., & Davis, C. G. (1999). "Thanks for sharing that": Ruminators and their social support networks. *Journal of Personality and Social Psychology, 77*(4), 801–814. https://doi.org/10.1037/0022-3514.77.4.801

Norman, S., Cissell, S., Means-Christensen, A., & Stein, M. (2006). Development and validation of an Overall Anxiety Severity and Impairment Scale (OASIS). *Depression and Anxiety, 23*(4), 245–249.

Novaes, P. H., da Cruz, D. T., Lucchetti, A. L. G., Leite, I. C. G., & Lucchetti, G. (2017). The "iatrogenic triad": Polypharmacy, drug–drug interactions, and potentially inappropriate medications in older adults. *International Journal of Clinical Pharmacy, 39*(4), 818–825. https://doi.org/10.1007/s11096-017-0470-2

Pagonabarraga, J., Kulisevsky, J., Strafella, A. P., & Krack, P. (2015). Apathy in Parkinson's disease: Clinical features, neural substrates, diagnosis, and treatment. *Lancet Neurology*, *14*(5), 518–531. https://doi.org/10.1016/S1474-4422(15)00019-8

Pedersen, K. F., Larsen, J. P., Alves, G., & Aarsland, D. (2009). Prevalence and clinical correlates of apathy in Parkinson's disease: A community-based study. *Parkinsonism & Related Disorders*, *15*(4), 295–299. https://doi.org/10.1016/j.parkreldis.2008.07.006

Phillips, L. J. (2006). Dropping the bomb: The experience of being diagnosed with Parkinson's disease. *Geriatric Nursing*, *27*(6), 362–369. https://doi.org/10.1016/j.gerinurse.2006.10.012

Piers, R. J., Farchione, T. J., Wong, B., & Cronin-Golomb, A. (2022). Telehealth cognitive behavioral therapy for depression in Parkinson's disease: A case study. Psychotherapy, *59*(2), 223–233. https://doi.org/10.1037/pst0000367

Pigott, H., Leventhal, A., Alter, G., & Boren, J. (2010). Efficacy and effectiveness of antidepressants: Current status of research. *Psychotherapy and Psychosomatics*, *79*, 267–279.

Pinquart, M., Duberstein, P. R., & Lyness, J. M. (2007). Effects of psychotherapy and other behavioral interventions on clinically depressed older adults: A meta-analysis. *Aging & Mental Health*, *11*(6), 645–657. https://doi.org/10.1080/13607860701529635

Pinquart, M., & Sorensen, S. (2001). How effective are psychotherapeutic and other psychosocial interventions with older adults? In *Database of Abstracts of Reviews of Effects (DARE): Quality-assessed Reviews* [Internet]. Centre for Reviews and Dissemination. https://www.ncbi.nlm.nih.gov/books/NBK68899

Poewe, W. (2008). Non-motor symptoms in Parkinson's disease. *European Journal of Neurology*, *15*(S1), 14–20. https://doi.org/10.1111/j.1468-1331.2008.02056.x

Pontone, G. M., Williams, J. R., Anderson, K. E., Chase, G., Goldstein, S. R., Grill, S., Hirsch, E. S., Lehmann, S., Little, J. T., Margolis, R. L., Palanci, J., Rabins, P. V., Weiss, H. D., & Marsh, L. (2013). Pharmacologic treatment of anxiety disorders in Parkinson disease. *American Journal of Geriatric Psychiatry*, *21*(6), 520–528. https://doi.org/10.1016/j.jagp.2012.10.023

Pontone, G. M., Williams, J. R., Anderson, K. E., Chase, G., Goldstein, S. R., Grill, S., Hirsch, E. S., Lehmann, S., Little, J. T., Margolis, R. L., Rabins, P. V., Weiss, H. D., & Marsh, L. (2009). Prevalence of anxiety disorders and anxiety subtypes in patients with Parkinson's disease. *Movement Disorders*, *24*(9), 1333–1338. https://doi.org/10.1002/mds.22611

Prediger, R. D. S., Matheus, F. C., Schwarzbold, M. L., Lima, M. M. S., & Vital, M. A. B. F. (2012). Anxiety in Parkinson's disease: A critical review of experimental and clinical studies. *Neuropharmacology*, *62*(1), 115–124. https://doi.org/10.1016/j.neuropharm.2011.08.039

Qato, D. M., Alexander, G. C., Conti, R. M., Johnson, M., Schumm, P., & Lindau, S. T. (2008). Use of prescription and over-the-counter medications and dietary supplements among older adults in the United States. *JAMA*, *300*(24), 2867–2878. https://doi.org/10.1001/jama.2008.892

Quelhas, R., & Costa, M. (2009). Anxiety, depression, and quality of life in Parkinson's disease. *Journal of Neuropsychiatry and Clinical Neurosciences*, *21*(4), 413–419.

Reijnders, M., Ehrt, U., Weber, W., Aarsland, D., & Leentjens, A. (2008). A systematic review of prevalence studies of depression in Parkinson's disease. *Movement Disorders*, *23*, 183–189.

Reiss, S., Peterson, R. A., Gursky, D. M., & McNally, R. J. (1986). Anxiety sensitivity, anxiety frequency and the prediction of fearfulness. *Behaviour Research and Therapy*, *24*(1), 1–8. https://doi.org/10.1016/0005-7967(86)90143-9

Reynolds, G. O., Saint-Hilaire, M., Thomas, C. A., Barlow, D. H., & Cronin-Golomb, A. (2020). Cognitive–behavioral therapy for anxiety in Parkinson's disease. *Behavior Modification*, *44*(4), 552–579. https://journals.sagepub.com/doi/abs/10.1177/0145445519838828

Rimes, K. A., & Chalder, T. (2010). The Beliefs About Emotions Scale: Validity, reliability and sensitivity to change. *Journal of Psychosomatic Research*, *68*(3), 285–292. https://doi.org/10.1016/j.jpsychores.2009.09.014

Robinson, M. S., & Alloy, L. B. (2003). Negative cognitive styles and stress-reactive rumination interact to predict depression: A prospective study. *Cognitive Therapy and Research*, *27*(3), 275–291. https://doi.org/10.1023/A:1023914416469

Saeed, U., Compagnone, J., Aviv, R. I., Strafella, A. P., Black, S. E., Lang, A. E., & Masellis, M. (2017). Imaging biomarkers in Parkinson's disease and parkinsonian syndromes: Current and emerging concepts. *Translational Neurodegeneration*, *6*(1), 8. https://doi.org/10.1186/s40035-017-0076-6

Salazar, R. D., Weizenbaum, E., Ellis, T. D., Earhart, G. M., Ford, M. P., Dibble, L. E., & Cronin-Golomb, A. (2019). Predictors of self-perceived stigma in Parkinson's disease. *Parkinsonism & Related Disorders*, *60*, 76–80. https://doi.org/10.1016/j.parkreldis.2018.09.028

Santangelo, G., Vitale, C., Trojano, L., Longo, K., Cozzolino, A., Grossi, D., & Barone, P. (2009). Relationship between depression and cognitive dysfunctions in Parkinson's disease without dementia. *Journal of Neurology*, *256*(4), 632–638. https://doi.org/10.1007/s00415-009-0146-5

Schrag, A. (2006). Quality of life and depression in Parkinson's disease. *Journal of the Neurological Sciences*, *248*(1), 151–157. https://doi.org/10.1016/j.jns.2006.05.030

Schrag, A., & Taddei, R. N. (2017). Depression and anxiety in Parkinson's disease. International *Review* of *Neurobiology*, *133*, 623–655. https://doi.org/10.1016/bs.irn.2017.05.024

Seppi, K., Chaudhuri, K. R., Coelho, M., Fox, S. H., Katzenschlager, R., Lloret, S. P., Weintraub, D., & Sampaio, C. (2019). Update on treatments for nonmotor symptoms of Parkinson's disease—An evidence-based medicine review. *Movement Disorders*, *34*(2), 180–198. https://doi.org/10.1002/mds.27602

Serfaty, M., Haworth, D., Blanchard, M., Buszewicz, M., Murad, S., & King, M. (2009). Clinical effectiveness of individual cognitive behavioral therapy for depressed older people in primary care: A randomized controlled trial. *Archives of General Psychiatry*, *66*, 1332–1340.

Shear, M. K., Rucci, P., Williams, J., Frank, E., Grochocinski, V., Vander Bilt, J., Houck, P., & Wang, T. (2001). Reliability and validity of the Panic Disorder Severity Scale: Replication and extension. *Journal of Psychiatric Research*, *35*(5), 293–296. https://doi.org/10.1016/S0022-3956(01)00028-0

Shiba, M., Bower, J. H., Maraganore, D. M., McDonnell, S. K., Peterson, B. J., Ahlskog, J. E., Schaid, D. J., & Rocca, W. A. (2000). Anxiety disorders and depressive disorders preceding Parkinson's disease: A case–control study. *Movement Disorders, 15*(4), 669–677. https://doi.org/10.1002/1531-8257(200007)15:4<669::AID-MDS1011>3.0.CO;2-5

Siddiqui, S. V., Chatterjee, U., Kumar, D., Siddiqui, A., & Goyal, N. (2008). Neuropsychology of prefrontal cortex. *Indian Journal of Psychiatry, 50*(3), 202–208. https://doi.org/10.4103/0019-5545.43634

Smith, S. J., & Souchay, C. (2013). Autobiographical memory in Parkinson's disease: A retrieval deficit. *Journal of Neuropsychology, 7*(2), 164–178. https://doi.org/10.1111/jnp.12014

Smith, S. J., Souchay, C., & Conway, M. A. (2010). Overgeneral autobiographical memory in Parkinson's disease. *Cortex, 46*(6), 787–793. https://doi.org/10.1016/j.cortex.2009.08.006

Spielberger, C., Gorsuch, R., Lushene, R., Vagg, P., & Jacobs, G. (1983). *Manual for the State–Trait Anxiety Inventory*. Mind Garden.

Spreng, R. N., Mar, R. A., & Kim, A. S. N. (2008). The common neural basis of autobiographical memory, prospection, navigation, theory of mind, and the default mode: A quantitative meta-analysis. *Journal of Cognitive Neuroscience, 21*(3), 489–510. https://doi.org/10.1162/jocn.2008.21029

Starkstein, S., Mayberg, H., Leiguarda, R., Preziosi, T., & Robinson, R. (1992). A prospective longitudinal study of depression, cognitive decline, and physical impairments in patients with Parkinson's disease. *Journal of Neurology, Neurosurgery, & Psychiatry, 55*, 377–382.

Starkstein, S., Merello, M., Jorge, R., Brockman, S., Bruce, D., & Power, B. (2009). The syndromal validity and nosological position of apathy in Parkinson's disease. *Movement Disorders, 24*(8), 1211–1216.

Stefanova, E., Potrebic, A., Ziropadja, L., Maric, J., Ribaric, I., & Kostic, V. S. (2006). Depression predicts the pattern of cognitive impairment in early Parkinson's disease. *Journal of the Neurological Sciences, 248*(1), 131–137. https://doi.org/10.1016/j.jns.2006.05.031

Sumner, J. A., Griffith, J. W., & Mineka, S. (2010). Overgeneral autobiographical memory as a predictor of the course of depression: A meta-analysis. *Behaviour Research and Therapy, 48*(7), 614–625. https://doi.org/10.1016/j.brat.2010.03.013

Suzuki, A., Hoshino, T., Shigemasu, K., & Kawamura, M. (2006). Disgust-specific impairment of facial expression recognition in Parkinson's disease. *Brain, 129*, 707–717.

Tickle-Degnen, L., Zebrowitz, L. A., & Ma, H. (2011). Culture, gender and health care stigma: Practitioners' response to facial masking experienced by people with Parkinson's disease. *Social Science & Medicine, 73*(1), 95–102. https://doi.org/10.1016/j.socscimed.2011.05.008

Tremblay, L., Worbe, Y., Thobois, S., Sgambato-Faure, V., & Féger, J. (2015). Selective dysfunction of basal ganglia subterritories: From movement to behavioral disorders. *Movement Disorders, 30*(9), 1155–1170. https://doi.org/10.1002/mds.26199

Troeung, L., Egan, S. J., & Gasson, N. (2013). A meta-analysis of randomised placebo-controlled treatment trials for depression and anxiety in Parkinson's disease. *PLoS One, 8*(11), e79510. https://doi.org/10.1371/journal.pone.0079510

Troeung, L., Egan, S. J., & Gasson, N. (2014). A waitlist-controlled trial of group cognitive behavioural therapy for depression and anxiety in Parkinson's disease. *BMC Psychiatry*, *14*(1), Article 19. https://doi.org/10.1186/1471-244X-14-19

Tysnes, O.-B., & Storstein, A. (2017). Epidemiology of Parkinson's disease. *Journal of Neural Transmission*, *124*(8), 901–905. https://doi.org/10.1007/s00702-017-1686-y

van den Hoven, E., & Eggen, B. (2008). Informing augmented memory system design through autobiographical memory theory. *Personal and Ubiquitous Computing*, *12*, 433–443. https://doi.org/10.1007/s00779-007-0177-9

Veazey, C., Cook, K. F., Stanley, M., Lai, E. C., & Kunik, M. E. (2009). Telephone-administered cognitive behavioral therapy: A case study of anxiety and depression in Parkinson's disease. *Journal of Clinical Psychology in Medical Settings*, *16*(3), 243–253. https://doi.org/10.1007/s10880-009-9167-6

Visted, E., Vøllestad, J., Nielsen, M. B., & Schanche, E. (2018). Emotion regulation in current and remitted depression: A systematic review and meta-analysis. *Frontiers in Psychology*, *9*. https://doi.org/10.3389/fpsyg.2018.00756

Voss, T., & Richard, I. H. (2011). Depression in Parkinson's disease. In C. W. Olanow, F. Stocchi, & A. E. Lang (Eds.), *Parkinson's disease: Non-motor and non-dopaminergic features* (pp. 183–192). Wiley. https://doi.org/10.1002/9781444397970.ch17

Watkins, E. R. (2008). Constructive and unconstructive repetitive thought. *Psychological Bulletin*, *134*(2), 163–206. https://doi.org/10.1037/0033-2909.134.2.163

Williams, J., Barnhofer, T., Crane, C., Herman, D., Raes, F., Watkins, E., & Dalgleish, T. (2007). Autobiographical memory specificity and emotional disorder. *Psychological Bulletin*, *133*, 122–148.

Yamanishi, T., Tachibana, H., Oguru, M., Matsui, K., Toda, K., Okuda, B., & Oka, N. (2013). Anxiety and depression in patients with Parkinson's disease. *Internal Medicine*, *52*(5), 539–545. https://doi.org/10.2169/internalmedicine.52.8617

Yang, S., Sajatovic, M., & Walter, B. L. (2012). Psychosocial interventions for depression and anxiety in Parkinson's disease. *Journal of Geriatric Psychiatry and Neurology*, *25*(2), 113–121. https://doi.org/10.1177/0891988712445096

Yesavage, J. A., Brink, T. L., Rose, T. L., Lum, O., Huang, V., Adey, M., & Leirer, V. O. (1982). Development and validation of a geriatric depression screening scale: A preliminary report. *Journal of Psychiatric Research*, *17*(1), 37–49. https://doi.org/10.1016/0022-3956(82)90033-4

Yoshimura, N., Kawamura, M., Masaoka, Y., & Homma, I. (2005). The amygdala of patients with Parkinson's disease is silent in response to fearful facial expressions. *Neuroscience*, *131*(2), 523–534. https://doi.org/10.1016/j.neuroscience.2004.09.054

Zhang, Q., Yang, X., Song, H., & Jin, Y. (2020). Cognitive behavioral therapy for depression and anxiety of Parkinson's disease: A systematic review and meta-analysis. *Complementary Therapies in Clinical Practice*, *39*, 101111. https://doi.org/10.1016/j.ctcp.2020.101111

11

Application of the Unified Protocol in Irritable Bowel Syndrome

ZAHRA ZANJANI AND SANAZ JOEKAR ■

INTRODUCTION

Irritable Bowel Syndrome: Definition and Prevalence Rates

Irritable bowel syndrome (IBS) is characterized by the disruption of the bowel movement accompanied by abdominal pain in which no single causative factor has been identified so far. This condition was traditionally known as a brain–gut interaction disorder, but it is increasingly evident that IBS embraces various pathologies. Currently, the gold standard for defining IBS is the Rome criteria. Using the Rome criteria (Table 11.1), IBS is diagnosed when the patient complains of experiencing recurrent abdominal pain (at least once per week and during the past 3 months) associated with defecation, change in frequency of defecation, or change in consistency of stool (Mearin et al., 2016).

IBS is one of the most common functional bowel disorders, but estimating the exact global prevalence is difficult due to significant variability between epidemiological studies in different countries. One systematic review and meta-analysis aimed to determine the global prevalence of IBS in adults found that even by applying uniform symptom-based criteria and identical methodology used in studies, the prevalence of IBS varies substantially between countries. According to this study, the pooled prevalence of IBS according to the Rome III criteria was 9.2%, and based on Rome IV criteria, it was 3.8% (Oka et al., 2020).

IBS is more prevalent in females than in males, and in most populations the IBS rates in women are approximately 1.5- to 3-fold higher than those seen in men (Drossman et al., 1990). This is particularly true for populations in the Western hemisphere. Whereas the female to male ratio in North America and Europe is

Zahra Zanjani and Sanaz Joekar, *Application of the Unified Protocol in Irritable Bowel Syndrome* In: *Applications of the Unified Protocol in Health Conditions.* Edited by: Jorge Osma and Todd J. Farchione, Oxford University Press. © Oxford University Press 2023. DOI: 10.1093/oso/9780197564295.003.0011

Table 11.1 The Different Rome Criteria

Iteration and Year Released	Symptoms	Duration for Diagnosis
Rome I (1992)	Abdominal pain and discomfort relieved with defecation, or associated with a change in stool frequency, and two or more of the following criteria on at least 25% of occasions or days: Altered stool frequency Altered stool form Altered stool passage Passage of mucus Bloating of distension	These criteria should be fulfilled for at least 12 weeks out of the preceding 12 months.
Rome II (1999)	Abdominal discomfort or pain with at least two of following three features: Relieved with defecation Onset associated with a change in stool frequency Onset associated with a change in stool form	These criteria should be fulfilled for at least 12 weeks (no need to be consecutive) out of the preceding 12 months.
Rome III (2006)	Recurrent abdominal pain or discomfort (defined as an uncomfortable sensation not described as pain), 3 days per month associated with two or more of the following criteria: Improvement with defecation Onset associated with a change in stool frequency Onset associated with a change in stool form	These criteria should be fulfilled for the past 3 months, with symptom onset at least 6 months prior to diagnosis.
Rome IV (2016)	Recurrent abdominal pain on average at least 1 day/week in the past 3 months, associated with two or more of the following criteria: Related to defecation (either increasing or improving pain) Associated with a change in stool frequency Associated with a change in stool form	These criteria should be fulfilled for the past 3 months, with symptom onset at least 6 months prior to diagnosis.

spread around 2:1, in South Asia, South America, and Africa, the rates of IBS in men are almost equal to those of women, and in some cases even higher (Lovell & Ford, 2012). It seems conceivable that cultural differences, sex difference in health care access, or normalization of symptoms in these regions may play a role in this phenomenon.

IBS occurs in diverse age groups, including children and the elderly. Approximately 50% of IBS patients experience their first symptoms before age 35 years; the prevalence is 25% lower in people older than age 50 years than in young people (Canavan et al., 2014). The risk of having IBS in people with a biological relative with IBS is twice as high. Still, it appears that social learning may exert an equal or even more significant influence (Levy et al., 2001). The role of socioeconomic status in IBS onset is controversial. Whereas some studies suggest that IBS is related to low socioeconomic status (Drossman et al., 1993), other studies demonstrate that the opposite is true (Howell & Talley, as cited in Canavan et al., 2014). An urban population seems to be at higher risk for IBS than a rural population, which may validate the argument that IBS is an industrialization and civilization disease (Usai et al., 2010). IBS is stable over time for the majority of afflicted people and is associated with significant disease burden. Many studies have documented decreased quality of life (Lea & Whorwell, 2001; Monnikes, 2011), elevated rates of psychological comorbidities (Singh et al., 2012), and high economic costs due to absenteeism and nonproductivity (Nellesen et al., 2013).

Emotional Difficulties in IBS

The role of negative emotions on health has been historically recognized; in particular, the physiological consequences associated with emotional arousal can lead to increased vulnerability to illness (Rosmalen et al., 2007). Possible contributing factors or associated features in IBS onset, course, and clinical manifestation include emotional and cognitive factors, psychopathology, psychological disorders, and chronic distress (Bruno et al., 2018). Therefore, psychological factors may be associated with the exacerbation of the symptom experience and contribute to impairment in quality of life and excessive use of health care resources in IBS patients (Hu et al., 2002; Kanazawa et al., 2004; Kumano et al., 2004). Research that has examined negative emotions associated with IBS has most commonly considered anger, anxiety, shame, and depression (Bouchoucha et al., 2013; Muscatello et al., 2010; Zoccali et al., 2006). These emotions have been consistently associated with visceral and pain hypersensitivity. The perception of pain is also influenced by the emotional mechanism (Wilder-Smith, 2011). When individuals experience negative emotions, they are more likely to pay attention to their visceral sensations and label them as painful (Gros et al., 2009).

Depression and anxiety are the most common emotional difficulties among IBS patients. The prevalence of depressive symptoms in IBS patients has been approximately 28–87% (Bruno et al., 2018; Zamani et al., 2019). The prevalence of IBS also is high in patients diagnosed with chronic depression (57.69%). In addition to major depression, anxiety disorders (panic disorder, social phobia, and generalized anxiety disorder) are among the most common psychiatric disorders observed in IBS patients (Lee et al., 2015; Van Oudenhove et al., 2016). Anxiety is one of the main reasons for medical consultation among IBS patients (Koloski et al., 2001). In one study of IBS in a large sample of university students (N = 1,021), researchers found that students with IBS were more likely to report higher rates of anxiety, anxiety sensitivity, neuroticism, and trait worry than students without IBS symptoms (Hazlett-Stevens et al., 2003). Therefore, it was suggested that IBS might reflect a vicious cycle of anxiety and anxious response in which fears and negative beliefs about gastrointestinal (GI) symptoms and visceral sensations increase vigilance toward somatic sensations. In turn, the visceral sensations themselves may further increase and subsequently lead to more anxiety.

Studies also show that anger is another emotion observed in IBS (e.g., Dibajnia et al., 2013; Stănculete et al., 2014). The mechanism and process by which anger influences IBS is yet unclear. IBS patients exposed to anger-provoking conditions became angrier than healthy controls, and their large intestine motor activity increased (Welgan et al., 1988).

Also, chronic patients, especially those with intestinal illnesses, are theoretically considered more prone to experience shame (e.g., Casati et al., 2000; Kellett & Gilbert, 2001). Individuals with IBS may also view their symptoms negatively, which leads to various emotions, including shame and embarrassment (Corsetti et al., 2018). In a study of 3,254 people with IBS, 39% of participants said they were embarrassed by their symptoms (American Gastroenterological Association, 2015). Individuals with IBS are often cautious about their symptoms and use a set of avoidance and safety behaviors because they are embarrassed by their IBS symptoms. For example, they often do not travel too far away from a bathroom, only go to places where there is a nearby bathroom, and avoid other people's bathrooms or public toilets. In some cases, the individual may even carry extra underwear in case they have an accident and need to change. People with IBS avoid dinner/social occasions with friends or try not to eat when they are not at home.

Not only negative emotional experience but also difficulty in identifying and describing feelings has been reported in IBS. Several studies have shown that many IBS patients obtain a high score in the alexithymia personality trait (Porcelli et al., 2003; Portincasa et al., 2003). Alexithymia in IBS affects treatment response (Porcelli et al., 2003; Portincasa et al., 2003) and is related to increased symptom severity (Endo et al., 2011). It has been suggested that individuals with high alexithymia have poor ability to recognize and process emotions (Kano & Fukudo, 2013). Therefore, alexithymia potentially leads to symptom persistence and decreases the positive effects of standard medical treatments by increasing the subjective pain experience and the likelihood of reporting high somatic symptoms (Carrozzino & Porcelli, 2018).

Generally, it is believed that emotions may influence thoughts and behaviors—for example, perceptions of threat, decisions to seek medical screenings or treatment, adherence to diet, and other health-related behaviors (Rothman & Salovey, 1997). It has been shown that health care–seeking behavior and treatment consequent in IBS patients are negatively related to anxiety, chronic social stress, acute stress, and maladaptive coping style (Videlock et al., 2009). Anxiety has been considered as an important determinant of health care–seeking behavior among patients with IBS (Koloski et al., 2001; Hu et al., 2002). However, negative emotions may not always facilitate care-seeking. The concurrent physical symptoms and stressful events may lead to the misattribution of symptoms to the stressor, thus postponing medical care-seeking (Cameron et al., 1995).

PSYCHOLOGICAL INTERVENTIONS IN IBS

Disorder-Based Psychological Interventions

Different models of IBS etiology and maintenance have led to the development and examination of varied psychological treatments in order to address the affective components in IBS, such as hypnotherapy (Ford et al., 2014; Hyphantis et al., 2009), relaxation training (e.g., Boyce et al., 2003; Lahmann et al., 2010), behavioral psychotherapy (Corney et al., 1991), systematic desensitization, biofeedback (Jeong, 2004), acceptance and commitment therapy (Ito, & Muto, 2020), cognitive–behavioral therapy (e.g., Ballou & Keefer, 2017; Craske et al., 2011), mindfulness-based interventions (e.g., Gaylord et al., 2011; Ljótsson et al., 2010), and interpersonal therapies (e.g., Hyphantis et al., 2009). These treatments effectively improve the symptoms of IBS (Olatunji et al., 2004). They decrease somatic symptom severity, depression, and anxiety, with small to moderate effect sizes, but they have limitations.

Limitations of Disorder-Based Psychological Interventions

Although disorder-specific treatments for any of the emotional difficulties in IBS have been shown to be effective, some limitations are still related to these protocols. One of them is due to the high comorbidity rates observed in emotion disorders (e.g., depression and anxiety disorders; Wittchen et al., 2011). These disorders are likely to be concurrent, with estimated lifetime comorbidity up to 76% (Brown et al., 2001). Despite high comorbidity of anxiety and depression in IBS patients, such treatments involve separate protocols for targeting each of these disorders. Another limitation is that a different protocol for each emotional disorder makes a training burden for therapists. In addition, disorder-based protocols often do not address patients characterized by a high degree of comorbidity (Cassiello-Robbins et al., 2020). Therefore, research and theorists have turned to transdiagnostic approaches to psychological intervention in response to these issues.

Unified Protocol as a Transdiagnostic Treatment

The Unified Protocol (UP) is a transdiagnostic treatment protocol developed by Barlow and colleagues (2017). This model suggested that emotion dysregulation plays an important and causal role in anxiety, depressive, and related disorders (e.g., somatic symptom disorders and dissociative disorders) (Bullis et al., 2019).

First, this approach could be of particular interest in public services, in which clinicians treat patients presenting with multiple diagnoses, making it challenging to select an adequate protocol (Sauer-Zavala et al., 2017). This treatment is also more time- and cost-efficient for patients because it can address multiple comorbidities at the same time (Bullis et al., 2015). Second, training clinicians in a single treatment protocol is easier and more likely to be implemented in large health care settings, where patients with IBS are most likely to seek treatment (Barlow et al., 2004). Third, comorbid mental disorders can be treated more adequately (Farchione et al., 2012).

Empirical studies support the efficacy of transdiagnostic treatments for anxiety (e.g., Reinholt & Krogh, 2014), depression (Sauer-Zavala et al., 2020), and concurrent anxiety and depression (e.g., McEvoy et al., 2009; Steele et al., 2018). A review of 77 studies in 2020 indicated that the UP had been applied to a wide range of problems, such as anxiety, depression, bipolar, traumatic-stressor, substance use, eating, borderline personality, insomnia, and physical health disorders. Furthermore, this review reported that the UP has also been used for nondiagnosable problems such as nonsuicidal self-injury, subclinical presentations, and sexual minority stress (Cassiello-Robbins et al., 2020).

The Efficacy of the UP on Different Health Conditions and IBS

Although the number of published studies on the efficacy of the UP for health conditions, particularly IBS, is limited, evidence is promising. A case study demonstrated the efficacy of the UP for pain and emotional symptoms in an adolescent population (Allen et al., 2012). Also, a study including 14 patients with psychosomatic disorders demonstrated that the UP is an effective treatment in improvement of emotional dysregulation (Mazaheri et al., 2014). The UP was also as effective as mindfulness-based stress reduction for treating anxiety and depressive symptoms among individuals with infertility (Mousavi et al., 2019).

Research also indicates that the UP is also effective for GI disorders. For example, the results of research on the efficacy of the UP on the emotional problems of patients with these disorders and psychosomatic patients revealed a significant reduction in emotion dysregulation, for instance, in catastrophizing as one measure of cognitive emotion regulation strategies (Mazaheri et al., 2014).

Johari-Fard and Ghafourpour's 2015 study showed that the UP improved quality of life and reduced symptoms in patients with IBS, and these effects persisted after 1-month follow-up.

We also conducted a study in 2018 to assess the efficacy of the UP in patients with IBS (Mohsenabadi et al., 2018). According to our results, it seems that patients with IBS tend to experience many negative emotions, such as anxiety, sadness, and distress. This study revealed that the UP was effective for patients with IBS and could decrease anxiety, depression, stress, and GI symptoms, as well as improve emotion regulation. We found that emotion regulation mediates the effect of the UP on changes in emotional and GI symptoms. Furthermore, results indicated that cognitive reappraisal (one of the components of emotion regulation) fully and the suppression (another component of emotion regulation) partially (not fully) mediated effects of the UP on emotional and GI symptoms.

UNIFIED PROTOCOL ADAPTATION FOR PATIENTS WITH IBS

The UP for IBS consists of eight modules that are delivered in 12 group sessions. The first 11 sessions are held weekly, and the 12th session is held 2 weeks after the 11th session to provide more time for patients to practice techniques from Modules 6 and 7, which are focused on interoceptive and situational emotion exposures. Considering the prominent visceral symptoms in IBS patients, 3 sessions (sessions 9–11) are devoted to these techniques. Several mindfulness techniques have also been added to the original UP. The description of modules is presented in Table 11.2.

CASE EXAMPLE

"F." is a 26-year-old postgraduate student. She is the only child in her family and used to be the top student in school. She was accepted with honors in sociology at the university 8 years ago.

Development of IBS Problems

F. reported having abdominal cramps specifically in the academic environment since she can remember. In elementary school, her abdominal pain and cramps were limited to exam days. Despite being an excellent student, she was always afraid to speak in public and worried about being embarrassed in social situations. She is reluctant to be the center of attention, and such situations make her anxious. The first year of university was highly stressful to her because she

Table 11.2 UP-IBS Module Descriptions and Adaptations from the Original UP

Module 1: Introduction, setting goals, and maintaining motivation (Session 1)	This module begins with an introduction to the treatment. This is followed by a report on IBS physical symptoms and related problems, including emotional changes that usually occur before and during the experience of IBS symptoms. Then, medication and psychological treatment are introduced and reasons for medication use are discussed. The rationale for the UP, general format (e.g., weekly, 90- to 120-minute group sessions), and group rules and procedures (the nature and importance of assessment and intersession practice) are also discussed. In addition, patients are taught how to complete the self-monitoring rating scale. This helps patients track change in symptoms during treatment and helps them reflect on how much their emotions, and related patterns of avoidance, may be interfering with their daily life on a week-to-week basis. The discussion on motivation usually begins by validating patients' doubts and fears about treatment. We also focus on evaluation of the advantages and disadvantages of treatment participation in order to increase their motivation. The treatment goal-setting exercise in Module 1 is used to provide patients with the opportunity to articulate goals for treatment.
Module 2: Understanding emotions (Session 2)	In this module, psychoeducation about emotions and their functions are explored to help patients develop greater awareness of their emotions as they occur. One of the most important goals in this module is to help patients gain a better understanding of the interactions between physical sensations, thoughts, and behaviors. Examples of emotion-provoking situations that are more relevant to IBS (i.e., antecedent: setting up a romantic date; physical response: palpitations and shortness of breath; cognitive response: "I will be ashamed by stomach growling"; behavioral response: refuse the romantic date) are discussed.
Module 3: Mindful emotion awareness (Session 3 and 4)	In this module, we introduce mindful emotion awareness, including a nonjudgmental, present-focused attention toward emotional experiences. The principles of mindfulness are used to develop a more open, approach-oriented relationship with emotions. The third and fourth sessions are dedicated to this module. Patients are exposed to guided meditation exercises to increase mindful emotion awareness. These include Thought Train, Leaves Floating on a Stream, A Beach Ball, and The Dandelion Metaphor.
Module 4: Cognitive flexibility (Session 5)	Module 4 (fifth session) focuses on helping patients (a) develop a greater awareness of how thoughts (or interpretations) influence emotions, (b) identify negative thinking patterns, and (c) increase flexibility in interpreting different situations. The fifth session is performed according to the original UP but with emphasis on IBS patients' examples (i.e., "I will never get married" and "No one can accept my illness and will leave me").

Module 5: Countering emotional behaviors (Session 6 and 7)	In this module, patients are guided to identify their maladaptive emotional behaviors and to then develop and engage in alternative behaviors. Based on the original UP, we introduce the concept and types of emotional behaviors. When patients identify their emotional behaviors, the paradoxical effects of these behaviors are discussed. Finally, patients are encouraged to develop and practice alternative actions (e.g., staying in the situation vs. avoiding people). The sixth and seventh sessions are dedicated to this module.
Module 6: Understanding and confronting physical sensations (Session 8)	The aim of this module is to help patients identify internal physical sensations (e.g., stomach growling and abdominal cramps) that contribute to their emotions. They also gain a greater understanding of how sensations contribute to their emotional experiences and how this may be an important part of what makes emotions difficult to tolerate. For example, a patient who restricts their diet to avoid experiencing abdominal pain because they think they will experience severe and unbearable pain is encouraged to gradually confront their physical sensations in order to increase tolerance of these sensations.
Module 7: Putting it into practice—emotion exposures (Session 9–11)	In this module, which is conducted across three sessions, the concept of emotion exposures and its rationale are introduced. Patients are then guided to gradually confront internal (especially physical sensations) and external stimuli that produce intense emotional reactions. One of the most important exposures in this module is the physical sensation emotion exposure, which involves confronting uncomfortable physical sensations that may be contributing to strong emotions and/or related to their IBS symptoms, consistent with Module 6. For example, we might focus on having the patient experience their distressing, intense physical sensations that typically arise during a romantic date (e.g., heart racing and abdominal cramp). They also will be coached to modify their responses to those emotions. We also emphasize applying the mindfulness skills to decrease any emotion avoidance that may hinder treatment progress. The mindfulness techniques taught earlier in treatment are also practiced.
Module 8: Recognizing accomplishments and looking to the future (Session 12 with 2-week interval)	The purpose of this module is to review key treatment concepts and help patients develop strategies for preventing "relapse." Treatment progress is reviewed by examining change in baseline emotions, avoidance, and behaviors. Also, we discuss improvements related to situations (and associated symptoms) that were confronted between sessions 11 and 12. Then, patient expectations regarding the recurrence of symptoms and potential risk situations in the future are identified to help them prepare for difficulties that might arise following treatment. Finally, patients are encouraged to set aside time each week for reviewing progress and developing or revising a plan to move forward.

had to present several lectures. She worried that her performance might not live up to the expectations of her professors. At that time, she began to experience symptoms including stomach growling, abdominal cramps, and pain that was most common in the morning and intensified in cold weather. Sometimes, the abdominal pain was so severe that she would use diclofenac suppositories to control it. She also experienced symptoms including constipation, chronic fatigue, increased appetite (leading to her becoming overweight), and sleep difficulties. She met a physician and took nortriptyline (10 mg TDS). It took her 3 years to enter the master's degree program after completing her bachelor's degree. During that time, she reported increased conflict with her parents and became increasingly concerned about how others would judge her performance. Two years ago, in the first year of her master's degree program, her symptoms intensified. She experienced the symptoms of constipation 4 days and the symptoms of diarrhea 2 days a week for 6 months.

Constipation and diarrhea worsen her abdominal pain and cramps, and whenever these symptoms worsen following excretion, she becomes extremely fatigued and prefers to sleep. Her stomach growling increased and made her embarrassed in the class. Her function was negatively affected by the symptoms. She could not concentrate in the class; her daily activities decreased, and she had suicidal ideation. Finally, she met a gastroenterologist and was diagnosed with IBS-M. Her treatment plan includes lifestyle and dietary advice followed by psychopharmacotherapy (nortriptyline [10 mg TDS], chlordiazepoxide [5 mg TDS], and propranolol [10 mg TDS]). Currently, she is attending virtual classes, which provides her with an easier situation to deal with academic tasks despite ongoing IBS symptoms.

Case Formulation with the UP

F.'s presenting complaints are described in Table 11.3. Her IBS problems were interfering with several areas of her life, including physical and basic necessities (i.e., balanced diet, sleep, medication side effects, etc.), work, daily life activities, pleasant activities, personal relationships, and life goals. She also reported experiencing strong emotions (e.g., anxiety, depression, and anger) that are interfering (score of 8 out of 10, with 0 being "nothing," 5 being "medium," and 10 being "extreme") and cause her to avoid many activities (e.g., social and physical activities, and praying) and stay at home, and she was very preoccupied with her problems and her future.

Psychological Assessment of Previous UP Application

Before the treatment, F. was asked to complete the following measures: Depression Anxiety Stress Scale (DASS-42), the Emotion Regulation Questionnaire, and the Gastrointestinal Symptoms Rating Scale (GSRS). She also completed these scales in modules 3, 5, and 8 and 1 month after treatment. F. reported extremely

Table 11.3 A Case Conceptualization with the UP in Irritable Bowel Syndrome

HEALTH CONDITION ANALYSIS						
Health condition description: Chronic symptoms of abdominal pain begin after eating as well as abdominal cramp and growling, which are more common in the morning and intensify by cold weather and stress. Intermittent constipation or diarrhea also occurs periodically, but the amount varies depending on the patient's stress and nutrition.						
How health condition (and its treatment) affects the patient's life?			**EMOTION ANALYSIS REGARDING HEALTH CONDITIONS AND ITS CONSEQUENCES**			
General life aspects		**Affectation/ interference** **0______10** **Nothing Very much**	**Strong uncomfortable emotions** Do patients feel strong emotions in any of these general life aspects?	**Intensity** **0______10** **Nothing Extreme**	**Aversive reactions**	**Emotional behaviors** (Situational avoidance/escape, subtle behavioral avoidance, cognitive avoidance, safety signals)
1. **Physical and basic necessities**	**Physical symptoms and pain**: Abdominal pain and cramps, bloating, fatigue following defecation Diarrhea or constipation, feeling of incomplete emptying Frequent urination, especially in stressful situations	10	Frustration, anxiety, fatigue Sadness, anxiety Anger, sadness	10 8 7	"I will never get better." "Why me?" "I shouldn't be in distressing situations."	Subtle behavioral avoidance: Stays at home; refuses to see a doctor Cognitive avoidance: Ruminates about death Situational avoidance: Avoids presenting a lecture in class
	Eat: Her appetite is good, but fear of experiencing IBS symptoms makes her avoid her favorite foods.	8	Anxiety, anger Anger, sadness	7 8	"I need to control everything I eat." "I can't eat foods like fast food, soda, and chewing gum."	Situational avoidance: Avoids foods with laxative or bloating effects, including beans and milk, especially during premenstrual period Subtle behavioral avoidance: Avoids eating before and during parties Situational avoidance: Avoids social situations (especially romantic date) because explaining dietary restrictions to others is distressing

(*continued*)

Table 11.3 CONTINUED

HEALTH CONDITION ANALYSIS					
Health condition description: Chronic symptoms of abdominal pain begin after eating as well as abdominal cramp and growling, which are more common in the morning and intensify by cold weather and stress. Intermittent constipation or diarrhea also occurs periodically, but the amount varies depending on the patient's stress and nutrition.					
How health condition (and its treatment) affects the patient's life?		**EMOTION ANALYSIS REGARDING HEALTH CONDITIONS AND ITS CONSEQUENCES**			
General life aspects	**Affectation/ interference** **0______10** **Nothing Very much**	**Strong uncomfortable emotions** Do patients feel strong emotions in any of these general life aspects?	**Intensity** **0______10** **Nothing Extreme**	**Aversive reactions**	**Emotional behaviors** (Situational avoidance/escape, subtle behavioral avoidance, cognitive avoidance, safety signals)
Sex: She worries about her future sexual function and that she is still single.	7	Depression, anxiety	6	"Sex will worsen my IBS symptoms." "Abdominal pain and cramps will prevent me from passionate and satisfying sex." "I'll never get married." "No one can accept my illness and will leave me." Ruminations about possible problems with the opposite sex	Situational avoidance: Avoids intimate relationships with the opposite sex Cognitive avoidance: Uses TV as a distractor to avoid negative thoughts Subtle behavioral avoidance: Resigned to being single forever

	Sleep: Sometimes her sleep is disturbed by diarrhea and the need to go to the bathroom frequently. Therefore, she is sleepy and fatigued the next day.	9	Fatigue, anger, anxiety	9	"This disease has deprived me of a good night's sleep." "I'm behind in my homework but I can't manage it with this fatigue."	Subtle behavioral avoidance: Stays in bed for long hours and misses classes Subtle behavioral avoidance: Preoccupied with unfinished tasks, which increases anxiety and leads to procrastination
	Activity: She is reluctant to be "in the spotlight"; avoids class participation, which led to academic difficulties; and restricts her social interactions to those who know about her IBS.	9	Anxiety, depression, shame	10	"Others will judge me as a wretched person." "My symptoms will embarrass me in social situations."	Subtle behavioral avoidance: Tries not to attract attention Situational avoidance: Avoids participating in group activities
	Energy: Very frequently feels fatigued, especially following defecation.	9	Depression	7	"This disease has made me weak and fatigued." "I can't deal with my problems. I'm useless."	Subtle behavioral avoidance: Procrastinating on academic tasks
	Medication side effects: Constipation (nortriptyline) and feeling drowsy (chlordiazepoxide)	8	Anger, worry	7	"The doctor did not diagnose my problem correctly." "All these efforts are useless."	Cognitive avoidance: Ruminates about stopping medication

(continued)

Table 11.3 CONTINUED

HEALTH CONDITION ANALYSIS					
Health condition description: Chronic symptoms of abdominal pain begin after eating as well as abdominal cramp and growling, which are more common in the morning and intensify by cold weather and stress. Intermittent constipation or diarrhea also occurs periodically, but the amount varies depending on the patient's stress and nutrition.					
How health condition (and its treatment) affects the patient's life?		**EMOTION ANALYSIS REGARDING HEALTH CONDITIONS AND ITS CONSEQUENCES**			
General life aspects	**Affectation/ interference** **0________10** **Nothing Very much**	**Strong uncomfortable emotions** Do patients feel strong emotions in any of these general life aspects?	**Intensity** **0________10** **Nothing Extreme**	**Aversive reactions**	**Emotional behaviors** (Situational avoidance/escape, subtle behavioral avoidance, cognitive avoidance, safety signals)
2. **Work/studies**: She is a postgraduate student but refuses to attend classes when feeling sick. She worries about possible embarrassing situations, which makes it difficult for her to concentrate.	10	Depression, shame, anxiety	10	"My stomach growling in class will embarrass me." "They will judge me as a rude person." "I am unable to meet all my obligations." "I will eventually be expelled from university. It is better for me to drop out of school myself."	Situational avoidance: Delays or fails to attend some classes Subtle behavioral avoidance: Tries to control the movements of the abdomen by clenching hands around stomach; maintains distance from others in the classroom Cognitive avoidance: Using TV as a distractor to keep her away from thinking; rumination about dropping out of school

3. **Daily life activities** (to buy, to cook, to clean, etc.): She sleeps more than she would like to and does not do the household chores. She experiences intrusive thoughts when shopping at the supermarket. Her self-confidence in different areas of functioning has decreased.	8	Sadness, anxiety	8	"I will never be able to eat delicious food, so why should I cook?" "What if I need a bathroom when I am in the supermarket?"	Subtle behavioral avoidance: Avoids cooking; worries about experiencing symptoms in outdoor or unfamiliar environments; performs safety behaviors such as using the bathroom frequently before leaving home
4. **Pleasant activities** (hobbies, sport, etc.): She has reduced activities such as jogging or going to the gym due to worries about her symptoms. She loves going to coffee shops and restaurants, but she always eats at home for fear of experiencing symptoms while she is out.	9	Shame, sadness, disappointment	7	"In the gym or restaurant, everyone will hear the sound of my stomach growling and I will be embarrassed." "When I am at a gym/restaurant, it embarrasses me that I have to go to the bathroom several times in a short time." "I can't enjoy the things I love."	Situational avoidance: Avoids going to the gym Subtle behavioral avoidance: Needs friends nearby for support and reassurance Avoidance/escape: Postpones doing athletic activities with her friends
5. **Personal relationships** (couple, family, friends, etc.): Her social relationships are limited to a few people who are aware of her condition. Despite her interest in living independently, being away from family and friends is a source of stress. Her relationships are affected by her aggressive reactions when experiencing symptoms, especially pain.	8	Depression, anger, shame	9	"People don't understand my pain." "My friends think I'm a weak or ridiculous person." "I'm ashamed by stomach growling."	Subtle behavioral avoidance: Avoids talking with family and friends about her feelings Situational avoidance: Avoids living in a university dormitory despite her interest to live with peers; rents a home to be alone; refuses to accept invitations for a romantic date

(*continued*)

Table 11.3 Continued

HEALTH CONDITION ANALYSIS					
Health condition description: Chronic symptoms of abdominal pain begin after eating as well as abdominal cramp and growling, which are more common in the morning and intensify by cold weather and stress. Intermittent constipation or diarrhea also occurs periodically, but the amount varies depending on the patient's stress and nutrition.					
How health condition (and its treatment) affects the patient's life?		**EMOTION ANALYSIS REGARDING HEALTH CONDITIONS AND ITS CONSEQUENCES**			
General life aspects	**Affectation/ interference** **0______10** **Nothing Very much**	**Strong uncomfortable emotions** Do patients feel strong emotions in any of these general life aspects?	**Intensity** **0______10** **Nothing Extreme**	**Aversive reactions**	**Emotional behaviors** (Situational avoidance/escape, subtle behavioral avoidance, cognitive avoidance, safety signals)
6. **Spirituality**: She is Muslim and has found worship useful as a way to calm herself down, but religious rituals that need ablution make her extremely upset.	7	Worry, anger	7	Obsessive thoughts about ablution	Avoidance/escape: Postpones praying
7. **Life goals**: She would like to actively participate in her classes, restart doing sports and going out with her friends without fear of embarrassment, travel more and meet new people, and ideally start a romantic relationship. She would like to graduate on time and start a job in her field.	9	Despair, depression	10	"I will never achieve my goals."	Subtle behavioral avoidance: Avoids planning due to the fear of not being adequate and being unable to achieve her goals
TREATMENT PLAN: FOCUS/APPLICATION OF CORE MODULES					
MODULE 1					
During this module, we will ask the patient to report her physical symptoms and their impact on different areas of her daily activities, as well as emotional changes usually occurring before and during the experience of IBS symptoms. Then, medication and psychological treatments will be introduced and reasons for medication use discussed. Regarding her negative expectation about treatment outcome (i.e., "I will never get better"), we will collaboratively evaluate the pros and cons of treatment participation. Then, treatment goals will be clarified (e.g., participating regularly in her classes). We will also introduce the self-monitoring rating scale and ask the patient to complete it.					

MODULE 2
Following psychoeducation about emotions, we will discuss the role of emotions (anxiety, fear of not being efficient, and depression) on her avoidant behaviors and general function. The aim is to help the patient achieve a more accurate understanding of the interaction between physical feelings associated with her emotions (shame and anxiety), thoughts ("Everyone will hear my stomach growling and I will be embarrassed"), and behaviors (avoid public situations such as class, dating, or the gym) and identifying emotional triggers (e.g., class presentation and meeting new people). Therefore, in this module, she will gain a greater understanding of her feelings and the situations that raise and reinforce them and learn to analyze her emotional responses.
MODULE 3
Because the patient uses avoidance as a predominant strategy in order to not experience negative emotions, which in turn limits her activities in general, in this module we will focus on encouraging her to observe her emotions (e.g., shame and despair) and subsequent reactions (e.g., avoidance) mindfully and not judge her physical and emotional sensations ("I will be ashamed by stomach growling"), herself ("I can't deal with my problems, I am useless"), or others (e.g., "My friends think I am a weak or ridiculous person," "People do not understand my pain"). In this module, the mindfulness techniques including Thought Train, Leaves Floating on a Stream, and Beach Ball metaphor will be trained. These visualization techniques are very useful for regulating emotions. Thought Train and Leaves Floating on a Stream exercises are used to help patients distance themselves from their flow of thoughts. Beach Ball metaphor helps patients understand that, sometimes, the more they fight a problem, the further they will sink and that often the solution lies in facing whatever it is they have been avoiding.
MODULE 4
In this module, rigid and nonadaptive appraisals of events (e.g., "If I attend this party, my stomach will definitely make noise and it will ruin my reputation") will be targeted by teaching the patient cognitive flexibility. The patient will gain skills to become more flexible in her thinking (e.g., "If I attend in this party/class, my stomach may or may not make some noise and others may or may not hear the noise. But I have some behavioral options to make the situation more comfortable for myself, such as explaining my condition or joking with the condition"; "I'll never get married. No one can accept my illness and will leave me" versus "I am not sure whether I will get married, but not getting married does not mean being miserable.")
MODULE 5
The concept and types of emotional behaviors will be introduced. Then patient will identify her emotional behaviors (e.g., procrastinating academic tasks), and the paradoxical effects of these behaviors (increasing her anxiety, which will intensify her gastrointestinal symptoms) will be discussed. She will plan for alternative actions. For example, she will be recommended to set up a hierarchy and perform it daily gradually. She will approach anxiety-provoking situations to practice engaging in alternative actions and to deal with her anxiety by practicing cognitive flexibility.

(*continued*)

Table 11.3 Continued

MODULE 6
She will work to increase her awareness of the role of physical sensations in emotional experiences. The focus in this module is on identifying physical sensations (e.g., stomach growling) associated with intense emotions (anxiety, shame, sadness, and despair). She will examine the way in which she experiences and thinks about her physical sensations, which contributes to her emotional experience. For example, because she does not eat before going to parties with friends, she will be encouraged to confront her physical sensations in order to increase her tolerance of them. In addition, imaginal exposures to stress-provoking situations will be used to help her become more aware and tolerant of her physical sensations.
MODULE 7
The concept of emotion exposures and its rationale will be introduced briefly. Then, the patient will be taught to gradually expose herself to internal (especially physical sensations such as stomach growling) and external stimuli (e.g., presenting a lecture) that tend to elicit intense emotional reactions. During these exposures, in order to help her become more tolerant of intense emotions while experiencing IBS symptoms, we will apply mindfulness skills from Module 3, such as the Beach Ball metaphor. The Beach Ball metaphor illustrates that the more she tries to bottle up her emotion, the harder it pops back up. In this metaphor, the ball symbolizes her emotions (e.g., anxiety, fear, anger, and shame) that she has been hiding for some time. She will imagine herself trying to sink the beach ball, and every time she pushes it under, it pops up to the surface again. She will understand that she is wasting her energy on an impossible and unhealthy task. In this module, the patient will be taught to approach her emotions and physical sensations and modify her responses to them by practicing other skills developed during treatment, including cognitive flexibility, and by applying mindful emotion awareness more directly. She will also develop a hierarchy of her fearful situations (class participation) and avoidance (participating in class group activities) and plan to conduct emotion exposures during the remainder of treatment. Physical sensation emotion exposures will be used for confronting uncomfortable physical sensations that may be contributing to strong emotions. For example, we will ask her to go to the hypermarket or gym and experience her physical sensations (e.g., heart racing and abdominal cramp) while being mindful of her emotional experience.
MODULE 8
In this module, we will review key treatment concepts and assess achievements. Symptoms and functional impairment at the end of treatment will be compared to baseline scores on measures of emotion and avoidance. Also, situations related to the disorder and its symptoms that occur between sessions 11 and 12, and the specific treatment techniques that she used to respond to her emotion, will also be discussed. To help reduce the possibility of setbacks following treatment, she will be helped to identify "high-risk" situations that are likely to elicit strong emotions (e.g., experiencing abdominal cramps while dating a man for the first time) and make a plan for responding to them using the treatment skills that she learned.

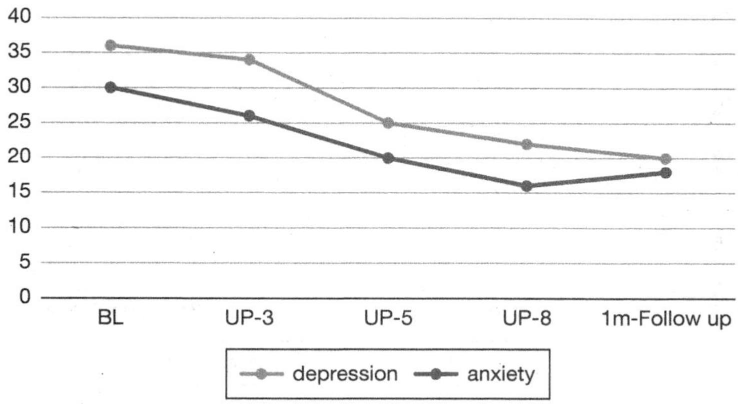

Figure 11.1 Changes in mood and anxiety during UP and 1-month follow-up. BL, baseline.

severe depression (36 of 126) and anxiety (30 of 126), based on a cutoff score of DASS-42. She showed high suppression (19 of 28) and partly low cognitive reappraisal (16 of 42) in her emotion regulation. In terms of the severity of GI symptoms, she achieved a score of 65 on GSRS, which indicates severe symptoms of GI IBS.

Changes in Mood and Anxiety During UP

Figure 11.1 shows F.'s mood variations from the baseline (BL) to the end of treatment. As observed, mood improved progressively from BL to the end of UP treatment, specifically after session 3. This decrease continued to a lesser extent until the follow-up period. Anxiety also decreased from BL (score = 30) to session 8 (score = 16). Anxiety then slightly increased at 1-month follow-up (score = 18) with issues in her exam.

Changes in Emotion Regulation Across the UP

As observed in Figure 11.2, emotion dysregulation also generally improved during treatment. The improvement in repression was more visible from the third session, but in terms of cognitive reappraisal, the improvement was more visible from session 5. These improvements remained stable from the last session until 1 month after treatment.

Changes in the Severity of Gastrointestinal Symptoms During the UP

F. reported the decrease of severity of her GI symptoms during all sessions of the UP treatment (score 64 at BL, 63 in session 3, 56 in session 5, and 50 at the end of

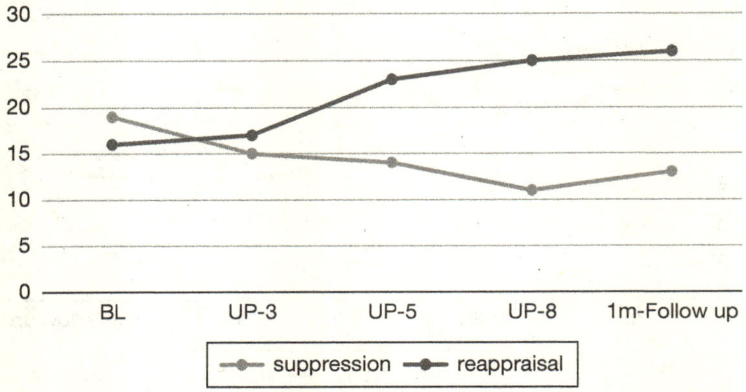

Figure 11.2 Changes in emotion regulation during UP and at 1-month follow-up.

treatment), and then slightly increased at 1-month follow-up (score = 53) when she was involved in preparing to take a final examination in one of her classes. Nevertheless, the symptoms were still less than the BL.

Case Example Conclusions

The patient reported severe anxiety and depression at BL. These emotions decreased during treatment, particularly after the implementation of Module 3 techniques. GI symptoms also showed a decreasing trend after this module. It seems that adding more exercises after Module 3 can play a role in this reduction. It is also possible that some of the reduction in symptoms is due to the patient's familiarity with the therapist and the treatment setting that occurs over time.

After treatment terminated, F.'s anxiety and GI symptoms recurred to some extent. At the 1-month assessment, we asked F. whether she had continued with mindfulness exercises as we assumed that this may have contributed to the brief recurrence of repression in the follow-up. F. confirmed that she had not been practicing mindfulness skills on a regular basis following treatment. Therefore, it seems that maintenance sessions can help her in this regard.

Regarding her educational activities, she reported that she engaged in these activities with less avoidance and had been able to attend her university classes, whereas she was not attending classes at the beginning of treatment.

CONCLUSION

Numerous studies have confirmed the co-occurrence of various psychological disorders among patients with IBS. Psychological comorbidities, especially depression and anxiety, can decrease social functioning, treatment adherence, and quality of life in patients with IBS. The psychiatric disease model suggests that the GI symptoms are a somatic expression of psychological problems. It has been suggested that IBS may reflect a vicious cycle of anxiety response in which fears and negative beliefs about somatic sensations lead to increased vigilance toward visceral sensations, which in turn may lead to a greater perception of visceral emotions. On the other hand, visceral emotions may be increased due to anxiety. Previous studies have also demonstrated that most IBS patients suffer from emotional dysregulation (Mazaheri et al., 2014; Porcelli et al., 2003) and may not use effective emotion regulation strategies. When patients with IBS cannot distinguish their emotions from physical states or suppress their emotions, they may be at greater risk of somatoform disorders and may experience more intense physical symptoms.

Given the high levels of emotional disorders in IBS, treatments that address psychological distress and IBS-specific symptoms and GI dysfunction may be especially appropriate to achieve positive outcomes in IBS patients. Therefore, applying treatments based on a transdiagnostic perspective seems to be useful. As mentioned previously, the UP is a transdiagnostic treatment of emotional disorders that focuses on targeting emotional dysregulation as a common maladaptive coping strategy across disorders. Regarding the fact that the UP targets emotion regulation as a common vulnerability in emotional disorders, it can be considered a potentially appropriate treatment for IBS patients who suffer from various comorbid emotional problems. Despite extensive evidence supporting the efficacy of UP in somatic and emotional disorders, the need for further investigations in the field of IBS still remains.

Limitations/Barriers Observed

Although co-occurrence of emotional disorders is well known as one of the most common problems in patients with IBS and despite the increasing knowledge about the promising effects of psychological interventions for improving the quality of life and daily functioning of IBS patients, there are still barriers to accommodating these therapies as part of a comprehensive treatment plan for the disease. Psychotherapy in some cultures, including Iran, may be highly unacceptable due to the stigma attached to any implication that patients may be "crazy" or "mentally ill." In addition, individuals with IBS, like many individuals with a chronic medical illness, often experience stigma related to their condition, and they believe that others have negative attitudes or beliefs about them or their condition (Taft et al., 2017). Stigmatization may come from health care providers, friends, and family and can lead to long-standing feelings of shame. Because IBS patients perceive their symptoms as shameful, it can be difficult or embarrassing to talk about them, and they may hide these symptoms from others, including their health care providers, and may postpone treatment and management of their symptoms (Ruddy, 2018). Even when they seek treatment for their problems, they prefer to see physicians and be attended at general hospitals that often do not include a psychologist and where physicians rarely refer these patients to a psychologist.

Poor knowledge about the effectiveness of different types of psychotherapeutic approaches and the format of intervention's delivery, especially for the Iranian population, is another important barrier that must be considered.

Additional barriers are the high cost of psychotherapy and the lack of insurance support in some countries, including Iran, which reduce the opportunity for people to receive psychotherapy for this disease.

Future Directions

Based on our clinical and research experience and regarding the barriers mentioned, the presence of a psychologist on the treatment team for patients with psychosomatic disorders, including IBS, and the use of psychotherapy UP, as a complementary treatment to medical treatments, are strongly recommended. To do this, it is necessary to make policy changes (e.g., to combine clinical and health psychologists in medical hospitals and provide insurance support for psychotherapy services) in evaluating and treating patients with IBS. Another solution is to disseminate information regarding the role of psychological factors in physical illnesses and the effectiveness of psychotherapy in improving them. Investigating the feasibility and effectiveness of different psychotherapies in general, and the UP in particular in an Iranian population, and adapting these interventions to specific cultural characteristics are recommended to enrich the comprehensive treatment plan for addressing IBS in Iran. In addition, while studying the effectiveness of this treatment on people with IBS, training and familiarizing clinicians can disseminate this protocol more broadly. Also, training psychologists with the UP in this treatment can also help reduce psychotherapy costs because they do not need to be trained and apply several specific-disorder protocols for emotional difficulties of IBS.

Tips/Advice to Clinicians

Based on our observations and experiences with IBS patients, we present some suggestions for clinicians adjusting the protocol for this population. Patients with IBS have been shown to struggle with assertiveness (e.g., difficulty in making needs known to others, discomfort in authoritative roles, and inability to be firm and assertive with others) and often experience social avoidance that can contribute to the aggravation of their IBS symptoms (Lackner & Gurtman, 2005). Therefore, we recommend focusing on these difficulties in treatment to help patients improve their ability to deal with social situations appropriately and improve their interpersonal relationships. In our experience, we find it useful to discuss difficulties related to interpersonal relationships before Module 5. During Module 5 in particular, we also help patients develop assertiveness skills and change patterns of avoidance related to social situations. Patients may also benefit from at least one additional follow-up session after treatment has concluded. During that session, patients will have further opportunities to raise concerns about applying the skills they learned and receive additional guidance on application of treatment skills to their daily lives. These additional sessions may also make it easier for some patients to cope with treatment termination. So, we propose adding two sessions to the program, one of which should follow the fifth session to train assertiveness and communication skills, and the other one should be added at the end of the protocol as a follow-up session to provide additional guidance.

REFERENCES

Allen, L. B., Tsao, J. C., Seidman, L. C., Ehrenreich-May, J., & Zeltzer, L. K. (2012). A unified, transdiagnostic treatment for adolescents with chronic pain and comorbid anxiety and depression. *Cognitive and Behavioral Practice, 19*(1), 56–67.

American Gastroenterological Association.(2015, December). *IBS in America: Survey Summary findings.*

Ballou, S., & Keefer, L. (2017). Psychological interventions for irritable bowel syndrome and inflammatory bowel diseases. *Clinical and Translational Gastroenterology, 8*(1), e214.

Barlow, D. H., Allen, L. B., & Choate, M. L. (2004). Toward a unified treatment for emotional disorders. *Behavior Therapy, 35*(2), 205–230. https://doi.org/10.1016/S0005-7894(04)80036-4

Barlow, D. H., Farchione, T. J., Fairholme, C. P., Sauer-Zavala, S., Latin, H. M., Ellard, K. K., Bullis, J. R., Bentley, K. H., Boettcher, H. T., & Cassiello-Robbins, C. (2017). *Unified Protocol for Transdiagnostic Treatment of Emotional Disorders: Therapist guide* (2nd ed.). Oxford University Press.

Bouchoucha, M., Hejnar, M., Devroede, G., Babba, T., Bon, C., & Benamouzig, R. (2013). Anxiety and depression as markers of multiplicity of sites of functional gastrointestinal disorders: A gender issue? *Clinics and Research in Hepatology and Gastroenterology, 37*(4), 422–430.

Boyce, P. M., Talley, N. J., Balaam, B., Koloski, N. A., & Truman, G. (2003). A randomized controlled trial of cognitive behavior therapy, relaxation training, and routine clinical care for the irritable bowel syndrome. *American Journal of Gastroenterology, 98*(10), 2209–2218.

Brown, T. A., Campbell, L. A., Lehman, C. L., Grisham, J. R., & Mancill, R. B. (2001). Current and lifetime comorbidity of the DSM-IV anxiety and mood disorders in a large clinical sample. *Journal of Abnormal Psychology, 110*(4), 585–599. https://doi.org/10.1037//0021-843X.110.4.585

Bruno, A., Zoccali, R. A., Pandolfo, G., Genovese, G., Merlino, M., Fries, W., Morace, C., Consolo, P., Mento, C., & Muscatello, M. R. A. (2018). Negative emotions in irritable bowel syndrome: Which differences among IBS subtypes? *Mediterranean Journal of Clinical Psychology, 6*(1). doi:10.6092/2282-1619/2018.6.1730

Bullis, J. R., Boettcher, H., Sauer-Zavala, S., Farchione, T. J., & Barlow, D. H. (2019). What is an emotional disorder? A transdiagnostic mechanistic definition with implications for assessment, treatment, and prevention. *Clinical Psychology: Science and Practice, 26*(2), e12278. https://doi.org/10.1111/cpsp.12278

Bullis, J. R., Sauer-Zavala, S., Bentley, K. H., Thompson-Hollands, J., Carl, J. R., & Barlow, D. H. (2015). The Unified Protocol for Transdiagnostic Treatment of Emotional Disorders: Preliminary exploration of effectiveness for group delivery. *Behavior Modification, 39*(2), 295–321.

Cameron, L., Leventhal, E. A., & Leventhal, H. (1995). Seeking medical care in response to symptoms and life stress. *Psychosomatic Medicine, 57*(1), 37–47.

Canavan, C., West, J., & Card, T. (2014). The epidemiology of irritable bowel syndrome. *Clinical Epidemiology, 6*, 71–80. https://doi.org/10.2147/CLEP.S40245

Carrozzino, D., & Porcelli, P. (2018). Alexithymia in gastroenterology and hepatology: A systematic review. *Frontiers in Psychology, 9*, 470. doi:10.3389/fpsyg.2018.00470

Casati, J., Toner, B. B., de Rooy, E. C., Drossman, D. A., & Maunder, R. G. (2000). Concerns of patients with inflammatory bowel disease: A review of emerging themes. *Digestive Diseases and Sciences, 45*, 26–31.

Cassiello-Robbins, C., Southward, M. W., Tirpak, J. W., & Sauer-Zavala, S. (2020). A systematic review of Unified Protocol applications with adult populations: Facilitating widespread dissemination via adaptability. *Clinical Psychology Review, 78*, 101852.

Corney, R. H., Stanton, R., Newell, R., Clare, A., & Fairclough, P. (1991). Behavioural psychotherapy in the treatment of irritable bowel syndrome. *Journal of Psychosomatic Research, 35*(4–5), 461–469.

Corsetti, M., Tack, J., Attara, G., & Sewell, M. (2018). *IBS global impact report 2018: Uncovering the true burden of irritable bowel syndrome (IBS) on people's lives.* GI Society. https://badgut.org/wp-content/uploads/IBS-Global-Impact-Report.pdf

Craske, M. G., Wolitzky-Taylor, K. B., Labus, J., Wu, S., Frese, M., Mayer, E. A., & Naliboff, B. D. (2011). A cognitive–behavioral treatment for irritable bowel syndrome using interoceptive exposure to visceral sensations. *Behaviour Research and Therapy, 49*(6–7), 413–421.

Dibajnia, P., Moghadasin, M., Madahi, M. E., & Keikhayfarzaneh, M. M. (2013). Depression, anxiety, stress, anger in IBS patients. *Journal of Pure and Applied Microbiology, 7*(1), 175–180.

Drossman, D. A., Li, Z., Andruzzi, E., Temple, R. D., Talley, N. J., Thompson, W. G., Whitehead, W. E., Janssens, J., Funch-Jensen, P., & Corazziari, E. (1993). U.S. householder survey of functional gastrointestinal disorders: Prevalence, sociodemography, and health impact. *Digestive Diseases and Sciences, 38*(9), 1569–1580. https://doi.org/10.1007/BF01303162

Drossman, D. A., Thompson, W. G., Talley, N. J., Funch-Jensen, P., Janssens, J., & Whitehead, W. E. (1990). Identification of subgroups of functional bowel disorders. *Gastroenterology International, 3*, 159–172.

Endo, Y., Shoji, T., Fukudo, S., Machida, T., Machida, T., Noda, S., & Hongo, M. (2011). The features of adolescent irritable bowel syndrome in Japan. *Journal of Gastroenterology and Hepatology, 26*, 106–109.

Farchione, T. J., Fairholme, C. P., Ellard, K. K., Boisseau, C. L., Thompson-Hollands, J., Carl, J. R., Gallagher, M. W., & Barlow, D. H. (2012). Unified Protocol for Transdiagnostic Treatment of Emotional Disorders: A randomized controlled trial. *Behavior Therapy, 43*(3), 666–678.

Ford, A. C., Quigley, E. M., Lacy, B. E., Lembo, A. J., Saito, Y. A., Schiller, L. R., Soffer, E. E., Speigel, B. M. R., & Moayyedi, P. (2014). Effect of antidepressants and psychological therapies, including hypnotherapy, in irritable bowel syndrome: Systematic review and meta-analysis. *American Journal of Gastroenterology, 109*(9), 1350–1365.

Gaylord, S. A., Palsson, O. S., Garland, E. L., Faurot, K. R., Coble, R. S., Mann, J. D., Frey, W., Leniek, K., & Whitehead, W. E. (2011). Mindfulness training reduces the severity of irritable bowel syndrome in women: Results of a randomized controlled trial. *American Journal of Gastroenterology*, *106*(9), 1678—1688.

Gros, D. F., Antony, M. M., McCabe, R. E., & Swinson, R. P. (2009). Frequency and severity of the symptoms of irritable bowel syndrome across the anxiety disorders and depression. *Journal of Anxiety Disorders*, *23*(2), 290–296.

Hazlett-Stevens, H., Craske, M. G., Mayer, E. A., Chang, L., & Naliboff, B. D. (2003). Prevalence of irritable bowel syndrome among university students: The roles of worry, neuroticism, anxiety sensitivity and visceral anxiety. *Journal of Psychosomatic Research*, *55*(6), 501–505.

Howell, S., Talley, N. J., Quine, S., & Poulton, R. (2004). The irritable bowel syndrome has origins in the childhood socioeconomic environment. *American Journal of Gastroenterology*, *99*(8), 1572–1578.

Hu, W. H., Wong, W. M., Lam, C. L., Lam, K. F., Hui, W. M., Lai, K. C., Xia, H. X., Lam, S. K., & Wong, B. C. (2002). Anxiety but not depression determines health care-seeking behaviour in Chinese patients with dyspepsia and irritable bowel syndrome: A population-based study. Alimentary *Pharmacology & Therapeutics*, *16*(12), 2081–2088. https://doi.org/10.1046/j.1365-2036.2002.01377.x

Hyphantis, T., Guthrie, E., Tomenson, B., & Creed, F. (2009). Psychodynamic interpersonal therapy and improvement in interpersonal difficulties in people with severe irritable bowel syndrome. *Pain*, *145*(1–2), 196–203.

Ito, M., & Muto, T. (2020). Effectiveness of acceptance and commitment therapy for irritable bowel syndrome non-patients: A pilot randomized waiting list-controlled trial. *Journal of Contextual Behavioral Science*, *15*, 85–91.

Jeong, I. S. (2004). Effect of progressive muscle relaxation using biofeedback on perceived stress, stress response, immune response and climacteric symptoms of middle-aged women. *Journal of Korean Academy of Nursing*, *34*(2), 213–224.

Kanazawa, M., Endo, Y., Whitehead, W. E., Kano, M., Hongo, M., & Fukudo, S. (2004). Patients and nonconsulters with irritable bowel syndrome reporting a parental history of bowel problems have more impaired psychological distress. *Digestive Diseases and Sciences*, *49*(6), 1046–1053. https://doi.org/10.1023/b:ddas.0000034570.52305.10

Kano, M., & Fukudo, S. (2013). The alexithymic brain: The neural pathways linking alexithymia to physical disorders. *BioPsychoSocial Medicine*, 7(1), 1

Kellett, S., & Gilbert, P. (2001). Acne: A biopsychosocial and evolutionary perspective with a focus on shame. *British Journal of Health Psychology*, *6*, 1–24.

Koloski, N. A., Talley, N. J., & Boyce, P. M. (2001). Predictors of health care seeking for irritable bowel syndrome and nonulcer dyspepsia: A critical review of the literature on symptom and psychosocial factors. *American Journal of Gastroenterology*, *96*(5), 1340–1349.

Kumano, H., Kaiya, H., Yoshiuchi, K., Yamanaka, G., Sasaki, T., & Kuboki, T. (2004). Comorbidity of irritable bowel syndrome, panic disorder, and agoraphobia in a Japanese representative sample. *American Journal of Gastroenterology*, *99*(2), 370–376. https://doi.org/10.1111/j.1572-0241.2004.04048.x

Lackner, J. M., & Gurtman, M. B. (2005). Patterns of interpersonal problems in irritable bowel syndrome patients: A circumplex analysis. *Journal of Psychosomatic Research*, *58*(6), 523–532.

Lahmann, C., Röhricht, F., Sauer, N., Noll-Hussong, M., Ronel, J., Henrich, G., von Arnim, A., & Loew, T. (2010). Functional relaxation as complementary therapy in irritable bowel syndrome: A randomized, controlled clinical trial. *Journal of Alternative and Complementary Medicine, 16*(1), 47–52.

Lea, R., & Whorwell, P. J. (2001). Quality of life in irritable bowel syndrome. *Pharmacoeconomics, 19*(6), 643–653.

Lee, S. P., Sung, I. K., Kim, J. H., Lee, S. Y., Park, H. S., & Shim, C. S. (2015). The effect of emotional stress and depression on the prevalence of digestive diseases. *Journal of Neurogastroenterology and Motility, 21*(2), 273–282.

Levy, R. L., Jones, K. R., Whitehead, W. E., Feld, S. I., Talley, N. J., & Corey, L. A. (2001). Irritable bowel syndrome in twins: Heredity and social learning both contribute to etiology. *Gastroenterology, 121*(4), 799–804.

Ljótsson, B., Falk, L., Vesterlund, A. W., Hedman, E., Lindfors, P., Rück, C., Hursti, T., Andreewitch, S., Jansson, L., Lindefors, N., & Andersson, G. (2010). Internet-delivered exposure and mindfulness-based therapy for irritable bowel syndrome: A randomized controlled trial. *Behaviour Research and Therapy, 48*(6), 531–539.

Lovell, R. M., & Ford, A.C. (2012). Global prevalence of and risk factors for irritable bowel syndrome: A meta-analysis. *Clinical Gastroenterology and Hepatology, 10*(7), 712–721.

Mazaheri, M., Daghaghzadeh, H., Afshar, H., & Mohammadi, N. (2014). The effectiveness of the Unified Protocol on emotional dysregulation and cognitive emotion regulation strategies in patients with psychosomatic disorders. *International Journal of Body, Mind and Culture, 1*(1), 73–82.

McEvoy, P. M., Nathan, P., & Norton, P. J. (2009). Efficacy of transdiagnostic treatments: A review of published outcome studies and future research directions. *Journal of Cognitive Psychotherapy, 23*(1), 20–33. https://doi.org/10.1891/0889-8391.23.1.20

Mearin, F., Lacy, B. E., Chang, L., Chey, W. D., Lembo, A. J., Simren, M., & Spiller, R. (2016). Bowel disorders. *Gastroenterology, 150*(6), 1393–1407. https://doi.org/10.1053/j.gastro.2016.02.031

Mohsenabadi, H., Zanjani, Z., Shabani, M. J., & Arj, A. (2018). A randomized clinical trial of the Unified Protocol for transdiagnostic treatment of emotional and gastrointestinal symptoms in patients with irritable bowel syndrome: Evaluating efficacy and mechanism of change. *Journal of Psychosomatic Research, 113*, 8–15.

Monnikes, H. (2011). Quality of life in patients with irritable bowel syndrome. *Journal of Clinical Gastroenterology, 45*(Suppl.), S98–S101.

Mousavi, E., Hosseini, S., Bakhtiyari, M., Mohammadi, A., Isfeedvajani, M. S., Arani, A. M., & Sadaat, S. H. (2019). Comparing the effectiveness of the Unified Protocol Transdiagnostic and Mindfulness Based Stress Reduction Program on anxiety and depression in infertile women receiving in vitro fertilization. *Journal of Research in Medical and Dental Science, 7*(2), 44–51.

Muscatello, M. R. A., Bruno, A., Pandolfo, G., Mico, U., Stilo, S., Scaffidi, M., Consolo, P., Tortora, A., Pallio, S., Giacobbe, G., Familiari, L., & Familiari, L. (2010). Depression, anxiety and anger in subtypes of irritable bowel syndrome patients. *Journal of Clinical Psychology in Medical Settings, 17*(1), 64–70.

Nellesen, D., Yee, K., Chawla, A., Lewis, B. E., & Carson, R. T. (2013). A systematic review of the economic and humanistic burden of illness in irritable bowel syndrome and chronic constipation. *Journal of Managed Care Pharmacy, 19*(9), 755–764. https://doi.org/10.18553/jmcp.2013.19.9.755

Oka, P., Parr, H., Barberio, B., Black, C. J., Savarino, E. V., & Ford, A. C. (2020). Global prevalence of irritable bowel syndrome according to Rome III or IV criteria: A systematic review and meta-analysis. *Lancet Gastroenterology & Hepatology*, *5*(10), 908–917. https://doi.org/10.1016/S2468-1253(20)30217-X

Olatunji, B. O., Tolin, D. F., & Lohr, J. M. (2004). Irritable bowel syndrome: Associated features and the efficacy of psychosocial treatments. *Applied and Preventive Psychology*, *11*(2), 125–140.

Porcelli, P., Bagby, R. M., Taylor, G. J., De Carne, M., Leandro, G., & Todarello, O. (2003). Alexithymia as predictor of treatment outcome in patients with functional gastrointestinal disorders. *Psychosomatic Medicine*, *65*(5), 911–918.

Portincasa, P., Moschetta, A., Baldassarre, G., Altomare, D. F., & Palasciano, G. (2003). Pan-enteric dysmotility, impaired quality of life and alexithymia in a large group of patients meeting ROME II criteria for irritable bowel syndrome. *World Journal of Gastroenterology*, *9*(10), 2293–2299.

Reinholt, N., & Krogh, J. (2014). Efficacy of transdiagnostic cognitive behaviour therapy for anxiety disorders: A systematic review and meta-analysis of published outcome studies. *Cognitive Behaviour Therapy*, *43*(3), 171–184. https://doi.org/10.1080/16506073.2014.897367

Rosmalen, J. G., Neeleman, J., Gans, R. O., & de Jonge, P. (2007). The association between neuroticism and self-reported common somatic symptoms in a population cohort. *Journal of Psychosomatic Research*, *62*(3), 305–311.

Rothman, A. J., & Salovey, P. (1997). Shaping perceptions to motivate healthy behavior: The role of message framing. *Psychological Bulletin*, *121*(1), 3–19.

Ruddy, J. (2018). From pretending to truly being OK: A journey from illness to health with postinfection irritable bowel syndrome: The patient's perspective. *Gastroenterology*, *155*(6), 1666–1669.

Sauer-Zavala, S., Bentley, K. H., Steele, S. J., Tirpak, J. W., Ametaj, A. A., Nauphal, M., Cardona, N., Wang, M., Farchione, T. J., & Barlow, D. H. (2020). Treating depressive disorders with the Unified Protocol: A preliminary randomized evaluation. *Journal of Affective Disorders*, *264*, 438–445.

Sauer-Zavala, S., Gutner, C. A., Farchione, T. J., Boettcher, H. T., Bullis, J. R., & Barlow, D. H. (2017). Current definitions of "transdiagnostic" in treatment development: A search for consensus. *Behavior Therapy*, *48*(1), 128–138.

Singh, P., Agnihotri, A., Pathak, M. K., Shirazi, A., Tiwari, R. P., Sreenivas, V., Sagar, R., & Makharia, G. K. (2012). Psychiatric, somatic and other functional gastrointestinal disorders in patients with irritable bowel syndrome at a tertiary care center. *Journal of Neurogastroenterology and Motility*, *18*(3), 324–331. https://doi.org/10.5056/jnm.2012.18.3.324

Stănculete, M. F., Pojoga, C., & Dumitraşcu, D. L. (2014). Experience of anger in patients with irritable bowel syndrome in Romania. *Clujul Medical*, *87*(2), 98–101.

Steele, S. J., Farchione, T. J., Cassiello-Robbins, C., Ametaj, A., Sbi, S., Sauer-Zavala, S., & Barlow, D. H. (2018). Efficacy of the Unified Protocol for transdiagnostic treatment of comorbid psychopathology accompanying emotional disorders compared to treatments targeting single disorders. *Journal of Psychiatric Research*, *104*, 211–216.

Taft, T. H., Bedell, A., Naftaly, J., & Keefer, L. (2017). Stigmatization toward irritable bowel syndrome and inflammatory bowel disease in an online cohort. *Neurogastroenterology & Motility*, *29*(2), e12921.

Usai, P., Manca, R., Lai, M. A., Russo, L., Boi, M. F., Ibba, I., Giolitto, G., & Cuomo, R. (2010). Prevalence of irritable bowel syndrome in Italian rural and urban areas. *European Journal of Internal Medicine, 21*(4), 324–326.

Van Oudenhove, L., Levy, R. L., Crowell, M. D., Drossman, D. A., Halpert, A. D., Keefer, L., Lackner, J. M., Murphy, T. B., & Naliboff, B. D. (2016). Biopsychosocial aspects of functional gastrointestinal disorders: How central and environmental processes contribute to the development and expression of functional gastrointestinal disorders. *Gastroenterology, 150*(6), 1355–1367. doi:10.1053/j.gastro.2016.02.027

Videlock, E. J., Adeyemo, M., Licudine, A., Hirano, M., Ohning, G., Mayer, M., Mayer, E. A., & Chang, L. (2009). Childhood trauma is associated with hypothalamic–pituitary–adrenal axis responsiveness in irritable bowel syndrome. *Gastroenterology, 137*(6), 1954–1962.

Welgan, P., Meshkinpour, H., & Beeler, M. (1988). Effect of anger on colon motor and myoelectric activity in irritable bowel syndrome. *Gastroenterology, 94*(5), 1150–1156.

Wilder-Smith, C. H. (2011). The balancing act: Endogenous modulation of pain in functional gastrointestinal disorders. *Gut, 60*(11), 1589–1599.

Wittchen, H. U., Jacobi, F., Rehm, J., Gustavsson, A., Svensson, M., Jönsson, B., Olesen, J., Allgulander, C., Alonso, J., Faravelli, C., Fratiglioni, L., Jennum, P., Lieb, R., Maercker, A., van Os, J., Preisig, M., Salvador-Carulla, L., Simon, R., & Steinhausen, H.-C. (2011). The size and burden of mental disorders and other disorders of the brain in Europe 2010. *European Neuropsychopharmacology, 21*(9), 655–679.

Zamani, M., Alizadeh-Tabari, S., & Zamani, V. (2019). Systematic review with meta-analysis: The prevalence of anxiety and depression in patients with irritable bowel syndrome. *Alimentary Pharmacology & Therapeutics, 50*(2), 132–143.

Zoccali, R., Muscatello, M. R. A., Bruno, A., Barillà, G., Campolo, D., Meduri, M., Familiari, L., Bonica, M., Consolo, P., & Scaffidi, M. (2006). Anger and ego-defence mechanisms in non-psychiatric patients with irritable bowel syndrome. *Digestive and Liver Disease, 38*(3), 195–200.

12

Treating Depression and Anxiety Disorders Simultaneously in Patients with Cardiovascular Diseases Utilizing the Unified Protocol

PHILLIP J. TULLY AND SUZANNE M. COSH ■

Cardiovascular diseases (CVDs) are the leading cause of mortality, morbidity, and disability globally (GBD 2017 Causes of Death Collaborators, 2018; GBD 2017 DALYs and HALE Collaborators, 2018; GBD 2017 Risk Factor Collaborators, 2018). CVDs portend diminished quality of life by comparison to that of persons without CVDs, including reduced social and occupational functioning (Le et al., 2018). Persons with CVDs comorbid with depression or anxiety are at an especially heightened risk for further death and disability, poor quality of life, and significantly higher costs for medical care (Baumeister et al., 2015; Carney & Freedland, 2017; Lichtman et al., 2014; Tully, Cosh, et al., 2014).

In the broadest sense, CVDs encompass conditions affecting the heart and vascular system (Verma et al., 2020). The most common CVDs include coronary heart disease (also referred to as coronary artery disease), heart failure (also referred to as cardiomyopathy), arrhythmia including atrial fibrillation and ventricular tachycardia, and disease of the aortic, mitral, tricuspid, or pulmonary heart valves. More than one CVD may occur in an individual due to common risk factors and different CVDs posing a risk for each other. Treatments for CVDs

Phillip J. Tully and Suzanne M. Cosh, *Treating Depression and Anxiety Disorders Simultaneously in Patients with Cardiovascular Diseases Utilizing the Unified Protocol* In: *Applications of the Unified Protocol in Health Conditions.* Edited by: Jorge Osma and Todd J. Farchione, Oxford University Press. © Oxford University Press 2023. DOI: 10.1093/oso/9780197564295.003.0012 typically necessitate pharmacological management and corrective surgery (e.g., coronary bypass surgery, coronary stent, ablation, and pacemaker insertion) that may be elective, urgent, or an emergency. Prior to surgeries, CVD patients experience heightened anxiety, worry, and fear of death (Hernandez-Palazon et al., 2018; Jackson et al., 2022; Tully et al., 2013). Postoperative phases are dominated by depression, anhedonia, somatic symptoms, pain, a period of limited physical mobility, and hypervigilance (Farris et al., 2019; Murphy et al., 2014; Simony et al., 2015). The CVD population with implanted cardioverter defibrillator devices or who experienced sudden cardiac arrest are particularly susceptible to enduring anxiety due to worries about device failure or death, post-traumatic stress disorder (PTSD) symptoms due to appropriate or inappropriate device "shocks," hypervigilance and preoccupation with cardiac symptoms, and avoidance (Berg et al., 2020; Habibovic et al., 2017; Hohls et al., 2020; Rosman et al., 2015). The dramatic and emergency nature of some cardiac events, such as a myocardial infarction, can lead to adjustment disorder and symptoms consistent with PTSD (Tully & Cosh, 2019; Wilder Schaaf et al., 2013). Fear of dying is especially linked with PTSD, anxiety, and depression in the longer term (Whitehead et al., 2005).

It is estimated that 15–20% of CVD patients meet criteria for major depression (Baird et al., 2018; Correa-Rodriguez et al., 2020; Lossnitzer et al., 2013; Thombs et al., 2008), comparable to the combined prevalence of single and recurrent major depressive episodes in the community (Kessler et al., 2012). Less is reported on dysthymia and bipolar disorders, although these appear to have a strong association with cardiometabolic risk factors and CVDs (Baune et al., 2006; Goldstein et al., 2015). Randomized control trial (RCT) data suggest that at least 50% of CVD patients with depression also meet criteria for anxiety disorder (Rollman et al., 2009), and psychiatric disorder comorbidity appears to be the norm rather than the exception (Celano et al., 2013; Grech et al., 2019; Tully, Wittert, et al., 2014), parallel to general presentations in community mental health care (Kessler et al., 2011). The point prevalence for some anxiety disorders may be lower in CVD populations, including obsessive–compulsive disorder (1.8% vs. 2.7%), social phobia (4.6% vs. 13.0%), and specific phobia (4.3% vs. 13.8%) (Kessler et al., 2012; Tully, Cosh, et al., 2014); however, evidence is sparse. Otherwise, anxiety disorder prevalence is marginally higher in CVD populations by comparison to general community samples for PTSD (12.0% vs. 8.0%), generalized anxiety disorder (8% vs. 6.2%), panic disorder (6.8% vs. 5.2%), and agoraphobia (3.6% vs. 2.6%) (Edmondson et al., 2012; Kessler et al., 2012; Tully, Cosh, et al., 2014).

There is consistent empirical evidence from meta-analyses that the association between CVDs with anxiety and depression disorders is bidirectional. That is, meta-analyses of etiological studies indicate that anxiety and depression disorders lead to the onset of CVDs (Edmondson et al., 2013; Nicholson et al., 2006; Tully et al., 2015) and, conversely, that the onset of CVDs is associated with incident anxiety and depression disorders, which in turn increase the risk for recurrent adverse cardiac events (Barth et al., 2004; Edmondson et al., 2012; Nicholson et al., 2006; Tully, Cosh, et al., 2014). Potential explanations for this bidirectional association include a preponderance of CVD risk factors, such as tobacco smoking, excessive alcohol use, illicit drug use, unhealthy diet, reduced physical activity, and obesity, which are commonly seen alongside depression and anxiety (Albus et al., 2019; Pedersen et al., 2017). In established CVD populations, additional psychosocial risk factors associated with depression and anxiety include reduced adherence to medications and lifestyle recommendations (e.g., cardiac rehabilitation) (Pogosova et al., 2015). Depression is universally associated with poorer adherence and unhealthy CVD behavioral risk factors, thereby increasing CVD risk (Carney & Freedland, 2017). Findings for anxiety appear mixed, with some research documenting an association with increased (Parker et al., 2011) as well as decreased adherence to recommended secondary prevention strategies (Husain et al., 2018; Taggart Wasson et al., 2018). Adherence behaviors attributable to anxiety are partly driven by attention, monitoring, and worry, whereas lower adherence behaviors are most strongly driven by avoidance and fear (Hohls et al., 2020; Sardinha et al., 2012). Research has linked PTSD and re-experiencing symptoms in particular with avoidance of cardiovascular medications post-cardiac event (Husain et al., 2018).

Collectively, the bidirectional association and multifactorial behavioral pathways involved in depression and anxiety within CVD populations underscore the importance of concerted mental health treatment in persons with established CVDs or CVD risk factors. Unfortunately, the majority of interventions in CVD are narrowly focused on depression or persons without clinically relevant symptoms, whereas interventions focusing on anxiety disorders in CVD populations remain scarce.

Transdiagnostic interventions are positioned at the forefront of new ways to improve mental health of CVD populations. Recent examples include metacognitive therapy (MCT) devised by Wells et al. (2018) and the Unified Protocol (UP) based on work by Barlow and colleagues (2011). Potential advantages of the UP over MCT in CVD populations include increasing awareness and tolerance of physical sensations such as through interoceptive symptom induction of cardiovascular symptoms. We further argue below that the UP's targeting of maladaptive emotion-driven behaviors can be conceptually broadened to include emotion-driven behaviors pertinent to cardiovascular health (binge eating, smoking, etc.). Moreover, attention training techniques in MCT aiming to increase a patient's executive control (Normann & Morina, 2018) may prove challenging in CVD populations who are prone to executive function deficits due to focal lesions in white matter tracts (Tully et al., 2020) and altered frontal–subcortical connectivity (Taylor et al., 2013). Nonetheless, MCT can be efficacious among somatic disease patients in as few as 6 sessions (Fisher et al., 2019), whereas the UP outlined by Barlow et al. (2011) may require between 12 and 18 sessions depending on severity of depression and anxiety. The application of UP to CVD populations is described next, noting, where relevant, some suggested adaptions for the UP with CVD patients. A clinical case example is also summarized to provide additional context for these adaptions.

ADAPTIONS OF THE UP FOR USE IN CVD POPULATIONS

Our team's work with the UP commenced in 2013 in a sample of general cardiovascular patients. Due to the highly medicalized nature of treating anxiety and depression in CVD populations and patient preference for shorter therapies (Skala et al., 2005), we refined the UP from 18 sessions, covering 8 modules (and the preliminary module), down to 12 sessions (Table 12.1), opting for 50- to 90-minute weekly sessions delivered individually and face-to-face at the cardiology outpatient clinic. General treatment format and procedures as outlined by Barlow and colleagues (2011) are adhered to with some important modifications specific to the nature of treating CVD patients with mental health concerns. To illustrate the adaptions of UP in the context of CVD, Table 12.2 describes further the modifications for a 56-year-old patient with atrial fibrillation and coronary artery disease, presenting with major depression and panic attacks. The patient presents after referral from the treating cardiologist with concerns about a slow recovery from the cardiac ablation procedure and myocardial infarction, with ongoing low energy and mood, diminished exercise capacity, and emergency department presentations for high heart rate and breathlessness that rapidly de-escalates without medical intervention (no cardiac biomarkers or electrocardiogram [ECG] indication of myocardial infarction). The patient reports an inability to cope and worry they might have another heart attack. A description of their pre- and post-treatment outcomes is provided in Table 12.3.

When devising a UP schedule for CVD patients, we implement the module on psychotropic drugs (formerly Module 8) in Week 1, opting to discuss how CBT can complement psychotropic medication use prior to UP. The case example was taking citalopram (a selective serotonin reuptake inhibitor) for anxiety and depression, thus necessitating acknowledgment by the therapist how CBT and medication may be used concurrently. The importance of emotional disorders in CVD was also described, utilizing information from the National Heart Foundation of Australia and the American Heart Association. A second modification during motivation enhancement (Module 1) involves developing a chest pain action plan to foster coping strategies and leave patients with something tangible from their early CBT sessions. A description of how to develop chest pain action plans is detailed elsewhere (Tully et al., 2017), and the aim is to provide clear instructions on seeking urgent medical help in the event of a probable myocardial infarction or other cardiac emergency. The chest pain action plan is a requisite step prior to situational or interoceptive exposures.

We also adapt the module pertaining to observing emotional experiences (Module 3) by instilling a suite of mindfulness techniques suitable for chronic pain, cancer, and other somatic diseases such as CVDs. The breathing space (5–10 minutes) and body scan (10–30 minutes) (Kabat-Zinn, 1990; Williams et al., 2007) exercises focus more on bodily sensations than thought activity, which we value as a formative and necessary step preceding Modules 4–7. Specifically, body scan may draw attention to CVD specific sensations involving breathing and heart

Table 12.1 Application of Transdiagnostic UP in CVD Populations Compared to Barlow's Original Model[A]

		Suggested UP Structure with Cardiovascular Populations				Barlow's Original UP Structure	
Week	Module	Focus	Content	Week	Module	Focus	Content
1	Prelim, 1-I	Introduction	Introduction to emotional disorders, CBT treatment format and procedures including monitoring, goal setting	1	—	Introduction	Introduction to emotional disorders, CBT treatment format and procedures including monitoring
2	1-II	Motivation enhancement for treatment engagement	Focusing on enhancing motivation and readiness for change and treatment engagement	2	1	Motivation enhancement for treatment engagement	Focusing on enhancing motivation and readiness for change and treatment engagement
3	2-I and 2-II	Psychoeducation	Understanding emotions, and recognizing and monitoring emotional responses	3	2-I	Psychoeducation	Understanding emotions
4	3-I	Emotion awareness training	Learning to observe emotional experiences and mindfulness	4	2-II	Psychoeducation	Recognizing and tracking emotional responses
5	3-II	Emotion awareness training	Learning to observe emotional experiences and mindfulness	5	3-I	Learning to observe experiences	Increasing present-focused emotion awareness
6	4-I and 4-II	Cognitive appraisal and reappraisal	Increasing cognitive flexibility	6	3-II	Learning to observe experiences	Increasing present-focused emotion awareness
7	5-I and 5-II	Emotion avoidance	Identifying and preventing patterns of emotion avoidance and maladaptive emotion-driven behaviors	7	4-I	Cognitive appraisal and reappraisal	Increasing cognitive flexibility
8	6	Awareness and tolerance of physical sensations	Increasing awareness and tolerance of emotion-related physical sensations	8	4-II	Cognitive appraisal and reappraisal	Increasing cognitive flexibility
9	7	Interoceptive and situational emotion exposures	Interoceptive and situation-based emotion-focused exposure	9	5-I	Emotion avoidance	Identifying and preventing patterns of emotion avoidance and maladaptive emotion-driven behaviors

(*continued*)

Table 12.1 CONTINUED

		Suggested UP Structure with Cardiovascular Populations				Barlow's Original UP Structure	
Week	Module	Focus	Content	Week	Module	Focus	Content
10	7	Interoceptive and situational emotion exposures	Interoceptive and situation-based emotion focused exposure	10	5-II	Emotion-driven behaviors	Identifying and preventing patterns of emotion avoidance and maladaptive emotion-driven behaviors
11	7	Interoceptive and situational emotion exposures	Interoceptive and situation-based emotion-focused exposure	11	6	Awareness and tolerance of physical sensations	Increasing awareness and tolerance of emotion-related physical sensations
12	8	Accomplishments, maintenance and relapse prevention	Summarizing the relevant techniques attained and developing relapse prevention strategies	12–17	7	Interoceptive and situational emotion exposures	Interoceptive and situation-based emotion-focused exposure
				18	8	Medications for anxiety and depression, accomplishments, maintenance and relapse prevention	Medications for anxiety and depression, summarizing the relevant techniques attained and developing relapse prevention strategies

[a]Patient self-assessment of symptoms completed before every session in the waiting room utilizing the Overall Anxiety Severity and Interference Scale (OASIS) and Overall Depression Severity and Interference Scale (ODSIS). For CVD patients, we recommend alternative monitoring forms for depression (Patient Health Questionnaire 9-item scale [PHQ-9]) and for anxiety (Generalized Anxiety Disorder 7-item scale [GAD-7]). The rationale is these are widely recommended and adopted in the CVD population (Albus et al., 2019; Huffman et al., 2013; Lichtman et al., 2014; Vaccarino et al., 2019). Cardiac-specific anxiety can also be assessed with the Cardiac Anxiety Questionnaire (Eifert et al., 2000)

CBT, cognitive–behavioral therapy; CVD, cardiovascular disease; HW, homework; UP, Unified Protocol.

Table 12.2 A Case Conceptualization with the UP in Cardiovascular Disease

HEALTH CONDITION ANALYSIS						
Health condition description: Male patient 56 years of age presenting with a history of atrial fibrillation (arrhythmia) requiring ablation procedure in the past 12 months. Cardiac symptoms include tachycardia, breathlessness, and fatigability secondary to a myocardial infarction in the past 6 months. The patient presents after referral from the treating cardiologist with concerns about a slow recovery from the cardiac ablation procedure and myocardial infarction, with ongoing low energy and mood, diminished exercise capacity, and emergency department presentations for high heart rate and breathlessness that rapidly de-escalates without medical intervention (no cardiac biomarkers or ECG indication of myocardial infarction). The patient reports an inability to cope and worry they might have another heart attack.						
How does the health condition (and its treatment) affect the patient's life?			**EMOTION ANALYSIS REGARDING HEALTH CONDITIONS AND ITS CONSEQUENCES**			
General life aspects		**Affectation/ interference** 0_____10 Nothing Very much	**Strong uncomfortable emotions** Do patients feel strong emotions in any of these general life aspects?	**Intensity** 0_____10 Nothing Extreme	**Aversive reactions**	**Emotional behaviors** (Situational avoidance/escape, subtle behavioral avoidance, cognitive avoidance, safety signals)
1. **Physical**	**Eat:** Monitoring food intake for salt and saturated fats. Binge eating when alone and anxious.	4 7	Worry Guilt	5 9	"If I do not watch what I eat I may have a heart attack." "I can't cope with anxiety and must eat to feel better."	Avoid cooking and leave this up to wife to monitor; secretly binge eat when alone
	Sex: Low sex drive and erectile problems,	4	Worthlessness	5	"I cannot satisfy my wife."	Sleep in separate bedroom to wife
	Sleep: Interrupted sleep duration and quality resulting in exhaustion and daytime sleepiness.	7	Irritable, restlessness	7	"I can never get enough sleep."	Stay up late reading in bed
	Activity: Limited exercise and physical activity.	6	Fear, panic	8	"Exercise leads to abnormal heart rate."	Avoid physical exertion; stop at any sign of breathlessness or fast heart rate
	Energy: High fatigability.	6	Tiredness, lethargy	7	"I am too tired to do anything."	

(*continued*)

Table 12.2 CONTINUED

HEALTH CONDITION ANALYSIS						
Health condition description: Male patient 56 years of age presenting with a history of atrial fibrillation (arrhythmia) requiring ablation procedure in the past 12 months. Cardiac symptoms include tachycardia, breathlessness, and fatigability secondary to a myocardial infarction in the past 6 months. The patient presents after referral from the treating cardiologist with concerns about a slow recovery from the cardiac ablation procedure and myocardial infarction, with ongoing low energy and mood, diminished exercise capacity, and emergency department presentations for high heart rate and breathlessness that rapidly de-escalates without medical intervention (no cardiac biomarkers or ECG indication of myocardial infarction). The patient reports an inability to cope and worry they might have another heart attack.						
How does the health condition (and its treatment) affect the patient's life?			**EMOTION ANALYSIS REGARDING HEALTH CONDITIONS AND ITS CONSEQUENCES**			
General life aspects		**Affectation/ interference** **0________10** **Nothing Very much**	**Strong uncomfortable emotions** Do patients feel strong emotions in any of these general life aspects?	**Intensity** **0________10** **Nothing Extreme**	**Aversive reactions**	**Emotional behaviors** (Situational avoidance/escape, subtle behavioral avoidance, cognitive avoidance, safety signals)
	Medication side effects: Palpitations from nitrates, bronchospasm from beta-blockers, chest pain from anti-arrhythmics.	6	Hopelessness, frustration	7	"Maybe I am too sick to be saved." "I dread taking these stupid pills."	Intentionally miss a dose of medications
2. **Work**	Multiple paid and unpaid absences from work for surgery and appointments.	4	Guilt	5	"I could lose my job."	Not talking to co-workers about health when asked
3. **Daily life activities**	Start driving to work rather than take public transport.	4	Anxiety, panic	6	"Help won't be available if I have a heart attack."	Avoid public transport; avoid congested driving routes as help might not be available
4. **Pleasant activities**	Playing golf.	3	Sadness	5	"I can't see my friends anymore on the golf course."	Avoid playing golf

5. **Personal relationships**	Co-dependent on wife for being present at doctor's appointments.	3	Guilt	5	"I cannot cope on my own."	Avoid doctor's appointments on own
	Not knowing what to say to friends about anxiety.	7	Shame	8	"My friends will think less of me."	Avoid phone calls from friends
TREATMENT PLAN						
MODULE 1						
The first module describes the prevalence and importance of emotional disorders in CVD and utilizes pamphlets on depression and anxiety from the National Heart Foundation of Australia and American Heart Association. The CBT and UP treatment format and procedures are described along with monitoring forms, opting for measures endorsed by several cardiac societies (e.g., PHQ-9, GAD-7). Goal setting is undertaken with the therapist while focusing on enhancing motivation and readiness for change and treatment engagement. Consideration is given to cardiologist notes to guide psychotherapy treatment focus (e.g., frequent emergency department visits). The first module acknowledges how CBT can complement psychotropic medication use. Also during the earliest module, we develop chest pain action plans to foster coping strategies and as a fundamental step prior to situational or interoceptive exposures.						
MODULE 2						
The second module requires psychoeducation about emotions and recognizing and monitoring emotional responses. Specific examples tailored to CVD patients include fear of a heart attack, anxiety about exercise, and depression-related emotions such as hopelessness, guilt, and shame about loss of dependence and physical activity restrictions as a result of CVD. Consideration is given to identify any resultant emotion-driven behaviors that have adverse cardiovascular effects (e.g., binge eating).						
MODULE 3						
Mindfulness practice orients patients to body scan and observing one's physical sensations, which is a formative step before any interoceptive symptom inductions can occur. The observation of emotions is facilitated with record forms and in session exercises. Cardiovascular-specific adaptions to body scan can incorporate mindful awareness of heart beating sounds, heart rhythm, and heartbeat intensity.						

(*continued*)

Table 12.2 Continued

MODULE 4
The increasing cognitive flexibility module requires exploration of alternates to maladaptive cognitions that are cardiac specific (e.g., "Exercise leads to abnormal heart rate" and "Help won't be available if I have a heart attack") and also those related to binge eating (e.g., "I can't cope with anxiety and must eat to feel better").
MODULE 5
This module works with CVD patients toward identifying and preventing patterns of emotion avoidance and maladaptive emotion-driven behaviors. The module works collaboratively with patients who identify any CVD-risky behaviors as emotion-driven behaviors or coping strategies. The case example has a history of binge eating that coincides with being alone and anxious, which parallels some anxieties (avoiding public transport) and cognitions concerning a myocardial infarction (e.g., "I cannot cope on my own" and "Help won't be available if I have a heart attack").
MODULE 6
Module 6 involves psychoeducation about the overlap between emotional disorder symptoms and CVDs, acknowledging the ambiguity in symptom origins as "mental," "cardiovascular," or "shared." The suite of mindfulness techniques are continued to foster a nonjudgmental attitude toward somatic symptoms and resisting trying to judge origins as "mental" or "cardiovascular." The *chest pain dilemma matrix* can be presented for patients who frequently present to emergency departments for benign reasons such as the case example.
MODULE 7
A great deal of therapist and patient time should be dedicated to this module to increase awareness and tolerance of emotion-related physical sensations, counter avoidance, and provide CVD symptom and situational exposures in order to provide habituation. The module may require 6 weeks for patients with severe anxiety and high avoidance. The module is presented with panic symptom induction maneuvers that are considered safe for CVD patients. Idiosyncratic exploration and challenging of panic-like anxiety with between-session homework tasks set in real-world situations are required for success in this module.
MODULE 8
Summarizing the relevant techniques attained and developing relapse prevention strategies. Psychotropic drugs omitted from this module and presented in Module 1.

Table 12.3 Self-Reported Psychological Rating Scale Outcomes for the Cardiovascular Case Study After Treatment with the UP

	Baseline	End of Treatment	6 Months After UP
Anxiety—GAD-7	17	4	5
Anxiety impairment and avoidance—OASIS	13	3	2
Depressive symptoms—PHQ-9	20	5	4
Stress—DASS	21	5	7

DASS, Depression Anxiety and Stress Scales; GAD-7, Generalized Anxiety Disorder 7-item scale; OASIS, Overall Anxiety Severity and Impairment Scale; PHQ-9, Patient Health Questionnaire 9-item scale; UP, Unified Protocol.

beats. For patients with a left ventricular device (i.e., an external device that takes over the pumping action of the heart), we redirect focus on the absence of heart sounds. In either case, the purpose of mindful body scan is to lay foundation work on the ambiguity of the origins of somatic symptoms as "mental," "cardiovascular," or "shared" (see Table 12.2, Module 6).

Our work in the adapted Module 5 posits that emotion-driven behaviors may include specific behaviors that are detrimental to cardiovascular health. Some CVD patients conceptualize their emotion-driven behaviors in this manner, which is somewhat analogous to maladaptive coping strategies observed in cardiovascular populations (Whitmarsh et al., 2003). For the purposes of treating CVD patients with the UP, we work with patients who describe emotion-driven behaviors in terms of CVD risky behaviors: binge eating, smoking, excessive alcohol intake, or illicit drug use. Our adapted module also conceptualizes exercise avoidance as emotion avoidance. Care should be taken here to address any surreptitious avoidance of physical sensations and exercise (Farris et al., 2019) in order to maximize the utility of Modules 6 and 7. Moreover, moderate-intensity exercise such as brisk walking forms a frontline exposure technique for anxious CVD patients (Tully et al., 2017).

In Module 6, we provide detailed psychoeducation about the overlap between emotional disorder symptoms and CVDs and delay symptom induction tasks until Module 7. Many symptoms of major depression overlap those of heart failure and coronary artery disease, namely fatigability and lethargy, concentration problems, insomnia or hypersomnia, and psychomotor retardation, whereas physical activity limitations imposed by CVDs may be misinterpreted by the psychologist as anhedonia (Martens et al., 2006). Likewise, anxious cardiac patients may attribute chest pain, palpitations, or dyspnea to CVD and impending myocardial infarction. Dizziness and derealization may be interpreted as a sign of imminent stroke. Other symptoms can also be targets for misinterpretation (e.g., postural hypotension or lower blood pressure when standing up quickly). CVD patients must evaluate such symptoms in terms of high medical risk (Schwartz

Table 12.4 The Chest Pain Dilemma Matrix for the Case Example with CVD Treated with the UP[a]

	The Dr. said . . .	
I **thought . . .**	"Yes it was a heart attack"	"No it was not a heart attack"
Yes it was a heart attack!	True positive	False positive
No it was not a heart attack	False negative	True negative

[a]UP therapist asks, "Which section of the table best represents your last visit to hospital?" The patient nominated a false positive.

CVD, cardiovascular disease; UP, Unified Protocol.

Reprinted with permission from Tully et al. (2017).

et al., 1999) under the caveat that it is improbable to distinguish between chest pain caused by anxiety and that caused by CVD (Dornelas, 2008).

Cognitive restructuring based on notions of catastrophic misinterpretation of bodily symptoms is reserved only for patients who present frequently to emergency departments for benign reasons, such as our case example. In these cases, we utilize the chest pain dilemma matrix (Table 12.4). This entails discussing a recent example of chest pain; exploring each of the four quadrants of the matrix; and, both before and after the in vivo exercise, rating the patient's belief they were having a cardiac event or heart attack.

For patients with anxiety and no emergency department presentations (for benign reasons), the uncertainty in knowing the origins of somatic symptoms is discussed. The mindfulness techniques instilled in Module 5 are drawn upon to explore the ambiguity in somatic symptom origins as mental, cardiovascular, or shared. Moreover, we utilize Socratic questioning and downward arrow techniques to explore the continuum of control over risk factors and explore positive meta-cognitions about anxiety and hypervigilance. Deeper cognitive restructuring is based on the perceived threat of somatic symptoms. Common examples include "I cannot cope," "I am weak," "I brought this on myself," and "I just cannot go through that again!" Problem-solving strategies and therapist reframing are well tolerated to address cardiovascular risk in such a broad manner, thereby increasing awareness and tolerance of emotion-related physical sensations.

A total of 3 weeks is allocated to Module 7, which should indeed be extended to six sessions in cases of severe anxiety dominated by emergency department presentations and overt avoidance of situations or behaviors that lead to CVD-like sensations (e.g., exercise). We previously outlined some special considerations to factor into CBT, including the UP, when devising in vivo symptom exposures and cognitive restructuring for anxiety symptoms that overlap those of CVDs, especially panic (Tully et al., 2017; Tully et al., 2022). Clinicians should familiarize themselves with these adaptions prior to commencing CBT for anxiety with a

CVD patient. Exposure and interoceptive symptom induction exercises provide an opportunity for habituation (Asmundson et al., 2013) but pose a risk to anxious cardiac patients by combining a mental stressor and physiological challenge to the cardiorespiratory system, which can induce myocardial ischemia (Rozanski et al., 1999). Possible serious complications include myocardial stunning, reversible left ventricular dysfunction (Wittstein et al., 2005), arrhythmia (Çiçek et al., 2012; Yavuzkir et al., 2007), and syncope and head injury (Ricci et al., 2015). Given these potential complications, we stress that interoceptive symptom induction maneuvers should be performed after consultation with the cardiologist or general physician (Sardinha et al., 2009). We conclude the UP with Module 8 on relapse prevention as described by Barlow et al. (2011), omitting the section on psychotropic drugs.

EFFICACY OF THE UP IN CVD PATIENTS

We performed the first pilot-feasibility study to implement the UP with CVD populations in the Cardiovascular Health and Mood Problems Study (CHAMPS). In CHAMPS (Tully et al., 2016), patients were eligible if they met criteria for a current depression or anxiety disorder (as defined by the Mini International Neuropsychiatric Interview) and had moderate or higher levels of current depression or anxiety symptoms (defined by the Patient Health Questionnaire 9-item scale [PHQ-9] and the Generalized Anxiety Disorder 7-item scale [GAD-7]). Assessments were made by trained assessors blind to treatment allocation, at baseline, post-treatment, and 6 months after the end of treatment. By 6-month follow-up, there was a significant reduction in anxiety symptoms among the patients randomized to the UP versus enhanced usual care (EUC) in linear mixed models (Table 12.5). Significant reduction in anxiety was evident for the GAD-7 in the UP post-treatment ($\Delta = -9.00 \pm 3.74$) and at 6-month follow-up ($\Delta = -6.16 \pm 3.43$), by comparison to change in the EUC post-treatment ($\Delta = -6.20 \pm 3.21$) and at 6-month follow-up ($\Delta = -4.85 \pm 4.43$) (Tully et al., 2022). Significant reduction in anxiety was also evident for the Overall Anxiety Severity and Interference Scale in the UP post-treatment ($\Delta = -3.89 \pm 4.30$) and at 6-month follow-up ($\Delta = -2.81 \pm 3.32$), by comparison to change in the EUC post-treatment ($\Delta = -2.52 \pm 2.48$) and at 6-month follow-up ($\Delta = -1.43 \pm 2.39$). No significant effects were evident for depression (PHQ-9), stress (Depression Anxiety and Stress Scales–21), or metacognitive worry beliefs (Tully et al., 2022). There was evidence favoring the UP intervention for greater improvement over 6 months in physical quality of life, as well as a reduction in harmful alcohol use (Tully et al., 2022). Reduction in CVD-related readmissions has not been established but is plausible based on similar work focusing on exposure and habituation to somatic symptoms common to CVD populations with depression and anxiety (Tully, 2015; Tully et al., 2015). Collectively, these encouraging results indicate that the UP may offer the most benefit to CVD patients with anxiety disorders (Tully et al., 2022) alongside well-established interventions for depression (Tully et al., 2021).

Table 12.5 Change in Psychological Outcomes for Patients Randomized to Unified Protocol Versus Enhanced Usual Care in the CHAMPS Trial

		Control		UP		*P*
		M (*SD*)	Δ (*SD*)	Pre *M* (*SD*)	Δ (*SD*)	
Anxiety (GAD-7)	Pre	9.50 (3.31)	—	10.67 (5.57)	—	0.011*
	Post	3.30 (5.16)	−6.20 (3.21)	1.67 (2.78)	−9.00 (3.74)	
	6-month	4.65 (6.61)	−4.85 (4.43)	4.51 (3.66)	−6.16 (3.43)	
Anxiety impairment and avoidance (OASIS)	Pre	4.32 (3.95)	—	4.11 (4.82)	—	0.013*
	Post	1.80 (3.91)	−2.52 (2.48)	0.22 (0.67)	−3.89 (4.30)	
	6-month	1.30 (2.21)	−3.02 (2.55)	2.89 (3.52)	−1.22 (2.91)	
Depressive symptoms (PHQ-9)	Pre	12.60 (6.22)	—	13.44 (4.59)	—	0.16
	Post	5.81 (7.99)	−6.79 (4.80)	4.03 (5.99)	−9.41 (3.60)	
	6-month	8.97 (10.16)	−3.63 (6.39)	7.67 (6.40)	−5.77 (3.88)	
Stress (DASS-stress)	Pre	4.76 (5.44)	—	6.11 (7.64)	—	0.59
	Post	2.60 (6.65)	−2.16 (3.99)	0.78 (1.39)	−5.33 (6.58)	
	6-month	2.60 (6.65)	−3.86 (4.08)	0.78 (1.39)	−2.44 (4.58)	
Positive metacognitive worry beliefs (MaSCS)	Pre	16.00 (14.68)	—	21.33 (8.76)	—	0.95
	Post	4.40 (10.01)	−11.60 (8.98)	8.56 (14.52)	−12.78 (9.17)	
	6-month	9.10 (14.88)	−6.90 (9.35)	15.44 (14.92)	−5.89 (9.50)	
Negative metacognitive worry beliefs (MaSCS)	Pre	13.60 (12.39)	—	19.00 (9.19)	—	0.17
	Post	3.00 (6.75)	−10.60 (8.08)	3.00 (4.58)	−16.00 (5.45)	
	6-month	5.70 (10.11)	−7.90 (7.44)	9.11 (9.87)	−9.89 (6.06)	

Quality of life (SF-12 PCS)	Pre	40.00 (5.10)	—	38.99 (8.67)	—	0.023*
	Post	42.23 (5.88)	2.23 (2.57)	47.74 (8.48)	8.75 (3.84)	
	6-month	43.18 (10.97	3.18 (7.54)	46.17 (11.83)	7.18 (7.14)	
Quality of life (SF-12 MCS)	Pre	35.47 (7.06)	—	34.80 (8.34)	—	0.59
	Post	37.84 (11.13)	2.37 (5.68)	41.60 (6.70)	6.80 (3.72)	
	6-month	40.49 (8.17)	5.02 (4.93)	40.41 (9.84)	5.61 (5.92)	
Physical activity, minutes	Pre	16.00 (13.42)	—	15.71 (9.25)	—	0.15
	Post	35.00 (17.00)	19.00 (7.64)	43.33 (12.38)	27.62 (5.72)	
	6-month	43.00 (19.33)	27.00 (11.78)	53.00 (15.56)	37.29 (9.87)	
Alcohol use (AUDIT-C)	Pre	2.10 (3.25)	—	3.44 (3.58)	—	0.011*
	Post	3.10 (2.64)	1.00 (1.44)	2.11 (2.93)	−1.33 (1.58)	
	6-month	2.60 (1.65)	0.50 (2.17)	1.67 (2.29)	−1.77 (2.22)	
Adherence (MOS-SAS)	Pre	2.61 (1.67)	—	2.78 (1.44)	—	0.35
	Post	2.80 (1.13)	0.19 (0.82)	3.30 (1.21)	0.52 (0.63)	
	6-month	3.67 (1.46)	1.06 (1.01)	3.44 (1.67)	0.66 (1.00)	

AUDIT-C, Alcohol Use Disorders Identification Test–Shortened Clinical version; DASS, Depression Anxiety and Stress Scales; EUC, enhanced usual care; GAD-7, Generalized Anxiety Disorder 7-item scale; MaSCS, Metacognitions About Symptoms Control Scale; MOS-SAS, Medical Outcomes Study Specific Adherence Scale; OASIS, Overall Anxiety Severity and Impairment Scale; PHQ-9, Patient Health Questionnaire 9-item scale; UP, Unified Protocol. *$p < 0.05$.

Reprinted with permission from Tully et al. (2022).

CONCLUSION

The UP provides a coherent conceptual and pragmatic approach to treating emotional disorders that are highly prevalent in CVD populations. Anxiety disorders in particular remain largely neglected by RCTs (Rollman & Huffman, 2013), likely due to procedural challenges in applying traditional CBT exposure therapies to CVD patients. Thus, the UP outlined here is well placed to afford immense benefits to patients with CVDs and comorbid emotional disorders. Moreover, the UP may offer a novel approach to dually treat emotional disorders and CVD risk behaviors (e.g., binge eating) when conceptualized as emotion-driven behaviors.

Limitations and Barriers

The foreseeable barriers to wider adoption of the UP for CVD patients include the lack of validation with this population, raising the likelihood that early adopters of the UP should follow more feasibility and efficacy trials. Notably, the CVD field's general reluctance to address emotional disorders other than depression poses a systemic barrier. Nonetheless, recent cardiology guidelines have highlighted anxiety among other psychosocial risk factors besides depression, suggesting that a greater awareness of psychosocial processes in CVD populations has been achieved (Lawton et al., 2022; Visseren et al., 2021).

Future Directions

Future avenues for research that may help consolidate this field in CVD patients are to examine transdiagnostic constructs and hierarchical conceptualizations of disorders. Specifically, greater understanding of the role that transdiagnostic constructs play in cardiovascular health could help bolster the rationale for employing the UP as opposed to disorder-specific interventions (e.g., Cheng et al., 2022; Frøjd et al., 2021; Habibovic et al., 2021; Luberto et al., 2021; Lukoševičiūtė & Šmigelskas, 2019; Trick et al., 2019; Velikanov et al., 2019). Likewise, epidemiological work on hierarchical conceptualizations of disorders and their structure, prevalence, comorbidity, and risk for incident CVD and prognosis would lead to a greater understanding of patient profiles requiring concerted mental health intervention (Grech et al., 2019; Roest et al., 2017). Moreover, in-depth qualitative work on patients' emotional needs would identify any gaps between current screening and intervention approaches with patient-perceived needs (Collopy et al., 2021; Cosh et al., 2022; Jbilou et al., 2019). Along these lines, research on patient emotion-driven behaviors that are detrimental to cardiovascular health could help refine the UP and improve its suitability for use alongside cardiac rehabilitation programs (Grech et al., 2019; Roest et al., 2017).

Advice for Clinicians

Successful implementation of the UP in CVD patients necessitates several minor adaptions tailored to the unique needs of this population. Requisite adaptions should factor in severity and type(s) of CVD(s) in each particular patient prior to undertaking any in vivo symptom exposures. Otherwise, Barlow's manualized UP protocol is a valuable tool for treating the emotional needs of CVD patients.

REFERENCES

Albus, C., Waller, C., Fritzsche, K., Gunold, H., Haass, M., Hamann, B., Kindermann, I., Kollner, V., Leithauser, B., Marx, N., Meesmann, M., Michal, M., Ronel, J., Scherer, M., Schrader, V., Schwaab, B., Weber, C. S., & Herrmann-Lingen, C. (2019). Significance of psychosocial factors in cardiology—Update 2018: Position paper of the German Cardiac Society. *Clinical Research in Cardiology, 108*(11), 1175–1196. https://doi.org/10.1007/s00392-019-01488-w

Asmundson, G. J., Fetzner, M. G., Deboer, L. B., Powers, M. B., Otto, M. W., & Smits, J. A. (2013). Let's get physical: a contemporary review of the anxiolytic effects of exercise for anxiety and its disorders. *Depression and Anxiety, 30*(4), 362–373.

Baird, D., Jackson, A. C., Higgins, R. O., Murphy, B. M., & Tully, P. J. (2018). Depression screening, assessment and treatment for patients with chronic heart failure. *British Journal of Cardiac Nursing, 13*(8), 386–393.

Barlow, D. H., Farchione, T. J., Fairholme, C. P., Ellard, K. K., Boisseau, C. L., Allen, L. B., & Ehrenreich-May, J. (2011). *The Unified Protocol for Transdiagnostic Treatment of Emotional Disorders: Therapist guide*. Oxford University Press.

Barth, J., Schumacher, M., & Herrmann-Lingen, C. (2004). Depression as a risk factor for mortality in patients with coronary heart disease: A meta-analysis. *Psychosomatic Medicine, 66*(6), 802–813. https://doi.org/10.1097/01.psy.0000146332.53619.b2

Baumeister, H., Haschke, A., Munzinger, M., Hutter, N., & Tully, P. J. (2015). Inpatient and outpatient costs in patients with coronary artery disease and mental disorders: A systematic review. *BioPsychoSocial Medicine, 9*, Article 11. https://doi.org/doi:10.1186/s13030-015-0039-z

Baune, B. T., Adrian, I., Arolt, V., & Berger, K. (2006). Associations between major depression, bipolar disorders, dysthymia and cardiovascular diseases in the general adult population. *Psychotherapy and Psychosomatics, 75*(5), 319–326. https://doi.org/10.1159/000093955

Berg, S. K., Rasmussen, T. B., Herning, M., Svendsen, J. H., Christensen, A. V., & Thygesen, L. C. (2020). Cognitive behavioural therapy significantly reduces anxiety in patients with implanted cardioverter defibrillator compared with usual care: Findings from the Screen-ICD randomised controlled trial. *European Journal of Preventive Cardiology, 27*(3), 258–268. https://doi.org/10.1177/2047487319874147

Carney, R. M., & Freedland, K. E. (2017). Depression and coronary heart disease. *Nature Reviews Cardiology, 14*(3), 145–155. https://doi.org/10.1038/nrcardio.2016.181

Celano, C. M., Suarez, L., Mastromauro, C., Januzzi, J. L., & Huffman, J. C. (2013). Feasibility and utility of screening for depression and anxiety disorders in patients with cardiovascular disease. *Circulation: Cardiovascular Quality and Outcomes, 6*(4), 498–504. https://doi.org/10.1161/circoutcomes.111.000049

Cheng, M. Y., Zhang, R. X., Wang, M. J., & Chang, M. Y. (2022). Relationship between cognitive emotion regulation strategies and coronary heart disease: An empirical examination of heart rate variability and coronary stenosis. *Psychology & Health, 37*(2), 230–245. https://doi.org/10.1080/08870446.2020.1859112

Çiçek, D., Gökay, S., Lakadamyali, H., Sapmaz, I., & Muderrisoglu, H. (2012). Effect of Obstructive Sleep Apnea on Heart Rate, Heart Rate Recovery and QTc and P-wave dispersion in newly diagnosed untreated patients. *The American Journal of the Medical Sciences, 344*, 180–185.

Collopy, C., Cosh, S., & Tully, P. J. (2021). Screening and referral is not enough: A qualitative exploration of barriers to access and uptake of mental health services in patients with cardiovascular diseases. *BMC Health Services Research, 21*, 49.

Correa-Rodriguez, M., Abu Ejheisheh, M., Suleiman-Martos, N., Membrive-Jimenez, M. J., Velando-Soriano, A., Schmidt-RioValle, J., & Gomez-Urquiza, J. L. (2020). Prevalence of depression in coronary artery bypass surgery: A systematic review and meta-analysis. *Journal of Clinical Medicine, 9*(4), Article 909. https://doi.org/10.3390/jcm9040909

Cosh, S. M., Pinto, R., Denson, L., & Tully, P. J. (2022). Understandings and experiences of adherence to secondary prevention for patients with cardiovascular disease and comorbid depression or anxiety. *Psychology, Health & Medicine*. https://doi.org/10.1080/13548506.2022.2060515

Dornelas, E. A. (2008). *Psychotherapy with cardiac patients: Behavioral cardiology in practice*. American Psychological Association.

Edmondson, D., Kronish, I. M., Shaffer, J. A., Falzon, L., & Burg, M. M. (2013). Posttraumatic stress disorder and risk for coronary heart disease: A meta-analytic review. *American Heart Journal, 166*(5), 806–814. https://doi.org/10.1016/j.ahj.2013.07.031

Edmondson, D., Richardson, S., Falzon, L., Davidson, K. W., Mills, M. A., & Neria, Y. (2012). Posttraumatic stress disorder prevalence and risk of recurrence in acute coronary syndrome patients: A meta-analytic review. *PLoS One, 7*(6), e38915. https://doi.org/10.1371/journal.pone.0038915

Eifert, G. H., Thompson, R. N., Zvolensky, M. J., Edwards, K., Frazer, N. L., Haddad, J. W., & Davig, J. (2000). The Cardiac Anxiety Questionnaire: Development and preliminary validity. *Behaviour Research and Therapy, 38*(10), 1039–1053.

Farris, S. G., Abrantes, A. M., Bond, D. S., Stabile, L. M., & Wu, W.-C. (2019). Anxiety and fear of exercise in cardiopulmonary rehabilitation: Patient and practitioner perspectives. *Journal of Cardiopulmonary Rehabilitation and Prevention, 39*(2), E9–E13. https://doi.org/10.1097/hcr.0000000000000401

Fisher, P. L., Byrne, A., Fairburn, L., Ullmer, H., Abbey, G., & Salmon, P. (2019). Brief metacognitive therapy for emotional distress in adult cancer survivors. *Frontiers in Psychology, 10*, Article 162. https://doi.org/10.3389/fpsyg.2019.00162

Frøjd, L. A., Papageorgiou, C., Munkhaugen, J., Moum, T., Sverre, E., Nordhus, I. H., & Dammen, T. (2022). Worry and rumination predict insomnia in patients with coronary heart disease: A cross-sectional study with long-term follow-up. *Journal of Clinical Sleep Medicine, 18*(3), 779–787. https://doi.org/10.5664/jcsm.9712

GBD 2017 Causes of Death Collaborators. (2018). Global, regional, and national age-sex-specific mortality for 282 causes of death in 195 countries and territories, 1980–2017: A systematic analysis for the Global Burden of Disease Study 2017. *Lancet*, *392*(10159), 1736–1788. https://doi.org/10.1016/S0140-6736(18)32203-7

GBD 2017 DALYs and HALE Collaborators. (2018). Global, regional, and national disability-adjusted life-years (DALYs) for 359 diseases and injuries and healthy life expectancy (HALE) for 195 countries and territories, 1990–2017: A systematic analysis for the Global Burden of Disease Study 2017. *Lancet*, *392*(10159), 1859–1922. https://doi.org/10.1016/S0140-6736(18)32335-3

GBD 2017 Risk Factor Collaborators. (2018). Global, regional, and national comparative risk assessment of 84 behavioural, environmental and occupational, and metabolic risks or clusters of risks for 195 countries and territories, 1990–2017: A systematic analysis for the Global Burden of Disease Study 2017. *Lancet*, *392*(10159), 1923–1994. https://doi.org/10.1016/S0140-6736(18)32225-6

Goldstein, B. I., Carnethon, M. R., Matthews, K. A., McIntyre, R. S., Miller, G. E., Raghuveer, G., Stoney, C. M., Wasiak, H., & McCrindle, B. W. (2015). Major depressive disorder and bipolar disorder predispose youth to accelerated atherosclerosis and early cardiovascular disease: A scientific statement from the American Heart Association. *Circulation*, *132*(10), 965–986. https://doi.org/10.1161/cir.0000000000000229

Grech, M., Turnbull, D. A., Wittert, G. A., Tully, P. J., & CHAMPS Investigators. (2019). Identifying the internalizing disorder clusters among recently hospitalized cardiovascular disease patients: A receiver operating characteristics study. *Frontiers in Psychology*, *10*, Article 2829. https://doi.org/10.3389/fpsyg.2019.02829

Habibovic, M., Denollet, J., & Pedersen, S. S. (2017). Posttraumatic stress and anxiety in patients with an implantable cardioverter defibrillator: Trajectories and vulnerability factors. *Pacing and Clinical Electrophysiology*, *40*(7), 817–823. https://doi.org/10.1111/pace.13090

Habibovic, M., Widdershoven, J., Wetzels, M., Piera-Jimenez, J., & Kop, W. (2021). Association between behavioral flexibility and psychological distress in patients with cardiovascular disease: Data from the Do Cardiac Health: Advanced New Generation Ecosystem Study. *Heart and Mind*, *5*(2), 33–39. https://doi.org/10.4103/hm.hm_15_21

Hernandez-Palazon, J., Fuentes-Garcia, D., Falcon-Arana, L., Roca-Calvo, M. J., Burguillos-Lopez, S., Domenech-Asensi, P., & Jara-Rubio, R. (2018). Assessment of preoperative anxiety in cardiac surgery patients lacking a history of anxiety: Contributing factors and postoperative morbidity. *Journal of Cardiothoracic and Vascular Anesthesia*, *32*(1), 236–244. https://doi.org/10.1053/j.jvca.2017.04.044

Hohls, J. K., Beer, K., Arolt, V., Haverkamp, W., Kuhlmann, S. L., Martus, P., Waltenberger, J., Rieckmann, N., Müller-Nordhorn, J., & Ströhle, A. (2020). Association between heart-focused anxiety, depressive symptoms, health behaviors and healthcare utilization in patients with coronary heart disease. *Journal of Psychosomatic Research*, *131*, 109958. https://doi.org/10.1016/j.jpsychores.2020.109958

Huffman, J. C., Beach, S. R., Suarez, L., Mastromauro, C. A., Dubois, C. M., Celano, C. M., Rollman, B. L., & Januzzi, J. L. (2013). Design and baseline data from the Management of Sadness and Anxiety in Cardiology (MOSAIC) randomized controlled trial. *Contemporary Clinical Trials, 36*(2), 488–501. https://doi.org/10.1016/j.cct.2013.09.012

Husain, S. A., Edmondson, D., Kautz, M., Umland, R., & Kronish, I. M. (2018). Posttraumatic stress disorder due to acute cardiac events and aversive cognitions towards cardiovascular medications. *Journal of Behavioral Medicine, 41*(2), 261–268. https://doi.org/10.1007/s10865-017-9906-3

Jackson, A. C., Rogerson, M. C., Amerena, J., Smith, J., Hoover, V., Alvarenga, M. E., Higgins, R. O., Grande, M. R. L., Ski, C. F., Thompson, D. R., & Murphy, B. M. (2022). Unraveling the complexity of cardiac distress: A study of prevalence and severity. *Frontiers in Psychiatry, 13*, 808904. https://doi.org/10.3389/fpsyt.2022.808904

Jbilou, J., Grenier, J., Chomienne, M. H., Talbot, F., Tulloch, H., D'Antono, B., & Greenman, P. (2019). Understanding men's psychological reactions and experience following a cardiac event: A qualitative study from MindTheHeart. *BMJ Open, 9*(9), e029560. https://doi.org/10.1136/bmjopen-2019-029560

Kabat-Zinn, J. (1990). *Full catastrophe living: Using the wisdom of your body and mind to face stress, pain and illness*. Random House.

Kessler, R. C., Ormel, J., Petukhova, M., McLaughlin, K. A., Green, J. G., Russo, L. J., Stein, D. J., Zaslavsky, A. M., Aguilar-Gaxiola, S., Alonso, J., Andrade, L., Benjet, C., de Girolamo, G., de Graaf, R., Demyttenaere, K., Fayyad, J., Haro, J. M., Hu, C., Karam, A., . . . Ustun, T. B. (2011). Development of lifetime comorbidity in the World Health Organization World Mental Health Surveys. *Archives of General Psychiatry, 68*(1), 90–100. https://doi.org/10.1001/archgenpsychiatry.2010.180

Kessler, R. C., Petukhova, M., Sampson, N. A., Zaslavsky, A. M., & Wittchen, H. U. (2012). Twelve-month and lifetime prevalence and lifetime morbid risk of anxiety and mood disorders in the United States. *International Journal of Methods in Psychiatric Research, 21*(3), 169–184. https://doi.org/10.1002/mpr.1359

Lawton, J. S., Tamis-Holland, J. E., Bangalore, S., Bates, E. R., Beckie, T. M., Bischoff, J. M., Bittl, J. A., Cohen, M. G., DiMaio, J. M., Don, C. W., Fremes, S. E., Gaudino, M. F., Goldberger, Z. D., Grant, M. C., Jaswal, J. B., Kurlansky, P. A., Mehran, R., Metkus, T. S., Nnacheta, L. C., . . . Zwischenberger, B. A. (2022). 2021 ACC/AHA/SCAI guideline for coronary artery revascularization. *Journal of the American College of Cardiology, 79*(2), e21–e129. https://doi.org/doi:10.1016/j.jacc.2021.09.006

Le, J., Dorstyn, D. S., Mpfou, E., Prior, E., & Tully, P. J. (2018). Health-related quality of life in coronary heart disease: A systematic review and meta-analysis mapped against the International Classification of Functioning, Disability and Health. *Quality of Life Research, 27*(10), 2491–2503. https://doi.org/10.1007/s11136-018-1885-5

Lichtman, J. H., Froelicher, E. S., Blumenthal, J. A., Carney, R. M., Doering, L. V., Frasure-Smith, N., Freedland, K. E., Jaffe, A. S., Leifheit-Limson, E. C., Sheps, D. S., Vaccarino, V., & Wulsin, L.; and on behalf of the American Heart Association Statistics Committee of the Council on Epidemiology and Prevention and the Council on Cardiovascular and Stroke Nursing. (2014). Depression as a risk factor for poor prognosis among patients with acute coronary syndrome: Systematic review and recommendations: A scientific statement from the American Heart Association. *Circulation, 129*(12), 1350–1369. https://doi.org/10.1161/CIR.0000000000000019

Lossnitzer, N., Herzog, W., Stork, S., Wild, B., Muller-Tasch, T., Lehmkuhl, E., Zugck, C., Regitz-Zagrosek, V., Pankuweit, S., Maisch, B., Ertl, G., Gelbrich, G., & Angermann, C. E. (2013). Incidence rates and predictors of major and minor depression in patients with heart failure. *International Journal of Cardiology, 167*(2), 502–507. https://doi.org/10.1016/j.ijcard.2012.01.062

Luberto, C. M., Crute, S., Wang, A., Yeh, G. Y., Celano, C. M., Huffman, J. C., & Park, E. R. (2021). Lower distress tolerance is associated with greater anxiety and depression symptoms among patients after acute coronary syndrome. *General Hospital Psychiatry, 70,* 143–144. https://doi.org/10.1016/j.genhosppsych.2021.01.011

Lukoševičiūtė, J., & Šmigelskas, K. (2019). Illness perception and its changes during six months after cardiac rehabilitation: Relevance of biopsychosocial factors. *European Journal of Health Psychology, 26*(3), 90–100. https://doi.org/10.1027/2512-8442/a000034

Martens, E. J., Denollet, J., Pedersen, S. S., Scherders, M., Griez, E., Widdershoven, J., Szabo, B., Bonnier, H., & Appels, A. (2006). Relative lack of depressive cognitions in post-myocardial infarction depression. *Journal of Affective Disorders, 94*(1–3), 231–237. https://doi.org/10.1016/j.jad.2006.04.023

Murphy, B. M., Ludeman, D., Elliott, P., Judd, F., Humphreys, J., Edington, J., Jackson, A., & Worcester, M. (2014). Red flags for persistent or worsening anxiety and depression after an acute cardiac event: A 6-month longitudinal study *European Journal of Preventive Cardiology, 21*(9), 1079–1089. https://doi.org/10.1177/2047487313493058

Nicholson, A., Kuper, H., & Hemingway, H. (2006). Depression as an aetiologic and prognostic factor in coronary heart disease: A meta-analysis of 146,538 participants. *European Heart Journal, 27*(23), 2763–2774. https://doi.org/doi:10.1093/eurheartj/ehl338

Normann, N., & Morina, N. (2018). The efficacy of metacognitive therapy: A systematic review and meta-analysis. *Frontiers in Psychology, 9,* Article 2211. https://doi.org/10.3389/fpsyg.2018.02211

Parker, G., Hyett, M., Hadzi-Pavlovic, D., Brotchie, H., & Walsh, W. (2011). GAD is good? Generalized anxiety disorder predicts a superior five-year outcome following an acute coronary syndrome. *Psychiatry Research, 188*(3), 383–389. https://doi.org/10.1016/j.psychres.2011.05.018

Pedersen, S. S., von Kanel, R., Tully, P. J., & Denollet, J. (2017). Psychosocial perspectives in cardiovascular disease. *European Journal of Preventive Cardiology, 24*(3 Suppl.), 108–115. https://doi.org/10.1177/2047487317703827

Pogosova, N., Saner, H., Pedersen, S. S., Cupples, M. E., McGee, H., Höfer, S., Doyle, F., Schmid, J.-P., & von Känel, R. (2015). Psychosocial aspects in cardiac rehabilitation: From theory to practice. A position paper from the Cardiac Rehabilitation Section of the European Association of Cardiovascular Prevention and Rehabilitation of the European Society of Cardiology. *European Journal of Preventive Cardiology, 22*(10), 1290–1306 https://doi.org/10.1177/2047487314543075

Ricci, F., De Caterina, R., & Fedorowski, A. (2015). Orthostatic hypotension. *Journal of the American College of Cardiology, 66*(7), 848–860.

Roest, A. M., de Jonge, P., Lim, C. W. W., Stein, D. J., Al-Hamzawi, A., Alonso, J., Benjet, C., Bruffaerts, R., Bunting, B., Caldas-de-Almeida, J. M., Ciutan, M., de Girolamo, G., Hu, C., Levinson, D., Nakamura, Y., Navarro-Mateu, F., Piazza, M., Posada-Villa, J., Torres, Y., . . . Scott, K. M. (2017). Fear and distress disorders as predictors of heart disease: A temporal perspective. *Journal of Psychosomatic Research, 96,* 67–75. https://doi.org/10.1016/j.jpsychores.2017.03.015

Rollman, B. L., Belnap, B. H., LeMenager, M. S., Mazumdar, S., Houck, P. R., Counihan, P. J., Kapoor, W. N., Schulberg, H. C., & Reynolds, C. F., 3rd. (2009). Telephone-delivered collaborative care for treating post-CABG depression: A randomized controlled trial. *JAMA, 302*(19), 2095–2103. https://doi.org/10.1001/jama.2009.1670

Rollman, B. L., & Huffman, J. C. (2013). Treating anxiety in the presence of medical comorbidity: Calmly moving forward. *Psychosomatic Medicine, 75*(8), 710–712. https://doi.org/10.1097/psy.0000000000000011

Rosman, L., Whited, A., Lampert, R., Mosesso, V. N., Lawless, C., & Sears, S. F. (2015). Cardiac anxiety after sudden cardiac arrest: Severity, predictors and clinical implications. *International Journal of Cardiology, 181*, 73–76. https://doi.org/10.1016/j.ijcard.2014.11.115

Rozanski, A., Blumenthal, J. A., & Kaplan, J. (1999). Impact of psychological factors on the pathogenesis of cardiovascular disease and implications for therapy. *Circulation, 99*(16), 2192–2217.

Sardinha, A., Araujo, C. G., & Nardi, A. E. (2012). Psychiatric disorders and cardiac anxiety in exercising and sedentary coronary artery disease patients: A case–control study. *Brazilian Journal of Medical and Biological Research, 45*(12), 1320–1326.

Sardinha, A., Nardi, A. E., & Zin, W. A. (2009). Are panic attacks really harmless? The cardiovascular impact of panic disorder. *Revista Brasileira de Psiquiatria, 31*(1), 57–62.

Schwartz, S. M., Trask, P. C., & Ketterer, M. W. (1999). Understanding chest pain: What every psychologist should know. *Journal of Clinical Psychology in Medical Settings, 6*(4), 333–351. https://doi.org/10.1023/A:1026215730296

Simony, C. P., Pedersen, B. D., Dreyer, P., & Birkelund, R. (2015). Dealing with existential anxiety in exercise-based cardiac rehabilitation: A phenomenological–hermeneutic study of patients' lived experiences. *Journal of Clinical Nursing, 24*(17–18), 2581–2590. https://doi.org/10.1111/jocn.12867

Skala, J., Freedland, K. E., & Carney, R. M. (2005). *Heart disease*. Hogrefe & Huber.

Taggart Wasson, L., Shaffer, J. A., Edmondson, D., Bring, R., Brondolo, E., Falzon, L., Konrad, B., & Kronish, I. M. (2018). Posttraumatic stress disorder and nonadherence to medications prescribed for chronic medical conditions: A meta-analysis. *Journal of Psychiatric Research, 102*, 102–109. https://doi.org/10.1016/j.jpsychires.2018.02.013

Taylor, W. D., Aizenstein, H. J., & Alexopoulos, G. S. (2013). The vascular depression hypothesis: Mechanisms linking vascular disease with depression. *Molecular Psychiatry, 18*(9), 963–974. https://doi.org/10.1038/mp.2013.20

Thombs, B. D., de Jonge, P., Coyne, J. C., Whooley, M. A., Frasure-Smith, N., Mitchell, A. J., Zuidersma, M., Eze-Nliam, C., Lima, B. B., Smith, C. G., Soderlund, K., & Ziegelstein, R. C. (2008). Depression screening and patient outcomes in cardiovascular care: A systematic review. *JAMA, 300*(18), 2161–2171. https://doi.org/10.1001/jama.2008.667

Trick, L., Watkins, E. R., Henley, W., Gandhi, M. M., & Dickens, C. (2019). Perseverative negative thinking predicts depression in people with acute coronary syndrome. *General Hospital Psychiatry, 61*, 16–25. https://doi.org/10.1016/j.genhosppsych.2019.06.012

Tully, P. J. (2015). A good time to panic? Premorbid and postmorbid panic disorder in heart failure affects cardiac and psychiatric cause admissions. *Australasian Psychiatry, 23*(2), 124–127.

Tully, P. J., Alpérovitch, A., Soumaré, A., Mazoyer, B., Debette, S., & Tzourio, C. (2020). The association between cerebral small vessel disease with antidepressant use and depression: Three-City Dijon MRI study. *Stroke*, *51*(2), 402–408.

Tully, P. J., Ang, S. Y., Lee, E. J. L., Bendig, E., Bauereiß, N., Bengel, J., & Baumeister, H. (2021). Psychological and pharmacological interventions for depression in patients with coronary artery disease. *Cochrane Database of Systematic Reviews*, *2021*(12), CD008012. https://doi.org/https://doi.org/10.1002/14651858.CD008012.pub4

Tully, P. J., & Cosh, S. M. (2019). Post-traumatic stress disorder in heart failure patients: A test of the cardiac disease-induced PTSD hypothesis. *Current Psychiatry Research and Reviews*, *15*(4), 290–296. https://doi.org/10.2174/2666082215666191113121558

Tully, P. J., Cosh, S. M., & Baumeister, H. (2014). The anxious heart in whose mind? A systematic review and meta-regression of factors associated with anxiety disorder diagnosis, treatment and morbidity risk in coronary heart disease. *Journal of Psychosomatic Research*, *77*(6), 439–448.

Tully, P. J., Cosh, S. M., & Baune, B. T. (2013). A review of the affects of worry and generalized anxiety disorder upon cardiovascular health and coronary heart disease. *Psychology, Health & Medicine*, *18*(6), 627–644. https://doi.org/10.1080/13548506.2012.749355

Tully, P., Pedersen, S. S., Cosh, S., & Foldes-Busque, G. (2022). Treating Anxiety Disorders in Patients with Cardiovascular Disease: How to Formulate Exposure Therapy When Anxiety Mimics the Heart. In Jasper A. J. Smits, Jolene Jacquart, Jonathan Abramowitz, Joanna Arch, & Jürgen Margraf (Eds.), *Clinical Guide to Exposure Therapy* (pp.161–182). Springer.

Tully, P. J., Sardinha, A., & Nardi, A. E. (2017). A new CBT model of Panic Attack Treatment in Comorbid Heart Diseases (PATCHD). *Cognitive and Behavioral Practice*, *24*(3), 329–341. https://doi.org/https://doi.org/10.1016/j.cbpra.2016.05.008

Tully, P. J., Turnbull, D., Horowitz, J. D., Beltrame, J. F., Selkow, T., Baune, B. T., Markwick, E., Sauer-Zavala, S., Baumeister, H., Cosh, S., & Wittert, G. A. (2016). Cardiovascular Health in Anxiety or Mood Problems Study (CHAMPS): Study protocol for a randomized controlled trial. *Trials*, *17*(1), 18.

Tully, P. J., Turnbull, D. A., Beltrame, J. F., Horowitz, J. D., Cosh, S., Baumeister, H., & Wittert, G. A. (2015). Panic disorder and incident coronary heart disease: A systematic review and meta-regression in 1,131,612 persons and 58,111 cardiac events. *Psychological Medicine*, *45*(14), 2909–2920.

Tully, P. J., Turnbull, D. A., Horowitz, J. D., Beltrame, J. F., Baune, B. T., Sauer-Zavala, S., Baumeister, H., Bean, C. G., Pinto, R. B., Cosh, S., & Wittert, G. A. (2022). Transdiagnostic cognitive–behavioral therapy for depression and anxiety disorders in cardiovascular disease patients: Results from the CHAMPS pilot-feasibility trial. *Frontiers in Psychiatry*, *13*, 741039. https://doi.org/10.3389/fpsyt.2022.741039

Tully, P. J., Wittert, G. A., Selkow, T., & Baumeister, H. (2014). The real world mental health needs of heart failure patients are not reflected by the depression RCT evidence. PLoS *One*, *9*(1), e85928. https://doi.org/10.1371/journal.pone.0085928

Vaccarino, V., Badimon, L., Bremner, J. D., Cenko, E., Cubedo, J., Dorobantu, M., Duncker, D. J., Koller, A., Manfrini, O., Milicic, D., Padro, T., Pries, A. R., Quyyumi, A. A., Tousoulis, D., Trifunovic, D., Vasiljevic, Z., de Wit, C., Bugiardini, R., & ESC Scientific Document Group Reviewers. (2019). Depression and coronary heart disease: 2018 position paper of the ESC Working Group on Coronary Pathophysiology and Microcirculation. *European Heart Journal, 41*(17), 1687–1696. https://doi.org/10.1093/eurheartj/ehy913

Velikanov, A. A., Boyarskaya, A. A., Stoljarova, A. A., Protasov, E. A., Lubinskaya, E. I., & Demchenko, E. A. (2019). Study of phobic manifestations and anxiety in patients with coronary heart disease after myocardial infarction in view of tasks of psychological rehabilitation. *RUDN Journal of Psychology and Pedagogics, 16*(4), 517–539. https://doi.org/10.22363/2313-1683-2019-16-4-517-539

Verma, M., Grover, S., Singh, T., Dahiya, N., & Nehra, R. (2020). Screening for cognitive impairment among the elderly attending the noncommunicable diseases clinics in a rural area of Punjab, North India. *Asian Journal of Psychiatry, 50*, 102001. https://www.scopus.com/inward/record.uri?eid=2-s2.0-85082840505&doi=10.1016%2fj.ajp.2020.102001&partnerID=40&md5=a1721cc1204ef23558af5717eb44c480

Visseren, F. L. J., Mach, F., Smulders, Y. M., Carballo, D., Koskinas, K. C., Bäck, M., Benetos, A., Biffi, A., Boavida, J.-M., Capodanno, D., Cosyns, B., Crawford, C., Davos, C. H., Desormais, I., Di Angelantonio, E., Franco, O. H., Halvorsen, S., Hobbs, F. D. R., Hollander, M., . . . ESC Document Group. (2021). 2021 ESC guidelines on cardiovascular disease prevention in clinical practice: Developed by the Task Force for Cardiovascular Disease Prevention in Clinical Practice with representatives of the European Society of Cardiology and 12 medical societies with the special contribution of the European Association of Preventive Cardiology (EAPC). European Heart *Journal, 42*(34), 3227–3337. https://doi.org/10.1093/eurheartj/ehab484

Wells, A., McNicol, K., Reeves, D., Salmon, P., Davies, L., Heagerty, A., Doherty, P., McPhillips, R., Anderson, R., Faija, C., Capobianco, L., Morley, H., Gaffney, H., Shields, G., & Fisher, P. (2018). Improving the effectiveness of psychological interventions for depression and anxiety in the cardiac rehabilitation pathway using group-based metacognitive therapy (PATHWAY Group MCT): Study protocol for a randomised controlled trial. *Trials, 19*(1), Article 215. https://doi.org/10.1186/s13063-018-2593-8

Whitehead, D. L., Strike, P., Perkins-Porras, L., & Steptoe, A. (2005). Frequency of distress and fear of dying during acute coronary syndromes and consequences for adaptation. *American Journal of Cardiology, 96*(11), 1512–1516. https://doi.org/10.1016/j.amjcard.2005.07.070

Whitmarsh, A., Koutantji, M., & Sidell, K. (2003). Illness perceptions, mood and coping in predicting attendance at cardiac rehabilitation. *British Journal of Health Psychology, 8*(2), 209–221.

Wilder Schaaf, K. P., Artman, L. K., Peberdy, M. A., Walker, W. C., Ornato, J. P., Gossip, M. R., & Kreutzer, J. S. (2013). Anxiety, depression, and PTSD following cardiac arrest: A systematic review of the literature. *Resuscitation, 84*(7), 873–877. https://doi.org/10.1016/j.resuscitation.2012.11.021

Williams, M., Teasdale, J., Segal, Z., & Kabat-Zinn, J. (2007). *The mindful way through depression*. Guilford.

Wittstein, I. S., Thiemann, D. R., Lima, J. A., Baughman, K. L., Schulman, S. P., Gerstenblith, G., Wu, K. C., Rade, J. J., Bivalacqua, T. J., & Champion, H. C. (2005). Neurohumoral features of myocardial stunning due to sudden emotional stress. *The New England Journal of Medicine, 352*(6), 539–548.

Yavuzkir, M., Atmaca, M., Dagli, N., Balin, M., Karaca, I., Mermi, O., Tezcan, E., & Aslan, I. N. (2007). P-Wave dispersion in panic disorder. *Psychosomatic Medicine, 69*(4), 344–347.

13

The Unified Protocol for Smoking Cessation

Conceptual Basis and Integrated Treatment Approach

AMANDA R. MATHEW AND CHELSEA COX ■

BACKGROUND

Tobacco use is the leading cause of preventable death and disability worldwide, and it is responsible for roughly 7 million deaths per year (Reitsma et al., 2017). Although more than half of smokers attempt to quit each year, only 5–10% of them maintain abstinence from cigarettes (Creamer et al., 2019). Given its chronic and recurring course, there is increased emphasis on treating tobacco use disorder with a chronic care approach that targets engagement in smoking cessation as a process rather than a discrete event.

Affective disturbance has an important role in maintaining smoking within many contextual accounts of smoking and nicotine dependence (Baker et al., 2004; Mathew et al., 2017). Periods of smoking abstinence reliably induce negative affective symptoms of depression, anxiety, and irritability associated with nicotine withdrawal (Hughes, 2007; Piper, 2015), which can occur in as little as 30 minutes without a cigarette (Hendricks et al., 2006). Low positive affect (i.e., anhedonia) is also increasingly recognized to be part of the nicotine withdrawal syndrome (Cook et al., 2015). Importantly, affective disturbance is associated with a higher risk of smoking lapse or relapse following a quit attempt (Cook et al., 2010; Leventhal et al., 2014; Schnoll et al., 2013).

Amanda R. Mathew and Chelsea Cox, *The Unified Protocol for Smoking Cessation* In: *Applications of the Unified Protocol in Health Conditions.* Edited by: Jorge Osma and Todd J. Farchione, Oxford University Press. © Oxford University Press 2023. DOI: 10.1093/oso/9780197564295.003.0013

CONCEPTUAL BASIS OF THE UNIFIED PROTOCOL FOR SMOKING CESSATION

The Unified Protocol for Transdiagnostic Emotional Disorders (UP; Barlow, Farchione, et al., 2011) is an emotion-focused, cognitive–behavioral treatment designed to target any disorder characterized by aversive reactions to frequent and intense negative affect. Given its primary treatment target of aversive and avoidant reactions to emotional experiences, we believe that the UP is well-suited to address affective symptoms as both a trigger for cigarette smoking and a symptom of nicotine withdrawal following smoking abstinence.

As shown in Figure 13.1, the overall rationale is that UP treatment will target psychological risk factors, reduce reliance on smoking for affective coping motives, and foster long-term engagement in the cessation process. Given the UP's modular approach (Brake et al., 2016; Sauer-Zavala et al., 2017), we focus on the most conceptually relevant treatment modules of Mindful Emotion Awareness (Module 3), Interoceptive Exposure (Module 6), and Countering Emotional Behaviors (Module 5). We specifically target three core psychological factors that underlie both nicotine dependence and affective disturbance (Leventhal & Zvolensky, 2015): distress intolerance (inability to withstand distressing states), anxiety sensitivity (fear of anxiety-related sensations), and anhedonia (diminished sense of pleasure or interest). These psychological factors commonly index an individual's tendency to smoke to regulate affect (i.e., to enhance pleasure or reduce distress). By reducing the tendency to smoke for affect regulation, we hope to foster greater engagement in the cessation process, indexed by better tolerance of withdrawal-related distress, greater number and length of attempts to quit smoking, and maintenance of smoking abstinence over time.

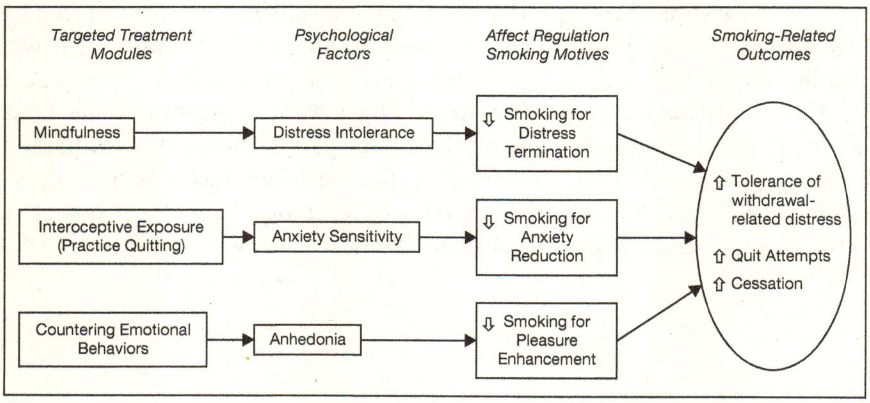

Figure 13.1 Unified Protocol for smoking cessation: Conceptual model.

TREATMENT DELIVERY OF THE UNIFIED PROTOCOL FOR SMOKING CESSATION

Overview of Treatment Approach

This adaptation of the UP for smoking cessation includes three modules that are connected within the standardized context of the UP framework (i.e., share a focus on the core components of thoughts, physical sensations, and behaviors) but are functionally distinct. Each module has individual goals (Table 13.1) and contributes to the overall treatment target of reducing smoking for affect regulation. Detailed session content is reviewed below and summarized in Table 13.2. The session content for each module has been designed to be delivered in three 45- to 60-minute individual sessions, which our group has delivered either in person or by telephone/videoconference. The material covered in each session and associated homework assignments are consistent with the published UP patient workbook (Barlow, Ellard, et al., 2011). Although the Interoceptive Exposure module was designed to be delivered prior to a quit attempt (i.e., as preparation counseling), the other modules may be delivered either for skill-building prior to a quit attempt or for maintaining abstinence/relapse prevention following a quit attempt. We deliver the treatment modules in the order presented below, and we also include one session of content specific to planning for quit date (Box 13.1), when the patient expresses readiness to set a quit date.

Interoceptive Exposure (i.e., Practice Quitting)

Session 1

The first session includes an assessment of the patient's smoking history, including number/length of prior quit attempts, reasons for quitting smoking, and

Table 13.1 Treatment Goals by Module

Interoceptive Exposure (Practice Quitting)	Mindful Emotional Awareness	Countering Emotional Behaviors
To gradually expose patients to nicotine withdrawal symptoms through a series of "practice quit attempts" (i.e., brief periods of smoking abstinence without the pressure to permanently quit) To reduce fear and avoidance of the physical sensations associated with nicotine withdrawal	To cultivate nonjudgmental, present-focused experience of emotions, thoughts, and physical sensations related to cigarette smoking To facilitate tolerance of the physical and emotional symptoms of nicotine withdrawal	To increase positive emotions by systematically introducing greater engagement with natural rewards To replace smoking with adaptive coping strategies to facilitate contact with and enjoyment of reinforcing activities that are incompatible with smoking

Table 13.2 Session Content by Module

Session 1	Session 2	Session 3
Interoceptive Exposure (Practice Quitting)		
Assess smoking/cessation history Introduce physical and emotional symptoms of nicotine withdrawal Discuss relationship between physical symptoms of nicotine withdrawal, smoking thoughts, and behaviors Introduce interoceptive exposure (i.e., practice quitting) Review rationale for practice quitting Complete exposure hierarchy adapted for nicotine withdrawal exposures Identify goals for the next week and encourage monitoring of these goals	Review rationale for practice quitting Review how thoughts, feelings, and smoking behavior are related, and how practice quitting can help break this cycle Introduce corrective information (i.e., challenging outcome expectancies) regarding smoking abstinence Provide psychoeducation on the avoidance of nicotine withdrawal symptoms and rationale as to why it can be harmful to avoid these symptoms Set goals for at-home practice Plan a period of nonsmoking prior to next week's session	Conduct in-session exposure to nicotine withdrawal symptoms and discuss the patient's experience (thoughts, feelings, and physical sensations of withdrawal) Identify and challenge outcome expectancies associated with nicotine withdrawal symptoms Review goals of practice quitting Review strategies to avoid practice relapsing Summarize take-home points Set goals for at-home practice
Mindful Emotional Awareness		
Provide psychoeducation on the purpose of emotions Discuss secondary reactions to initial emotion, and how these reactions can lead to the unhealthy coping strategy of smoking Introduce the concept of mindfulness	Review components of mindful emotion awareness Discuss consequences of judgmental reactions to emotions Discuss common smoking traps	Conduct listening to music exercise Debrief Review benefits of mindfulness Discuss translation of formal mindfulness practice into adopting a more mindful style in everyday life

Conduct mindful emotion awareness exercise Debrief Provide psychoeducation on the components of mindful emotion awareness Set goals for at-home practice	Review rationale of mindfulness strategies to break the link between emotional triggers and responses Conduct anchoring in the present exercise Debrief Set goals for at-home practice Ask patient to identify a song for next week's session that will bring up strong emotions	Review use of mindfulness to avoid smoking traps Summarize take-home points Set goals for at-home practice
Countering Emotional Behaviors		
Provide psychoeducation on emotion-driven behaviors Introduce smoking as an emotion-driven behavior Introduce alternative actions Review alternative actions that are incompatible with smoking Set goals for at-home practice	Review smoking as an emotion-driven behavior Discuss how repeatedly pairing certain emotions with reaching for a cigarette makes the association between these two stronger Provide psychoeducation on smoking and avoidance Introduce alternative actions as an approach cycle Review alternative actions list Set goals for at-home practice	Review smoking and avoidance cycle Review benefits of alternative actions Brainstorm additional alternative actions Summarize take-home points Set goals for at-home practice

Box 13.1

Prior to Planned Quit Day

- Review smoking cessation medication options.
  - Review nicotine replacement therapy (NRT; nicotine gum, patches, nasal spray, inhaler, and lozenges) and non-nicotine-based medications (bupropion and varenicline), and how these medications work.
  - Help the patient make a plan to follow up with their doctor regarding smoking cessation medications or to purchase NRT over the counter.
- Prepare for challenges.
  - Provide education on symptoms of nicotine withdrawal.
  - Discuss what the patient identifies as the most challenging part of quitting smoking and coping strategies.
  - Identify any negative thoughts that the patient may have about quitting smoking, and how to address these.
- Review benefits of quitting smoking.
  - Discuss health effects and other benefits of quitting smoking.
  - Ask patient to discuss their most important reasons for quitting smoking and how they can remind themself of their reasons for quitting.
- Prepare for quit day.
  - Instruct patient to remove ashtrays, lighters, and cigarettes from their home or any other places they smoke (e.g., vehicle).
  - Discuss who the patient has informed about their quit date, and encourage the patient to tell others when their quit date is so they can obtain support and encouragement from others.
  - Plan enjoyable activities for quit day to keep the patient busy and to have something to look forward to.
  - Remind patient to refrain from smoking (not even a puff) starting at midnight the night before.

interest in smoking cessation pharmacotherapy. The therapist then introduces physical and emotional symptoms of nicotine withdrawal and encourages the patient to identify withdrawal symptoms that they have experienced in the past. Although nicotine withdrawal symptoms can be highly unpleasant, the therapist underscores that these symptoms are not medically dangerous. The therapist then provides psychoeducation on how feelings of nicotine withdrawal are related to thoughts and behaviors, consistent with the UP's three-component model of emotion. For example, the physical sensations of nicotine withdrawal leads to the thought, "I need a cigarette right now," which triggers the action of reaching for a cigarette. The more this cycle is repeated, the stronger the link becomes between smoking-related feelings, thoughts, and behaviors. The therapist then introduces the concept of interoceptive exposure, which we refer to as "practice quitting." Practice quitting is defined as spending more time without cigarettes, without the pressure to quit permanently. Practice quitting is beneficial for several reasons: (a) It allows the patient to learn more about the situations, withdrawal symptoms, and thoughts that accompany smoking; (b) it helps reduce cigarettes per day and nicotine dependence over time; (c) it can help break the link between smoking-related thoughts, feelings, and behaviors; and (d) it increases the patient's self-efficacy for smoking cessation. The patient can practice quitting by delaying the first cigarette of the day, increasing the amount of time between cigarettes during the day, and/or omitting cigarettes in specific situations. The therapist helps the patient develop an interoceptive exposure hierarchy, adapted specifically for nicotine withdrawal exposures. The therapist encourages the patient to identify 5–10 situations in which they usually smoke, and how difficult (from 0 [not difficult at all] to 100 [extremely difficult]) it would be to skip the cigarette in each situation. The session ends with the patient selecting a moderately difficult situation from their exposure hierarchy to engage in for at-home practice.

Session 2

The therapist reviews material from the previous session, assesses patient understanding, and addresses any questions. The therapist then reviews at-home practice and addresses what went well and any challenges the patient experienced. The therapist then introduces the concept of how engaging in practice quitting can provide corrective information about what happens when the patient does not smoke. Patients often have outcome expectancies regarding the severity/duration of cravings if they do not smoke (e.g., "This will be awful," "I can't handle it," and "The cravings will drive me crazy"). The therapist highlights how practice quitting (i.e., exposure to nicotine withdrawal symptoms) gives patients the opportunity to learn from their own experience about what will happen when they refrain from smoking and to challenge their expectations. Next, the therapist reviews the common tendency of smokers to avoid or escape from any signs of nicotine withdrawal. This avoidance cycle creates problems because it maintains smoking and prevents the patient from learning about the symptoms of nicotine withdrawal and how to cope with them. The last portion of the session includes a review of strategies to minimize the reward value of smoking after practice quitting. Specifically, this means the patient's next cigarette should be smoked in the most boring way possible; the cigarette should not be paired with things the patient enjoys (e.g., drinking coffee or socializing with others), and the patient should do nothing but smoke the cigarette. The session ends with a review of the nicotine exposure hierarchy and a selection of goals for practice quitting for the upcoming week. The patient is encouraged to include a nonsmoking period prior to the next week's session for an in-session exposure exercise.

Session 3

Following review of key concepts and at-home practice, the in-session nicotine withdrawal exposure is conducted. The therapist and patient conduct a detailed review of the patient's experience of nicotine withdrawal symptoms (thoughts, feelings, and physical sensations). The patient is presented with a list of physical and emotional symptoms of nicotine withdrawal and asked to rate the intensity of each. The patient is also asked to describe the time course of withdrawal symptoms over time (e.g., "Which symptom did you notice first?" and "Were the symptoms constant, or did they come and go?"). If the patient did not abstain from smoking prior to the session, the therapist should encourage the patient to recall their most recent practice quitting exercise. After debriefing about the in-session exposure, the next portion of the session involves identifying and challenging outcome expectancies associated with nicotine withdrawal. The therapist reviews how patients sometimes expect the physical symptoms of nicotine withdrawal to be worse than they actually are and highlights how practice quitting gives patients the opportunity to learn from their own experience about what happens to withdrawal symptoms and cravings when patients do not smoke. Alternatively, the practice quitting exercise may have been as challenging as expected, or even more challenging than expected, but provided patients with information about their own ability to tolerate the symptoms. The session ends with a review of the goals of practice quitting and the patient's nicotine withdrawal hierarchy and a selection of goals for the upcoming week.

Mindful Emotion Awareness

Session 1

First, the therapist provides psychoeducation on the purpose of emotions (i.e., how emotions give us helpful information about the world around us), with an example of how the patient might respond after hearing a loud noise while walking alone at night, and how the emotions of anxiety or fear could lead to the adaptive response of taking protective action. Second, the therapist then introduces secondary reactions to initial emotions, which are often unhelpful. Secondary reactions can often be judgmental, and negative self-judgments can trigger unhealthy coping strategies such as smoking. Third, the therapist introduces the in-session exercise from the UP workbook (p. 66) designed to practice present-focused, nonjudgmental awareness of emotions through mindfulness. Fourth, the therapist leads the patient through the scripted mindful emotion awareness exercise for approximately 15 minutes, followed by time for debriefing. Fifth, the therapist provides psychoeducation on the different components of mindful emotion awareness, including allowing the patient to experience emotions as they happen, with a focus on being in the present moment rather than "living" in the future or past. The therapist highlights how being mindful includes allowing emotions to come and go, without trying to push away or hold on to certain feelings. The therapist also discusses how being aware of one's emotions allows the patient to respond thoughtfully, without overreacting or reacting out of habit. Last, the patient is asked to identify a goal for engaging in at-home practice of mindful awareness.

Session 2

Following review of at-home practice, the therapist reviews mindful emotion awareness and consequences of judgmental reactions. The therapist then introduces the concept of "smoking traps," such as smoking out of strong habit or "autopilot," or smoking to escape or avoid negative feelings, which is discussed further in the Countering Emotional Behaviors module. The therapist highlights how mindfulness can help the patient sidestep these smoking traps by paying attention to the feelings they are having instead of zoning out, and inviting their feelings in rather than pushing them away. The therapist then conducts an anchoring in the present exercise for approximately 10 minutes. The exercise consists of a "three-point check," in which the patient identifies the feelings in their body, the thoughts running through their mind, and any emotions they may be experiencing. The patient is then asked to identify any urges to act, and practices mindfully responding versus reacting out of strong habit or emotion. Following debriefing, the therapist and patient discuss at-home practice. The patient is encouraged to try anchoring in the present at least once per day, particularly during a time when they would usually have a cigarette. The therapist also asks the patient to think of a song that will bring up strong emotions, for use in next week's session.

Session 3

An in-session mood induction exercise is conducted by listening to the song that the patient identified. The therapist encourages the patient to notice any thoughts, physical sensations, and feelings that come up during this experience. After debriefing, the therapist reviews the benefits of mindfulness and how the patient can translate formal mindfulness practice into a more mindful style in everyday life. The therapist should encourage the patient to use mindfulness anytime they catch themself getting carried away with a strong emotion or having thoughts that are critical or judgmental. The latter part of the session involves a review of smoking traps, including smoking out of strong habit and smoking in response to an emotional trigger. The patient and therapist then set goals for at-home practice. The patient is encouraged to practice mindfulness while listening to music, as well as trying exercises twice throughout the day: before smoking the first cigarette in the morning and during a time when the patient would smoke out of habit or in response to an emotional trigger.

Countering Emotional Behaviors

Session 1

The therapist introduces emotion-driven behaviors (EDBs), or actions taken in response to intense emotions. The therapist explains how EDBs can be helpful in the short term but become unhelpful in the long term. The therapist then introduces smoking as an EDB, with a key distinction of short-term versus long-term effects of smoking. In the short term, a common motive for smoking is "to relax," especially when experiencing stress or negative mood. However, as smoking leads to increased nicotine dependence over time, smokers typically experience frequent bouts of nicotine withdrawal symptoms between cigarettes, which are characterized by marked irritability and anxiety. Thus, nicotine addiction can be seen as the *cause* of stress and negative mood, rather than the solution to it. The therapist then introduces *alternative actions*, which are actions the patient can take in response to negative emotions that are incompatible with smoking. For example, when the patient is feeling stressed, they could choose to go for a walk, spend time with family, or call a friend instead of reaching for cigarettes. The therapist should address how alternative actions take more effort in the short term but have more positive consequences in the long term. Good alternative actions are within the patient's control and do not depend on other people. The session ends with an identification of what emotion tends to trigger the patient's smoking, and brainstorming what alternative action the patient could take instead, the next time that emotion comes up. The patient should be encouraged to try out an alternative action once a day, at a time when they would usually have a cigarette, and record their experience.

Session 2

The therapist reviews smoking as an EDB and short-term versus long-term consequences of smoking. The therapist should highlight that smoking as an EDB strengthens the belief that individuals are unable to cope with that emotion without having a cigarette. The next part of this session focuses on the role of smoking and avoidance. The therapist should highlight how many people use smoking to avoid or escape from negative emotions or stressful situations. This avoidance cycle is problematic because it maintains the smoking habit and is ineffective in the long term because it does not lead to effective problem-solving. The therapist then introduces the idea of alternative actions as an opportunity to approach, rather than avoid, a situation. Although alternative actions can include enjoyable activities, they can also include activities that convey a sense of mastery or accomplishment. The therapist should then facilitate a discussion of situations that the patient may be currently avoiding but that they would like to work on approaching. Next, the therapist and patient review a list of alternative actions, and the patient selects activities that they would either like to do more of or would like to try for the first time. The patient is encouraged to add any additional activities they are able to identify to this list. Last, the therapist and patient work to identify goals for the upcoming week, including identifying an alternative action that they enjoy and one they have been putting off or avoiding. It is important to remind the patient that these activities should be incompatible with smoking, meaning that the patient does not bring cigarettes with them during these activities, and the activity should be scheduled during a time when the patient usually smokes.

Session 3

After reviewing the key concept of the smoking avoidance cycle, the therapist next reviews alternative actions that the patient has used so far and any barriers to completing these alternative actions. The therapist should assist the patient in addressing barriers and brainstorming additional alternative actions. These could include hobbies the patient has enjoyed in the past but has not done recently, activities they have been putting off but would like to check off their to-do list, and activities that align with the patient's values. Last, the patient and therapist work to identify the patient's goals for the upcoming week, and the patient is encouraged to consider alternative actions that will benefit their health (e.g., going for a walk, brushing their teeth, and making a healthy snack).

Planning for Quit Day

When patients express readiness to make a permanent attempt to quit smoking, we recommend devoting a session to planning for a quit date. The therapist should review smoking cessation medications with the patient and highlight how nicotine replacement therapy (NRT) or non-nicotine medications (i.e., varenicline or bupropion) can increase the patient's chances of quitting for good. The therapist should encourage the patient to make a plan to meet with their health care provider to discuss smoking cessation medications and obtain a prescription, if necessary. In addition, the therapist should facilitate a discussion regarding possible physical symptoms the patient may experience as they break their addiction to nicotine. The therapist should also have the patient identify what they anticipate being most challenging and the strategies they will employ to cope with these challenges. It is also important that this session address the health benefits that occur soon after quitting (e.g., improved sense of taste and smell), as well as the health benefits that occur over time (e.g., fewer colds and respiratory infections). The therapist should have the patient identify their reasons for quitting smoking and how they can remind themselves of these reasons (e.g., leaving notes around the home). The patient should also prepare their home to be smoke-free; the therapist should encourage the patient to get rid of any ashtrays, lighters, and cigarettes that they may have in their home or any other places where the patient smokes. The therapist should also encourage the patient to tell family and friends about their quit date and make specific requests to let others know how to help, such as "Please do not smoke around me or offer me cigarettes" or "Please give me space while I'm working on quitting smoking and my patience is thin." Last, we recommend that the patient plan enjoyable activities for their quit date to have something to look forward to and keep their mind off of smoking.

CASE EXAMPLE

Ms. Smith is a 64-year-old African American female who smokes 10–15 cigarettes per day and smokes her first cigarette within 5 minutes of waking. She has been smoking for nearly 50 years and is interested in quitting smoking to better manage her chronic health conditions and save money.

In the first several sessions, the therapist introduced the concept of practice quitting, which involves spending more time without cigarettes, without the pressure to quit for good. The therapist worked with Ms. Smith to create an exposure hierarchy adapted for nicotine withdrawal, and Ms. Smith identified several situations in which she usually smokes and rated how difficult (from 0 to 100) it would be to skip her cigarette in each situation. Ms. Smith rated her first cigarette in the morning with coffee as the most difficult to skip (100), whereas her cigarette after dinner was rated as the easiest (30). For at-home practice, Ms. Smith initially decided that she would omit smoking after dinner. After successfully skipping this cigarette 5 of the 7 days of the week, Ms. Smith moved on to more difficult situations on her hierarchy, such as skipping a break-time cigarette while watching her granddaughter (50) and skipping a cigarette while driving her car (50). Ms. Smith reported that each of these goals felt challenging but doable and that she felt proud of herself that she was able to meet her goals for at-home practice.

Next, the therapist introduced mindful emotion awareness and explained how mindfulness allows the patient to experience her emotions in a nonjudgmental and present-focused way. The therapist conducted an in-session mindfulness exercise and debriefed with Ms. Smith afterward. The therapist worked with Ms. Smith to identify her goals for practicing mindfulness over the next week, which include completing mindfulness exercises before her first cigarette of the day. Initially, Ms. Smith expressed concern about when she would be able to engage in mindfulness practice at home, as she shared space with several family members and watches her granddaughter throughout the day. The patient and therapist problem-solved a time of day that was typically available for mindfulness practice (i.e., in the evenings or while her granddaughter is napping). The therapist also underscored the importance of adopting a more mindful style in everyday life and bringing the principles of mindfulness to everyday activities such as conversations with family members, preparing meals, and completing tasks at work. Ms. Smith was successfully able to listen to mindfulness recordings between sessions, and she ultimately used mindfulness to delay her smoking throughout the day.

Last, the therapist introduced the concept of EDBs, or actions taken in response to intense emotions. The therapist discussed how smoking can be an EDB because many patients smoke to avoid intense emotions and stressful situations. The therapist introduced the idea of alternative actions, which are actions that Ms. Smith can take in response to negative emotions instead of smoking. The therapist worked with Ms. Smith to brainstorm alternative actions, and Ms. Smith decided that she would try listening to music, reading, cooking, or organizing her home the next time that she faces a stress trigger for smoking.

In discussing smoking cessation, Ms. Smith expressed an interest in using the nicotine patch. She discussed her goal of quitting smoking with her partner, who was also a smoker and interested in quitting. As shown in Figure 13.2, Ms. Smith reduced her smoking from approximately 13 to 1 cigarette per day following her quit date, and she was abstinent for 12 of the past 14 days at her last treatment session. She also reduced her level of smoking for affect regulation (i.e., to enhance pleasure or reduce distress) over the course of treatment. She voiced strong motivation to continue using the tools she had gained in treatment to remain smoke-free.

EFFICACY/CLINICAL UTILITY OF THE UNIFIED PROTOCOL FOR SMOKING CESSATION

To date, some evidence suggests that cognitive–behavioral treatment strategies may be used to target psychological risk factors of distress intolerance, anxiety

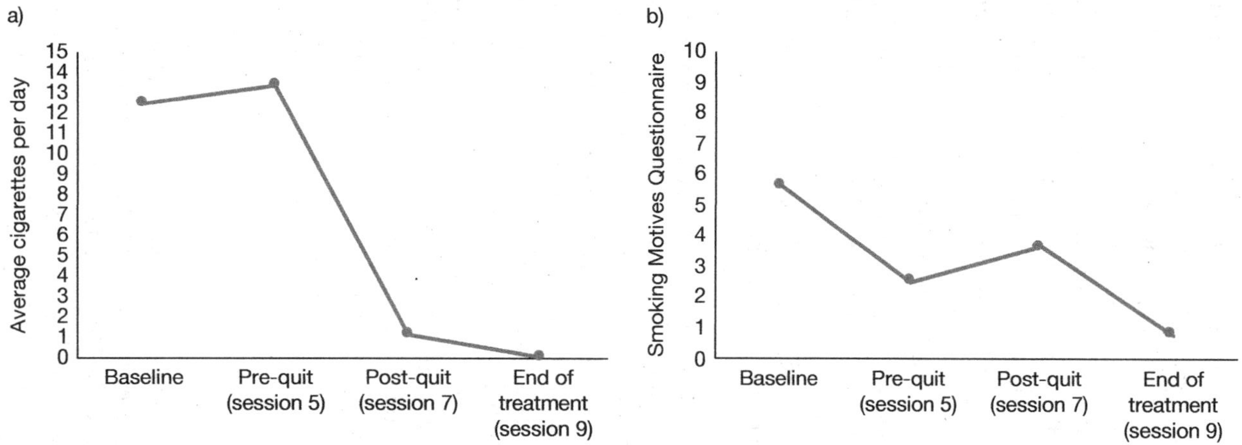

Figure 13.2 Case example data for (a) cigarettes per day and (b) smoking for affect regulation over the course of treatment.

sensitivity, and anhedonia among selected populations of cigarette smokers (i.e., those with anxiety disorders or elevated anxiety sensitivity; Farris et al., 2016; Feldner et al., 2008). These treatment strategies are shown to reduce reliance on smoking for affect regulation (Brown et al., 2013; Feldner et al., 2013) and provide skills to cope with acute nicotine withdrawal after quitting (Brown et al., 2013; MacPherson et al., 2010; Zvolensky et al., 2014).

A next step is to build on these findings with a modular, transdiagnostic treatment approach, such as the UP, which can be applied to a range of smoking populations. Furthermore, it is important for treatment research to be designed "with the end in mind" by incorporating rigorous assessment of hypothesized treatment mechanisms and clinically significant endpoints. We are currently conducting a study to test the feasibility and initial efficacy of the UP for smoking cessation among individuals with chronic obstructive pulmonary disease. Our study framework is guided by the Obesity-Related Behavioral Intervention Trials model (Czajkowski et al., 2015), which is focused on the early, pre-efficacy stages of treatment development. We are specifically interested in establishing proof of concept of the UP modules on psychological risk factors (i.e., distress intolerance, anxiety sensitivity, and anhedonia) to examine whether these factors are modifiable by targeted treatment and whether reducing psychological risk factors impacts smoking behavior. We will assess the behavioral target of smoking for affect regulation, as measured by the Smoking Motives Questionnaire–Revised (Comeau et al., 2000; Grant et al., 2009). Next, we will assess early cessation milestones to tailor treatment to relapse vulnerability factors within the initial days of a quit attempt. Evidence suggests that the majority of smoking lapses occur within the first 2 weeks following a quit attempt (Fiore et al., 2008), and smokers with psychological risk factors are particularly vulnerable to early lapse (Brown et al., 2005, 2009). A focus on the early abstinence period maximizes sensitivity to preliminary treatment effects and is strongly related to long-term cessation outcomes (Ashare et al., 2013; Garvey et al., 1992). Through this work, we hope to better understand the mechanisms by which emotion-focused treatment impacts smoking cessation outcomes and contribute to the literature on behavioral health applications of the UP treatment.

CONCLUSION

In this chapter, we have outlined the conceptual model guiding use of the UP for smoking cessation and presented a detailed treatment description and case study of this approach. Because the UP is targeted to aversive and avoidant reactions to emotional experiences across diagnoses, we believe that it is uniquely well-suited to address affective disturbances that are common triggers for cigarette smoking and are exacerbated by nicotine withdrawal. By integrating the UP treatment with standard behavioral counseling for smoking cessation, we hope to reduce smoking for affect regulation, build skills for targeting the aversive symptoms of nicotine withdrawal, and foster long-term smoking abstinence.

Directions for Future Research

Although we have focused on the three UP modules that are most strongly conceptually linked to cigarette smoking, there may also be value to using other modules (i.e., Psychoeducation and Cognitive Flexibility) with patients interested in quitting smoking. Especially for smokers with co-occurring emotional disorders, a greater emphasis on the role of emotions and thinking patterns as they relate to smoking outcome expectancies (i.e., catastrophizing) may be warranted. Second, refining treatment techniques for interoceptive exposure through practice quitting exercises is an active area of treatment development research (Cox et al., 2022). In particular, it is unclear if practice quitting should incorporate use of NRT. NRT sampling may be valuable in engaging smokers in higher quality, evidence-based quit attempts, rather than attempting to quit "cold turkey." However, if viewed through the lens of practice quitting as a nicotine withdrawal exposure (i.e., in a parallel fashion to graduated exposure therapy for anxiety disorders; Otto et al., 2005), NRT use would likely not be indicated. Because NRT products blunt the symptoms of acute withdrawal, they may prevent patients from habituating to withdrawal-related distress and experiencing the full benefit of the practice quitting exercise. Given the absence of studies that directly test this question, we advise patients to consider practice quitting without the aid of NRT, but ultimately defer to patient preference.

Limitations/Barriers Observed

Traditionally, smoking cessation treatment programs have allocated nearly all resources to only those smokers willing to set a quit date (Fiore et al., 2008). This is a problem because few smokers are ready to set a quit date at any given time (Wewers et al., 2003), and many smokers engage in as many as 30 quit attempts before achieving lasting abstinence (Chaiton et al., 2016). Behavioral treatments such as the UP are needed to offer strategies that appeal to smokers regardless of their willingness to set a quit date. In addition, standard treatment using an individual, in-person delivery format limits the potential reach of health-focused interventions using the UP. More work is needed to assess whether telehealth platforms and digital health technologies can be used to scale up UP treatment delivery for population health, while maintaining treatment potency.

Tips/Advice to Clinicians

It is important for the clinician to assess patient understanding of topics throughout (e.g., by asking how they would explain the treatment strategy to a friend), to draw on the patient's own experiences with smoking in generating examples of key concepts, and to develop a strong working alliance with the patient. With regard to the Interoceptive Exposure module, it is important to have patients identify a wide range of situations that vary in level of difficulty when creating the nicotine withdrawal exposure hierarchy, to allow for calibrating an exposure of the right degree of difficulty. One challenge inherent to the Interoceptive Exposure module is that the initial cigarette following a practice quit may be especially reinforcing, and the enhanced reward value of this cigarette could be potentially countertherapeutic. We counsel patients not to allow practice quitting to turn into "practice relapsing" and to make the return to smoking as boring as possible. In delivering the Mindful Emotion Awareness module, we have found that some patients have difficulty with their connotations of mindfulness (e.g., it is a practice for New Age hippies or Buddhist monks) and respond better to descriptions such as centering or grounding. In delivering the Countering Emotional Behaviors module, it is important for the therapist to assist the patient in selecting realistic goals that are feasible in the patient's everyday life. Especially for patients with chronic health conditions, we have found it helpful to incorporate principles of activity pacing (e.g., by setting time-based goals with planned rest time). Last, for providers new to smoking cessation treatment, high-quality resources are available from the Association for the Treatment of Tobacco Use and Dependence (https://www.attud.org) and the University of Wisconsin Center for Tobacco Research and Intervention (https://ctri.wisc.edu/providers/education/tobacco-treatment-training).

REFERENCES

Ashare, R. L., Wileyto, E. P., Perkins, K. A., & Schnoll, R. A. (2013). The first seven days of a quit attempt predicts relapse: Validation of a measure for screening medications for nicotine dependence. *Journal of Addiction Medicine, 7*(4), 249–254.

Baker, T. B., Piper, M. E., McCarthy, D. E., Majeskie, M. R., & Fiore, M. C. (2004). Addiction motivation reformulated: An affective processing model of negative reinforcement. *Psychological Review, 111*(1), 33–51.

Barlow, D. H., Ellard, K. K., & Fairholme, C. P. (2011). *Unified Protocol for Transdiagnostic Treatment of Emotional Disorders: Workbook*. Oxford University Press.

Barlow, D. H., Farchione, T. J., Fairholme, C. P., Ellard, K. K., Boisseau, C. L., Allen, L. B., & May, J. T. E. (2011). *Unified Protocol for Transdiagnostic Treatment of Emotional Disorders: Therapist guide*: Oxford University Press.

Brake, C. A., Sauer-Zavala, S., Boswell, J. F., Gallagher, M. W., Farchione, T. J., & Barlow, D. H. (2016). Mindfulness-based exposure strategies as a transdiagnostic mechanism of change: An exploratory alternating treatment design. *Behavior Therapy, 47*(2), 225–238.

Brown, R. A., Lejuez, C., Kahler, C. W., Strong, D. R., & Zvolensky, M. J. (2005). Distress tolerance and early smoking lapse. *Clinical Psychology Review, 25*(6), 713–733.

Brown, R. A., Lejuez, C., Strong, D. R., Kahler, C. W., Zvolensky, M. J., Carpenter, L. L., Niaura, R., & Price, L. H. (2009). A prospective examination of distress tolerance and early smoking lapse in adult self-quitters. *Nicotine & Tobacco Research, 11*(5), 493–502.

Brown, R. A., Reed, K. M. P., Bloom, E. L., Minami, H., Strong, D. R., Lejuez, C. W., Kahler, C. W., Zvolensky, M. J., Gifford, E. V., & Hayes, S. C. (2013). Development and preliminary randomized controlled trial of a distress tolerance treatment for smokers with a history of early lapse. *Nicotine & Tobacco Research, 15*(12), 2005–2015.

Chaiton, M., Diemert, L., Cohen, J. E., Bondy, S. J., Selby, P., Philipneri, A., & Schwartz, R. (2016). Estimating the number of quit attempts it takes to quit smoking successfully in a longitudinal cohort of smokers. *BMJ Open, 6*(6), e011045.

Comeau, N., Stewart, S., Loba, P., Rhyno, E., & Loughlin, H. (2000). Adolescents' motives for smoking and marijuana use: Factor structure and relations to motives for alcohol use [Paper presentation]. Joint Meeting of the British Experimental Psychology Society and the Canadian Society for Brain Behavior and Cognitive Science, Cambridge, UK.

Cook, J., Spring, B., McChargue, D., & Doran, N. (2010). Effects of anhedonia on days to relapse among smokers with a history of depression: A brief report. *Nicotine & Tobacco Research, 12*(9), 978–982.

Cook, J. W., Piper, M. E., Leventhal, A. M., Schlam, T. R., Fiore, M. C., & Baker, T. B. (2015). Anhedonia as a component of the tobacco withdrawal syndrome. *Journal of Abnormal Psychology, 124*(1), 215–225.

Cox, C. M., Westrick, J., McCarthy, D. E., Carpenter, M. J., & Mathew, A. R. (2022). *Practice quit attempts: Scoping review of a novel intervention strategy. Journal of Studies on Alcohol and Drugs, 83*(1), 115–125.

Creamer, M. R., Wang, T. W., Babb, S., Cullen, K. A., Day, H., Willis, G., Jamal, A., & Neff, L. (2019). Tobacco product use and cessation indicators among adults—United States, 2018. *MMWR Morbidity and Mortality Weekly Report, 68*(45), 1013–1019.

Czajkowski, S. M., Powell, L. H., Adler, N., Naar-King, S., Reynolds, K. D., Hunter, C. M., Laraia, B., Olster, D. H., Perna, F. M., Peterson, J. C., Epel, E., Boyington, J. E., & Peterson, J. C. (2015). From ideas to efficacy: The ORBIT model for developing behavioral treatments for chronic diseases. *Health Psychology, 34*(10), 971–982.

Farris, S. G., Leyro, T. M., Allan, N. P., Øverup, C. S., Schmidt, N. B., & Zvolensky, M. J. (2016). Distress intolerance during smoking cessation treatment. *Behaviour Research and Therapy, 85*, 33–42.

Feldner, M. T., Smith, R. C., Monson, C. M., & Zvolensky, M. J. (2013). Initial evaluation of an integrated treatment for comorbid PTSD and smoking using a nonconcurrent, multiple-baseline design. *Behavior Therapy, 44*(3), 514–528.

Feldner, M. T., Zvolensky, M. J., Babson, K., Leen-Feldner, E. W., & Schmidt, N. B. (2008). An integrated approach to panic prevention targeting the empirically supported risk factors of smoking and anxiety sensitivity: Theoretical basis and evidence from a pilot project evaluating feasibility and short-term efficacy. *Journal of Anxiety Disorders, 22*(7), 1227–1243.

Fiore, M. C., Jaén, C. R., Baker, T. B., Bailey, W. C., Benowitz, N. L., Curry, S. J., Dorfman, S. F., Froelicher, E. S., Goldstein, M. G., Healton, C. G., Henderson, P. N., Heyman, R. B., Koh, H. K., Kottke, T. E., Lando, H. A., Mecklenburg, R. E., Mermelstein, R. J., Mullen, P. D., Orleans, C. T., . . . Wewers, M. E.; Tobacco Use and Dependence Guideline Panel. (2008). *Treating tobacco use and dependence: 2008 update*. U.S. Department of Health and Human Services.

Garvey, A. J., Bliss, R. E., Hitchcock, J. L., Heinold, J. W., & Rosner, B. (1992). Predictors of smoking relapse among self-quitters: A report from the Normative Aging Study. *Addictive Behaviors, 17*(4), 367–377.

Grant, V. V., Stewart, S. H., & Mohr, C. D. (2009). Coping-anxiety and coping-depression motives predict different daily mood-drinking relationships. *Psychology of Addictive Behaviors, 23*(2), 226–237.

Hendricks, P. S., Ditre, J. W., Drobes, D. J., & Brandon, T. H. (2006). The early time course of smoking withdrawal effects. *Psychopharmacology, 187*(3), 385–396.

Hughes, J. R. (2007). Effects of abstinence from tobacco: Etiology, animal models, epidemiology, and significance: A subjective review. *Nicotine & Tobacco Research, 9*(3), 329–339.

Leventhal, A. M., Piper, M. E., Japuntich, S. J., Baker, T. B., & Cook, J. W. (2014). Anhedonia, depressed mood, and smoking cessation outcome. *Journal of Consulting and Clinical Psychology, 82*(1), 122–129.

Leventhal, A. M., & Zvolensky, M. J. (2015). Anxiety, depression, and cigarette smoking: A transdiagnostic vulnerability framework to understanding emotion-smoking comorbidity. *Psychological Bulletin, 141*(1), 176–212.

MacPherson, L., Tull, M. T., Matusiewicz, A. K., Rodman, S., Strong, D. R., Kahler, C. W., Hopko, D. R., Zvolensky, M. J., Brown, R. A., & Lejuez, C. W. (2010). Randomized controlled trial of behavioral activation smoking cessation treatment for smokers with elevated depressive symptoms. *Journal of Consulting and Clinical Psychology, 78*(1), 55–61.

Mathew, A. R., Hogarth, L., Leventhal, A. M., Cook, J. W., & Hitsman, B. (2017). Cigarette smoking and depression comorbidity: Systematic review and proposed theoretical model. *Addiction, 112*(3), 401–412.

Otto, M. W., Powers, M. B., & Fischmann, D. (2005). Emotional exposure in the treatment of substance use disorders: Conceptual model, evidence, and future directions. *Clinical Psychology Review, 25*(6), 824–839.

Piper, M. E. (2015). Withdrawal: Expanding a key addiction construct. *Nicotine & Tobacco Research, 17*(2), 1405–1415.

Reitsma, M. B., Fullman, N., Ng, M., Salama, J. S., Abajobir, A., Abate, K. H., Abbafati, C., Abera, S. F., Abraham, B., Abyu, G. Y., Adebiyi, A., Al-Aly, Z., Aleman, A., Ali, R., Al Alkerwi, A., Allebeck, P., Al Raddadi, R., Amare, A., Amberbir, A., . . . Gakidou, E.; GDB 2015 Tobacco Collaborators. (2017). Smoking prevalence and attributable disease burden in 195 countries and territories, 1990–2015: A systematic analysis from the Global Burden of Disease Study 2015. *Lancet, 389*(10082), 1885–1906.

Sauer-Zavala, S., Cassiello-Robbins, C., Conklin, L. R., Bullis, J. R., Thompson-Hollands, J., & Kennedy, K. A. (2017). Isolating the unique effects of the Unified Protocol treatment modules using single case experimental design. *Behavior Modification, 41*(2), 286–307.

Schnoll, R. A., Leone, F. T., & Hitsman, B. (2013). Symptoms of depression and smoking behaviors following treatment with transdermal nicotine patch. *Journal of Addictive Diseases, 32*(1), 46–52.

Wewers, M. E., Stillman, F. A., Hartman, A. M., & Shopland, D. R. (2003). Distribution of daily smokers by stage of change: Current Population Survey results. *Preventive Medicine, 36*(6), 710–720.

Zvolensky, M. J., Bogiaizian, D., Salazar, P. L., Farris, S. G., & Bakhshaie, J. (2014). An anxiety sensitivity reduction smoking-cessation program for Spanish-speaking smokers (Argentina). *Cognitive and Behavioral Practice, 21*(3), 350–363.

14

Unified Protocol Application in Patients with Long COVID-19 Condition

VERÓNICA MARTÍNEZ-BORBA, ÓSCAR PERIS-BAQUERO, LAURA MARTÍNEZ-GARCÍA, JORGE OSMA, AND ESTHER DEL CORRAL-BEAMONTE ■

INTRODUCTION

Incidence and Impact of the COVID-19 Pandemic

COVID-19 is an infectious disease caused by the SARS–CoV-2 virus (severe acute respiratory syndrome coronavirus 2), which became a global pandemic in March 2020. Since then, it is estimated that it has caused the death of more than 6 million people, and more than 657 million people worldwide have been infected (World Health Organization [WHO], 2022a).

Regarding the symptoms caused by the virus, people who contracted this infection presented various symptoms with different severity, including fever, dry cough, and fatigue; others such as loss of smell and taste; and more severe symptoms such as respiratory insufficiency (WHO, 2021). Symptoms last approximately 3–7 days and disappear entirely within 10–14 days after infection (WHO, 2021).

In addition to the physical symptoms associated with the infection, the pandemic situation and the actions taken to prevent its transmission (i.e., confinements) greatly impacted the mental health of the population worldwide—specifically, a high prevalence of symptomatology related to the presence of mental disorders in the general population (Rodríguez-Fernández et al., 2021). More precisely,

Verónica Martínez-Borba, Óscar Peris-Baquero, Laura Martínez-García, Jorge Osma, and Esther del Corral-Beamonte, *Unified Protocol Application in Patients with Long COVID-19 Condition* In: *Applications of the Unified Protocol in Health Conditions.* Edited by: Jorge Osma and Todd J. Farchione, Oxford University Press.
DOI: 10.1093/oso/9780197564295.003.0014

Rodríguez-Fernández et al. (2021) reported a prevalence of between 8.3% and 45.1% in anxiety symptomatology and between 14.6% and 46.4% in the case of depressive symptomatology. Moreover, in both cases, the incidence was higher in women and young people.

Special Case of COVID-19 Survivors: Long COVID-19 Condition, Definition, and Prevalence

Although COVID-19 symptoms disappear entirely within a short time, some patients continue to present symptoms over time. According to the WHO European Observatory on Health Systems and Policies (Rajan et al., 2021), one-fourth of infected persons presented symptoms 1 month after diagnosis, and 1 in 10 presented symptoms 12 weeks later. This condition has been described as a post-COVID-19 condition or long COVID-19, and it is defined as the presence of symptoms or the development of new symptoms of COVID-19 3 months after the initial COVID-19 infection (WHO, 2022b).

In the recent literature, several systematic reviews have analyzed the prevalence of long COVID-19 in the population. Studies such as the one carried out by Fernández-de-Las-Peñas et al. (2021), which included more than 24,000 patients, found the presence of more than one COVID-19 symptom in 45.9% of patients more than 90 days after infection. As for the main symptoms shown, they included fatigue and dyspnea in 35–60% of cases, followed by others such as cough (20–25%) and anosmia (10–20%). Other studies, such as that of Zeng et al. (2023), which included data from 1,285,407 participants from 32 countries, found at least one symptom in COVID-19 survivors 12 months after infection. The most prevalent symptoms were abnormalities on lung computed tomography and pulmonary function in 45.6% and 56.9% of patients, respectively, followed by fatigue (28.7%).

In addition to physical symptoms, mental health problems are highly prevalent in people suffering from long COVID-19, with depressive and anxiety disorders being the most common (approximately 20%; Deer et al., 2021). In addition, a reduction in activities of daily living and a decrease in quality of life are also observed in these people (de Oliveira Almeida et al., 2023).

Psychological Interventions for Long COVID-19 Patients

Enormous efforts have been conducted to understand the psychological processes of patients suffering from COVID-19 condition (Ahmed et al., 2021; Bekele et al., 2021) and to provide psychological interventions that allow the amelioration of psychological suffering. Several systematic reviews summarize the practices developed to address emotional suffering in COVID-19 patients (Chennapragada et al., 2022; Tasleem et al., 2022; Uzunova et al., 2021). However, the low number of studies that have focused on long COVID-19 condition is also noteworthy. In Spain, the ARACOV-01 project, promoted by Dr. Del Corral and financed by Solutex GC S.L. (idmf7202170008), aimed to (a) characterize the sociodemographic, clinic, psychological, and biological profile of a sample of patients who suffer long COVID-19; and (b) study the efficacy of a transdiagnostic psychological intervention for long COVID-19 patients who present comorbid emotional disorders (i.e., anxiety, depressive and related disorders) (Bullis et al., 2019).

In this context, our team is working on a systematic review to explore the main characteristics of the psychological interventions provided to patients with COVID-19 or long COVID-19 condition and comorbid emotional disorders or symptoms (PROSPERO: CRD42022367227). The preliminary results of this systematic review indicated that interventions mainly focus on COVID-19 patients, especially when hospitalized. Only two studies have applied a psychological intervention to long COVID-19 patients. In the study of Bogucki and Sawchuck (2022), cognitive processing therapy was implemented in a case of a 30-year-old female patient. A reduction in post-traumatic, anxiety, and depressive symptoms was observed after the intervention. The second study, conducted by Compagno et al. (2022), used a pre–post design to provide a cognitive–behavioral therapy and Eye Movement Desensitization and Reprocessing (EMDR)-based intervention to 30 patients presenting long COVID-19 syndrome. The authors found a reduction in anxiety and depressive symptoms after four sessions according to the specific psychological symptoms of the patients. Although the aforementioned studies provided valuable information to understand the management of psychological suffering in long COVID-19 patients, it is important to highlight some of their limitations. First, both studies described utilized a randomized clinical trial design to establish the efficacy of the interventions. Second, the studies reported changes in different emotional symptoms (i.e., anxiety and depressive symptoms). However, they implemented specific-symptom programs that did not consider the transdiagnostic nature of emotional disorders and did not address the shared etiological and maintenance factors that underlined the emotional disorders.

The Unified Protocol for Transdiagnostic Treatment of Emotional Disorders

Given that most of the mental health problems presented by people with long COVID-19 are related to mood and anxiety disorders, which are included in the so-called emotional disorders, it is necessary to apply psychological treatments that address these disorders. One treatment specially designed for emotional disorders is the Unified Protocol for the Transdiagnostic Treatment of Emotional Disorders (UP; Barlow et al., 2018). Its focus on underlying mechanisms instead of disorder-specific symptoms allows application across different contexts and problems, including health conditions (Osma et al., 2021). Considering this versatility, and the transdiagnostic approach to treating emotional disorders, it is believed that the UP may also be effective for addressing emotional disorders in people suffering from long COVID-19. Moreover, its transdiagnostic character allows it to intervene on the vulnerability factors shared by all emotional disorders, thus allowing its use regardless of the specific emotional symptoms or emotional disorder (e.g., mood or anxiety disorder) presented by the patients or the presence of comorbidity. However, so far, no studies have evaluated the efficacy of the UP for treating emotional disorders in people with long COVID-19.

USING THE UP TO TREAT PEOPLE LIVING WITH LONG COVID-19

Previous Considerations

The case we present is part of the research study our team is conducting in the autonomous community of Aragon in Spain. Thus, cultural characteristics may have influenced our UP intervention program. Because the autonomous community of Aragon has a vast expanse of land, with small cities and towns far away from general hospitals, we decided to apply the psychological assessment and intervention through the internet. Another consideration is that the UP intervention we describe is based on our experience treating people attending the Spanish Public Health System. As a result, the UP may need to be adapted by clinicians treating people from other contexts—for example, by COVID-19 associations in the community. Finally, because many public health settings prefer intervention programs with fewer sessions to reduce cost, we decided to implement the UP in eight sessions (as opposed to the recommended 12–16 sessions; Barlow et al., 2018), one per module, each with a duration of 50–60 minutes.

When clinicians apply the UP in a shorter, more intensive fashion, such as the one described in this chapter, they should indicate from the beginning that the intervention will be conducted over two phases. The first phase will focus on understanding how the patient experiences emotions, identifying behaviors (i.e., maladaptive emotion regulation strategies) they are using to try to feel better when an intense emotion appears, and learning and practicing new ways to tolerate their intense emotions while maintaining their personal goals. This first phase will last eight weekly sessions. The second phase will focus on repeatedly practicing the new emotion regulation strategies, and follow-up assessments—for example, at 3, 6, and 12 months after the end of the first phase—are recommended.

Description of the UP Intervention to Treat People with Long COVID-19

The UP allows clinicians to personalize the modules and techniques to their patients depending on sociodemographics, clinical characteristics, personal resources, and preferences. As we have seen throughout this book, this personalization also applies to individuals with health conditions where their health issues must also be considered. Considering that clinicians should personalize the UP to their specific patients, in the following sections, we describe a general adaptation we have made to treat people with long COVID-19 and comorbid emotional disorders.

Module 1: Setting Goals and Maintaining Motivation

This module introduces the connection between physical symptoms (e.g., pain and brain fog) and emotional and cognitive aspects (e.g., focusing on the symptoms and catastrophizing) in humans. This relationship is more relevant to individuals suffering from a health condition because physical symptoms are more frequent and intense. These aspects are discussed in-depth in the following modules, but a brief introduction at the intervention's beginning can help patients adjust their expectations. To maintain their motivation, it is necessary to help them focus on aspects they can change by themselves.

In this regard, people with long COVID-19 constantly live with intense uncertainty. It is unclear whether the physical and cognitive symptoms they experience will decrease or remit. This uncertainty can affect a person's ability to establish personal goals. Clinicians should validate these difficulties and work with their patients to adjust their expectations and help them clarify their goals. This is done through different explanations and questions; for example, if a patient is reporting debilitating feelings of fatigue, the therapist might ask, "When you're feeling exhausted, it feels like you can't do anything at all; but is it possible to find some middle ground between being able to do what you used to do in the past and doing nothing?" or "What specific behaviors can you do but are not doing because of your mood state?" or "Nobody knows if you will be able to run again as you did before COVID-19, but what do you think about starting with low intense physical training as a first goal?" Special attention is needed when patients have children because they usually feel guilty about being unable to do activities with them, such as doing homework together, going to the park, playing football or basketball, etc. In these cases, it can be helpful for patients to generate more realistic and attainable personal goals related to their families. A decisional balance exercise can be done following the recommendations of the original manual.

Module 2: Understanding Emotions and Following the Antecedents, Responses, and Consequences of Emotions

In our experience, we have found that patients with long COVID-19 present frequently with emotions of sadness, anxiety, guilt, and anger. It is also difficult for them to connect with "positive" emotions. As in the original manual, we discuss the functions of different emotions and the common response to them (physical, cognitive, and behavioral). We also explain the antecedents, responses, and consequences (ARC) of emotional experiences, focusing mainly, as we introduced in the previous session, on the association between physical symptoms (e.g., pain), the emotion that triggers them (e.g., sadness), and the cognition ("I will always feel that way" or "I cannot do anything"), physical sensations (e.g., dizziness), and emotion-driven behaviors (EDBs; e.g., stay in bed all morning). Some characteristic EDBs for individuals suffering from long-COVID include not doing enjoyable activities, work, or physical exercise and not going out with friends.

Patients with a primary diagnosis of a mood disorder with minimal daily activity and no pleasant activities may find an explanation about the relationship between activity and improvements in mood state beneficial. We recommend that clinicians consider if some behavioral activation exercises can be recommended at this point. We have observed that patients with more cognitive impairment are used to delegating to others some activities that require attention or concentration, such as reading, cooking, or driving. This reduction in daily activities can significantly limit their lives and affect their emotional state.

In this module, patients are taught to recognize both the short- and long-term consequences of their emotional responses. The clinician would try to help the patient recognize that although they may feel some relief from their physical symptoms in the short term by staying in bed, this may make them feel worse in the long term and can contribute to additional difficulties related to their job. Some patients may find this problematic. For example, a patient might say, "In the short term I do not feel any relief, I feel worse staying in bed than going to work." The therapist could explore this "trade-off" using questions or comments; for example, the therapist might inquire, "What do you think would happen if you went to work in this state?" or "I understand that staying in bed is not making you feel better but think about when you are feeling very sad because of the pain and what happens as soon as you decide to stay in bed and not go to work in this condition."

Another important recommendation for clinicians is that patients sometimes do not differentiate between physical symptoms related to their health condition and those associated with intense and unpleasant emotions. Four tips can be helpful in this regard:

1. Consult with the patient's physician about the physical symptoms to determine the extent to which they may be a consequence of the infection or an existing identified health condition and whether there are health recommendations to consider (this will also be helpful in Module 6, "interoceptive exposures").
2. Ask patients to describe their physical symptoms in detail since the beginning of the infection until the present. This can help the clinician better understand the patient's physical symptoms and evolution over time. It can also help identify potential triggers, including specific times during the day, that exacerbate them (e.g., tiredness at night).
3. Explain in this module, with multiple examples, the similarities between physical symptoms related to COVID-19 and those triggered by intense emotions (e.g., tachycardia).
4. Explain how patients can observe, through the ARC, components of an emotional response, as occurs. This includes the antecedents or triggers of intense emotions; the cognitive, physical, and behavioral components of the emotion itself; and the (short- and long-term) consequences of the response. The ARC can be useful for observing the patient's emotional patterns and helping them identify which physical sensations are associated with particular emotions and antecedents.

Module 3: Mindful Emotion Awareness

We follow the same content of the original UP manual for Module 3, but because it is covered in only one session in our shortened program, just two of the three exercises are conducted in this module. First, we conduct a mindful emotion awareness meditation. Patients with long COVID-19 will benefit especially from exercises focused on describing physical sensations as they are currently occurring, in the "present moment" (e.g., "I feel fatigue"), without judgment (e.g., "I hate these feelings"), and without projecting into the future (e.g., "I'll never feel better"). Second, we use the anchoring in the present exercise. This exercise is beneficial because patients with emotional disorders often react emotionally based on thoughts about the past (e.g., "I used to do this quickly") or future (e.g., "I won't be fully independent anymore"). For example, a patient said,

> I felt happy seeing my daughter winning a literature award at high school last weekend, but at that moment, I started thinking how I used to feel so much better. Then I started wondering if I would ever feel like that again and if I could help my daughter in the future now that my memory is shot.

This patient then described the physical sensations they were experiencing, stating, "I started to feel sad and dizzy. Then I had breathing difficulties. I couldn't pay attention to the ceremony anymore. I just wanted to go home." If the patient had used anchoring in the present at that moment, taking a deep breath to anchor, and then reviewing his thoughts, physical sensations, and EDBs, he might have realized that he was reacting to thoughts about the past and the future. In turn, he may have been able to pay attention to the present moment, to his daughter. Clinicians should decide if it is also possible to introduce the mindful mood induction exercise in this session.

Module 4: Cognitive Flexibility

We can also follow the manual for this session. As we have seen over the previous modules, patients with long COVID-19 often present with thinking traps such as thinking the worst (e.g., "The pain will remain forever") and jumping to conclusions (e.g., "My boss won't understand my health condition"). In addition, they describe "I should" and "what if" type statements (e.g., "I should be able to enjoy it" or "What if I never recover from this tiredness?"). In this module, patients are taught how to think more flexibly, as the manual recommends, and to rely more on objective and realistic thoughts (e.g., "I do not know how my health condition is going to progress") rather than thinking traps (e.g., "I won't be able to work again"). The ability to recognize one's thoughts and consider situations more flexibly can be crucial for developing solutions to problems that may result from the physical difficulties that the patient is experiencing. For example, reducing working hours may be a more favorable outcome for someone than not working anymore due to physical and cognitive symptoms.

Module 5: Countering Emotional Behaviors

This module can be applied the same as in the original UP. Some examples of emotional behaviors in people with long COVID-19 are not going out, not exercising, not driving (overt avoidance), postponed activities, and not talking about how they feel in a conversation (subtle behavioral avoidance). Also common are rumination, distraction, worry (cognitive avoidance), and being with a "safe person" in an uncomfortable situation or carrying the medication (safety signals). Regarding EDBs, some examples are returning home when experiencing intense and unpleasant emotions, yelling at their loved ones, and staying in bed or at home. In this session, patients can analyze the short- and long-term consequences of their emotional behaviors. We use the traditional exercise about the *white bear* to make them experience what happens when using avoidance behaviors; in this case, they cannot suppress an image of a white bear. As a result of this module, patients begin generating alternative and healthier behaviors.

Module 6: Understanding and Confronting Physical Sensations

Due to the previous work with the ARC and by focusing on describing physical sensations without judgment and without projecting into the future, patients have increased their awareness of their physical symptoms derived from the long COVID-19 health condition and those physical sensations experienced because of their emotional reactions to intense and unpleasant emotions. If clinicians have doubts about this difference, they can consult the patient's doctors. During this module, patients work to increase tolerance of physical sensations associated with intense and unpleasant emotions through interoceptive exposure exercises (hyperventilation, running in place, breathing through a thin straw, etc.). While practicing these exercises, patients identify thinking traps triggered by physical sensations and use more realistic interpretations.

Module 7: Putting It into Practice: Emotion Exposures

The UP aims to help patients become more tolerant of intense emotions and respond to emotional experiences more adaptively, consistent with personal goals. In this module, patients use all emotion regulation strategies learned previously while completing exposures to intense emotions such as sadness, anxiety, depression, or guilt. We recommend building the emotion exposure hierarchy by adding as many items/stimuli as possible (memories or images, thoughts, objects, people, places, situations, and physical sensations) and by considering different factors that may influence the intensity of the emotional response, such as duration, number of people, distance, time of day, etc. Clinicians should show patients how to prepare the emotion exposures through the appropriate record. Furthermore, we recommend that the therapist review the first emotion exposure record with the patient as soon as possible (by telephone if necessary) to guarantee that the patient understands how to conduct an exposure exercise before continuing with additional exposures on the emotion exposure hierarchy.

Module 8: Moving UP from Here: Recognizing Accomplishments and Looking to the Future

This module can be applied following the UP manual. After only 8 weeks of intervention, many patients may not fully recover and will need more practice. Therefore, we remind patients at the end of the session that this is the last session of the first phase of the intervention. They must continue practicing all emotion regulation strategies to achieve their goals and internalize the skills. We recommend clinicians conduct follow-up assessments at 3, 6, and 12 months over the second phase.

UNIFIED PROTOCOL FOR THE MANAGEMENT OF EMOTIONAL DISORDERS: A CASE STUDY

Case Description

S. is a 38-year-old woman who has worked as a store clerk in Spain for the past 11 years. She is married and has two daughters, aged 8 and 4 years. Regarding health habits, she reported no smoking or alcohol consumption. She also explained that she has healthy eating habits (i.e., a balanced diet that includes vegetables, fruits, meat, and fish).

She reported not having previous physical or psychological antecedents. She is adopted and does not know her biological family's physical and mental health history.

COVID-19 Description

In January 2021, she was on her way to work when she realized she had a nosebleed. She tried to stop the bleeding but was unsuccessful, so she went to a pharmacy. Once there, the pharmacist plugged her nose. She also had her blood pressure checked and was informed that it was "high." She decided to go to work and tried to finish her working day. However, her nosebleed had not stopped after an hour, and she began to feel dizzy. In response, she decided to go to the hospital, where she tested positive for COVID-19.

After the diagnosis, she was under observation for 24 hours. She then requested a voluntary discharge from the hospital and planned to continue her recovery while isolating herself at home. The following week, she experienced fever, oxygen deficiency, low heart rate, headaches, muscle pain, and weakness. She reported being unable to even walk to the shower and was resting in bed for long periods without walking. She was on sick leave for 18 months, returning to work in June 2022. In September 2022, she was reinfected with COVID-19, with the predominance of physical symptoms being muscle pain, headache, and fatigue. Three months after the second infection, she had not recovered from related physical symptoms and was diagnosed with a long COVID-19 condition by her physician.

At the time of the first contact with the psychologist (January 2023), she reported many physical consequences of COVID-19 infection. Specifically, she described asthenia, weight loss (-1.5 kg in the past 3 months), shortness of breath, arthralgia, myalgia, skin dryness, dizziness, headache, paraesthesia of hands, memory and attention issues, thoracic pain, and disorientation (temporary loss of spatial memory).

Psychological Assessment

Table 14.1 shows the measures administered over the course of the program. Assessment points included eligibility criteria, pretreatment assessment, baseline assessments (BL; six consecutive daily assessments before implementation of the UP), continuous assessments (weekly assessments over the course of the UP-based program), and post-treatment.

Psychological Status of the Patient Before Application of the UP

Clinical Diagnosis

Based on the Anxiety and Related Disorders Interview Schedule for DSM-5 (ADIS-5; Brown & Barlow, 2014), in January 2023, S. met criteria for the following emotional disorders:

Major depressive disorder: During the previous months, S. had been feeling constantly depressed (i.e., intense daily feelings of sadness and hopelessness), and she felt a diminished interest in almost all activities she used to do (e.g., going to the gym, going to the park with her daughters). She had lost 1.5 kg in the previous month and suffered from insomnia nearly daily. She also reported psychomotor retardation, fatigue, and feelings of worthlessness. With regard to cognitive symptoms, she reported a diminished ability to think and concentrate.

Panic disorder: S. reported experiencing unexpected panic attacks characterized by a sudden rush of intense fear accompanied by many physical symptoms, including palpitations, sweating, sensations of shortness of breath, nausea, dizziness, chest pain, and fear of losing control. After her first panic attack, she reported more than 1 month of persistent worry about having additional panic attacks. Consequently, she modified some of her behaviors to reduce the likelihood of additional attacks (i.e., not going out alone with her daughters).

Agoraphobia: During the first assessment, S. explained that she constantly felt intense fear in a crowd and when outside of the home alone. Due

Table 14.1 Description of the Psychological Measures Administered Throughout the Study

Measure	Variable	No. of Items (Total Score Range)	Interpretation	Assessment
ADIS-5	Clinical interview to establish clinical diagnosis of anxiety, mood, and related disorders (i.e., obsessive–compulsive, trauma, etc.)	NA	NA	Eligibility criteria, Post
ODSIS	Frequency, severity of depressive symptoms, anhedonia, and interference	5 (0–20)	Higher scores indicate higher depressive symptoms.	Pre, BL Treatment, Post
OASIS	Frequency and severity of anxiety symptoms, avoidance, and interference	5 (0–20)	Higher scores indicate higher anxiety symptoms.	Pre, Post
MEDI	Dimensions of emotional disorders *Subscales*: neurotic temperament (NT), positive temperament (PT), depressed mood (DM), autonomic arousal (AA), somatic anxiety (SOM), social anxiety (SOC), intrusive cognitions (IC), traumatic re-experiencing (TRA), avoidance (AVD)	Total items = 49 NT = 5 (0–40) PT = 5 (0–40) DM = 5 (0–40) AA = 5 (0–40) SOM = 5 (0–40) SOC = 5 (0–40) IC = 6 (0–48) TRA = 5 (0–40) AVD = 8 (0–64)	Higher scores indicate higher impact in each emotional disorder dimension.	Pre, Post
EuroQol	Perceived quality of life *Subscales*: mobility, self-care, daily tasks, pain/discomfort, anxiety, depression Visual analogue scale to assess perceived general health	Five items response rate (1 = no impairment; 2 = moderate impairment; 3 = great impairment) 1 (0–100)	Higher scores indicate higher quality of life.	Pre, Post

(*continued*)

Table 14.1 CONTINUED

Measure	Variable	No. of Items (Total Score Range)	Interpretation	Assessment
DERS	Difficulties in emotion regulation when facing stressors *Subscales*: confusion, inattention, lack of control, interference, rejection	Total items = 28 (28–140) Confusion = 4 (4–20) Inattention = 4 (4–20) Lack of control = 9 (9–45) Interference = 4 (4–20) Rejection = 7 (7–35)	Higher scores represent higher emotion dysregulation.	Pre, Post
DTS	Perceived ability to manage distress *Subscales*: tolerance emotional distress, subjective appraisal of distress, attention absorber by negative emotions, regulation efforts to alleviate distress	Total = 15 (15–75) Tolerance = 3 (3–15) Appraisal = 6 (6–30) Absorption = 3 (3–15) Regulation = 3 (3–15)	Higher scores indicate lower ability to tolerate distress.	Pre, Post
CSQ-8	Adaptation of the original questionnaire: 6 items were maintained (i.e., quality of the program, utility of the program, recommendations, utility of the content to solve problems, general satisfaction, and desire to participate in this kind of intervention in the future). An additional item was included to assess discomfort generated by the intervention.	7 (each item ranges from 0 to 10)	Higher scores indicate greater satisfaction. Item of discomfort: Greater scores indicate greater discomfort.	Post
UP satisfaction	Patients' general satisfaction with the psychological program received and specific satisfaction with each of the modules.	7 (each item ranges from 0 to 10)	Higher scores indicate greater satisfaction.	Post

ADIS-5, Anxiety and Related Disorders Interview Schedule for DSM-5; BL, baseline; CSQ, Client Satisfaction Questionnaire (adapted); DERS, Difficulties in Emotion Regulation Scale; DTS, Distress Tolerance Scale; EuroQol, health-related quality of life; MEDI, Multidimensional Emotional Disorder Inventory; NA, not applicable; OASIS, Overall Anxiety Severity and Impairment Scale; ODSIS, Overall Depression Severity and Impairment Scale; Post, post-treatment; Pre, pretreatment; Treatment, weekly treatment assessment; UP, Unified Protocol; .

to these fears, she avoided going to crowded restaurants or leaving her home alone. She sometimes asked her husband to go with her when leaving home.

Emotional Symptoms (ODSIS, OASIS, and MEDI)

As indicated in Table 14.2, scores at pretreatment on the Overall Depression Severity and Impairment Scale (ODSIS; Bentley et al., 2014; Osma et al., 2019) and Overall Anxiety Severity and Impairment Scale (OASIS; Norman et al., 2006; Osma et al., 2019) remained above the clinical cut-off of 10 points established for Spanish populations (Osma et al., 2019). Congruently, these scores were higher than those obtained in the Spanish nonclinical population (approximately 3 and 4 points for depressive and anxiety symptoms, respectively; Osma et al., 2022).

Figure 14.1 shows the participant's scores in the nine dimensions of the Multidimensional Emotional Disorder Inventory (MEDI; Rosellini & Brown, 2019; see also Osma et al., 2023). The most impaired areas were somatic anxiety, depressed mood, autonomic arousal, social anxiety, and avoidance. In these five dimensions, S. showed higher scores (represented by the figure with gray bars) than nonclinical populations (represented by the figure with a black line). On the contrary, the less affected dimensions of emotional disorders were intrusive cognitions and traumatic re-experiencing. As shown in Figure 14.1, both scores were much lower than those reported by nonclinical samples.

Particular attention should be paid to temperament on this measure, given the UP's focus on targeting core temperamental processes in emotional disorders. In the case of S., the score in neurotic temperament was below the mean for nonclinical populations. Similarly, the score for positive temperament in the case of S. (mean = 72.50) was very similar to that obtained by the nonclinical sample (mean = 72.50; Osma et al., 2023). This may indicate a protective temperament profile in this case.

Quality of Life (EuroQol)

As shown in Table 14.2, some subscales of the EuroQol (Brooks, 1996; Herdman et al., 2001)—namely mobility, self-care, and ability to conduct daily tasks—were not affected before the UP program implementation. However, other areas, such as physical (i.e., pain/discomfort) and mental health (i.e., anxiety/depression), were highly impacted at pre-assessment (scores of 3 and 2, respectively). In addition, S. scored 40 on global perceived health status (visual analogue scale). This score was much lower than those reported by the normative population (perceived global health mean = 80.70; Hernandez et al., 2018), indicating that her perceived health status was significantly impacted.

Distress (DTS)

As reported in Table 14.2, compared with normative populations, S. presented higher scores on the Distress Tolerance Scale (DTS; Simons & Gaher, 2005; see

Table 14.2 Evolution of Psycological Measures from Pre- to Post-Treatment Assessments

Outcome	ND [mean (*SD*)]	Reliability (Chronbach's α)	Pre RS	Post RS (PCP)	RCI	Interpretation
ODSIS	2.91 (3.90)	0.95	10	3 (70)	−5.68	SC, improvement
OASIS	3.81 (4.09)	0.94	11	4 (63.64)	−4.94	SC, improvement
MEDI						
Neurotic temperament	44.96 (22.15)	0.80	42.50	40.00 (5.88)	−0.18	Non significant
Positive temperament	71.23 (16.28)	0.74	72.50	73.00 (0.69)	0.04	Non significant
Depressed mood	22.55 (21.15)	0.87	67.50	35.00 (48.15)	−3.01	SC, improvement
Autonomic arousal	18.63 (19.35)	0.79	67.50	25.00 (62.96)	−3.39	SC, improvement
Somatic anxiety	33.35 (19.20)	0.75	70.00	40.00 (42.86)	−2.21	SC, improvement
Intrusive cognitions	20.79 (20.81)	0.87	14.58	12.00 (17.70)	−0.24	Non significant
Social anxiety	34.70 (25.55)	0.92	52.50	32.00 (39.05)	−2.01	SC, improvement
Re-experiencing	17.78 (19.98)	0.87	2.50	2.00 (20.00)	−0.05	Non significant
Avoidance	30.69 (17.08)	0.77	50	26.00 (48.00)	−2.07	SC, improvement
EuroQol			-			
Mobility	NA		1	1 (0.00)	NA	
Self-care	NA		1	1 (0.00)	NA	
Daily tasks	NA		1	1 (0.00)	NA	
Pain/discomfort	NA		3	2 (33.33)	NA	
Anxiety/depression	NA		2	1 (50.00)	NA	
Visual analogue scale	80.7 (16.8)	0.82	40	60 (50.00)	NA	Non significant

DTS total	3.41 (0.84)	0.83	46	22 (52.17)	−47.62	SC, improvement
Tolerance	3.20 (1.09)	0.84	11	5 (54.55)	−9.44	SC, improvement
Appraisal	3.81 (0.89)	0.89	17	9 (47.06)	−25.95	SC, improvement
Absorption	3.22 (1.18)	0.83	11	5 (54.55)	−10.84	SC, improvement
Regulation	3.00 (1.24)	0.93	5	3 (40.00)	−2.76	SC, improvement
DERS total	59.1 (17.50)	0.78	85	49 (42.35)	−5.49	SC, improvement
Confusion	7.9 (3.1)	0.73	10	5 (50.00)	−2.43	SC, improvement
Inattention	−9.6 (3.4)	0.91	6	4 (33.33)	−.080	Non significant
Lack of control	−16.5 (7.5)	0.87	22	12 (45.45)	−3.14	SC, improvement
Interference	−10.2 (3.9)	0.90	14	8 (42.86)	−3.02	SC, improvement
Rejection	−14.9 (6.5)		33	20 (39.39)	−4.47	SC, improvement

DERS, Difficulties in Emotion Regulation Scale; DTS, Distress Tolerance Scale; EuroQol, health-related quality of life; MEDI, Multidimensional Emotional Disorder Inventory; NA, not applicable; ND, normative data; OASIS, Overall Anxiety Severity and Impairment Scale; ODSIS, Overall Depression Severity and Impairment Scale; PCP, percentage of change from pre-test; RCI, Reliable Change Index; RS, raw score; SC, significant change.

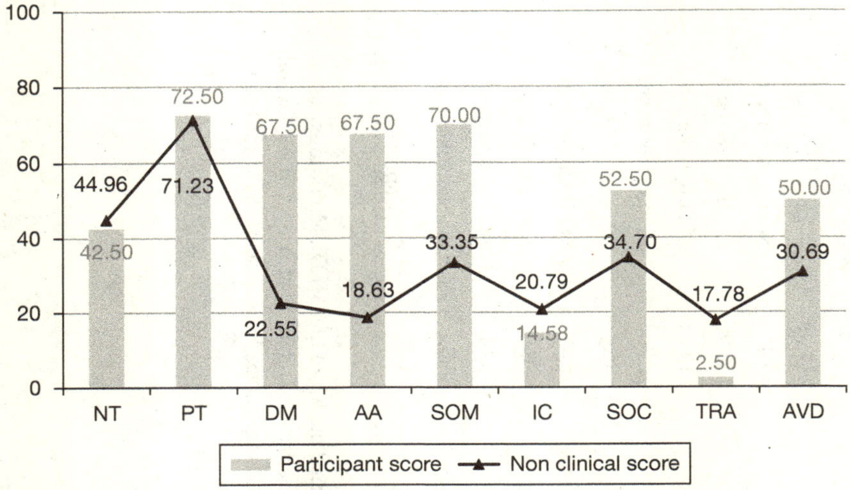

Figure 14.1 MEDI scores at pretreatment assessment. AA, autonomic arousal; AVD, avoidance; DM, depressed mood; IC, intrusive cognitions; MEDI, Multidimensional Emotional Disorder Inventory; NT, neurotic temperament; PT, positive temperament; SOC, social anxiety; SOM, somatic anxiety; TRA, traumatic re-experiencing.

also Sandín et al., 2017). Specifically, before the implementation of the UP-based psychological intervention, the participant found difficulties mainly in tolerance (i.e., "inability to handle feeling distressed"; a score of 11 points out of a total of 15), appraisal (i.e., "feeling scared of distress"; a score of 17 out of a total of 30), and absorption of stress (i.e., "distress being so intense that it takes over the patient"; a score of 11 out of a total of 15).

Emotion Dysregulation (DERS)

The total score on the Difficulties in Emotion Regulation Scale (DERS; Gratz & Roemer, 2004; Hervás & Jódar, 2008) was 85 out of 140. As shown in Table 14.2, this score is higher than those reported by normative populations (mean = 59.10; *SD* = 17.50; Hervás & Jódar, 2008). Specifically, it seems that at pretreatment, the most affected areas were rejection (score = 33 out of 35 possible points) and interference (score = 14 out of 20 possible points). The least affected domain was attention to emotions (i.e., "I pay attention to my emotions"; score = 6 out of 20 possible points).

Case Formulation with the UP

As shown in Table 14.3, the physical symptoms S. suffered in the context of long COVID-19 have impacted different vital areas of her life. As explained in Table 14.3, the most affected areas were physical and basic necessities (e.g., sleep, pain, medical side effects, and general physical issues), work, daily life activities, cognitive functions, pleasant activities, personal relationships, and life goals.

Table 14.3 Case Conceptualization According to UP

HEALTH CONDITION ANALYSIS						
Health condition description: The patient presents long COVID-19 condition which is described as the persistence or development of new COVID-19 symptoms three months after the initial diagnosis (WHO, 2022). In the case of "S," she was first diagnosed with COVID-19 in January 2021 and re-diagnosed in September 2022. Physical symptoms of COVID-19 (i.e., shortness of breath, arthralgia, myalgia, headache, etc.) have remained present since January 2021.						
How does the health condition (and its treatment) affect the patient's life?			**EMOTION ANALYSIS REGARDING HEALTH CONDITIONS AND ITS CONSEQUENCES**			
General life aspects		**Affectation/ interference** **0______10** **Nothing Very much**	**Strong uncomfortable emotions** Do patients feel strong emotions in any of these general life aspects?	**Intensity** **0______10** **Nothing Extreme**	**Aversive reactions**	**Emotional behaviors** (Situational avoidance/scape, subtle behavioral avoidance, cognitive avoidance, safety signals)
1. **Physical and necessities**	**Eat:** The patient does not present alterations in this area.					
	Sleep quality: Frequent awakening during the night and difficulties in sleeping again.	7	Frustration	7	**Thoughts**: "Tomorrow I will feel worse."	**Subtle behavioral avoidance**: Going to bed late
	Pain: Intense muscle and joint pain (due to long COVID-19 condition).	10	Anger Sadness Helplessness	8 9 9	Tachycardia and suffocation **Thoughts**: "I should already accept my physical condition"; This pain is going to kill me".	**Cognitive avoidance**: Rumination about their pain and their physical limitations **Emotion-driven behaviors**: Stays in bed during the whole day
	Medical side effects: She feels burdened because she is having several medical procedures (i.e., lung plaques, electrocardiogram, oxygen saturation measure).	8	Sadness Worry	9 8	Crying **Thoughts**: "I will always feel this way"; "I will be always having medical procedures."	**Subtle behavioral avoidance:** She does not talk with her family about her physical health.

(*continued*)

Table 14.3 CONTINUED

HEALTH CONDITION ANALYSIS						
Health condition description: The patient presents long COVID-19 condition which is described as the persistence or development of new COVID-19 symptoms three months after the initial diagnosis (WHO, 2022). In the case of "S," she was first diagnosed with COVID-19 in January 2021 and re-diagnosed in September 2022. Physical symptoms of COVID-19 (i.e., shortness of breath, arthralgia, myalgia, headache, etc.) have remained present since January 2021.						
How does the health condition (and its treatment) affect the patient's life?			**EMOTION ANALYSIS REGARDING HEALTH CONDITIONS AND ITS CONSEQUENCES**			
General life aspects		**Affectation/ interference** **0________10** **Nothing Very much**	**Strong uncomfortable emotions** Do patients feel strong emotions in any of these general life aspects?	**Intensity** **0________10** **Nothing Extreme**	**Aversive reactions**	**Emotional behaviors** (Situational avoidance/scape, subtle behavioral avoidance, cognitive avoidance, safety signals)
	General: She feels constantly tired and fatigued.	8	Disappointed Frustrated	7 8	**Thoughts:** "I cannot handle this situation anymore"; "I cannot stop, I should do all my duties without help."	**Emotion-driven behaviors**: She does all the tasks impulsively and then she feels more muscle pain and tiredness.
2. **Work**	She feels overwhelmed when the shop is full of people. She has problems with co-workers and bosses because of these situations.	7	Anger Anxiety	7 8	Tachycardia, muscle tension **Thoughts**: "I should be able to manage my emotions."	**Subtle behavioral avoidance**: She avoids as much as possible interacting with her co-workers and bosses. **Subtle behavioral avoidance**: She does not talk with them about her health and worries.

3. **Daily life activities** (shopping, cooking, cleaning, etc.)	She tries to clean the house on the weekend, but she cannot do it as quickly as usual.	7	Frustration	7	Crying. **Thoughts**: "I am useless."	**Cognitive avoidance**: Worrying about the possibility that her family will abandon her.
4. **Cognitive functions**	She is in the street with her daughters and has forgotten how to get home (memory problem regarding spatial orientation).	9	Panic	9	Tachycardia, sweat, nausea, dizziness **Thoughts**: "I am going to lose control."	**Situational avoidance**: Not to go out with her daughters. **Safety signals**: Asks her husband to go out with them.
5. **Pleasant activities** (hobbies, sport, etc.)	She used to go to the gym. However, she stopped going to the gym because of her tiredness. Feeling overwhelmed when being in a crowded place (i.e., restaurants).	7 8	Worthlessness Anxiety	7 8	Chest tightness **Thoughts**: "I am a weak person." Tachycardia, choking sensations **Thoughts**: "I am going to have a panic attack"; "This is dangerous."	**Cognitive avoidance**: Rumination with self-punishment thoughts. **Safety signal**: She tries to go to crowded places with a loved one. **Situational avoidance**: She did not meet with people in potentially crowded places. **Emotion-driven behaviors**: She goes home if restaurants are overcrowded.

(*continued*)

Table 14.3 Continued

HEALTH CONDITION ANALYSIS						
Health condition description: The patient presents long COVID-19 condition which is described as the persistence or development of new COVID-19 symptoms three months after the initial diagnosis (WHO, 2022). In the case of "S," she was first diagnosed with COVID-19 in January 2021 and re-diagnosed in September 2022. Physical symptoms of COVID-19 (i.e., shortness of breath, arthralgia, myalgia, headache, etc.) have remained present since January 2021.						
How does the health condition (and its treatment) affect the patient's life?			**EMOTION ANALYSIS REGARDING HEALTH CONDITIONS AND ITS CONSEQUENCES**			
General life aspects		**Affectation/ interference** 0_____10 Nothing Very much	**Strong uncomfortable emotions** Do patients feel strong emotions in any of these general life aspects?	**Intensity** 0_____10 Nothing Extreme	**Aversive reactions**	**Emotional behaviors** (Situational avoidance/scape, subtle behavioral avoidance, cognitive avoidance, safety signals)
6. **Personal relationships** (couple, family, friends, etc.)	Trouble communicating with her husband and daughters that results in arguments in the family. Not knowing how to respond when friends ask about physical health and worries. She is not able to play with her daughters in the park because she feels extremely fatigued.	9 8 8	Sadness Guilt Anxiety Guilt Sadness	9 9 8 8	**Thoughts**: "I do not understand because I am feeling so upset"; "I cannot control my emotions." **Thoughts**: "They will judge me"; "They will ask about my health." **Thoughts**: "I am feeling depressed again"; "I hate feeling this way"; "I am a horrible mother."	**Emotion-driven behaviors**: Shouts at her daughters and husband. **Situational avoidance**: Telling friends that she cannot meet them next weekend. **Subtle behavioral avoidance**: Not talking with her daughters about her physical and mental health.
7. **Life goals**	Despite following all medical recommendations, her physical symptoms of long COVID-19 do not improve.	10	Sadness Frustration	9 8	**Thoughts**: "I should accept my illness"; "I will always feel this way"; "It is horrible."	**Situational avoidance**: She is reducing the activities she used to do (e.g., going out with friends, weekend trips with her family, exercise).

TREATMENT PLAN
MODULE 1: Setting goals and maintaining motivation
S. agreed to participate in the study because she feels sad and anxious, and wants to do whatever it takes to be the person she was before the COVID-19 infection. Even though she is motivated to change, her expectations regarding the psychological intervention and the recovery from physical symptoms are unrealistic. In the first session, I will introduce the interrelationship between physical symptoms and emotions, and I will try to help S. understand that we do not know if physical symptoms will recover (it does not depend only on what we do) but we can work with variables depending on ourselves (behaviors, thoughts, attitudes, etc.). It will probably be difficult to clarify S.' goals because she wants to function at a level that is similar to where she was before the COVID-19 infection, as a worker, mother, and wife. As her clinician, I will prepare some questions and comments to help her define realistic goals despite her physical symptoms. In the decisional balance exercise, I will make sure that she generates arguments in both the cons/cost of "change" part of the form and in the pros/benefits of "stay the same" part of the form, those ones used to be the most difficult ones.
MODULE 2: Understanding emotions
In this module, the clinician will introduce the nature and function of emotions, the three-component model of emotions, and functional assessment using the ARC. S. presents depressive and anxious symptoms, but if she is maintaining her job and doing all of the activities she can, then behavioral activation will not be needed. Two important aspects in this session are, first, to understand the difference between a physical symptom because of the long COVID-19 condition and the physical sensations associated with intense and unpleasant emotions. I will use some examples that S. noted during the assessment; for example, she told me that sometimes she feels muscle pain that makes her stop working and change her physical position, to lie down and rest. This situation makes her feel sad and useless. Another time, she told me that she feels sad when her daughters ask her husband for help with their homework when she was the one to help them in the past; at that moment, she starts to feel tired, dizzy, and experiences a headache. In that moment, she thinks she is useless and leaves the room. I will need some time in this session to explain the similarities and differences of those two emotional experiences. Second, we will examine the different short- and long-term consequences of her emotional response. I will probably need to use some questions to help S. become aware of the relief she experiences in the short term when engaging in an avoidant behavior (e.g., leaving the room). I will provide S. a summary of the most important content of each session because she has difficulties maintaining concentration while reading.
MODULE 3: Mindful emotion awareness
I will use the ARCs of the past week to talk about the "thoughts" she had because of an intense emotion. Probably, I will find thoughts related to the past (e.g., "I used to do it quickly") and especially to the future (e.g., "I will always feel this way"). Using these examples, I will introduce mindful emotion awareness. I will explain two exercises in the module, mindful emotion awareness meditation and anchoring in the present. Due to the physical symptoms she is experiencing because of the long COVID-19 condition, she will probably benefit from describing physical sensations occurring in the "here and now" (e.g., "I feel joint pain"), without judgment (e.g., "This is horrible"), and without projecting into the future (e.g., "This is not going to change"). I will record the exercises conducted in session and send it to her to facilitate further practice for homework.

(*continued*)

Table 14.3 Continued

MODULE 4: Cognitive flexibility
S. will likely report a tendency to fall into thinking traps when experiencing intense and unpleasant emotions. During this module, she will practice how to generate new and more objective interpretations of her most common thinking traps, for example, thinking the worst (e.g., "This pain is going to kill me"), jumping to conclusions (e.g., "They will judge me"), and those starting with "I should" (e.g., "I should be able to manage my emotions"). I will help S. question her automatic thoughts to generate more realistic interpretations of herself, her situation, her medical condition, her emotional experiences, etc. She can read and concentrate sufficiently for now so we will use the paper-and-pencil format to do the homework. Sometimes S. has difficulties related to spatial memory so it is likely that we will have to implement a problem-solving technique to think about how to manage this problem. For example, instead of not going anywhere with her daughters, she can use the map app on her telephone. I will facilitate the homework practice by asking S. to record thinking traps and the new interpretations in her telephone instead of writing them on the session form. Another tip for her will be to write the new, more flexible, interpretations on Post-it notes or note cards to easily see them and remember them (e.g., "I do not know how my physical condition will evolve" or "I can still have a worthwhile life").
MODULE 5: Countering emotional behavior
During the assessment, I identified several maladaptive emotional behaviors S. uses to try to manage her emotions. In this session, I will revisit these behaviors with S. and ask her to write down additional ones. Some examples of her emotion behaviors are overt avoidance (e.g., not going out, not doing exercise), subtle behavioral avoidance (e.g., not talking about how she feels), cognitive avoidance (e.g., rumination and worry), safety signals (e.g., going out with her husband), emotion-driven behaviors (EDBs; e.g., yelling at her loved ones). Some of her probable opposite or alternative behaviors will be going out, exercising, talking about her feelings and symptoms, focusing on the present moment instead of ruminating, going out with her daughters without her husband, and being assertive in her communication. We will also analyze the short- and long-term consequences of these new behaviors.
MODULE 6: Understanding and facing physical sensations
In this session, we will focus on the physical sensations associated with S.'s intense and unpleasant emotions. I will remind her how intense emotions are associated with physical sensations, thoughts and EDBs, and explain the increasing tolerance of physical sensations. I will provide a rationale for interoceptive exposures and discuss some exercises we can practice in session and at home. I will select several exercises to expose her to bodily sensations associated with intense and unpleasant emotions (e.g., tachycardia, dizziness, redness). As she experiences breathing symptoms associated with her health condition, we will avoid exercises such as hyperventilation or breathing through a thin straw. We will probably practice running in place, spinning while standing, and sitting in front of a space heater.

MODULE 7: Emotional expositions
The most frequent intense emotions S. is experiencing are anxiety and sadness (typically related to other feelings of depression). Thus, we will design an exposure hierarchy focusing on these two emotions, starting with the one she would consider the most problematic. To design a complete hierarchy, I will ask her about memories or images, thoughts, objects, people, places, situations, and physical sensations that trigger these (and other) emotions. After generating an initial list of potential exposures, I will ask her to rate avoidance and distress for each one and then reorder the list from least to most distressing. After that, I will suggest some modulators such as distance, number of people, time, among others. This process will result in a longer list of items which we will order again. Finally, we will choose the item to start the exposure (distress and avoidance around 4–5 points from a 0–10 scale) and I will help S. to prepare it through the correspondent form. I will remind her that it is important to review this first exposure as soon as possible so I will tell her to call me once she has finished it. In this case, S. wants to get her old life back desperately so I will make sure that the different levels of the hierarchy are well defined in terms of avoidance and distress to practice step by step without hurrying too much.
MODULE 8: Recognizing accomplishments and looking to the future
For this module, I will review the takeaway messages of the UP intervention, I will evaluate S.'s progress and the treatment goals defined at the beginning of the intervention and I will talk about the start of the second phase of the intervention. Following treatment (and during what we consider the "second phase"), we will ask S. to continue practicing the emotion regulation strategies learned during treatment. If S. is unable to achieve her personal treatment goals, or her treatment response is suboptimal (i.e., she continues to experience clinical levels of anxiety or depression), we will discuss the importance of continued practice and use the practice plan form to develop a long-term plan for implementing treatment skills. I will conduct three follow-up assessments 3, 6, and 12 months after the end of the first phase of the treatment.
OTHER MODULES IF NECESSARY
Not applicable.

Changes During the UP

Figure 14.2 depicts changes in ODSIS and OASIS scores during treatment. Fluctuations in ODSIS and OASIS were observed during the baseline period before treatment began. Similar slopes are found in ODSIS and OASIS scores (e.g., higher ODSIS scores are accompanied by higher OASIS scores).

During the baseline period, ODSIS scores ranged from 5 to 15 points (the mean during the baseline assessments was 9.33 points). A similar tendency was observed during weekly treatment assessments. ODSIS scores during treatment oscillated between 3 and 13 points. However, the mean score of ODSIS was 7.63 points, slightly lower than scores during baseline.

Regarding anxiety symptoms; OASIS ranged from 5 to 13 points during the baseline period (the mean was 9 points). During treatment assessments, scores ranged between 3 and 15 points, but again, mean scores during baseline (7.25 points) were somewhat lower than during baseline.

Psychological Status of the Patient After the UP Application

Clinical Diagnosis

After the intervention, the clinical interview ADIS-5 (Brown & Barlow, 2014) was readministered to explore whether diagnoses established before the intervention

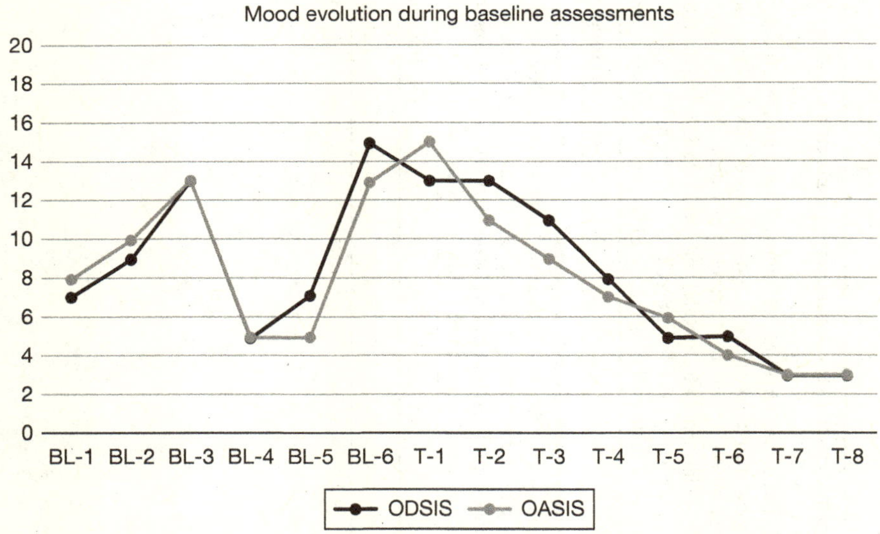

Figure 14.2 Change in depressive and anxiety symptoms at BL and during treatment. The dashed line indicates the clinical cut-off established for Spanish clinical populations (Osma et al., 2019). BL, baseline assessment; OASIS, Overall Anxiety Severity and Impairment Scale; ODSIS, Overall Depression Severity and Impairment Scale; T, weekly treatment assessment.

were still present once the psychological intervention was completed. According to this interview, S. no longer met criteria for agoraphobia or panic disorders at post-treatment. At the end of treatment, S. expressed feeling somewhat anxious about being in a crowd; however, she could keep herself in those situations without using avoidance behaviors (e.g., safety signals). Also, she no longer avoided going out with her daughters. S. denied having any additional panic attacks and, perhaps more important, was no longer worried about the possibility of experiencing an attack in the future.

S. still met the diagnostic criteria for major depressive disorder at the end of treatment, although she noted a reduction in related symptoms. For instance, S. explained that although she had felt sad during the previous weeks, she was also more interested in engaging in pleasant activities (i.e., going to the gym, going to the park with her daughters or meeting friends). Her insomnia symptoms had improved (i.e., she woke up in the middle of the night with less frequency), as did her attention and concentration.

Emotional Symptoms (ODSIS, OASIS, and MEDI)

Table 14.2 indicates the scores obtained across different psychological measures at post-treatment. After the intervention, the total score on ODSIS and OASIS was 3 and 4 points, respectively. The Reliable Change Index (RCI; Jacobson & Truax, 1991) showed a significant improvement in ODSIS (RCI = –5.68, $p < .050$) and OASIS scores (RCI = –4.94, $p < .050$).

With regard to the psychological profile according to MEDI dimensions, we observed a significant improvement in depressed mood (RCI = –3.01, $p < .050$), autonomic arousal (RCI = –3.39, $p < .050$), social anxiety (RCI = –2.01, $p < .050$), somatic anxiety (RCI = –2.21, $p < .050$), and avoidance (RCI = –2.07, $p < .050$). Moderated and nonsignificant reductions in intrusive cognitions (RCI = –0.24, $p > .050$) and traumatic re-experiencing (RCI = –0.05, $p > .050$) were also observed. Although there was some improvement in neurotic (RCI = –0.18, $p > .050$) and positive temperament (RCI = 0.04, $p > .050$), these changes were not significant.

Quality of Life (EuroQol)

At the end of the intervention, two of the subscales of the EuroQol were improved specifically, pain/discomfort reduced from "a lot" to "moderate" levels. Mental health (i.e., anxiety/depression) also decreased from "moderately anxious and/or depressed" to "not anxious and/or depressed." Moreover, an improvement was found in the visual analogue scale (from 40 to 65 points).

Distress (DTS)

The patient reported a significant improvement in tolerance (RCI = –9.44, $p < .050$), appraisal (RCI = –25.95, $p < .050$), absorption (RCI = –10.84, $p < .050$), and distress regulation (RCI = –2.76; $p < .050$).

Emotion Dysregulation (DERS)

DERS total score at post-treatment was 49 points, indicating a significant reduction in emotion dysregulation (RCI = −5.49; $p < .050$). This reduction in emotion dysregulation was observed across some DERS subscales, namely confusion (RCI = −2.43; $p < .050$) lack of control (RCI = −3.14; $p < .050$), interference (RCI = −3.02; $p < .050$), and rejection of emotions (RCI = −4.47; $p < .050$). Although inattention was enhanced, this difference was not significant (RCI = −0.80; $p > .050$).

Program Satisfaction

Client Satisfaction Questionnaire

S. completed the Client Satisfaction Questionnaire (Larsen et al., 1979) to report her satisfaction with the UP. She scored 9 points (scores range from 0 = "no quality" to 10 = "highest quality") for her general satisfaction with the program, indicating great satisfaction with the program. According to her responses, she scored the quality of the program 8 points. Regarding the utility, she stated it was highly useful (score of 8), and it helped her solve problems more adaptively (score of 8). She expressed her intention to participate in a similar intervention in the future (score of 8) and will recommend it to friends or relatives who need it (score of 8).

Regarding the discomfort generated by the intervention, she scored 2 points (scores range from 0 = "no discomfort" to 10 = "maximum discomfort"), which indicates that she experienced minimal discomfort.

Satisfaction with the UP-Based Program

Once the program had ended, the participant manifested that the UP-based psychological intervention helped her regulate her emotions better (score 8 out of 10 possible points). Then, she was asked about satisfaction with each of the specific modules that were presented over the course of the treatment. In general terms, S. reported feeling highly satisfied with all the UP modules. Scores for each of the modules ranged from 7 to 10. The modules that obtained the highest scores were cognitive flexibility (satisfaction = 9) and identifying EDBs (score = 8). The patient reported high satisfaction with the remaining modules, with the emotional awareness module obtaining the lowest satisfaction score (score = 7).

CONCLUSION

Limitations and Advice to Clinicians

In addition to the specific tips we added in each session when describing the UP intervention, we share some barriers that are usually faced in patients with long COVID-19 condition and possible solutions and considerations for clinicians working with people with long COVID-19 condition.

One barrier for patients with long COVID-19 condition to receive psychological treatment is that some health professionals still think that the appropriate intervention for these patients is only medical; therefore, they will not refer these patients to a clinical psychologist. A clear, brief, and reasonable screening process by family doctors could provide psychological assistance to those in need. For this to happen, health professionals must work as a team. Once patients with long COVID-19 condition are referred to a clinician, the most common situation is the comorbidity between emotional disorders and physical health symptoms. Accessing the patient's medical records to gain information about their physical symptoms and health limitations can be helpful. If this is not possible, clinicians should consider assessing existing medical conditions in addition to a clinical and psychosocial assessment. Regarding the treatment of choice, we have presented a structured transdiagnostic psychological intervention (the UP) as an alternative due to its cost-effectiveness. If clinicians want to use this intervention, appropriate training is also recommended to ensure the program is applied with fidelity.

We highlight some other barriers already mentioned throughout the chapter. It is important to understand three common characteristics that can be present in people living with long COVID-19 condition and may act as a barrier to treatment adherence: Some patients present cognitive inflexibility, they often experience uncertainty about the future, and they feel hopeless. All three characteristics may result in the experience of unpleasant emotions, which may in turn result in behavioral inactivity and reduced adherence to treatment. First, patients experiencing long COVID-19 condition usually think they cannot do the same things they used to and will not enjoy life until they completely recover from their physical symptoms. Consequently, they can reduce pleasant activities (e.g., leisure time, exercise, traveling, being with loved ones) and may believe that they do not need psychological treatment and instead should only focus on eliminating their pain. Second, long COVID-19 patients cannot be sure if total recovery of physical symptoms will occur. In this context of uncertainty, when doubts arise (e.g., "What if I never recover from these symptoms?" "What if this psychological treatment does not help me?"), they may choose not to adhere to psychological interventions because the possibility of failing is perceived as being worse than not trying the interventions. The third case has to do with a special situation that occurs when the patient responds to the aforementioned doubts "Will my pain ever be reduced?" with negative catastrophizing thoughts, "I will never recover from this physical or psychological suffering." Patients who feel hopeless may think that no matter what they do, because they will never recover from physical symptoms, their sadness will never be reduced, and they will never experience happiness again. These feelings may discourage patients from seeking psychological treatment (e.g., "I will never improve, so it makes no sense to make any effort"). In this context, clinicians should, from the beginning of the treatment, express an understanding of the situation and validate the intense and unpleasant emotions their patients are experiencing due to long COVID-19. In the context of long COVID-19 condition, it is reasonable for patients to feel uncertainty about the future because it is unclear whether the symptoms will improve or remit. Through this approach of acceptance and validation, the therapist can help the patient identify whether their current cognitive, emotional, and behavioral responses help them achieve their goals or not (e.g., "It is true that we cannot know whether your physical symptoms will disappear in the future. However, do your current thoughts, emotions, and behaviors allow you to achieve your goals in the present?"). Then the therapist can also help the patient develop realistic goals for treatment. For example, a patient may describe experiencing physical symptoms that interfere with their ability to enjoy pleasant activities as frequently as in the past. In this case, the therapist could recognize the patient's experience and draw from several treatment modules to help the patient consider whether they can do similar or other activities to achieve their goals or enjoy life. Then, patients can use the emotion regulation strategies they have learned to make their life worthwhile despite their health situation.

Another potential limitation to implementing the UP intervention is the cognitive impairment of some patients, especially with symptoms such as memory loss, "brain fog," or concentration and attention difficulties. Because of these cognitive symptoms, it may be difficult for some patients to read or comprehend the manual, follow a 60-minute session, and do homework using paper-and-pencil formats. In these cases, some practical adaptations include shorter sessions, a slower communication pace when talking with the patient, and the use of support material instead of the complete original manual (if possible, more visuals and fewer words). In this regard, clinicians should also consider using technology instead of using the UP workbook and the paper forms and records. For example, patients may find it easier to use a mobile recording app or a WhatsApp contact (they can create a contact to do this work) to register their emotional experiences and complete exercises between sessions instead of using paper forms. Also, some clinicians record the audio of the session to share it later with their patients with cognitive difficulties (after a confidentiality agreement is signed), allowing them to listen to the sessions as often as needed.

Future Directions

As previously discussed, only two studies have been conducted demonstrating the efficacy of psychological interventions in patients with long COVID-19, both with research design limitations. Thus, the first step to providing effective psychological treatment to these patients will involve further examining the medical, psychological, and psychosocial aspects of long COVID-19, particularly from the patient's perspective. This knowledge will help us identify the variables associated with this medical condition and its consequences from a biopsychosocial model of health. Second, more studies are needed regarding the cost-effectiveness of psychological interventions for people living with long COVID-19. Finally, as mentioned in Chapter 3 and previously in this chapter, technological tools have the potential to improve the psychological assessment and treatment of people suffering from health conditions and emotional disorders or symptoms.

Summary

As presented in this chapter, people suffering from long COVID-19 condition usually experience comorbid emotional disorders. Although the scientific community has made some attempts to manage these psychological issues, we believe that there is still ample room for improving these interventions. To demonstrate the utility of the UP in managing emotional disorders that occur in several health conditions, we have presented the adaptations and outcomes when the UP has been applied in the case of a patient with long COVID-19 diagnosed with depression, agoraphobia, and panic disorder.

The results presented in this chapter informed us about the UP's preliminary clinical utility in managing emotional disorder in long COVID-19 patients. As observed, depressive and anxiety symptoms were reduced at post-treatment. We also observed improved quality of life, distress, and emotion dysregulation. These outcomes suggest that the patient learned adaptive emotion regulation skills that allowed her to better manage challenging situations associated with the long COVID-19 syndrome. This can also be seen in the patient's opinion about the intervention. She stated that the program helped her learn emotion regulation skills and solve her problems better.

These promising results in terms of clinical utility and satisfaction with the intervention encourage us to believe that this intervention, applied in the context of public health services, could help reduce the psychological burden of the long COVID-19 condition. Health care providers may benefit from information and communication technologies, especially the internet, to provide or support psychological interventions, especially when there are barriers such as long distances to hospitals, reduced mobility, or difficulties in combining self-care with family and work demands. We hope that the considerations explained in this chapter help professionals and the health care system provide psychological treatments to COVID-19 survivors who are suffering the physical and emotional consequences of the long COVID-19 condition.

REFERENCES

Ahmed, A., Aqeel, M., & Aslam, N. (2021). COVID-19 health crisis and prevalence of anxiety among individuals of various age groups: A qualitative study. *Journal of Mental Health Training, Education and Practice, 16*(1), 58–66. https://doi.org/https://doi.org/10.1108/JMHTEP-07-2020-0046

Barlow, D., Farchione, T., Sauer-Zavala, S., Latin, H., Ellard, K., Bullis, J., Bentley, K., Boettcher, H., & Cassiello-Robbins, C. (2018). *Unified Protocol for Transdiagnostic Treatment of Emotional Disorders: Therapist guide* (2nd ed.). Oxford University Press.

Bekele, F., Mechessa, D. F., & Sefera, B. (2021). Prevalence and associated factors of the psychological impact of COVID-19 among communities, health care workers and patients in Ethiopia: A systematic review. *Annals of Medicine & Surgery, 66*, 102403. https://doi.org/10.1016/j.amsu.2021.102403

Bentley, K., Gallagher, M., & Barlow, D. (2014). Development and validation of the Overall Depression Severity and Impairment Scale. *Psychological Assessment, 26*(3), 815–830. https://doi.org/10.1037/a0036216

Bogucki, O. E., & Sawchuk, C. N. (2022). Cognitive processing therapy for posttraumatic stress disorder due to COVID-19-related traumas: A case study. *Psychological Services*. Advance online publications. https://doi.org/https://doi.org/10.1037/ser0000630

Brooks, R. (1996). EuroQol: The current state of play. *Health Policy, 37*(1), 53–72. https://doi.org/10.1016/0168-8510(96)00822-6

Brown, T., & Barlow, D. (2014). *Anxiety and Related Disorders Interview Schedule for DSM-5 (ADIS-5)–Adult and Lifetime version: Clinician manual.* Oxford University Press.

Bullis, J. R., Boettcher, H., Sauer-Zavala, S., & Barlow, D. H. (2019). What is an emotional disorder? A transdiagnostic mechanistic definition with implications for assessment, treatment, and prevention. *Clinical Psychology: Science and Practice, 26*(2), e12278. https://doi.org/10.1111/cpsp.12278

Chennapragada, L., Sullivan, S. R., Hamerling-Potts, K. K., Tran, H., Szeszko, J., Wrobleski, J., Mitchell, E. L., Walsh, S., & Goodman, M. (2022). International PRISMA scoping review to understand mental health interventions for depression in COVID-19 patients. *Psychiatry Research, 316*, 114748. https://doi.org/10.1016/j.psychres.2022.114748

Compagno, S., Palermi, S., Pescatore, V., Brugin, E., Sarto, M., Marin, R., Calzavara, V., Nizzetto, M., Scevola, M., Aloi, A., Biffi, A., Zanella, C., Carretta, G., Gallo, S., & Giada, F. (2022). Physical and psychological reconditioning in long COVID syndrome: Results of an out-of-hospital exercise and psychological-based rehabilitation program. *International Journal of Cardiology: Heart and Vasculature, 41*, 101080.

Deer, R. R., Rock, M. A., Vasilevsky, N., Carmody, L., Rando, H., Anzalone, A. J., Basson, M. D., Bennett, T. D., Bergquist, T., Boudreau, E. A., Bramante, C. T., Byrd, J. B., Callahan, T. J., Chan, L. E., Chu, H., Chute, C. G., Coleman, B. D., Davis, H. E., Gagnier, J., . . . Robinson, P. N. (2021). Characterizing long COVID: Deep phenotype of a complex condition. *EBioMedicine, 74*, 103722. https://doi.org/10.1016/j.ebiom.2021.103722

de Oliveira Almeida, K., Nogueira Alves, I. G., de Queiroz, R. S., de Castro, M. R., Gomes, V. A., Santos Fontoura, F. C., Brites, C., & Neto, M. G. (2023). A systematic review on physical function, activities of daily living and health-related quality of life in COVID-19 survivors. *Chronic Illness, 19*(2), 279–303. https://doi.org/10.1177/17423953221089309

Fernández-de-las-Peñas, C., Palacios-Ceña, D., Gómez-Mayordomo, V., Florencio, L. L., Cuadrado, M. L., Plaza-Manzano, G., & Navarro-Santana, M. (2021). Prevalence of post-COVID-19 symptoms in hospitalized and non-hospitalized COVID-19 survivors: A systematic review and meta-analysis. *European Journal of Internal Medicine, 92*, 55–70. https://doi.org/10.1016/j.ejim.2021.06.009

Gratz, K. L., & Roemer, L. (2004). Multidimensional assessment of emotion regulation and dysregulation: Development, factor structure, and initial validation of the Difficulties in Emotion Regulation Scale. *Journal of Psychopathology and Behavioral Assessment, 26*(1), 41–54. https://doi.org/10.1023/B:JOBA.0000007455.08539.94

Herdman, M., Badia, X., & Berra, S. (2001). El EuroQol-5D: Una alternativa sencilla para la medición de la calidad de vida relacionada con la salud en atención primaria. *Atención Primaria, 28*(6), 425–429. https://doi.org/10.1016/s0212-6567(01)70406-4

Hernandez, G., Garin, O., Pardo, Y., Vilagut, G., Pont, À., Suárez, M., Neira, M., Rajmil, L., Gorostiza, I., Ramallo-Fariña, Y., Cabases, J., Alonso, J., & Ferrer, M. (2018). Validity of the EQ-5D-5L and reference norms for the Spanish population. *Quality of Life Research, 27*(9), 2337–2348. https://doi.org/10.1007/s11136-018-1877-5

Hervás, G., & Jódar, R. (2008). The Spanish version of the Difficulties in Emotion Regulation Scale. *Clinica y Salud, 19*(2), 139–156.

Jacobson, N. S., & Truax, P. (1991). Clinical significance: A statistical approach to defining meaningful change in psychotherapy research. *Journal of Consulting and Clinical Psychology, 59*(1), 12–19. https://doi.org/10.1037//0022-006x.59.1.12

Larsen, D. L., Attkisson, C. C., Hargreaves, W. A., & Nguyen, T. D. (1979). Assessment of client/patient satisfaction: Development of a general scale. *Evaluation and Program Planning, 2*(3), 197–207. https://doi.org/10.1016/0149-7189(79)90094-6

Norman, S. B., Hami Cissell, S., Means-Christensen, A. J., & Stein, M. B. (2006). Development and validation of an Overall Anxiety Severity and Impairment Scale (OASIS). *Depression and Anxiety, 23*(4), 245–249. https://doi.org/10.1002/da.20182

Osma, J., Martínez-García, L., Quilez-Orden, A., & Peris-Baquero, Ó. (2021). Unified Protocol for the Transdiagnostic Treatment of Emotional Disorders in medical conditions: A systematic review. *International Journal of Environmental Research and Public Health, 18*(10), 5077. https://doi.org/10.3390/ijerph18105077

Osma, J., Martínez-Loredo, V., Díaz-García, A., Quilez-Orden, A., & Peris-Bequero, O. (2022) Spanish adaptation of the overall anxiety and depression severity and impairment scales in university students. *International Journal of Environmental Research and Public Health, 19*(1), 345. https://doi.org/10.3390/ijerph19010345

Osma, J., Martínez-Loredo, V., Quilez-Orden, A., Peris-Baquero, O., Ferreres-Galán, V., Prado-Abril, J., Torres-Alfosea, M. A., & Rosellini, A. J. (2023). Multidimensional Emotional Disorders Inventory: Reliability and validity in a Spanish clinical sample. Journal of Affective Disorders, *320*, 65–73. https://doi.org/10.1016/j.jad.2022.09.140

Osma, J., Quilez-Orden, A., Suso-Ribera, C., Peris-Baquero, O., Norman, S., Bentley, K., & Sauer-Zavala, S. (2019). Psychometric properties and validation of the Spanish versions of the Overall Anxiety and Depression Severity and Impairment Scales. *Journal of Affective Disorders, 252*, 9–18. https://doi.org/10.1016/j.jad.2019.03.063

Rajan, S., Khunti, K., Alwan, N., Steves, C., MacDermott, N., Morsella, A., Angulo, E., Winkelmann, J., Bryndová, L., Fronteira, I., Gandré, C., Or, Z., Gerkens, S., Sagan, A., Simões, J., Ricciardi, W., de Belvis, A., Silenzi, A., Bernal-Delgado, E., . . . McKee, M. (2021). In the wake of the pandemic: Preparing for long COVID [Internet]. European Observatory on Health Systems and Policies.

Rodríguez-Fernández, P., González-Santos, J., Santamaría-Peláez, M., Soto-Cámara, R., Sánchez-González, E., & González-Bernal, J. J. (2021). Psychological effects of home confinement and social distancing derived from COVID-19 in the general population—A systematic review. *International Journal of Environmental Research and Public Health, 18*(12), 6528. https://doi.org/10.3390/ijerph18126528

Rosellini, A. J., & Brown, T. A. (2019). The Multidimensional Emotional Disorder Inventory (MEDI): Assessing transdiagnostic dimensions to validate a profile approach to emotional disorder classification. *Psychological Assessment, 31*(1), 59–72. https://doi.org/10.1037/pas0000649

Sandín, B., Simons, J., Valiente, R., Simons, R., & Chorot, P. (2017). Psychometric properties of the Spanish version of the Distress Tolerance Scale and its relationship with personality and psychopathological symptoms. *Psicothema*, *29*(3), 421–428.

Simons, J. S., & Gaher, R. M. (2005). The Distress Tolerance Scale: Development and validation of a self-report measure. *Motivation and Emotion*, *29*(2), 83–102. https://doi.org/10.1007/s11031-005-7955-3

Tasleem, A., Wang, Y., Li, K., Jiang, X., Krishnan, A., He, C., Sun, Y., Wu, Y., Fan, S., Boruff, J. T., Markham, S., Rice, D. B., Bonardi, O., Santo, T. D., Li, L., Thombs-Vite, I., Agic, B., Fahim, C., Martin, M. S., . . . Thombs, B. D. (2022). Effects of mental health interventions among people hospitalized with COVID-19 infection: A systematic review of randomized controlled trials. *General Hospital Psychiatry*, *77*, 40–68.

Uzunova, G., Pallanti, S., & Hollander, E. (2021). Presentation and management of anxiety in individuals with acute symptomatic or asymptomatic COVID-19 infection, and in the post-COVID-19 recovery phase. International Journal of Psychiatry in Clinical Practice, *25*(2), 115–131.

World Health Organization. (2021). Coronavirus disease (COVID-19). https://www.who.int/health-topics/coronavirus#tab=tab_3

World Health Organization. (2022a). Post COVID-19 condition (*long* COVID). https://www.who.int/europe/news-room/fact-sheets/item/post-covid-19-condition

World Health Organization. (2022b). WHO *coronavirus* (COVID-19) *dashboard*. Global situation on December 23, 2022. https://covid19.who.int/?adgroupsurvey=%7Badgroupsurvey%7D&gclid=CjwKCAiAk--dBhABEiwAchIwkTxwO_flMPCZfaAqdl48BHUzrr1W4NBZD-lze-166WYgiS2BM7ZXQxoCULsQAvD_BwE

Zeng, N., Zhao, Y.-M., Yan, W., Li, C., Lu, Q.-D., Liu, L., Ni, S.-Y., Mei, H., Yuan, K., Shi, L., Li, P., Fan, T.-T., Yuan, J.-L., Vitiello, M. V., Kosten, T., Kondratiuk, A. L., Sun, H.-Q., Tang, X.-D., Liu, M.-Y., . . . Lu, L. (2023). A systematic review and meta-analysis of long term physical and mental sequelae of COVID-19 pandemic: Call for research priority and action. *Molecular Psychiatry*, *28*(1), 423–433. https://doi.org/10.1038/s41380-022-01614-7

INDEX

For the benefit of digital users, indexed terms that span two pages (e.g., 52–53) may, on occasion, appear on only one of those pages.

Tables, figures, and boxes are indicated by *t*, *f*, and *b* following the page number

accomplishments, recognizing
  endometriosis, 220
  following bariatric surgery, 161
  HIV (human immunodeficiency virus), 108
  long COVID-19 condition, 335
  type 2 diabetes mellitus, 86
antecedents, responses, and consequences (ARC) of emotions, 78–79
anxiety symptom dimensions, 46–47
assessment and case formulation
  bariatric surgery (BS), 162*t*
  cardiovascular diseases (CVDs), 289*t*, 291*t*
  case example, 53–60, 54*t*
  case formulation in health conditions, 50–53, 52*t*
  challenges of, 43–44, 60
  conclusion, 62–63
  dimensional-categorical profile approach to classification, 47–50
  dimensions associated with emotional disorders, 44–47
  endometriosis, 208*t*
  fertility problems, 182*t*, 189*t*
  HIV (human immunodeficiency virus), 110*t*
  irritable bowel syndrome (IBS), 258*t*, 265*t*, 267*t*
  long COVID-19 condition, 343*t*
  pain management, 54*t*, 140*t*
  Parkinson's disease (PD), 235*t*
  self-report questionnaires, 47, 48*t*
  smoking cessation, 311*t*, 312*t*
  technology-based assessment, 60–62
  type 2 diabetes mellitus (T2D), 88*t*, 92*t*
autonomic arousal, 47

bariatric surgery (BS)
  assessment instruments and constructs, 167*t*
  case analysis, 161–69
  case example, 161
  case formulation, 162*t*
  future directions of UP treatment, 171–72
  impact of obesity, 155–56
  limitations/barriers of UP treatment, 170–71
  pre- and post-treatment assessment scores, 168*t*
  preliminary results, 169–70
  psychological treatments for people who have undergone, 156–58
  tips and recommendations for clinicians, 172
  Unified Protocol adaptions for patients after, 158–61
behavioral inhibition, 44–45
behavioral medicine, 10
behavioral pathogens, 8
behavioral suppression strategies, 45–46

biomedical model, 2, 5–8
biopsychosocial model, 2, 7, 8–9

cardiovascular diseases (CVDs)
  case conceptualization, 291*t*
  chest pain dilemma matrix, 296*t*
  conclusion, 300
  definition and prevalence of, 285–86
  efficacy of Unified Protocol in, 297, 298*t*
  emotional disorders in, 286–87
  future directions of UP treatment, 300
  limitations and barriers observed, 300
  post-treatment scores, 295*t*
  tips and recommendations for clinicians, 301
  transdiagnostic interventions for, 287
  Unified Protocol adaptions for, 288–97, 289*t*
case analysis tables
  bariatric surgery (BS), 162*t*
  cardiovascular diseases (CVDs), 289*t*, 291*t*
  endometriosis, 208*t*
  fertility problems, 182*t*, 189*t*
  HIV (human immunodeficiency virus), 110*t*
  irritable bowel syndrome (IBS), 258*t*, 265*t*, 267*t*
  long COVID-19 condition, 343*t*
  pain management, 54*t*, 140*t*
  Parkinson's disease (PD), 235*t*
  smoking cessation, 311*t*, 312*t*
  type 2 diabetes mellitus (T2D), 88*t*, 92*t*
case formulation. *See* assessment and case formulation
chronic pain. *See* pain management
clinical health psychology. *See also* health psychology
  definition of term, 14
  development of, 13–15
  future of, 15–17
  history of, 1–2
  relationship of mind and body, 2–5
clinical psychology, 13–15
cognitive flexibility
  endometriosis, 215–16
  following bariatric surgery, 160
  HIV (human immunodeficiency virus), 105–6
  long COVID-19 condition, 333
  overview of UP module, 29–30
  pain management, 147
  type 2 diabetes mellitus, 81–82
cognitive suppression strategies, 45–46

dairy/assessment apps, 60–61
determinants of health, 8
Diabetes Distress Scale (DDS), 75–76, 76*t*

EBPTs (evidence-based psychological treatments), 72
ecological momentary assessment (EMA), 60–62
Effective Skills to Empower Effective Men-Sexual Compulsivity (ESTEEM-SC), 103
EMA (ecological momentary assessment), 60–62
embedded biosensors, 60–61
emotional behaviors, countering
  endometriosis, 216–17
  following bariatric surgery, 160
  HIV (human immunodeficiency virus), 106–7
  identifying and altering, 23–24
  long COVID-19 condition, 334
  overview of UP module, 30–31
  pain management, 147–48
  smoking cessation, 317–19
  type 2 diabetes mellitus, 82–83
emotional disorders (EDs)
  comorbidity between, 22–24, 33
  dimensional-categorical profile approach to classification, 47–50
  dimensions associated with, 44–47
  functional model of, 26–27
  and physical health, 24–26
  transdiagnostic assessments, 47
  transdiagnostic treatment of, 27–32
emotion-driven behaviors (EDBs), 30–31
emotion dysregulation
  as component of chronic physical health conditions, 32–33
  fertility issues case study, 186, 188, 194–96, 195*f*
  irritable bowel syndrome (IBS), 262–63, 275, 276*f*
  long COVID-19 condition, 342, 352, 355
  role in anxiety, depressive, and related disorders, 262
  role in maintenance of psychopathology, 32–33
  transdiagnostic treatment and, 27
emotion exposures
  endometriosis, 218–20

following bariatric surgery, 160–61
HIV (human immunodeficiency virus), 106–7
long COVID-19 condition, 334
overview of UP module, 31
pain management, 148–49
type 2 diabetes mellitus, 84–85
emotion regulation dimensions, 45–46
emotions, understanding
endometriosis, 213–14
following bariatric surgery, 159
HIV (human immunodeficiency virus), 104
long COVID-19 condition, 331–32
overview of UP module, 29
type 2 diabetes mellitus, 78–79
endometriosis. *See also* fertility problems
case conceptualization, 208*t*
case example, 206–21
case example OASIS scores over 18 sessions, 221*f*
conclusion, 222
definition and diagnosis, 204
efficacy and clinical utility of UP, 221–22
emotional effect of, 205
future directions of UP treatment, 222
limitation of UP treatment, 222–23
relevance of Unified Protocol for, 205–6
tips and recommendations for clinicians, 223
Engel, G. L., 7, 8, 9
ESTEEM-SC (Effective Skills to Empower Effective Men- Sexual Compulsivity), 103
evidence-based psychological treatments (EBPTs), 72
experiential avoidance, 45–46
experimental psychophysiology, 10

fertility problems. *See also* endometriosis
assisted reproduction techniques (ART), 178
case conceptualization, 189*t*
case example, 187–97
case example change in mood and anxiety, 195*f*
case example psychological evolution, 194*t*
case study emotion dysregulation evolution, 195*f*
change in quality of life related to fertility problems, 185*t*
conclusion, 197
definition and prevalence of, 177–78
emotional impact of ART, 178
future directions of UP-PP, 198
limitations and barriers of UP-PP, 197
pilot study of UP-PP (UP–Prevention Program), 181–87
psychological aspects in women undergoing ART, 179–80
tips and recommendations for clinicians, 198–99
Unified Protocol as preventive intervention, 180
Unified Protocol modifications, 181, 182*t*
figures, list of, vii
functional case analysis tables
bariatric surgery (BS), 162*t*
cardiovascular diseases (CVDs), 289*t*, 291*t*
endometriosis, 208*t*
fertility problems, 182*t*, 189*t*
HIV (human immunodeficiency virus), 110*t*
irritable bowel syndrome (IBS), 258*t*, 265*t*, 267*t*
long COVID-19 condition, 343*t*
pain management, 54*t*, 140*t*
Parkinson's disease (PD), 235*t*
smoking cessation, 311*t*, 312*t*
type 2 diabetes mellitus (T2D), 88*t*, 92*t*

GAD-7 (Generalized Anxiety Disorder 7-Item Scale), 76*t*
goals and motivation
endometriosis, 207–13
following bariatric surgery, 158–59
long COVID-19 condition, 331
overview of UP module, 28
people living with HIV, 103
smoking cessation, 311
type 2 diabetes mellitus, 77–78

health conditions analysis tables
bariatric surgery (BS), 162*t*
cardiovascular diseases (CVDs), 289*t*, 291*t*
endometriosis, 208*t*
fertility problems, 182*t*, 189*t*
HIV (human immunodeficiency virus), 110*t*
irritable bowel syndrome (IBS), 258*t*, 265*t*, 267*t*
long COVID-19 condition, 343*t*

health conditions analysis tables (*cont.*)
pain management, 54*t*, 140*t*
Parkinson's disease (PD), 235*t*
smoking cessation, 311*t*, 312*t*
type 2 diabetes mellitus (T2D), 88*t*, 92*t*
health psychology. *See also* clinical health psychology
broad acceptance of as a subdiscipline, 17
constitution as a subdiscipline, 11–13
definition of term, 12–13
development of clinical health psychology, 13–15
future of, 15–17
history of, 1–2
origins of, 9–10
higher order emotion regulation dimensions, 45–46
HIV (human immunodeficiency virus)
case analysis, 109–20
case example, 108–9
case formulation, 110*t*
conclusion, 120–22
emotional impact of, 101
future directions for treatment, 123
key clinical aspects, 99–101
psychological treatments for people living with, 102–3
reliable change index pre- and post-treatment, 149*t*
tips and recommendations for clinicians, 123–24
treatment limitations and barriers, 122–23
Unified Protocol adaptation for people living with, 103–8
human immunodeficiency virus. *See* HIV (human immunodeficiency virus)

interoceptive exposure (smoking cessation), 311–16, 312*t*
irritable bowel syndrome (IBS)
case conceptualization, 267*t*
case example, 263–76
case formulation, 266
changes in emotion regulation during and post-treatment, 276*f*
changes in mood and anxiety during and post-treatment, 275*f*
conclusion, 276–77
definition and prevalence of, 257–59
emotional difficulties in, 259–61
future directions of UP treatment, 278
limitations and barriers observed, 277–78
psychological interventions in, 261
Rome criteria, 258*t*
tips and recommendations for clinicians, 278–79
Unified Protocol as transdiagnostic treatment, 262–63
UP adaptations for IBS, 263, 265*t*

list of figures, vii
list of tables, ix–x
long COVID-19 condition
case conceptualization, 343*t*
case study, 335–52
case study change in emotional symptoms pre- and during treatment, 350*f*
definition and prevalence of, 328
description of psychological measures administered, 337*t*
future directions of UP treatment, 354
incidence and impact of COVID-19 pandemic, 327–28
limitations and barriers observed, 352–54
MEDI scores at pretreatment assessment, 342*f*
psychological interventions for, 328–29
quality of life scores pre- and post-treatment, 340*t*
summary, 355
tips and recommendations for clinicians, 332, 352
Unified Protocol for treatment, 329–35

medical illnesses, 1–2
medicalization, 8
medical sociology, 2
mind/body dualism, 4, 15
mindful emotion awareness
endometriosis, 214–15
following bariatric surgery, 159
HIV (human immunodeficiency virus), 104–5
long COVID-19 condition, 333
overview of UP module, 29
pain management, 146
smoking cessation, 316–17
type 2 diabetes mellitus, 79–80
mindfulness, 45–46

mood dimensions, 46–47
moral model, 5
Multidimensional Emotional Disorder Inventory (MEDI), 49–50, 50*f*

natural model, 3–5
negative affectivity, 44–45
neuroticism
  aversion/avoidance tendencies and, 23
  contribution to co-occurrence of mental disorders, 24, 33, 44–45
  definition of term, 23
  economic burden associated with, 24
  emotional disorders functional model, 26–27
  higher levels of associated with worse medical outcomes, 25–26
  links to mental health conditions, 23–24, 25
neurotic/negative temperament (NT), 44–45

obesity, impact of, 155–56

pain management
  case conceptualization, 139, 140*t*
  case example, 138–39
  cognitive-behavioral treatment of, 132–33
  conclusion, 150–51
  impact of chronic pain, 131–32
  modifications to unified protocol, 149
  outcome measures, 149–50
  outcome monitoring, 149*t*, 149–50
  treatment overview, 146–49, 149*t*
  unified, transdiagnostic approach to treatment, 133–35
  Unified Protocol overview, 135–38
Parkinson's disease (PD)
  anxiety in, 228
  case examples, 233–43
  case example scores pre- and post-treatment, 242*f*, 245*f*
  case formulation, 235*t*
  clinical characteristics, 227–28
  clinical utility of UP treatment for anxiety and depression, 243–46
  conclusion, 246–47
  current treatment of anxiety and depression, 231–32
  depression in, 228–29
  emotional and cognitive factors of, 230–31
  physcosocial factors of, 229–30
  tips and recommendations for clinicians, 246–47
  Unified Protocol treatment for anxiety and depression, 232–33
Parsons, T., 2
personality dimension, 44–45
PHQ-9 (Patient Health Questionnaire-9), 76*t*
physical health/illness, emotional disorders and, 24–26
physical sensations, understanding and confronting
  endometriosis, 217–18
  following bariatric surgery, 160
  long COVID-19 condition, 334
  overview of UP module, 31
  pain management, 148
  type 2 diabetes mellitus, 83–84
physiological parameters, 10
positive temperament (PT), 45
post-COVID-19 condition. *See* long COVID-19 condition
psychophysiological reactions, 10
psychosomatic illnesses, 9–10, 11
PT (positive temperament), 45

"quit day" planning, 314*b*, 319. *See also* smoking cessation

recommendations for clinicians
  bariatric surgery (BS), 172
  cardiovascular diseases (CVDs), 301
  endometriosis, 223
  fertility problems, 198–99
  HIV (human immunodeficiency virus), 123–24
  irritable bowel syndrome (IBS), 278–79
  long COVID-19 condition, 332, 352
  Parkinson's disease (PD), 246–47
  smoking cessation, 323–24
relapse prevention
  endometriosis, 220
  HIV (human immunodeficiency virus), 108
  long COVID-19 condition, 335
  overview of UP module, 32
  type 2 diabetes mellitus, 86
Rome criteria, 257, 258*t*

Schofield, William, 12
Selye, Hans, 10
smartphone-based EMA, 60–61

smoking cessation
affective disturbance due to, 309
case example, 319–20
case example cigarettes per day and affect regulation, 321*f*
conceptual basis for Unified Protocol, 310*f*, 310
conclusion, 322
efficacy and clinical utility of UP, 320–22
future directions of UP treatment, 323
limitations and barriers observed, 323
mortality and morbidity due to smoking, 309
"quit day" planning, 314*b*, 319
session content by module, 312*t*
tips and recommendations for clinicians, 323–24
treatment delivery of Unified Protocol, 311–19
treatment goals by module, 311*t*
social factors, 8–9
somatic anxiety, 47
supernatural model, 3

T2D. *See* type 2 diabetes mellitus (T2D)
tables, list of, ix–x
technology-based assessment, 60–62
temperament dimension, 44–45
transdiagnostic treatment. *See* Unified Protocol for Transdiagnostic Treatment of Emotional Disorders (UP)
type 2 diabetes mellitus (T2D)
affective components of diabetes versus diabetes health outcomes, 70–71
anxiety and depressive symptoms, 70
baseline and post-treatment descriptive data, 76*t*
case conceptualization, 88*t*
case example, 73–76
clinical outcomes, 76*t*, 86–87
conclusion, 87
integrative approach to management, 72
prevalence and cost of, 69
relationship between symptomatology, affective components, and health behaviors, 77*f*
shortcomings of existing adherence and self-management programs, 71–72
transdiagnostic conceptualization, 76, 80*f*
transdiagnostic treatment for diabetes and distress, 73
treatment, 77–86
UP module modifications, 92*t*

Unified Protocol for Transdiagnostic Treatment of Emotional Disorders (UP)
bariatric surgery (BS), 162*t*
benefits of, 33, 157–58
cardiovascular diseases (CVDs), 288–301, 289*t*, 291*t*, 295*t*, 296*t*, 298*t*
case example, 53–60
case formulation form, 52*t*
case formulation in health conditions, 50–53, 54*t*
endometriosis, 205–23, 208*t*, 221*f*
evidence for, 32–33
fertility problems, 180–97, 182*t*, 185*t*, 189*t*, 194*t*, 195*f*
HIV (human immunodeficiency virus), 103–8, 110*t*
irritable bowel syndrome (IBS), 258*t*, 262–79, 265*t*, 267*t*, 275*f*, 276*f*
long COVID-19 condition, 329–55, 337*t*, 340*t*, 342*f*, 343*t*, 350*f*
modules included in, 28*t*, 28–32
overview of, 27
pain management, 54*t*, 135–51, 140*t*, 149*t*
Parkinson's disease (PD), 232–47, 235*t*, 242*f*, 245*f*
self-report questionnaires assessing, 47, 48*t*
smoking cessation, 310*f*, 310–24, 311*t*, 312*t*, 314*b*, 321*f*
type 2 diabetes mellitus (T2D), 73–87, 88*t*, 92*t*
UP–Prevention Program (UP-PP), 181, 182*t*, 183. *See also* fertility problems

wearable devices, 60–61
Work and Social Adjustment Scale (WSAS), 75–76, 76*t*